Manufacturing Africa

Manufacturing Africa

Performance & Prospects
of Seven Countries
in Sub-Saharan Africa

Roger C. Riddell

**with Peter Coughlin • Charles Harvey • Igor Karmiloff •
Stephen Lewis jnr • Jennifer Sharpley • Christopher Stevens**

James Currey • LONDON
Heinemann • PORTSMOUTH (N.H)

Overseas Development Institute
Regent's College, Regent's Park, London NW1 4NS

James Currey Ltd
54b Thornhill Square, Islington, London N1 1BE

Heinemann Educational Books Inc
361 Hanover Street, Portsmouth, New Hampshire 03801–3959

British Library Cataloguing in Publication Data
Riddell, Roger, *1947–*
    Manufacturing Africa: performance and prospects of Seven
    Countries in Sub-Saharan Africa.
    1. Africa. Manufacturing industries
    I. Title
    338.4767096

    ISBN 0–85255–120–7   (James Currey Cloth)
            0–85255–119–3   (James Currey Paper)

    ISBN 0–435–08046–6   (Heinemann Cloth)
            0–435–08050–4   (Heinemann Paper)

Typeset in 9pt English Times by Colset Private Limited, Singapore
Printed in England by Villiers Publications, London N6

Contents

Part II
The Seven Case-Studies   69

Preface

The words 'Africa' and 'crisis' have become increasingly linked over the past decade as outside donors and funding agencies and groups within Africa such as the Organisation for African Unity and the Economic Commission for Africa have watched a succession of forces – internal and external, natural and man-made – batter the continent. The sub-Saharan region, in particular, enters the 1990s poorer than it was in the 1980s and the 1970s and with few knowledgeable people optimistic that its economic problems will be eased, let alone solved, in the first half of the new decade. Some 30 years ago, when many countries in Africa were gaining their independence and thoughts of economic growth and progress were becoming the principal focus of attention, the words 'development' and 'industry' were practically synonymous. Independence was to be followed by rapid and sustained development (the 1960s were dubbed the 'development decade') and this was to be achieved through the basis of industrialisation.

In the intervening period much has been learnt about the development process even if, as in other disciplines, policy issues have been influenced by fads and fashions. One enduring element, however, has been the link between development and industrialisation, as the much-respected Hollis Chenery confirmed in the opening of his important book *Industrialization and Growth* (Chenery *et al.*, 1986: ix, 1):

> Development is now conceived as the successful transformation of the structure of an economy. In his historical studies of modern economic growth, Kuznets (1966) identified the shift of resources from agriculture to industry as the central feature of this transformation . . .
> Historically, the rise in the share of manufacturing in output and employment as per capita income increases, and the corresponding decline in agriculture, are among the best documented generalizations about development.

It comes, therefore, as a surprise to find that in the recent efforts to come to grips with the 'African crisis' the role of industry has tended to be ignored or underplayed, at least by Western donors and the international institutions. What is even more astonishing is that this apparent disregard for the role of industry in the development of the sub-continent appears to have been based not on contemporary analysis of the progress of the industrial sector but more upon ignorance. There has been little recent work done on the performance of manufacturing in sub-Saharan Africa (SSA) and even less to attempt to link trends across key countries of the area. Is SSA an exception to the general evidence that industrial expansion and deepening are corner-stones of development or does this neglect mean that its prospects for development are more remote than even the pessimists would have us believe?

The present book is an attempt to fill some of these gaps and answer some of these critical questions through an analysis of the industrialisation process in Botswana, Cameroon, Côte d'Ivoire, Kenya, Nigeria, Zambia and Zimbabwe. These seven countries account for some 60 per cent of total manufacturing production and are amongst the most advanced and 'successful' of all countries in SSA.

The book is based on a major research project initiated and co-ordinated by the Overseas Development Institute, London and funded by the Economic and Social Committee for Research (ESCOR) of the Overseas Development Administration. It is divided into two distinct parts. Part I opens with an overview which introduces the general themes, places the industrialisation process of SSA in its broader context and summarises available trends of manufacturing growth in all the countries of the sub-continent for which data are available. Most importantly, however, Part I contains a lengthy reflection upon the industrial process in SSA and its potential future role based on the evidence provided in the seven case-studies which form Part II. The individual authors of Part II are not responsible for either the generalised conclusions or the other views expressed in Part I – even though their views and comments on earlier drafts have influenced the final text. Final responsibility for these opinions lies with myself as the overall editor.

Each of the case-study chapters should be viewed as a self-contained piece with its own bibliographical references. A general bibliography of works cited in the first three chapters is contained at the end of Part I and there is thus no overall bibliography at the end of the book. The index, however, has been compiled in relation to the entire text.

The book's conclusions challenge a number of assumptions commonly made about African development and its prospects. While the analysis neither diminishes the seriousness of Africa's development crisis nor maintains that expansion and promotion of the manufacturing sector provide 'the' solution, it does suggest that underplaying the role of industry has been a mistake. The failure to integrate medium- and longer-term objectives of development with policies to address short-term problems has concealed the role that manufacturing is likely to be called upon to play with increasing prominence as the 1990s proceed. What is more, in a number of countries competitive and far from weak industrial enterprises have been established and these – and the whole future of manufacturing in SSA – could be under threat if short-term market-dominated policies commonly associated with the World Bank's structural adjustment policies dictate the pattern and structure of future development.

Rejecting both the old 'import-substitution' approach to industrialisation (which, it is argued, is notable in SSA more by its absence than its failure) and the export-oriented approach, *Manufacturing Africa* argues that the future prosperity of SSA is likely to be enhanced by a new three-pronged approach to industrialisation. Policies to promote the expansion of non-traditional manufactured exports *and* a more systematic approach to further import substitution need to be vigorously implemented, not in isolation but in conjunction with policies which seek to raise the efficiency of existing manufacturing enterprises. Closing down factories is not rejected but, unlike proposals currently advocated by the World Bank, this is seen as a last, rather than a first, choice option to be taken if other efficiency-promoting measures have consistently failed. What is more, evidence in the book suggests that, although the environment is far from optimal, not a few African countries will be able to develop, expand and deepen their manufacturing sectors in the 1990s, particularly if present negative attitudes are reversed and support is given to the promotion of manufacturing by international institutions and donors. This in itself would help to facilitate the inflow of private foreign investment, which, the study also concludes, is vital in the present environment.

This book is the work of many hands. In the first place I would like to thank the individual researchers who have ably carried out the case-studies. Many of the wider insights drawn have been based on careful analysis contained in them. Their names and short biographical details follow this Preface. Besides those who have commented upon the details of individual country studies, I would also like to thank officials at both the World Bank in Washington and at the United Nations Industrial Development Organisation (UNIDO) in Vienna for their co-operation and for providing access to data and reports. In addition, thanks go to Walter Elkan, Stanley Please, Sanjay Lall, Herman Muegge, Colin Stoneman, Laurence Cockcroft, John Roberts and Job Ohiorhenuan as well as to Adrian Hewitt and John Howell at the ODI who have provided comments on project documents and draft chapters. Thanks are also due to Margaret Cornell who has managed to trim down the final document as well as to improve the text through her invaluable editorial skills.

Even though the book is long there are clearly major gaps both in the country coverage and in the theme chosen for analysis. These are readily acknowledged. Thus *Manufacturing Africa* should be viewed more as the re-starting of in-depth cross-country research on an area of crucial importance to the future development of SSA rather than the final word.

To begin with, more in-depth country studies are clearly needed. There are two broad types of approach. One would be to examine the industrial performance and prospects of other 'leading' countries such as Mauritius, Ghana, Senegal, Sudan and Ethiopia (the latter being of importance because of its successes in operating state-run enterprises, acknowledged, among others, by the World Bank). Another approach could be to analyse those countries which have decisively failed in their efforts to industrialise over the last 15 or more years. These would include, for instance, Zaire, Mozambique, Uganda, Chad and Liberia.

But research should by no means be restricted to this or any other country-study approach. *Manufacturing Africa* has highlighted the inadequacy of current statistics on African industry, inconsistencies between data used by different organisations and the almost entire absence of data on small-scale/informal sector activities. There is a need to pinpoint with greater accuracy than has been possible here the degree and range of these problems and to draw clearer implications of these inadequacies for policy debates. In relation, particularly, to the informal/small-scale element, there is also a need to understand better the potential for future development, the handicaps and constraints and the links which exist and could be furthered between medium and large and small-scale manufacturing.

The present book's analysis has also pinpointed other areas of importance to manufacturing growth as well as revealing gaps in existing knowledge. Further work clearly needs to be done linking more orthodox economic questions of manufacturing development to the important issues of technology, engineering capability, skills and management training, plant maintenance and the 'art' of export promotion – all crucially important issues which have an intricate role in manufacturing sector development.

Finally, more work is needed to determine in greater detail the manner in which foreign aid resources (financial, manpower and technological) could be utilised to further the development of Africa's manufacturing base and – of interest to donors – the manner in which the needs of Africa can be better harmonised with the profit-oriented interests of private business in donor countries. The present research has clearly identified the need, but has only provided an overview of the types of assistance which could be provided by foreign aid agencies.

Despite all these inadequacies, it is hoped that the book's publication will act as a stimulus to other researchers to fill these gaps and help to revive serious debate about the role of industry in African development.

Roger Riddell

Notes on Contributors

Peter Coughlin, Kenya.
Senior lecturer in the Department of Economics, University of Nairobi and co-ordinator of a major research project on industrialisation in Kenya: *Industrialization in Kenya: In Search of a New Strategy*, James Currey (London) and Heinemann (Nairobi), 1989 (co-authored by Gerrishon Ikiara).

Charles Harvey, Botswana.
Fellow at the Institute of Development Studies at Sussex University. He has had long professional experience in Africa, including advising a number of African governments. Co-author with Stephen Lewis of *Policy Choice and Development Performance in Botswana*, London: Macmillan, 1989.

Igor Karmiloff, Cameroon and Zambia.
He has worked for many years with UNCTAD, specialising in trade and broader development questions. Much of his work since the early 1960s has been on African development planning including advice to several African governments, both French- and English-speaking. He has recently been working on issues of African industry and structural adjustment with UNIDO.

Stephen Lewis Jnr, Botswana and Kenya.
He has acted as economic adviser to both the Kenyan and Botswanan governments in recent years. He has also made an important contribution to the theoretical analysis of third world industrialisation, for example with his book *Economic Policy and Industrial Growth in Pakistan*. His recent African publications include a study on the SADCC states, a book on the South African economy and, with Charles Harvey, *Policy Choice and Development Performance in Botswana*, London: Macmillan, 1989. Since 1989 he has been President of Carleton College, Minnesota, USA.

Roger C. Riddell, Côte d'Ivoire and Zimbabwe and general editor.
A Research Fellow at the Overseas Development Institute, London since 1984. He lived in southern Africa for ten years and worked on industrial questions in Africa for over six years, most recently in relation to the Preferential Trade Agreement for Eastern and Southern Africa. He has been a consultant for UNIDO and in 1981–83 was the Chief Economist of the Confederation of Zimbabwe Industries after serving as the Chairman of the Commission of Inquiry into Prices, Incomes and Conditions of Service under President Mugabe.

Jennifer Sharpley, Botswana and Kenya.
A London-based consultant, who has worked on macroeconomic and sectoral issues in both Africa and the Caribbean. She is a specialist on the Kenyan economy and has been an adviser and consultant to the Government of Kenya. Among her publications are 'Economic Policies and Agricultural Performance: The Case of Kenya' for the OECD Development Centre and contributions to *The Quest for Economic Stabilization*, and *The IMF and Stabilization* (T. Killick et al.), resulting from previous ODI research work.

Christopher Stevens, Nigeria.
A Research Fellow at the Overseas Development Institute since 1975. He has wide experience of African economies covering food, agricultural, aid, energy, external trade and industrial issues. Most recently he has worked with the FAO on its major report on African agriculture and with the UN Economic Commission for Africa on its report for the 1986 UN Special Session on Africa. He is the author of *Nigeria: Economic Prospects to 1985*, London: Economist Intelligence Unit, 1982.

1 Introduction

Whither SSA development?

As the 1990s begin, the problem of development in sub-Saharan Africa (SSA) stands out as a critical unresolved human issue to be faced by the international community[1]. Towards the end of the 1970s, the World Bank began work on a series of reports on the region which revealed that from the 'first development decade' of the 1960s a whole generation across an entire continent had experienced a stagnation in *per capita* incomes, in stark contrast to the steady rise in income levels in all other regions of the developing world. Together with the African Development Bank and the Finance Ministers of the Organisation for African Unity, the Bank began to argue that there was little hope of overall improvement unless there was to be, among other things, a massive increase in the inflow of external resources. The initial response from donors, foreign investors and commercial lenders was minimal.

In the mid-1980s, the widespread publicity associated with, and the international sympathy generated by, the famines in Ethiopia and Sudan, massive crop losses in West Africa and the rise in the numbers of refugees and displaced persons in southern Africa raised the profile of the plight of the subcontinent still higher on the international agenda. In response, both official and voluntary aid to SSA rose significantly in 1985. Yet this increase in aid flows was due more to an expansion of disaster and relief efforts rather than of assistance earmarked for medium and long-term development and, in the event, it was not sustained[2]. But even if it had been, the quantities would still have been insufficient to halt the erosion of living standards and reduce the numbers of people living in poverty and squalor. In addition, SSA's need for external financial resources rose because of other adverse trends such as the fall in world commodity prices, failure to resolve the region's growing debt problems and the channelling of resources into defensive and offensive uses as military conflict spread to more countries across the continent.

If the 1980s failed to provide SSA with the external resources adequate to address its massive and growing development problems, what they *did* bring was the most profound change in development policy to have taken place since the independence era of the late 1950s and early 1960s. Twenty-five years of emphasis on long-term development and grand projects and programmes to achieve these distant objectives gave way to serious attempts to solve the short-term macroeconomic problems; 'adjustment' and 'stabilisation' became the buzzwords of the decade as the painful challenge of reducing budget and balance of payments deficits was taken up by a majority of countries[3]. What is more, it was not only the donors and external international agencies which voiced their doubts about past approaches to development; cries of *mea* – or at least *nostra* – *culpa* were heard from many individual African leaders. Long-held tenets of development practice were overturned if not overnight then in a comparatively short period of time: food subsidies were abandoned or markedly reduced as the prices of basic foodstuffs were raised and price regulations reduced; private foreign investment was again welcomed to the continent and an almost obsessive drive to 'privatise' public or semi-public enterprises and institutions was set in train[4].

The dust from this first wave of upheaval is now beginning to settle and it is time to step back and evaluate afresh some fundamental questions both about these recent events and about prospects for Africa's longer-term future. For all the turmoil at the policy level over the past ten years, it would not be too harsh to say that few people or institutions – inside or outside the African continent – are confident that SSA is now set fair on a course of rapid and progressive development. In the words of the World Bank's long-term perspective report (1989: 185): 'The outlook for Africa is potentially devastating . . . there are no quick fixes and no simple blueprints.'[5]

In part this is understandable because the structural adjustment policies of the 1980s were put in place more to attempt to iron out the short-term problems of the immediate crisis than to lay out a detailed blueprint for the longer term. More and more voices have been raised, however, to question even their short-term effectiveness[6]. As the 1980s ended, donor governments and international agencies, such as UNICEF, together even with senior officials in the World Bank and the Managing Director of the IMF, began to express their concern about the efficacy of some of the recent measures taken[7]. Doubts include the over-optimistic time-frame in which distortions in economic structures were to be corrected, the political conse-quences of too rapid execution of policies and the substantial welfare costs and frequently adverse ripple effects on poverty of the programmes being implemented[8].

If doubts have been raised about the efficacy of the short-term measures taken or advo-cated, increasingly pressing questions need to be voiced about the long term. Clearly, it is not possible to 'adjust' *in vacuo*: if adjustment policies are meant to correct distortions so as to improve the chances of longer-term development there has to be some sort of longer-term conceptual framework – however vague – to which the short-term adjustment process relates. While no one (perhaps wisely!) was bold enough in the 1980s to write a blue-print for sustained African development for the 1990s and beyond, a few dominant themes have been emerging – especially in the World Bank's long-term perspective study (1989).

A major concern remains the inadequacy of financial resources required to achieve any sort of sustainable development. In its 1986 report, *Financing Adjustment with Growth in Sub-Saharan Africa, 1986–90*, the World Bank stated that Africa's attempts to help itself would simply fail without the addition of significant amount of new financial resources; for 'low-income Africa' (the poorest 29 countries) the Bank estimated that an additional $2.5 billion would be needed each year from 1986 to 1990, over and above that already committed, if *per capita* incomes were to be any higher than at the start of the 1980s. Two years later, the report of the United Nations Advisory Group on Financial Flows for Africa, *Financing Africa's Recovery*, (The Wass Report) came to the gloomy conclusion that the financing gap for economic recovery in SSA had widened further still (1988: vi):

> On the basis that the African countries implement and persevere with their programmes of structural adjustment, we judge their need for help for the next few years to be $5 billion a year over and above what, in the middle of 1987, they were expected to receive in the rest of the decade. This amount is simply to restore the prospects for development and growth as of the early 1980s, which were already constrained in many countries of the region . . . We believe this assessment to be conservative.

Besides the shortage of funds, another basic policy issue to be highlighted has been agricul-ture, now viewed as the key sector into which available resources should be channelled. This is hardly a remarkable emphasis as over 80% of Africa's adult population is engaged in agriculture – even if carrying out agriculturally-biased policies will entail for many countries of SSA a quite radical shift in resource allocation compared with what occurred in practice during the past quarter century. In some variants, however, and especially in relation to those (few) countries with large populations and small areas of farming land and/or meagre water resources, the emphasis is wider than agriculture and extends to what is termed 'resource-based' development, embracing, for instance and where relevant, mineral, oil, forestry and fishing resources.

When agriculture or, more generally, resource-based development is married to key ele-ments in adjustment programmes then other parts of what is being proposed for the longer-term development strategy for the 1990s begin to take shape. These can best be seen, initially, in relation to reversing a series of what are now widely perceived as key 'negative' policies which have adversely influenced African development since the early 1960s, incorporating, too, the main policy lessons from those developing countries outside Africa which performed exceptionally well in the last 30 years.

Thus, within the framework of resource-based development, what is being suggested for the 1990s and beyond is a type of development concerned more with export-orientation than in the past, responding more to market forces, price signals and price incentives, with a greater role for the private (local and foreign) sector, the retreat and even possible removal of the state from directly productive activities and from much of the service sector together with a less interventionist role for the state overall – all in the context of raising economic effi-ciency and reducing fiscal deficits. In addition, what is being proposed is a form of deve-lopment which gives far greater prominence than in the past to the development of human capital. Finally (as these particular issues have become fashionable), it will be a type of development which addresses the problems of women and which is both ecologically and environmentally sustainable, as made clear in World Bank (1989: 37–88).

THE ROLE AND PLACE OF INDUSTRY

In both the adjustment policies undertaken in the 1980s and the emerging strategies for the 1990s articulated by Western agencies, the place of industry – currently and in the future – is notable by its absence from discussion and policy prescription or by the minor role that it is given. For instance, in its first report on SSA, the World Bank proposed an agriculturally-oriented strategy with 'industry in a supporting role', stressing that 'the pace of industrialisation should not be forced' (1981: 95). In its penultimate report of the decade (World Bank and UNDP, 1989), industry is hardly mentioned at all: in the key chapters on 'Policy Reforms' and 'The Impact of Reforms', discussion of industry is entirely absent.

The World Bank's long term perspective report (1989) would appear to be an exception, suggesting – at least initially – a fresh approach and more prominent role for industry in African development in the 1990s. Not only does this report devote a whole chapter to industry (together with mining and energy) but it suggests that the 'stress on agriculture does not imply a minor role for industry' in the future (1989:39). While its analysis of industry-specific problems[9] are to be heartily welcomed – many coinciding with those highlighted in this book – there is, sadly, no evidence to suggest that these words will be translated in practice into effective, consistent and reoriented policy recommendations to African governments which the Bank is hoping to influence. While the report does indeed refer to interventionist policies to promote industrial expansion, it also emphasises the pre-eminence of the market in future industrial development (ibid.: 9). What is more, in its list of six key strategies for African development in the 1990s (ibid.: 62), the role and place of industry is simply not mentioned. Finally, industrial sector country studies produced by the World Bank in the late 1980s were still dominated by policy advice based on macroeconomic management issues, the overriding importance of market and price signals and the eclipsing of more interventionist strategies of industrial promotion, as highlighted in Chapters 6 and 10 of this book.

There are three reasons why this effective down-playing of industry in both short-term adjustment policies and in discussion of longer-term development in Africa is surprising. First, industry and industrial development were given pride of place in almost all former long-term strategies drawn up by individual countries, often with the advice and consultation of the international agencies. Few argued in 1968 with Ewing who opened his book *Industry in Africa* with the words, 'The main thesis of this book is that industry is the main lever of African development' (1968: xiii). But if practice is the hallmark of acceptance, few advisers, governments and institutions outside Africa would appear to agree with Ewing today. Second, and relatedly, the pre-eminence (or bias) given to industry in the development process did not arise from the whim of either African scholars or the newly independent governments: it was rooted in mainstream analyses and theoretical insights of the development literature and has persisted to the present day. Finally, the 1980s have witnessed no lessening of the emphasis placed on the role of industry in debates and strategies for long-term development *within* Africa. Indeed, the 1980s have been termed the 'Industrial Decade for Africa'. In fact it is no exaggeration to argue that over the past decade, in parallel with a process of de-industrialisation at work in a number of African countries, industry appears to have been given an even more prominent role in consensus policy statements emanating from African leaders. Not only have these continued to reaffirm in general terms the importance of industry but the two key initiatives proposed by African leaders in the 1980s – *The Lagos Plan of Action for the Economic Development of Africa, 1980–2000* and *A Programme for the Industrial Development Decade for Africa* – have both highlighted its central place in Africa's long-term development[10].

The strong contrasts between the emphasis given to the role of industry within Africa by African governments and their advisers, its virtual absence in policy debate emanating from outside Africa[11], and the implicit downgrading of industry in structural adjustment programmes, all raise a series of questions for African development for the 1990s.

Are these differing views merely differences in emphasis or do they represent differences of substance? If the latter, is this a reflection of new theoretical insights into the process of development? If not, then the question arises whether the downgrading of the role of industry, apparent in so much contemporary policy discussion, might leave Africa *more* underdeveloped and backward at the end of the 1990s than if an alternative pro-industry strategy were to be adopted.

Although the problems of African development have attracted increasing attention among donors it is surprising that these questions hardly appear to have been addressed in any depth. The most recent book in English on industry in SSA, *Industry and Accumulation in Africa*, was published in 1982 utilising data that is now 10 to 15 years old. While studies of industry in a number of countries have been produced in the last few years, there has been no recent attempt to provide a perspective across the sub-continent and little examination of the effects of, and consequences for industry of, structural adjustment programmes in Africa[12].

This raises the possibility that the lack of any firm conclusions about the role and place of industry in African development has been due to the absence of detailed information on recent cross-continent industrial performance and on the realistic options open for the 1990s, given the range of constraints under which *any* alternative scenarios will need to be placed – such as shortages of foreign exchange, probable continued decline in and certain volatility of commodity prices, infrastructural and especially transport difficulties and less than adequate inflows of official development assistance (oda) and private foreign investment. Support for such a view comes, for instance, from Killick who concluded a 20 year survey of African industry from 1960 to 1980 with the words (1982: 51):

> . . . it may be that the only firm conclusion to be drawn from this study is that the data base is to poor for any firm generalisations at all, so that governments have to form policy in a state of ignorance.

Certainly the provision of up-to-date information on industrial performance and the parameters around which the choice of future paths must needs be drawn should help to clarify controversies between those within Africa who have continued to maintain the primacy of industry in development and the external sceptics who have downgraded its role.

The present book is an attempt to fill this important gap in the literature on recent African development and future prospects for the region by providing in-depth analyses of manufacturing industry in seven key countries of sub-Saharan Africa.

INDUSTRY AND MANUFACTURING INDUSTRY – A QUESTION OF SEMANTICS?

Observant readers will have noticed that the title of this book uses the word manufacturing and not industry, yet the preceding section of this chapter ended by stating that the book attempts to provide an in-depth analysis not of the industrialisation process but of manufacturing industry in SSA. It is thus time to ask whether the words 'manufacturing' and 'industry' are interchangeable or whether they refer to different things and, if so, whether these differences matter.

Most recent publications on Africa which use the terms 'industry' or 'industrialisation' have usually been discussions either exclusively or predominantly of the *manufacturing* sector of various SSA economies[13]. Similarly, the United Nations Industrial Development Organization (UNIDO) applies almost all its energies to analysing aspects of the manufacturing sector – indeed its *Handbook of Industrial Statistics* is devoted exclusively to statistics of manufacturing: manufacturing value added, manufacturing production, employment and trade. All this would not much matter if 'industry' and 'manufacturing' *were* synonymous. Strictly speaking, however, they are not.

According to the widely used United Nations *Systems of National Accounts (SNA)* series F. No. 2, revision 3, *industry* embraces extractive mining, construction, electricity, water and gas as well as the more narrowly-focused sector, *manufacturing*. To the extent that the non-manufacturing parts of industry make only a small contribution to GDP, manufacturing could serve as a good proxy for industry as a whole. Regrettably, however, this is neither universally true nor true for either SSA as a whole or for many of the key (larger) countries of the sub-continent. Countries which have large mineral or oil processing facilities and smaller manufacturing industries tend to show a wide divergence between share of GDP arising from industry and that arising from manufacturing. An illustration of the usually very marked differences between the broad category 'industry' and the narrower one 'manufacturing' is shown in Table 1.1.

In relation to the SSA region in particular, not only are the relative contributions of manufacturing and industry to GDP very different, but the gap between the two has widened over the past two decades. In 1965, the share of manufacturing in GDP for SSA was 9% while that of industry was 19% (World Bank 1988: 227).

The case-studies in this book are concerned almost exclusively with the evolution, performance and potential of the manufacturing part of industry, where manufacturing is defined

Table 1.1 *Origin of GDP accounted for by industry and manufacturing, 1986*

	Industry as % of GDP	Manufacturing as % of GDP
Low-income economies	35	24
Lower middle-income	30	22
Upper middle-income	40	25
Sub-Saharan Africa	25	10
of which:		
Zambia	48	20
Sierra Leone	22	4
Zimbabwe	46	30
Nigeria	29	8
Botswana	58	6
Congo	54	6

Source: World Bank, *World Development Report 1988*, Table 3.

as the mechanical or chemical transformation of inorganic or organic substances into new products whether the work is performed by power-driven machines or by hand, whether it is done in a factory or in the workers' home and whether the products are sold wholesale or retail[14]. Following the UN *International Standard Industrial Classification of All Economic Activities (ISIC)*, and unless otherwise specified, the manufacturing sector will be sub-divided thus: food and agriculture, division 31; textiles and clothing, division 32; machinery and transport equipment, major groups 382–4; chemicals, major groups 351 and 352; wood and related products, division 33; paper and related products, division 34; petroleum and related products, major groups 353–6; basic metals and mineral products, divisions 36 and 37; fabricated metal products, major groups 381 and 385 and all other industries, major group 390. Where the term 'industry' refers to a classification wider than manufacturing, reference to this will normally be made.

THE STRUCTURE OF THE BOOK

The bulk of the book (Part II) is devoted to an examination of the role and place of manufacturing in seven countries: Botswana, Cameroon, Côte d'Ivoire, Kenya, Nigeria, Zambia and Zimbabwe. Although the case-studies vary in length, each is divided into two sections. The first examines the performance of the manufacturing sector over the past 15 to 20 years (or in some cases over an even longer period) in the context of the overall development of the respective countries. This is followed by a discussion of the prospects and options which exist for the sector into the 1990s, not so much in relation to the goals and objectives commonly outlined in documents such as national development plans – however desirable it may be to achieve these – but in the context of the macroeconomic constraints facing each country.

How does one go about selecting a group of countries within the SSA region for a study such as the present one? Certainly the countries which have been chosen are both sufficiently diverse and also sufficiently important in terms of their contribution to the whole SSA region as (potentially at least) to form the basis for important insights to be drawn. Thus, the seven countries combined account for some 40% of the total population and for 60% of the total GDP of the region[15]. In addition they include both English- and French-speaking countries, big and small economies, those characterised by substantial differences in the contribution of agriculture, different degrees of urbanisation and different patterns of growth. In relation to manufacturing in particular, they include those in which development has occurred in the context of widespread controls and interventionist policies and those in which the policy context has been far more open and market-oriented.

It would, however, be a mistake to draw the conclusion that they therefore in some way 'represent' the general situation of manufacturing in SSA and that common features from them can be readily applied to the other 40 or so countries of the sub-continent. In part this is because one of the conclusions emanating from the case-studies is that the pattern of manufacturing development has differed greatly from country to country and that particular circumstances have had a significant impact in the evolution of the sector in each of them. While such a conclusion does not mean that no generalisations can be made across the continent, it does suggest that one needs to be particularly wary of detailed policy prescriptions across the entire sub-continent or, perhaps more importantly, of belief that the conclusions drawn from this (or any other group of countries in SSA) can be applied willy-nilly to countries which have not been the subject of analysis.

More substantially, however, a warning light needs to be displayed for those wishing to use these particular case-studies as a means of understanding the process of industrialisation in other African countries. This is for the simple reason that the choice of the majority of countries was deliberately biased towards *'successful'* manufacturing development. One of the most important criteria for country selection was to pick countries in which significant manufacturing capacity exists and/or where, over the past 25 years, expansion and progress *have* occurred – in the overall context of a continent which, in aggregate, has singularly failed to industrialise. Thus, out of 10 countries in SSA with a ratio of Manufacturing Value Added (MVA) to GDP of over 12% in 1986, five are included in the current case-studies. Together, the seven selected account for 60% of the total MVA of the 47 countries of SSA (40% if Nigeria is excluded)[16].

Of course, to group these countries together as 'successful' is not meant to imply either that the process of industrialisation has been without blemish or that problems have not arisen which could/might impede the continuation of expansion and/or deepening of the manufacturing sector. Indeed in some cases, for instance Côte d'Ivoire, it is argued that the widely-held perception of industrial success is largely misplaced. Nonetheless, as will be elaborated in Part II, almost all of the seven countries (with the partial exception of Zambia) have achieved industrial expansion on a par with the best in the sub-region. Past success, however, is by no means a guarantee of success in the future. Indeed, another conclusion is that unless policies are altered, in some cases quite dramatically, it is likely that the successes which have been achieved will be at risk in almost all the countries.

On the other hand, cautioning against misuse of the data and country-specific analysis presented in this book should not be taken to imply that the data presented will be of little use beyond the countries examined. On the contrary, one of the reasons for embarking upon this particular exercise was to help in understanding better the process of development in the SSA region as a whole.

More specifically, it is to be hoped that the evidence provided will help to throw light on two important questions for African development. First and rather negatively, in isolating those factors which have led to expansion of the manufacturing sectors in the selected countries, we should be better able to understand why the majority of African countries have failed to set in motion a process of sustained industrialisation. Second, by analysing in some detail the evolution of manufacturing in these (mostly) 'vanguard' countries, together with their prospects for further expansion into the 1990s, we should be in a better position to appraise the extent to which, in the context of the constraints facing African development as the 1990s begin, the route to development which provides a more prominent role for industrialisation is a realistic strategy to be followed.

While each case-study describes the evolution of the manufacturing sector, a major purpose of the research has been to attempt to increase understanding of the constraints and opportunities impeding and stimulating manufacturing and to isolate features common or unique to these countries. In striving to achieve these objectives, there has been a trade-off between working within a common framework of analysis across countries, by examining similar variables in each, and looking at each country separately and attempting to isolate the common and distinct features separately. The problem with the first approach is that important causes of industrial success or failure may be left out or insufficiently analysed, the problem with the second is that the results would tend all the more to be influenced by subjective judgement.

In practice, and as far as data and individual time commitments permitted, this dilemma was resolved by approaching the case-studies within the framework of a loose common perspective: the evolution of and future prospects for the expansion and deepening of the manufacturing sector have been evaluated within the context of each country's broad macroeconomic framework. Some of the more specific issues addressed include the following: identifying the links (or lack of them) between manufacturing and other sectors of the economy, particularly those with agriculture; examining the degree of export-orientation of the manufacturing sector and the causes of failures to expand manufactured exports; and, finally, isolating those aspects of particular importance to or constraints inhibiting manufacturing expansion in each country.

The data available for Botswana, Kenya and Zimbabwe permitted time series 'sources of growth' analysis to be carried out specifically for this research, while 'sources of growth' analysis under a different recent research project in Nigeria was also utilised (see Ohiorhenuan, 1988). This is probably the first time that this particular mode of analysis has been used in a cross-country study of African manufacturing, although it has been used in other parts of the developing world[17]. Finally, the comparative nature of the study has benefited from the fact that for six out of the seven countries individual researchers each analysed the manufacturing experience of two of them, while both the French-speaking countries were examined by researchers who also worked on two of the English-speaking countries[18].

In this first part of the book the different themes of past industrialisation and prospects for the future from the case-studies are brought together in Chapter 3. The purpose here is not so much to summarise the conclusions of the individual case-studies but rather to reflect on what the combined evidence suggests about the process of industrialisation up to the late 1980s and the prospects for further industrialisation in the 1990s and the appropriateness of adopting different policies. Before this, Chapter 2 gives a more general introduction to the case-study material by providing an overview of manufacturing, initially by comparing the performance of SSA with other regions of the developing world and then by examining in greater detail the statistical trends of the manufacturing performance of all countries within sub-Saharan Africa.

Notes

1. As Kitchen wrote in late 1988 (Kitchen, 1988): 'The next US administration cannot ignore the bleak prospects facing many African countries without turning its back on the values most Americans hold dear.'
2. Net disbursements of official aid from all sources to SSA at 1986 prices and exchange rates was as follows (OECD, 1988: 202):

Year	$m.
1983	9,788
1984	10,452
1985	11,851
1986	11,515
1987	11,096.

3. The World Bank's first 1989 report on the economic plight of the continent was called *Africa's Adjustment and Growth in The 1980s*.
4. See Page and Riddell (1988) for more detail on the issues of foreign investment and privatisation.
5. This final World Bank report on SSA for the 1980s, *Sub-Saharan Africa. From Crisis to Sustainable Growth* acknowledges both that the economic crisis is continuing and that the obstacles to raising growth levels are formidable. It calls (p. 62) for 'bold action'.
6. See, for instance, *IDS Bulletin*, Vol. 19, No. 1, 1988 for an assessment and review of structural adjustment policies in Africa and particularly the editorial by Colclough and Green entitled 'Do Stabilisation Policies Stabilise?' For both a more general and analytically tight critique of the Bank and Fund's approaches to stabilisation see Taylor (1988b).
7. See for instance World Bank (1989: 37) for comments on the need for a new approach.
8. As Colclough and Green write (1988: 1):

   Critical questions include the following: Does the combination of classical IMF macroeconomic demand management plus liberalisation lead to stabilisation? If so, does it do so at the price of frustrating adjustment and renewed growth? Are conventional ways of adjusting macroeconomic balances remotely good enough if other human imbalances – such as high infant mortality, malnutrition, lack of access to basic health and education services and absolute poverty – become more extended as a result? Or is it that 'stabilisation with an inhuman face' must be judged to be professionally (as well as humanly) irresponsible? . . .
   The seven case studies in this volume (Algeria, Ghana, Madagascar, Malawi, Sierra Leone, Togo, Zambia) . . . cannot claim to answer these questions definitively. They do, however, pose them sharply; they also throw light on the probable range of answers and cast grave doubt on claims that – in any general sense – 'stabilisation is working.'

9. These include shortages of foreign exchange, poor maintenance, lack of skills, inappropriate technological transfer and low levels of domestic demand for manufactured products.
10. Although these two documents came out at the start of the 1980s they have been reconfirmed in subsequent policy statements through to the end of the decade (see for instance UNIDO, 1986).

11. One, of course, excludes from this generalisation those institutions which either work for or are sympathetic to the African perspective such as UNIDO in Vienna or, in Britain, the Institute for African Alternatives.

12. It might be argued that the 1984 World Bank Technical Paper No. 25 (Steel and Evans 1984) is an exception. This, however, only uses data up to 1980 and does not explicitly address the problems of the 1980s. In a brief but useful paper, Hawkins (in Berg and Whitaker, 1986) begins to cover some of the issues – even if he terms the designation of the 1980s as the Industrial Decade for Africa 'unfortunate' (1986: 304). A recent French book which discusses industrialisation in three African countries in the context of a wider study is that edited by de Bandt and Hugon (1988). The book *Industrial Adjustment in Sub-Saharan Africa*, edited by Meier and Carroll and produced in 1987 by the Economic Development Institute of the World Bank (published by Oxford University Press in 1989) consists of extracts of papers related (more or less closely) to the theme of African industrialisation from other sources rather than providing a fresh analysis of the issues.

13. For instance, a 1986 publication with the title *African Industrialization* on the front cover turns out to be almost entirely about the manufacturing sector in Tanzania! (Barker et al.: 1986.)

It is important to make clear whether one is discussing the whole of the continent (Africa) or a part of it, such as the sub-Saharan region. In practice there is often much confusion over this point as a number of recent, and particularly more popular, texts which use the term 'Africa' are in fact concerned solely with countries of sub-Saharan Africa – a region which usually excludes North Africa (Algeria, Egypt, Libya, Morocco, Sudan and Tunisia). In contrast, UN organisations, in particular, refer to *all* the countries of the continent when they use the term 'Africa'. Thus the Industrial Decade for Africa refers to the *whole* continent and not just to those countries south of the Sahara. For further discussion of geographical groupings within Africa see Chapter 2, note 2.

As the sub-title of this book indicates, the present study's geographical coverage embraces seven countries selected exclusively from the sub-Saharan region. Following UN practice, when the term Africa is used it refers to the whole continent, sub-Saharan Africa to those countries of Africa excluding the northern six and also excluding South Africa.

14. See *International Standard Classification of all Economic Activities*, Department of Economic and Social Affairs, Statistical Office of the United Nations, New York, 1968, Statistical Papers Series M. No. 4, Rev. 2.

15. Excluding Nigeria, the six countries account for 18% of the (non-Nigerian) population of SSA and for 32% of the respective GDP. Both sets of figures exclude South Africa. They are taken from World Bank statistics.

16. World Bank data base. The importance of referencing the particular source of statistical data will be explained in Chapter 2.

17. 'Sources of growth' analysis has been used in *individual* industry sector studies carried out by the World Bank. This material is, however, neither widely available nor, because the Bank has not provided a detailed description of the methodology used or of the raw data utilised, is it entirely clear whether the same identical approach has been used from country to country. In addition, the 'sources of growth' analyses undertaken specifically for this study cover a longer time period than that reproduced in the relevant World Bank reports.

18. As the chapter headings of Part II reveal, Botswana and Kenya were analysed by Lewis and Sharpley, Cameroon and Zambia by Karmiloff and Côte d'Ivoire and Zimbabwe by myself.

PART I

The Role & Place
of Manufacturing
in African Development

2 Overview

Manufacturing Development in Sub-Saharan Africa

Warnings about statistical inadequacies

Perhaps the best way to sketch the trends in manufacturing both between different regions of the developing world and within sub-Saharan Africa (SSA) is to take a Cook's tour of the appropriate indicators of performance. It is necessary at the outset, however, to erect 'warning signs' around the discussion because of the woeful inaccuracy and/or unreliability of much of the data available for comparisons, most notably those published by the international agencies. While the figures given in this chapter certainly provide an indication of the magnitude of the relative manufacturing performance of SSA and other parts of the world and trends within the sub-continent, many of them remain little more than crude estimates.

Perhaps the most fundamental problem with the available SSA data is that these are widely known to be inaccurate but the degree of inaccuracy cannot easily be judged – itself a sign of the underdevelopment of the region. Little can be done in a book of this nature to rectify this problem except to state at the outset that it throws considerable doubt on *all* the aggregate data used subsequently! Difficulties are exacerbated, however, because the main time-series data collected and analysed by different international organisations, such as the United Nations, the World Bank, the UN Industrial Development Organisation (UNIDO), the Economic Commission for Africa (ECA), the International Monetary Fund (IMF) and the UN Conference on Trade and Development (UNCTAD), not only use different sources on which to base their aggregate figures but they also classify the region of sub-Saharan Africa differently[1]. As a result it will be necessary to go through the rather tedious process of referencing the various sources for the data given; one also needs to caution against the practice of drawing firm (policy) conclusions from data obtained from different sources or even from the same sources but over different time periods.

More specific data problems arise in relation to the derivation of statistics for the manufacturing sector. One difficulty relates to the definition of manufacturing and, in particular, to the sometimes hazy distinctions between manufacturing and mineral and agricultural processing[2]. Relatedly, the definition of what constitutes manufactured exports also varies significantly between different international and national organisations – a point illustrated by the data reproduced in Table 2.A5. Of major importance, too, all the published SSA data comparisons are eventually based on official statistics emanating from the different countries. For manufacturing industry this means that the data will refer almost exclusively to *formal* sector industries (but by no means all of these) and tend to give a disproportionate view of the range, scale and number of small-scale manufacturing operations[3]. *Informal* activities are omitted, even though in many countries – such as Nigeria and Kenya of the case-studies considered here – it is apparent that a significant proportion of manufacturing activity takes place within the informal sector (see, for instance, Liedholm and Mead,1987). In Uganda, recent estimates suggest that in the mid-1980s over 70% of manufacturing value added originated in small-scale industrial operations, most within the informal sector.

SSA manufacturing performance in the international context

An initial 'way in' to an examination of manufacturing in sub-Saharan Africa is to compare the aggregate performance of the sub-continent with that of other parts of the developing world. This reveals both the low level of manufacturing development reached and (at least in reference to some indicators) a relative deterioration in the performance of SSA especially in the period since 1970. To the extent that the growth of the manufacturing sector can be taken to be a key indicator of overall development performance – an issue to be discussed more fully in Chapter 3 – not only is SSA the least developed region but over the past 30 years the 'development gap' has widened between it and the rest of the developing world.

TRENDS IN GDP AND MVA

With these introductory words of caution the ground is – somewhat roughly – prepared for a discussion of the aggregate data trends which are available.

In 1985, the population of SSA (418 m.) accounted for 9.5% of world population and 11.4% of the population of the developing world[4]. Yet the gross domestic product (GDP) of the countries of SSA came to only 1.3% of global GDP and only 7% of the GDP of the developing countries. While this disproportionate level of overall development suggests that a smaller share of global manufacturing would be likely to be a characteristic of SSA, the region's level of manufacturing is even lower in comparison with other regions of the world than its smaller GDP *per capita* levels would suggest.

An initial indicator of this is the share of manufacturing in GDP. In 1986 for the countries of SSA combined, manufacturing contributed only 10% to the sub-continent's GDP compared with over 30% for industrial market economies and nearly 30% for all developing countries: 24% for all low-income and 22% for all middle-income developing countries[5]. Not surprisingly therefore, given its lower level of overall development, in that year SSA contributed only 0.76% to world Manufacturing Value Added (MVA)[6] and 3.8% to the total MVA of the developing economies. Whereas GDP *per capita* in SSA was $384 in 1985, compared with $550 in all developing countries and $2,900 globally – ratios, respectively, of 1 to 1.4 and 1 to 7.6 – MVA *per capita* in SSA stood at $45 compared with $137 in all developing economies and $2,730 in industrial market countries, giving ratios, respectively, of 1 to 3.0 and 1 to 60.0.

In 1985, the total MVA of all the countries of the SSA region amounted to just over $19 bn. This was only just over half the MVA of India and less than one-third of the MVA of Brazil. Excluding Nigeria, the MVA of the remaining SSA countries came to just under $12 bn, similar to that of Turkey, Finland or Indonesia (World Bank, 1988: 236–7).

If SSA's contribution to manufacturing value added is considered pitifully low, its performance in relation to manufactured exports is even worse. In 1986, SSA contributed just

Figure 2.1 *Manufacturing Value Added, $ bn*
Industralised and Developing Countries

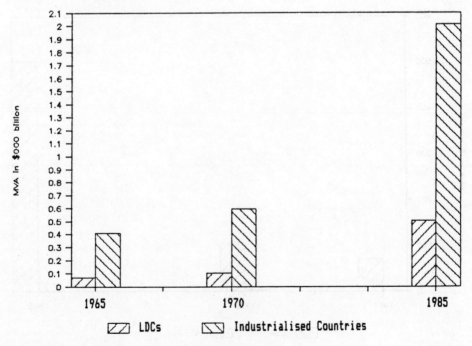

Source: World Bank, *World Development Report*, 1987 and 1988, Tables 3 and 8.

0.23% of world exports in manufactures and only 1.5% of total manufacturing exports from all developing economies. Manufacturing exports *per capita* from SSA in 1986 came to a mere $8 compared with $57 from all developing economies and $1,552 from industrial market countries – ratios, respectively, of 1 to 7.1 and 1 to 194.

This brief overview of some recent key indicators of manufacturing performance clearly throws some light on the extremely small contribution SSA plays in world manufacturing production and exports, but its static nature precludes all but the crudest comparisons. More revealing is an analysis of longer-term trends because this shows the changing relative position of SSA in the world economy. Four sets of indicators will be examined: changes in value added and production structure, trade in manufactures and the relationship between manufactured output and manufactured exports.

Figures 2.1 and 2.2 show the trends in MVA by different sub-groups from the mid-1960s to the mid-1980s. Figure 2.1 reveals that while MVA from the industrialised world has increased substantially in absolute terms over the period, the *rate* of expansion of MVA from developing countries has been even more rapid. As a result, whereas in 1965 the developing economies accounted for 13% of global MVA, by the mid-1980s their share had risen to 20%[7].

In sharp contrast, Figure 2.2 shows that MVA (at current prices) has risen substantially in the developing world as a whole compared with only a small rise for the SSA region. Relatedly, manufacturing in SSA plays no greater part in overall development today than it did in 1965: between 1965 and 1986, the ratio of MVA to GDP for SSA has remained at 10%, while it has risen from 20 to about 30% for all developing countries[8].

When trends at fixed rather than current prices are examined, the differences are even more striking. Thus, *per capita* MVA from a sample of 21 countries of SSA[9] rose from $27 in 1970 (at 1980 prices) to $53 in 1984, a rise of only $1.70 a year. This compares, for example, with a rise from $264 in 1970 to $337 in 1984 (at 1984 prices) for the countries of Latin America, a rise of $5 a year[10].

Figure 2.2 *Manufacturing Value Added, $ bn*
All LDCs and Sub-Saharan Africa

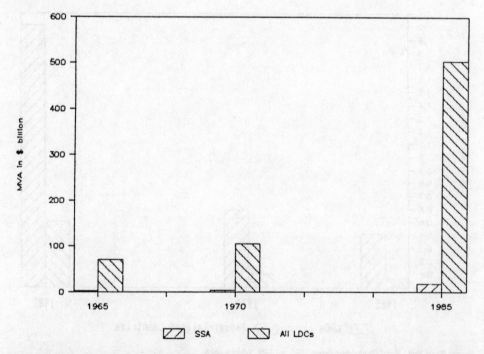

Source: World Bank, *World Development Report,* 1987 and 1988.

While it is clear from Figure 2.2 that the absolute gap between SSA and the rest of the developing world has certainly increased over the past 20 years, has the relative gap also widened? This is certainly a widely-held view. A more cautious answer, however, is probably necessary because of the unreliability of the data from which to draw such a conclusion. For what they are worth, the data from Figures 2.1 and 2.2 combined appear to suggest that the *share* of SSA's MVA in both developing country and global MVA has remained at much the same – very low – level over this entire period: about 3.5% of the former and about 0.6% of the latter[11].

Long-term trends in annual growth rates of MVA by region and grouping of developing countries tend also to confirm the relatively poor SSA performance, especially in the post-1970 period, and most strikingly in the 1980s as Table 2.1 reveals. Nonetheless, as the top part of the table suggests, in the 1960s, the growth rate for SSA appeared to be greater than the average for all developing economies and this spurt led to a slightly higher than average performance for SSA over the entire period 1965–80. It appeared to be in the 1970s that the performance of SSA began to lag behind other regions (except uniquely the Indian subcontinent). Then, finally, in the 1980s, SSA again lagged behind all other developing regions – except for Latin America – with, in this latter period, the Indian subcontinent experiencing rapid growth rates[12].

Another notable feature derived from Table 2.1 is that the performance of the middle-income SSA countries appears to have been better than average for both the 1960s and the 1970s; it was only in the 1980s that high growth rates among this group of countries were not sustained.

Table 2.1 *Annual growth rates of MVA by developing country grouping*

Region/Area	1960–70	1970–80	1965–80	1980–86
Low-income – SSA	8.6	1.1		
Low-income – All	6.3	3.7	4.8[c]	4.8[c]
Middle-income – SSA	8.2	7.1		
Middle-income – All	6.8	6.4	8.2	2.5
All SSA	8.3	4.9	8.5	0.3
All developing countries[b]		6.25	8.0	5.9[a]
Developing Africa		4.5		2.1
Latin America		5.53		1.1
North Africa		5.28		6.6
West Asia		7.12		6.9
Indian subcontinent		2.20		5.1
South-east Asia		11.95		7.7

Source: World Bank, *World Development Reports*, 1986–1988, Tables 1–3, UNIDO, *Industry and Development Global Report 1987*, pp. 6, 7, 8 and 69 and Steel and Evans (1984:82).

Notes: [a] For this and all remaining figures in this column the 1986 figures are UNIDO estimates.
[b] These and all subsequent figures are from the UNIDO source.
[c] These figures exclude India and China. With India and China they are 7.6 and 11.2 respectively.

It is necessary, however, to caution against drawing anything but tentative conclusions from these trend figures and to point out that some of the data appear strikingly contradictory. For instance, Table 2.1 shows that according to the World Bank the average annual growth rate of MVA among SSA countries in the period 1980–86 was 0.3% a year, whereas UNIDO data for developing Africa give a figure of 2.1% – seven times higher than the World Bank's estimates[13]!

Nonetheless, the (apparently) better performance of the middle-income SSA countries and the relatively poorer performance of the low-income countries of the subcontinent are confirmed by analysis of the changes in the composition of MVA between SSA and Asian countries. As Table 2.2 shows, low-income African countries have a far greater concentration of

Table 2.2 *Percentage composition of MVA by income groups in Africa and Asia*

	Low-income Africa		Low-income Asia		Middle-income Africa		Middle-income Asia		World	
	1973	1984	1973	1984	1973	1984	1973	1984	1973	1984
1. Food, beverages & tobacco	37.7	35.0	12.5	12.7	32.6	27.5	20.3	12.3	12.4	11.2
2. Textiles, apparel & leather	22.3	15.9	24.2	14.7	13.2	9.9	22.6	28.0	10.2	8.4
3. Wood and wood products	5.9	3.4	2.2	2.0	3.7	6.1	4.1	1.4	4.1	3.2
4. Paper and paper products	4.9	5.0	4.4	3.5	4.8	6.5	5.0	4.6	6.3	8.1
5. Chemicals, petroleum & prod.	11.7	28.5	14.5	19.7	16.2	14.2	18.9	14.4	14.0	17.7
6. Non-metallic mineral products	4.1	2.8	4.7	4.9	4.5	5.3	4.2	2.2	5.3	4.7
7. Basic metals	2.9	1.5	9.5	17.0	11.8	5.2	5.0	4.9	8.7	8.1
8. Metal prod. machinery & equip.,	9.8	7.5	24.8	22.8	12.5	21.7	18.3	29.9	37.1	38.9
9. Other manufactures	0.6	0.3	3.2	2.6	0.8	3.5	1.6	2.2	1.8	1.8
Total manufacturing	100.0	100.0	100.0	100.0	100.0	100.0	100.0	100.0	100.0	100.0
Traditional industries (1–3)	65.9	54.3	38.9	29.4	49.5	43.5	47.0	41.7	26.7	22.8
Non-traditional industries (4–9)	34.1	45.7	61.1	70.6	50.5	56.5	53.0	58.3	73.3	77.2
Consumer goods industries (1,2,9)	60.6	51.2	39.9	30.0	46.6	40.9	44.5	42.5	24.4	21.4
Intermediate goods industries (3–7)	29.6	41.3	35.3	47.1	40.9	37.4	37.2	27.6	38.5	39.7
Capital goods industries (8)	9.8	7.5	24.8	22.8	12.5	21.7	18.3	29.9	37.1	38.9

Source: Lall (1987:17) from World Bank data base.

production in traditional/consumer goods production than their Asian equivalents, whereas in the middle-income grouping the performance of SSA appears in a number of respects to have been better in the 1973–84 period. The dominance of the food industry, however, appears to be a feature across both groups of countries in SSA[14].

TRENDS IN EXPORTS
Moving from production data to export trends, there seems to be more consistent evidence to show not only the poor performance of the SSA region but also a serious deterioration in the relative position of the subcontinent. Using UNCTAD trade data, the overall contribution of the SSA countries to total world trade has fallen steadily from about 2.6% in 1960 to about 1.6% in 1985[15]. In relation to total exports from developing countries, however, SSA's contribution has fallen even more rapidly over time: from 14% in 1960, to 9% in 1980 and to a low of 7% by 1985. The details are given in Appendix Table 2.A2.

Manufacturing exports from SSA have performed even more poorly than is apparent from the picture of aggregate exports. This is confirmed by both World Bank and United Nations data – even if the two sets of figures differ markedly in relation to the totals for SSA. According to 1988 World Bank data (from the *World Development Report 1988*: 248–9), while the ratio of manufactured exports from developing economies to world manufactured exports rose from 8.4% to 15.6% over the period 1965–86, the ratio of manufactured exports from SSA to manufactured exports from all developing countries fell from 4.6 to 1.5%; similarly, the ratio of manufactured exports from SSA to world manufactured exports fell from 0.38 to 0.23% over the same period.

Of particular additional interest is that the UNCTAD data[16] suggest that in the first half of the 1960s, although the absolute gap in manufactured exports between SSA and other regions of the world widened significantly[17], manufactured exports from SSA appeared both to maintain their share of world manufactured exports and of manufactured exports from all developing economies. In addition, the ratio of manufactured to total exports within SSA appeared to rise during the 1960s. Thereafter, however, these positive trends were dramatically reversed as SSA's manufactured exports fell as a share of world manufactured exports, of total manufactured exports from developing economies and of total SSA exports. The UNCTAD data reveal a far more severe relative fall in the position of SSA than do the World Bank figures[18]. Thus according to UNCTAD, in 1960 African manufactured exports accounted for 0.36% of world manufactured exports and 9.3% of total manufactured exports from developing countries, but by 1984 these ratios had fallen to 0.05 and 0.39% respectively. The distinctive trends are shown well in Figure 2.3, the data from which this picture is derived being reproduced as Appendix Table 2.A3.

Figure 2.3 *LDC and SSA manufactured exports*
Ratios, 1965 to 1984

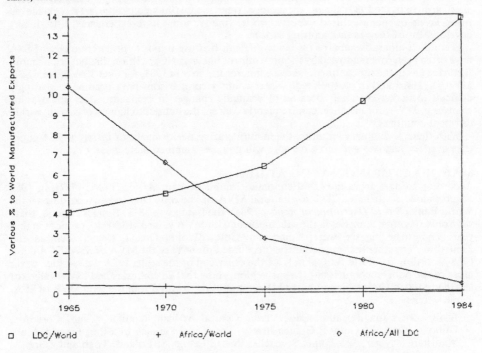

Source: Appendix Table 2.A3.

Finally, available data on trends in the ratio of manufactured exports to manufactured output in the 1970s also suggest a less dynamic performance for SSA countries in contrast to Asian countries especially. Whereas the ratio of manufactured exports to manufactured output rose from 8.1 to 10.3% for countries in the Indian subcontinent and from 10.4 to 25.8% for those of South and South-East Asia, for SSA the ratio fell from 6.1 to 5%[19].

In general, then, and in spite of the caution which must always go with examining the available comparative data, there seems to be little doubt not only that the level of manufacturing development in SSA is the lowest in the developing world but that, combining the main indicators of performance, the gap between SSA and the rest of the world appears to have widened considerably, especially in recent years.

Manufacturing within Sub-Saharan Africa

We now move from comparisons of manufacturing performance with other parts of the world to focus explicitly on the evolution and status of manufacturing among the different countries of SSA. Again we need to begin with a warning. If 'warning signs' had to be raised around the previous discussion, 'danger signs' need to be erected around the present one, such are the dubious nature of the data available and also the often substantial differences in the same indicators provided by the leading international agencies. Indeed, it is to be hoped that this particular section of the book will not only give an initial insight into the status and evolution of manufacturing in the SSA region but will also instil a healthy scepticism into all those who may be tempted to draw firm conclusions from the data published by the international agencies on the economic performance of sub-Saharan Africa. Thus this part of our Cook's tour might be better termed a statistical mystery tour!

Besides cautioning about data inaccuracy, three particular initial comments need to be made. First, the evolution of manufacturing within SSA has been extremely varied, making it very difficult – probably impossible – to make reliable generalisations applicable to all countries of the region. Some countries have had manufacturing growth rates as high as any in the world and over substantial periods of time, some have suffered severe de-industrialisation, a few have experienced quite considerable deepening of manufacturing[20], some have experienced growth in the 1980s against the regional trend, some (the small minority) have achieved rising levels of manufactured exports, while, finally, some have experienced little if any development of their manufacturing sectors.

Second, comparative analysis is made difficult because trends in other countries of SSA have often been overshadowed by the pre-eminent but changing position that Nigerian manufacturing has in the subcontinent (accounting, for instance in 1983, for over 30% of total SSA MVA[21]). Third and in part relatedly, inter-country comparisons have become increasingly difficult to make, especially because of dramatic changes in exchange rates: dollar value changes in MVA, for instance, can frequently conceal the domestic changes occurring within different countries.

With these preliminary remarks, the manufacturing performance of different SSA countries over the last two and more decades will now be examined more closely.

MANUFACTURING VALUE ADDED

According to data from the UN Economic Commission for Africa (ECA: 1987), in 1985 Nigeria alone contributed 28% to the total MVA of the SSA countries. According to the World Bank (*World Development Report 1988*), the figure was 38%. Besides Nigeria, there were only six other countries in the subcontinent with MVA valued at $500 m. or more in that year. These (the big six) were: Cameroon, Côte d'Ivoire, Ghana, Kenya, Zambia and Zimbabwe. Together the seven countries accounted for 66% of the MVA of SSA (ECA data; 61% according to World Bank data). At the other end of the scale, ECA data, which cover more of the poorest countries of the sub-region, show that 23 countries had MVA values of less than $100 in 1985, their combined MVA amounting to only 7% of the total MVA of SSA. These were[22]:

Benin, Botswana, Burundi, Cape Verde, Central African Republic, Chad, Comoros, Djibouti, Gambia, Guinea, Guinea Bissau, Equatorial Guinea, Lesotho, Liberia, Mali, Mauritania, Niger, Sao Tomé, Seychelles, Sierra Leone, Swaziland, Togo and Zaire.

The remaining 15 countries achieved value added in manufacturing in the range of $100 m. to $500 m. in 1985, amounting, in aggregate, to 28% of the total MVA of SSA, almost exactly the same amount of value added as that of Nigeria (on ECA not World Bank estimates). These 15 countries were the following:

Angola, Burkina Faso, Congo, Ethiopia, Gabon, Madagascar, Malawi, Mauritius, Mozambique, Rwanda, Senegal, Somalia, Sudan, Uganda, and Tanzania.

Not only are the levels of manufacturing and the shares of aggregate MVA very different among the countries of SSA but there is also a disproportionate relationship between manufacturing and population distribution. Thus, accounting for 28% of the share of total MVA in 1985, Nigeria contained approximately 22% of the population of SSA, while the top seven countries in terms of their contribution to MVA (some 66% of the total) contained only 53% of SSA's population. On the other hand, the smallest 23 countries in terms of MVA (7% of total MVA) accounted for 20% of the population, with the middle grouping of 15 countries (contributing 27% of total MVA) with 40% of the population.

So much for the static and relatively recent picture of manufacturing between the different countries of SSA. An examination of the longer-term trends provides a better grasp of the more dynamic aspects of manufacturing in the subcontinent. Nearly 25 years ago, in 1965, Nigeria's contribution to the total MVA of SSA was just 9% and that of the other 'big six' 22%. By 1985, however, as noted above, their combined contribution had more than doubled to between 61 and 66%. All of these countries, except for Ghana, are included in the case-studies contained in Part II of this book where explanations for this better performance are analysed.

Trends in MVA shares by the different country groupings listed above in the 12-year period 1973–85 are shown in Figure 2.4[23]. This reveals that although the contribution of the smallest 23 countries in terms of MVA has been minimal it has been fairly stable over time. For the middle 15 countries, however, their share of total MVA has progressively declined over time, falling from 42% in 1973 to 27% by 1985[24].

Further insights into the long-term trends in the evolution of the manufacturing sector can be obtained by examining the growth rate of MVA of individual countries over different

Figure 2.4 *Total Sub-Saharan Africa MVA*
Broken down by Different Groupings

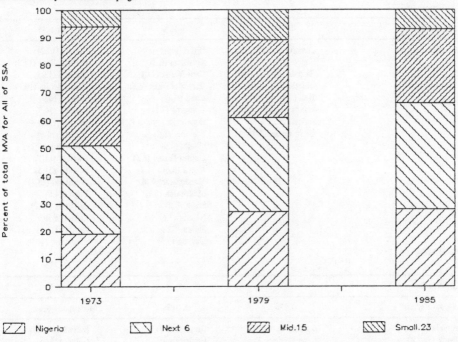

Source: World Bank, *World Development Report 1988*, Tables 3 and 8; UNIDO, *Africa in Figures 1985 and 1986*; ECA, *Survey of Economic and Social Conditions in Africa 1985–86*, Table 9.

periods. Available data for 43 different SSA countries (this time almost exclusively from UNIDO) permit the 23 years from 1963 to 1986 to be broken down into three separate periods: 1963–73, 1973–9 and 1979–86. The great variety in country performance is shown in Table 2.3.

It might be useful to comment, briefly, on some of the trends. If a somewhat arbitrary (but in international terms quite respectable) 5% annual increase in MVA is taken as a norm against which to judge performance, then only four countries (out of 43 for this exercise[25]) exceeded this rate of growth in each of these periods. These were Botswana, Burundi, Mauritania and Rwanda, all small countries in terms of their absolute level of MVA – combined it came to less than 3% of total MVA of the region in 1985, up from 1% in 1973[26].

The increasingly poor performance of most countries in the region in terms of manufacturing is revealed by the fact that whereas in the first period (1963–73) 34 out of 43 of the countries had annual growth rates of MVA in excess of 5%, in 1973–9 the number dropped to 13 and in 1979–86 had fallen to just 10 countries. As these figures suggest, the most significant overall change in growth performance occurred from the 1960s to the 1970s. Thus in the period 1973–9, 30 countries recorded annual growth in MVA of 5% or less compared with only 9 countries in 1963–73; in the 1979–86 period, this number had only risen to 33. Similarly, in the period 1963–73, the rate of growth of manufacturing value added decelerated in 33 out of the 43 countries whereas in the following two periods it slowed in only 20 countries. For 13 it slowed in both periods. In stark contrast, for only 5 countries – Botswana, Cameroon, Congo, Mauritania and Mauritius – did the growth rate of MVA rise from the first to the second period and again from the second to the third.

A different picture emerges, however, when analysis is based not on performance based on numbers of countries but on the respective contribution that each makes to the total MVA of the region. On this score (as summarised in the figures given at the end of each time period in Table 2.3), the most significant changes in the growth of MVA occurred from the 1970s to the 1980s. Thus in the period 1963–73, those countries with growth rates of MVA higher than 5% a year accounted for 87% of total regional MVA; their contribution to total MVA fell to 53%

Table 2.3 *Trends in growth rates of MVA, 1963–86*

A. Period 1963–73

Negative growth	0–5%	5–10%	More than 10%
Réunion (− 1.9)	Cameroon (2.5)	Benin (6.0)	Angola (10.2)
	Congo (0.3)	Botswana (6.2)	Burkina Faso (18.3)
	Gambia (3.5)	Cape Verde (9.0)	Burundi (13.8)
	Guinea (3.3)	Central Af Rep (6.6)	Côte d'Ivoire (10.7)
	Mali (4.8)	Chad (5.4)	Gabon (10.9)
	Mauritius (2.8)	Comoros (7.2)	Lesotho (34.3)
	Senegal (4.2)	Equatorial Guinea (5.1)	Liberia (12.8)
	Sierra Leone (4.5)	Ethiopia (8.2)	Malawi (14.9)
		Ghana (6.9)	Mozambique (13.6)
		Guinea Bissau (8.4)	Rwanda (15.5)
		Kenya (8.6)	Somalia (21.5)
		Madagascar (9.0)	Swaziland (18.1)
		Mauritania (5.1)	Togo (14.0)
		Niger (8.0)	Tanzania (10.2)
		Nigeria (7.6)	Zaire (12.5)
		Sudan (5.6)	Zambia (12.7)
		Uganda (5.3)	Zimbabwe (10.9)

% of MVA[a]

0	14	54	33

B. 1973–9

Negative growth	0–5%	5–10%	More than 10%
Angola (− 16.8)	Burkina Faso (4.6)	Burundi (5.7)	Botswana (10.3)
Benin (− 7.4)	Cape Verde (0.8)	Cameroon (6.4)	Gabon (13.0)
Chad (− 4.8)	Central Af Rep (4.3)	Côte d'Ivoire (5.8)	Kenya (10.8)
Comoros (− 8.9)	Congo (2.5)	Liberia (7.2)	Nigeria (13.2)
Equatorial Guinea (− 16.8)	Ethiopia (1.0)	Malawi (5.4)	
Ghana (− 1.9)	Gambia (1.1)	Mauritania (7.8)	
Mozambique (− 11.2)	Guinea (3.2)	Réunion (7.3)	
Sudan (− 3.1)	Guinea Bissau (4.2)	Rwanda (6.0)	
Togo (− 1.7)	Lesotho (4.0)	Swaziland (7.1)	
Uganda (− 12.1)	Madagascar (3.4)		
Zaire (− 5.9)	Mali (3.3)		
Zambia (− 2.2)	Mauritius (4.3)		
Zimbabwe (− 1.3)	Niger (0.0)		
	Senegal (4.5)		
	Sierra Leone (1.8)		
	Somalia (4.6)		
	Tanzania (4.3)		

% of MVA

28	19	17	36

C. 1979–86[b]

Negative growth	0–5%	5–10%	More than 10%
Angola (− 1.7)	Benin (3.2)	Burundi (8.7)	Botswana (11.7)
Burkina Faso (− 2.2)	Cape Verde (2.6)	Congo (6.2)	Cameroon (24.6)
Central Af Rep (− 1.4)	Comoros (3.6)	Mauritania (8.4)	Gambia (13.9)
Chad (− 12.1)	Ethiopia (4.8)	Mauritius (7.6)	Lesotho (12.9)
Côte d'Ivoire (− 0.4)	Gabon (2.9)	Rwanda (9.1)	
Equatorial Guinea (− 0.8)	Guinea (4.1)	Somalia (6.9)	
Ghana (− 2.4)	Kenya (4.9)		
Guinea Bissau (− 1.0)	Malawi (2.7)		
Liberia (− 6.0)	Mali (2.7)		
Madagascar (− 6.3)	Niger (0.2)		
Mozambique (− 5.5)	Nigeria (1.6)		
Tanzania (− 4.5)	Réunion (1.1)		

Table 2.3 *contd*

C. Period 1976–86			
Negative growth	0–5%	5–10%	More than 10%
Uganda (− 0.8)	Senegal (3.6)		
Zaire (− 0.7)	Sierra Leone (1.7)		
	Swaziland (2.9)		
	Sudan (1.5)		
	Togo (1.3)		
	Zambia (1.0)		
	Zimbabwe (4.5)		
% of MVA			
21	66	6	7

Source: UNIDO, *Africa in Figures* 1985 and 1986, and World Bank, *World Development Report* 1988.

Note: ᵃ These percentage figures refer to the contribution of the above listed countries to the total MVA of SSA. They are based on 1985 MVA data.
ᵇ Figures only up to 1985 for the following: Equatorial Guinea, Gabon, Gambia, Guinea, Guinea Bissau, Lesotho, Madagascar, Malawi, Mali, Mauritania, Mozambique, Niger, Réunion, Sao Tomé, Somalia and Swaziland.
Figures only to 1984 for Angola, Burkina Faso, Cape Verde, Chad, Comoros and Côte d'Ivoire.

in the period 1973–9 and to a very small 13% in the 1980s. Perhaps surprisingly, the data also suggest that whereas in the period 1973–9 those countries which recorded negative MVA accounted for 28% of the MVA of the region, in the 1979–86 period, although slightly more countries experienced negative growth of MVA, their total contribution to regional MVA was only 21%.

THE CONTRIBUTION OF MANUFACTURING TO OVERALL PRODUCTION

Further insights into the performance within different countries can be obtained by examining trends in the MVA/GDP ratio. In 1985, just 6 countries of the region had MVA/GDP ratios in excess of 15%: Mauritius, Rwanda, Senegal, Swaziland, Zambia and Zimbabwe[27]. Twelve years previously, the number had been only 4 – in the intervening period the ratios for Mauritius and Senegal increased respectively from 13.1 to 18.3% and from 13.2 to 16.3%. However, the number of countries whose MVA/GDP ratio was 5% or less or 10% and more remained remarkably constant over the period: the former remaining at 9 and the latter at 16 in both 1973 and 1985. The details are shown in Appendix Table 2.A4[28].

A comparison of contributions to total MVA and shares of MVA in GDP by country reveals that it is by no means true that those countries with a high MVA/GDP ratio are among the leading contributors to the MVA of the region. Thus out of 22 countries with MVA values in excess of $100 m. in 1985, only 12 had MVA/GDP ratios of 10% or more (Appendix Tables 2.A1 and 2.A4.) Nigeria, Uganda and Tanzania all had MVA/GDP ratios of 5% or less but their individual MVAs were in excess of $100 m., whereas Djibouti, Gambia and the Seychelles all had MVA/GDP ratios of over 10% but manufacturing sectors of a very small absolute size – each valued at less than $30 m. in 1985.

Further complexities are revealed when country data on trends in MVA growth rates are compared with changes in the MVA/GDP ratios. *Ceteris paribus*, one would expect the MVA/GDP ratio to fall when the growth rate of MVA is lower than that of GDP and vice versa. Zaire is an example which illustrates well these sorts of trends; it has experienced a process of both relative and absolute de-industrialisation in the past 30 years. In 1986, manufacturing value added totalled 835 m. zaires (at 1980 prices); 17 years previously, in 1969, it stood at 1,081 m. zaires (also at 1980 prices) – a value 30% higher. MVA growth was − 12.5% a year in the period 1963–73, − 5.9% in 1973–9 and still a negative value of − 0.7% a year in 1979–86. Thus, as one would expect, Zaire's MVA/GDP ratio fell from 16% in 1965 to 8% in 1973 and was down to 1.2% by 1985. The reverse trends appear to have taken place in Rwanda. From 1969 to 1985, MVA in Rwanda rose by 230% while the annual rate of growth of MVA rose from 6% in 1973–9 to over 9% in 1979–86. As one would also expect, the share of MVA to GDP went up from 16% in 1969 to 18% in 1985.

The complete picture for the 46 SSA countries over the past 12 years, however, reveals far more complex results. Thus, of the 20 countries which recorded a lower annual rate of growth of MVA from the period 1973–9 to 1979–86, 8 had a higher MVA/GDP ratio in 1985 than in 1973. On the other hand, of the 26 countries whose annual average MVA growth rate was higher in 1979–86 than in 1973–9, a full 15 recorded a fall in their MVA/GDP ratios. In other words, the aggregate evidence by no means supports what might initially be thought to be the obvious relationship between the growth of MVA and trends in the MVA/GDP ratio. Clearly events more complex than those related exclusively to manufacturing influenced the majority of African economies in a manner which led to these seemingly perverse trends.

MANUFACTURED EXPORTS

We now shift attention to manufactured exports, a dimension of manufacturing in which in aggregate, as noted above, the performance of SSA appears to have been profoundly disappointing. Analysis of manufactured export trends is hampered not only because of data inaccuracies but also because of lack of international agreement about what precisely constitutes manufactured as opposed to, say, mineral or agricultural exports. Table 2.A5 reproduces the data on manufactured exports published by the World Bank, UNCTAD and ECA. In relation to the different definitions used by these agencies[29], one would expect ECA data to record the largest quantity of manufactured exports and UNCTAD data the smallest.

As Table 2.A5 reveals, however, for 8 out of 30 countries, World Bank data show lower export figures than those published by UNCTAD and for 21 out of 32 countries, the Bank records manufactured exports higher than does ECA. In addition, some of the differences in manufactured exports recorded by the different sources are very great; for instance, manufactured exports from Ghana in 1981 varied from $5 m. to $424 m., from Zambia in 1985 from $20 m. to $587 m. and from Nigeria in 1985 from $26 m. to $86 m. A large part of the cause of *these* very significant differences lies in the incorporation or non-incorporation of processed minerals in the statistics for manufactured exports, highlighting the care with which one should use and derive conclusions from these different published figures. They do not, however, provide a complete explanation. It appears, for instance, that some oil and some diamond exports have crept in to some of the World Bank data for manufactured exports in the cases of the Congo, Gabon and the Central African Republic[30].

For the purposes of the present discussion – and in the context of the errors and discrepancies just revealed – we shall use the World Bank figures[31]. These suggest that in 1986 manufactures constituted only 11% of total SSA exports. They totalled a mere $3.2 bn. for the entire SSA region, lower than the value of manufactured exports from individual developing countries such as Thailand or Malaysia, less than half of India's manufactured exports and less than one third of manufactures exported by Brazil.

Within this overall context, however, some important trends within SSA need to be highlighted. Appendix Table 2.A6 provides data on manufactured exports for 31 SSA countries (accounting for nearly 80% of total manufactured exports from SSA) for the years 1966, 1976 and 1986. On a positive note, the data suggest that manufactured exports have been less volatile than non-manufactured exports, as indicated by the progressive increase in the ratio of manufactured to total exports, a rise from 5.8% in 1966 to 9.7% in 1986[32]. On a country-specific basis the rise has been quite marked: thus whereas in 1966 the ratio of manufactured to total exports exceeded 15% for only 3 countries of the sub-region, the number had doubled to 6 by 1976 and again to 13 by 1986.

As with the breakdown of total MVA by country, the bulk of manufactured exports originates in only a handful of SSA countries. In 1986, only 8 countries had manufactured exports greater than $100 m., which together contributed 63% of all manufactured exports from the region. In contrast, however, while the share of total MVA originating in the leading 7 countries has been rising over time (see Figure 2.4, above), the share of manufactured exports of the leading 8 countries in total SSA manufactured exports has remained fairly static: it was also 63% in 1966.

Furthermore, there are differences between those countries which have made the greatest contribution to aggregate MVA and those that have made the greatest contribution to total exports of manufactures from the region. Thus in the mid-1980s, Nigeria, responsible for some 30% of the MVA of the entire SSA region, was ninth in the league of SSA manufacturing exporters. Nonetheless, of the 7 leading countries in terms of MVA, 4 are amongst the 7 leading manufacturing exporters: Zimbabwe, Côte d'Ivoire, Cameroon and Kenya.

Another trend to note is that for the vast majority of countries for which data are available there seems to be a strong association between changes in the share of manufactured to total exports and in the ratio of MVA to GDP. Thus a comparison of the figures in Appendix

Table 2.A6 with those in Table 2.A4 shows that from 1965/6 to 1985/6, out of 24 countries, 15 had rising ratios of manufactured to total exports and 14 had rising ratios of MVA/GDP. Moreover, Nigeria, Sierra Leone, Uganda and Zaire all recorded falls in both the ratio of manufactured to total exports and in their MVA/GDP ratios.

THE STRUCTURE OF MANUFACTURING

A final important area to examine is the changing structure of the manufacturing sector within different SSA countries. Regrettably substantial analysis is hampered not merely by the poor quality of the statistics available but also because of the absence of data on internationally comparable sub-sectoral changes within the manufacturing sector in a large number of African countries. UNIDO publishes time series data by industrial sub-sector for only 7 SSA countries while the World Bank's figures provide sub-sectoral data for only 16 countries for its 1970 analysis, accounting for only 40% of total MVA, and for only 25 countries for its 1985 data-base.

Nonetheless it has been possible to use the World Bank's 1985 data for these 25 countries (which together account for just over 80% of the total MVA of the region) to give a crude breakdown of manufacturing by broad sub-sectoral grouping. As expected, this confirms the low level of diversity and depth of manufacturing in much of SSA, the almost complete absence of machinery and transport equipment manufacture (ISIC branches 382–4) and the dominance of food, beverages, textiles and clothing manufacture. The aggregate data are summarised in Table 2.4 with the country-specific breakdown reproduced in Table 2.A7.

Almost exactly half of manufacturing in SSA in the mid-1980s was concentrated in the food, beverages and textile branches, 8% in chemicals[33] and 10% in the manufacture of machinery and transport equipment. In addition, it is the top 7 countries in terms of MVA – Nigeria, Cameroon, Côte d'Ivoire, Ghana, Zambia and Zimbabwe – which dominate the chemical and machinery manufacture in the region. Together, in 1985, these 7 countries accounted for $2.7 bn (75%) of the total SSA value added in these sub-sectors, the remaining 25% ($0.9 bn) originating in the remaining 40 countries[34].

Table 2.4 *Breakdown of MVA in SSA by broad sub-sectoral[a] division, 1985 ($m.)*

	Food & Agriculture	Textiles & Clothing	Machinery & transport Equipment	Chemicals	Other	Total MVA
Total, SSA[b]	7,074.9	2,588.3	1,997.8	1,633.8	5,835.5	19,130
% of total	37.5	13.5	10.4	8.5	30.5	100
of which:						
Low-income SSA	3,763.4	1,289.1	453.4	723.9	2,283.2	8,513
% of total	44.2	15.1	5.3	8.5	26.7	100
Middle-income SSA	3,311.4	1,299.2	1,544.4	909.8	3,552.2	10,617
% of total	31.2	12.2	14.5	8.6	33.5	100
Top 7 countries[c]	4,063.0	1,434.6	1,667.6	1,034.1	4,043.5	12,243
% of total	33.1	11.8	13.6	8.5	33.0	100
Total 7 as % all SSA	57.4	55.4	83.5	63.3	69.3	63

Source: World Bank, *World Development Report 1988*; ECA, *Survey of Economic and Social Conditions in Africa, 1985–1986*.

Notes: a Caution needs to be expressed even about the accuracy of these data because the 'other' category includes data for textiles, machinery or chemicals when national data do not disaggregate these elements. The classification is based on the UN's International Standard Industrial Classification as follows: Food and Agriculture: Division 31; Textiles and Clothing: Division 32; Machinery and Transport Equipment: Major Groups 382–4; Chemicals: Major Groups 351 and 352.
b World Bank data give complete 1985 MVA data for only 22 countries. Individual data for Côte d'Ivoire, Burkina Faso and Madagascar were estimated from the ECA and UNIDO data-bases and included in the country aggregation. As the source of these World Bank figures is the UNIDO data-base it would appear legitimate to combine the figures from these sources in the one table. This provided total MVA of $15.6bn out of the total of $19.1bn for SSA in 1985. The figures were then scaled up proportionately using separate shares for middle-income and low-income countries of SSA.
c Cameroon, Côte d'Ivoire, Ghana, Kenya, Nigeria, Zambia and Zimbabwe.

The dominance of consumer rather than intermediate or capital-oriented manufacture in present-day SSA would suggest not only that manufacturing is relatively simple in technique but also that there has been little structural change in the post-independence period. Although the aggregate data of sub-sectoral trends are insufficient to make a firm judgement on this issue, more detailed analysis of what is termed 'apparent consumption' data would tend to add considerable strength to this viewpoint.

Apparent consumption is the term used to describe domestic production plus imports less exports. A closely related ratio – production as a percentage of apparent consumption (P/AC) – indicates the degree to which consumption of manufactured products is derived from domestic production. Thus a (P/AC) score of 100 suggests that domestic consumption is the result entirely of domestic production and a score of 0 that domestic consumption results completely from importing. A score in excess of 100 shows that the country is an exporter, as more of the product in question is being produced than consumed[35].

UNIDO data on apparent consumption cover a wide cross-section of countries in SSA and a range of products analysed down to the four-digit level of ISIC classification. Comparative data of the P/AC ratio for 11 products from the early 1970s to the early 1980s have been brought together in Table 2.5. They reveal four sets of disturbing trends. First, and consistent with the data in Table 2.4 above, they show that production of more sophisticated metal/machinery in SSA is at a very low level.

For instance, some 90% of pig iron requirements are imported together with some 20% of the more common types of steel products, even if these ratios have shifted slightly in a more favourable direction over the ten-year period[36]. For many other products (not shown in the table), there is no production capability at all except in a handful of countries of the region. These ratios confirm the view expressed some years ago by Fransman (1984: 4):

In most African countries the capital good sector (which produces the means of production) is at present either practically non-existent or in the early stages of infancy.

The second disturbing feature of the data in Table 2.5 is the low and decreasing level of the P/AC ratio for the main, nitrogenous and phosphatic, fertilisers[37]. These figures, however, almost certainly underestimate the degree of dependence upon agricultural imports. Thus, data on fertiliser consumption and imports available from studies carried out by the Food and Agriculture Organisation (FAO) of the UN show that in the years 1980–85, SSA imported some 88% of its total requirements, totalling 910,700 tonnes of nutrients, rising

Table 2.5 *Production as a percentage of apparent consumption, 1973–5 to 1981–3, various products*

Selected Products	1973–5			1981–3		
	No. of Countries	% of SSA MVA[b]	P/AC[a] %	No. of Countries	% of SSA MVA[b]	P/AC %
Milk/cream[c]	22	22	36	17	11	26
Butter	27	74	82	25	68	64
Vegetable oil	39	99	110	40	99	90
Cotton woven fabric	25	73	86	25	79	91
Footwear	22	66	93	19	61	106
Soaps	23	48	91	22	71	90
Cement	29	92	79	25	90	74
Nitrogenous fertiliser	38	98	18	38	99	13
Phosphatic fertiliser	37	92	26	37	99	20
Pig iron	32	96	10	24	86	11
Angles, shapes & sections	31	58	15	22	44	19

Source: UNIDO (1986) *Africa in Figures 1986*, Vienna, UNIDO, Table 6 and ECA (1987) *Survey of Economic and Social Conditions in Africa 1985–1986*, Addis Ababa, United Nations.

Notes: [a] Ratio of production over apparent consumption.
[b] MVA figures used here are those from ECA.
[c] The sub-sectoral classification of products listed here is as follows, with ISIC numbers in brackets: Milk and cream condensed (3112–01); Butter (3112–07); Vegetable oil (3115–10, 13, 16, 19, 22, 25, 28, 31, 34, 37); Cotton woven fabrics (3211–28); Footwear, excluding rubber footwear (3240–00); Other printing and writing paper (3411–22); Soap (3523–01); Cement (3692–04); Nitrogenous fertilizer (3512–01); Phosphatic fertiliser (3512–04, 07); Pig iron (3710–07, 10); Angles, shapes and sections (3710–35).

from 82% at the start of the period to an astounding 93% by 1985, most of which were obtained from the OECD countries and Eastern Europe (FAO, 1987: 5–7). While the falling ratios (revealed in Table 2.5) may, in some small way, help to explain the poor performance of regional agriculture over the decade, the more worrying policy implication is that, unless fertiliser production capacity can be expanded significantly, higher levels of agricultural production will require even larger amounts of imports, putting further strains on already over-stretched import bills. FAO estimates suggest that by 1995 the total fertiliser imports of the SSA will have almost doubled from 1985 levels to 1.8 m. tonnes of nutrients (ibid: 6).

There has, thirdly, been a marked deterioration in the P/AC ratio of those intermediate products for which SSA has had a relatively high level of domestic production capacity. For soap, minimally, and also for cement, more significantly, the P/AC ratios have been falling. The top group of products in Table 2.5 are all within the foodstuffs sub-sector. Here, fourthly, the data reveal even greater falls in the P/AC ratio and, in the case of vegetable oil, there has been a decisive swing from aggregate surplus to overall deficit.

The single optimistic feature of Table 2.5 relates to the high and rising A/PC ratios for two major elements of the textile and footwear industries, leading in the latter period to an aggregate surplus for footwear manufacturing. This aside, the sub-sectoral data confirm the overall picture of low level and deteriorating manufacturing performance throughout much of the SSA region.

Clearly the amount of information on manufacturing performance that can be gleaned from national comparisons within the subcontinent is severely restricted. We therefore turn now to the light that can be shed from the seven case-studies on three key issues: reasons for the past performance of manufacturing, prospects for manufacturing expansion in the 1990s, and the implications that this discussion has for the place that industry could play in the future development of the subcontinent.

Notes

1. The African continent contains some 53 separate countries, including island states. Sub-Saharan Africa (SSA) is the term commonly applied to the group of independent African countries south of the Sahara but excluding South Africa. This group is made up of 47 countries including the island states of Cape Verde, Comoros, Mauritius and Madagascar, Réunion, Sao Tomé and Principe and Seychelles.

   There is some ambiguity, however, over the grouping of a country to the north-west of the continent called, variously, 'Western Sahara', 'Former Spanish Sahara' and the 'Saharawi Republic'. But as no international agency publishes statistical data on it in its international statistics, it has also been omitted from the present discussion. A further initial complication arises in relation to the Sudan. The ECA which, unlike the UN in New York, tends not to use the term 'sub-Saharan Africa', divides its statistics into four groupings: North, West, Central and Eastern and Southern Africa. In this division, Sudan is classified under North Africa, its western neighbour Chad under Central Africa and its eastern neighbour Ethiopia under Eastern and Southern Africa. Following the World Bank and the IMF, Sudan will be classified here under SSA.

   In addition to these classification difficulties more substantial problems arise from the countries used by different agencies for the compilation of statistics referring to the SSA region. The IMF usually uses 44 countries – South Africa, Namibia, Cape Verde and Réunion are omitted, while its tables also usually omit Nigeria. The World Bank's 1988 *World Development Report* omits from its detailed tables Cape Verde, Comoros, Djibouti, Equatorial Guinea, Gambia, Namibia, Réunion, Seychelles and Swaziland. But its 1988 publication *World Tables 1987* does include the Gambia and Swaziland. Nonetheless, aggregate SSA figures from the World Bank claim to use data from all SSA countries with the sole exception of Namibia which the Bank explicitly states is omitted. UNCTAD's 'Developing Africa' trade data frequently exclude Zimbabwe while the *Global Report* produced by UNIDO excludes Angola from its list of 'Tropical Africa'. However UNIDO's 1985 and 1986 publications entitled *Africa in Figures* include Angola but omit Namibia. ECA data include 44 countries of SSA in their country statistics; this excludes North African countries but includes Sudan (for reasons explained above). ECA data, however, omit Réunion and Cape Verde as well as South Africa. Influential World Bank reports on SSA such as *Accelerated Development in Sub-Saharan Africa* (1981) and *Financing Adjustment with Growth in sub-Saharan Africa 1986–1990* (1986) only use 39 countries for their detailed country tables; Cape Verde, Comoros, Equatorial Guinea, Seychelles, Djibouti, Sao Tomé, Réunion, Namibia and, of course, South Africa, are all omitted.

   Different international agencies frequently publish different estimates also for key variables such as total population and (important for international comparisons) exchange rates, trade, production and employment.

An illustration of the problem of data inaccuracy would be population statistics. In its 1987 *WDR*, the World Bank gave the population of Nigeria as 99.7 m., ECA 95.6 m. and the UN *Demographic Yearbook* 95.2 m. Similarly the figures for Tanzania were 22.2, 21.2 and 21.7 m. respectively.

Particular care also needs to be taken in using historical statistics because of the continual and often dramatic alterations made to past data in subsequent years. For instance, the UN *Demographic Yearbook* for 1984 gives the 1982 Nigerian population as 82.39 m., whereas the 1985 edition gives a revised figure of 86.126 m. For an example of altered statistics outside the SSA region see Notes 5 and 13, below.

Of perhaps even greater relevance to the present study, it is important to be aware of the great variety in the estimates of the key figure for manufacturing, Manufacturing Value Added (MVA). Appendix Table 2.A1 shows the wide differences in the estimates provided for 1983 by UNIDO and ECA, and for the year 1985 between the World Bank and ECA. Even wider discrepancies are found in relation to statistics for manufactured exports, exacerbated – but in no way entirely explained – by differences in defining what manufactured exports are. Some of these differences are shown in Appendix Table 2.A5.

2. For instance in Zimbabwe, where the quality of the statistics is among the best on the continent, processing of minerals which takes place at the mine is (arbitrarily) denoted as a mining operation and that which takes place in a geographically different location is included as manufacturing. The loose way in which the term 'industry' is commonly used to denote 'manufacturing' was discussed in Chapter 1.

3. For instance Zimbabwe's industrial statistics only include establishments with a gross output of over Z$2,000 ($1,080 in mid-1988). Of more than passing interest, this particular cut-off point has been operating for at least the past 10 years: in 1978, the cut-off point would have been around Z$4,000 at 1988 prices, equivalent to $5,600 at current prices. The bias of the statistical base is shown by the fact that according to the official statistics the number of manufacturing firms with a gross output of Z$2,000 or more (at current prices) rose from 23 in 1979 to 29 in 1985. See Government of Zimbabwe, *The Census of Production 1979/80 and 1984/85*, Harare, Central Statistical Office, 1981 and 1988.

4. All the data in this and the following paragraph are from the 1987 and 1988 editions of the World Bank's *World Development Report*.

5. Low-income developing economies are those which according to the World Bank and its data-base had *per capita* incomes of $425 or less in 1986. Lower middle-incomes are those with *per capita* incomes between $460 and $1,570 in 1986.

An indication of the dangers of comparing statistics by world region or economic grouping is provided by examining World Bank data on 'structure of production' for low-income economies over the three years 1984, 1985 and 1986, provided in *WDR* 1986, 1987 and 1988 respectively. The details are as follows:

Ratio of MVA to GDP	1984	1985	1986
a. all low-income economies	15%	26%	24%
b. India and China	15%	29%	27%
c. Other low-income economies	15%	12%	11%

6. The term 'manufacturing value added', abbreviated to MVA, will be used extensively in this book. In brief, MVA is the difference between the gross output of the manufacturing sector and the sum of physical purchases and service inputs before any provision is made for depreciation. Gross output is equal to total turnover plus the value of capital work done by own employees adjusted for change in the value of stocks of own-produced goods and work in progress.

7. These figures are based on data from the 1987 and 1988 *WDR*.

8. Figures for SSA and for all developing economies in 1965 are from *WDR* 1988, Table 3. The 1988 figure for all developing economies is an approximate estimate.

9. Accounting for over 85% of the total MVA of SSA in 1984.

10. Figures calculated from World Bank *WDR* 1986/88, *World Tables 1987* and Inter-American Development Bank, *Economic and Social Progress in Latin America 1986 Report*, Tables 1 and 11.

11. Fransman (1982: 1–2) argues, on the basis of UNIDO statistics, that the African share of world MVA rose from 0.7% in 1960 to 0.8% in 1975. For what they are worth, World Bank (1987 and 1988) data show the following for SSA:

Ratio of Manufacturing Value Added

Year	SSA/Global	SSA/all ldcs
1965	0.60	3.4
1970	0.47	3.1
1985	0.76	3.7
1986	0.56	

These figures show that the largest fall in the SSA/global ratio occurred between 1985 and 1986. This, however, was explained largely by the massive devaluation of the Nigerian Naira, reducing the value of Nigerian value added from $7,373 m. in 1985 to $3,929 m. in 1986. If the 1985 figure is taken the figures show a rise in the SSA/global MVA ratio from the mid-1960s but if the 1986 figure is taken the ratio has fallen. In contrast, the World Bank's *World Tables 1987* record a fall in MVA from Naira $6,580 m. in 1985 to only 5,470m. in 1986.

Of greater significance, the 1987 ECA report gives a figure for the MVA of Nigeria in 1985 as $3,389 m., compared (as we have seen) with the World Bank's $7,373 m., while their respective figures for total MVA for SSA in 1985 differ by over 60%: $19,130 m. for the *WDR* and $11,577 m. for ECA. Such differences in basic data render almost meaningless attempts to derive firm general conclusions. For differences in both country and aggregate assessments of MVA see Table 2.A1.

12. One needs, however, to continue to be sceptical about making firm conclusions. The figures reproduced in Note 11 would appear to contradict this view: it shows that the SSA/global and SSA/All ldc ratio for MVA *fell* from the mid-1960s to 1970.

13. Of more than passing interest, the *WDR* for 1988 gives a figure of 0.3% for the annual average growth of MVA in SSA from 1980 to 1986 whereas the *WDR* for 1987 gives a figure of 3.5% for 1980–85. If both sets of figures are accurate it would indicate a fall in aggregate MVA in 1986 of 18.9%, whereas the UNIDO data give a *rise* of 4% for MVA in 1986!

14. This point is developed further in the next section of this chapter.

15. UNCTAD's aggregate external trade data are classified under 'Developing Africa' rather than 'sub-Saharan Africa'. For clarification of how the different definitions and statistics were used for the present discussion see Note 16, below.

16. The data from which this part of the discussion on international trade are based come from UNCTAD's *Handbook of International Trade and Statistics 1972, 1983* and *1986 Supplement*. Although this is the most comprehensive international trade information available it has had to be adapted for use in the present context. UNCTAD trade data for Africa are aggregated under the group 'Developing Africa', which includes the North African countries of Algeria, Egypt, Libya, Morocco and Tunisia. Using the World Bank's *World Tables 1987* and the IMF's *International Financial Statistics Yearbook 1987*, the overall and manufactured export data of these North African countries were subtracted from the UNCTAD figures. In addition, the UNCTAD data do not include Zimbabwe – presumably because of the secret nature of trade data during the 1965–80 period of UDI. The respective data obtained from Zimbabwe trade data have been added to the UNCTAD data.

A final – and central – issue concerns the definition of manufactured exports. Although the UNCTAD *Handbook* calls its Table A.9 'exports of manufactured goods (excluding iron and steel and non-ferrous metals', embracing SITC groups $(6+8) - (67+68)$, the definition of manufactured exports used in the present discussion includes in addition UNCTAD's: Table A.7, Exports of iron and steel, SITC 67; Table A.9, Exports of manufactured goods, SITC $(6+8) - (67+68)$; Table A.10, Exports of machinery and transport equipment, SITC 7.

17. From $58 bn to $89 bn between SSA and world manufactured exports and from $2 bn to $3 bn between manufactured exports from SSA and all developing countries.

18. As will be discussed below, the World Bank data suggest that within SSA the ratio of manufactured to total exports could have risen in the 1970s, and probably did so if aggregate data excluding Nigeria are analysed.

19. It is particularly difficult to locate international comparative data on levels of manufactured output – most data relate to MVA. The UN *Statistical Yearbook* does have such data, however, for a limited number of countries. The figures quoted here are based on comparisons between 1969 and 1979 for all those countries in the regions specified for which output data were published by the UN for 1975 and 1983/4 (published respectively in 1976 and 1986), supplemented by manufacturing export data from the World Bank's *World Tables 1987*. For SSA, data from 12 countries (accounting for over 70% of SSA MVA) were in a form sufficient to use; for the Indian subcontinent data from Sri Lanka, India and Pakistan were usable and for the remaining countries of Asia from the following countries: Indonesia, South Korea, Philippines, and Hong Kong. No more recent data were available.

20. The term 'deepening' is used here to refer to an increase in the number and complexity of manufacturing establishments operating in a particular country, producing a wider range of manufactured products, as well as to an increasing level of inter-linkage both between sub-sectors of manufacturing industry and, importantly, between manufacturing and other sectors of the economy.

21. Based on UNIDO data from *Africa in Figures 1986*, Table 1.

22. Réunion, officially a 'department' of France, is excluded here because its MVA is recorded by neither the World Bank nor the ECA. UNIDO's 1986 data record Réunion's MVA for 1984 at $57 m.; however, more recent data give, for 1985, an MVA value of $168 m. accounting for 8.8% of its GDP (UNIDO, *Africa in Figures, 1988*, Vienna, UNIDO, November 1988).

23. The details are as follows:

Contribution to the MVA of SSA, 1965–85

	Nigeria	Other Big 6[a]	Middle 15[b]	Lowest 23[c]
1965[d]	12	22		
1973[e]	19	32	42.17	8.68
1979[e]	27	34	28	11
1985[f]	28	38	27.01	6.99

Source: World Bank, *World Development Report 1988*, Tables 3 and 8, UNIDO, *Africa in Figures 1985 and 1986*, UNECA, *Survey of Economic and Social Conditions in Africa 1985–86*, Table 9.

Notes: [a] Cameroon, Côte d'Ivoire, Ghana, Kenya, Zambia and Zimbabwe.
[b] Benin, Botswana, Burundi, Cape Verde, Central African Republic, Chad, Comoros, Djibouti, Gambia, Guinea, Guinea Bissau, Equatorial Guinea, Lesotho, Liberia, Mali, Mauritania, Niger, Sao Tomé, Seychelles, Sierra Leone, Swaziland, Togo and Zaire.
[c] Angola, Burkino Faso, Congo, Ethiopia, Gabon, Madagascar, Malawi, Mauritius, Mozambique, Rwanda, Senegal, Somalia, Sudan, Uganda, and Tanzania.
[d] World Bank figures.
[e] UNIDO figures.
[f] UNECA figures.

24. The population ratios do not seem to have changed substantially over the period. Between 1973 and 1985 the proportionate breakdown was as follows:

	Nigeria	Other Big 6	Middle 15	Lowest 23
1973	22	18	40	20
1985	21	17	40	22

25. Data were incomplete for Djibouti, Sao Tomé and Seychelles.
26. The absolute figures for MVA in recent years are shown in Appendix Table 2.A1.
27. One needs to be particularly careful not to read too much into the figures, most especially of Rwanda and Swaziland. For instance, the 1985 edition of UNIDO's *Africa in Figures* gives the MVA/GDP ratio for Rwanda as 3.86% in 1973 and 3.63% in 1981. However, the 1986 edition gives figures of 18.4% and 15.5% for these *same* years. For Rwanda, most industry consists of relatively simple forms of food processing. Similarly for Swaziland, still dominated by sugar. In its country survey of Swaziland, UNIDO writes that the figures of Swazi industry 'ought to be viewed with extreme caution. They contain errors of omission and incorporate assumptions which might be unrealistic. Also there are significant problems with aggregation.' (UNIDO, *Industrial Development Review Series, Swaziland*, Vienna, Regional and Country Studies Branch, Division of Industrial Studies, UNIDO, 6 February 1985, UNIDO/IS. 516, p. 7).
28. Caution, however, is needed when comparing the World Bank's estimates for the years 1965 and 1986 with those of UNIDO for the intervening years recorded in the table.
29. According to the respective organisations, manufactured exports are defined as follows:

> World Bank: SITC groups 5 to 9 minus 68;
> UNCTAD: SITC groups 5 to 8 minus (67 + 68);
> UNECA: SITC groups 5 to 8.

30. According to the *World Tables* of the World Bank, the manufactured exports of the Central African Republic totalled $31.47 m. in 1984, yet according to the UNIDO country report *total* exports, excluding cotton, diamonds, coffee, timber and tobacco, amounted to no more than $12 m. (p. 16). Similarly, for the Congo, it is apparent that manufacturing exports now include both re-exports and petroleum products from the petroleum refinery which in 1984 accounted for over 50% of 'manufactured' exports. Similarly the Congo's next largest export of manufactures consists of more simple wood products. But even when these are included, the World Bank's data are still high. According to the UNIDO country report on the Congo (p. 26), the ratio of manufactured to all exports was, respectively: in 1981, 3.6; in 1982, 3.9; 1983 6.9 and in 1984 7.9%; according to the World Bank's *World Tables*, the figures were as follows: for 1981, 9; 1982, 10.3; 1983 9.7; and 1984 9.4%.
31. In theory, these are not as restrictive as those provided by UNCTAD but have the merit of excluding processed non-ferrous metals in their definition of manufactured exports.
32. From 6.4 to 12.7% if Nigeria is excluded.
33. According to both the ISIC definitions and the breakdown used by the World Bank, 'chemicals' do not include petroleum products – ISIC Division 34 – which are included under 'Other'.

34. In the same year, India's MVA for machinery, transport equipment and chemicals came to $11 bn, Brazil's to $19 bn.
35. This is not strictly true, for the same P/AC percentage score would be recorded if a country exports an amount equal to that which it imports in a defined product category. Similarly, it would be possible for a P/AC score to exceed 100 and for no exporting to take place if a product was being stockpiled. The theoretically possible but highly unlikely occurrence of a negative score is discounted in the present discussion.
36. The combined P/AC ratios given in the table provide the aggregate figures for the number of countries in the region indicated. These particular aggregate numbers do *not* distinguish between the source of imports. Thus the 19% P/AC score for angles, shapes and sections does not distinguish between those countries which import this product from within Africa and those which import it from outside the region. As Zimbabwe, for instance, exports steel products to over 15 countries in Africa it is apparent that domestic shortfalls in a number of countries are met, at least in part, by supplies from within Africa.
37. UNIDO data, not reproduced in the table, show that SSA has no production facility for potassic fertilisers and that the P/AC ratio has been zero in both time periods.

Statistical Appendix 2.A

Table 2.A1 *Different estimates of MVA 1983 and 1985, $m.*

	ECA 1985	W. Bank 1985	UNIDO 1983	ECA 1983
Angola	127		75.9	98
Benin	53	43	62	55
Botswana	36	49	108	70
Burkina Faso	116		122.5	119
Burundi	85	87	130.6	90
Cameroon	790	952	659.4	622
Cape Verde	4		5.5	4
Central Af Rep	44	55	49.3	42
Chad	50		45.4	52
Comoros	5		5.4	5
Congo	127	128	126.1	128
Côte d'Ivoire	631	889	747.5	606
Djibouti	28		27.3	27
Equatorial Guinea	2		1	2
Ethiopia	482	492	559.5	475
Gabon	175		225	170
Gambia	20		13.8	15
Ghana	726	526	596	341
Guinea	71	41	80.1	61
Guinea Bissau	2		1.3	2
Kenya	705	631	721.1	702
Lesotho	16	26	28.1	17
Liberia	55	49	44.6	63
Madagascar	230		311.8	296
Malawi	140	126	174.7	136
Mali	81	82	75.6	49
Mauritania	38		50.4	51
Mauritius	160		183.4	143
Mozambique	119		351.2	128
Niger	60	58	107.7	62
Nigeria	3,389	7,373	4,483.2	3,652
Rwanda	299	260	263.4	222
Sao Tomé	3		2.3	3
Senegal	345	474	371.6	331
Seychelles	15		17.5	14
Sierra Leone	30	71	127.9	67
Somalia	112	138	159.6	122
Sudan	394	498	495.1	461
Swaziland	76		142.7	111
Togo	29	49	45.4	30

Table 2.A1 *contd*

	ECA 1985	W. Bank 1985	UNIDO 1983	ECA 1983
Uganda	165	130	44.1	141
Tanzania	219	393	360	308
Zaire	32	59	91.8	65
Zambia	529	513	553.1	478
Zimbabwe	1,126	1,314	1,370.5	1,365
TOTAL MVA	11,941		14,218.4	12,001
Total (Bank ctries)	10,771	15,506		
less Nigeria	7,382	8,133		

Source: World Bank, *World Development Report 1988*; UNIDO, *Africa in Figures 1986*, and ECA, *Survey of Economic and Social Conditions in Africa, 1985–1986*.

Table 2.A2 *Total world exports*

Year	Total world exports $ bn	All ldc total exports $ bn	Developing Africa total Exp. $ bn	Ratio of ldc to total world exports %	Ratio of African to total world exports %	Ratio of African to total ldc exports %
1960	127.8	23.7	3.3	18.5	2.6	14.0
1965	185.6	35.9	4.9	19.3	2.6	13.6
1970	312.0	54.9	7.1	17.6	2.3	12.9
1975	872.6	210.9	18.8	24.2	2.2	8.9
1980	1,994.7	559.0	48.3	28.0	2.4	8.6
1985	1,932.9	456.7	30.3	23.6	1.6	6.6

Source: UNCTAD, *Handbook of International Trade and Development Statistics 1983 and 1986 Supplements*, New York, United Nations, 1983 and 1986, Table a. IMF, *International Financial Statistics Yearbook 1987*, various tables, World Bank, *World Tables 1987*, various tables and Zimbabwe, *Monthly and Quarterly Digest of Statistics*, various months.

Note: The high figure for 1980 was abnormal, due in large measure to the rise in oil prices. Averaging out 1979 and 1981 trade data for Africa would reveal a more consistent downward trend in the ratio of African to total world trade.

Table 2.A3 *World manufactured exports*

Year	Total world manuf. exports $ bn	All ldc total manuf. exports $ bn	Developing Africa manuf. exp. $ bn	Ratio of ldc to total manuf. exp. %	Ratio of African manuf. to total manuf. exp. %	Ratio of African manuf. to total ldc manuf. exp. %
1960	58.0	2.2	0.21	3.84	0.36	9.31
1965	90.0	3.7	0.38	4.11	0.43	10.39
1970	167.8	8.4	0.56	5.04	0.33	6.59
1975	438.9	28.0	0.76	6.38	0.17	2.71
1980	943.2	90.5	1.46	9.60	0.15	1.61
1984	983.6	135.8	0.54	13.81	0.05	0.39

Source: Ibid.

Table 2.A4 *Ratio of MVA/GDP, SSA countries, 1965, 1973 and 1985*

	1965	1973	1984	1985	1986
Angola		4.3	2.8	2.9	
Benin		9.6	6.8	6.36	4
Botswana	12	5.5	5.3	6.01	6
Burkina Faso		13.8	11.9	13.78	
Burundi		7.2	9.9	8.4	10
Cameroon	10	10.2	10.2	11.03	12
Cape Verde		5.6	5.5	5.18	
Central Af. Rep.	4	6.2	5.9	7.4	4
Chad	12	12.1	7.7	8.53	
Comoros		7.1	5.5	5.84	
Congo		6.9	6.1	7.33	6
Côte d'Ivoire	11	11.6	11.7	11.6	16
Djibouti		8.4	8	10.21	
Equitorial Guinea		5.2	5	4.61	
Ethiopia	7	10.4	11.6	10.27	10
Gabon		5.2	6.6	5.97	
Gambia		3.5	5.1	10.3	
Ghana	10	9.3	6.1	13.61	12
Guinea		3.5	3.2	3.55	
Guinea Bissau		1.7	1.8	1.6	
Kenya	11	9.6	12.5	12.56	12
Lesotho	1	5.2	7.2	7.18	13
Liberia	3	8.3	8.3	7.57	5
Madagascar	11	13.9	12	11.17	
Malawi		13.2	14.5	14.84	12
Mali		8.6	7.1	7.57	7
Mauritania	4	4.5	8.3	6.21	
Mauritius	14	13.1	16.5	18.28	23
Mozambique		11.5	7.7	6.43	
Niger	2	6.3	3.7	4.01	4
Nigeria	7	2.7	5.5	5.14	8
Réunion		8	7.7		
Rwanda	2	18.4	18.1	18	16
Sao Tomé		4.9	5.6	9.34	
Senegal	14	13.2	17.2	16.27	17
Seychelles		3.3	8.3	11.12	
Sierra Leone	6	7.1	6.9	4.11	4
Somalia	3	8.9	8.9	7.78	6
Sudan	4	8.8	7.8	9.14	7
Swaziland		18.7	20.2	22.23	
Togo	10	14.4	8.2	4.75	7
Uganda	8	7.6	3.7	4.5	5
Tanzania	8	13.4	5.3	5.23	6
Zaire	16	3.9	2.7	1.25	
Zambia	6	20.7	18.4	20.01	20
Zimbabwe	20	22.6	21.1	27.74	30

Source: World Bank, *World Development Report 1988*, UNIDO, *Africa in Figures 1986* and ECA, *Survey of Economic and Social Conditions in Africa, 1985–86*.

Note: Figures for 1965 and 1986 at current prices from World Bank, for 1973 and 1984 at 1980 prices from UNIDO and for 1985 at current prices from ECA.

Table 2.A5 *Varying estimates of value of manufactured exports: World Bank, UNCTAD and ECA data*

	YEAR	Source of Data:			YEAR	Source:	
		UNCTAD	ECA	W. BANK		ECA	W. BANK
Angola	1981	225	150		1985	179	
Benin	1982	20		6	1985	24	16
Botswana					1985	566	462
Burkina Faso	1981	10	11	23	1985	4	19
Burundi	1982	1		5	1985	2	8
Cameroon	1982	77		84	1985	74	109
Cape Verde	1980	0			1985	0	
Central Af. Rep.	1980	29		39	1985	39	38
Chad	1975	3			1985	2	
Comoros					1985	13	
Congo	1980	64		64	1985	83	117
Côte d'Ivoire	1981	240	251	262	1985	219	225
Djibouti					1985	0	
Equitorial Guinea					1985	0	
Ethiopia	1981	2	2	5	1985	3	3
Gabon	1983	87		86	1985	79	142
Gambia	1977	0		1	1985	0	2
Ghana	1981	5	424	25	1985	125	10
Guinea					1985	0	
Guinea Bissau					1985		0
Kenya	1981	124	130	154	1985	125	169
Lesotho					1985	9	5
Liberia	1982	3		17	1985	7	20
Madagascar	1982	24		23	1985	19	19
Malawi	1981	20	20	31	1985	14	33
Mali	1979	25		33	1985	9	38
Mauritania	1981	0	2	5	1985	4	8
Mauritius	1981	115	115	121	1985	162	190
Mozambique	1984	1			1985	2	
Niger	1981	9	8	10	1985	8	2
Nigeria	1979	49		92	1985	26	86
Réunion					1985		
Rwanda	1980	0		1	1985	0	1
Sao Tomé					1985	0	
Senegal	1981	109	109	98	1985	86	108
Seychelles	1981	0.4	1		1985	3	
Sierra Leone	1983	27		51	1985	47	62
Somalia	1981	0.5	1		1985	0	
Sudan	1981	4	8	10	1985	15	28
Swaziland					1985	44	
Togo	1981	30	32	24	1985	16	43
Uganda	1976	1		1	1985	11	1
Tanzania	1981	58	76	71	1985	35	45
Zaire	1978	2		129	1985	543	88
Zambia	1982	28		9	1985	587	20
Zimbabwe	1982	104		313	1985	323	384

Source: World Bank, *World Development Report 1988*; UNECA, *Survey of Economic and Social Conditions in Africa, 1985–1986*; and UNCTAD, *Handbook of International Trade and Development Statistics, 1986 Supplement*.

Note: According to the respective organisations, manufactured exports are defined as follows:
World Bank: SITC groups 5 to 9 minus 68;
UNCTAD: SITC groups 5 to 8 minus (67 + 68);
UNECA: SITC groups 5 to 8.

Table 2.A6 *Trends in manufactured exports, 1966–86 (World Bank data & definitions)*

	Manufactured exports $ m.			Ratio Manufactured to Total Exports		
	1966	1976	1986	1966	1976	1986
Botswana	2.27	11.36	20.36	12	13.2	21.7
Burkina Faso	0.83	4.88	17.98	4	5.9	12.6
Burundi	0.54	0.66	19.36	5.4	1.2	11.6
Cameroon	3.8	49.6	120.9	2.8	9.3	5.9
Cen Af. Repub.	20.39	12.26	47.4	53.7	17.6	32.7
Côte d'Ivoire	12.5	121.7	289	4	7.5	9
Congo	18.96	23.46	133.78	54.8	12.4	18.6
Ethiopia	1.4	5.8	3	1.3	2.1	0.7
Gabon	9.47	13.02	140.18	9	1.1	12.6
Gambia	0	1.07	3.28	0	3	6.8
Ghana	9.62	26.49	22.23	3.9	3.5	2.6
Kenya	18.1	169.2	191.7	7	20.5	15.8
Lesotho	0.52	2.85	8.86	8.7	20.4	36.4
Liberia	4.99	11.8	5.92	3.3	2.5	1.5
Madagascar	6.06	22.11	40.97	6.2	7.8	12.3
Malawi	2.74	11.64	39.09	5.6	7	16.1
Mali	0.21	1.18	56.97	1.6	1.4	29.7
Mauritania	0.61	4.12	8.92	0.9	2.3	2.6
Mauritius	0.7	52.53	276.56	1	19.8	41.8
Niger	1.38	3.31	6.87	4	2.5	3
Nigeria	21	68.1	99	2.7	0.6	1.5
Rwanda	0.02	1.75	1.39	0.2	1.5	0.8
Senegal	8.2	64.2	184.7	5.5	13.2	28.8
Sierra Leone	42.96	68.33	71.65	57.5	64.1	56.4
Sudan	2.2	6.9	32.3	1.1	1.2	6.5
Togo	1.37	8.46	51.84	2.8	5.3	20.8
Uganda	1.08	1.51	0.96	0.6	0.4	0.2
Tanzania	30.6	57.1	58	13.9	11.6	16.9
Zaire	30.4	32.9	88.2	6.6	4.1	5.8
Zambia	4.98	8.13	21.4	0.7	0.8	3
Zimbabwe	228	241	365.2	10	24.7	36.7
Totals:	285.9	1,107.42	2,427.97	5.8	4.8	9.7
– Nigeria	264.9	1,039.32	2,328.97	6.4	8.3	12.7

Source: World Bank, *World Tables 1987*.

Table 2.A7 *Country breakdown of MVA by broad sub-sector, 1985*

	MVA $m.	A. % breakdown of MVA					B. Breakdown of MVA in $m.				
		Food	Textiles	Mach & Tport Eq.	Chem	Other	Food	Textiles	Mach & Tport Eq.	Chemicals	Others
Benin	43	58	16	0	5	21	24.94	6.88	0	2.15	9.03
Botswana	49	52	12	0	4	32	25.48	5.88	0	1.96	15.68
Burkina Faso	116	62	18	2	1	17	71.92	20.88	2.32	1.16	19.72
Burundi	87	75	11	0	5	9	65.25	9.57	0	4.35	7.83
Cameroon	952	50	13	7	6	23	476	123.76	66.64	57.12	218.96
Central Af. Rep.	55	44	19	0	7	30	24.2	10.45	0	3.85	16.5
Congo	128	47	13	3	9	29	60.16	16.64	3.84	11.52	37.12
Côte d'Ivoire	889	40	13	8	8	31	355.6	115.57	71.12	71.12	275.59
Ethiopia	492	51	23	0	3	22	250.92	113.16	0	14.76	108.24
Ghana	526	53	6	2	4	35	278.78	31.56	10.52	21.04	184.1
Kenya	631	35	12	14	9	29	220.85	75.72	88.34	56.79	182.99
Lesotho	26	12	20	0	0	68	3.12	5.2	0	0	17.68
Madagascar	230	35	47	3	0	15	80.5	16.45	1.41	0	34.5
Malawi	126	49	13	2	11	25	61.74	16.38	2.52	13.86	31.5
Mauritius	185	37	34	4	5	21	68.45	62.9	7.4	9.25	38.85
Nigeria	7,373	29	11	17	9	35	2,138.17	811.03	1,253.41	663.57	2,850.55
Rwanda	260	77	1	0	12	9	200.2	2.6	0	31.2	23.4
Senegal	474	48	15	6	7	24	227.52	71.1	28.44	33.18	113.76
Sierra Leone	71	36	4	0	38	22	25.56	2.84	0	26.98	15.62
Somalia	138	46	21	0	2	31	63.48	28.98	0	2.76	42.78
Sudan	498	22	25	1	21	31	109.56	124.5	4.98	104.58	154.38
Tanzania	393	28	26	8	7	31	110.04	102.18	31.44	27.51	121.83
Zaire	59	40	16	8	8	29	23.6	9.44	4.72	4.72	17.11
Zambia	513	44	13	9	9	25	225.72	66.69	46.17	46.17	128.25
Zimbabwe	1,314	28	16	10	9	36	367.92	210.24	131.4	118.26	473.04
TOTAL MVA	15,628						5,559.68	2,060.6	1,754.67	1,327.86	4,869.01
Percent	100	35.57	13.18	11.22	8.5	31.16					

Source: World Bank, *World Development Report 1988*, Table 8.

3 Manufacturing Africa

Reflections from the Case-Studies

The purpose of this chapter is to draw together some threads of argument and analysis woven within the chapters of the detailed case-studies contained in Part II of this book. It does not attempt to duplicate the discussion and detailed analysis, save for a summary account of the main factors which appear to explain the deteriorating performance of most of the countries during the 1980s, and the contrasting expansion of manufacturing in Botswana, provided at the end of the first section. It attempts both to make some broader generalisations and to interpret some of the main trends within the constraints of considerable data inadequacy and the inevitable uncertainties in social science analysis in trying to draw firm links between cause and effect.

The discussion is divided into three parts. The chapter starts by examining the growth and evolution of manufacturing in the seven countries from the early 1960s (in some instances earlier and in some, regrettably, later) to the end of the 1980s, and seeking explanations for the varying performance between countries and over time. It attempts to highlight both the differences and similarities which help to explain the pattern of manufacturing development in these more 'successful' seven countries and, more specifically, to throw light on contemporary and more recent problems of their manufacturing sectors. Building upon this analysis and in the context of the constraints present and likely to persist over the next few years, the second part of the chapter discusses the potential for the expansion of manu-facturing into the 1990s and the major problems which need to be addressed. The chapter ends with some reflections on what analysis of the past and a hopefully realistic assessment of the future might shed on some theoretical questions being debated about the role of manu-facturing in the future development of sub-Saharan Africa.

Manufacturing up to the late 1980s

HIGH RATES OF GROWTH AND THE IMPORTANCE OF DOMESTIC DEMAND

Rates of growth of Manufacturing Value Added (MVA) and the share of MVA in Gross Domestic Product (GDP) are two key indicators commonly used to evaluate performance and to judge success. On this basis, the seven countries selected for detailed analysis in this book – Botswana, Cameroon, Côte d'Ivoire, Kenya, Nigeria, Zambia and Zimbabwe – would be judged successes, certainly in the SSA context and, at least in relation to growth rates of MVA, internationally. This is confirmed by the trends shown in Table 3.1. All the countries except Botswana and Nigeria have MVA/GDP ratios higher than the SSA average of 10, Zambia double and Zimbabwe three times the regional average, while Botswana and Nigeria have experienced the longest sustained expansion of MVA of all SSA countries. All seven have had higher annual growth rates of MVA than the SSA average in the 1980s, four out of the seven having higher growth rates of MVA in the 1965–80 period – an average figure itself raised significantly by the inclusion of Nigeria.

Even though (as will become clearer below) rates of growth of MVA and the MVA/GDP ratio in isolation give a partial and, in the end, wholly inadequate basis for judging 'success', it is still important to try to understand why for the selected countries these particular indicators have been amongst the highest in SSA from the 1960s to the end of the 1980s[1]. This question is approached, and the subsequent discussion structured, by examining the different sources of growth of manufacturing output.

For the purposes of the sources of growth analysis[2], manufacturing output growth is broken down into three elements: domestic demand, import substitution and export growth. Difficult though it often is to gather long-term sources of growth data, these were calculated or made available for five of the seven countries (Botswana, Cameroon, Kenya, Nigeria and

Table 3.1 *Growth rate of MVA and ratio of MVA to GDP: case-study countries and SSA averages*

Country	MVA/GDP 1986	Growth Rate of MVA 1965–1980	1980–1986	Comment
Botswana	6	13.5	6.2[a]	Highest growth rate of MVA in SSA
Cameroon	12	7.0	5.4[b]	Given its size, most rapid increase in MVA in SSA post-1980
Côte d'Ivoire	16	9.1	0.9[c]	Higher than average on all three scores
Kenya	12	10.5	4.1	Higher than average on all three scores
Nigeria	8	14.6	1.0	Greatest growth in absolute MVA in all SSA
Zambia	20	5.3	0.6	Largest increase of MVA/GDP ratio in SSA 1965–80 (6% to 20%)
Zimbabwe	30	4.0	1.3	Highest MVA/GDP ratio in SSA
All Sub-Saharan Africa	10	8.5	0.3	

Source: World Bank, (1988) *World Development Report 1988*, Tables 2 and 3.

Notes: [a] See text below for discussion of these particular estimates.
[b] World Bank data not used, rather EIU and country case study estimates for 1985 and 1986.
[c] Own calculations from national sources, see Part II.

Zimbabwe)[3]. Across all these economies, the results consistently show that the predominant source of growth of manufacturing has been *domestic demand*; for Botswana 54%, for Cameroon about 55%, for Kenya 69%, for Nigeria 76% and for Zimbabwe 72%[4], while for Côte d'Ivoire and Zambia (where these particular data could not be derived or were unavailable for more than a short period) the case-studies suggest that domestic demand has been no less important[5].

There are two ways in which the dominance of domestic demand in aggregate growth could be broadly interpreted: either the growth of manufacturing was predominantly determined by the growth of demand from within the sector itself to which the wider (domestic) economy could and did respond favourably, or it resulted from positive changes within the wider domestic economy, with manufacturers supplying an increasing quantity of goods to the domestic market. There are a number of reasons why the latter explanation is likely to be of greater importance. First, the overall share of manufacturing in total output in the seven countries, while significant, is far from dominant[6]. Furthermore, as the case-studies confirm, manufacturing expansion has originated predominantly at the consumer-products end of the manufacturing process. In addition, any substantial generation of domestic demand from within manufacturing would be confirmed if there had been a high and rising level of import substitution in the different countries; the data, however, provide little support for such a conclusion. Finally, the interpretation tends to be corroborated by comparing World Bank data for trends in MVA and GDP growth rates: the four countries which had higher than the SSA average growth rates for MVA in 1965–80 – Botswana, Côte d'Ivoire, Nigeria and Kenya – each also had rates of GDP growth higher than the SSA average (see Table 3.2, below).

We would thus seem able to make some important initial generalisations about manufacturing expansion. Growth in manufacturing appears to have been predominantly dependent upon the growth of domestic demand, rather than upon either import substitution or export growth: its pace seems to have been critically determined by the dynamics of the wider domestic economy. Relatedly, as the case-studies also stress, it has been dependent on access to sufficient amounts of foreign exchange required in order to finance the purchase of plant and equipment and a significant proportion of inputs, which the manufacturing sector itself has in large measure been unable to earn. In the pre-1980s period, as most of the case-studies suggest, rapid growth of MVA was significantly enhanced by expansion of the more dominant productive sectors, led most frequently by agriculture[7]. In the 1980s, however, as discussed briefly below, it was policies adopted to address broad macroeconomic distortions (and therefore largely external to either agriculture or the extractive industries) which played a major role in the slowdown in manufacturing growth in six of the seven countries, while, in the case of Botswana, it was a combination of a favourable macroeconomic climate and rapid expansion of the leading (non-manufacturing) productive sectors which boosted manufacturing sector growth.

It would thus appear that a major cause of manufacturing growth in SSA has been rooted in the establishment of an environment conducive to steady expansive growth outside the sector itself and principally primary product-related. As this conclusion seems to be confirmed for those SSA countries with the most advanced manufacturing sectors, it would seem safe to add that for countries with even smaller manufacturing sectors (the vast majority), substantial growth of manufacturing would be highly unlikely to occur unless their leading productive sectors were also experiencing sustained growth and expansion.

It is important, however, not to *over-emphasise* the role of domestic (and, as we shall see, sub-regional) demand in stimulating the expansion of manufacturing output: predominant does not mean exclusive. The figures quoted above of the share of growth attributable to domestic demand also imply that a far from insignificant part of output growth originated in import substitution and/or export growth – ranging from 24% for Nigeria to 46% for Botswana – with the data suggesting, too, that the absolute size of a country's manufacturing sector does not appear necessarily to have provided either a particular benefit or impediment to achieving high relative shares of these items in overall output growth. We therefore need to examine trends in these particular sources of growth in more detail.

THE POOR RECORD OF MANUFACTURING EXPORTS

When the contribution to total manufactured output of export growth and import substitution is analysed over different time periods, what is particularly striking is the manner in which key features have been common to all the countries for which data are available, with a number of them also occurring in similar historical sequence. For instance, after domestic demand the next most important source of output growth has always been import substitution, frequently accounting in all countries for four and five times the contribution made by export growth. In addition, it has not been uncommon (in Nigeria, Kenya and Zimbabwe, for instance) for export growth to make a negative contribution for certain manufacturing sub-sectors, particularly over more recent time periods. Not only is the share of output originating in export growth extremely small but the case-study data for all the countries show that manufactured exports make only a minor contribution to total output – indeed in most of the countries (Botswana is the exception here and Cameroon for a short period) manufactured exports have declined in fixed price terms over long periods since the early 1960s.

Other trends also indicate that the relative importance of export growth in overall production has consistently declined in countries for which these trends can be analysed with some reliability[8]. Thus for Cameroon, for instance, export growth accounted for 17% of manufacturing output growth in the early 1965–70 period but more than halved to 8% in 1970–75. For Kenya, the export/output ratio dropped from over 20% in the early 1980s to only 7% by the mid-1980s, while in the case of Zimbabwe the ratio fell rapidly from around 17% in 1978/9 to 10% by 1982/3 following a trend begun in the early 1960s.

Not only have manufactured exports constituted a small and falling proportion of total output growth but these exports have tended to be dominated by further processed (largely agriculturally-linked) goods destined for markets outside SSA, thus to many analysts not, strictly speaking, manufactured exports at all. In contrast, if the major processed primary product exports are excluded, the remaining and far smaller quantities of manufactured exports have predominantly been destined for countries within SSA, usually going to near neighbours. It is more than coincidence that for the three countries (both from the case-studies and in the SSA region as a whole) with the largest value of manufactured exports over the post-1960s period – Côte d'Ivoire, Kenya and Zimbabwe[9] – all were initially the most industrially developed in their respective regions. For each of them, in the early years especially, these regional markets were often little more than an extended domestic market, an advantage originating in their being administrative centres in the pre-Independence period and enhanced, but probably not critically determined, by the establishment of regional trade agreements[10].

It has, however, become increasingly difficult for these 'regional export-leaders' to maintain their share – and in some cases even the absolute amounts – of regional trade in manufactures. Two main factors would appear to have contributed to these trends. First, non-African countries have grown increasingly successful in recent years in supplying the African market with manufactured goods. Thus between 1970 and 1984, for instance, imports of manufactures to developing African countries (UNCTAD definition) increased more than fivefold to $40.5 bn. Of this amount, only $650 m. (a mere 1.5%) were supplied from within Africa, compared with a still small, but significantly larger, 4% which developing Africa supplied in 1970 (UNCTAD, 1987: 104–5). The second factor relates to the small, yet in African terms significant, rise in manufacturing industry in other countries of the continent which have expanded the manufacture, in particular, of more simple, consumer-oriented products already manufactured by their neighbours[11]. The main industries here would include basic food industries, textiles and/or clothing, wood and furniture, beer and beverages. The recent expansion of manufactured exports from Zambia into regional markets would, for instance, be part of the phenomenon of largely replacing products from third African countries. Equally the case of Cameroon is of interest because it managed to expand its regional manufactured exports up to the mid-1970s, exploiting markets before its neighbours began their own import-substituting industries. But in recent years it, too, has lost market shares: the ratio of manufactured to total exports had fallen to a low of just over 1% by 1982 and, at least in proportional terms, failed subsequently to recover.

In brief, the longer-term trends in the role and position of manufactured exports in the evolution of the sector in SSA (a slightly more complex relationship than is often thought) can be generalised in the following manner. The absolute quantity of manufactured exports from SSA has remained minute, especially when processed primary products (including refined petroleum products or copper) are excluded. In addition, at least over the past 20 years, not only has there been no marked movement from production for the domestic market to production for the regional and finally for the overseas market[12], but there has tended to be a retreat in recent years to a more exclusive reliance on the domestic market.

It is one thing, however, to isolate common trends, another to establish their causes. Is it possible to explain such deteriorating export performance and particularly to isolate factors unique to particular countries and those common across all or most countries? In attempting to answer these questions we move into the area of policy analysis.

The conventional and widely-shared explanation for these trends runs along the following lines. The failure of manufacturing industry in sub-Saharan African to become more export-oriented lies in the fact that it is not competitive internationally – probably because it never was and certainly because it has tended to become ever more high-cost over the past two to three decades. In addition, it is argued that its high-cost structure has been due to inefficiencies originating in and perpetuated by rising levels of protection and the erection of other barriers to external competition, such as the persistence of overvalued exchange rates but, most especially, through quantitative restrictions placed on competing imports. The conclusion commonly drawn is that if the trend is to be reversed then priority should be given to policies aimed at reducing tariffs, eliminating quantitative restrictions and ensuring that there is far closer alignment between nominal and real exchange rates.

Does the evidence in the case-studies confirm this conventional explanation and its policy conclusions? The answer is: only partially! To begin with, it is of more than passing interest to know that until recently (from the 1980s onwards), there was little if any concerted effort put into promoting manufactured exports, especially to destinations overseas, except for processed agricultural and mineral products. As a result a 'climate' encouraging manufacturers to look for, promote and expand into markets beyond their borders or those of their near neighbours was never established. Indeed, a frequent combination of the absence of trade promotion activities targeted to manufacturers and few or minimal export incentives was self-reinforcing and effectively dampened any ambitions manufacturers might have had to try to penetrate and obtain a sure foothold in export markets.

The principal role apparently assigned to manufacturing in SSA was to establish plants and factories in order to manufacture goods predominantly for the domestic (and regional) markets in the attempt to replace imports and hence reduce the overall import bill. That this provides an important element in explaining the low level of manufacturing exports is confirmed by policy changes initiated in the 1980s. In a number of countries – Kenya, Zambia and Zimbabwe – this period saw the expansion of non-traditional manufacturing exports, especially in the mid- to late 1980s, as a result of explicit export promotion policies and the establishment or extension of export incentives. Important though these developments have been, however, they need to be placed in a broader context. Thus, it has to be acknowledged that the overall effect on raising the export/output ratio has been at best modest, at worst negligible. Moreover, in those countries where manufacturing industry has been relatively 'long-established' – all of the case-studies, with the exception of Botswana – and where some successes in expanding into the export field in recent years have occurred, there have been only very few examples of firms originally oriented to the domestic market switching significantly to the export market – an important issue, to be discussed further below. For most enterprises, exporting has been possible only on a 'marginal cost basis' with overall costs covered by charging higher prices on the domestic market or else, as appears to have occurred in Zambia, as a result of government subsidies[13].

Does, then, the evidence confirm that a major reason for the increasing inward-looking nature of manufacturing arises from its increasingly high-cost structure vis-à-vis competitive imports? Here the case-study evidence is far from unambiguous. While for a range of industries in most of the countries comparative price data indicate that domestic prices are higher (often considerably higher) than border prices, the evidence from a number of countries, including Zimbabwe, Cameroon, Kenya and Côte d'Ivoire indicates some contradictory trends. In these countries international competitiveness across a range of industries has been maintained in a climate of *rising* protectionism; indeed there is evidence to suggest that competitiveness between firms in the same industry differs often quite markedly and that the degree of competitiveness has increased for certain firms over time. For a number of firms, albeit the minority, production has always been export-oriented with well over 50% of output destined for export, and not solely, to the extra-regional market. What this sort of evidence suggests is that the prevailing policy framework and trade and tariff regime in these countries provide nothing like a complete explanation for the internal/external orientation of manufacturing in SSA. Other factors are clearly involved: in all these countries other policy measures (particularly export incentives) have been able to narrow price differentials considerably. In addition, in regard to the exchange rate, the evidence from Kenya and Zimbabwe and from the francophone countries suggests that this has not been 'excessively' overvalued.

It is in the context of this discussion that the Botswana case needs to be considered. Botswana appears to be an exception to the general trends in three significant ways. First, the growth of manufactured exports in the ten-year period to the mid-1980s accounted for a higher share of output growth than for any of the other countries in the same, and in some cases in any other, period. Second, manufactured exports (excluding meat slaughtering) have expanded at a rate of over 15% a year in the 1980s (to 1987, at least). Finally, the environment for the development of manufacturing in Botswana is characterised both by minimal external protection and by policies which determine that the prices of manufactures domestically produced should be similar to those of competing imports. To deduce, however, that Botswana's manufacturing export successes have been due to its trade and tariff policies would be premature. Three other factors need to be considered. One is that, in contrast with the other case-study countries, there has always been a 'climate' of exporting in Botswana. In addition, it is important to remember that its manufacturing base and, even more, its non-traditional exports constitute a tiny volume of goods. Most important, however, is the fact that not even Botswana has managed to break out of its dependence on regional markets for its manufactured exports – less than 5% of its non-beef manufactured exports went to destinations other than Zimbabwe or South Africa, a share not dissimilar to most of the other case-study countries. It does not seem, therefore, that in Botswana minimal tariff barriers and a competitive exchange rate provide exclusively or even predominantly an adequate basis for the creation, or expansion, of export-oriented manufacturing.

Returning to the establishment of manufacturing in the other countries studied, it is critically important for policy purposes to note the *sequence* in which change occurred and policies were drawn up and implemented. Thus it was not so much the climate of creeping protectionism which *led* to industries becoming high-cost in relation to international competition; rather, the problem of the lack of international competitiveness was aggravated by more deep-seated structural and institutional problems. The drive to establish manufacturing enterprises in the hope of saving foreign exchange by reducing the importation of final products tended to lead, in part because of geography and backward communications systems, to the increasing isolation of these SSA enterprises from the dynamics of efficient change occurring elsewhere. These would include technical adaptation, management advances and insights and, more recently, developments in computer-assisted manufacture and ancillary services. As a result, in comparative terms, productive efficiency in SSA lagged behind that of its potential competitors and was increasingly determined by what were becoming obsolete techniques, using out-dated machinery and frequently operated by personnel out of touch with new techniques and without the skills to alter or adapt machinery. The jacking-up of protective tariffs and the extension of quantitative restrictions tended to be the quick-fix but prolonged *response*, implemented in preference to closing down what little manufacturing there was – an option which was as likely, in the 1960s and 1970s as in the 1980s, to be ruled out or be extremely difficult because of political and social concerns.

What has all this to do with the specific issue of manufactured exports? Simply that understanding the sequence of the origin of the problem and the policy response in relation to the current lack of international competitiveness of much of SSA manufacturing has important implications for attempts to address the problem and to diversify the structure of manufacturing. Thus, if recent events are any guide to current policy decisions, *it would appear that efforts to alter the structure of manufacturing and, in particular, to raise the share of exports in total output, are highly unlikely to succeed by tinkering with tariff levels and rapidly opening up manufacturing to internationally competitive forces unless and until changes are made to address the problems of comparative inefficiency at the enterprise level.* What is more, there is little in the case-studies to suggest that drives to create more domestic competition and to remove the power and control of large firms in particular industrial sub-sectors will be likely to lead to a rapid expansion of manufactured exports. Indeed, recent cross-sectional evidence would tend to confirm the view that such an approach is likely to be counter-productive[14]. Even the Botswanan experience shows that a liberal trade regime is inadequate, in isolation, to create a strong manufacturing sector capable of competing internationally. What would appear to be needed, in general terms, is an overall commitment by management, and supported by politicians and financial institutions, to improve efficiency through implementing a range of policies aimed at raising productive efficiency[15]. This would include the following: more appropriate machinery, 'new' management techniques, research and technological capabilities, innovative ways of raising labour productivity, systematic attempts to enter new non-domestic markets with higher quality products packaged more attractively, attempts to reduce comparative transport disadvantages, the provision or extension of export credit guarantees and facilities to minimise foreign-exchange risks.

The importance of this conclusion is confirmed by examples from some of the case-studies which show that manufacturing firms (in the textile sub-sector especially, but also in others) with, until recently, little or no previous tradition of exporting outside Africa have now succeeded in establishing themselves, especially in European Community markets, following some or all of the following changes: the re-equipping of their factories with new or less antiquated plant and machinery, the mounting of a sustained export drive, often with state assistance in penetrating new markets, substantive changes in worker/machine relationships and new management techniques[16]. What is more, international experience suggests that such a conclusion is far from unique to SSA[17].

IMPORT SUBSTITUTION:
HAS IT FAILED OR NOT REALLY BEEN TRIED?
Returning to the sources of growth analysis, we need to consider the third element, namely import substitution. Two initial features should be noted. First, in the countries for which evidence is available, import substitution has been a *significant* source of growth in manufacturing output in at least one phase of the industrial history: it accounted for 30% of output growth in Nigeria from 1963 to 1973; for 37% in Botswana from 1973/4 to 1984/5 and for 18% in Kenya from 1970 to 1975. In two countries, for particular (albeit relatively short) periods of time, import substitution constituted the major source of growth, accounting for 55% of output growth in Zambia in the late 1960s and for 54% of growth in manufacturing in Zimbabwe from 1952/3 to 1964/5. Secondly, however, while the degree of import substitution has varied from country to country, the overall impact appears to have been minimal in all but one of the countries (the exception being Zimbabwe). It has resulted neither in a very significant degree of inter-linkages with other sub-sectors of manufacturing, or to other productive sectors of the economy (excepting, of course, further processing of primary products), nor to a significant fall in the importation of even the simpler consumer goods. What this suggests is that the process of import substitution has tended to be arbitrary, confirmed by other evidence which also indicates that in many of the countries a large and, not unusually, a growing absolute quantity of manufactured imports still consist of consumer goods[18].

How does one explain this limited progress and patchy performance? A conventional view is that import substitution was aimed initially at replacing the high level of the simpler consumer-good imports, its advocacy being linked to the substantial and/or expanding level of domestic demand for these products and to the fact that their manufacture required fairly simple machinery and production techniques, few skills and frequently (though not always) a proportion of locally available inputs. SSA has not advanced far along the road of import substitution, it is argued, because this 'easier' phase has been completed in increasing numbers of countries in the region and import – substitution policies pursued in relative insularity tend to 'get stuck'[19]. In the literature, this view has been frequently propounded as a *complete and sufficient* explanation for both the shallowness of African industrialisation and the fall-off in the relative importance of import substitution over time.

This interpretation, however, leaves a range of questions unanswered. Why, for instance, has the extent of import substitution achieved tended to vary so markedly from one country to another, why, as just noted, does such a high quantity of consumer goods still have to be imported, and why is it that the process of import substitution has been sustained for far longer periods in some countries than in others? To what extent has the 'slowdown' in the process been due to 'natural' factors rather than to the absence or decline of additional steps to promote the establishment of new and non-consumer-oriented industries? To which also needs to be added the question of the alternative on offer. Lance Taylor, for instance, argues that there is no theoretically persuasive case in favour of the export-led growth alternative and that 'the neoclassical case for export promotion runs into an empirical cul-de-sac' (1988a: 19)[20].

But perhaps the first question to ask is whether this simple view of import substitution is borne out by the facts. The case-study evidence throws this into some doubt. To start with, import substitution, for instance, in Nigeria, Côte d'Ivoire, Kenya, Zambia and Zimbabwe was by no means exclusively confined to the replacement of simple consumer goods: there was a deliberate policy to establish more sophisticated industries, at different periods in the case of the first three countries.

In addition, the evidence fails to show that the share of output growth attributable to import substitution declined over time. In Kenya, for instance, its relative contribution to overall output expansion appears to have risen from the late 1960s to the early 1970s and, after a period of decline in the late 1970s, to have continued expanding in the early 1980s, with some sub-sectors recording their highest relative expansion in import substitution in the later period. Nonetheless, and in spite of these apparent advances, even by the early 1980s Kenyan industry was not markedly diversified. In Nigeria, although the overall figures tend to confirm a relative decline over time in the share of import substitution in overall growth, they probably conceal more than they reveal because, as the case-study argues, import substitution in Nigeria has been very shallow, with the rise in the expansion of investment goods in the period 1973–83 (compared with 1963–73) due predominantly to the setting up of (high-cost) vehicle assembly plants. For Botswana, in the period 1973–4 to 1984–5 and following annual growth rates of 13% for the previous eight years, import substitution accounted for nearly 40% of output growth excluding meat products. The Zambian study is also of relevance here; in spite of the high degree of import substitution, especially in the late 1960s, and a rapid and prolonged rise in the MVA/GDP ratio (see Table 3.1), dependence upon imports in the more sophisticated sub-sectors has tended to rise over time, while during the past two decades there would appear to have been few if any substantial structural shifts.

The most interesting results, however, come from Zimbabwe where the degree of inter-industry linkages is high and the level of imported to total inputs is low, at least in contrast with other SSA countries. A quite complex level of inter-action has developed both between and within different manufacturing sub-sectors and forward to the agricultural, mining, construction and transport sectors, while, in addition, the imported to total inputs ratio has declined progressively at least over the last two decades[21].

These characteristics and the fact that the manufacturing sector accounts for upwards of 25% of GDP point to considered and relatively comprehensive import substitution having taken place in Zimbabwe. What is more, the sources of growth analysis strongly supports this conclusion. In the period 1952/3 to 1964/5, import substitution was the *major* source of manufacturing growth, accounting for 54% of output growth, while in the next period, from 1964/5 to 1978/9, it accounted for 30%. Furthermore, 20% of all manufacturing output growth in the 30-year period from the early 1950s originated in the metals sub-sector of manufacturing, and of that, as much as 70% was attributable to import substitution. Thus at least over this period, and almost certainly for a significantly longer period[22], import substitution has been a key element in overall manufacturing output growth. The Zimbabwean experience also shows that the process of import substitution has managed to lead to the production of a range of products of a quality high enough for them to be internationally traded. Finally, evidence at the level of the firm shows that import substitution has continued throughout the 1980s saving large amounts of foreign exchange, even though in aggregate the decomposition of the sources of growth data tends to suggest that it has now all but ceased[23].

Clearly, if Zimbabwe has been able to develop its industrial base in this way there would appear to be no *a priori* reason why other SSA countries could not also have initiated strategies of sustained and comprehensive import substitution with an equally high (30% and over) proportion of industrial growth. The Zimbabwe case-study discusses in some depth the reasons for its successes as well as stressing some of the weaknesses, inadequacies, unique historical circumstances and elements of good fortune which played a part in the evolution of the manufacturing sector. Some of these relate to developments within the sector itself, others to policies and incentives within the wider economy. The most important factors highlighted (albeit at different points of time) would include the following:

> government support for industrial promotion and expansion, a sustained period without balance of payments problems, a long period of overall growth and continued diversification in the rest of the economy, a fairly developed and efficiently operating supporting physical, transport and financial infrastructure, a developed capital market, high levels of local management and engineering skills, knowledge of production processes and ability to adapt machinery to local conditions, international confidence in the economy leading to inflows of foreign investment and technology (in the crucial pre-UDI period), trade agreements which ensured relatively captive neighbouring and larger markets for goods, tariffs and quantitative restrictions which provided protection to newly-established firms and, in the case of some firms, the payment of subsidies.

What seems to have been important for Zimbabwe was not so much that one or other characteristic featured more strongly at one point of time but rather the convergence of so many supportive elements for long periods, together with the ability of both the government and manufacturers to adapt as circumstances, internal and externally-induced, changed – shown most clearly during the phase of the Unilateral Declaration of Independence (UDI). Thus, prior to and during the Federal period (1952/3 to 1964/5), the economy was characterised by relatively low tariffs and few quantitative controls. On the other hand, the UDI period (1964/5–78/9) was dominated by almost all-embracing controls and regulations, including prohibition of a wide range of competing imports and limited access to foreign exchange. Yet in *both* periods the share of import substitution in overall growth exceeded 30%, a share not equalled by any SSA country over such a long period of time[24].

In contrast, most of the other case-studies point to particular weaknesses in their own manufacturing history. For instance, the Botswanan, Kenyan and Zambian studies refer to the crucial role of management. In Côte d'Ivoire, the expansion of manufacturing was due in no small measure to competent management, the weakness being its expatriate nature. Failures in Cameroon's attempts to expand heavy industry are attributed to poor technical design and inadequate infrastructure, especially power supplies, while for Kenya the fragility of the engineering base is mentioned as an important constraint. For Nigeria, inadequate high-level manpower, an over-dependence upon oil revenues, politically-motivated decisions and the availability of greater incentives to entrepreneurs engaged in commerce are all highlighted as causes of failure to expand industry and develop successful import substitution industries – the lack of incentives for entrepreneurs also being highlighted in the case of Kenya. In Côte d'Ivoire, in a generally protection-free environment in the early post-independence years, the incentive system discriminated against the establishment and expansion of intermediate and capital goods industries.

There were also more widespread problems contributing to the particular pattern of industrialisation which developed. Thus in Kenya, Nigeria, Côte d'Ivoire, Cameroon and Zambia, pressures to expand the sector more rapidly in the face of inadequate domestic skills and markets and an unreliable supply of inputs led to an unco-ordinated establishment of enterprises and a number of substantial failures, often concealed (until the 1980s when cost-cutting exercises became more urgent) by government bail-outs and escalating subsidies. In countries like Côte d'Ivoire, Zambia, Cameroon and Nigeria, at different periods, politically-inspired pressures to promote state-owned industries without adequate overall planning, or infrastructure, and with inadequate local and, not infrequently, foreign personnel, played a significant role in establishing and perpetuating inefficient industries. These pressures have by no means disappeared in the late 1980s, as seen, for instance, in the Ajaokuta steel plant in Nigeria[25].

One final, although more tentative, comment based on the data provided in Table 3.1 could be made in this context. For all of Zimbabwe's achievements, it is notable that in the period 1965–80, its MVA growth rate was the lowest of all the case-study countries and in the early 1980s was the third lowest. There is no doubt that, with more efficient policies, and a more favourable external, particularly regional, environment, manufacturing growth rates could have been higher. For example, long-term MVA growth rates were certainly pulled down significantly by the adverse effects of the 1974–9 war years[26]. The question remains, however, whether industrial expansion – linked more to developing inter-linkages and deepening the structure rather than to expanding the supply of current products in response to increases in effective demand – led to *lower* rates of growth than if the latter path of manufacturing sector expansion had been pursued. If this were proved to be the case – and the case-studies, sadly, throw little additional light on the subject – then not only would the commonly-used measures of manufacturing performance – rates of MVA growth and changes in the MVA/GDP ratio – prove inadequate, because they omit key variables, but they would tend to over-exaggerate the long-term strength of the sector.

1980s CLOSE-UP: SEEKING EXPLANATIONS FOR THE SLOWDOWN

An important set of questions is raised by the apparent abrupt changes in overall industrial performance in SSA in the 1980s compared with the 1960s and 1970s, as summarised in Table 3.2. Why was it that, in general, growth rates in manufacturing fell dramatically in the 1980s? Relatedly, however, why was it that, against this general trend, growth rates in Cameroon and Botswana remained buoyant, Botswana's growth rate (according to World Bank data) amounting to over twice the rate of growth of manufacturing of all middle-income developing countries. Again, why did Zimbabwe's manufacturing sector not return to its steady pre-independence rate of growth? Finally why, as the data in Figures 3.1 and 3.2 show so well, do the 1980s appear to have been characterised by so much *volatility* in growth rates in so many of the case-study countries, while the expansion in Cameroon and Kenya appears, in contrast, to have been smooth and steady?

An initial explanation for the dramatic fall in growth rates of MVA lies beyond SSA in the performance of the major actors in the world economy. In the period, 1980–86, the average growth rates of the leading industrial economies dropped by 30% to 2.5% a year compared with the previous period, 1965–80, with the drop in their annual import growth being even greater, falling off by 36% to 4.3% a year (World Bank, 1988, Tables 2–16). This slowdown in world production and trade itself adversely affected world prices of commodities leading to an even greater deceleration in industrial growth in the developing economies: the index of agricultural raw material prices fell from 100 in 1980 to 79.0 in 1986, metal prices from 100 to 65.5 (IMF, *International Financial Statistics Yearbook 1988*, pp. 184–5). For all middle-income economies, average growth of MVA fell from 8.2% for the period 1965–80 to 2.5% for 1980–86, with growth rates falling by more than half in 25 out of 29 countries for which World Bank data were available. The slowdown in manufacturing growth in SSA was clearly part of a far wider phenomenon.

For the SSA countries, with their manufacturing sectors oriented predominantly to domestic demand and their inputs of both raw materials and machinery, spares and equipment highly dependent upon imports, the effects of trade volume and price contractions on the overall level of imports and on aggregate growth were particularly adverse. As Table 3.2 shows, substantial contractions in GDP growth rates and in export and import expansion coincided with major falls in MVA for most countries. In the case of Cameroon, however, MVA expanded as did GDP growth rates and exports, while annual GDP growth still remained astonishingly high in Botswana, above 11%, coinciding with a rate of growth of MVA higher than 6%.

It is thus apparent that for most of the countries studied a part of the explanation for both the lower rates of MVA growth and the greater volatility lies *outside* their manufacturing sectors, a fact which confirms the vulnerability of manufacturing to external influences. Lower levels of export earnings together with more restrictive access to investment and commercial

Table 3.2 *Growth rates of selected indicators, 1965–80 and 1980–86: case-study countries*

Country	1965–80 growth rates				
	GDP	MVA	AVA	Imports	Exports
Botswana	14.3	13.5	9.7	24.5[b]	37.0[b]
Cameroon	5.1	7.0	4.2	5.6	5.2
Côte d'Ivoire	6.8	9.1	3.3	8.0	5.6
Kenya	6.4	10.5	4.9	1.7	0.3
Nigeria	8.0	14.6	1.7	15.1	11.4
Zambia	1.8	5.3	2.2	−5.5	1.7
Zimbabwe	4.4	4.0	15.5[a]	−1.8	3.5
SSA average	5.6	8.5	1.6	4.9	6.6

	1980–86 growth rates				
	GDP	MVA	AVA	Imports	Exports
Botswana	11.9	6.2	−9.8	2.9[b]	14.7[b]
Cameroon	8.2	5.4	2.0	−0.5	13.8
Côte d'Ivoire	−0.3	2.8	0.9	−5.4	3.5
Kenya	3.4	4.1	2.8	−5.2	−0.9
Nigeria	−3.2	1.0	1.4	−17.2	−6.0
Zambia	−0.1	0.6	−2.8	−7.3	−2.1
Zimbabwe	2.6	1.3	3.4	−6.7	−2.7
SSA average	0.0	0.3	1.2	−7.5	−2.1

Source: World Bank, *World Development Report 1988*, *World Tables 1987* and country case-study (for Cameroon and Côte d'Ivoire).

Notes: [a] 1969 to 1980, national data.
[b] Botswana trade data from *World Tables 1987*, for all other countries from *World Development Report 1988*.

finance and little if any increase in development assistance coincided with lower levels of agricultural and mining production. The effects were felt on both the demand and supply side of manufacturing: resultant falls in domestic demand were accompanied by lower levels of real imports which restricted the supply of inputs, the provision of spare parts and the availability of funds needed for rehabilitation, reinvestment or expansion. Capacity utilisation levels dropped and the overall climate put paid to much hope of new foreign investment to help bridge the growing gap in external resource requirements. For many countries – Côte d'Ivoire, Kenya, Nigeria, Zambia and Zimbabwe and eventually Cameroon – increased macroeconomic dislocation (rising balance-of-payments and fiscal deficits and high and rising rates of inflation) led to pressures, internal and external, to introduce further deflationary policies through either World Bank-promoted or less formalised structural adjustment programmes. The result was to depress manufacturing still further, with the varying effectiveness of the measures adopted and their differing duration contributing to the often substantial annual swings in MVA as the 1980s proceeded.

In general, however, it took till the latter half of the decade for more substantial policies directed specifically at manufacturing to be either introduced or seriously considered in an attempt to address the more substantial structural problems inherited, and perhaps worsened, during the previous 15 years. As a result it is probably too early to be able to analyse with any certainty the effects of these initiatives, both in tackling the problems of the past and in preparing manufacturing to face the problems and challenges of the 1990s – even if initial indications suggest that much will need to be done if high and sustained growth rates are to be attained in the 1990s.

For Zimbabwe, the 1980s began not only with great optimism for the future but also with impressive initial economic expansion. The ending of the war, the removal of the sanctions premium and excellent rains all reinforced each other to produce initially, in 1980 and 1981[27], record rates of growth of the economy. Manufacturing benefited from pent-up domestic demand while supply constraints were eased with the rapid expansion of import allocations underwritten first by aid flows but increasingly by external commercial borrowing. In many respects, however, the initial success had the effect of diverting attention away from the

Figure 3.1 *Annual changes in MVA 1980–86 (1979 = 100)*

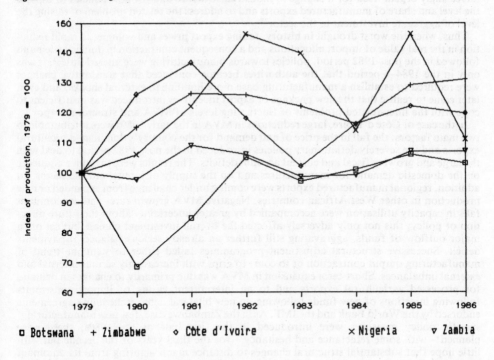

Figure 3.2 *Changes in MVA, 1980–86 (1979 = 100)*

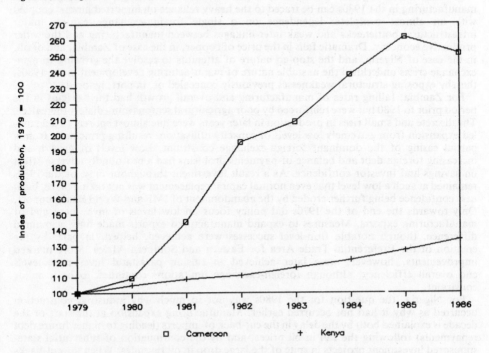

Source: World Bank, *World Tables 1987*, except for Côte d'Ivoire and Cameroon data from national sources.

increasingly urgent need for a change in industrial structure and for new policies to expand the level and share of manufactured exports and to address the related problem of raising the level of aggregate investment in the sector[28].

Thus, when the worst drought in history, falling export prices and volumes, a rapid reduction in the real value of import allocations and a consequent contraction in domestic demand followed in the post-1982 period, policies towards manufacturing were altered little[29]. It was only in the 1984-6 period that the authorities became convinced that substantive changes were required to establish a manufacturing base more immune to external shocks, and even later came to realise that the new package of export incentives introduced was insufficient to cope with the inter-related problems of fluctuating levels of MVA and structural torpor.

In the case of Côte d'Ivoire, large reductions in MVA in the early 1980s were attributable to two main factors: the fall in the price of and demand for the country's dominant agricultural exports and the severely deflationary policies introduced in the post-1982 period to deal with the large and growing fiscal and current account deficits. The results were to induce a squeeze on the domestic demand for manufactures and on the supply of inputs into the sector. In addition, regional manufactured exports were coming under challenge from expanded or new production in other West African countries. Negative MVA growth rates and concomitant falls in capacity utilisation were accompanied by greater uncertainty about the future direction of policy; this not only adversely affected the overall investment climate but set off a major outflow of funds, aggravating still further an already serious balance-of-payments deficit. Successive structural adjustment programmes failed either to stem the trend of manufacturing output contraction or to come to grips with increasingly serious internal and external imbalances. Short-term expansion in MVA was due primarily to changes in demand for processed agricultural exports and to an intermittent easing of import constraints following injections of new funds following on new bilateral debt rescheduling agreements endorsed by the World Bank and the IMF. As in the Zimbabwe case, few new manufacturing-specific policy measures were introduced in the first half of the 1980s; these were planned – with some reluctance and hesitancy – for the final years of the decade but with little hope that substantial structural changes to distance manufacturing from its dominant dependent links on agriculture would be achieved.

In Zambia and Nigeria, volatile and, in general, very low average levels of growth in manufacturing in the 1980s can be traced to the heavy reliance on imported inputs, coupled with an almost complete dependence on a single foreign-exchange earner, major infrastructural bottlenecks and weak inter-linkages between manufacturing and the wider productive economy. Dramatic falls in the price of copper, in the case of Zambia, and of oil, in the case of Nigeria, and the stop-go nature of attempts to resolve the growing foreign-exchange crises underlined the unstable nature of manufacturing development in the 1980s, thereby exposing structural weaknesses previously concealed or, in part, ignored.

For Zambia, falling rates of manufacturing and overall growth had their origins in the period prior to 1980 but were reinforced by poor agricultural seasons immediately thereafter. The discrete and small rises in production in later years were due almost entirely to demand-led expansion from extremely low levels of capacity utilisation, resulting principally from a partial easing of the dominant foreign-exchange constraint. Low levels of growth and increasing foreign debt and balance-of-payments problems had a profoundly adverse effect on savings and investor confidence. As a result investment throughout most of the 1980s remained at such a low level that even normal capital replacement was not taking place, business confidence being further eroded by the abandonment of IMF and World Bank support. Only towards the end of the 1970s did policy focus on low levels of investment and of manufacturing exports. Measures to expand manufactured exports made only a minimal difference, though notable firm-level successes were achieved, helped, in part, by the creation of the Preferential Trade Area for Eastern and Southern Africa. More marked improvements, however, were later achieved in raising parastatal investment levels and overall efficiency, although foreign-exchange limitations continued to be a major constraint.

For Nigeria, the question for the 1980s was not so much why industrial contraction occurred as why it had not occurred earlier. Manufacturing expansion at the start of the decade is explained both by the delay in the cut-back of imports (leading to higher future debt repayments) following the fall in oil prices, and by the continuation of substantial state-sponsored investment projects in spite of the large drop in oil revenues. When the cut-backs were eventually made, the effects were severe; contractions in domestic demand for manufactured products became especially acute in the mid-1980s and massive lay-offs of workers took place. On the policy front little effective action had been taken by the mid-1980s to address the structural problems of manufacturing, although there was some reduction in the high level of imported inputs. It was only in the second half of the 1980s that a resolution of the major distortions of the economy appeared possible and that any substantially different policies appeared on the agenda. New initiatives included attempts to raise investment levels through the twin policies of privatisation and radically altering the investment code, efforts to improve the efficiency of sub-sectors like vehicle assembly through rationalising the number of makes of vehicles and, more generally, through the effects of exchange-rate devaluations, an economy-wide tariff reform and incentives to stimulate the expansion of manufactured exports. With MVA estimated to have risen by 8% in 1988, it might seem that there had been some success at reversing the longer-term stagnation. Yet these achievements have had little to do with tariff reform, for instance, which has effectively been shelved. The growth spurt was due more to an expansion from very low (perhaps 25%) levels of capacity, to a partial easing of foreign-exchange shortages, and to a spurt in domestic demand, not expected to be repeated in any sustained fashion. Over the medium term, therefore, manufacturing industry in Nigeria will continue to be constrained by the country's poor infrastructure, weak management and foreign-exchange shortages.

Cameroon's manufacturing performance in the 1980s has been far less rosy than the steady growth rate during the first fix years would suggest. By the second half of the decade the low-and-volatile-growth syndrome of so many other SSA countries had also gripped manufacturing in Cameroon.

The initial successes in the 1980s of the entire domestic economy are attributable almost solely to oil exports. Oil propelled the economy forward as it rose rapidly to achieve a (short-lived) prominence in the post-1978 period. Oil exports accounted for a mere 3% of total export earnings in 1978 but they had risen to over 65% by 1984, rising from $25 m. to $1.5 bn, easing foreign-exchange shortages, and stimulating overall domestic demand. Thus the prevailing supply and demand constraints on manufacturing industry were overcome – at least while the oil boom lasted. But there was more. Massive expansion of public investment across the domestic economy, including the manufacturing sector, together with a linked and unprecedented boom in the construction industry further helped to boost manufacturing growth.

While some new import substitution did take place during the first half of the 1980s, it followed the historical pattern and was predominantly agriculturally-based. At the same time, regional manufactured exports suffered increasingly from competing import substitution efforts in neighbouring countries. What is more, the investment-led boom had a sting in its tail: vast sums were spent on several disastrous public investment projects, some of which had to be totally abandoned and others could only be maintained through substantial and rising state subsidies. When, after 1985, the fall in oil output aggravated that in oil prices, these burdens became increasingly difficult to shoulder and signalled a rapid drop in the rate of growth of manufacturing and of GDP. Compared with its rapid rise from 1979 to 1984, MVA grew by around 4% in 1985 and fell to nearly zero the year after. These aggregate rates, however, conceal more violent swings in performance in the different industrial sub-sectors: textiles and clothing contracted by over 15% as early as 1985, grain milling by over 30% in 1985, while, by 1987, falls of over 20% in food processing and an even greater contraction in the manufacturing-linked construction sector had taken place.

The story of industrial development in Kenya in the 1980s is less dramatic but provides only marginally more encouragement. The steady, albeit fairly low, expansion of manufacturing can also be explained principally by events in the wider economy together with the continued increase in tariff protection (especially after 1974) which thus stimulated manufacturing expansion. While a series of stabilisation measures had to be introduced to tackle the problems of macro-dislocation, they did not need to be so intense since the degree of distortion was not as high as in many other SSA countries. It was thus easier to attract adequate amounts of external funding while comparatively high levels of official aid flows continued[30]. In addition, agriculture, to which manufacturing was strongly linked, continued to expand, albeit at a slower rate than in the previous decade[31]. This, plus the shift in the internal terms of trade from agriculture and towards the manufacturing sector, allowed manufacturing to continue to expand (but more slowly[32]) in the first half of the 1980s without major disruption.

But the small amount of structural change which then occurred favoured the further expansion of consumer goods industries and reinforced the inward-looking nature of the sector.

The Kenyan story does not end here, however, for the sectoral aggregates tend to conceal some important sub-sectoral differences. Thus the early 1980s were also a period when the system of import licensing was tightened; with the drop in domestic demand, this helps to explain why the share of output growth attributable to import substitution was at its highest in this period. In addition, the chemical, rubber and petroleum refining sub-sectors benefited from oil price movements at the end of the 1970s and beginning of the 1980s, while the contracting volumes of imports available to manufacturing led to a relative weakening in the contribution to growth of those sub-sectors highly dependent upon imported inputs: machinery, metal products, transport equipment, textiles and clothing. As a result, under-utilisation of capacity became an increasing and more widespread feature of manufacturing as the 1980s progressed. As for manufactured exports, by the mid-1980s they constituted only 7.5% of total manufactured output compared with 22% in 1972 (*Financial Times*, 12 December 1988, p. 16).

What the Kenyan case also suggests is that, far from being an example for others to follow, the macroeconomic deterioration which became increasingly apparent in the 1980s was due in no small measure to the nature of past manufacturing growth. As a result, manufacturing expansion remained predominantly linked to external beneficial factors such as agricultural expansion, improved international terms of trade and capital inflows sufficient to finance the increasing costs of a protected manufacturing sector. This tends to explain the even more bullish events characterising 1987-8[33]. It was equally apparent, by the end of 1988, that the stated objective of reorienting manufacturing to a more export-oriented growth path had not yet led to any substantial changes in the structure of the sector[34].

In sharp contrast with both Kenya and Cameroon, Botswana provides a refreshingly different picture. Indeed, the case-study suggests that the aggregate figures reproduced here significantly understate the development of manufacturing and its contribution to overall growth and development. Between 1979 and 1980, MVA fell by a record and abnormal 33% following a similar rise between 1978 and 1979 as a result of a uniquely high level of cattle slaughters. Discounting this abnormality, and considering the growth rates of manufacturing from 1974 (the first year much reliable data on manufacturing were collected) into the 1980s, annual MVA growth accelerated from around 10% in the 1970s to about 17% in the 1980s[35]. Furthermore, the fastest rate of manufactured export expansion and the highest levels of manufacturing investment, including foreign investment inflows to the sector, also occurred in the 1980s[36]. The 1980s have been a period of pronounced success in terms of aggregate manufacturing growth, import substitution, expansion of exports and overall structural change.

This impressive performance can be explained by the convergence of four sets of positive factors: the ability to earn increasing amounts of foreign exchange through expanding primary exports, favourable regional developments, macroeconomic management which maintained high levels of domestic demand and, finally (but almost certainly of lesser relative importance), increased incentives for the manufacturing sector.

Continued high levels of overall export growth, due principally to an expansion of mineral exports, together with high levels of foreign investment inflows, meant that Botswana did not suffer from severe balance-of-payments problems in the 1980s. What is more, the current account deficits of the early 1980s did not lead to policies resulting in a substantial drop in either domestic demand or government expenditure because of successful counter-cyclical measures. Prudent exchange-rate management enabled high levels of domestic demand to be maintained while foreign investment was stimulated, in particular by policies restricting profit repatriation in neighbouring Zimbabwe which encouraged a number of firms to relocate to Botswana.

It was in this context that a series of measures favouring expansion of manufacturing had an impact. First was the switch away from state investment in infrastructural projects in the post-1975 period towards more productive investment. Second, use was beginning to be made of the protection of local industry clause of the Southern African Customs Union agreement to which Botswana was a signatory. But of more direct importance was, thirdly, the Financial Assistance Policy (FAP) which provided subsidies largely to manufacturing enterprises involved in import substituting and exporting.

The combination of these domestic measures, together with a climate favouring investment in stable Botswana as a result of adverse developments in most other southern African countries, goes a long way towards explaining Botswana's manufacturing successes in the 1980s. What is more, this convergence of favourable factors has striking similarities to those which characterised Zimbabwe's success in import substitution prior to 1964. Botswana's manufacturing expansion was achieved with a minimum of regulations and little direct protection although, also like Zimbabwe, developments occurred within the context of a protected trade area. More generally, the period after the mid-1970s paralleled, in many ways, the circumstances prevailing in the 1960s in so many other African countries: rapid industrialisation was made possible by the relative absence of foreign-exchange constraints and the prospect of a range of early import-substituting opportunities.

It is important, however, not to over-play the importance of the Botswana case-study for, however notable its successes, the manufacturing sector still remains minuscule not only in respect to other middle-income countries but also in comparison with others in the SSA region[37].

CONCLUDING OBSERVATIONS
Analysing trends in rates of growth of MVA and of the share of manufacturing in aggregate growth, provides only a partial measure for judging industrial success. Lack of inter-linkages within manufacturing, weak forward linkages to other productive sectors, shallow consumer goods-dominated manufacture, partial and patchy progress in import substitution, and low and deteriorating shares of exports in total manufacturing output, are all characteristics of manufacturing in almost all of the 'successful' countries examined in this book. They highlight profound weaknesses in their manufacturing structures and the inadequacies of the 'supporting' infrastructure.

The 1980s have seen little change in the structure of manufacturing, the most striking characteristic being the sharp slowing down of industrial growth, more dramatic than that in the 1970s and in marked contrast with the performance of the 1960s. Botswana is the single and, in terms of the size of its manufacturing sector, minor exception to these predominant trends. If restructuring of industries was to have been the priority for the 1980s then the decade has certainly been a failure (see Steel and Evans, 1984: v).

The decade should not be viewed solely as a failure, however. Part II of this book not only pinpoints some of the underlying weaknesses of the sector which influenced perceptions and decisions at the policy level but also reveals ways in which a number of countries have found solutions to some of the problems of industrial expansion and deepening. As a result, analysts and African governments are in a better position to understand both why more distinct manufacturing development, and different from the other productive sectors, has not taken place and why the level of manufacturing exports remains so pitifully low.

But the case-studies have done more. They have enabled us to look more positively at the problems and to search for more substantial and durable solutions to the weaknesses highlighted. For instance, they have isolated a series of factors which go a long way towards explaining specific successes at particular points of time in several countries, highlighting the importance not only of incentives in the wider economy, but also of those tailored to the specific needs of the manufacturing sector. One implication is that what 'works' in one country will not necessarily 'work' in another: the case-studies suggest that there does not appear to be one particular road to industrialisation or mould into which either these or other SSA countries could or should be made to fit. Another lesson is to warn of the dangers of trying to force the pace of industrial expansion and/or structural change when conditions within the sector or the broader economy are clearly not conducive to such promotional stimulation.

But there is an important difference between *forcing* change inappropriately and providing the optimal conditions for manufacturing development and deepening to be accelerated. In this regard, the comments made earlier about the role of domestic demand in inducing the growth of manufacturing output need to be qualified. It was argued that the dominance of domestic demand in contributing to the growth of manufacturing output suggested that a rise in such demand was a necessary condition for sustained manufacturing development. This conclusion now appears too constrictive: import substitution and export growth can also sustain the expansion of manufacturing to a significant extent. In other words, the evidence tends to suggest that there is scope for a more complex view of industrial development than that maintained in the past. The path chosen must be rooted in the particular strengths of the economy in question, sound assessments of external constraints and potential, and the political will to execute often painful adjustment.

The opportunities for the SSA region for manufacturing expansion and restructuring in the 1990s is the subject to which we now turn.

Manufacturing into the 1990s:
prospects, constraints and opportunities

LOWER GROWTH RATES FOR MANUFACTURING
TO THE MID-1990s

What are the prospects for the manufacturing sector in the 1990s? If these are to be judged in terms of steady expansion of MVA (and unless this happens there will be little substantial progress) then it would appear that they are not bright, especially in the first half of the decade: growth rates are likely to be as low (on average) as during the dismal 1980s, with year-to-year changes continuing to follow the volatile path characteristic of the recent past. Botswana, Kenya and Zimbabwe are the countries most likely to see further expansion of their manufacturing sectors but for none of these – probably not even Botswana[38] – is rapid growth going to be easy to achieve, given the inherited structural problems outlined above. For the others, growth rates are more difficult to predict but, barring fortuitous, significant but unexpected rises in the prices of their leading primary product exports, even lower and more volatile growth is likely to characterise their manufacturing sectors.

Given these poor prospects, there is even less chance that over the medium term the manufacturing sector could provide the 'answer' to their current economic crises. What is more, as these seven countries collectively hold out the best hopes for manufacturing expansion in SSA, there is not the remotest hope that in the medium term the manufacturing sector can be a major force in solving the economic malaise which pervades the subcontinent.

This pessimism is sharply at variance with official and semi-official assessments of the sector for the future. Development plans, official forecasts and projections and what are frequently referred to as 'medium-term policy frameworks'[39] drawn up for these countries, particularly by the World Bank, suggest both growth rates in the years ahead higher than the average achieved in the 1980s and steady and sustained expansion, albeit mostly at rates lower than those achieved in the heady days of the 1960s. In sharp contrast, all the case-studies argue that the figures provided in such forecasts/scenarios range from being suspect[40] to being totally unreliable guides to future performance: in most cases *best* estimates range between a half and two thirds of these forecast/projected figures.

Table 3.3 is thus reproduced here with some hesitancy. While it attempts faithfully to summarise the 'best–case' official and semi-official scenarios for the first half of the 1990s, it cannot be stressed too strongly that these figures are likely to bear little or no relation to reality. The eerie similarity of the majority of the MVA growth rates clustered in the 7.5–8% range is itself probably sufficient to indicate that the figures constitute little more than the

Table 3.3 *Hoped-for or target scenarios for manufacturing into the 1990s*

Country	MVA growth 1980–86 Actual/Estimate	MVA growth 1990–95 (Target) Scenario	MVA/GDP 1986 Estimate	Ratios 1995 (Target) Scenario
Botswana	6.2	8.3[a]	6	7[a]
Cameroon	5.4	8.0	12	14
Côte d'Ivoire	2.8	8.0	16	18
Kenya	4.1	7.5	12	14
Nigeria	1.0	7.5[b]	8	10
Zambia	0.6	3.1[c]	20	22
Zimbabwe	1.3	6.5	30	31

Source: Table 3.1, country case-studies and own estimates.

Notes: [a] Based on 1985-91 government plan.
[b] Estimates made prior to the publication of the Fifth National Development Plan.
[c] Based on the Fourth National Development Plan.

targets one might like to see achieved rather than the outcome of realistic assessment of what can be expected to happen in the real world with the constraints most likely to affect economic performance.

Nonetheless, one point of interest and importance can be derived from these figures. Even if these high rates of growth of MVA were to be achieved up to the middle of the 1990s, the contribution of manufacturing to GDP in each of the seven countries would still be small, except for Zambia and Zimbabwe. As a result, one can dismiss as mere conjecture any notion that the 1990s will herald the era when the SSA region begins to catch up with the pace of industrial development in other regions of the developing world.

For each of the case-study countries, the predominant cause of this pessimistic assessment of manufacturing growth lies *outside* the manufacturing sector and beyond the changes occurring there. As in the past, it appears that over the next few years manufacturing growth will continue to be most profoundly affected by events in other parts of the economy, eclipsing any changes occurring within the sector itself, and in the relationship between these economies and the international economy.

Pessimism about the performance of the manufacturing sector is therefore rooted in unfavourable assessments of overall growth prospects in these economies. Reasons for this revolve around a number of common threads across most of the countries. The principal one is that the case-study authors argue that export prospects are likely to be poor during this period and, in particular, to be substantially worse than those contained in official and semi-official documents to which manufacturing growth rates are critically related. This is largely because of the over-optimistic assumptions made for relevant primary product prices, particularly by those agencies supporting structural adjustment policies under the aegis of the World Bank and IMF.

Levels of real export earnings far lower than projected would adversely affect manufacturing in a number of direct and indirect ways. They would heighten the already severe foreign debt problems crippling most of these countries (Botswana excluded), exacerbating foreign-exchange shortages. Not only would this push back well into the 1990s the time when debt-servicing obligations fall, but low commodity prices would perpetuate the supply-related restrictions that have increasingly constrained manufacturing growth in the 1980s. These problems are likely to be particularly acute in Zambia, Cameroon, Zimbabwe and Nigeria, but still serious for Côte d'Ivoire and Kenya.

In addition, lower levels of traditional export earnings would induce a general slowdown in income and thereby reduce the demand for domestically produced manufactures. Furthermore, balance-of-payments constraints are likely to exacerbate already strained public sector finances and, at least in the cases of Cameroon, Zambia, Nigeria, Zimbabwe and Côte d'Ivoire, to lead to a slowdown in public sector demand for domestically-made consumer goods (for instance through budget constraints in relation to education and health spending), as well as further reductions in public sector capital development projects from which manufacturers have significantly benefited, dramatically so in the case of Cameroon.

Admittedly, manufacturing demand could be stimulated to the extent that a range of policies aimed at expanding agricultural sector development achieve their objectives. Most importantly, production increases of small-scale farms would lead to increases in incomes of at least middle-income farmers, raising the demand for consumer goods and, to some extent, for manufactured inputs to the agricultural sector.

The overall impact of this type of effect, however, is not likely to be very great over the next few years for a number of reasons. First, in most of the countries effort still seems to be directed at expanding export rather than domestic food crops, the effective demand for which, as we have suggested, is likely to stagnate in the near term. Even in Zimbabwe, where increases in production by small-scale farmers have been dramatic in the 1980s and where the linkages between manufacturing and agriculture are the most developed of all the countries considered, the overall impact on manufacturing has not been significant. In large part this has been because foreign-exchange constraints have continued to limit production even when money demand has risen. For a majority of the other countries, average rural incomes progressively deteriorated in at least the first six years of the 1980s and there remains little optimism that sustained reversals in these trends are immediately within grasp[41]. Even if average rural incomes *were* to rise quickly, it would take several years before the demand effect upon manufacturing would induce anything more than an expansion in what are extremely low levels of capacity utilisation. In West Africa in particular, when rises in rural incomes have occurred in recent years, these have tended to lead to dramatic rises in inflows of smuggled goods rather than to a stimulation of domestic manufactures. Furthermore, in Zimbabwe as elsewhere, rural incomes have fluctuated wildly from year to year as a result of varying rainfall patterns, resulting in swings in demand for manufactured goods – and if the 1990s are anything like the 1980s then they will be characterised by substantially lower than former long-term average rainfall levels. Overall, therefore, it does not seem likely that, even if there is a dramatic rise in agricultural production, this in itself would suffice to overcome the constraints on domestic demand for manufactured goods and lead to an acceleration in the rate of MVA growth.

Finally in a number of countries (particularly Nigeria, Zimbabwe, Cameroon and Botswana) manufacturing growth is likely to be held back by an increasingly inadequate physical infrastructure, lack of financial intermediation to support manufacturing expansion and the growing gap between the demand for and supply of these services[42].

As if these problems were not enough, a Catch-22 type scenario is also likely to develop, to add another dose of gloom to the near-term prospects for manufacturing. In almost all the case-study countries – most notably Nigeria, Zimbabwe, Zambia, Côte d'Ivoire and Cameroon – potential growth in manufacturing has been increasingly constrained by extremely low and (in recent years) declining levels of investment. Levels of domestic investment are likely to continue to be constrained both by low income growth rates and rising pressures to rein in public expenditure programmes: as a result significant inflows of foreign investment will be required even to maintain past growth rates and to ease the overall foreign-exchange constraints besetting manufacturing. But the expected slowdown in traditional commodity export earnings and in aggregate growth will add yet a further disincentive to would-be foreign investors, as the case studies of Nigeria, Zimbabwe and Côte d'Ivoire suggest[43].

To end this particular discussion, we need to ask what are the immediate and realistic prospects for boosting manufacturing growth through further import substitution and/or export expansion. The case-studies list a considerable number of specific opportunities when discussing further import substitution in more general terms. Yet in most of the countries examined, substantial and systematic expansion is likely to be constrained in the near term both by shortages of foreign exchange necessary for the import of a high proportion of new plant and equipment[44], together with the poor investment climate and, in some countries, skill shortages. As for the prospects for an expansion of manufacturing exports, the constraints highlighted in the previous section of this chapter are likely to continue into the first half of the 1990s. Continuing budgetary constraints will be likely to inhibit any major new financial initiative to subsidise manufactured exports, while sensitive fields like health and education are also bound to suffer. Thus no sustained near-term expansion of manufactured exports sufficient to make a major impact on overall growth of the sector is likely in any of the case-study countries.

GROUNDS FOR OPTIMISM IN THE LONGER TERM

If the prospects for manufacturing development in SSA were to be judged exclusively in comparison with past growth rates of MVA and if the bearish short-term time-horizon were to be projected further into the future, then the prospects would indeed be bleak. Other elements however, need to be considered which, while not casting doubt on pessimistic near-term assessments, place them in a wider and more bullish perspective. A majority of the case-studies – Kenya, Zimbabwe, Côte d'Ivoire, Botswana – view the longer-term future in anything but gloomy terms.

The starting point for such an alternative view has its origins, somewhat ironically, in the deteriorating economic fortunes of the 1980s. As the 1980s were drawing to a close, and in sharp contrast with any other time in the post-independence period, fundamental changes have increasingly been taking place and/or been seriously discussed in all the case-study countries. These embrace some of the key constraints which have inhibited the growth and development of the manufacturing sector or which have led to its becoming an increasing burden on the rest of the economy. They concern both issues specific to the sector and the manner in which manufacturing relates to the wider national and international economy and include the following: the high-cost nature of manufacturing; inefficiencies in production;

the narrow domestic focus of the sector and its lack of international competitiveness; low levels of investment and the battery of controls that inhibit management decision-making; the haphazard evolution of different industries as well as the high-cost nature of much import substitution.

It has been the acuity of the problems facing their economies as the 1980s have progressed, and the resulting elimination of short-term palliatives, which have created the climate for fundamental change to appear and remain on the political agenda in so many SSA countries. What is more, the poor overall prospects for the early 1990s and the foreclosing of many past policy options provide the grounds for believing that more substantive problems will be addressed in the 1990s rather than ignored or shelved as in the past. The implications could be profound: for the first time since the 1960s, substantive changes could well take place which would provide the conditions in the longer term – that is, roughly, after 1995 – for accelerated development of, and substantial structural change in, manufacturing.

Before developing this idea further, it is important to put it in perspective. It would be mistaken to believe either that the late 1990s will necessarily be a more buoyant era for manufacturing or that there is a sequential link between generally poor short-term prospects for manufacturing and more rapid and profound development in the longer term – even if such an outlook permeates official policy documents and if the theme of hope-arising-from-despair (death-and-resurrection) has its roots deep in the human psyche.

What is more, while embarking on a process of fundamental change is a start, it remains only a start: one also needs to be clear that the objectives are indeed the correct ones and that the means of achieving them will be available and are the most appropriate. In many of the case-study countries, there remains considerable controversy not so much about the objectives of industrialisation (although this is not totally absent) but particularly about the best means of achieving them and whether the necessary instruments can be effectively utilised. As a result, there is no guarantee that, even if fundamental changes are initiated, they will result in as beneficial an outcome as their proponents would suggest. Finally, even if it is agreed that change should take place, even if the targets are accepted, and even if a particular course of action is embarked upon, we are still not home and dry. This is because success in achieving agreed objectives will also be dependent upon factors external to the policy package drawn up.

In summary, then, a note of optimism is appropriate in evaluating the prospects for manufacturing in SSA in the 1990s because – and in strong contrast with the start of the 1980s – more and more countries have realised that, together with other aspects of their economies, their manufacturing sectors are in trouble and require major surgery[45]. Yet even if the correct diagnosis has been made and surgery is prescribed, the environment is far from supportive for convalescence. Furthermore, there is considerable uncertainty about the efficacy of various types of instruments envisaged at this point of time, both because their long-term effects have not been sufficiently assessed and also because of the high risk of contracting other infections in the post-operative ward. Thus – to complete the analogy – patients are faced with a succession of dilemmas as it is recognised that, although there are severe risks in not undergoing surgery, profound doubts remain about the type of surgery to be applied together with deep concern about post-operative recuperation.

STRUCTURAL CHANGE AND THE POTENTIAL FOR SUSTAINED GROWTH IN THE MEDIUM AND LONGER TERM

The longer-term prospects for the development and deepening of the manufacturing sector in SSA, in general, and for the seven case-study countries, in particular, will be critically determined by the nature of the policy environment, the incentive system in which manufacturing enterprises operate, and by policies and stimuli targeted specifically at firms within the manufacturing sector. While the policy environment and incentive structure will clearly play a role in accelerating or constraining the immediate rate of growth of MVA, what is of particular interest here is the way in which different policy choices are likely to affect structural changes within the sector and the relationship between manufacturing and the rest of the economy. This section is thus intended to provide a brief overview of the various policy options facing the different countries, based largely upon the more in-depth country-specific analysis contained in Part II. More specifically, the discussion is intended to shed light upon the prospects for manufacturing development under these different alternatives and, if substantive change is indeed to occur, to form a view on the appropriateness of each.

For the purposes of the present discussion, the various approaches have been narrowed down and grouped together into four options. This breakdown is intended to highlight the differing nature of the alternatives being debated in the often blurred world of practical decision-making: each is likely to lead to a substantially different type of structural change of manufacturing. The four options can be briefly summarised as follows.

Option 1. Continue to promote the expansion of the manufacturing sector, but in a manner substantially similar to that adopted in the expansive post-independence period.

Option 2. Leave the manufacturing sector to itself by neither introducing new policies nor re-vamping old approaches to make them work more effectively in the changing circumstances of the 1990s.

Option 3. Embark on a system of economy-wide reforms to which the manufacturing sector (like all others) will respond, which work to eliminate (at a varying pace) price and other financial and economic distortions. Open up the economy and its constituent sectors to international competition and, by eliminating distortions in the incentive system, re-order the structure of the whole economy and within it the manufacturing sector.

Option 4. Embark on a series of reforms targeted specifically at the manufacturing sector which, through a system of interventionist measures, attempt to correct specific inherited weaknesses in the context of an incentive structure whose objectives are to accelerate the growth, expand the exports and deepen the inter-linkages of the sector through further selective import substitution. Ensure, as far as possible, that reforms and incentives in the wider economy are in harmony with those devised for the sector.

Two brief initial observations must be made. The first is the simple observation that Options (1), (3) and (4) are all active approaches, while Option (2) is a passive 'do nothing' approach to industry's future. The importance of Option (2) in practical terms will become clearer in a moment. Secondly, this schematic breakdown is not meant to be a prelude to 'fitting' particular case-study countries neatly into one of these groupings. Nonetheless, and as should already be apparent from a reading of the chapter to this point, none of the seven countries could now be said to subscribe in practice (or almost certainly in theory either) to Option (1)[46]. In historical terms this needs to be acknowledged as a significant feature of policies towards industrialisation in SSA. It is, at least implicitly, a recognition that past approaches – long-term protective, high-cost, internationally uncompetitive, domestically-focused manufacturing[47] – have been a drain on national resources and should therefore not be pursued in the future. As a result, it appears unlikely that such an approach will feature on the policy agenda in the 1990s.

Before dismissing Option (1) completely, however, we need to consider explicitly the case of Botswana. As already mentioned, in relation both to the rapid growth of its manufacturing sector and its pursuit of new import-substitution policies, Botswana's recent performance could be said to mirror the early pattern of post-independent industrial development of several other SSA countries. Yet it differed crucially from almost all the other case-study countries[48] as its manufacturing expansion was based largely on an externally-open and market-based policy environment, not markedly at variance with the approach encapsulated in Option (3). Whether Botswana will or should maintain its present approach is taken up below.

Returning to the general discussion, an abandonment of option (1) – an active and pro-industry approach – has by no means meant that this has been replaced by any consensus within or between the different countries to opt for or adopt an alternative *active* approach – of which, broadly, options (3) and (4) present, rather sharply, the two central but markedly different alternatives before the SSA countries as they enter the 1990s. Indeed, a reading of the case-studies indicates quite clearly that *none* of the countries has committed itself fully to either Option (3) or Option (4). On the contrary, there are forces at work in most of them pulling opinion and influencing policy in the directions indicated by all the final three theoretical options, including therefore, and importantly, Option (2).

Options (3) and (4), as presented here, are brief schematic summaries of the two main and differing approaches to industrialisation which are influencing policy most profoundly in SSA today[49]. Option (3) encapsulates the approach most closely associated with and promoted by the World Bank, (and, to a lesser extent, the IMF[50]) under the umbrella of its various structural adjustment programmes. As indicated, it places manufacturing industry and its development within a broader macroeconomic framework and gives little attention to manufacturing-specific policies and incentives. Thus the structure of manufacturing, under this scenario, would change predominantly in response to policies implemented at the macro-level[51]. In practice these structural changes are likely to be profound.

In contrast, Option (4) comes closest to the alternative most readily associated generally with Africa-wide statements of the future role of manufacturing industry as well as those in country-specific development plans, particularly those not influenced by the structural adjustment thinking of the World Bank. It has tended, however, to be an approach articulated more at the level of generalities than one outlining more detailed sectoral and sub-sectoral policies. (In recent years the World Bank's approach and perspective on policy have become increasingly incorporated into official national policy documents[52].) Option (4) is an active interventionist approach which explicitly attempts to encourage both the expansion of manufacturing and structural change of the sector. Importantly, however, it is not a pro-industry approach blind to the demands of and constraints imposed by the 'real economy'[53] and thus, like Option (3), the outcome of following through an Option (4) policy package would result in substantial structural changes for the sector. Like Option (3), but unlike Option (1), it is concerned with the establishment of more efficient industries and the creation of a more export-oriented manufacturing sector and, in general, it shares the same objective of creating an industrial sector that is dynamic and less of a burden on the rest of the economy[54]. Unlike Option (3), however, one of Option (4)'s basic tenets is that these objectives can *best* be achieved by moulding market signals through the tempered use of interventionist policies by planned[55] or carefully worked out strategies for a future stretching well beyond the short term.

Under Option (4), the general objectives of economic growth and development are assumed to be enhanced by policies which promote an expanding and gradually more efficient and export-oriented manufacturing sector as well as further (efficient and integrated) import substitution[56]. Under Option (3) there is no such underlying pro-industry assumption: manufacturing industry would continue to exist and expand and manufacturing exports to be maintained and to grow to the extent that they can survive and swim in the increasingly internationally price-competitive world to which they are to be exposed. A process of de-industrialisation, the closing down of enterprises and the contraction of particular industrial sub-sectors are by no means excluded under Option (3); indeed to the extent that industry is unable to survive in the increasingly competitive world, these consequences are to be expected. This outcome *could* result under Option (4); it would, however, only do so as a last resort after attempts had been made to raise the efficiency of those enterprises and industries whose non-viable nature had been exposed and after the wider costs of closure had been assessed. In short, it would occur if these new manufacturing-specific policy initiatives had failed the test of time.

Having summarised (or caricatured) the two alternative active approaches on the current policy agenda, we can now ask which of the different case-study countries best fit into the approaches of Option (3) or Option (4) in regard to the future of their manufacturing industry. It appears – and this is an important conclusion – that *none* of the countries fits comfortably into the mould of either Option (3) or Option (4). At first sight this seems a conclusion considerably at variance with the facts, as a majority of the case-study countries are either implementing policies in large measure designed by the World Bank or pursuing policies in relation to their manufacturing sectors influenced strongly by the 'liberalisation' approach of the Bank and the IMF. Thus Option (3) does appear not only to be influential but, overwhelmingly, to be making the running.

This interpretation, however, remains narrow and partial and on its own is an unreliable guide to policy approaches one might anticipate for the 1990s. The pressures and financial inducements (largely of external origin) brought to bear on almost all the case-study countries to adopt some form of Option (3) initiative have – in varying degrees – been challenged by elements and groupings within them. In no country has Option (3) been totally accepted by the government, and in those in which the World Bank's hand in policy execution has been apparent longest – Côte d'Ivoire, Kenya, Nigeria – resistance to these policies has persisted and been influential, leading (in Côte d'Ivoire and Nigeria most clearly) to both long delays in agreements being reached, as well as to reversals of policy.

This resistance is manifested in a number of ways. One element can be understood in relation to the dynamics of political change. Thus, while any form of new policy initiative is bound to disturb the prevailing balance of political forces and be subject to some sort of political constraint, domestic opposition to Option (3), which is highly likely rapidly to set off fundamental changes in economic structure the extent of which is not known beforehand, has been and will continue to be strong. What is more, as political power is currently held disproportionately by those who have gained from past patterns of economic development, resistance from this group to Option (3)-type changes is likely to continue to be significant. The owners of manufacturing establishments benefitting from protection will not only continue to have an influential role in determining policies related to their sectoral interests but, in most of the case-study countries, their view is likely to be the dominant one emanating from the manufacturing sector. These issues are discussed more generally in Nelson (1989).

In general, there are few if any signs that the slowdown in growth rates of MVA which, as argued above, is to be expected in the early 1990s, will do anything but maintain, if not stiffen, this domestic opposition. In Cameroon, for instance, the political elite has successfully continued to extend its influence in the 1980s by utilising the oil surpluses to establish a wide range of parastatal organisations which, with the majority of manufacturing enterprises (some with foreign links), have a major interest in resisting Option (3)-type changes. While Cameroon's agreement with the World Bank in late 1988 is therefore unlikely to lead to a vigorous pursuit of liberal policies, the immediate closure of some profoundly inefficient parastatals was to be expected with more competitive manufacturing imports being allowed into the country with the abolition of quantitative restrictions.

For Côte d'Ivoire, resistance to the World Bank's radical proposals on tariff levels and protection, of direct immediate interest to the manufacturing sector, was manifested in the 1980s primarily by repeated delays in implementing measures apparently agreed. While major manufacturing interests, including foreign companies, were opposed to the process of liberalisation, more influential opposition has come from the farming community (tracing its support right up to the President's Office) which vigorously opposed the Bank's proposals for reducing the producer prices principally of coffee and cocoa products. More recently, and with implications for the future, the disarray in public finances resulting particularly from the decline in export commodity prices in 1988 and early 1989 and controversy about both policy targets and economic strategies drawn up and agreed by the World Bank[57] mean that the Bank will continue to find it difficult to persuade the Ivorians to implement policies which radically alter the status quo, at least until a change in the presidency, and possibly thereafter.

In Nigeria, the manufacturing sector is of less relative importance but the debate about the overall direction of policy is no less vigorous. What is more, the manufacturing lobby wields considerable influence and, as the case-study argues, substantial reversals of liberalisation policy in the late 1980s owed much of their success to 'the onslaught of pressure from the industry lobby'. What appears to distinguish Nigeria is its more overt opposition to SAP-type initiatives[58] and the manner in which even its willingness to sit round and talk is related critically to the fortunes of the oil market. Given the continued volatility of oil prices in the future, the perennial expectation that world prices will rise again, the lack of substantial progress to date in addressing the fundamental problems of the manufacturing sector, and the undoubted political influence of the protection-dominated industrial sector, there would appear to be little hope that a sustained restructuring of the sector along Option (3) lines will occur in Nigeria for many years to come.

Zambia and Zimbabwe are of particular interest to this discussion as they have recently implemented policies which encourage further efficiencies in manufacturing – Zambia through improving the management and accounting system of INDECO and stimulating regional exports, Zimbabwe through export incentive schemes and, at least indirectly, through price squeezes. Yet these changes should more appropriately be viewed in relation to an Option (4) rather than an Option (3)-type approach to industrial policy – they were implemented *without* World Bank and IMF programmes and in the context of macro-policies characterised by the maintenance of key interventionist and non-market-based structures. In both countries, *domestic* support for radical liberalisation policies, while certainly present, is far from dominant[59], so a rapid switch to an Option (3)-type approach is unlikely to be implemented without considerable domestic hostility.

In both countries, however, the need for change does now appear to be widely accepted and this has important implications. Manufacturers appear to have more political influence than their counterparts in Cameroon and Nigeria (and probably than in Côte d'Ivoire[60]) although in neither are they as important as, in the case of Zambia, copper interests and, of Zimbabwe, the commercial farming lobby. The Zambian case-study argues that the degree of political homogeneity and lack of social and political unrest in face of severe economic contraction and the country's 'go-it-alone' policies are both remarkable and an important element in assessing the ability of external actors to persuade Zambia to implement policies with which it disagrees. For Zimbabwe, the 1980s have seen large numbers of the politically influential black middle class move into the private sector, often via the civil service, where they have tended to take over the conservative outlook as well as the highly paid jobs of those they have replaced. Increasing numbers of the new political elite have also exploited (legally and illegally) their privileged position in the largely administered economy where short-cuts can bring windfall gains[61]. As a result, support for any sort of radical change from the political elite – seen as a realistic possibility at Independence in 1980 – has been on the wane as the decade progressed. Thus a more cautious approach to structural change is more likely to receive domestic support in the 1990s rather than the untried and highly risky approach implicit in an Option (3)-type strategy – and acknowledged as such in the honest discussion contained in the World Bank's 1987 report *Zimbabwe – A Strategy for Sustained Growth*.

The Botswana case is strikingly different. Its tiny manufacturing sector commands minimal political influence at the national level. Farming (cattle) interests are dominant in parliament, followed at some distance by the influence of the (diamond) mining lobby, both of which have benefited from the predominantly liberal and open macro-policies that have characterised the economy to date. While elements of an interventionist approach to manufacturing have not been entirely absent in recent years, the case-study argues that, if the sector is to maintain its expansion in the 1990s, a deepening process needs to occur, together with a significant expansion of manufacturing exports. Yet, it is argued, this will require a shift to a far more interventionist approach – through increasing subsidies. What remains seriously in doubt is whether sufficient political support can be mustered, especially if external institutional pressures continue to eschew such an approach.

Domestic political pressures are by no means the only ones opposing Option (3)-type solutions. Opposition is also grounded in the post-independence process of industrialisation. In a number of the case-study countries the advantage of hindsight challenges the conclusion that market-based solutions are preferable and that interventionism and the explicit promotion of industrial expansion are incompatible with efficiency. In their various ways, the case-studies (particularly of Zimbabwe, Kenya, Zambia and Botswana) point to the following conclusions:

- that efficient manufacturing production can occur under a far from liberal trade regime;
- that factors other than price play a major role in determining the extreme variations in efficiency occurring within different industrial sub-sectors – in particular management, machine design and engineering skills;
- that sustained manufactured exports require far more than short-run cost advantages;
- that management and machinery-choice questions are vital to the creation of viable industries and that in these small economies they require state intervention and careful planning;
- that a sheltered regional market can assist the drive to create efficient manufacturing units;
- that the development of manufacturing depends critically upon the presence and promotion of an adequate base of domestic skills;

and finally,

- that sustained import substitution and the development of linkages between sub-sectors of manufacturing and with other productive sectors are unlikely without recourse to specific incentives, and (far from costless) industrial promotion activities implemented in the context of a long-term perspective.

Given these experiences and the creation of a substantial industrial base in countries like Kenya and Zimbabwe, it is understandable why a gradualist approach has so much appeal and why the Option (3)-type approach, which has tended to address short-term structural problems rather than to approach structural change through a longer-term perspective, is received with so much reserve in Africa[62].

But Option (3)-type solutions concern SSA policy-makers for three other reasons. First, under such an approach the extent and development of manufacturing would be largely taken out of their hands: there would be no assurance that expansion would proceed or that a process of de-industrialisation would not wipe out major parts of the industrial base of a country, leaving it more vulnerable, exposed and dependent for growth upon an even narrower economic base.

Second, influencing the structure of industry and the pattern of future industrialisation predominantly by short-run price signals runs the risk that the already fragile manufacturing base will be even more vulnerable to the effects of those signals, for instance by exposure to the adverse effects of dumping and other externally-induced disruptive trade practices. The most likely outcome would be that industry would thus be in a weak position either to build up a comparative advantage in the manufacture of particular products or to respond to the technological innovations and market changes in part engineered by subsidisation and other non-market force mechanisms used in other parts of the world.

Three of the country case-studies well illustrate these fears. The first is Botswana where, as we have seen, it is argued that a greater degree of interventionism and explicit encouragement of manufacturing will become an increasingly urgent necessity if past gains are to be built upon and the overall economy strengthened. The second is Côte d'Ivoire. Here the 'open' policies of the past have not only played a major role in creating the present structure of the manufacturing sector (still predominantly linked to the further processing of agricultural export crops) but, it is argued, the structural adjustment policies promoted by the World Bank have been a major force *preventing* a restructuring of industry away from this weak dependent link. Thirdly, the Kenya case-study suggests that the major gaps in that country's industrial base, particularly the lack of manufacturing capability to supply inputs to the agricultural sector, are unlikely to be addressed in the context of further liberalisation.

The final reservation about adopting an Option (3)-type policy framework flows from the generally pessimistic assessment of the prospects for manufacturing growth in the first half of the 1990s. Not only is there considerable resistance to implementing far-reaching change when the consequences are substantially uncertain, but this resistance is compounded by the clearly over-optimistic scenarios for growth which the proponents of Option (3) have tended to link to their particular assessment of the future. In this regard the Zimbabwe and Cameroon case-studies not only reveal the wide margin of error in World Bank assessments of future growth paths but, of even more relevance here, the Zimbabwe study also indicates that, during a period in the 1980s, *without* adopting Option (3)-type policies, *higher* rates of industrial growth were achieved than the Bank judged would have been possible *with* the adoption of such policies.

What are the implications for the future of this resistance? At minimum it means that these policies will continue to be pursued only under varying degrees of duress – never a sound basis for a successful outcome. But it also means that alternative approaches grounded in less domestic opposition, or even in substantial domestic support, are more likely to be adopted where possible.

But what are these alternatives and what are the prospects of their influencing policy decisions in the 1990s? In many ways reservations about Option (3)-type policies for the future provide the context for understanding the type and range of support in SSA for Option (4)-type approaches. These are widely perceived as less risky and more in tune with efforts to promote longer-term and sustainable expansion. They are also seen as easier to execute as they are more similar to past approaches, more predictable in outcome and more controllable in evolution. Finally, they are supported because, in relation to a range of industrial objectives across many of the countries, interventionist approaches have met with not inconsiderable success[63]. To these advantages (and, in part, because of them) must be added the important dimension of political acceptability. An Option (4)-type approach would be far less likely to challenge entrenched interest groups[64].

There are, however, a number of factors constraining the wholesale adoption of such an approach. One is that the liberalisation/open/market-dominated approach of the World Bank (and the IMF) does have its frequently influential supporters within the different African countries. There is little to suggest, however, either that their view predominates or commands sizeable domestic political support.

A more significant constraining factor would arise if Option (4) policy approaches do not turn out in practice to be sufficiently different from Option (1) approaches. Risks remain of the *status quo ante* being perpetuated. In effect this could mean that, to a greater or lesser degree, the Option (4) approach would be still-born, giving rise to the apparently sterile but, in practice, retrogressive outcome emanating from the passive Option (2)[65].

Of most importance, however, is the fact that at present far greater potential domestic support for Option (4)-type policies contrasts sharply with far less international support for this particular approach. Opposition comes from the World Bank but also from the significant and increasing number of bilateral agencies which have agreed to link their financial support for SSA countries to arrangements made with the Bank[66]. Significant amounts of external finance under an Option (4)-type approach would thus be far more difficult to secure than for an Option (3)-type approach, while an Option (4)-type future is likely to need *greater* quantities of foreign exchange, in the medium term at least. Additional external funds would be needed to purchase plant and equipment to replace old and inefficient production methods (a *sine qua non* for expanding manufacturing exports) and to finance the foreign-exchange costs of further import substitution and, in the shorter term, the accelerated skills training programme necessary to improve the efficiency of current undertakings and ensure that new enterprises become cost-effective more rapidly.

Access to Bank and Fund facilities undoubtedly opens up a major direct source of external funds – clearly shown in the case of Côte d'Ivoire during almost all the 1980s – as well as giving access to other funds, concessional and not, and providing a climate more conducive to encouraging the inflow of new foreign investment and the reinvestment of profits of existing companies. It should not be thought, however, that either the failure to adopt Bank and Fund programmes precludes access to either concessional or commercially-linked external financing, or that the adoption of such programmes will necessarily provide funds sufficient for sustained expansion. The Bank was among the first to acknowledge its concern during the second half of the 1980s that Africa's external financing gap has been widening, throwing up major problems for any attempt to reverse the long-term decline in per capita incomes[67].

As for aid flows, concessional aid continued to flow into Zambia after it severed links with the Bank and IMF, albeit in far lower amounts, while aid to Zimbabwe has been sustained in spite of its having had no formal Bank or Fund agreements for most of the 1980s[68]. As for access to non-concessional finance it should be noted that Zimbabwe has also managed to maintain access to international commercial bank borrowing. It is important, however, not to overplay these points: SSA countries without Bank or IMF programmes, and with high external debts and poor export prospects, are unlikely to attract funds in sufficient quantities to address either their medium or longer-term structural problems.

In this context we need to examine the role of foreign private investment. Providing its inflow can be sustained[69], private foreign investment has a range of positive attributes. First and foremost, it injects foreign exchange. In addition, it has the potential to further the expansion of manufacturing exports and to contribute to industrial deepening by exploiting import-substitution opportunities. Equally it can assist the achievement of other crucial goals such as developing a skills base and assisting in technological upgrading or adaptation and learning.

Given the scarcity of external finance, *any* viable long-term industrial path for the SSA region would be boosted significantly by major inflows of new private investment. However, inflows into manufacturing are unlikely to be adequate even under an Option (3)-type approach. Thus while Fund and Bank programmes, improvements in domestic investment codes and multilateral investment guarantees enhance the host country's attractiveness, these measures have not managed to change the unfavourable environment in any of the case-study countries. On the other hand, the absence of Bank programmes and ambiguous investment codes have not been an insurmountable obstacle, as the recent evidence from Zambia and Zimbabwe confirm[70]. In general, however, to the extent that the international institutions and bilateral donors fail to support an Option (4)-type approach, the filling of the external resource gap through foreign private investment is likely to be of even greater importance.

It is difficult to be sanguine either that the overall external funding problems of the countries of SSA will easily be solved or, more particularly, that significant increases in private foreign financial flows will occur in the early 1990s. In large part this is because SSA is caught in a downward spiral of gloom: poor commodity prospects for the next few years mean that the foreign financing gap will remain and probably increase and private commercial investors are unlikely to inject substantial amounts of new funds when future prospects are so poor. To the extent that current trends continue, the prospects for manufacturing will be adversely affected. The crucial question for the 1990s is how this apparently self-perpetuating cycle can be replaced with a new optimism built on firm and lasting foundations. The melding of many of the themes in this book suggests that seeds of hope can be found through shifting priorities and giving greater emphasis to the sustained growth of an efficient and expanding manufacturing sector.

In this context there are three important additional reasons for favouring an Option (4)-type approach. Besides the successes already achieved[71], it is a long-term approach which, in contrast to much of the previous record, is based on addressing the main structural problems which have led to the evolution of large areas of inefficient manufacturing and the sector's disproportionate use of scarce and, in particular, foreign-exchange resources.

There are, however, a number of pre-requisites for these seeds of optimism to germinate. One would be for the Bank and the bilateral agencies to look afresh at the manufacturing sector in the SSA leading countries and revise their adverse views on both its place in overall development strategies and the role of efficiently-targeted interventionist policies in the light of *all* the evidence of past performance. A second would be for these donors and guarantors to join the minority supporting such approaches by injecting additional resources into manufacturing. Importantly in this context, increased foreign aid resources could assist the expansion, restructuring and efficiency-oriented approach to manufacturing outlined here in the following ways:

- funding and, perhaps assisting in the execution of, sectoral and firm-based studies of inefficiencies, particularly intra-firm differences;
- helping to establish training assistance programmes;
- helping to expanding the technical skills base;
- evaluating weaknesses in management and entrepreneurial skills and providing both stop-gap replacement and the training of indigenous staff;
- helping to build up a domestic competence to assess reinvestment needs and appropriate machinery purchase;
- assistance in embarking upon and sustaining export programmes including pinpointing gaps in product range, quality and packaging, and monitoring current and anticipated trends in world trade;
- finally, encouraging the more rapid inflow of appropriate private foreign investment.

A third pre-requisite would be for private foreign investors to be encouraged to invest in a re-ordered manufacturing sector[72]. As just noted, while external agencies can play an important facilitating role in this area, it is crucial to the success of this last element that African governments should reverse (or at minimum supplement) their passive attitude to foreign investment (by improving the general climate). At minimum, this would require them to decide what type of external investment is required and then go out to woo particular international concerns[73].

Thoughts on theoretical themes

One of the principal objectives of this book is to raise the level of debate about manufacturing industry in the future development prospects of sub-Saharan Africa. Hence policy issues, rather than questions of theory, have been the main focus of attention. We can end this chapter with a brief overview of factors emerging from the overall study which do relate to some of the theoretical questions posed, such as the extent to which industry should be the main lever of development (in SSA or elsewhere)[74], or whether further industrialisation is a necessary condition for countries to develop and for poverty to be eliminated[75].

TO PROMOTE OR NOT PROMOTE MANUFACTURING DEVELOPMENT?

One might say that the findings of the case-studies are all very well in the abstract. The question they raise, however, is whether the structure of manufacturing *in practice can* be altered, and in the virtuous manner indicated. While it is argued that it might be preferable, in the ideal world, for manufacturing growth and deepening to be pursued, in practice this is not likely to happen and it should not therefore feature on practical policy agendas. If manufacturing development is to occur at all, the best prospects lie in resource-based industrialisation, linked to the further expansion of the sector with the greater immediate comparative advantage, most commonly agriculture. Thus (the argument concludes) while it would be nice to think that there could be an alternative – and faster – way for SSA to develop, this is not going to occur in practice: to force the pace of manufacturing development would, sadly, be self-defeating.

This, however, is only part of the story. The evidence also suggests that manufacturing sector growth has not been *exclusively* dependent upon rising domestic demand. The overall growth of the economy, and the expansion of agriculture in particular, do not constitute an *a priori* and binding pre-requisite for its expansion: import substitution and export growth have both been important sources of growth of manufacturing output and could continue to be. Moreover, the parasitic nature of substantial segments of manufacturing in SSA and the manner in which it has frequently evolved to become a net user of scarce foreign exchange is, at bottom, a problem of inefficient production, often associated with poor – or plain bad – initial decision-making. Constraints impeding manufacturing expansion and inhibiting increases in efficiency of production have not been *entirely* foreign-exchange dominated. They often relate in a critical manner to questions of skills (managerial, technical and engineering), to technology and its adaptation and to the level of information available. Quite substantial differences in efficiency between firms in the same sub-sector point to factors other than the price, tariff and overall incentive structure playing a crucial role in determining the efficiency of manufacturing units. The conclusion to be drawn from this – equally important – evidence is that many key constraints to growth and the deepening of manufacturing, and which perpetuate inefficiencies, can be tackled without having, beforehand, to solve the overall foreign-exchange constraint.

But there is more. The evidence also suggests that even in circumstances in which countries do have severe foreign-exchange constraints, the option of stimulating manufacturing growth through further import substitution and/or promoting the expansion of manufacturing exports is not necessarily foreclosed. The experience with export revolving funds indicates that manufactured exports can rise rapidly over a short period (even in less than a year), while the time-period for 'saving' foreign exchange through efficient import substitution can also occur within a year or two[76].

Two other related points need to be made. In the immediate context, where the prospects for rapid rises in both overall domestic demand and primary product exports are so poor, it would seem a sensible (risk-averting) idea to attempt to promote alternative paths to raising aggregate growth: efficient import substitution and the expansion of non-traditional exports would appear to fit this particular bill. Looking further ahead, it is uncontroversial that countries diversify their export base by growing a wider range of crops. Similarly, it would also appear sensible to welcome the further processing of primary products prior to export (in order to maximise foreign-exchange earning) and to encourage diversification away from over-dependence upon primary product processing to embrace a wider range of products. Again, there is evidence in Africa to prove that this can be done[77].

At minimum this suggests that foreign-exchange shortages and low levels of overall growth do not have to rule out either promotion or achievement of manufacturing sector growth. More strongly, the argument could perhaps be turned on its head: not to force the pace of manufacturing growth and diversification would be likely to perpetuate the low-growth/high dependence syndrome which still characterises so much of SSA today.

IMPORT-SUBSTITUTING OR EXPORT-ORIENTED INDUSTRIALISATION?

Although the studies in this book were not written with a view to informing this particular debate[78], they do suggest that posing the question import substitution *versus* export-oriented industrialisation is rather irrelevant to the countries of SSA at the start of the 1990s. With few exceptions, SSA is characterised by countries in which widespread import substitution has not really occurred. The crucial question for most of those embarking on the promotion of their manufacturing sectors is how to do this in the context of their foreign-exchange constraints.

The answer appears to be that neither import substitution nor export-oriented industrialisation seems a very appropriate basis for embarking on further industrialisation. Rather, it lies in an approach which blends in elements of both so that (although probably in relation to different industries and sub-sectors) further inter-linked import substitution industries are established at the same time as short-, medium- and longer-term comparative advantage in selected manufactured exports is developed in an overall environment which addresses (with care and gradualism) the current inefficiencies of the inherited manufactured sector. Thus what is needed is a path of industrialisation in which higher rates of growth are promoted through a mix of policies (the ratios of which can only be determined in relation to particular countries) which aim to maximize the benefits of expanded domestic demand and to stimulate both substantial import substitution and increased export orientation. As elaborated earlier, this mix is likely to embrace price factors, training and skill elements, technology questions, policies related to foreign-exchange saving, earning and usage as well as broader questions of promoting the wider efficiency of the physical and financial infrastructure.

Perhaps it is unfair to talk of this approach as a particular strategy. For many years to come grand theories of manufacturing in SSA are likely to be eclipsed by the prior need to raise the efficiency of those units currently operating, to ensure that potential manufacturing enterprises are assessed in relation to their ability to produce efficiently and all in the context of policies to enhance the domestic skills base and the capability to adapt to and initiate technological change[79].

Such an approach is not radically different from that suggested by the case-study evidence of a selection of middle-income (and non-African) countries analysed in the most important volume on industry to be published in over a decade: *Industrialization and Growth: A Comparative Study* (Chenery *et al.*, 1986: 358).

> . . . (An) examination of the experiences of countries which have successfully pursued export-led growth policies shows that their governments followed active interventionist policies, albeit with heavy reliance on market incentives.

The one qualification to be made would be to omit the word 'heavy'. As Westphal (1981) argues, the joint import substitution/export orientation approach is far from impossible to achieve but is particularly likely to occur if incentives are tied to export performance[80].

The final word needs to be reserved for reiterating the problems of statistical gaps and data inadequacies. Any discussion of development and development policies in SSA must necessarily be tentative because of the dubious nature of the statistics available, the major gaps in our knowledge of what has been happening (and thus of the processes of change that have been taking place) and the often unaccountably large differences in data-bases used both by different 'authorities' and by the same agencies in different publications and, indeed, over relatively short time-periods. Both the analysis of past patterns of industrial development and the proposals for future industrial policies in SSA contained in this book suffer from these inadequacies. Thus appropriate caution should be exercised when agreeing with or challenging the views expressed.

Notes

1. Clearly if MVA is not expanding and the ratio of MVA to GDP is not increasing then little manufacturing expansion or deepening is taking place.
2. A description of the sources of growth analysis is provided in the chapter on Botswana.
3. There are, of course, also theoretical problems associated with the whole 'sources of growth' approach, such as the inter-linkages and inter-relationship between the three elements. Some of these issues are addressed specifically in the different case-studies.
4. Details are found in the respective country chapters. The time periods for these figures are as follows: Botswana: 1973/4–1982/3; Kenya: 1970–84; Nigeria: 1963–83; Zimbabwe: 1964/5–82/3. The Zimbabwe figure for this particular time period is not shown in the case-study chapter but has been calculated from the original sources for purposes of comparison.
5. In the case of both Côte d'Ivoire and Zambia, however, it is apparent that import substitution was an important source of growth in the 1960s with, in the case of Zambia, import substitution exceeding domestic demand in the respective ratios of 55% and 44%.
6. The ratio of manufacturing to total output in all low-income economies in 1986 was 24% (11% if China and India are omitted) and 22% for all middle-income economies (World Bank, *World Development Report 1988*, Table 3).
7. Botswana provides an exception here especially in the post-1980 period where mining development has been a significant 'motor' of development, while in Zambia the importance of agriculture has been eclipsed continually by the vagaries of the copper mining industry.
8. The data for Botswana, however, suggest a different picture especially in the 1980s when regional exports are judged to have expanded by about 15% a year to 1987. Reasons why this might have occurred are summarised below and discussed more fully in Chapter 4.
9. The rise in manufactured exports from Mauritius only occurred from the late 1970s onwards and

even by 1983 manufactured exports from Côte d'Ivoire, Kenya and Zimbabwe still exceeded the value of its manufactured exports.

10. As Zehander comments in this context (1988: 57): 'The relative export success of countries like Côte d'Ivoire, Cameroon, Kenya, Nigeria and Zimbabwe in their respective regions has less to do with the regional "economic community" machinery (which at best has a strengthening role) than with the historical structure of their industrial sectors.'

11. Mention should also be made of South Africa which not only dominates manufactured exports within the southern African region but has made increasing inroads into countries further north even though accurate trends are difficult to analyse because of the secrecy surrounding such trade.

12. Particularly, but not exclusively, if trade preferences are excluded.

13. 'Indeco products, such as maize meal, sugar and cooking oil are all sold near or below cost price . . . So cheap are Indeco products in comparison with goods available in neighbouring countries that up to 20% of production is smuggled out.' (*Financial Times*, 30 December 1988.)

14. As Jebuni, Love and Forsyth comment (1988: 1518):

> Where market power is positively related to export performance, policy emphasis on eliminating monopolistic elements or creating small competitive establishments to promote exports of manufactured goods may be misplaced. Measures to restrict the development of large firms in favor of small competing firms may be counterproductive. The simultaneous positive influence on export performance of economies of scale suggests that export success may depend on having a concentrated domestic market structure which allows companies to enjoy scale economies domestically and thereby to achieve unit costs at which companies can compete abroad. . . .

15. The importance of radical changes in management and human resources as well as in technology is discussed in detail in Caulkin (1989) and in UNIDO (1989).

> Human resource development is the starting point in discussing policy areas relevant for the development and application of new technologies . . .
> Human resources did not always receive the strong attention they deserve as crucial determinants of economic development. Specifically in the sixties and early seventies a widespread fallacy has been to explain economic development basically in terms of capital and technology inputs and to treat the concomitant development of human resources largely as a residual – as such considered more a social concern than an economic variable. Meanwhile, however, it has become widely accepted that it is human beings and the skills they command which are decisive to promote development and that investment in human capital can in fact yield higher returns than does real capital formation.

16. In Zimbabwe, Central African Cables (CAFCA) could be considered an example of a manufacturing company which in the 1980s has changed from being domestically to export-oriented. It expanded exports fourfold to over $4.5 m. from 1986 to 1988 and was expecting to raise the value by a further 16% in 1989; 35% of production was geared to exports in 1988. The company attributes its successes, *inter alia*, to a massive investment programme, management commitment to exporting and a sustained export drive. While almost all exports are to the regional market these markets have been secured by overcoming both South African and overseas competition.

17. 'Why do some companies grow rapidly to operate on an international scale, while others remain small and tied to their local market,' began an article at the end of 1988 in the *Financial Times*, entitled 'When Late Developers Produce Rapid Growth'. Reporting the results of a conference, a number of common themes emerged from work carried out by academics, businessmen and venture capitalists (*Financial Times*, 20 December 1988, p. 18):

> What became apparent from the companies surveyed was that . . . sometimes these companies slumbered for decades before the arrival of an entrepreneurial family member or professional manager led to an acceleration of growth . . .
> Success does not depend on a single formula or even on a small number of readily identifiable factors. It is the result of welding an almost infinite number of variables into an effective combination. It is the skill with which they are mixed together rather than the raw ingredients which holds the secrets of growth.

18. See the end of Chapter 2 and Table 2.5 for a general discussion of this little appreciated characteristic of manufacturing in SSA.

19. 'Import substitution is by its very nature a dead-end strategy, especially in a small market like Kenya' writes Professor Hawkins in an analysis of industrialisation in Kenya for the *Financial Times*, 12 December 1988.

20. His criticism of the World Bank and the IMF is even harsher. He adds that (1988: 33):

> On the basis of the foregoing arguments, it is fair to say that in the mid-1980s the trade liberalisation strategy is intellectually moribund, kept alive by life support from the World Bank and the International Monetary Fund.

21. This is not to argue, however, that the ratio has reached a 'satisfactory' level: reducing it further remains a major policy objective into the 1990s.
22. Clearly, too, considerable import substitution was occurring in the period prior to 1952/3 when the data permit analysis to be conducted. Thus, as long ago as 1938, 10% of GDP originated in the manufacturing sector and over the next 15 years the MVA/GDP ratio rose to 14%.
23. A factor supporting those sceptical of sources of growth analysis.
24. Botswana is the exception in purely statistical comparisons; however, the level of its industrialisation, even today, is far lower than Zimbabwe's even in the early 1950s.
25. 'One of Africa's grandest white elephants is taking shape in Nigeria's Kwara State. The Ajaokuta steel plant lies beside the River Niger and has so far cost $3 bn. It is still incomplete and a further $1 bn is needed to finish the first phase, now years behind schedule. If and when it is ever completed the scheme will, in the words of a confidential government report drawn up in 1984, be "uneconomic and will incur recurrent losses to the end of the century" ' (*Financial Times*, 1 March 1989, p. 16).
26. In the period 1965–74, the growth rate of MVA averaged 8%, while it averaged 0.9% in the 1974–9 period.
27. Growth rates of both MVA and GDP began to pick up in 1979, prior to the formal granting of Independence in April 1980, because of expectations that the war would soon be over, a rise in exports and an increase in allocations of foreign exchange to manufacturers.
28. In contrast the UDI period began inauspiciously with the worst contraction of the economy for over a decade and a concomitant fall in manufacturing output, events which heralded substantial changes in policy enabling the process of structural change in manufacturing to be maintained.
29. Thus the sector was buffeted by fluctuations in the wider economy without the underlying inherited structural problems being sufficiently addressed. Perceptions of hostility to external investment among current and potential foreign investors together with increased tension in the region originating in the apartheid policies of South Africa aggravated an already poor investment climate, frustrating substantial foreign investment inflows.
30. These totalled $2,976 m. over the five years 1983–7 (OECD, *Development Cooperation 1988 Report*, 1988: 207).
31. Notwithstanding, too, the 1984 drought which resulted in negative agricultural growth in that year.
32. The slowdown in manufacturing growth can, as in the case of Zambia, be traced back to the post-1977 period.
33. Thus in 1987, manufacturing growth, estimated at 5.7%, was close to the higher than average 5.9% recorded in 1986 (Republic of Kenya, *Economic Survey 1988*: 5), spurred by higher agriculturally-led GDP growth of 4.8 and 5.5% respectively, an easing of import restrictions and an overall rise in domestic demand. The annual growth rate for 1988 was expected to be even higher.
34. In mid-1988 imports in 3 out of 5 separate categories were liberalised. But, more generally, as the government's 1988 *Economic Survey* tersely put it (1988: 117): 'Liberalisation policies aimed at creating efficiency through competition have not yet borne fruit.'
35. Latest reliable figures at the time of writing go up to 1987.
36. In the 18 months to March 1989, the UK's Lonrho and Metal Box and the US's Heinz and Colgate Palmolive had all made investments in Botswana's manufacturing sector.
37. In 1985, Botswana's MVA totalled just $49 m., the lowest level of all 26 SSA countries for which World Bank data are provided in the 1988 *World Development Report*, with the sole exception of tiny Lesotho, whose MVA is given as $26 m. In contrast with Botswana, of the six other case-study countries the next smallest is Zambia whose MVA rose (in 1980 prices) from 575 m. kwacha in 1984 to 621 m. in 1986, a rise of some 47 m. kwacha.
38. Botswana's growth in the early 1990s is expected to be higher than initially forecast although lower than over the past 30 years. As the case-study suggests, the rate of growth of MVA is likely to remain very high by African standards even if its slowdown is likely to accelerate as the 1990s proceed.
39. Which are, as Mosley and Toye have argued (1988: 402): 'development plans in all but name'.
40. Projections/forecasts of rates of growth of MVA in the different countries – even those produced by the World Bank – are based on extremely flimsy data. They are commonly spin-offs from more general macroeconomic projections and forecasts and not based on manufacturing-specific analysis, perhaps itself a sign of the way in which the importance of manufacturing in overall development is judged.
41. For a general discussion of the effects of economic recovery programmes on rural incomes in a number of African countries see International Fund for Agricultural Development (IFAD) and Overseas Development Institute (ODI) 1989.
42. Not all these problems refer to all countries. For instance, Zimbabwe's financial infrastructure is both adequate and efficiently run. A recent example of infrastructural problems comes from Nigeria's National Electric Power Authority which, in the first quarter of 1989, needed to raise tariffs by over 350% to recoup current losses.
43. Although, as discussed below, this attitude could be changed if the international institutions and bilateral aid donors were to change their current, rather negative, view on manufacturing development.

For an analysis of the prospects for and constraints on foreign investment in Africa in the 1990s see Cockcroft and Riddell (1990).

The Catch-22 situation is already occurring in the case of Nigeria. Analysts in early 1989 were all agreed that low levels of foreign investment were stunting the growth of the economy. What is more, as an official of the Bank of Netherlands has argued, the economic reconstruction objectives of the structural adjustment programme may well go unfulfilled without adequate inflows of foreign investment, thereby exacerbating the economic crisis and providing a further disincentive to foreign investors. (See *West Africa*, 9 January 1989, p. 8).

44. Even in Zimbabwe, the share of foreign exchange in new investment projects in manufacturing was estimated in the mid-1980s to be over 60% of the total cost of investment.

45. The term 'surgery' is defined (in the Oxford dictionary) as 'manual treatment of injuries or disorders of the body, operative therapeutics, surgical work'. It does not necessarily imply the *removal* of parts of the body. As we shall see, the nature of Botswana's manufacturing problems are rather different from those of the other case-study countries.

46. In the sense described below, Botswana never has.

47. The issue of the role of the public and private sectors in industrial development is not one that has been resolved in the case-study countries with unanimity so it is not included in this particular listing.

48. Colonial Zimbabwe perhaps being the exception in the Federal and pre-Federal period.

49. More complete descriptions of what these different approaches mean in practical terms are given in the case-studies, especially those of Côte d'Ivoire and Zimbabwe.

50. In 1986 the IMF set up a new Structural Adjustment Facility (SAF), replaced in 1987 by an Enhanced Structural Adjustment Facility. It should also be noted that the IMF's Extended Fund Facility, set up in 1974, 'was a precursor of the SAF, not the least because, for the first time, it engaged the IMF in medium-term policy programmes addressed to the strengthening of the productive structure' (Killick, 1989: 53).

51. As noted in Chapter 1, although the World Bank's long-term perspective study on Africa (1989) is different from previous Africa-wide studies produced in the 1980s in that it *does* highlight manufacturing-specific policies, there is little to suggest that these will receive prominence in practice.

52. These issues are discussed in Mosley and Toye in which, *inter alia*, the senior author of the World Bank's 1981 report *Accelerated Development in Sub-Saharan Africa*, is quoted thus (1988: 412):

Structural adjustment loans are not intended as relief for the balance of payments of the (recipient) country. Instead the money is mainly intended to help bring Bank representatives to the borrowers' policy-making high table, where basic policy issues are decided by policy-makers, not merely explored by technical analysts.

53. For a wide-ranging discussion of the term 'real economy' see Killick et al. (1984).

54. Option (4) needs to be differentiated sharply from Option (1) where neither efficiency nor explicit promotion of manufactured exports receive prominent attention.

55. The term 'planning' is used here with some hesitation; it is not meant to imply the re-adoption of a system of central planning more characteristic of the 1960s.

56. Accepting the principle of infant-industry tariff protection for a certain limited period of time.

57. These include differences of opinion about future overall economic strategy between especially the Bank and France and differences over future policy towards industry between the Bank and UNIDO's advisers to the government.

58. This has been seen, for instance, in a number of contradictions between verbal agreements to conform to such policies and the embarking in practice on policies at variance with the whole approach. In the 1989 budget, Nigeria decided to raise tariffs and increase domestic protection for a range of products manufactured domestically at the same time as agreeing to implement structural adjustment policies.

59. In both it is important to distinguish between support for private enterprise and support for radical liberal policies: support for the former is strong, for the latter substantially weaker.

60. Given the importance of the agricultural lobby in Côte d'Ivoire.

61. As was made transparent in the public proceedings and aftermath of the Sandura Commission of Inquiry.

62. The World Bank's own evaluations of its structural adjustment programmes (World Bank, 1986a) concluded that structural change in Africa tends to take longer than had earlier been envisaged.

63. Neither Option (3) nor Option (4) approaches necessarily have particular advantages in terms of a range of issues currently under debate in SSA, such as private versus public sector investment, small versus large-scale initiatives, the problems of regional markets and regionally based industrial production strategies and inadequacies in the financial market for sustained industrial expansion. A number of these particular issues are taken up in the case-studies.

64. This is not to argue, of course, that entrenched group interests would not be challenged. For instance the Côte d'Ivoire study suggests that radical restructuring of manufacturing industry would be likely to challenge directly those Ivorian and, especially, French interests which have benefitted from past industrial growth patterns.

65. It would not be entirely unfair to argue that the vigour with which (in the early 1980s) the Bank underplayed the future role of manufacturing in SSA and in later years increasingly pursued its own Option (3)-type approaches has, in part, been related to its belief that this would be the most likely outcome.

66. This move towards a closer linkage between aid funds and World Bank initiated, sponsored or approved programmes is also apparent in relation to aid programmes.

67. These issues are discussed, for instance, in *Financing Africa's Recovery*, Report and Recommendations of the Advisory Group on Financial Flows for Africa, United Nations Publications, February 1988 (The Wass Report), World Bank (1986) and in Mistry (1988).

68. In announcing the lifting of a two-year freeze on aid to Zimbabwe in August 1988 (following diplomatic not economic differences between the two countries), the US Ambassador in Harare stated that his country recognised that Zimbabwe's economy was healthy and dynamic, and with the potential for greater growth based on past successes.

69. The Côte d'Ivoire study highlights a series of problems thrown up by an economy whose growth has been propelled by foreign investment inflow for a considerable period of time, which then slowed and went into reverse.

70. In December 1988, the US food giant, Heinz, announced it was planning to expand its investments in Zimbabwe by $184 m. to the year 1994, an increase of over 200%, while, in March 1989, a $40 m. investment in commercial agriculture in Zambia was announced involving Masstock of Ireland and 3 US companies, following investment from Tata of India in 1988.

71. Successes which have tended to remain unknown, ignored or overlooked in much of the literature on African development.

72. It is not being argued here that private foreign investment is *always* necessary for manufacturing expansion and deepening to occur or that the need for it is the same in each of the case-study countries. The argument is that at this particular time, especially given the structural problems of manufacturing and the desirability to re-orient it towards earning more foreign exchange, the need for foreign investment inflow becomes compelling.

Links with international companies are also likely to become even more important both as the 1990s progress and if SSA countries are to achieve their goals of expanding non-traditional exports. See 1989 'World Industrial Review' comments (*Financial Times*, 23 January 1989).

73. Ideally this approach would lead to a number of international companies becoming interested in investing which would itself lead to a certain amount of competitive bidding to obtain the best deal. This is discussed more fully in Cockcroft and Riddell (1990).

74. As noted in Chapter 1, Ewing argued in 1968 that industry *should* be the main lever of African development. Fourteen years later, in Fransman (1982: 27), Singh wrote thus:

. . . in order to achieve fast economic growth, the African countries should aim to change the structure of their economies by substantially increasing the share of manufacturing in national output and by corresponding changes within the structure of manufacturing industry itself.

More recently, in 1989, Stoneman maintained that industrialisation was *necessary* for development and poverty alleviation in southern Africa (C. Stoneman, article in *Southern African Economist*), Vol. 1, No. 6, December 1988-January 1989.

75. Two observations of Chenery are relevant to this point (Chenery in Chenery *et al.* (1988: 4, 358)):

Krueger (1984) points out that the main issue between proponents of neoclassical trade policy and its critics is not whether to industrialize but what form the industrialization should take.

In studying the semi-industrial economies which have grown rapidly in the postwar period, it is difficult to sort out necessary conditions from the sets of sufficient conditions that underlie the successful cases.

76. See Note 16, above, and the Zimbabwe case-study for other specific examples.

77. For instance, the Japanese investment in a zip-fastener factory in Swaziland.

78. See for instance the various essays in Fransman (1982), Hawkins in Berg and Whitaker (1986) and, more generally, Kirkpatrick, Lee and Nixson (1984) and Weiss (1988) and the journal published out of UNIDO: *Industry and Development*.

79. This is not meant to imply either that infant industry protection should be abandoned or that in some strategic sectors there could well be a necessity for more permanent protection, especially if this provided the opportunity for the products of other sub-sectors to be exported in significant quantities. For theoretical discussion of technological questions see especially Bell *et al.* (1984) and Dahlman and Sercovich (1984) and for explicit treatment of this in SSA see Lall (1987).

80. Nishimuzu and Robinson in Chenery *et at.* (1988: 308). See also Bell *et al.* (1984).

References and Bibliography for Part I

Bailey, R. (1976), *Africa's Industrial Future*, Blandford (Dorset), Davison Publishing.

Barker, C.E. *et al.* (1986), *African Industrialisation*, London, Gower.

Bell, M., Ross-Larson, B. and Westphal, L.E. (1984), *Assessing The Performance of Infant Industries*, World Bank Staff Working Papers, No. 666, Washington DC, World Bank.

Berg, R.J. and Whitaker, J.S. (1986), *Strategies For African Development*, Berkeley, University of California Press.

Caulkin, S. (1989), *The New Manufacturing: Minimal IT for Maximum Profit*, Economist Special Report, London, Economist Publications and Computer Weekly.

Chenery, H., Robinson, S. and Syrquin, M. (1986), *Industrialization and Growth: A Comparative Study*, New York, Oxford University Press for the World Bank.

Cockcroft, L. and Riddell, R.C. (1990), 'Foreign Direct Investment in Sub-Saharan Africa', paper prepared for World Bank Symposium on African External Finance in the 1990s, London, Overseas Development Institute (mimeo).

Colclough, C. and Green, R.H. (1988), 'Do Stabilisation Policies Stabilise?', *IDS Bulletin*, Vol. 19, No. 1.

Coughlin, P. and Ikiara, G.K. (eds) (1989), *Industrialization in Kenya: In Search of a New Strategy*, London, James Currey and Nairobi, Heinemann.

Dahlman, C.J. and Sercovich, F.C. (1984), *Local Development and Exports of Technology*, World Bank Staff Working Papers, No. 667, Washington DC, World Bank.

De Bandt, J. and Hugon, P. (Eds) (1988), *Les Tiers Nations en Mal D'Industrie*, Nanterre, Centre d'Etude et de Recherche pour une Nouvelle Economie Appliquée (CERNEA).

Diejomaoh, V.P. and Iyoha, M.A. (1980), *Industrialization in the Economic Community of West African States (ECOWAS)*, Ibaden, Heinemann for the West African Economic Association.

Economic Commission for Africa (ECA) (various years), *Survey of Economic and Social Conditions in Africa*, Addis Ababa, UNECA.

—— Organisation for African Unity (OAU) and United Nations Industrial Development Organisation (UNIDO) (1982), *A Programme for The Industrial Development Decade For Africa*, New York, United Nations.

Economist Intelligence Unit (EIU) (1989), *World Outlook 1989*, London, Business International.

Elkan, W. (1986), *Policy for Small-Scale Industry: A Critique*, Uxbridge, Discussion Papers in Economics, No. 8701, Brunel, The University of West London.

Ewing, A.F. (1968), *Industry in Africa*, London, Oxford University Press.

Food and Agriculture Organization of the United Nations (FAO) (1987), *Supplement to the Report of the Feasibility Study on Expanding the Provision of Agricultural Inputs as Aid-in-Kind*, (C.87/20-Sup. 1. September), Rome, FAO.

Fransman, M. (ed.) (1982), *Industry and Accumulation in Africa*, London, Heinemann.

—— (1984), *The Capital Goods Industry in Africa: A General Review and Elements for Further Analysis*, Vienna, UNIDO, Division for Industrial Studies.

Ghai, D. (1987), *Economic Growth, Structural Change and Labour Absorption in Africa: 1960–85*, Geneva, United Nations Research Institute for Social Development (UNRISD), Discussion Paper No. 1.

Hawkins, A.M. (1986), 'Can Africa Industrialize?' in Berg and Whitaker.

Inter-American Development Bank (IDB), (various years), *Economic and Social Progress in Latin America*, New York, IDB.

International Fund for Agricultural Development (IFAD) and Overseas Development Institute (ODI) (1989), *The Impact of Economic Recovery Programmes on Smallholder Farmers and the Rural Poor in Sub-Saharan Africa*, Working Paper No. 1, Rome, April.

International Monetary Fund (IMF), (various years), *Direction of Trade Statistics*, Washington DC, IMF.

—— (various years), *International Financial Statistics*, Washington DC, IMF.

—— (various years), *World Economic Outlook*, Washington DC, IMF.

Jebuni, C.D., Love, J. and Forsyth, D.J.C. (1988), 'Market Structure and LDCs' Manufactured Export Performance', *World Development*, Vol. 16, No. 12, December.

Killick, T. (1981), *The Role of the Public Sector in the Industrialisation of African Developing Countries*, Vienna, UNIDO, ID/WG.343/7.

—— (1982), 'African Experiences with Industrial Policies and Performance, 1960–1980', Report prepared for UNIDO, London, ODI (mimeo).

—— (ed.) (1984), *The Quest for Economic Stabilisation: the IMF and the Third World*, London, Overseas Development Institute and Gower Publishing.

—— (1989), 'Structure, Development and Adaptation', London, Overseas Development Institute (mimeo).

Kirkpatrick, C.H. (1987), 'Trade Policy and Industrialisation in LDCs' in Gemmell, N. (ed.) *Surveys in Development Economics*, Oxford, Basil Blackwell.

—— Lee, N. and Nixson, F.I. (1984), *Industrial Structure and Policy in Less Developed Countries*, London, George Allen and Unwin.

—— and Nixson, F.I. (1983), *The Industrialisation of Less Developed Countries*, Manchester, Manchester University Press.

Kitchen, H. (1988), *Some Guidelines on Africa for the Next President*, Washington DC, Center for Strategic and International Studies, Significant Issues Series, Vol. X, No. 4.

Krueger, A.Ó. (1984), 'Comparative Advantage and Development Policy Twenty Years Later' in Syrquin, M., Taylor, L. and Westphal, L.E. (eds), *Economic Structure and Performance: Essays in Honour of Hollis B. Chenery*, New York, Academic Press.

Kuznets, S. (1966), *Modern Economic Growth*, New Haven, Conn., Yale University Press.

Lall, S. (1987) 'Long-Term Perspectives on sub-Saharan Africa: Background Paper, Industry', Washington DC, World Bank (mimeo).

—— (1988), *Learning To Industrialise: The Acquisition of Technological Capability by India*, London, Macmillan.

Liedholm, C. and Mead, D. (1987), *Small Scale Industries in Developing Countries: Empirical Evidence and Policy Implications*, East Lansing, Michigan, MSU International Development Papers, No. 9, Department of Agricultural Economics.

Meier, G.M. and Steel, W.F. (eds) (1987), *Industrial Adjustment in Sub-Saharan Africa*, Washington DC, Economic Development Institute; subsequently published (1989), New York, Oxford University Press.

Mistry, P.S. (1988), *African Debt: The Case for Relief for Sub-Saharan Africa*, Oxford, Oxford International Associates.

Mosley, P. and Toye, J. (1988), 'The Design of Structural Adjustment Programmes', *Development Policy Review*, Vol. 6, No. 4, December.

Nelson, J.M. *et al.* (1989), *Fragile Coalitions: The Politics of Economic Adjustment*, Washington DC, Overseas Development Council.

Nishimuzu , M. and Robinson, S. (1986) 'Productivity Growth in Manufacturing' in Chenery *et al.*

Nixson, F. (1982), 'Import-Substituting Industrialisation' in Fransman.

Ohiorhenuan, J.F.E. (1988), 'The Industrialisation of Very Late Starters: Historical Experience, Prospects and Strategic Options for Nigeria', Ibadan, Department of Economics, University of Ibadan (mimeo).

Organisation for Economic Cooperation and Development (OECD) (Various Years), *Development Cooperation: efforts and policies of the members of the Development Assistance Committee 1981 to 1989 Reports*, Paris, OECD.

Organisation for African Unity (OAU) (1982), *Lagos Plan of Action for the Economic Development of Africa, 1980-2000*, Geneva, International Institute for Labour Studies.

Pack, H. and Westphal, L.E. (1986), 'Industrial Strategy and Technological Change: Theory Versus Reality', *Journal of Development Economics*, Vol. 22, No. 1, June.

Page, S.B. and Riddell, R. (1988), 'Opportunities and Impediments to Foreign Direct Investment in Africa', Paper Prepared for the United Nations Centre on Transnational corporations, London, July Overseas Development Institute, July (mimeo), published in abridged form in *UNCTC Reporter*, April 1989.

Ravenhill, J. (1988), 'Adjustment with Growth: A Fragile Consensus', *The Journal of Modern African Studies*, Vol. 26, No. 2.

Rose, T. (ed) (1985), *Crisis and Recovery in Sub-Saharan Africa*, Paris, Organisation for Economic Cooperation and Development.

Singh, A. (1982), 'Industrialization in Africa: A Structuralist View' in Fransman.

Steel, W.F. and Evans, J.W. (1984), *Industrialization in Sub-Saharan Africa: Strategies and Performance*, Washington DC, World Bank, Technical Paper No. 25.

Taylor, L. (1988a), *Economic Openness – Problems to the Century's End*, World Institute for Development Economics Research of the United Nations University, Working Paper WP.41, April.

—— (1988b) *Varieties of Stabilization Policies: Towards Sensible Macroeconomics in the Third World*, Oxford, Clarendon Press.

United Nations (UN) (Various Years), *Demographic Yearbook*, New York, United Nations.

—— (various years), *Monthly Bulletin of Statistics*, New York, Statistical Office, United Nations.

—— (various years), *Statistical Yearbook*, New York, United Nations.

United Nations Advisory Group on Financial Flows for Africa (1988), *Financing Africa's Recovery*, New York, United Nations (the Wass Report).

United Nations Conference on Trade and Development (UNCTAD) (Various Years), *Handbook of International Trade and Development Statistics (supplement)*, New York, United Nations.

United Nations Industrial Development Organisation (UNIDO) (1985), *A Programme for the Industrial Development Decade for Africa: Initial Integrated Industrial Promotion Programme at the Sub-regional Level*, Vienna, UNIDO, UNIDO/OED.138, 19 March.

—— (various years), *Africa in Figures*, Vienna, UNIDO.

—— (various years), *Industry and Development Global Report*, Vienna, UNIDO.

—— (various years), *Handbook of Industrial Statistics*, Vienna, UNIDO.

—— (1986), *Report on the Eighth Conference of African Ministers of Industry*, Vienna, UNIDO, 3 November, CMI/8/17/rev.2.

—— (1989), *New Technologies and Industralisation Prospects for Developing Countries, Main Policy Issues*, Issue Paper Prepared for Expert Group on Prospects for Industrialisation Policies in Developing Countries Taking into Account the Impact of Developments in the Field of New and High Technologies, Vienna, UNIDO, April 1989.

Weiss, J. (1988), *Industry in Developing Countries*, London, Croom Helm.

Westphal, L.E. (1981), *Empirical Justification for Infant Industry Protection*, World Bank Staff Working Papers, No. 445, Washington DC, World Bank.

Wheeler, D. (1984), 'Sources of Stagnation in Sub-Saharan Africa', *World Development*, Vol. 12, No. 1, January.

World Bank (various years) *World Debt Tables*, Washington DC, World Bank.

—— (various years), *World Development Report*, Oxford, Oxford University Press.

—— (1981), *Accelerated Development in Sub-Saharan Africa: An Agenda for Action*, Washington DC, World Bank.

—— (1984), *Toward Sustained Development in Sub-Saharan Africa*, Washington DC, World Bank.

—— (1986a), *Structural Adjustment Lending: A First Review of Experience*, Washington DC, World Bank, Operations Evaluation Department, Report No. 6409.

—— (1986b), *Financing Adjustment with Growth in Sub-Saharan Africa 1986–90*, Washington DC, World Bank.

—— (1988), *World Tables 1987*, Washington DC, World Bank.

—— (1989), *Sub-Saharan Africa: From Crisis to Sustainable Growth*, Washington DC, World Bank.

—— and United Nations Development Programme (1989), *Africa's Adjustment and Growth in the 1980s*, Washington DC, World Bank.

Zehander, W. (1988), 'Regional cooperation in perspective: some experiences in sub-Saharan Africa', *The Courier*, No. 112, November-December.

PART II

The Seven Case-Studies

4 Botswana

STEPHEN LEWIS, JENNIFER SHARPLEY & CHARLES HARVEY

Introduction – Why Botswana?

With a population of only one million people and an economy apparently dominated by mining, a question may arise as to the usefulness of studying the development of manufacturing in Botswana. Several factors suggest that a review of its experience may be of some general value. First, it had the most rapid rate of real economic growth, whether measured by GNP per capita or GDP, of any country in the world between 1965 and 1985 (World Bank, 1987). More importantly for this discussion, its rate of growth of manufacturing value added (MVA) over two decades is among the highest reported in the World Bank's figures; indeed, only China, South Korea, Singapore, Indonesia and Libya achieved faster rates. And UNIDO data place Botswana at the top of the league in sub-Saharan Africa. So, perhaps there is a story to tell. In addition, a number of studies of mineral-rich developing countries (World Bank, 1979; Nankani, 1979; Lewis, 1984) have suggested that the dynamics of mineral-led growth may result in strong discrimination against other sectors producing tradeable goods, both manufacturing and agriculture. Furthermore, there is continuing debate about the role of trade policy, particularly of protection, in promoting both manufacturing growth and economic development more generally (Chenery, et al., 1986). Botswana is in a Customs Union with Lesotho, South Africa and Swaziland, has a free trade arrangement with Zimbabwe, and has made relatively little use of import controls or protective tariffs. A study of its experience might provide some insight into the continuing discussion on trade policy and industrialisation.

This chapter examines the performance of Botswana's manufacturing sector since Independence in 1966 and its prospects for development into the 1990s. In the next section we review the aggregate record of economic growth and structural change over the past two decades, and discuss briefly the overall approach of government policy toward manufacturing. Next follow analyses of the pattern of manufacturing growth, including the changing importance of different sub-sectors, the growth of employment relative to output and value added, and the growth of manufacturing in relation to both exports and the growth of competing imports. While many of the data are incomplete, this section does give a broad view of the 'sources' of growth in relation to the expansion of domestic demand, import substitution, and export growth. The principal features of economic policy affecting the manufacturing sector are then analysed, including the general macroeconomic framework, particular elements of foreign trade and protection policy, and other policies affecting manufacturing, such as infrastructure development, taxation and land policies. This is followed by some episodes or case-studies related to specific issues of government policy and the promotion of manufacturing growth[1].

The final three sections look to the future[2], highlighting first those features of past performance of importance to policy debate. Then follows a discussion of the prospects for the medium and the longer term in which possible new policy initiatives and orientations are discussed. Finally new policy approaches to a more outward-oriented structure of manufacturing are outlined.

The aggregate record of development 1965–85[3]

As Table 4.1 indicates, Botswana's record compares favourably with that of other low-income countries and with the rest sub-Saharan Africa. In terms of economic structure, Botswana had a slightly lower share of manufacturing in GDP in 1985 than both other groups. The improvement in its investment ratio and ratio of domestic savings to GDP over

Table 4.1 *Botswana in comparative perspective (all figures in percentages unless noted otherwise)*

	Botswana		Low-income other than India & China		Sub-Saharan Africa	
Annual growth of GNP per capita, 1965-86	8.8		0.5		0.9	
1986 GNP per capita in US$	840		200		370	
1986 oda net receipts per capita in US$	92.3		19.6		23.1	
1985 Gross international reserves in months of import cover	15.0		2.2		2.1	
Annual growth rates:	1965-80	80-86	1965-80	80-86	1965-80	80-86
Total GDP	14.3	11.9	3.1	2.9	5.6	0.0
Inflation	8.0	7.6	11.3	19.1	12.5	16.1
Agricultural GDP	9.3	-9.8	1.9	2.0	1.6	1.2
Manufacturing GDP	12.5	6.2	4.8	4.8	8.5	0.3
Govt. consumption	12.0	12.8	4.1	1.7	8.1	-1.0
Gross investment	21.0	-6.9	3.7	0.4	8.8	-9.3
Share of Total GDP	1965	1986	1965	1985	1965	1985
Agriculture	34	4	43	38	45	36
Industry	19	58	18	20	19	25
Manufacturing	12	6	10	11	9	10
Govt consumption	24	28	10	12	11	13
Investment	6	26	15	15	15	14
Domestic saving	-13	26	12	7	15	11
Exports of goods & non-factor services	32	63	19	14	23	19
Debt Service and Industrial Labour Force						
Debt service as share of exports	0.9	4.3	7.6	20.9	5.3	19.3
% of labour force in Industry	4	13[a]	8[a]	10[a]	8	9

Source: World Bank, *World Development Report, 1988.*

Notes: . . . negligible (a) −1980.

the period was relatively good, and government consumption as a share of GDP was almost twice as large as in the other comparative groups. Botswana is a relatively open economy, and its exports of goods and net-factor services as a share of GDP doubled, whereas those of the other groups declined. Foreign aid per capita, and gross foreign reserves in months of import coverage, were also four to five times higher, and the debt-service ratio was relatively low.

At Independence in 1966, Botswana was one of the poorest countries in the world. It was suffering from a drought which caused the death of about one third of the total national cattle herd, the only major domestic resource at that time. Half the government's recurrent budget and all of its development or capital budget were met from Grants-in-Aid from the British government. Through a combination of good fortune and good management (Harvey and Lewis, 1989), an exceptional rate of economic progress was achieved over the next two decades; the compound growth rate of real GDP was over 12.5% per year, though there were significant year-to-year fluctuations[4].

The leading growth sectors were cattle and non-cattle agriculture during the early years, but principally mining: a large copper-nickel mine and three major diamond mines were developed between 1969 and 1982. Renegotiation of the revenue-sharing formula under the Southern African Customs Union Agreement, careful negotiations with the mining companies, and the active pursuit of concessional finance from bilateral and multilateral aid agencies, contributed to a very high rate of growth of both government revenue and expenditure.

The picture of the economy which had emerged by the mid 1980s was totally different from that at Independence (Table 4.2). Agriculture had declined from 39 to 4% of GDP in 1986 (another drought year), while the share of broadly-defined industry (manufacturing, mining, construction, electricity, and water) rose from 19 to 58%, largely because of the growth of the mining sector. Manufacturing, which in 1966 had consisted principally of processing beef for

Table 4.2 *Key economic indicators (all figures in percentages unless noted otherwise)*

1. *Sectoral Growth Rates* increase in real GDP (1979/80 prices) over previous year	average 1965–68/9	average 1973/4–79/80	average 1979/80–85/6
Agriculture	2.8	8.0	9.4
Mining	–	28.8	15.3
Manufacturing	2.9	9.9	17.5
Central government	3.2	19.5	10.3
Total	0.6	12.0	10.3

2. *Sectoral Shares of GDP*	average 1965–68/9	average 1973/4–79/80	average 1979/80–85/6
Agriculture	40.8	22.4	8.2
Mining	0.7	15.8	30.8
Manufacturing	8.6	6.8	6.5
Central government	11.1	14.5	15.7
Total	100.0	100.0	100.0

3. *Use of Resources* Total GDP-current	average 1965–68/9	average 1973/4–79/80	average 1979/80–83/4
Gross investment	26.1	34.7	34.3
Domestic savings	– 15.3	12.5	17.4
External savings	41.4	22.3	16.9
Exports of goods (+)	30.8	51.9	53.5
Imports of goods (–)	– 72.1	– 61.9	– 61.3
Net imports of goods and services	– 41.4	– 22.3	– 16.9

4. *Government Revenue and Expenditure* total GDP-current		average 1973–4/78/9	average 1979/80–84/5
Recurrent revenue		27.0	37.8
Total expenditure		32.8	37.3
Financing requirement		– 5.8	+ 0.5

5. *Commercial Bank Credit* annual increase		average 1974–9	average 1979–85
		27.1	17.8

6. *Inflation* increase over previous year (1979/80 = 100)			
Consumer Price Index		12.4	11.5
GDP deflator		13.6	10.3

7. *Formal Sector Employment* annual increase		average 1973–9	average 1979–85
Agriculture		– 1.0	– 2.4
Mining		19.4	8.5
Manufacturing		9.0	13.1
Central government		18.8	16.9
Total citizens:		9.1	8.5
in South African Mines		– 9.2	– 3.8

8. *Share of Total Employment*		1972	1985
Agriculture		8.0	4.7
Mining		7.2	7.0
Manufacturing		6.5	7.7
Central government		8.0	4.5
Total		100	100

Table 4.2 *Cont'd*

9. International Terms of Trade (1979/80 = 100)	1975	1979	1984
Export unit prices	44.9	98.9	129.3
Import unit prices	49.9	89.6	179.1
Barter terms of trade	89.2	109.3	71.5
10. Foreign Reserves	1976	1979	1985
As % imports	35.9	49.6	150.2
Weeks equivalent	18.7	25.8	78.1
11. Population (million)	0.69	0.75	1.0

Source: *National Accounts of Botswana*; *Statistical Bulletin*; *Tables and Estimates of Recurrent Revenue* (various years).

export, declined slightly as a share of total GDP because of the latter's even more rapid growth. However, as a share of non-mining GDP, manufacturing rose from 8.6 to 11.4% over two decades, and in relation to agricultural GDP, from 20 to 154%[5]. The growth of total employment in the modern sector was also extremely rapid. At Independence, there were more citizens employed in South Africa than in domestic wage employment (52,000 as against 23,000). By 1985, the position had reversed completely, with 112,000 employed domestically in the modern sector, whereas only 24,000 were employed in South Africa. The increase in manufacturing employment, from around 2,000 to 10,000, provided an annual growth rate of 8.4% over the two decades, and over 10% from 1973 to 1985[6].

In the major macroeconomic aggregates, Botswana was also transformed. Domestic saving was negative at Independence; grants supported the government budget and the consumption requirements of the population were met by drought relief assistance. Government revenue as a share of GDP also rose dramatically from 23 to 50% between 1973 and 1983, though government expenditure as a share of GDP did not increase as rapidly, rising from 30 to 39%. Nonetheless, Botswana had the most rapid rate of growth of real general government expenditure (12% a year) of any country in the world. Domestic investment was only 10% of GDP in 1966, but because of the mining booms and investment in other sectors, it was around 34% by the mid-1980s, with domestic saving averaging over 20% of GDP.

At Independence, a good share of the very large current account deficit was financed by remittances from workers in South Africa. Because the leading productive sectors were export-oriented and the degree of openness of the economy increased, the ratio of commodity exports to GDP more than doubled from under 30 to over 60%, while the share of imports rose from 51 to 57%.

Inflows of private and public foreign capital have been extremely important in Botswana's development, at times exceeding 30 or even 40% of GDP. The entire copper-nickel mine and its infrastructure were financed by foreign capital. All the diamond mining investments prior to 1979 were financed by private foreign capital, as was the bulk of the investment in the Jwaneng diamond mine, with the government purchasing 20% of the equity investment, largely funded from its own sources. Private capital has also been important in the development of the manufacturing sector (apart from the parastatal Meat Commission). The government, through the Botswana Development Corporation, has made significant investments in the sector, but the most recent data suggest that in 1984 over 60% of all manufacturing establishments were wholly foreign-owned[7].

The performance of the manufacturing sector to the mid-1980s

SOME CHARACTERISTICS OF THE SECTOR

At Independence, manufacturing was dominated (perhaps 95% of MVA) by the Botswana Meat Commission (BMC) in Lobatse, which is an abattoir producing chilled and frozen de-boned beef for the high-quality international market. As late as 1984/5, the BMC's operations still accounted for 28% of value added and 36% of output from the manufacturing sector, but less than 20% of employment. Over the 20 years since Independence a variety of other activities has been developed in response to different stimuli. The second largest single enterprise (after the BMC) is the Kgalakgadi Brewery in Gaborone, which was established in the mid-1970s. Operations have been established in textiles, food products such as grain milling and bakeries, building supplies (concrete products, metal-working for door and window frames and galvanised iron products, etc.). Traditional village industries, such as beer brewing, have declined in relative importance, while the workshops associated with the mining industry have added a variety of miscellaneous metal working and chemical activities. There are no petroleum refining, cement making, or large metal-working activities. Apart from the BMC, the larger establishments tend to be those which are foreign owned or in partnership with local firms, particularly the Botswana Development Corporation (BDC).

By 1985, the manufacturing sector provided 12.6% of total wage employment in the private and parastatal sector, up from 7.4% in 1975. Manufacturing activities are highly concentrated geographically, with over 60% of all manufacturing jobs in Gaborone and Lobatse in both 1975 and 1985, while half of all manufacturing jobs created in that decade were located in Gaborone.

Since the early 1970s, manufacturing has risen from around 8% to over 11% of non-mining GDP and from less than 20% of agricultural GDP to over 150% (a calculation affected in part by the drought of the early 1980s). The explanation of this rapid growth rate in absolute terms and the fairly substantial rate of structural change within the non-mining sectors of the economy, would appear to be of some interest.

PATTERNS AND SOURCES OF GROWTH

Because of the close relationship between industrialisation and foreign trade, it is useful to analyse the growth of manufacturing in relation to import substitution and export expansion. For the years 1973/4–84/5, it was possible to construct estimates of gross output, value added, imports and exports for 11 sub-groups of manufacturing by ISIC sectors. The total supply of an industry's output is the sum of gross output and imports, while domestic demand (for consumption, intermediate use, and investment, including 'inventory changes) can be calculated as total supply minus exports.

Using these measures for each industry, three sets of fairly aggregative statistics can be compiled for each sub-sector and for manufacturing as a whole. One of these is the ratio of output to total supply, or its complement, imports as a ratio of total supply. This gives an indication, sector by sector, of the relative importance of imports and competing domestic output. One would expect that the process of import substitution in most industries would produce a rising ratio of output, or a falling ratio of imports, to total supply. How rapidly these ratios change, and in what industries, would be determined in part by investment patterns, comparative advantage, and industrial incentives.

Another measure is the ratio of exports to total supply (or of exports to output). This would give some indication of the extent to which the expansion of output in each sub-sector came from the expansion of export markets relative to the domestic market.

The third aggregate statistic – of less interest in the case of Botswana – is the ratio of value added to gross output. While 'import substitution' might take place due to an increasing ratio of domestic output to total supply in any given industry, import substitution could also take place through a rising ratio of domestic value added to total output within any given sector.

It may be useful to attempt a quantitative measure of the different 'sources' of industrial growth, estimating the relative importance of domestic demand, import substitution, and exports in accounting for the growth of manufacturing and its major sectors. The general approach was first developed by Chenery (1960) and later refined by Lewis and Soligo (1965) in their analysis of industrial growth in Pakistan. Since we are interested in the changes in the structure of the economy, it is assumed that growth would be proportional among all sectors, unless there are particular reasons for some deviation.

In our model O_i is the value of output of industry i, M_i is the value of imports of the same industrial classification, Z_i is the value of total domestic supply ($Z_i = Oi_i + M_i$), and X_i is the value of exports from industry i; then by subtraction D_i ($= Z_i - X_i$) is domestic demand for goods of the i'th industry. We can define u_i as the ratio of domestic production to total supply. All the values are at domestic market prices. The change in output (ΔO) for any industry between year 1 and year 2 can then be broken down as follows:

$$\Delta O = u_1 (D_2 - D_1) + u_1 (X_2 - X_1) + (u_2 - u_1)Z_2$$

We are interested not only in manufacturing output but also in MVA, and can partition the sources of value added growth in the same way, into domestic demand, exports and import substitution, plus an additional term, which measures the effect on value added of changes in its ratio to domestic output. The term is essentially a residual, and captures, among other things, the effect of intra-industry changes in the composition of output as well as changes in technical efficiency. If V_i is the value added in industry i, then we could use r_i to denote its ratio to gross output ($r_i = V_i/O_i$).

The change in value added (ΔV) for an industry group between periods 1 and 2, can be partitioned as follows:

$$\Delta V = u_1 r_1 (D_2 - D_1) + u_1 r_1 (X_2 - X_1) + (u_2 - u_1) r_1 Z_1 + (r_2 - r_1) u_2 Z_2$$

Figure 4.1 shows the behaviour of the aggregate ratios of imports, exports and output to total supply, as well as the ratio of exports to output, for the manufacturing sector as a whole. (The extreme variations of exports/output from 1978/9 to 1980/81 are related to outbreaks of foot and mouth disease, which affected cattle movement and slaughter and beef output and exports). Overall the manufacturing sector appears from these figures to have grown less rapidly than the supply of manufacturing imports, and manufactured exports appear to have grown more slowly than manufacturing output. These aggregates suggest that imports displaced domestic production in terms of market shares, and that exports lagged. Disaggregation by industry will show a different story, however.

Figure 4.1 *Manufacturing exports and imports as % of output and total supply*

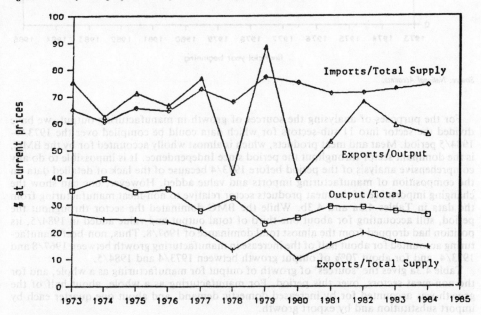

Source: National Accounts.

The ratios of value added to gross output in the three major goods-producing sectors are shown in Figure 4.2. The declining ratio of value added to output in agriculture is fairly typical of the development for that sector in most countries, reflecting the increased importance of purchased inputs as agriculture is modernised. In Botswana it is also affected by the drought in the early 1980s, during which investments in purchased inputs failed to result in increased output. The sharply rising ratio of value added to output in mining reflects the growing importance of the highly profitable diamond sector relative to the much less profitable copper-nickel and coal sectors. Manufacturing shows little change in aggregate, though there appears to have been some increase relative to the early 1970s.

Figure 4.2 *Value added as a share of output in agriculture, mining and manufacturing*

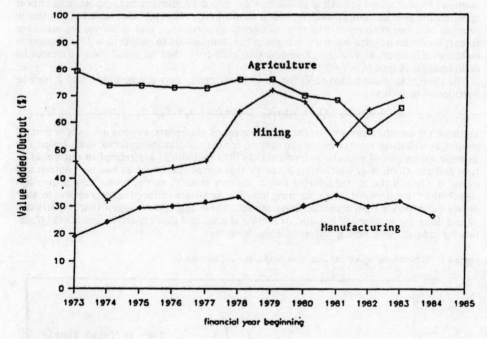

Source: *National Accounts*.

For the purposes of analysing the sources of growth in manufacturing output, we have divided the sector into 11 sub-sectors for which data could be compiled over the 1973/4–1984/5 period. Meat and meat products, which is almost wholly accounted for by the BMC, is the dominant sector throughout the period since Independence. It is impossible to do any comprehensive analysis of the period before 1973/4 because of the lack of detailed data on the composition of manufacturing imports and value added. However, one can show the changing importance of the meat products sector relative to non-meat manufacturing from the data in Tables 4.3a and 4.3b. While the BMC dominated the sector throughout the period, still accounting for about one third of total output and value added in 1984/5, its position had dropped from the almost total dominance of 1967/8. Thus, non-beef manufacturing accounted for about half of the increase in manufacturing growth between 1967/8 and 1973/4, and for about 70% of output growth between 1973/4 and 1984/5.

Table 4.3a gives the 'sources' of growth of output for manufacturing as a whole, and for the non-meat sectors, over this period. For manufacturing as a whole, about half of the growth was accounted for by increased domestic demand, and about one quarter each by import substitution and by export growth.

For manufacturing excluding meat and meat products, export growth was of less importance and import substitution and domestic demand of greater importance than for the sector as a whole. On a sectoral basis, the pattern indicates considerable variability (Table 4.3b). Both meat and meat products and textiles showed export growth as an important source of output growth, while import substitution was of considerable importance in beverages, chemical products, paper products, metal products and miscellaneous manufactures.

These more detailed figures for individual industries explain the overall 'sources' of manufacturing growth. The dominance of meat and meat products in overall output growth (about 30% of the total) and the importance of exports as a source of that growth largely explains why 24% of total manufacturing growth was due to export expansion, while only 8% of the non-meat manufacturing growth was accounted for by export growth. Among the non-meat sectors only textiles show exports as an important source of growth. The disproportionate share of import substitution as a source of growth in the non-meat sectors is explained by its strength in several sectors, e.g. beverages, chemicals, and miscellaneous. Given the rapid growth of the domestic market as total GDP grew at world-record rates, it is not surprising that domestic demand was a major source of manufacturing growth, and that, for the non-meat sectors, export growth was not. It is somewhat more surprising to find that import substitution was an important source of growth, given the open trading system and the lack of a generally protectionist approach to industry. We shall discuss this further below in relation to the overall policy regime. However, we note that the importance of import substitution as a source of manufacturing growth was higher than for Kenya (see Chapter 7), and approximately the same as for Zimbabwe (see Chapter 10) during the UDI period.

Tables 4.4a and 4.4b show the sources of growth of MVA. By and large the same pattern appears as for output growth: domestic demand accounts for about half the increased value added, while import substitution is much more important than export growth for the

Table 4.3a *Sources of growth of manufacturing output as share of total output growth*

	Growth 1973/4–1984/5			
	Output	Domestic demand	Exports	Import substitution
Meat and meat products	29.2	12.5	17.8	−1.2
Dairy and agro products	−0.1	5.8	0.0	−5.9
Beverages etc. (excl. tobacco)	24.3	6.4	0.0	17.9
Bakery products	1.9	2.2	0.0	−0.3
Textiles clothing	9.0	3.6	3.7	1.7
Tanning leather	−0.1	1.7	0.6	−2.4
Chemicals excl. petrol	5.4	0.3	0.0	5.1
Wood products	2.2	1.7	0.3	0.2
Paper products	4.7	2.0	0.0	2.6
Metal excl. machinery and vehicles	6.3	4.0	0.2	2.1
Miscellaneous [a]	17.2	10.5	0.8	5.9
Total all sectors	100.0	50.9	23.4	25.6
Total excluding meat	100.0	54.4	7.9	37.7

Table 4.3b *Sources of growth of manufacturing output as share of sector output growth*

	Growth 1973/4–84/5			
	Output	Domestic demand	Exports	Import substitution
Meat and meat products	100.0	42.7	61.0	−4.0
Dairy and agro products	100.0	*	*	*
Beverages etc. (excl. tobacco)	100.0	26.5	0.0	73.5
Bakery products	100.0	114.0	0.0	−14.0
Textiles clothing	100.0	40.2	41.0	18.8
Tanning leather	100.0	*	*	*
Chemicals excl. petrol	100.0	5.8	0.0	94.2
Wood products	100.0	77.6	15.5	6.9
Paper products	100.0	43.8	0.8	55.4
Metal excl. machinery and vehicles	100.0	64.4	2.5	33.1
Miscellaneous [a]	100.0	61.3	4.5	34.2
Total all sectors	100.0	50.9	23.4	25.6
Total excluding Meat	100.0	54.4	7.9	37.7

Source: National Accounts, Statistical Bulletin, External Trade Statistics.

Note: * Not meaningful because output was virtually unchanged.
[a] Includes tobacco, petrol, machinery, vehicles, other manufacturing.

Table 4.4a *Sources of growth of MVA as share of total value added*

	Growth 1973/4–84/5				
	Value added	Domestic demand	Exports	Import substitution	Residual
Meat and meat products	25.4	6.7	9.5	−0.1	−9.4
Dairy and agro products	−0.4	1.8	0.0	−1.8	−0.4
Beverages etc. (excl. tobacco)	22.8	7.2	0.0	19.0	−3.5
Bakery products	1.3	0.1	0.0	0.0	1.2
Textiles clothing	7.3	2.1	2.1	0.9	2.3
Tanning leather	−0.1	1.2	0.4	−1.7	0.0
Chemicals excl. petrol	6.4	0.0	0.0	4.2	2.2
Wood products	2.1	1.0	0.3	0.1	0.6
Paper products	4.9	1.7	0.0	2.1	1.2
Metal excl. machinery and vehic.	11.8	3.2	0.1	1.7	6.8
Miscellaneous[a]	18.5	22.6	1.7	12.6	18.4
Total all sectors	100.0	47.6	14.0	37.0	−17.4
Total excluding Meat	100.0	54.8	6.0	49.8	−10.7

Source: Ibid.

Note: [a] Includes tobacco, petrol, machinery, vehicles, other manufacturing.

Table 4.4b *Sources of growth of MVA as share of sector value added*

	Growth 1973/4–84/5				
	Value added	Domestic demand	Exports	Import substitution	Residual
Meat and meat products	100.0	26.3	37.4	−0.5	−36.9
Dairy and agro products	100.0	*	*	*	*
Beverages etc. (excl. tobacco)	100.0	31.6	0.0	83.6	−15.3
Bakery products	100.0	10.0	0.0	90.0	
Textiles clothing	100.0	28.1	28.1	12.3	31.6
Tanning leather	100.0	*	*	*	*
Chemicals excl. petrol	100.0	0.0	0.0	66.0	34.0
Wood products	100.0	50.0	12.5	6.3	31.3
Paper products	100.0	34.2	0.0	42.1	23.7
Metal excl. machinery and vehicles	100.0	27.2	1.1	14.1	57.6
Miscellaneous[a]	100.0	122.2	9.0	68.1	−99.3
Total all sectors	100.0	47.6	14.0	37.0	−17.4
Total excluding Meat	100.0	54.8	6.0	49.8	−10.7

Source: Ibid.

Note: * not meaningful because output was virtually unchanged:
[a] Includes tobacco, petrol, machinery, vehicles, other manufacturing.

non-meat manufacturing industries. Due to the different ratios of value added to output in various industries, import substitution seems to have been considerably higher as a source of value added growth than as a source of output growth. For two sectors, meat and meat products and miscellaneous manufacturing, the declining ratio of value added to gross output over the period resulted in a sizeable negative contribution to value added growth. Both these changes were due to very specific factors which we believe were not indicative of problems of industrial policy or efficiency[8].

In summary, Botswana's pattern of manufacturing growth showed an increasing diversification away from its initial nearly total dependence on meat and meat products, and an interesting balance of 'sources' between the growth of domestic demand, import substitution and export growth. In order to evaluate the efficiency and the sustainability of the growth of the sector it is necessary to examine the framework in which this growth took place and the extent to which it was due to an incentive structure and other factors that were, or were not, viable in the longer term.

The policy framework

We have divided the discussion of the policy framework developed into four parts. A number of issues cut across several of these areas, but most will fall in one or another.

i) ATTITUDES TOWARD THE PRIVATE SECTOR
Since Independence, the government has regarded the development of the enterprise sectors of the economy as an activity primarily for the private sector. It saw its own role as one of providing infrastructure and services, including basic education and training for the labour force. A basic statement of policy, first given in the Transitional Plan for Social and Economic Development published at Independence in 1966, and repeated with minor changes in all six National Development Plans, reads in part:

A rationally planned and guided economy is the objective of government policy. However, a balance must be struck where private initiative has ample scope within the general confines laid down by government. It is government's duty to set forth its objectives and priorities, to frame its policies accordingly, and to assist the private sector in every way consistent with the attainment of these goals.

. . . Private enterprise will only be interested in investing in Botswana if there is a profit to be made . . . . . The government's policy will be, in the case of every proposal (for added incentives), to examine the balance of advantages to Botswana; the costs and benefits will be studied, and decisions made on that basis alone.

In 1970, the government established the Botswana Development Corporation to be its operational arm in promoting industrial and commercial development, either in partnership with the private sector or, where private initiative was not forthcoming, on its own. The BDC was established to be a commercial enterprise and to operate on strict commercial lines, though with a bias toward projects which would lead to further development within Botswana[9].

As explained in some detail elsewhere (Harvey and Lewis, 1989), the lack of basic physical and social infrastructure at Independence, as well as the initial dependence on foreign grants to balance the recurrent budget (which caused decisions about government spending to be made in London rather than in Gaborone), meant that the government's efforts in the first decade of independence were focused primarily on the public sector. It concentrated on the development of water, roads, communications, basic health services, and, in general, a public sector that could deliver services to the population, especially in the rural areas where the majority of citizens and voters resided. In the mid-1970s, attention began to shift within the government towards more active measures to promote the diversification of the economy away from beef and the newly found minerals exports, and to encourage the creation of employment opportunities in manufacturing and other sectors. A comprehensive study of employment policies (Lipton, 1978) and a series of policy initiatives in the next few years (Financial Assistance Policy, 1982; National Policy on Economic Opportunities, 1982) showed the increased attention paid to the development of the manufacturing sector in particular. The protection of local industry clause in the Southern African Customs Union Agreement was first used in 1976; a Local Preference Scheme was introduced in government purchasing and tendering arrangements in 1976; and a variety of additional measures were introduced in the early 1980s to promote particular industries and to provide (with price and quality guarantees) protection from imports for specified industries.

ii) MACROECONOMIC POLICY
Under macroeconomic policies we include budgetary or fiscal policy (including counter-cyclical policy), monetary policy (including money, credit and interest rates), exchange-rate policy and wages/incomes policy.

At the time of Independence, Botswana had no opportunity to exercise any kind of independent macroeconomic policy. It was still in a monetary area using the South African currency, and it had no independent budgetary policy, since, as noted earlier, government expenditure plans had to be approved by the British government as a condition of receiving annual grants-in-aid. After Independence high priority was given to developing its own

Figure 4.3 *Government revenue and expenditure as % of total GDP at current prices*

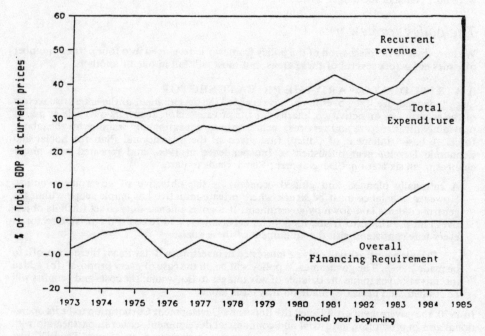

Source: National Accounts.

revenue base and achieving 'financial independence'. Through the successful renegotiation of the terms of revenue-sharing in the Southern African Customs Union and through revenue from the new mining projects, particularly diamonds, a position was achieved where recurrent costs were fully covered from its own revenue sources in the financial year 1972/3. A significant indication of the government's overall financial policy is that in the same year two special funds were created: the Revenue Stabilisation Fund (RSF) and the Public Debt Service Fund (PDSF). The RSF was to provide a vehicle for balancing year-to-year fluctuations in revenue with long-term growth in public expenditure and the PDSF was to be invested in domestic projects which would yield a flow of interest and principal repayments to match Botswana's debt-service obligations abroad. Financial prudence and a long-term view of the budget were early parts of the macro-management system.

An indication of the general macroeconomic picture is provided by Figures 4.3 and 4.4 which show the aggregates for the government budget and domestic saving and investment since 1973. The overall financing requirements of the budget have always been considerably below the gap between domestic investment and saving. Indeed, after the opening of the Jwaneng diamond mine in 1982 the budget went into overall surplus (though the Development Plan makes it clear that this would be temporary). Maintaining a growth rate of total government expenditure that could be financed on a long-term basis has been a part of the overall fiscal strategy, and the lower increase in the share of total expenditure than in that of total revenue in GDP shown in Figure 4.3 reflects that approach. The large negative figure for net imports of goods and services shown for most years in Figure 4.4 is the result of the substantial role of foreign private financing of mining projects and of many manufacturing ventures which added to the capital inflow provided by foreign loans and grants to the government. As compared with many developing countries, however, Botswana's fiscal policy was not one which added substantially to domestic aggregate demand and created an unsustainable level of imports. The large excesses of imports over exports in some years were a reflection of project financing in the public, private and parastatal sectors, not the result of increased domestic demand brought about by excessive borrowing from the banking sector to hold up general government or private spending.

Figure 4.4 *Investment and saving as a % of total GDP at current prices*

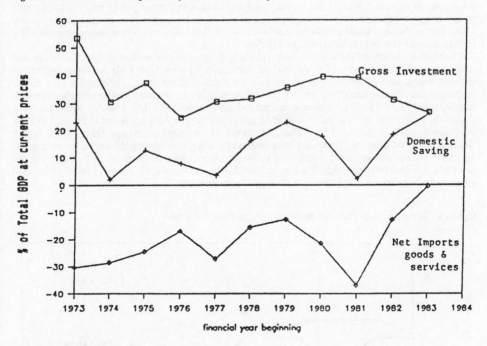

Source: *National Accounts*.

The story of Botswana's countercyclical macroeconomic and budgetary policy is an interesting and extended one, covered in detail elsewhere (Harvey 1984; Harvey, 1987; Harvey and Lewis, 1989). What it managed to achieve in its overall budgetary stabilisation policy was a rate of growth of government expenditure that fluctuated much less than that of revenue, with the consequence that the level of government cash balances at the Central Bank (and, to some extent as a counterpart, the level of foreign-exchange reserves) were used as a buffer to absorb differentials in the growth of government revenue and planned spending (Lewis and Mokgethi, 1983). Even in its only major balance-of-payments 'crisis' of 1982, Botswana was able to avoid the need to depress domestic demand excessively in order to meet balance-of-payments constraints. Further, in 1981, the government began a process of making annual wage adjustments in the public sector after consultation with the tripartite consultative National Employment Manpower and Incomes Commission, on which government, trade unions and employers were represented. Public sector wage rate decisions then became more closely integrated into general budgetary policy, though ad hoc approaches through public service salary commissions were reintroduced in 1985/6.

It is in exchange-rate policy that Botswana has been most active in its macroeconomic management. In 1975, it decided to establish its own currency and central bank, and in 1976 the Pula was introduced. From that time on, it had its own independent monetary and exchange-rate system and policies. From the first the government made clear that it intended to use general macroeconomic policies rather than exchange controls or import controls to manage its external balance of payments. Only nine months after introducing the new currency, it made the first of what became a number of adjustments in the exchange rate as a tool for influencing general economic conditions and macroeconomic policy.

The authorities have tried to maintain a balance between using the exchange rate as a tool for influencing the general rate of domestic inflation (given that inflation in southern Africa has been above world levels for most of the last decade) and the need to maintain competitiveness for domestic sectors producing tradeable goods and services (other than mining and beef, both of which would be competitive at a wide range of exchange rates). The fact that the share of imports in the consumption basket of the poorest groups in the country is higher than that of the richest, has meant that exchange-rate policy has important distributional implications as well. Finally, the authorities have considered wage policy and exchange rate policy together, recognising the importance of the need to maintain competitiveness in new economic activities, particularly in manufacturing, both for potential import-substituting industries and for potential export industries.

Through a variety of measures (discretionary changes in the exchange rate, the adoption and adjustment of the mix of a 'basket' of currencies to which the Pula has been pegged at various times, and combinations of the two devices), Botswana has followed a very active exchange-rate management policy. Its determination is complicated by the fact that the vast majority (85% in 1985) of exports are priced in and sold for US dollars, while the vast majority of imports are priced in and sold for either South African Rand (75% in 1985) or Zimbabwe dollars (about 8%). Thus, movements in cross exchange rates, over which Botswana has no control and which have been very large, complicate the exchange rate management issue considerably[10]. Figure 4.5 shows the movement of nominal exchange rates for the Pula relative to the Rand, the Zimbabwe dollar, and the SDR from 1976 to 1986, and gives an indication of the extremely divergent movements.

Figure 4.5 *Nominal exchange-rate trends foreign currency per Pula, 1980 = 100*

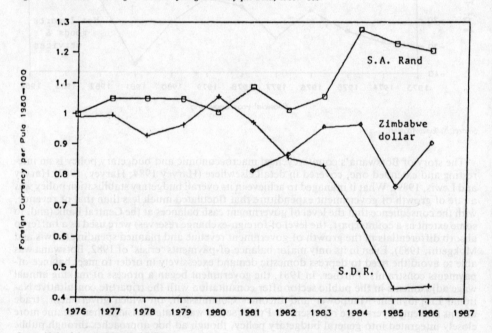

Source: *National Accounts, Statistical Bulletin.*

Botswana has managed to maintain a real effective exchange rate between the Pula and other major trading currencies which has not eroded its competitive position (indeed, this has improved in SDR and Zimbabwe dollar markets), and at the same time has been able to maintain a rate of inflation substantially less than that of other countries in the region (though above that of the industrial countries). These developments are shown in Figures 4.6 and 4.7. The manufacturing sector has been able to operate in a situation of relatively stable competitiveness with respect to the South African Rand, the currency of the principal competitive markets in the Southern African Customs Union Area.

Figure 4.6 *Real exchange rate foreign currency per Pula, 1980 = 100*

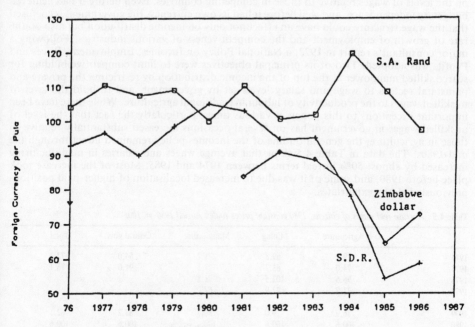

Source: *National Accounts*; IMF, *International Financial Statistics*.

Figure 4.7 *Relative rates of inflation Botswana's Consumer Price Index/that of major trading partners*

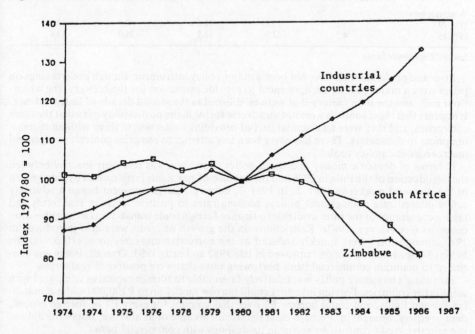

Source: *National Accounts, Statistical Bulletin*, IMF, *International Financial Statistics*.

But competitiveness depends not only on general price/exchange rate movements but also on the levels of wages relative to those in competing countries. Even before it had achieved budgetary independence, and well before it had its own currency, the government recognised that the wage structure could have an effect not only on income distribution but also on the rate of growth of employment and the competitiveness of various industries. Following a major consultant's report in 1972, a National Policy on Incomes, Employment, Prices and Profits was adopted. Two of its principal objectives were to limit competitive bidding for scarce skilled manpower at the top of the income distribution by restricting the private and parastatal sectors to wage and salary levels set by government, and to hold the level of unskilled wages to the productivity of labour in traditional agriculture. While there have been important exceptions to this policy at various times, particularly the fact that the level of unskilled wages in government has on several occasions increased substantially relative to those in agriculture, the general outline of the incomes policy remained intact through the mid-1980s. The data in Table 4.5 show that average wages and salaries in manufacturing increased by almost 50% in real terms between 1974 and 1985. Most of the increase took place before 1980, and some of it was due to increased localisation of higher-paid positions previously held by expatriates.

Table 4.5 *Average real wages of citizens, 1980 constant prices (index August 1980 = 100)*

	Agriculture	Mining	Manufacture	Central govt.	Total
1974	79.4	69.8	71.7	84.0	72.4
1975	74.0	63.7	71.1	91.0	76.1
1976	96.6	102.5	71.8		
1977	71.7	72.9	67.9		
1979	76.9	79.0	80.7	83.2	82.1
1980	100.6	100.6	100.6	100.6	100.6
1982	102.2	127.0	95.7		
1983	132.5	122.0	86.8		
1984	109.5	118.9	101.5		
1985	80.1	112.6	107.0	62.4	98.2
% increase between					
1974–79	− 3.2	13.2	12.6	− 0.9	13.4
1979–85	4.2	42.5	32.5	− 25.0	19.6

Source: *Employment Survey*.

Price and profit controls have not been a major policy instrument, though undertakings on prices were a major part of the agreement to provide protection for the brewery, the wheat-flour mill, and the soap factory that were established in the second decade of Independence. It appears that these controls were not an adverse factor in the profitability of two of the three enterprises, and they were an essential part of providing protection to them without increasing prices to consumers. There has never been any attempt to use price controls as a general macroeconomic policy tool.

In terms of domestic money and credit policy, Botswana was relatively inactive between the introduction of the Pula in 1976 and the balance-of-payments crisis caused by a downturn of the diamond market in 1981–2. In 1981–2, however, the government began a relatively active interest-rate management policy, pushing rates to positive levels in real terms and taking cognizance of the rates available to finance foreign trade transactions in neighbouring countries (see Harvey, 1987). Restrictions on the growth of credit were also introduced in 1982, though these were quickly reduced as the corrective measures took effect and the balance-of-payments position improved in late 1982 and early 1983. Overall, Botswana continued to maintain commercial bank borrowing rates that were positive in real terms.

Botswana's monetary policy was relatively favourable to foreign capital as compared with some other countries. Foreign investors could borrow locally up to P100,000 without matching foreign funds, and could borrow P1 over that amount for every P1 of foreign capital, debt or equity, brought in. Perhaps most significant because of its absence, Botswana did not use selective credit controls by sector in its dealings with commercial banks.

iii) TRADE POLICY AND PROTECTION

The three most important elements of Botswana's foreign trade policy are the preferential trading arrangements that it has through its membership of the Southern African Customs Union, the free trade agreement with Zimbabwe, and its preferential trading arrangements with the EEC/ACP countries under the Lomé Conventions.

Southern African Customs Union (SACU).   Botswana, Lesotho and Swaziland (BLS) were joined with South Africa in a Customs Union at the time of the establishment of the Union of South Africa in 1910. The arrangements provided for duty-free movement of goods among the four member countries with the responsibility to set external tariffs resting with the government of South Africa. The three smaller countries received a fixed share of the customs revenue pool each year.

Following their Independence in the 1960s, the three smaller countries renegotiated the arrangements with South Africa, culminating in an agreement in 1969 which provided both for a new basis for revenue sharing and for a variety of measures designed to enable them both to share in the growth of the regional economy and to protect new local industries from competition from other producers within the Customs Union (principally South African). There were also a variety of provisions dealing with marketing arrangements for agricultural commodities which permit quantitative restrictions to ensure orderly marketing, but which prohibit the use of such restrictions to protect one country's producers at the expense of another.

The BLS countries have made relatively limited use of these special provisions (see below). The Customs Union arrangements have been significant for Botswana in several respects, not least of which has been the revenue provided by the revenue-sharing formula[11]. This was a major source of government income in the early 1970s as imports rose rapidly during the construction periods of the Orapa diamond mine and the Selebi-Phikwe copper-nickel project. The customs revenue was still 15% of government recurrent revenue even in 1985/6, despite the rapid increase in revenues from diamond mining.

In addition to the revenue benefits (these being off-set by the fact that it has to pay protected prices for South African goods) Botswana enjoys a reciprocal advantage on its exports to South Africa. The largest single item benefiting from this is beef from the BMC and by-products of cattle slaughter, but there are increasing numbers of other manufactured exports. In addition, the Customs Union also provides free rights of transit for Botswana traffic to and from world markets via South African routes. In view of the difficulties experienced by other countries in the region, notably Zambia and Zimbabwe, this benefit is of considerable importance.

While SACU provides for duty-free movement of goods among the four member countries, with the responsibility for external tariffs resting with the government of South Africa, that government has limited the number of producers allowed to supply the protected domestic market. At times, producers in the BLS countries were blocked from exporting to South Africa, and South African pressure also prevented some industries from being started in the three smaller countries[12]. Nevertheless, there were increasing numbers of manufactured goods which benefited from access to the South African market.

The 1969 treaty also allowed Botswana to provide tariff protection for new local industries from SACU imports, for a maximum of eight years. If, however, the new firm could not compete with imports even with this protection, so that some imports continued, the additional revenue was paid into the common pool rather than to Botswana. This made it expensive to protect an industry which was too small or too unsuccessful to capture the local market, since Botswana consumers paid tariffs on imports from which Botswana received only a small share[13].

For this reason, and perhaps also because farmers and consumers were well represented in Parliament and the Cabinet, the government was basically against using tariff protection to promote local industry. In addition, the relatively small number of cases of protective tariffs or quantitative restrictions on imports were conditional on producers maintaining their selling prices at the same level as would have prevailed for duty-free imports. In the case of tariffs, which were only used twice (for a beer and a soap factory), consumers had to pay more for imports but faced approximately the same price as before for the new, domestically produced products[14]. The government also resisted pressure to subsidise water and electricity (itself a major user of water) for industry, on the grounds that underpricing important inputs would distort the economy and probably be unsustainable in the long run. Although the country has enormous coal reserves, to the point where 20 million tons a year could be exported for a long period without affecting domestic supply, it would be exceptionally damaging to underprice such a scarce commodity as water[15]. Exceptions to this unwillingness to protect local manufacturing were a local preference scheme and grants and tax relief under the Financial Assistance Policy (see iv) below.

Finally, the Customs Union arrangements provide a framework under which Botswana can discuss matters of trade and commercial policy with its most important trading partner. Regular meetings at the technical level provide an opportunity to work out arrangements to overcome practical difficulties and have also provided opportunities for Botswana to take some of the initiatives noted below in providing modest additional protection for its domestic industries.

The Zimbabwe Trade Agreement.   Trade with Zimbabwe has fluctuated over the years, but in the mid-1980s it constituted approximately 8% of Botswana's imports and 4% of its exports. The free trade arrangements with Zimbabwe predate Independence in both countries, and therefore also the renegotiation of the Customs Union Agreement in 1969. As a result, Zimbabwe's exports to Botswana are duty-free (though they have been subject to temporary import surcharges imposed by South Africa from time to time). This means that Zimbabwe has access to a portion of the Southern African Customs Union market and is able to sell its exports in Botswana at prices protected by the Customs Union's external tariff. At the same time, Botswana is able to accrue revenue from the Customs Union revenue-sharing formula on those imports.

Following the legal Independence of Zimbabwe in 1980, there was at first an increase in exports to Zimbabwe, reaching a high of 13% of total exports in 1982. At the same time, a number of manufacturing investors moved from Zimbabwe to Botswana, mainly to take advantage of more liberal exchange-control rules in Botswana which made imported inputs freely available, and to take advantage of differentials in the rules of origin for determining duty on the import of goods into Botswana from Zimbabwe and into Zimbabwe from the Customs Union area. As Zimbabwe moved into balance-of-payments difficulties, import quotas against imports from Botswana were imposed. Zimbabwe also began to 'dump' a number of products, including steel doors and window frames, on the Botswana market, using South African steel sold in Zimbabwe (a non-Customs Union country) at lower prices than in Botswana (a Customs Union country). In late 1987, after unhappiness expressed by Zimbabwe over the terms of the agreement[16], discussions took place regarding the terms of a revised trade agreement that would provide for a restatement of the rules of origin. Zimbabwe had been attempting to raise the local content requirements for its duty-free imports, which would have reduced the volume of Botswana's exports that could enter Zimbabwe's markets. A new agreement was signed in September 1988[17].

ACP/Lomé Agreements.   The third important set of trading arrangements affecting Botswana's exports are the privileged access it has to European Community markets through the Lomé agreements. The most important single benefit is the 90% abatement of the variable import levy enjoyed by 17,000 tons of Botswana's beef exports to the EC each calendar year. In view of the fact that EC prices are considerably above world market prices in most years, this abatement added as much as 15–20% to the value of Botswana's exports and an even higher percentage to cattle producers (since BMC operates as a non-profit organisation and distributes surplus revenues to its suppliers). Further, the relatively high EC prices for quality beef have encouraged the BMC to increase the degree of processing that is done domestically and, thereby, the value added (discussed below).

Botswana also receives duty concessions on other exports to the European Community, but the amount of trade in manufactures, principally textiles, actually affected by the Lomé agreement has been very small. As shown in Table 4.10 (p. 94), only 9% of Botswana's manufactured exports went to countries other than South Africa and Zimbabwe. The fall in the value of the Pula against non-regional currencies, from SDR 1.05 at the end of 1980 to SDR 0.45 at the end of 1987, was much larger than the inflation differential. This gave a greatly increased financial incentive to export to Europe and elsewhere outside the region, but Botswana's predominantly small manufacturing companies were, not surprisingly, mostly unable to take advantage of this.

Concluding comments.   The framework of international agreements, particularly the Customs Union agreement and the free trade agreement with Zimbabwe, have placed general constraints on Botswana's trade policy with regard to protecting local industries through tariffs or quantitative restrictions. Especially in the case of the Customs Union, there are provisions for the application of protective duties and in practice quantitative restrictions of various kinds have been used as well. Nonetheless, the agreements do provide a constraint on the use of such protective devices.

However, there has generally been an aversion to the use of restrictive trade policies by the government. After the renegotiation of the Customs Union agreement in 1969, internal procedures were developed for the evaluation of proposals for protection (few of which have ever been received). The approach taken to the analysis was in line with the statement of policy quoted earlier that 'the costs and benefits will be studied, and decisions made on that basis alone'. There has never been a rush to subsidise manufacturing jobs by raising prices to consumers, though there have frequently been questions raised as to whether the relative lack of restrictive trade policies has been the wisest course of action. As noted below, cases of both tariff protection and use of quantitative restrictions to protect local producers have always provided for undertakings by them to maintain their selling prices at the same level as for duty-free imports. The same principle governed the development of two other policies to promote local manufacturing activity: the Local Preference Scheme and the Financial Assistance Policy.

iv) OTHER POLICIES TO PROMOTE MANUFACTURING

The government introduced a Local Preference Scheme for domestic producers selling to the central government beginning in 1976. The Scheme basically provides for a maximum 12.5% price preference on any commodity which has a minimum of 25% local content (the numbers having been chosen to provide a maximum of around 50% effective rate of protection or subsidy). It was extended to parastatal bodies following the Report of the Presidential Commission on Economic Opportunities in 1982. The principal difficulty with the Scheme seems to be that it has operated in conjunction with a system of open tendering, though there have been a number of experiments with other methods to encourage local suppliers. It seems to have been most effective in supply contracts for government furniture and various types of uniforms, though it is not possible to associate the growth in the textile or furniture sectors with the policy in any specific way.

In 1982, a new approach was introduced, the Financial Assistance Policy (FAP), which provides for a system of grants and tax relief to new and/or expanded business. FAP is provided on a capital grant-only basis for small-scale projects. For medium-scale investments, the investor has two options. 'Automatic' FAP receives a tax holiday for up to five years on a declining share of its profits; a reimbursement of part of documented wage costs for unskilled and semi-skilled citizen labour, also on a decreasing basis over five years; and a grant for documented off-the-job training costs. This automatic package is available only to new ventures in manufacturing.

The other opportunity for medium-scale projects is available on a case-by-case basis for an initial capital grant based on the number of jobs expected to be created, reimbursement of a declining fraction of the wages of unskilled and semi-skilled employees and of portions of off-the-job training costs, and grants, which decline over time, related to the value of sales from the project regardless of whether they are in export or domestic markets. Large-scale projects (those with investments of Plm. or more) can apply for FAP but may be refused if the project appears to be sufficiently profitable already. Applications for financial assistance are analysed according to a set of well publicised criteria, principally that the projects should show a minimum 6% real rate of return when evaluated at social costs, including a discount for unskilled labour costs and an enhancement for the value of tradeable output produced and an enhanced deduction from benefits for the value of tradeable inputs used.

FAP was designed to do a number of things: provide additional cash flow in the earlier stages of projects, subsidise the use of unskilled and semi-skilled labour, particularly in the first five years of a project, and provide a modest cash subsidy on the basis of total sales, regardless of whether the projects are import-substituting or export-creating. Since assistance is limited to manufacturing and non-cattle agriculture, and since the parameters involved in analysing projects provide a premium for import substitution and exporting, FAP is to some extent a substitute for protection via tariffs or quantitative restrictions. In the government paper which introduced the policy in 1982, it was stated that 'the same criteria for analysis would be applied to applications for protection under the Customs Union'. Thus, the FAP was intended not only to be a specific instrument but also to establish the general rules by which costs and benefits would be weighted in judging other forms of protection or subsidy to local ventures. 6,250 jobs had been created in FAP assisted projects at a cumulative cost of P3m. disbursed and P14m. committed by 1985. There was no way, however, of knowing how many of these would have been created in any case.

A variety of other policies (some of them unique to Botswana) have affected the incentives facing the manufacturing sector, some positively and others negatively. With significant exceptions (expanded upon below), a policy of negotiating arrangements with individual foreign (or domestic) investors on the terms under which they would undertake projects has not been pursued. The Working Group which recommended the introduction of FAP rejected proposals for subsidising water and power (which are priced at full economic cost including replacement cost of capital in urban areas) as well as other specific subsidies proposed from time to time. Thus, the overall system is relatively even among different types of sectors (e.g. any new project is eligible for assistance from FAP).

The income tax system inherited at Independence was revised in 1972 and has undergone a number of modest changes since then. Individual tax is of the usual type found in English-speaking countries, with a basic exemption for taxpayers (no exemptions for children) and a rising marginal rate structure which moves fairly quickly through the middle and upper-middle income ranges. In the late 1970s and early 1980s, individuals in management or professional positions in the private sector were likely to be in brackets with a marginal rate in excess of 50%.

In the late 1970s the tax-free housing allowance for civil servants was abolished, and the value of free or subsidised housing was made subject to tax for all individuals. For expatriate employees, who constitute a large share of the management and technical personnel in the private sector, the increase in tax was very large. Most companies, who recruit on an opportunity cost basis with other countries in the region, 'grossed up' the incomes of their employees to cover this (and the tax on the gross-up). As a result, unit costs of senior expatriate personnel rose dramatically. The view of the private sector was that they would prefer a higher rate of corporate tax to the combination of high marginal individual rates and the taxation of housing benefits[18]. How much investment, if any, was actually lost through this disincentive is not known, but the issue had an effect on the 'climate' for investment from the late 1970s through the mid-1980s[19].

Company tax is relatively straightforward and the rate (initially 30%, raised in the late 1970s to 35%) is low compared with other countries in the region[20]. Up to 1982, investment allowances permitted accelerated depreciation of capital in manufacturing. During the discussion of FAP the government concluded that this was encouraging capital intensity of production unnecessarily, and it was discontinued. Provisions under FAP relate capital grants to numbers of jobs created and provide grants in the first five years of production related both to employment and to sales, with a partial tax holiday under 'automatic' FAP. The law allows 'Development Approval Orders' which can provide special tax treatment for particular enterprises or classes of expenditure, but little use has been made of this. The only other significant tax factor affecting manufacturing is that 200% of training expenditures can be deducted from taxable income, thus providing a 70% effective subsidy for such spending.

A number of other elements of the 'investment climate' involve government procedures or regulations. The private sector had complained for some years about everything from the relatively high charges for power and water to the difficulties in finding housing for employees and the obstruction of various licensing procedures. While the physical scarcity of land and housing appears to be of some importance in limiting the rate of manufacturing growth, there is no hard evidence that the other elements in the 'investment climate' have had a measurable effect on the growth of the sector[21].

During several periods in the late 1970s and 1980s infrastructure constraints – on water, power connections, serviced land, railway sidings, housing for employees – have been the principal obstacle to expansion of the manufacturing sector. Especially in Gaborone, the growth in supply of serviced land has been spasmodic, and there have been periods of months or even years when investors could find no place to locate. Severe drought, which threatened the Gaborone water supply, brought construction almost to a halt in 1982–3, which worsened the problems already felt by the lack of serviced land. Limited telephone and telex connections also were reported to be a serious deterrent at some times. Most of these factors were mentioned in the report of the Working Group on FAP in 1982[22].

Land is available outside the main urban areas, but most of it is held communally and cannot be sold as freehold land. It is allocated by Land Boards and can be leased for commercial or industrial uses by citizens or non-citizens, including companies[23]. The process of land-use planning and allocation may take longer than that in the urban areas because of both staff shortages and the necessity of balancing local needs and traditional local use rights. A number of smaller industrial ventures, and one large one (a wheat flour mill) have located on tribal land, which is much cheaper than urban land, although generally without much supporting infrastructure. The tribal areas adjacent to Gaborone have been used increasingly for commercial activities and as residential areas, and some smaller manufacturing enterprises have also set up there.

Some episodes or cases of manufacturing growth

In this short section we consider a few examples from the major manufacturing sectors, and focus on the extent to which government policy affected them and the nature of their interaction with the international economy.

The BMC, a statutory corporation which slaughters cattle and markets meat and by-products, has been the dominant enterprise in the manufacturing sector since before independence. It distributes to the cattle owners all revenues in excess of its operating costs plus some appropriations to reserve accounts. Cattle prices are determined by the price BMC can get for Botswana beef and by-products in international markets. It has resisted pressures to sell by-products to local industries at lower than export market prices. The European market has been important to the BMC for many years. High transport costs led to the decision to increase the de-boning of beef prior to shipment in order to increase net returns. A canning line was added to process low-quality cuts, and a tannery was built to process hides and skins through to the wet-blue stage. Both processing projects were completed in the late 1970s.

The BMC might have expanded its operations more rapidly but for the fact that sales in its two principal and highest-priced markets (the European Community and South Africa) are limited by quota. Marginal sales are made in lower-priced world markets. Increased sales would reduce the BMC's average price, which would reduce average prices paid to producers, even though total producer incomes would rise. The BMC's management resisted pressures for additional abattoir capacity in the northern parts of Botswana, despite the fact that this would have saved transport costs (beef being cheaper to transport than live cattle) and would have provided insurance for both drought and veterinary emergencies. Had the BMC moved more quickly (a small abattoir was built in Maun in the early 1980s, and a second larger one is being planned for Francistown), the growth of manufacturing in the meat and meat products sub-sector would have been more rapid.

This sub-sector does receive 'protection', in European and South African markets, but not at the expense of other sectors[24]. However, if the protection were removed, the pricing arrangements for cattle are such that the decrease in revenue would accrue to cattle producers, not to value added or employment in the meat manufacturing sectors.

The second largest source of employment and output in manufacturing is the Kgalakgadi Breweries, established in 1975 as a joint venture with a German group (which brought in its own brands) and the BDC. Protection was provided under the Customs Union arrangements by the imposition of a 100% 'Additional Duty' on all imports of beer (which principally affected imports from South Africa). The arrangement with the brewery provided for beer to be priced in Botswana at the same levels as prevailed in South Africa, so that consumers of domestic beer would not pay the tariff-protected price. However, the quality of the local beer proved to be so poor, and brand loyalties to the traditional brands so strong, that after some initial successes in establishing the local brands in 1976, beer imports flooded in, local sales fell, and there were substantial outflows of payments of Additional Customs Revenues to the customs revenue pool[25]. By 1979, the brewery was reorganised with a new technical partner, and there was a switch back to the traditionally popular brands now produced locally, which again became available at cross-border prices. As a result, imports declined to minimal levels, as indicated in Figure 4.8. This episode illustrates that fully competitive import substitution can and did take place, but that the right mix of incentives and choice of management was necessary to achieve that result. The government and the BDC placed constraints on the brewery management, and ultimately limited the losses to Botswana by insisting on pricing guarantees and by changing the management rather than simply restricting imports in order to ensure the profitability of the local industry. Indeed, since the brewery was a major

Figure 4.8 *Additional Customs Revenues Quarterly Collection – Pula, thousands*

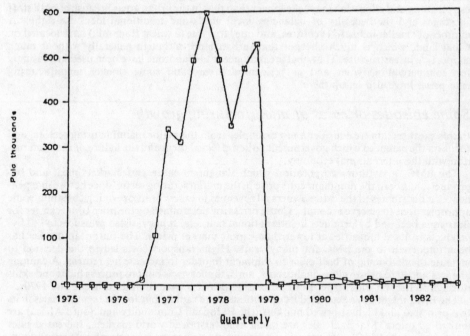

Source: External Trade Statistics.

consumer of Botswana's scarcest resource, water, it was of more than passing importance that it should be an efficient producer.

The textile sector is the third largest identifiable manufacturing group. Located mainly in Francistown, much of it processes for the export market, principally to Zimbabwe. In some of the largest firms, goods are processed at different stages in both Botswana and Zimbabwe, taking advantage of the free trade arrangements. There are advantages to Botswana producers at some manufacturing stages, since they can import intermediate goods from South Africa duty-free. Provided there is 25% value added in Botswana, the processed goods can then enter Zimbabwe on a duty-free basis.

There was fairly rapid growth in textiles in the 1970s, and a major increase in investment occurred immediately after Zimbabwe's independence in 1980, and exports from Botswana increased substantially. However, Zimbabwean restrictions on imports in 1983 and 1984 led to a sharp reduction with a consequent drop in output and employment in the Botswana textile sectors. Textiles have been exported to other markets as well, including Europe, but the vulnerability of manufacturing to a single large regional market has been considerable. On several occasions textile producers approached the government for financial subsidies or some form of protection with the explicit threat that failure to provide assistance would result in job losses. The government consistently refused such proposals, making it clear that private enterprises were expected to stand on their own. In the mid-1980s the BDC did provide some financing to the sector during the period of export cut-backs, but it was on a commercial basis.

The metal products industries, linked largely to construction activity, also had difficulties in the 1980s as Zimbabwean firms dumped goods in the Botswana market, and also because they were able to purchase steel more cheaply from South Africa than Botswana producers could (due to Customs Union pricing practices). The Botswana government responded by drawing up rules under which the Local Preference Scheme for government contracts could be extended to local manufacturing sub-contractors, thus providing some price preference to local producers on government-related contracts.

Another BDC joint venture of some interest and success was a wheat flour mill, established on tribal land in Ramotswa, about 20 miles from Gaborone. The choice of site was in part dictated by the scarcity of land in the existing urban industrial estates. The technical partners and foreign investors were a Zimbabwean firm with considerable regional expertise. They undertook to produce according to price and quality standards fully competitive with imports, and in return were provided with exclusive access to the Botswana market. The project resulted in nearly total import replacement (based entirely on imported wheat, since Botswana produces no wheat) and with no measurable welfare losses to Botswana consumers, since both price and quality guarantees were fully met.

One protected sector on which the jury was still out (in late 1987) was a soap factory (Kgalakgadi Soap Industries) established in Gaborone in the early 1980s without BDC partnership. The project obtained protection under the Customs Union agreement, with guarantees that prices would exceed import parity by only a small percentage. As with the first brewery project, the brands were new, not traditional. The first two years of operation turned out better than for the brewery, though imports continued to occupy a substantial market share despite the price premium. It remained to be seen whether the management could meet the necessary quality standards, capture a sufficiently large share of the market to be financially viable, and replace enough imports to eliminate payments into the customs pool[26].

This brief listing does not include a number of ventures that arose without any government intervention. A glance at the 11 industrial sectors in Tables 4.3a or 4.4a shows there was substantial import substitution in a range of industries, including paper products, miscellaneous manufacturing, wood products, and even chemicals (the soap factory had not opened by 1984/5). What was happening was a 'normal' development of the domestic market in response to the increased competitiveness of potential local firms. Where government intervention did occur, it did not involve 'protection' of one kind or another that imposed a drain on other sectors of the economy or on the government budget in order to support the manufacturing sector.

The context of future manufacturing growth

As noted above, manufacturing output in Botswana grew extremely fast in the 20 years after Independence. In part this was simply because the whole economy grew at an exceptional rate, led by mining. But Botswana avoided the common adverse effects of a mineral boom – the 'Dutch Disease' – which is symbolised by a rising real rate of exchange, making agriculture and manufacturing increasingly unprofitable (unless increasingly protected). In contrast, manufacturing output grew very rapidly, faster than in all but five other countries from 1965 to 1985. Moreover, the beef product sub-sector, which accounted for more than 90% of manufacturing in 1965, grew relatively slowly, so that the rest of manufacturing grew even more rapidly than the manufacturing sector as a whole.

This rapid growth was achieved with very little protection from the government; producers mostly had to be able to compete successfully with imports. It was also notable that there were few large-scale manufacturing projects in the public sector of the sort common elsewhere in Africa–manufacturing was mostly small-scale and privately owned apart from the BMC.

The government-owned Botswana Development Corporation, which was commercially oriented and profitable, participated in only a small number of manufacturing enterprises. Indeed, it was criticised for investing mainly in urban property and commercial businesses, and for neglecting manufacturing industry, although it did develop industrial estates and factory shells. By 1986, the bulk of its investment was still in the commercial rather than the industrial sector, although the overwhelming dependence on commercial property investments had fallen from 73% in 1976 to 20% in 1986. 'Commerce and industry' rose from 12 to 29% of BDC investments over the same period (BDC Annual Reports).

Discussion of the future of the manufacturing sector, therefore, revolves around quite different questions from those which are important in many other African countries:

• There was no need to find ways of reducing an overvalued exchange rate, because the real exchange rate had been roughly constant for the last 20 years, with a slight tendency to fall in the 1980s.

- There was no prospect of firms not being able to buy imported spare parts or raw materials because of a shortage of foreign exchange: there were no import controls and the foreign-exchange reserves were equivalent to nearly two years' imports (cif inclusive) at the end of 1987 (Bank of Botswana, 1988).
- There was no question of privatisation or closure of loss-making or inefficient government-owned firms because there were very few manufacturing parastatals, and none was in receipt of subsidies to cover losses.
- There was no need to liberalise the economic system to make it attractive to foreign investors, since there were no extensive controls or nationalisations, and foreign investment had always been welcome.

The main question investigated in the rest of this chapter is whether these conditions are likely to continue, and whether the policies that caused the success of the first decades of independence are likely to be as appropriate in the future as they apparently were in the past.

GROWTH OF MANUFACTURING OUTPUT AND EMPLOYMENT

In 1972, the BMC still accounted for 78% of value added in manufacturing. So apart from transforming live cattle into chilled deboned beef, Botswana had almost no manufacturing industry 20 years ago, and very little for some years after that. From the mid-1970s, however, the non-BMC manufacturing sector began to grow very fast (Table 4.6) at just over 20% a year to 6% of non-mining GDP. For the rest of this chapter, the discussion is concerned mainly with the manufacturing sector *excluding* BMC.

Table 4.6 *Manufacturing output, BMC and other, selected years (Pm. 1979/80 constant prices)*

	1971/2	1979/80	1983/4
BMC[a]	12.0	9.0	7.8
Other	3.3	20.2	36.2
Total	15.3	29.2	44.0
Other as % of non-mining GDP	1.4	4.1	6.3

Source: *National Income Accounts* (value added in the meat product sub-sector only given in certain years).

Note: [a] The statistics of value added at BMC give a false impression because BMC was not a profit maximiser, seeking instead to maximise payments to farmers. Figures in some years were affected by the timing of price changes for sales of beef abroad and purchases of cattle in Botswana. Thus the decline in statistics of value added does not necessarily reflect a fall in output. Employment, for example, did not decline over the period, and the number of cattle slaughtered more than doubled from 1966 to 1982 before falling because of the drought.

Table 4.7 *Value added in manufacturing 1980, 1982 and 1984 (Constant 1980 prices, BMC excluded)*

Sub-sector	1979/80	1981/2	1983/4	1986/7
Dairy and agro-based	1.1	2.4	0.2	
Beverages	3.2	9.6	7.7	
Bakery products	0.3	0.4	0.4	
Textiles	4.5	5.9	6.4	
Tanning and leather	0.7	− 0.4	0.3	
Chemical products	0.6	0.8	1.7	
Wood and wooden products	0.5	0.4	0.3	
Paper products	0.6	0.8	1.7	
Metal products[a]	− 0.3	1.4	5.3	
Other manufacturing[a]	4.3	10.9	6.4	
Village industries	4.7	5.2	5.6	
Total	20.2	38.2	36.2	
Manufacturing employment	5,600	7,200	9,500	12,200

Sources: *National Income Accounts*; *Employment Surveys*.

Note: [a] Some output was reclassified from other manufacturing to metal products between 1982 and 1984.

The breakdown by sub-sector in the most recent period for which the figures are available, is given in Table 4.7. This shows all the growth in the early 1980s occurring in the first two years, with none thereafter. But the *employment* figures suggest that growth was maintained at an average rate of 14% from 1980 to 1986, having been just under 10% a year from 1972 to 1980.

The registration of new firms, although a doubtful indicator because it is not weighted by size nor adjusted for firms that did not begin production, also appeared to show an acceleration of manufacturing growth in the 1980s: the average number of registrations was only six a year from 1966 to 1980, but 43 a year from 1981 to 1984 (GOB 1985: 239). Much of the output growth from these new firms is unlikely to have shown up yet in the output statistics. Yet another indicator of continuing growth in manufacturing is the severe shortage of serviced industrial land in the major urban centres[27].

Table 4.8 shows the distribution of firms by number, employment and capital invested in 1984. It is notable that investment and employment were much more widely spread across sub-sectors than exports; only meat and textiles had as much as 20% of employment and eleven sub-sectors had 2% or more.

Table 4.8 *Manufacturing sector 1984: number of firms, employment and investment*

	No of Firms	Employment	Investment (Pm.)
Meat and meat products	2	1,997	19.2
Dairy and agro-based	8	55	7.3
Beverages	13	606	16.4
Bakery products	13	397	2.1
Textiles	48	2,519	21.5
Tanning and leather	7	442	3.8
Chemicals and rubber products	16	425	15.7
Wood and wooden products	12	470	1.9
Paper and paper products	6	250	2.0
Metal products	37	1,569	10.9
Building materials	26	1,101	6.8
Plastics	8	278	4.6
Electrical	10	351	2.4
Handicrafts	3	56	0.4
Totals	209	10,526	115.1

Source: GOB, 1985: 236–7.

EXPORTS

Since, as noted earlier, the government offered relatively little protection or subsidy to local industry, most parts of the manufacturing sector had to be internationally competitive, which for most producers meant being able to compete with imports. Some, however, also managed to export and the total of manufactured exports grew rapidly (see Table 4.9). The

Table 4.9 *Exports[a] of manufactured goods 1972–86 (excluding beef) (Pm., current prices)*

	Textiles	Other	Total		Textiles	Other	Total
1972		5.6	5.6	1980	15.7	25.6	41.3
1973	1.5	5.2	6.7	1981	16.0	36.6	52.6
1974	1.7	8.3	10.0	1982	27.4	45.6	73.0
1975	2.5	10.4	12.9	1983	33.0	49.1	82.1
1976	6.1	11.4	17.5	1984	40.4	58.8	99.2
1977	6.0	13.3	19.3	1985	28.9	77.8	106.7
1978	8.2	20.2	28.4	1986			152.0
1979	12.9	26.2	39.1	1987			174.0

Source: External Trade Statistics.

Note: [a] Includes some goods re-exported after use in Botswana; excludes beef products.

ability of at least some sub-sectors to export was an important positive indicator of the potential for future growth, since the domestic market was so small. It should be noted that the figures for manufactured exports are gross, with no deduction for the import content, which was very high, or for re-exports. Value added in the export of goods actually manufactured in Botswana was thus much less than indicated in the table. There is no particular reason for thinking that this factor changed over time, however, so that the trend shown is probably correct.

No figures were available for manufactured exports in constant price terms. However, if the Consumer Price Index is used to deflate the Pula value (which then reflects the local buying power of export earnings) 'real' exports of manufactured goods increased from P12.3m. in 1972, to P82.8m. in 1986, at 1980 prices, an average annual rate of increase of about 15%.

Exports were, however, very dependent on regional markets, overwhelmingly Zimbabwe (66%) and South Africa (25%) as shown in Table 4.10. They were vulnerable, therefore, to changes in trade policy or in demand in those particular countries, or to a failure by Botswana to maintain competitive bilateral exchange rates.

Table 4.10 *Direction of manufactured exports 1983 (US$m., excluding beef)*

	Textiles	Clothes	Drugs	Other	Total
South Africa	3.7	0.5	0.3	6.6	11.1
Zimbabwe	15.5	6.9	1.1	5.7	29.2
Other		3.5	0.4		
Total		30.1	14.1		44.2

Source: External Trade Statistics and Granberg, 1986.

Only a relatively few sub-sectors of manufacturing, however, derived a significant part of their growth from exporting. As analysed above, the domestic market was the source of 54% of output growth (excluding BMC) from 1974 to 1985. Import substitution accounted for a further 38%, and exports for only 8%. Only textiles (41%) and wood products (16%) derived more than 10% of their growth over this period from exports (see Tables 4.3a and 4.3b).

EXCHANGE-RATE AND INCOMES POLICY

As already noted, the government was careful to maintain a real rate of exchange enabling manufacturers to compete with imports and in export markets. In practical terms, this meant preventing it from rising in terms of Zimbabwe and South Africa, the former being the most important market for manufactured exports, and the latter the most important source of manufactured imports.

Maintenance of competitiveness was based on control of government spending (since allowing excessive increases during the mineral boom would have driven up costs), incomes policy designed among other things to prevent an escalation of salaries for the very scarce categories of skilled labour, and a willingness to alter the nominal exchange rate if required. To some extent, the nominal rate could be allowed to rise against the Rand, for example, if this was then reflected in lower inflation and lower wage increases. On some occasions, though, the Pula rose against the Rand faster than could be reflected in domestic prices, making a nominal devaluation necessary.

Botswana had of course no control over the exchange rate between the Rand and the Zimbabwe dollar, so that it would have been very difficult to maintain a steady real exchange rate against both those currencies if they had moved significantly against each other. Fortunately for Botswana, when the Rand fell steeply against non-regional currencies in the 1980s, the Zimbabwe dollar moved roughly in line with it, with only minor fluctuations. Thus the import-weighted exchange-rate index conceals relatively small fluctuations in the bilateral position with Zimbabwe and South Africa (see Figures 4.5 to 4.7). For the same reason, though, Botswana's exchange rate against the SDR fell by much more than the inflation differential between Botswana and the industrialised countries, resulting in the steep improvement in price competitiveness with Europe and elsewhere already mentioned.

FOREIGN INVESTMENT
Most manufacturing firms were foreign-owned. More than half were wholly foreign-owned, and fewer than 20% were wholly owned by Botswana citizens[28]. Most foreign investment came from elsewhere in the region, mainly South Africa and Zimbabwe. Dividends were freely remittable to foreign shareholders. There were some restrictions on local borrowing by foreign firms – up to P100,000 could be borrowed, plus P1 for every P1 brought into the country in loans or equity, plus any additional amount allowed on application to the Bank of Botswana; these rules were not a significant constraint. The BDC, as already noted, had a share in some manufacturing firms. But the government never nationalised a manufacturing firm compulsorily[29]. In general, the official welcome to foreign investment was supported by action, although many investors (local and foreign) complained of the time spent on complying with the large number of government regulations.

CONCLUSIONS
The basic reasons behind the growth of the manufacturing sector appeared, therefore, to be based on the following factors.

- Rapid growth in domestic demand, based on a succession of mining projects which were very large in relation to GNP.
- Relatively little use of protection, so that most producers had to be internationally competitive (at least within the region).
- An exchange-rate policy which maintained a constant or falling real rate of exchange, so that the cost of foreign exchange was not a constraint on manufacturers' competitiveness.
- A rather less successful incomes policy, which nevertheless imposed some constraint on urban skilled and unskilled wages.
- Almost complete avoidance of large, public sector, protected projects, and therefore of the inefficiency, need for government subsidy and high-cost outputs commonly associated with such projects.
- A healthy balance of payments and foreign-exchange reserve position, so that imported inputs were always freely available.
- A willingness to accept foreign investment without threat of nationalisation, restrictions on the remission of dividends, or significant constraints on local borrowing by foreign companies.

On the other hand, some policies had negative effects. The cumulative effect of regulations imposed on business (including of course manufacturing) by various government agencies was frequently cited as an important investment disincentive[30]. Attempts to reduce or ease the process of acquiring all the necessary licences and other official papers were not notably successful. There were also periodic breakdowns in the infrastructure, partly caused by the rapid growth of the economy in general, and of urbanisation in particular: Botswana had the fastest rate of urbanisation in sub-Saharan Africa from 1965 to 1980, at 15%, although the rate slowed right down, to 4.5%, thereafter (World Bank, 1987: 267). But the government did not do all it might have done to improve matters, notably by not allowing the private sector to develop serviced land for industry and for housing, and insisting that it all be done by public sector agencies.

Questions for the future, then, were the following:

- would Botswana's rapid overall economic growth continue?
- if not, would it be possible to increase import substitution to the point where it could take over from growth in the domestic market as the primary source of growth in manufacturing?
- if not, would it be possible for manufactured exports to increase, which in turn would require firms capable of penetrating export markets, and growth and openness to Botswana manufactured goods in those markets?

Growth prospects for the economy

ABSENCE OF LARGE NEW MINING PROJECTS
The most recent development plan (1985–91) projected that real growth in GDP would be much slower, at 4.8%, than in the past 20 years. The main reason for expecting a slowdown was that there were no large new mining projects to be implemented.

Even if a new diamond mine were to be discovered, it is unlikely that it would be developed until the world market recovers further: worldwide sales of diamonds by De Beers' Central Selling Organisation (CSO) peaked at $2.7 bn in 1980, and fell to a low of $1.3 bn in 1982. They recovered thereafter, and in 1987 were higher than their previous peak, in money terms, for the first time. But they still had a long way to go to recover their 1980 real value.

The large coal project at Kgaswe looked quite promising until 1980. It would have ensured another ten years of rapid modern sector growth if it had been implemented, as well as a new railway outlet to the sea across the Kalahari to the west. It became a non-starter because of the fall in energy prices.

The decision to go ahead with the soda-ash project at Sua Pan, known about and picked over without results by several investors over the last 20 years, was at last taken in 1988. But whereas the total capital cost of the project would have been larger than GNP in the early 1970s, by 1988 it was only 20% of GNP and therefore not large enough on its own to generate rapid economic growth. The government also had to forgo some tax revenues in order to induce a foreign investor to participate; it was clear that the deposit was marginal because of the prolonged reluctance of a series of investors to commit themselves to the project. Moreover, the nature of the deposit meant that it would employ relatively few Batswana. There was also some revival of the gold mining sub-sector in the North-East, but again on a relatively small scale.

Significant growth in the export of beef could not be expected. On the contrary, there was a severe problem of overgrazing. The traditional solution was for people and cattle to move into new areas; but by the late 1980s, very little unutilised or under-utilised land was still available. The national cattle herd will recover as a result of the ending of the long drought in 1987/8; but there is no prospect of any long-term upward trend in beef exports until new and improved grazing techniques are found and successfully introduced.

PLAN FORECASTS COMPARED WITH ACTUALS

The static prospect for exports, and therefore also for government revenue, was recognised explicitly in the Plan. A flat line for government revenue and grants is shown as being crossed from below by a rising expenditure line, in 1989 in the 'base case', and in 1986 in the 'conservative case' (GOB, 1985: 42–3). Similarly, the balance-of-payments current account deficit is shown as increasing from P20m. in 1985/6 to P104m. in 1990/91, and the overall surplus as deteriorating by much more over the same period, from P243m. to P20m. because of the expected decline in capital inflows[31].

Actual out-turn since the NDP forecasts were prepared was better than expected. The forecasts assumed that the drought would end before it did, but the impact of a continuing drought was swamped in financial terms by two other events. The diamond market recovered more rapidly than expected, and, partly as a result, Botswana sold in 1987 the diamonds stockpiled after the downturn in the market in 1981, for some P400m.[32].

Secondly, the Rand fell sharply against the US dollar and other non-regional currencies, from US$1.34 at the end of 1980 to less than $0.40 in 1985, and was still only $0.50 in 1988[33]. Botswana buys some 85% of its imports from South Africa, and sells most of its exports in US dollars and other non-regional currencies, so that the fall of the Rand (and to a much

Table 4.11 *Balance of payments 1983-7: NDP forecasts and actuals (Pm.)*

	1985	1986	1987[a]
Current account: NDP forecast[b]	− 20	− 65	− 71
Actual	+ 251	+ 323	+ 1,062
Actual deflated by CPI	+ 251	+ 291	+ 887
Overall balance: NDP forecast[b]	+ 243	+ 258	+ 213
Actual	+ 501	+ 566	+ 942
Actual deflated by CPI	+ 501	+ 511	+ 787

Source: forecasts from National Development Plan 1985-91: 44; actuals from Bank of Botswana, 1988.

Notes: [a] Preliminary.
[b] NDP forecast was at constant prices.

lesser extent the accompanying fall in the Zimbabwe dollar) created large windfall gains[34]. As a result, the balance of payments showed record surpluses in the first years of the Plan instead of the decline referred to above. The differences were almost as large even when a crude adjustment is made for inflation as in Table 4.11[35].

For the same reasons, GDP at constant prices increased much faster than the annual 4.8% forecast in the Plan, as shown in Table 4.12. Moreover, the figures shown exclude the effect of selling the diamond stockpile, which occurred on the first day of the 1987/8 National Income Accounts year: another year of rapid growth in GDP was expected for 1987/8.

Table 4.12 *Growth of GDP, forecast and actual: 1985/6 and 1986/7 (annual rates of growth at constant prices, percentage)*

	1985/6	1986/7
NDP forecast	4.8	4.8
GDP growth[a]	14.0	14.7
Non-mining GDP growth[a]	9.4	7.8

Source: NDP 1985-91; Bank of Botswana, 1988.

Note: [a] 1985/6: preliminary; 1986/7: flash estimates.

Although diamond revenue and exchange-rate changes were the main causes of growth being so much better than expected, non-mining growth was also nearly twice as fast as forecast, with construction, trade and hotels, government, and manufacturing, in that order, growing at rates ranging from 17 to 8% in 1986/7. Output of the construction sector stagnated during the early years of the drought, only recovering to the level of 1981/2 in 1985/6.

Finally, the government budget (see Table 4.13) had a much higher surplus than forecast in the first years of the Plan, in spite of higher than forecast increases in government spending, because of the impact of diamond sales on revenue.

As a result of these large financial windfalls, the government not only continued to have no domestic debt at all, but at the end of 1987, had cash on deposit at the Bank of Botswana equivalent to 177% of government spending, including development spending and net lending, in 1986/7.

Table 4.13 *Government budget, forecast and actual: 1985/6 and 1986/7 (Pm.)*

	1985/6	1986/7
Revenue and grants: forecast (1985/6 prices)	753	742
Actual (deflated using CPI)	1,023	1,293
Total spending: forecast (1985/6 prices)	671	694
Actual (deflated using CPI)	649	843
Cash balances: forecast (1985/6 prices)	+126	+95
Actual (deflated using CPI)	+386	+518

Sources: Ibid.

MEDIUM-TERM PROSPECTS

It was clear, therefore, that the crossover points, of the government budget and the balance of payments, had been postponed for some years. In addition, the accumulated surpluses were large enough to enable the government to maintain a higher rate of growth than forecast. Indeed, the real rate of growth in the first two years of the Plan was actually higher than the 11% average of the previous 20 years, but that was mainly because of the windfall gains from diamond recovery and exchange-rate changes.

It seems very unlikely that comparable gains will accrue from diamonds in future. But the trend of worldwide gem diamond sales was still upwards in 1987, so the immediate future was promising. In the longer run, a collapse in the world market for gem diamonds such as occurred in 1981 could recur. The exchange-rate gains could also be reversed; for example, if the Rand were to recover on the back of a rise in the price of gold.

Botswana needs, therefore, to maintain a high level of reserves, against these and other possible financial contingencies. But even allowing for exceptionally large 'precautionary' holdings, the reserves are undoubtedly large enough to sustain several more years of rapid growth, led by government spending, even without a matching growth in export earnings[36]. There is a danger that the cash situation will encourage the government to expand its own spending faster than can be sustained in the long run, which would force a painful adjustment on the economy in the future; but that point would appear to be some years away.

The probability of several years of rapid growth led by government spending was greatly increased in 1987, when the government announced a 'major development initiative'. This consisted of a set of projects proposed by the Ministry of Finance and Development Planning (MFDP) additional to those in the 1985–91 Plan. At the same time, the government announced a set of criteria for any other new projects, additional, that is, to those in the Plan and those being proposed by the MFDP.

The MFDP's proposals included:

- a large addition to the supply of serviced urban land, for commerce, industry and housing;
- tarring part of the road west from Jwaneng towards Ghanzi;
- a tannery, attempts to attract a private investor having failed;
- the government's share of the infrastructure, plus a share of the equity finance, for the Sua Pan soda ash project;
- a new international hotel in Gaborone;
- a centre for training personnel for a diamond cutting industry.

The criteria set out by the MFDP for other new project proposals were that projects should as far as possible: have a (social) rate of return comparable to that on regular development projects; be self-liquidating in terms of government finance, and self-sustaining financially in the long run; focus on under-utilised resources and not add to the pressure on scarce resources; not create price distortions; be an integrative force in the economy, that is, not create enclaves; help to diversify the economy, and be attractive to donors. Most of the above criteria meant no more than that projects should be soundly conceived, although even that apparently obvious criterion was important because of the evidence of mis-spending during periods of financial surplus elsewhere in Africa. The interesting conditions which, if adhered to, would make the proposed programme crucially different, were that projects should where possible repay the government finance put into them initially, and should not be a burden on recurrent spending in the long run. Some at least of the proposed projects appeared to have one or the other of these features, most obviously the servicing of urban land for future sale, but also, with rather less certainty, the hotel, the tannery and the investment in Sua Pan.

The 'major initiative' could be seen either as further evidence of loss of control by the government of the growth in its own spending or, on the contrary, as a (mainly self-financing) initiative which was evidence of forward thinking and control of the situation. It did mean that rapid growth would continue in the immediate future. This, in turn, meant that in the medium term the manufacturing sector could be expected to rely on the same main source of growth, namely increasing domestic demand, as in the previous 14 years.

LONGER-TERM PROSPECTS

In the longer run, the absence of new large mining projects, the poor prospects for increasing beef exports, the extreme unreliability of rainfall and thus of rainfed arable agriculture, and the impossibility of relying on government spending without a new source of export growth, mean that growth appears certain to slow down, to levels far below the rates of the last 20 years. For the manufacturing sector, this means that growth will no longer be able to be based on growth in domestic demand; the sector must increase its ability to substitute for imports, and to export.

Putting this argument the other way round, the longer-term growth of the economy will have to be based on the growth of non-traditional, meaning manufactured, exports. Thus the future role of the manufacturing sector will be much more important than its present share of total exports or of GDP indicates. Other sectors have grown fast, and could continue to do so in the future. But, with the exception of tourism, tertiary sectors such as banking, water supply, trade and construction depend on primary and secondary sectors producing tradable goods for their continued growth. In other words, growth in such a small and open economy as Botswana generates demand for increased imports, which in turn require a dynamic export sector; import substitution is also important but cannot of itself be enough. Growth cannot be based entirely on the growth of service sectors selling to the domestic market.

But the manufacturing sector was still very small in the late 1980s, in absolute terms and in relation to the whole economy (6% of GDP in 1986). It was not possible, therefore, to rely on manufacturing to provide the sort of rapid growth Botswana enjoyed up to the mid-1980s. For example, a continued 15% per annum growth in the non-BMC sub-sector of manufacturing would initially add less than 1% a year to GDP (though it would add 1.5% to formal sector employment). So while overall growth in GDP can be expected to fuel manufacturing growth in the medium term, manufactured exports cannot be the prime source of rapid growth until the relative size of the sector has increased.

In the longer term, though, manufactured exports will have to take over from mining as the engine of growth. Relying on the Botswana market would condemn the manufacturing sector and therefore the economy to an ever-diminishing rate of growth. So it is important to ask what policy changes, if any, will be required to enable greater import substitution and export penetration to be achieved.

Policy for the longer term

Botswana has been very successful as regards manufacturing growth because of a relative *lack* of specific policy towards the manufacturing sector. Cautious macroeconomic policy, allied to giving the sector a relatively free hand to develop according to market forces, appeared to have produced remarkably good results.

In particular, the government offered very little protection to manufacturers, discouraged no doubt by the initial failure of the brewery, which was the first of only two firms to be offered tariff protection (Harvey, 1981a). And its policy towards foreign investment in manufacturing was essentially neutral: no specific tax incentives, but no nationalisations, a stable macroeconomic environment and therefore no restrictions on imports or on the remittance of dividends. Indeed, as noted above, the ability of firms to buy imported inputs without restriction was thought to be a specific reason (together with the Botswana-Zimbabwe trade agreement) for a number of Zimbabwean businesses deciding to invest in Botswana.

Any suggestions for changes in policy should be careful, therefore, not to spoil something which has worked well over a long period, and should be concentrated on removing some of the (quite numerous) constraints rather than on more 'positive' initiatives, such as large-scale direct investments in manufacturing by the government itself.

The circumstances in which manufacturing will have to operate are expected, however, to change in the medium term, if the analysis of the previous section is correct. Although growth of GDP over the period 1985–91 is now expected to be much higher than forecast in the last Plan, domestic demand will eventually cease to be such a major source of growth, so that the manufacturing sector will have to increase its ability to compete with imports, and to export, if it is to continue to grow significantly at all.

The unexpected extension of the period of rapid growth in domestic demand gives the country a breathing space in which to act. It means that the manufacturing sector should be larger, both absolutely and in relation to GDP, before the point is reached where it has to rely on import substitution and exporting for its own growth, and before the economy as a whole has to rely on manufacturing for overall growth.

DOMESTIC CONSTRAINTS

The government is already acting or planning to act on a number of domestic constraints. The new initiative on government spending will tackle the tremendous shortage of industrial land. The burden of various government regulations is to be reviewed once more by a revived Regulations Review Committee; although it is difficult for different agencies and ministries within the government to agree on changing their own regulations, the problem is at least recognised as important.

The government recognised in the early 1980s that it was itself employing too high a proportion of trained and educated manpower[37], and accepted the recommendation of the

Presidential Commission on Economic Opportunities 'to secure a larger share of (trained) manpower for the private sector' (1982: 39). The flow of skills and skilled people to the private sector is also helped by the rule that civil servants may retire at the age of 45, and by the absence of a 'leadership code' (of the type introduced into Tanzania and Zambia) preventing public sector employees from having business interests. The principle that public decisions should be independent of private interests is of course important and should be enforced. But preventing the entrepreneurial and managerial talents of public sector employees from being used in the private sector is too drastic a way of achieving that end; it can be done by other means, as it is in Botswana, for example, through the Public Tender Board.

There was, of course, no *overall* shortage either of credit or of foreign exchange for industry in Botswana: the availability of nearly two years' imports in the foreign-exchange reserves was mentioned above, and the commercial banks were so liquid that the Bank of Botswana had to act as deposit-taker of last resort (Harvey and Lewis, 1989: Chap. 9). However, there were some gaps in the type of finance available. The commercial banks were effective in supplying short-term working capital, but very slow to supply long-term finance or to act as agents in obtaining other types of finance for borrowers. Various public sector financial institutions expanded to fill part of the gap, as shown in Table 4.14, to the point where their combined lending was almost as large as that of the commercial banks by 1987, having been only a fifth as large 12 years earlier.

Table 4.14 *Growth of lending by financial institutions (Pm.)*

	1966	1975	1987
Commercial banks	7	56	265
Other financial institutions (f.i.):			
Botswana Building Society	–	2	36
Botswana Co-operative Bank	–	–	7
Botswana Development Corporation	–	6	115[a]
Botswana Savings Bank	–	1	11
Financial Services Company	–	1	19
National Development Bank	1	2	47[a]
Sub-total: other f.i.	1	12	235
Ratio: other f.i./commercial banks (%)	14	21	89

Source: Bank of Botswana, *Annual Reports*.

Note: [a] BDC, June 1987, NDB, March 1987; all others, December 1987.

In addition, the government itself was a major supplier of long-term loans and equity, mainly of course to parastatals, as shown in Table 4.15. Government investment in financial parastatals involves double counting with some of the lending shown in Table 4.14, and 'investment' in the Bank of Botswana was simply the government's cash balances on deposit; nevertheless, government investment in non-financial parastatals was nearly as large as the loans of all the financial institutions combined.

There was still not enough long-term finance, though, for the private sector, and within that available, there was not enough equity. With only a few exceptions, the BDC tended only to lend to companies in which it had share-holdings, and provided only 11 manufacturing companies with equity finance (out of 84 to which it provided finance). The National Development Bank concentrated on lending to the agricultural sector (the NDB also had some internal problems to the point that it needed to consolidate rather than expand). And the government lent only to parastatals.

There were several reasons for suggesting the more rapid development of equity financing. Firstly, although a small number of companies had made public share issues by 1988, and in 1984 the BDC issued shares in an investment trust with holdings in some BDC companies, there was virtually no secondary equity market, which limited the attraction of equity investment to investors. In general, companies were unable to finance themselves by acquiring

Table 4.15 *Government lending and equity investment (Pm.)*

	1970	1975	1980	1985	1986
Lending:					
Non-financial parastatals	0	59	98	291	386
Financial parastatals	1	2	5	66	70
Equity:					
Non-financial parastatals [a]	0	1	25	72	78
Financial parastatals [b]	0	2	19	159	474
Total domestic assets	1	64	147	588	1,008

Source: Bank of Botswana, *Annual Reports*.

Notes: [a] Includes investments in commercial undertakings.
[b] Includes equity in the Bank of Botswana, which was P460m. in 1986.

additional equity finance locally. As a result, many tended to have dangerously high debt to equity ratios.

Secondly, the insurance companies and pension funds had long-term savings to invest for which there were very few outlets. Institutional savings tended therefore to go disproportionately into urban property investments (as the government did not borrow domestically, there were not even any long-term government bonds available). If opportunities to invest in equity had been more widely available, the institutions, and the savers and future pensioners whose savings they held, could have had a hedge against inflation and some participation in the growth of the economy.

Thirdly, the manufacturing sector was, as already noted, excessively dependent on foreign investment. This created a risk that the government would react overhastily at some point in the future by moving against the foreign ownership of manufacturing industry. The development of equity finance, for manufacturing and other sectors of the economy, would make it possible for Botswana institutions and individuals to participate gradually in foreign-owned businesses, and so make disruptive action less likely. While a secondary market in shares would increase the attractions of equity investment, it was not absolutely necessary. Considerable progress could be made simply by making institutional savings available to those businesses interested in acquiring additional equity finance, without necessarily developing a fully fledged stock exchange.

It appeared, therefore, as if there was a need for some private sector financial institutions to provide a number of missing links: private provision of longer-term loans, underwriting of new share issues, acting as an intermediary between the institutions wishing to invest long-term savings and those companies in need of additional equity finance.

In principle, these functions could be performed by existing financial institutions (or in the case of intermediation by professional firms of accountants or lawyers). The most obvious candidates seemed to be the commercial banks, which had the largest network of branches[38] and other facilities such as accounting staff; but prolonged attempts to get them to do anything but provide short-term finance were unsuccessful. The explanation appeared to be the ease with which they made high profits from their traditional activities, together with the training and incentives which would have to be offered to their staff. In other words, they had neither the incentive nor apparently the capacity to take on new types of business. It seemed that the authorities needed to encourage a new type of private sector financial institution, such as merchant or investment banks, to set up, whose functions would be, among other services, to provide long-term loans and to act as intermediaries in the development of equity finance.

The role of foreign aid donors in finance for industry is likely to be indirect rather than direct, through assistance for education and training (see below), through help for BDC, and through technical assistance.

The dominance of foreign ownership and management could also be reduced by the provision of (even more) technical and managerial training. Industry, commerce, private vocational centres, parastatals and government already provided training for 9,000 people in about 70 centres by the mid-1980s (GOB, 1985: 151). The skilled manpower constraint (and other constraints such as the availability of housing and school places for expatriate children) applies to the training of more skilled manpower as to every other activity in the country, so that there were limits to the rate of expansion of technical training. Nevertheless, the 1985–91 Plan included, among other new facilities, the introduction of a new higher Diploma Course in accountancy and business studies which should help in the long run.

More generally, if Botswana is to increase manufactured exports, in more products and more markets than at present, it will need to be exceptionally active and flexible in order to cater for changing conditions in foreign markets. This will require not only training in specific skills, but as good a basic education as can be provided. The expansion of basic education was impressive after independence, as in many other African countries. What is unusual about Botswana is that in the late 1980s it has the financial resources to sustain that improvement. Moreover, the government is giving priority to education, including planned universal access to nine years of basic education by the mid-1990s. Education was allocated the highest planned real growth rate of government spending (11%) in the 1985–91 Plan (GOB, 1985: 125).

MANUFACTURED EXPORTS
Manufactured exports, at present very dependent on the two markets of Zimbabwe and South Africa, are therefore vulnerable to two risks. One is that demand or the availability of foreign exchange might fall in the two markets. The other is that Botswana's exports might be seen as a threat by their competing producers in Zimbabwe and South Africa, or by their governments. Some combination of these two factors seems to have caused Zimbabwe to reduce imports from Botswana in the mid-1980s, and then to try and end the Trade Agreement.

Table 4.16 *Relative importance of Botswana to South African and Zimbabwean economies (1985 statistics)*

	GDP (Pm.)	Botswana Relative Size (%)	Share of Botswana's exports in imports of South Africa and Zimbabwe (%)
Botswana	1,512	100	
South Africa	101,937	1.5	0.3
Zimbabwe	9,863	15.3	2.9

Source: IMF, *International Financial Statistics*; Reserve Bank of Zimbabwe; *Botswana Statistical Bulletin*.

Exports to South Africa may be slightly less vulnerable, for two reasons. They are a considerably smaller proportion of South Africa's imports, as shown in Table 4.16. Secondly, Table 4.17 shows that South Africa's annual trade surplus with Botswana in the mid-1980s was quite large, being of the same order of magnitude as the foreign currency component of its foreign-exchange reserves. These also included gold valued at several times the foreign currency reserves, but it was almost impossible for South Africa to sell significant quantities of its gold reserves, because of the depressing effect on the price of gold, which remained its leading export. In the past, it borrowed foreign currency using gold as collateral,

Table 4.17 *South Africa: trade surplus with Botswana and foreign currency reserves 1983-6 (Pm.)*

	Botswana's exports to S. Africa[a]	Botswana's imports from S. Africa[a]	Trade balance	South Africa foreign currency reserves[b]
1983	58	670	612	490–1,003
1984	76	700	624	311– 792
1985	78	814	737	595– 950
1986	91	1,022	931	492–1,524
1987	111	1,251	1,140	1,042–1,808

Source: Ibid.

Notes: [a] Figures are for trade with the Common Customs Area, but trade with Lesotho and Swaziland was negligible compared with trade with South Africa.
[b] Range of reserves from quarterly figures; includes holdings of SDRs.

but that became more difficult and at times impossible as financial sanctions were applied by international banks in the 1980s.

Cutting off trade with Botswana would thus eliminate South Africa's usable foreign-exchange reserves within a year, if nothing else changed. There were other benefits to South Africa in maintaining the status quo, including the income gained from Botswana's transit trade and the use of Botswana's railway system for South Africa's own transit trade (some 60% of goods traffic on Botswana Railways was in transit, all by definition going to or from South Africa).

The existence of a large trade surplus with Botswana did not by any means guarantee that South Africa would not put barriers in the way of Botswana's exports, or otherwise disrupt trade. Military, strategic and political factors could, as they have in the past, outweigh economic calculations. But the loss of foreign currency earnings from a trade boycott (threatened on several occasions as a response to sanctions) did give Botswana rather more bargaining power in maintaining its rights under the Customs Union than it would otherwise have. In the case of both Zimbabwe and South Africa, and indeed of other trading partners, it is in Botswana's interest that exports should not be concentrated in a small number of products, since that sharply increases the threat to competing producers in export markets and the risk of retaliation. It is important, therefore, for Botswana to continue to have a number of sub-sectors with significant exports.

There is a problem in that small firms in general face certain difficulties in exporting, since there are economies of scale in acquiring knowledge of distant markets and export markets can demand larger quantities than they can supply. But Botswana's manufactured exports have succeeded so far in selling to regional markets, so this difficulty may apply less to the relatively nearby markets of Zimbabwe and South Africa.

Because of foreign-exchange shortages, other regional markets are too volatile to be relied on for significant growth, although they should obviously not be neglected. The size of the Botswana import market, together with the country's ability to pay cash in hard currency, has potential for opening up some opportunities in, for example, Zambia. But those African economies with extreme foreign-exchange shortages tend to spend most of their export earnings on debt service and oil imports, relying on aid for other imports. Unless donors are willing to allow aid receipts to be spent on imports from Botswana, and on consumer goods which are mostly what Botswana has to offer, then these markets will tend to be closed to it so long as current conditions continue.

Larger-scale producers may be required if Botswana is to export manufactured goods to non-regional markets. This conflicts, however, with the argument that Botswana's growth of manufacturing derives partly from the avoidance of single, large, government-supported producers in most sub-sectors. It might therefore be better to try and find some way of overcoming the handicaps faced by small-scale producers in selling to distant markets. Some large firms capable of exporting to non-regional markets may develop independently; there is already some evidence of Botswana manufacturers exporting to Europe and elsewhere (including some of the firms shut out of the Zimbabwe market by tightening restrictions). The point is that the country should also try and take advantage of the fairly spontaneous growth in Botswana of small-scale manufacturing firms.

One possibility is that relatively large trading companies could buy from small-scale producers in Botswana in order to export to Europe and other non-regional markets (Europe is the obvious first choice because of access for manufactured goods through the ACP/Lomé agreements). There is a minor precedent for this in the activities of Botswanacraft, a subsidiary of BDC, which buys handicrafts from large numbers of rural producers and exports successfully to non-regional markets. Such trading companies would have to be large enough to research the detailed technical demands of export markets, and producers would have to be induced to meet those demands, presumably through the trading companies' buying prices. This type of marketing structure would enable Botswana to reach distant export markets without losing the benefits of domestic competition among small-scale producers.

The reason for preferring this type of approach, rather than the setting up of larger-scale producers to capture the necessary economies of scale and meet the demands of export markets, is that large-scale firms set up with government subsidy or protection would be unlikely to develop the efficiency needed to be successful exporters, on the evidence of such initiatives elsewhere in Africa. It would be preferable for Botswana to try and interest private investment in such trading companies. However, public sector investment would have a better chance of success in marketing rather than in production. The evidence of public sector initiative in export *marketing* in Africa is mixed. Botswana's own BMC and Botswanacraft are successful public sector exporters; evidence from elsewhere in Africa suggests that, in agricultural marketing, success depends heavily on there being a strong element of control by producers (Harvey, 1988: 238–42). This would suggest that a public sector initiative would need to build in a strong producer influence , to control the costs of marketing and to prevent a gap developing between border prices and those received by producers.

CONCLUDING PERSPECTIVES

The basic conclusion of this chapter is that policy in Botswana towards the manufacturing sector has been fundamentally correct, as witnessed by the rapid growth of output, employment, the number of manufacturing firms, and, to a lesser degree, of manufactured exports. Macroeconomic policy has delivered a fairly constant real exchange rate and a structure of wages which enables manufacturers to compete. Sector-specific policy has been to provide a minimum of protection, and a small amount of subsidy.

In future, it would seem that the government should maintain the same basic set of policies, with, if anything, a greater emphasis on ensuring that manufacturers are internationally competitive. It should also tackle such constraints as the burden of regulations, difficult though that has proved, and gaps in the supply of appropriate finance. It also has the financial resources to increase the supply of industrial land and to reduce the periodic shortages of telephone and telex services, electricity and water connections. These shortages, which are themselves symptoms of success, cannot be entirely removed by spending money; other constraints operate in turn, such as the rate of growth at which parastatals and the civil service can expand without losing efficiency. But the availability of cash will make a significant difference.

Botswana is faced with an inevitable slowdown in the rate of economic growth, although probably not in the next few years, because of the absence of large new mining projects of the type and size that caused exceptionally rapid economic growth in the last 20 years. Manufacturing industry has a few more years in which it can expect to derive most of its growth from domestic demand as in the past. In the medium term, though, it will have to rely more on import substitution. And in the long term, the small size of the domestic market means that manufacturing must depend on exporting if it is to grow rapidly; and the same absence of new mining projects means that overall growth will depend on manufactured exports as the leading sector.

Basically that requires the government to avoid protection of industry, in order that it will be able to compete successfully with imports and in export markets. In addition, because tax revenue from manufacturing is bound to be much less than from diamond mining, the government will have to plan for its own spending to grow less fast than in the past. If direct assistance is to be given to manufacturers, it would be preferable for it to be provided in the form of subsidies, as at present through the FAP, than by means of protection, for the simple reason that governments find it easier to reduce subsidies, which are a charge on the budget, than to reduce tariff protection which contributes to revenue. If tariff or quota protection is provided, as it has been in a few cases, it is equally essential that, as before, protected producers continue to be obliged to sell at tariff-free border equivalent prices so that there is some longer-term prospect of the development of exports.

The hardest question of all for Botswana, in deciding on a long-term strategy for manufacturing, is how much to rely on the South African market. Geographically, it makes no sense to de-link. The closeness of South Africa has been seen in the past as a handicap: how, it was asked, could Botswana compete with producers in such a relatively advanced economy? But in the longer term, the existence of such a large market nearby, to which Botswana producers have access (to the extent that South Africa keeps to the terms of the Custom Union Agreement), could be seen as a major bonus. This is especially important for a land-locked country distant from other large markets. But there is an obvious risk of political upheaval in South Africa, or of action by present or future South African governments, which would reduce or eliminate it as a market for Botswana exports.

This political risk adds to the economic arguments for diversification of export markets. Over-dependence on any export market, however politically stable, is an economic risk; the likelihood of political problems affecting trade merely adds to the need to diversify. Since it takes a long time to build up the knowledge and expertise required for successful export of manufactured goods to new markets, especially to distant ones, it is important for Botswana to start on the process as soon as possible. The decline of the Pula against non-regional currencies at the time of writing (1989), provides a strong financial incentive.

Notes

1. This first part of the chapter was written by Stephen Lewis and Jennifer Sharpley. A fuller version is to be found in Lewis and Sharpley (1988).
2. This second part of the chapter was written and researched by Charles Harvey.
3. More extensive discussion and documentation are found in Colclough and McCarthy (1980) for the earlier years and Harvey and Lewis (1989) for the entire period.
4. Growth rates of over 14% were recorded in 1986 and 1987 with an estimated growth rate of 8.7% in 1987/8 (*African Economic Digest*, 27 March, 1989).
5. Drought resulted in low levels of agricultural GDP from 1981/2 through 1985/6. Manufacturing GDP surpassed agriculture for the first time in 1982/3.
6. The 1964 figure of 2,400 is a census figure and includes small-scale, informal sector activity, while the 1985 figure comes from the annual employment surveys of establishments. The earliest employment survey, in 1967/8, showed 1,358 employees in manufacturing, while the 1971 survey showed 2,315. The estimate of 2,000 at Independence is probably generous.
7. The government has had a number of programmes aimed at the development of citizen entrepreneurs – recognising that at Independence few Batswana participated in any aspect of the modern sector other than some of the larger-scale cattle raising. The Botswana Enterprises Development Unit (BEDU), under the Ministry of Commerce and Industry, has provided a 'comprehensive support package' of factory space, finance, technical assistance, purchasing services, and a generally 'hothouse' atmosphere mainly on estates for small entrepreneurs in a variety of ventures such as jewelry, pottery, textiles, leather working, metal work and welding and construction.
8. For meat and meat products, the BMC pursued a policy of increasing the degree of processing in order to increase the total value added accruing to Botswana. Since this involved increased use of purchased inputs it probably was the major contributor to the declining ratio of value added to gross output, even though the practice increased overall domestic value added. Miscellaneous manufacturing is a very mixed bag of industries, dominated in the early years by village industries, which have extremely low ratios of purchased inputs to gross output. Thus, as the composition of this sub-sector changed over time by the addition of new and more 'normal' manufacturing industries, one would expect a decline in the ratio of value added to gross output.
9. The BDC has developed a large portfolio of projects, and is a participant in most of the major industrial and many commercial developments: the brewery, a chain of hotels, maize and wheat flour milling, insurance, liquor distribution, sugar packing and the national airline, Air Botswana. BDC provides both long-term loan capital and equity, but in almost all cases seeks a technical partner in its ventures. It operates mainly on commercial terms, but some of its activities (such as Botswanacraft, a marketing outlet for handicrafts mainly from rural areas) are run on a sub-commercial basis where there are distinct development advantages. Foreign investors have frequently sought BDC as a partner either to absorb some risk they did not wish to bear, to provide long-term financing, or to ensure that there was some local participation. BDC has been frequently criticised for not selling its profitable ventures directly to private citizens.
10. Lewis (1987) estimated that between 1984 and 1986 Botswana gained over $500 m. from movements in the Rand/dollar cross rate as the dollar price of South African, Rand-priced goods fell by 13%, 34% and 25% in 1984-5-6 relative to 1983. While this represented a national gain, it greatly complicated exchange-rate and other macroeconomic policies. And it is a movement that could be reversed, as happened between 1978 and 1980, when the dollar price of South African goods rose by 44% due to a combination of cross exchange-rate movements and South African inflation.
11. The revenue-sharing formula basically provides each of the BLS countries with an amount of revenue based on: their level of imports from all sources, the average rate of customs and excise collections and the share of imports plus exercisable production in the entire customs area, an 'enhancement' of that revenue rate by 42% to reflect the disadvantages to the BLS from being in a Customs Union with a larger partner, and finally a 'stabilisation factor' which provides that the rate of duty payable on BLS imports, including the enhancement factor, can never fall below 17% nor rise above 23%. Revenue is calculated and paid two years after the imports take place, so that during rising periods of imports there has been a substantial lag in the payment to the BLS from the common customs pool.
12. Several cases were cited in Selwyn (1975: 119) and Jones (1977: 31), as quoted in Colclough and McCarthy (1980: 164).
13. For a numerical example see Hudson (1981: 154-5).
14. Provided that the agreement was successfully monitored by the government. Even if it was, consumers had to pay more for any but the local brands of beer and soap. The soap producer was allowed a slightly higher price than the tariff-free import parity.

15. It was reported that all currently known potential sources of water would be needed just to satisfy urban demand within 20 years, with the exception of the Zambezi river in the extreme North, which would require a very large investment in infrastructure if it were to be made available.

16. Overall, Zimbabwe would lose foreign exchange from ending trade with Botswana. Its position was that it had a bilateral trade *deficit* with Botswana, but in fact it was a net earner of foreign exchange from this trade in the late 1980s. This was because it imported some of Botswana's copper-nickel matte for refining, and then re-exported the refined metals, resulting in net earnings of foreign exchange from these transactions. Excluding the trade in copper-nickel matte, Zimbabwe had a bilateral trade surplus with Botswana.

17. The new agreement, in theory at least, left the terms of trade regulations between the two countries relatively untouched. Thus goods qualifying for import to Zimbabwe from Botswana under the Open General Import Licence (OGIL) require 25% of final value to be local content. Local content, however, has been more tightly defined as direct labour involved in manufacture, and locally produced raw materials. Together these must amount to 25% of the ex-factory cost of the product from Botswana. The new agreement also stipulates that the manufacturing process must not include repacking goods from one container to another, assembly of imported kits or painting imported goods. In addition, adding colourings to food or mixing in new ingredients is held not to result in a new product. The new regulations were effective from November 1988.

18. The situation was exacerbated by the general scarcity of housing, particularly in Gaborone, which increased the economic value of any housing provided free by a company. General land scarcity is discussed further below.

19. A combination of decreases in the marginal tax rate structure over several budget years and modifications of the rules for valuation of the housing benefit significantly eased the problem by 1986.

20. The BMC is taxed at the company tax rate, but on the basis of a separate formula to determine taxable income. The tax works out effectively at a rate of around 10% of gross sales after deduction of freight, selling and distribution costs. Since BMC distributes (by statute) any surplus of its revenues over its costs (after appropriations for capital replacements and to a stabilisation fund), this is effectively a tax on cattle producers, not on the BMC.

21. Botswana has a system of industrial, including 'exclusive', licensing. All potential manufacturers must have a licence, all applications being published with invitations for public comment. The exclusive licence arrangement has been used selectively, generally but not solely in connection with some other aspect of government encouragement (e.g. protection under the Customs Union arrangements). Work Permits are required for non-citizens. As localisation is an extremely sensitive issue, the Department of Labour exercises care and caution, which are sometimes seen as delay and obstruction by employers. The Immigration Department has independent responsibility for granting Residence Permits, both are resented by much of the private business community.

22. Land development has been undertaken almost exclusively by the central government, with allocation of plots carried out by the Department of Surveys and Lands. Several government reports and White Papers have expressed a desire to speed up the development process for serviced land. The White Paper on Housing Policy (1981) made the point that the problem of high rents and plot prices in Gaborone in particular, was due to a failure to develop land fast enough to meet the demand from the public and private sectors for industrial, commercial and residential land.

23. Because a lease may not be transferred without Land Board approval, and because the title to structures goes with the lease, banks have been reluctant to lend against the security of land and buildings in tribal areas.

24. Since domestic prices are set by the prices in the BMC's principal markets, however, domestic consumers face higher prices than they would without favourable trading arrangements.

25. Botswana would recover only that part of the duty payments arising from the revenue-sharing formula – roughly 20%, and even that would be received two years after the initial payments into the pool had been made.

26. The factory was purchased by the US firm H.J. Heinz in 1988.

27. The discrepancy between output figures on the one hand and other indicators of growth on the other could be because the national income accounts have a less complete coverage of manufacturing firms; this is especially likely to occur when there is rapid growth, as in Botswana, of new and small-scale firms.

28. Weighted by size of firm, the proportion was almost certainly even less.

29. The government had share-holdings in the diamond and copper-nickel mines. The increase in its share in Debswana, to 50%, was negotiated with some difficulty since it was part of a package to increase the government's share of diamond mining profits; but there was no suggestion that this affected attitudes of potential investors in manufacturing.

30. 'What commerce and industry – workers, employers and frustrated would-be participants – most need from government is a huge shift from restriction, control and licensing towards promotion, training and competition' (Lipton, 1978 Vol 2: 111). The situation did not improve significantly in the following ten years.

31. The terms of aid are also expected to harden.

32. The sale took place at the beginning of July 1987; foreign-exchange reserves rose by P435 m. from end-June to end-July (Bank of Botswana, 1988).
33. It fell again subsequently, reaching $0.39 by the end of April 1989.
34. The gains were twofold. Annual balance-of-payments surpluses were increased; and the paper gains on existing foreign-exchange reserves were also nearly all real gains, in that the reserves (nearly all invested in major currencies and not in Rand) could be expected to be spent eventually on goods priced in Rand.
35. The balance of payments recorded a current account surplus of P798m. in 1988 and an overall surplus of P692m. (Bank of Botswana, *Annual Report* 1988).
36. Foreign currency reserves were at 28 months' import cover at end-1988 (Bank of Botswana, *Annual Report 1988*).
37. There had been some earlier recognition of the excessive demands of government for the existing supply of skilled people, for example in the 1972 Report on Localisation, but the argument that people whose education or training had been paid for by the government should work for the government was still being used throughout the 1970s.
38. In 1987, the three commercial banks had 35 branches and 46 agencies (Bank of Botswana, 1988). The National Development Bank had 6 regional and 12 district offices, but was in no position to take on new business (NDB, Annual Report 1985/6); no other financial institution had a significant number of branches.

References and Bibliography

Bank of Botswana, *Annual Report* 1988.
Botswana Development Corporation (BDC), *Annual Reports*.
Chenery, H.B. (1960), 'Patterns of Industrial Growth', *American Economic Review*, Vol. 50, September.
—— Robinson, S. and Syrquin, M. (1986), *Industrialization and Growth: a Comparative Study*, Washington DC, Oxford University Press for the World Bank.
Colclough, C. and McCarthy, S. (1980), *The Political Economy of Botswana: A Study of Growth and Distribution*, Oxford, Oxford University Press.
Government of Botswana (1982), 'Report of the Presidential Commission on Economic Opportunities', Gaborone, Government Printer.
—— (1985), *National Development Plan 1985 to 1991*, Gaborone, Government Printer.
Granberg, P. (1986) *Some Recent Trade Estimates for Angola, Botswana, Mozambique, Zambia and Zimbabwe*', DERAP Working Papers A351, Bergen, Christian Michelsen Institute.
Harvey, C. (1981a) 'Foreign investment in manufacturing: the case of Botswana's brewery' in Harvey, C. (ed.) (1981b), *Papers on the Economy of Botswana*, London, Heinemann.
—— (1985), *The use of monetary policy in Botswana, in good times and bad*, Discussion Paper No. 204, Institute of Development Studies at the University of Sussex.
—— (1987), *Successful macroeconomic adjustment in developing countries: Botswana, Malawi and Papua New Guinea*, Development Policy Case Series Economic Development Institute, Washington DC, World Bank.
—— (ed.), (1988) *Agricultural Pricing Policy in Africa: Four Country Case Studies*, London, Macmillan.
—— and Lewis, S.R. Jr. (1989), *Policy Choice and Development Performance in Botswana*, London, Macmillan.
Hudson, D.J. (1981), 'Botswana's Membership of the Southern African Customs Union', in Harvey (1981b).
Jones, D. (1977), *Aid and development in Southern Africa*, London, Croom Helm.
Lewis, S.R. Jr. (1971), *Economic Policy and Industrial Growth in Pakistan*, London, George Allen and Unwin.
—— (1984), 'Development problems of the mineral-rich countries', in Syrquin M. et al. (eds), *Economic Structure and Performance: Essays in Honour of Hollis B. Chenery*, New York, Academic Press.
—— (1987), *Economic Realities in Southern Africa (or, 100 m. futures)*, Discussion Paper No. 232, Institute of Development Studies, at the University of Sussex.
—— and Mokgethi, N.D. (1983), 'Fiscal Policy in Botswana', in Oomen et al., *Botswana's Economy since Independence*, New Delhi, Tata McGraw-Hill.
—— and Sharpley, J. (1988), *Botswana's Industrialisation*, Discussion Paper No. 245, Institute of Development Studies, at the University of Sussex.
—— and Soligo, R. (1965), 'Growth and Structural Change in Pakistan's Manufacturing Industry, 1954-1964', *The Pakistan Development Review*, Vol. V. No. 1. Spring; reprinted as Economic Growth Centre Paper, No. 99, Yale University, 1967.
Lipton, M. (1978), 'Employment and Labour Use in Botswana' (2 Vols), Ministry of Finance and Development Planning, Gaborone, (mimeo).
Nankani, G. (1979), *Development Problems of Mineral Exporting Countries*, World Bank Staff Working Papers No. 354, Washington DC, World Bank.

Republic of Botswana (1982), Government Paper 'National policy' on economic opportunities', Gaborone, Government Printer.

Republic of Botswana, Ministry of Finance and Development Planning, Central Statistical Office (various years), Gaborone, Government Printer:

> *National Accounts of Botswana*
> *Statistical Bulletin*
> *External Trade Statistics*
> *Financial Statements, Tables and Estimates of Recurrent Revenue*
> *Employment Survey*
> *National Development Plans.*

Selwyn, P, (1975), *Industries in the Southern African Periphery*, London, Croom Helm.

Sharpley, J. and Lewis, S.R. Jr. (1988), *Kenya's Industrialisation 1964–84*, Discussion Paper No. 242, Institute of Development Studies at the University of Sussex.

United Nations Industrial Development Organisation (UNIDO) (1987), *Industrial Development Review Series: Botswana*, Vienna, UNIDO, March.

World Bank (1979) *World Development Report 1979*, Oxford, Oxford University Press.

—— (1985) *Economic Memorandum on Botswana*, (Report No. 5238-BT), Washington DC, World Bank, October.

—— (1986), *Public Expenditure and Development in Botswana*, (Report No 6031-BT), Washington DC, World Bank, June.

—— (1987), *World Development Report 1987*, Washington DC, World Bank.

5 Cameroon

IGOR KARMILOFF

Introduction

Situated along the Gulf of Guinea, between 2° and 12° north of the Equator, Cameroon is a country of just under half a million km^2 and a population of just under 10m. in 1984, which enjoys a variety of climates and of vegetation because of its diversified topography. It also has one of the highest demographic growth rates in Africa. Rainfall is abundant in all but the North, bordering Chad, which provides it with a large hydroelectric potential and the possibility not only of staying virtually self-sufficient in basic foodstuffs, but also of having large exportable surpluses of tropical timber and several industrial crops. (The country's main economic characteristics are shown in Appendix Table 5.A1.)

For more than a decade after independence in 1960, the socio-economic climate was disturbed by political reunification problems between the two federal states – one English-speaking, bordering Nigeria in the West and the other, French-speaking, in the South and East. Because of high rates of economic growth and urbanisation, the proportion of townspeople shot up from 14% at independence, to 37% in 1984, bringing in its wake serious problems of imbalance between the rural and the urban areas – principally located in the South – urban unemployment, overcrowding and inadequate social infrastructure.

Cameroon's mineral wealth includes hydrocarbons, bauxite and as yet unexploited reserves of iron ore. Oil began to be marketed in 1978, but known deposits have a time horizon of only ten more years at current rates of extraction.

In broad terms, the country's development strategy up to 1985 aimed at enhancing economic self-reliance, under the slogan of 'communitarian liberalism'. Industrialisation rested on the twin pillars of consolidating food self-sufficiency by import substitution and more processing of domestic raw materials for export. The on-going sixth five-year plan (1986–91) adds the aims of developing national standards for improving the quality of domestic production, and of making more use of available patents and manufacturing licences. Drawing lessons from the past, the physical and financial infrastructure is to be strengthened and judicious use made of policy instruments that involve subsidies and affect factor prices.

The currency – the CFA Franc – is pegged to the French franc at the fixed rate of CFAF 1 = FFr 0.02 so that foreign-exchange transactions are based on Paris exchange rates. (The CFAF-dollar market exchange rates from 1960 to 1988 are set out in Table 5.A4.) Purchases/sales of foreign currencies are not subject to any tax or subsidy. All payments over CFAF 500,000 to France and to countries linked to the French Treasury by an Operations Account are free from control. All exports require documents to be deposited with authorised banks and the proceeds speedily repatriated. Non-franc export earnings have to be surrendered. Prior authorisation is needed for foreign credit operations.

Under the 1984 Investment Code, four types of fiscal benefits are available for new projects in areas listed as strategic in the development plan, and which generate employment, foreign exchange and help to decentralise economic activities. The nature and duration of the benefits vary according to size of investment, location, structure, technology and factor mix. They are comparable to those found in most francophone African countries[1].

The customs tariff is based on Customs Co-operation Council Nomenclature, 6-digit, 5-column and includes the customs duty plus complementary fiscal taxes as well as some other levies. Rates of duty are generally low (< 30%) and mostly ad valorem[2]. But when the cascading additional taxes and charges are taken fully into account, the resulting levels of nominal protection become substantial. Since African transport costs and commercial margins are relatively high, the wholesale price of imported goods in Cameroon averages out at 155% of their cif value (200% fob).

Trade with South Africa is prohibited. Special authorisation is required for the import of some 'controlled' goods, in addition to an import licence. All other imports, irrespective of origin, are subject to licensing when over specified levels, but licences are issued freely[3].

Industrialisation has been the subject of a series of specialised investigations in recent years[4]. These have focused variously on: Cameroon's singularly robust growth; after the coming on stream of oil, and its rising importance for the balance of payments, on the 'Dutch disease'[5]; the procrastination of the authorities in utilising the windfall gains from favourable oil prices and volumes for domestic investment; and, more recently, with the depletion of the monetary reserves, the liquidity shortage, stagnating investment and inflationary pressures.

Cameroon's overall economic performance stands up well to comparison with the African average and, in respect of per capita income, imports and investment, surpasses that of developing countries in general. The notable exception is its relatively low ratio of exports to gross domestic product (GDP) (see Table 5.1).

Fieldwork for Phase I of this study took place in the Spring of 1987 and the ensuing analysis of the industrialisation experience since independence ended with data covering the years 1984–5. The following year saw the Cameroonian economy sink into a deepening state of crisis. The follow-up field trip to Cameroon in March 1988 coincided with the application of several austerity measures and reforms, as well as negotiations with the IMF and the World Bank on a structural adjustment programme. The new Minister of Economic Reform at the Presidency had established working parties for the preparation of far-reaching administra-

Table 5.1 *International comparison of Cameroon's economic performance, 1970–84 at 1980 prices*

Indicator	Year	Cameroon	All Africa	All Developing Ctrs.
GDP per capita (US$)	1970	737	654	722
	1975	786	719	860
	1980	1,007	762	971
	1984	1,172	692	947
MVA per capita (US$)	1970	84	46	112
	1975	80	51	139
	1980	97	59	165
	1984	116	59	163
Recorded exports per capita (US$)	1970	149	289	221
	1975	169	217	241
	1980	218	251	262
	1984	204	185	243
Total imports per capita (US$)	1970	174	166	129
	1975	182	211	182
	1980	259	237	240
	1984	293	193	226
Exports/GDP %	1970	20.2	44.2	30.7
	1975	21.5	30.2	28.0
	1980	21.6	32.9	26.9
	1984	17.4	26.7	25.6
Imports/GDP %	1970	23.6	25.4	17.9
	1975	23.2	29.4	21.2
	1980	25.7	31.1	24.7
	1984	25.0	27.8	23.8
Capital formation per capita (US$)	1970	162	101	127
	1975	165	150	183
	1980	247	175	221
	1984	267	151	200
GFCF/GDP (%)	1970	22.0	15.5	17.7
	1975	21.0	20.9	21.3
	1980	24.6	23.0	22.8
	1984	22.8	21.8	21.1

Source: United Nations Industrial Development Organisation (UNIDO), based on data from the UN Statistical Office.

tive and institutional changes based on audits and diagnoses by external consultants financed by the United Nations Development Programme (UNDP).

The layout of the rest of this chapter is as follows. The next section presents an overview of the economy's development since the early 1960s. This is followed by an examination of the part played by the manufacturing sector, with the food industry being the subject of a closer examination. This is followed by a discussion of inter-sectoral linkages – with particular attention to agro-industrial ones – as well as the efficiency of resource use in manufacturing.

The final sections discuss at some length the scope and nature of the economy's present plight and medium-term outlook, and analyse the data-base used by various consultants and international agencies which, in 1987 and 1988, have assisted in the design of a master plan for industrial development to the year 2000 – *Le Plan Directeur Industriel* (DPI). Recent developments which plunged the economy into recession are examined, setting out the quantitative framework for macroeconomic projections and ending with a reference to the 'pathological' diagnosis that foreshadowed the official proclamation of World Bank-cum-IMF-sponsored adjustment measures. Next the sectoral ramifications of the latest changes in the external environment and their likely impact on the industrial sector are considered and in that context, trade figures are looked at for clues as to the sources of demand for Cameroon's manufactures and the most recent direction of import substitution. The demand and price assumptions subsumed in available macroeconomic projections are examined with an eye to the robustness of the policies and projects proposed for the industrial master plan (DPI), particularly as regards agro-industry. This is followed by an examination of the institutional, infrastructural and other bottlenecks to industrial development and the likelihood of corrective steps being taken in the near future to address them – given the country's commitment to regional integration within the UDEAC (Union Douanière Economique de l'Afrique Centrale) and to membership of the Franc Zone. The concluding section attempts to weave together the various findings and suggested initiatives which, it is believed, should lead to a self-sustaining expansion and further diversification of manufacturing in Cameroon.

Manufacturing performance: sub-sector structure and growth

Overall industrial output, defined in Cameroon to include primary processing of agricultural and forestry products, as well as public utilities, expanded over the period 1960/1–84/5 by a very healthy 9% a year on average, much higher than GDP growth. Within industry, manufacturing was the star performer. Its average annual growth during the first 15 years (10.7%) was double that of GDP. But in the following nine years, expansion slowed down considerably and just kept pace with the then oil-propelled domestic gross output (7.5% a year)[6].

The principal sources of industrial output growth during 1965–75, as estimated by the World Bank, are shown in Table 5.2.

Table 5.2 *Sources of growth, manufacturing sector, 1965–75 (%)*

	1965/6–70/1	1970/1–75/6
Domestic demand	58	51
Import substitution	25	41
Exporting	17	8

Source: World Bank (1980: 26).

Calculations by UNIDO of the sources of growth of manufacturing value added (MVA) during the 1975–80 and 1980–82 periods concluded that, for the sector as a whole, during the first period the main impetus was provided by the growth of domestic demand, followed by exports in a proportion of 4: 1, with little contribution from import substitution. In contrast, during the subsequent period, the propulsive role of the latter rose considerably, with exports constituting a drag on growth as their volume shrank in relative terms.

The shares of manufactured and semi-processed goods in exports for the years 1970/71–81/2 are summarised in Table 5.3. In the course of these eleven years their combined share dropped from 23 to 6% in 1981/2 when petroleum products' share came to 72% of commodity export earnings.

Table 5.3 *Value and structure of exports, 1970/1–81/2*

	1970/1	1975/6	1979/80	1981/2
Total export value				
(Current CFAF bn)	60.2	112.3	297.0	578.5
Of which (%)				
Petroleum products	0.2	0.2	28.1	71.7
Other goods n.e.s.	3.3	8.0	5.4	1.8
Agricultural products	73.1	70.3	50.8	20.9
Semi-processed goods	17.8	14.7	11.7	3.9
Manufactured goods	5.6	6.9	3.9	1.7

Source: World Bank (1984: Annex table 6).

Data on manufactured exports, labelled *produits industriels* in Cameroon's *Note Annuelle de Statistique, 1984/5*, show a slight rise in their share of total exports in 1983/4 to 3.2%, but a drop to 2.7% in the following year.

These developments underscore the difficulties faced by Cameroon's industrial goods in maintaining their shares in the external market including neighbouring countries, whose import-substituting strategies narrowed the industrial complementarities which existed in colonial times.

Up to the mid-1970s import substitution in Cameroon progressed farthest with the manu-facture of consumer goods; by then about three-quarters of their apparent consumption was met from domestic supply. The production of intermediate and capital goods expanded rapidly but from a very small base, leaving the industrial sector dependent on importing over one-half of the value of its intermediate consumption. Only in food, beverages and tobacco were dependency ratios in the 10 to 20% range.

Capacity utilisation in industry as a whole was estimated to have been in the range of two-thirds to three-quarters in 1975–7 and 1981, when the highest rates were in the beverages and tobacco industries and the lowest in base metals and fabricated metals production. No published data are available for subsequent years but numerous industry-specific studies point to a substantial reduction in these rates – as has been the case in most SSA countries. Lack of local supplies has been an important constraint on capacity use in the food sub-sector. 'Disloyal competition' on the domestic front because of smuggling plus consumer bias has depressed capacity use in several lines of consumer goods. Some heavy industries were poorly designed technically from the outset; others were based on faulty demand studies. Still others were bedevilled by power failures. The more common problems included inadequately trained personnel and the long delays in getting official approval for adjusting producer prices to rises in input costs.

As might be expected, fast growth of industrial output was unevenly spread among sub-sectors. The largest sub-sector (beer and soft drinks manufacturing – ISIC 313) succeeded in steadily improving its growth performance and in raising its share of total MVA to 20% (see Tables 5.4 and 5.5). The next largest sub-sector – food industries (ISIC 311) – did well only in years when domestic agriculture expanded strongly. Several poor harvests in the second

Table 5.4 *Capital and ownership structures of manufacturing enterprise, 1984/5*

Activity	Capital	National Public	Private	French	Other
	CFAF Bn.	Percentages			
Agro-food	98.8	64	12	17	7
Wood/paper	24.3	42	10	16	32
Metals	27.4	30	3	64	4
Chems. Plast.	12.6	21	35	32	12
Text. Leather	9.1	36	23	10	31
Other indus.	8.6	39	15	32	14

Source: International Financial Corporation, reproduced in UNIDO (1986b: Table 9).

Table 5.5 *Manufacturing growth, ISIC structure and employment 1975–85 (%)*

Growth rates			1975–84
Manufacturing value added (MVA)			5.03[a]
Employment in manufacturing			3.50

Subsector's share in MVA	1975	1980	1985
Food products (ISIC 311)	8.0	10.3	11.2
Beverages (313)	24.9	22.1	31.2
Tobacco (314)	10.8	9.3	8.1
Textiles (321)	11.4	9.6	6.6
Apparel (322)	3.1	3.9	2.2
Leather products (323)	1.1	0.5	1.4
Footwear (324)	4.3	4.1	2.9
Wood products (331)	1.2	7.2	1.6
Furniture, wooden (332)	0.1	1.6	0.2
Paper & products (341)	0.5	0.0	1.1
Printing etc. (342)	1.0	2.1	1.3
Industr. chemicals (351)	1.4	0.5	1.5
Other chemicals (352)	7.9	4.2	4.6
Petroleum refining (353)	0.0	0.9	..
Misc. hydrocarbons (354)	0.0	0.0	0.3
Rubber products (355)	0.0	0.1	0.5
Plastic products (356)	2.1	0.9	2.1
Pottery, china etc (361)	1.5	1.4	1.1
Glass & products (362)	1.1	1.4	0.9
Other non-metallic miner. (369)	3.1	3.3	2.3
Base metal products (371)	1.9	5.1	5.3
Non-ferrous metals (372)	4.8	4.4	4.0
Fabricated metal prod. (381)	0.6	..	0.0
Non-elect. machinery (382)	6.1	..	5.0
Electrical machinery (383)	1.6	..	1.4
Transport equipment (384)	0.7	1.3	0.6
Other manufactured prod. (390)	0.7	1.6	2.6
MANUFACTURING VALUE ADDED	100.0	100.0	100.0

Source: UNIDO, *A Statistical Review of Economic and Industrial Performance*, January 1987, tables 4, 5 and 8.

Note: [a] See Appendix for details.

half of the 1960s slowed down its earlier high rate of growth so that, over the whole period to 1984/5, the sub-sector just maintained its share of total MVA. Base metals manufacturing (ISIC 371) put in a strong performance throughout the last decade – the reverse of the path traced by textiles (ISIC 321). Chemicals for other than industrial use (ISIC 352) and non-ferrous metals (ISIC 372) both played a dynamic part in the industrialisation process until 1980, when a general slowdown set in.

At this juncture, the ownership structure of manufacturing activities, set out in Table 5.4, needs to be highlighted.

The particularly high proportion of non-French foreign participation in the wood/paper and textile/leather subsectors is in the former case due to CELLUCAM's financial structure, in which Austrian interests are substantial, and in the latter to the preponderance of Lebano/Syrian capital.

To elucidate the reasons for this structural pattern, the more important manufacturing sub-sectors are examined in turn, with food industries left for a separate and more detailed consideration further on.

BEVERAGES

Per capita consumption of beer in Cameroon is high even by African standards, having reached some 60–70 litres per annum in the early 1980s – propelled by an estimated income elasticity of 0.6. Breweries, also manufacturing soft drinks, have doubled in number (to 8) over the last 20 years. They have their own distribution and transport facilities. In 1985 they accounted for no less than 18% of total employment in manufacturing and growth in their value added (1975–84) averaged 15% a year. Local purchases of inputs were limited to sugar, bottles, plastic cases, crown corks and labels, in addition to water and electricity. With a high share of imported inputs, several import–substituting projects had been germinating for years, for example, growing barley locally and producing cassava starch. At the time of writing no more than 7% of the total barley residue of about 18,000 tonnes was being sold as livestock feed. Another by-product of brewing – unrefined yeast – amounting to some 12,000 tonnes awaits the installation of facilities for processing it into an animal feed additive. Thus two promising import–substituting opportunities are still to be exploited.

Return on capital in brewing has been good, with a steady 5% net profit on turnover. The World Bank study mentioned earlier found brewing activities in Cameroon to be very efficient, well managed, and price and quality competitive. Indeed ex-factory prices of beer have, on occasion, been below those officially allowed. But since beer is a differentiated product, brewing has not made a net contribution to the trade balance, as the quantity exported has been roughly matched by imported beers in recent years.

TEXTILES

Employing some 2,600 workers (1985) and with two large plants located in an under-industrialised area in the North, this strategic sub-sector expanded strongly for about a decade after 1968 and then entered a declining phase. Yet domestic demand has been growing on average at 10% a year for cotton piece-goods and at 16% for cotton-based undergarments, with average per capita consumption estimated to be about two kilograms a year. All the weaving, spinning and finishing plants have substantial government participation through the holding company, *Société Nationale d'Industrialisation* (SNI). The raw cotton, of good quality, is grown domestically, under the supervision of a public joint venture that receives technical support from abroad. Hence the only problem with supply is the price to be paid for ginned cotton – which follows world market quotations – and the high cost of electricity in the North. Labour productivity in the mills is on a par with that in Europe and finished fabrics are competitive in quality.

At the industry's zenith, in 1980/1, when the CICAM spinning and weaving mill operated briefly at full capacity, 57m. metres of cotton fabric were produced of which no less than 37% were exported, leaving a net profit of 3.2% on turnover. Decline ensued as the need for replacement of obsolescent machinery coincided with high world cotton prices, which the authorities did not cushion for some time, as well as with high dollar costs of imported inputs.

Both of CICAM's subsidiaries, engaged in downstream processing and blending, have been loss-makers for almost a decade. SOLICAM developed an endemically negative cash flow, notwithstanding that half of its output of house linen and towelling had once been exported. It had been over-sized at the outset and debt servicing built up to almost one-fifth of turnover. The rise in the cost of cotton thread resulted in the cessation of its exports to Europe, dismissal of 20% of its workforce and very low capacity utilisation. To float it anew, a merger followed with CICAM's second subsidiary SYNTECAM, manufacturing fabrics from imported synthetic thread. Its chief problems had been its obsolete machinery, the poor handling of cloth – resulting in a high proportion of defects – and the commonly shared inability to compete against fraudulently imported (Asian) fabrics that were believed to comprise over one-third of total apparent consumption.

Two other textile firms, SICABO and SAFIL, were unable to face up to competition from authorised imports, let alone illegal ones, and carried losses even with reduced personnel. Their capacity utilisation oscillated at around 50%. SCS was the country's sole 'manu-facturer' of jute bags (from imported materials, two thirds jute cloth and one third jute yarn). It had been burdened with poor management and procurement, with over-staffing and a negative cash flow in the face of market inroads by polyethylene sacks. Since 1985, it has passed into new hands and may yet undertake weaving jute cloth from imported thread and diversifying its product mix. Until recently its exports to UDEAC markets have not exceeded 2% of total sales. An attempt to replace jute with locally grown kenaf fibre was stultified by its high labour cost relative to cotton and food crop prices.

In general, the chief problem areas for textiles can be identified as follows:

- the magnitude of uncontrolled imports;
- the issue of import licences without good knowledge of domestic availabilities and

inadequate customs control over the exact nature of authorised imports;
- 'sticky' price setting and adjustment procedures;
- inadequate specialisation leading to uneconomically short production runs;
- poor marketing and promotional knowhow.

Finally it should be noted that, as with breweries, textile plants have their own transport and maintenance facilities.

CLOTHING[7]

Clothing enterprises have been in a critical state for well over a decade. In contrast to textiles, productivity has remained very low. They have been losing market shares both at home and abroad – mainly to goods of Asian origin. A UNIDO estimate of apparent consumption and trade dependence in the early 1980s gives 29.2% for imports and 24.1% for exports, nearly all of the latter to neighbouring markets. But it should be borne in mind that unauthorised imports of clothing have been very large, raising the effective import dependence to probably 35%. As the consumption of *pagnes* in Cameroon is only one third of UDEAC average, there is a large potential surplus in this product line with existing installations.

There have been numerous closures of industrial-sized garment firms in the past – as shown in Table 5.6 – and more were about to take place in 1987/8.

Table 5.6 *Performance of clothing manufacturing firms, 1970–82*

	1970	1978	1982
Number of firms operating	10	6	4
Turnover (CFAF 10⁹)	3	2.2	0.9
Employees (10³)	2.5	1.2	0.5

Source: GICAM, *L'économie camerounaise, 1982–83*, vol. II.

Hosiery producers, relying on European inputs, have had difficulty in obtaining import licences, forcing at least one firm (with labour productivity at 30% of standard) to operate at 10% of capacity and to envisage liquidation. Another, producing outer garments and impregnated cloth yielding a high proportion of value added, with a strong linkage to the upstream producer of its major input and already established in the UDEAC market, was in a similar situation because of a price squeeze, the loss of market shares from new import–substituting activities abroad and fraudulent imports at home. Another establishment in trouble had poor procurement practices and too little marketing expertise to draw upon.

In general, the volume of clothing exports – mainly to UDEAC countries and totalling 442 quintals only in 1984 – has fluctuated widely from year to year.

A common problem for many clothing manufacturers was competition from artisanal producers for government tenders. The latter group have no overheads to worry about, pay salaries below the legal levels, keep no accounts, pay hardly any taxes, and are exempt from having to provide formal guarantees of quality and delivery times. The clothing firm with the highest record of capacity utilisation in 1986 was an export-oriented joint venture, but it acquired only 10% of its inputs locally and had a negative cash flow.

LEATHER AND FOOTWEAR

Except for areas in the North, Cameroon's ecology and climate are not ideal for large-scale animal husbandry. Total animal population in 1984/5 was estimated at about 4m. head of horned cattle – many in nomadic herds moving freely between frontier areas of Nigeria, Chad and the Central African Republic – and a similar number of small ruminants, plus 0.9m. pigs. Exports of unprocessed hides and skins have dropped from an average of 2,000 tonnes in 1973–4 to about 900 tonnes in 1983–5.

Only one parastatal tannery (the STPC) has been established to date, located in the cattle-rearing area at a great distance from the country's two industrial abattoirs. It had to reduce its operations mainly to the collection and export of raw hides and skins, since prime costs of its finished leather were uncompetitively high even for domestic consumers. Debts mounted, followed by bankruptcy and privatisation in 1985.

Value added by semi-artisanal manufacturers of travel goods and accessories did expand at a healthy rate (13.9%) in the 1975–85 decade and employment at 2.7% a year. Import displacement by this branch, however, was not significant as the negative trade balance for this category of products more than doubled in value in the early 1980s. The US$0.6 m. of exports went principally to SSA markets.

Shoe manufacturing was also dominated by a parastatal – Bata. Its productivity reached European standards and the quality of its output made it competitive in neighbouring markets. But these have become progressively more self-sufficient through import substitution which, on occasion, involved the same technology (acquired from the same source), manufacturing articles of like design and quality. The quantities of footwear exported declined as a consequence from 790 tonnes in 1970 to 370 tonnes in 1980 and to a mere 100 tonnes in 1983, halving its share in the export value of all Cameroonian manufactures.

Several recent years were loss-making ones for Bata – ascribed by the holding parent (SNI) to the swamping of the domestic market by a conjunction of *authorised* imports of shoes at dumped prices (ostensibly of a different quality and type from those produced in Cameroon) and extensive contraband. The *recorded* negative trade balance on footwear reached US$10 m. in 1980, coming down to $8.3 m. by 1984/5. Because of uncertainty regarding the total supply of footwear, only a part of the shrinkage in the trade deficit can be ascribed to import substitution.

Total employment in shoe-making fell by 18% between 1975 and 1985. The employment elasticity for this group of industries (0.25 as computed by the World Bank's 1980 mission) was the *lowest* among all the manufacturing sub-sectors.

WOOD PRODUCTS, PAPER AND PRINTING

Cameroon's forest resources are vast. They cover 24m. hectares – of which over 30% is dense tropical forest – and rank it fourth in the whole of Africa. Over 350 different species have been identified but they are interspersed, requiring logging to be selective and, hence, costly. This natural wealth has been underutilised for reasons listed in numerous studies carried out under the auspices of the United Nations' Food and Agriculture Organisation (FAO), UNIDO and the World Bank:

- the absence of a comprehensive timber strategy;
- low technical proficiency and obsolete machinery in most of the 70 foreign-owned sawmills;
- high production losses and very little waste recuperation;
- the inadequate secondary road network in the timberland causing deliveries to be unreliable and costly;
- because of low profitability in logging, disappointing levels of investment.

The proportion of logs delivered to domestic processors – most often of *second* quality – has hardly risen, having been 54.7% in 1975/6 and 57.6% in 1983/4. Wood manufacturing enterprises included three match factories, one woodpulp mill which was shut down in 1985, five cutting and shaping units, two plywood and veneer plants, and a multitude of semi-artisanal manufacturers of building timber, furniture etc.

None of the four large parastatals in this sub-sector made a consistent profit in the five years to 1987, although domestic demand for their products has been growing at a healthy 8% a year. Import substitution is complete in veneers, plywood and improved wood, with consumption increasing from 26,000 square metres in 1975 to 46,000 square metres in 1984. But it has been only partial in manufactured wood products and hardly traceable in furniture during recent years. Domestic supplies to these enterprises have been unsatisfactory in quantity and quality, good logs being pre-empted by exports – chiefly to the European Community. But the quality of finished local products has also been found wanting. The sub-sector unquestionably presents the case of a 'missed opportunity'.

Losses by the parastatals have been nothing short of astronomical, mainly as a result of the stoppage of the pulp mill's operations two years after start-up. In 1980, CELLUCAM was the showpiece of Cameroon's industrialisation strategy and a turnkey model for Central Africa. (Excerpts from the firm's publicity brochure are reproduced in Table 5.A2.) The story is one of political motivations prevailing over economic considerations. The original feasibility study turned out to have been seriously at fault in respect of market demand, technical practicability, and the levels of fixed and operating costs. Located in the same geographical area as Zaire's very competitive pulp mill, CELLUCAM boasted being the first in the world to convert *all* species of timber into paper pulp. It also had the misfortune of having a section of its process chain blow up in the first year of operation. The initial investment in this monument to North-South co-operation came to more than US$400 m. Two years after it had been handed over to the government its debts amounted to CFAF 80 bn. By mid-1982 its total sales covered only one-third of variable costs[8]. The firm's cumulated losses by mid-1985 amounted to CFAF 160 bn – roughly equal to the investment required for forestry development in Cameroon for the next 15 years. The plant was put up for sale or disposal in July 1986.

The more common problems of the wood processing branch include:

- non-standardised, low quality domestic raw materials that are not 'pre-cut' to meet commercial needs;
- timber concessions are hard to come by and the periods granted (5 years) too short to recoup investment or get long-term bank loans, thus preventing vertical integration:
- inadequately weathered timber, (unsuitable for direct use as cement casing) requiring users to immobilise capital in drying inventories;
- lagging adjustment of authorised prices to real costs.

The sub-sector's employment elasticity has been very high (0.95) and its work force expanded from 1,370 in 1975 to 2,560 by 1985. Yet the value of furniture imported, chiefly from Europe, came to US$11.6 m. in 1982.

CHEMICALS, PETROCHEMICALS AND PLASTICS

This sub-sector is of especial interest because it comprises a number of enterprises which have been profitable and competitive in the regional and UDEAC markets. Yet they imported all their capital and over 95% of their intermediate inputs, and did not receive blanket protection from competing imports or other forms of subsidy.

Chemicals. Cameroon's natural endowment of *inorganic* raw materials for the chemical industry (1985 data) is limited to the refractory ingredient disthene, kaolin, limestone, pouzzolane, coarse silicate sand not suitable for window glass, rock and sea salt. The *organic* resource base for a chemical industry is much broader, with crude petroleum and good natural gas deposits, as well as abundant vegetable oils and fats. Should oil refining continue apace, the deficit in sulphates could be narrowed, but that in phosphates and chlorides would still remain.

The volume of deficit chemical imports has remained stable over the five years to 1987 and no new investment has taken place since 1982. Import substitution has made itself felt only in container glass and has not affected the import ratios of glass tableware or rubber tyres. Dependence on imports of fertilisers rose after the closure in 1981 of the parastatal factory – SOCAME – whose brief existence is instructive in many respects.

Like the ill-fated CELLUCAM, it was one of the centrepieces of the 1971–6 Plan and began operating in 1975 with a labour force of 500. It had been designed to produce 50,000 tonnes of ammonium sulphate (which acidifies soil), 20,000 tonnes of single superphosphate (for which there was no demand), and 27,000 tonnes of (expensive) complex fertilisers – all from imported inputs. No market study is known to have preceded the decision to go ahead with the investment, on which debt servicing alone amounted to CFAF 3 bn a year. Utilisation of plant capacity never exceeded 50% and the parastatal's deficit had to be financed out of public funds until it was closed down in 1981.

The following factors had come into play:

- delay in site preparation exceeded the contractual period in the original costing of the plant, requiring considerable upward adjustments;
- in the meantime, the value of supplier credits (denominated in DM and Florins) appreciated *vis-à-vis* the CFAF by about 50%;
- the plant's technology was faulty. The absence of a dryer in the steam granulation segment produced frequent congestion, and had to be replaced at higher cost – all to produce a diluted end product;
- its intermediate consumption (principally imported) came to 92% of output value;
- the cost of imported inputs in 1981 was greater than the *landed* price of competing *final products*;

– for some of the products, even their *variable* costs exceeded the duty-paid prices of competing imports;
– the common external UDEAC tariff had zero duties on all fertiliser imports, hence the plant could receive no tariff protection nor enjoy *preferential* access to member countries' markets. This fact sanctioned a direct subsidy out of the presidential extra-budgetary fund.

After the closure, 65% of the cif cost of fertilisers (and of pesticides) continued to be subsidised from this fund. Thanks to this, consumption of fertilisers in Cameroon has expanded by more than 6% a year, even though handling and transport costs add 100% to the cif price.

Mineral oil refining. The only parastatal in the chemicals sub-sector – SONARA – began operating in 1981 and worked for three years at below 50% capacity before the government agreed to cede to it Cameroon crude at a preferential price. After two years, its output of fuel oil reduced the country's import deficit of SITC 332 products by US$132 m. In addition, the quantities of sulphate by-products have been large enough to help improve the chemicals' trade balance. Given the world petroleum situation and Cameroon's limited *known* oil reserves, no cracking unit has been added to the refinery for producing higher value distillates such as kerosene and diesel oil. Nor is any envisaged to the early 1990s.

The natural gas associated with refining has been mostly flared. The substantial proven reserves of *non-associated* natural gas have not begun to be exploited for the manufacture of either ammonia or methane.

In 1986 a bitumen plant of 20,000 tonnes capacity was inaugurated. At least one half of its potential output should be available for export, even with a continued 6% growth rate in the domestic consumption of asphalt.

PHARMACEUTICALS AND PERFUME EXTRACTS

Domestic demand for medicines etc. has been growing fast and their import value doubled between 1977/8 and 1981, when it amounted to over CFAF 10bn. But only one (private) pharmaceutical firm has been established so far – limited to the manufacture of *medicinal herb extracts* and perfusion liquid[9]. This firm's export performance has been outstanding, having jumped from 61 tonnes in 1971 to 790 tonnes in 1983. Medicinal plants are plentiful in Cameroon and provide a good base for further expansion. Also successful has been the manufacture, for both local and regional markets, of perfumery and cosmetics by two private firms (one entirely foreign-owned). Over the 1982–5 period the level of their exports has averaged around 1,800 tonnes.

Soaps and detergents. This group of consumer goods, produced in several modern factories, was hampered in evolving out of import substitution to competitive exporting by the frequent pre-emption of the raw material input by domestic exporters of their chief ingredient – palm oil – on the one hand, and by the establishment of competing plants in most of the neighbouring countries, on the other. The supply constraint on soap manufacturing caused the export quantum to drop from 6,520 tonnes in 1982/3 to 1,942 tonnes in 1984/5. Detergents do not even figure among Cameroon's 15 top-ranking exports of industrial goods.

Plastics. There were 22 different-sized processors of polymers in 1985/6, with a combined capacity of 32,000 tonnes, of which only two-thirds was being exploited[10]. Per capita consumption of plastics (2.6 kg a year) was about one-third of that in near-by Gabon and in North African countries. The principal reason lies in the competition of aluminium and wood as building materials. At current UDEAC rates of consumption, the level of regional demand, even 15 years hence, would not justify – on economic grounds – the production of polystyrene or other base polymers.

PVC extruding and moulding operations have been functioning at about 35% of their rated capacity. A major contributing reason was their inability to satisfy the government's and donors' tendering condition that supply of the products be coupled with their installation. Multinational bidders were reportedly successful because they reduced the prices of materials while inflating the cost of the product. What is puzzling is why domestic contractors failed to invest in broadening their range of services in this respect. Labour productivity is about two-thirds of the European level.

Although all of the inputs of the firms in this branch were imported, several have achieved profitable operations and stable footholds in neighbouring markets. These were characteristically small, modern, well-managed units, adapting their output to narrow or specific segments of demand. In the most successful firm 50% of its output was exported. Another successful unit had polyvalent machinery allowing its output to be customised.

The loss-making producers had the common problems of not being price-competitive with cheaper, *duty-paid* articles from abroad and government's unwillingness to grant them a 'buy local' price differential. The cost of their commercial borrowing (rates of interest of up to 40%) was too burdensome. Administrative approval of price adjustments to reflect their rising costs was too tardy. The absence of rigorous in-plant quality control was another common shortcoming.

NON-METALLIC MINERALS

The manufacture of cement was carried out by a joint venture; the original Italian partner disposed of its shares to the SNI in 1981/2. Production is based on imported clinker plus local limestone and marble, and shared between one large, modern installation in Douala and a small plant near the border with Chad. Not only has import replacement been efficient, but the volume of exports to Chad and other neighbours has *tripled* between 1982/3 and 1984/5. Several plant extensions have taken place to keep up with the growth of building construction. By 1984/5 the combined annual output came to almost one million tons. The activity has been generally profitable and downstream linkages have increased.

The experience of a large parastatal brick and hollow-tile factory, CERICAM, stands out in sharp contrast. Technical and managerial problems proved intractable. It was bailed out of bankruptcy in 1982 with a CFAF 500m. government grant and, after further losses, was closed down for good.

A private firm manufacturing glass tableware and ceramic tiles has done well by broadening its product mix. But its activities were not reflected in reduced levels of imports during the last few years.

Local building material suppliers have often been edged out of large public tenders by foreign contractors who enjoy ready access to credit through their parent companies and/or close ties with foreign banks. Furthermore, as the World Bank's June 1984 Memorandum pointed out (p. 27), no pressure has been exerted by the authorities on foreign contractors to associate with Cameroonian firms, particularly with the small and medium-sized enterprises (SMEs).

A presidential admonition had to be delivered to the public sector (in May 1986) to placate complaints from local contractors about inordinate delays in the settlement of their contractual claims on the administration, causing them serious cash flow problems. In the following month the authorities settled CFAF 50 bn worth of outstanding bills. They explained the delays by the large number of decision-takers involved in processing claims – on average 15 to 20 busy officials.

BASE METALS, FABRICATED METAL PRODUCTS AND MACHINERY

Internal demand for base metals and their fabricated products grew at a 10% rate, approximating that of gross capital formation and considerably higher than GDP growth during the 1972–85 period, to the level of 125,000 tonnes. This yielded a per capita consumption of 18 kg a year of ingot equivalent – slightly below the all-African average (20 kg).

There were four main reasons for this relatively low ratio for a middle-income country. One was the absence of downstream manufacture of heavy agricultural and industrial machinery, transport equipment, and durable consumer goods until quite recently. Secondly, there was the high final price of base metal products; the ex-warehouse prices of base metals were on average 200% of their fob prices, while their retail prices were three times their cif prices. This resulted from duties and border taxes adding 50% to the declared cif price, wholesale and retail margins another 32–45%, and the turnover tax about 10%, plus the cost of inland transport. The third reason was the widespread availability of substitute construction materials such as hardwood and aluminium and the absence of a steel mill. Fourth, the authorised cost-plus distribution margins encouraged the importation of relatively high-priced products.

The processing of imported ingots and billets gave rise to the following structure of base metal intermediates in the early 1980s: long products – 38%, flat products – 15%, piping – 21%, building steel, containers, etc. – 26%.

These covered 75% of domestic demand. Exports of these products in 1984 (free of export tax but limited to UDEAC countries and Chad) constituted a mere 8% of total output. The resulting negative trade balance amounted to more than US$100 m. Import substitution in this branch has not spread beyond the manufacture of steel sheets and strips, cement reinforcing bars, welded pipes, nails and bolts.

Three parastatal firms operated as a group (SCDM) and accounted for some 40% of the sub-sector's output. The largest – SOLADO – producing reinforcing bars, worked to full capacity thanks to quantitative restrictions on competing imports, but its high production costs precluded exporting. A modern, efficiently-run plant, TROPIC, manufactured a wide spectrum of good quality spare parts and agricultural hand tools, but was over-sized even for the whole UDEAC market. A foundry, COFREM, – the third parastatal – manufactured mechanical spare parts and forged implements.

Among private firms, CAMSTEEL was the largest unit, meeting four-fifths of domestic requirements of welded pipe and zinc tubing and 100% of demand for strip steel. Other fabricators of metal intermediates produced scaffolding, boilers, containers, trailers, building steel, wheelbarrows, wagons and chassis, barges, and assembled equipment for off-shore oil platforms and rigs.

The domestic manufacture of machinery and consumer goods still remains embryonic, covering the assembly of bicycles, mopeds and motorcycles, air conditioner housing, electric stoves, ovens and refrigerators, as well as the manufacture of enamelled kitchen-ware.

RAW AND PROCESSED ALUMINIUM, INCLUDING ALLOYS

In contrast to iron and steel manufacturing, Cameroon has a metallurgical base in non-ferrous metals – the alumina smelting plant ALUCAM. It manufactures aluminium ingots from imported Guinean ore and is adjacent to a rolling mill. The primary smelter, employing some 1,300 workers, has been working at near full capacity (82,000 tonnes in 1984) and exporting between 66 and 75% of its output – chiefly to France and Japan. Yet even though it benefits from reduced electricity rates and is well located for ore deliveries, it has made losses during the financial years 1983–7 because of the depressed world price for its output[11] and the dollar-denominated cost of the alumina it purchases. On a per capita basis, Cameroon's consumption of unprocessed aluminium is one of the highest in the Third World. However, the consumption of *processed aluminium products* has been relatively low: 2.8 kg per head in 1980 and 3.1 kg in 1984, as it involved a narrow range of items (corrugated sheets, kitchenware, wire and cable, bars and tubes). Except for thin foil, specialised cables and wire, import substitution of processed aluminium goods has been clear in the trade figures. The nominal tariff protection received by this category of domestic goods was high – averaging 75% *ad valorem*.

As shown in Table 5.7, the level of exports of processed aluminium products has been dropping since the late 1970s in the face of sharpening competition for market shares in Cameroon's traditional foreign outlets, which UDEAC's *taxe unique* privilege could not

Table 5.7 *Exports of raw and processed aluminium products, 1977–84 (tonnes)*

Product/market	1977	1980	1982	1983	1984
Aluminium ingots (all)	20,244	9,708	59,014	52,515	60,998
of which to:					
France	..	9,625	33,088	36,404	..
Japan	..	–	19,765	11,129	..
Sheets, strips, disks	11,240	10,373	8,559	9,208	7,778
of which to:					
Côte d'Ivoire	5,406	5,264	2,536	2,316	..
Cen. Afr. Rep.	1,087	1,336	672	1,031	..
P.R. Congo	161	1,024	33	–	..
Gabon	–	1,079	2,163	3,420	..
Household articles	240	68	83	92	37
Other alumn. goods	35	32	13	19	13

Source: Note Annuelle de Statistique, 1978–1983 and UNIDO data.

offset[12]. Cameroon's exporters of these products found themselves at a disadvantage because of the absence of export financing and of insurance against foreign exchange risks.

The primary smelter and rolling mill, ALUCAM, undertook a CFAF 7 bn investment at the end of the 1970s, the servicing of which became ever more burdensome as interest rates rose. By 1981/2 it owed CFAF 4 bn in bank overdrafts and ended the year with a net CFAF 6.4 bn loss. In the following years rising costs of production and stagnant demand both at home and abroad prevented the firm from improving its performance.

The processing mill – SOCATRAL – was similarly unable to operate profitably during the early 1980s, principally because of lax licensing of competing imports as well as inefficient customs controls over the nature of goods actually entering under licence.

As several SNI *Annual Reports* have pointed out, much remains to be done by aluminium-based manufacturers to trim overheads and their variable costs, which tend to rise steadily even after cuts in their labour force.

The food processing industries

Cameroon's diversified agricultural production provides food processing with a wide and relatively stable base, although periods of drought (as in 1982/3 and again in 1984/5) have caused capacity utilisation to fall significantly. Virtual food self-sufficiency has been reached in recent years, but the high population growth (2.8% per annum) is bound to make its maintenance progressively more difficult.

When lumped with beverages and tobacco, the food sub-sector is the largest manufacturing activity and, in 1975/6, accounted for almost one-half of MVA and one-quarter of total modern sector employment. Subsequently, because of raw materials supply constraints, this strong growth decelerated, but the workforce in 1985 still made up about 8% of manufacturing employment and its value added more than 11% of MVA. There was only a small increment in employment and a large rise in capital assets per employee.

During the early period, 1969–75, most of the increase in processed food output was absorbed by domestic consumption, not exports. But thereafter, food products' share in total exports rose to almost three-quarters in 1978, to drop to 33% in 1982, again because of supply-side bottlenecks. The 1984/5 structure of domestically-produced raw materials for the local food industries and for export are given in Table 5.8, along with estimated deficit ratios (domestic output to apparent consumption).

Although the target of food self-sufficiency may be within reach, the figures in Table 5.8 point to the relative paucity of food processing in Cameroon. Several such activities have been given priority in successive five-year plans without the necessary investment being mobilised. The absence of secondary processing of fish and crustaceans is particularly regrettable in view of the very derivation of the country's name (Portuguese: *camaroes*) and the remunerative fishing operations of several coastal states in surrounding waters.

The total number of fishing craft has fallen in recent years, and the volume of maritime industrial fishery output has shrunk by two-thirds. Although shrimp output has improved over the four years 1983–7, import dependence in all fish products has become more pronounced. The tonnage of imported frozen fish products rose from 17,000 to over 20,000 tonnes between 1975/6 and 1982/3. An international agreement to regulate fishing rights in off-shore waters is urgently needed in view of the inadequacy of the in-shore fishing potential.

Another major gap is in cassava processing and in fruit-based products. Furthermore, exports of cocoa-based food products have wavered between 12,000 and 24,000 tonnes during the early 1980s without any apparent growth trend, while raw cocoa bean exports roughly doubled between 1977 and 1984. There is also an obvious import-substitution potential in the fabrication of animal fodder from the many by-products of existing primary processing activities.

Import substitution in the meat, dairy and fish sector has been disappointing. The Fifth Plan (1980–85) had targeted a reduction of import dependence in terms of per capita meat equivalents. The out-turn, however, showed a *rise* from 2.7 to 4.4 kg per person per year. By 1984/5, imports made up 14% of apparent consumption of all animal food products (see Table 5.9).

Production growth in food-based industries (ISIC 311) accelerated at the beginning of the

Table 5.8 *Production (10³ tons in 1984/5) & 1983 deficits (%) of raw food products*

Product	Quantity	Deficit	Remarks
CEREALS			
Millet/sorghum	207	41.6%	subsistence production
Maize	410	24.0%	7% in modern sector
Paddy	111	..	processing & importation
STARCHY FOODS			
Macabo-taro	188	64.5%	no processing activity
Cassava	1,375	surplus	(> 700,000 T) planned proc.
Yams	96	..	no processing
Sweet potatoes	50	62.0%	no processing
Irish potatoes	42	64.0%	no processing
Plantain	1,001	..	no processing
LEGUMES		43.2%	
Groundnuts	99	..	crushing for oil
Beans & peas	70	..	one canning plant
Sesame seed	13	..	
Courge seeds	56	..	
FRUITS & VEGETABLES	..	surplus	
Bananas	703	surplus	(> 340,000 T)
Pineapple	32	..	small juice factory
Other fruit	23	..	
Vegetables	185	44.6%	
VEGETABLE OILS		51.0%	
Palm oil	82	surplus	5 mills & plantations
Cotton-seed oil	10	..	3 crushers & 1 refinery
INDUSTRIAL CROPS	..	surplus	
Sugar cane	71	6.3% (1984)	SOSUCAM refinery
Cocoa	120	surplus	processing up to choc.
Coffee Arab. & Rob.	139(?)	surplus	processing started
Tea	2.3	..	3 CDC factories
ANIMAL PRODUCTS			
Cattle (meat equiv.)	91)		2 abattoirs, 1 tannery
Small ruminants	16)	26.0%	processing planned
Pork	19)		processing planned
Poultry	11)		
(TOTAL)	(137)	(95.0%)	(1984/5 imports 8,000 T)
Game etc.	26	..	
Milk & eggs	15	..	processing by 2 plants
Fish & shrimps	115	..	freezing only; + imports

Source: *Sixth Plan* and UNIDO data.

Note: .. data unavailable.

Table 5.9 *Consumption of animal products by origin, 1984/5 (kg per person per year of meat equivalent)*

Year	National output						Import	Apparent Consum.
	Cattle	Goats	Pigs	Poultry	Fish	Other		
1984/5	9.3	1.6	1.9	1.2	9.0	4.2	4.5	31.7

Source: *Sixth Plan*, p. 86.

1980s thanks to new capacities in grain and vegetable processing, as well as in 'other' food fabrication as shown in Table 5.10.

During the 1970s, the annual growth rate of MVA in food processing was 6% and that of employment under 2%. In 1980–84, MVA in food manufacturing just about doubled its past rate of growth, while the level of employment dropped in absolute terms. The acceleration in

Table 5.10 *Output index of food processing industries (1974/5 = 100)*

Process. Activity	1976/7	1980/1	1983/4	1984/5
Grains & vegetables	142	168	240	288
Industrial food crops	105	267	197	229
Bakeries & confectionery	82	121	150	..
Other foods	188	650	1,723	..

Source: Sixth Plan, pp. 128-9.

Note: .. not available.

output growth reflected particularly good returns on capital. The newly created industries processed agro-pastoral products as well as fruit – producing some yeast and alcohol, cereal foods and canned pineapples. Product diversification and reduced import-dependence are reflected in the drop of 'other' foods imports between 1982 and 1985 from 4,103 tonnes to 2,604 tonnes.

This development stands in sharp contrast with imports of refined sugar which, notwithstanding the existence in Cameroon of three refineries, sky-rocketed in 1984/5 to 14,487 tonnes. Much of this was re-exported to UDEAC and other neighbours, however.

A noteworthy fact is the far lower use of fertilisers in food crops than in industrial ones. The two ratios in 1984 were about 1: 6 kg per farm per year. Traditionally produced foodstuffs continued to be plagued by:

- inadequate transport and cool storage facilities, and the irregular supply of domestic raw materials to industries and to marketing centres;
- the absence of industrial-scale primary producing units (except for palm oil, sugar and wheat);
- an unstructured internal marketing network, giving rise to severe price distortions and periods of glut and scarcity with large, uncontrolled shifts of regional surpluses triggered by unco-ordinated cross-border prices;
- the frequent differences between real costs and the authorised market prices of processed goods:
- inefficient protection of domestic industries;
- poor control over the quality of marketed products;
- absence or scarcity of vocational training e.g. in baking, butchering etc., giving rise *inter alia* to misuse of machinery;
- the small size of the domestic market in terms of effective purchasing power, and the relatively high unit cost of transporting foodstuffs to neighbouring markets;
- no complementarity in food import substitution between UDEAC member states.

Production of industrial crops, as well as of processed foods – whether domestically-oriented or exported – is to a great extent controlled by the SNI through minority shareholdings. Considering only *secondary* food industries, the following picture emerges of parastatal activities during two recent years – 1981/2 (in brackets) and 1984/5:

- SIC-CACAOS and CHOCOCAM started to turn in profits. They employed over 500 workers in 1984/5 (800 three years earlier). Their combined turnover was CFAF 17.4 bn (11.4 bn) and their value added came to CFAF 3.8 bn (2.0 bn) equal, in 1984/5, to their total medium- and long-term debt. That same year fiscal payments made up 100% of value added so that the other constituents of VA had to come out of carried-over provisions and profits. In 1981/2 bank charges added up to two-thirds of value added. Existing price controls prevented the firms from passing the additional costs on to domestic consumers. Cashflow in 1984/5 was positive at about 10% of turnover (only 5% in 1981/2). Cost and quality controls have been their Achilles' heel in recent years.
- SCM comprised flour mills and has recently been making losses, primarily because of tightly fixed bread prices[13], on the one hand, and unwarranted imports of EC (subsidised) flour, on the other. Thus, in 1981/2 imports covered three-quarters of national consumption, leaving the flour mills with demand requiring the use of only one-half of their installed capacity. Capacity utilisation in 1984/5 was only a little higher (65%) and in 1985/6 flour imports came to 122,000 tonnes, allowing only 45% of the *newly-extended*

domestic capacity to be exploited. The mills carried out sharp cuts in their personnel in the five years to 1987, raising their capital intensity and value added per employee. Working capital has been very inadequate throughout. The ratio of value added to turnover was 15% in 1981/2 and only 10% four years later. The level of medium- and long-term debt came to 8% of turnover in 1984/5, having been close to 20% in 1981/2.

CAMLAIT offers a not untypical example of the structure and operation of a private, profitable, food processing SME, enjoying the attendant fiscal privileges but lacking easy access to bank credit. The company's output covers a full range of dairy products and milk-based desserts. Its value added coefficient in 1985/6 was 28.5% of which salaries added up to 42%, before-tax profits came to one-fifth, taxes to merely 3%, bank charges to 11% and amortisation to one quarter of turnover. The tax rate on profits that year was just over 50%. Although its sales were limited to the domestic market, less than one-twentieth of its intermediate requirements were direct imports, pointing to very substantial linkages with other domestic activities. This topic is considered across all manufacturing sub-sectors in the following section.

Linkages and efficiency

Inter-sectoral linkages.   The data on which the following discussion is based do not permit comprehensive and detailed treatment. The only attempt at putting together an input/output table resulted in an unofficial document of the Ministry of Planning for which no technical descriptions could be located by the author. The table covers 8 productive sectors, plus construction, commercial and non-commercial services. As with many other SSA countries' input/output exercises, intermediate consumption is not differentiated at the sectoral level between imported and domestically produced goods and services, since few firms make such a distinction in their own accounts. The values in the table are at factor cost.

Data on intermediate consumption at a disaggregated level for a sample of 18 manu-facturing firms were also made available to the author in the course of interviews. Although an industrial census had been carried out in Cameroon in 1985/6, the raw data had not been processed or checked by May 1987 for lack of resources within the Directorate of Statistics and National Accounts.

The input/output table for 1979/80 shows that, for the economy as a whole, only one-quarter of intermediate consumption was accounted for by *direct* imports of goods and services and the value added coefficient stood at about two-thirds of the value of output. The structure of intermediate consumption, according to the sectoral breakdown used for the above-mentioned input/output exercise, is set out in Table 5.11.

Given its high level of aggregation, there is little in Table 5.11 that distinguishes the Cameroonian economy from the typical African middle-income case. In 1979/80, the share

Table 5.11 *Structure of intermediate consumption in industry, 1979/80 (% of output value)*

SECTORS	Manufacturing sub-sectors					
	1	2	3	4	5	6
Primary agriculture	41.7	2.5	4.0	–	–	–
Industry, of which:						
1 Food processing	4.5	2.2	0.6	–	–	–
2 Consumer goods manuf.	0.0	10.6	0.6	–	–	–
3 Intermed. goods manuf.	5.8	16.7	33.2	30.9	5.7	29.1
4 Cement & metal fabri.	16.5	9.9	7.6	45.0	40.7	35.6
5 Capital goods & equip.	0.1	2.5	7.5	3.5	18.2	5.2
6 Construction	14.8	3.4	7.0	0.0	0.0	2.7
Services (commercial)[a]	15.1	51.5	31.9	19.6	35.1	26.6
Services (non-commercial)	0.1	0.1	1.3	0.1	0.0	0.1
TOTAL INTERMED. CONSUM.	100	100	100	100	100	100
of which domestic inputs	62	39	39	28	–	52

Source: Author's calculations based on Cameroon's input/output table.

Note: [a] Including transport and communications.

of imported inputs was lowest in the *food processing* sector, with over 40% of all inputs coming from primary agriculture. The bulk of capital and intermediate inputs was acquired through the commercial network, whose share of deliveries was about the same as those of cement and metal manufactures, and of construction. Over one-half of *consumer goods* supplies came through distribution services, about two-thirds of whose intermediate purchases were imported goods and services. Direct procurement of intermediate goods came to about 17% of all consumer goods inputs, and that of intra-sectoral purchases around 11%.

The intermediate goods sector acquired as many direct inputs from *within* the sector as from local traders (32%). These, on average, purchased 36% of their total requirements from abroad. The balance of inputs needed by the sector (around 22%) was evenly spread over cement and metals, capital goods, and construction. As could be expected, neither of the remaining three sectors made *direct* purchases of primary agricultural products, processed foods or consumer goods. The bulk (45%) of the intermediate needs of the *cement and metals fabrication* sector was met by intra-sectoral purchases, followed by 31% of inputs from direct deliveries by the capital goods and equipment manufacturing sector. Only one-fifth of its total intermediate consumption was serviced by local traders, making it almost as import-*independent* as food processing.

The *capital goods and equipment sector's* intermediate consumption structure showed that two-thirds of inputs came from only 3 producing sectors. As with the foregoing sector, it carried out almost all of its construction work by its own means.

These findings suggest that the three activities with the greatest *direct* multiplier effects on the Cameroonian economy in 1979/80 were food processing, cement and metals manufacturing, and construction. The 18-firm sample data for 1985/6 on *direct* procurement of intermediate inputs confirm the view that resource-based manufacturing activities are strategically the most important for advancing industrialisation in countries with endowments similar to those of Cameroon. The sample enterprises are ranked in Table 5.12 according to the intensity of direct domestic procurement of intermediate industrial inputs, including electricity and water. Because the output of the local refinery does not extend to fuel and lubricants, domestic purchases of these items are treated as direct imports.

The following are the salient features of the sample firms' procurement profiles. For *dairy products* (ISIC 311/2), intermediate inputs were almost entirely (93.6%) of domestic origin, with milk, sugar and plastic containers accounting for 70% of the total, followed by locally produced bottles and aluminium strips. The firm's operations were profitable. Added value came to 28.5% of sales. Two *textile-based*, household goods manufacturers (ISIC 321) had distinctly different procurement patterns. For *blankets and bed linen*, almost 90% of inputs

Table 5.12 *Intensity of direct input procurement, 1985/6 in a sample of 18 manufacturing firms (%)*

ISIC	Products	Value Added	Main Domestic Inputs	Domestic input share	Export share
311/2	Dairy produce	28	milk, sugar, plastics	94	nil
321	Blankets, bed linen	29	packaging materl., yarn, thread	11	4
332	Wood furniture	33	timber, paint, synth. sponge	98	nil
352	Soap, detergent	36	palm oil, kernels, packing mat.	43	19
352	Matches	40	timber, proc. wood, packing mat.	37	..
355	Tyres	42	latex, veget. oil, cartons	31	23
356	Plastics	44	chemicals, tools, apparel etc.	11	2
356	Plastics	42	spare parts, chemicals etc.	22	nil
362	Glassware	43	sand, clay, spares, apparel	19	6
369	Reinf. Concrete	19	cement, sand, gravel, steel bars	92	nil
369	Cement	27	packing mat. pouzzolane, spares	30	1
372	Alum. houseware	34	alum. disks & sheets, packing	85	11
372	Alum. processing	14	alum. sheet, chemicals, packing	98	35
381	Agric. handtools	32	iron & steel semis, paint, spare parts	13	6
383	Batteries	22	paper & cartons, chemicals	22	69
383	Electr. assembly	18	nil	0	5
384	Transp. equipment	29	iron & steel semis, hardware	98	nil
390	Household goods	61	packing mat. enamel, metals	11	3

Source: Interview information and UNIDO.

were imported, of which 60% were yarn and sewing supplies. Another 36% was in imported cloth. These items are probably good candidates for early import substitution. The local purchases were concentrated on packaging material (33%), thread and yarn (19%), sewing accessories (12%), with the balance of inputs undefined. Only 3.6% of output was exported and solely to UDEAC markets. The manufacture of *mattresses and canvas covering*, in contrast, filled 95% of its input requirements from domestic supplies: about one-half from the textiles sub-sector, one-fifth from plastics, and one-tenth from local metal fabricators. The final quarter comprised unidentified local goods. One-quarter of total sales were in UDEAC countries.

All intermediate inputs of the only large *furniture* manufacturer (ISIC 332) in the sample, except for fuels and lubricants, were domestically produced. Raw timber made up over 40% of the total, while the other inputs were spread over some 10 sub-sectors, with heavier purchases of paint, synthetic foam and items produced by others in the woodworking sub-sector. Hence the multiplier effects of wooden furniture-making in Cameroon are very considerable, with value added coming to 33% of sales. The firm had no exports in 1985/6 and its pre-tax profit was small.

Upstream linkages of one sampled firm manufacturing *soaps, oils, and detergents* (ISIC 352) were neither strong nor varied, although its by-products were sold as cattle cake to domestic animal husbandry. The enterprise was resource-based – palm oil and kernels making up about three-quarters of all domestic inputs. Yet more than one-half of *total* inputs were imported, with high shares occupied by animal fats (43.4%), chemicals required for soap-making (43.2%) and packaging materials (9%). This relatively high import-dependency points to other import-substituting opportunities, at least in the last-mentioned products, small amounts of which were already being purchased locally by the firm (about 10% of total domestic inputs). Almost one-fifth of output in 1985/6 was disposed of in UDEAC and other neighbouring markets.

The manufacture of *matches* (ISIC 352) was mainly aimed at satisfying domestic demand and was based on local raw and processed timber (58%), domestic packing materials, tyres and spare parts. These and other minor inputs came to 40% of total intermediate consumption. Value added comprised a similar proportion of output. Heavy imports of match-boxes invite a possible import-substituting investment.

Less than one-third of total inputs for the manufacture of *tyres (ISIC 355)* originated in Cameroon and were dominated by purchases of natural rubber, vegetable oils, cartons and boxes. The value added in this activity was 42% and exports to neighbouring countries (exclusively) made up 23% of final sales. The two *plastic goods (ISIC 356)* manufacturers met 11 and 22% of their respective intermediate requirements from local goods. Both generated high (40% plus) added value, with little or no exports. The domestic purchases included chemicals, hand-tools, cover-alls and spare parts. Both were heavy users of electricity and water. *Glassmaking (ISIC 362)* was also heavily import-dependent, notwithstanding the availability of local mineral resources, which made up about one-third of all local purchases, followed by spare parts (19%). The activity also made heavy use of public utilities (41% of all domestic inputs). Exports (6% of sales) did not go beyond the UDEAC area. The value added ratio was high – 43.5%.

Two *non-metallic minerals producers (ISIC 369)* had quite different input profiles by virtue of being at two levels of the processing chain. The *cement manufacturer* procured only 30% of total inputs from domestic sources, as its major input – clinker – had to be imported. Domestic links were with producers of lined bags, pouzzolane, spare parts, hardware and electricity. Only 1% of output was exported – all to Chad. The production of *reinforced concrete items*, on the other hand, was a large downstream consumer of local cement, gravel, sand and iron/steel rods. Most of its minor inputs were also manufactured locally, raising the share of domestically procured inputs to 92%. Value added was relatively low (19%) and no exports were made in 1985/6. A similar situation prevailed in respect of two aluminium-based firms *(ISIC 372 – non-ferrous metals fabrication)*. The upstream *processor of primary aluminium* had a small value added coefficient, exported over one-third of its output and only imported some chemicals, fuel and lubricants, leaving local products to meet 98% of its intermediate needs. The manufacturer of *aluminium utensils* etc. had a much higher value added (34%), but exported only 11% of its output. Its inputs were dominated by local aluminium semis (such as disks) and packaging material.

The production of *agricultural hand tools (ISIC 381)* was highly import-dependent as domestic inputs constituted a mere 13% of the total. However, they were widely distributed among manufacturing sub-sectors and public utilities. Added value reached almost 32% of turnover, only 6% of which came from sales abroad (UDEAC). *Electric battery* manufacture (ISIC 383), although as import-dependent (only 12% of all inputs procured in Cameroon), was able to export 69.2% of its output to several markets other than the UDEAC. Local purchases were confined mainly to paper-based items and packaging materials, plus some chemicals. The value added coefficient was 22%. Within the same ISIC category, but limited to *electronic assembly*, another firm recorded no locally purchased inputs whatsoever (except for electricity). Its value added came to 18.3% and exports to about 5% of turnover. *The metal products fabricating sub-sector* (ISIC 384) was represented in the sample by the manufacture of simple transport equipment, chassis etc., situated well downstream of existing industries which could supply it with all but fuel and lubricant inputs. Value added came to 29.5% of sales, which were limited to the domestic market, although in previous years small quantities had been exported.

The last of the sample firms – manufacturing household goods *(ISIC 390 – other manufactures)* – was also very import-dependent. Locally produced inputs made up only 10.5% of its intermediate consumption, heavily weighted by enamel supplies and packaging materials. The variety of its imported intermediates, for example, handles, metal sheeting and some articles similar to locally made ones, again present scope for substitution. The firm's value added coefficient was the highest in the sample – 66.3%.

EFFICIENCY

The review of sectoral and firm linkages and their direct multiplier potential concluded that domestic resource processing offered the best leverage for furthering industrialisation in Cameroon *within the existing policy and institutional framework*. It also detailed the generally poor competitiveness of Cameroon's manufactures, as reflected in the fall of the share of all manufactures, that is, including semi-processed goods, in total exports from about 20% in the late 1960s to below 10% in the early 1980s.

The first of these findings is consistent with those concerning changes in relative labour productivity in manufacturing in a recent study on Cameroon by UNIDO[14]. The five highest performance ratings (expected productivity gains/observed ones) were in the following order: processing of non-ferrous metals; processing and fabricating wood products; food processing and, finally, leather processing and fabrication.

An earlier comparison of ex-factory prices of a sample of manufactured Cameroonian products with those of duty-paid competing imports concluded affirmatively as to the economic efficiency of such food and drink industries as chocolate and pasta making, and beer brewing. These items were frequently sold at *less* than the maximum prices allowed by the tariffs so as to face up to the competition of contraband supplies. The prevailing incentive (protective) regime provided only negligible support to many other resource-based processing activities and, in the case of frozen shrimps, penalised their manufacture by taxes on inputs and exports. The studies of the incentive system carried out for the World Bank in 1977–80 concluded that the relatively greatest material and financial encouragements were being received by the *most import-dependent* manufacturing activities but these still failed to help them win or even maintain market shares abroad.

It is important to note that the protective/incentive regime has not changed significantly from the time of independence in 1960, save that the Investment Code of 1986 extended customs and fiscal advantages to SMEs. New investment continues to be provided with exemptions from import duties on capital and intermediate inputs, tax holidays on profits and other tax 'breaks'. Upon the expiry of the franchises, enterprises usually receive 'regional *taxe unique* status' under which tariff exemptions are *not time-bound*. More importantly, quantitative restrictions on competing imports – *when correctly applied* – provide industries with 'tailor-made' protection. The net effect of the prevailing regime still encourages import substitution at a substantially high cost to the taxpayer. Over time, the protective system must have acted to the detriment of the efficient use of resources in manufacturing and of the competitiveness of Cameroonian products by encouraging the use of up-market, capital-intensive technology in mainly inwardly-oriented activities[15].

Several food industries were found to have been efficient in the late 1970s, in the sense that the domestic resource costs of their products were less than the benefits in terms of the foreign exchange saved (earned) by their activities. Direct resource cost coefficients (DRCs),

Table 5.13 *Domestic resource cost coefficients (DRCs) of sampled manufacturing activities in 1975/6*[a]

Sub-sector & product	DRC
Food processing:	
– wheat flour	negative
– cocoa butter (for export)	1.03
– chocolate for the UDEAC market	0.50
– pasta for domestic & UDEAC sale	0.27
– frozen shrimps for export	0.65
Beverages:	
– beer for domestic sales	0.17–0.19
Textiles:	
– cotton goods for export	1.97
– cement bags for domestic sale	1.36
– jute sacking	negative
Chemicals:	
– soap for the UDEAC market	0.89
– matches for the UDEAC market	0.85
– fertilisers	negative
– flashlight batteries for export	1.53
Non-metallic mineral products:	
– cement (for South Cameroon)	0.14
– cement (for North Cameroon)	0.83
Base metal products:	
– steel reinforcing rods	negative
Fabricated metal products:	
– agricultural tools for export	0.75
Other manufactures:	
– assembly of radios & appliances	negative

Source: World Bank (1984: Table 4 and references).

Note: [a] For a definition of DRCs, see Note 16. These values were based on the capacity levels then being utilised and subsumed a shadow wage rate equal to 3/4 of the going one, and an 11% discount rate as the opportunity cost of capital.

calculated for the World Bank[16], pointed to efficient operations in frozen shrimps, pasta, chocolate, beer, soft drinks and cocoa butter – provided their capacity utilisation could reach acceptable levels. The major exception in the sampled food and beverage industries was flour milling, whose operations resulted in *net foreign exchange losses* (negative value added and DRC). As we have seen, the industry was also financially insolvent during the early 1980s.

At the other end of the efficiency spectrum are a number of import-dependent and/or capital-intensive industries. Those for which DRC values have been estimated include some textile manufacturing and the production of cement bags and flashlight batteries, all of whose DRCs in 1975/6 were above 1.3, that is, they were on the borderline of inefficiency (See Table 5.13). Those with a negative value added and DRC – hence patently wasteful of productive resources – included wheat flour, jute bags, fertilisers, reinforcing bars and the assembly of electronic goods, whose handicaps and inefficiencies have been noted earlier.

The deepening economic and financial crisis

Thanks to the steady expansion of oil output and in spite of the serious drought of 1982/3 which adversely affected the agricultural sector, the economy grew at a very healthy average annual rate of over 10% in real terms over the 1979–85 period[17] (see Table 5.A5). Manufacturing and utilities provided a powerful impetus, growing very strongly between 1980 and 1982 and contributing to an average growth rate of 7.8% of non-oil real GDP from 1980/81 to 1984/5. Thus, in the quinquennium that preceded the onset of the 1985/6 recession, the share in GDP of the manufacturing sector rose from 8.8 to 11%, largely at the expense of agriculture.

The recession which started in 1985/6 resulted principally from the fall of commodity prices on world markets. The average petroleum price per barrel in dollar terms dropped by

21% and that of cocoa, cotton and rubber by 23%, 35 and 17% respectively (see Table 5.A8). In 1986/7, all the country's major agricultural exports, except tobacco, saw their world prices fall by substantial proportions: cocoa by 22%, Arabica and Robusta coffee by 34%, cotton by 23%, rubber by 3%, while the average dollar price of Cameroon petroleum in 1986/7 was 32% lower than that of the previous year[18]. Unofficial estimates of GDP indicate negative growth of 8% for 1987, followed by a staggering 20% fall in 1988. Since the Franc/dollar rate also slumped[19], disposable income and import capacity were reduced by significant amounts, particularly as there was no offsetting rise in external aid flows or direct foreign investment.

Government revenue suffered not only from stagnating oil royalties and falling tax liabilities of oil company profits, but also from the reduction in the government's share of the public oil company's pre-tax revenue which, in the years prior to 1985/6, went into extra-budgetary reserves earmarked mainly for social and infrastructural projects, although they were also reportedly for operational subsidies of public sector enterprises[20]. This monetary cushion – estimated to have amounted to about one-quarter of budget revenue – disappeared during 1986/7. A very sharp cut in public sector investment outlays followed, aggravated by a fall in private capital spending.

A further negative factor was the persistence of liquidity shortages in the banking system, burdened as it was with bad debts which became more serious as Treasury and public enterprise deposits shrank. The foreign assets of commercial banks (estimated at about CFAF 170 bn in mid-1985) began to be repatriated in massive amounts to meet the private sector's *expanding* demand for credit to cover poorly-performing past investment decisions and to compensate for inordinate delays in the settlement of outstanding claims on the public sector. In parallel, demand and time deposits declined by as much as CFAF 138 bn between 1985 and 1987, when total money supply was 12% below its previous level.

These developments were mirrored in the overall decline in the external reserves from a peak of over CFAF 200 bn in 1985 to only 64 bn in 1987 and in the rise of the Central Bank's (BEAC's) external liabilities. Not only did oil-related receipts shrink by some CFAF 200 bn in the financial year 1986/7, but other non-tax revenues also fell significantly, resulting in an overall 28% drop in total revenue. Although current public expenditure was cut, investment outlays – many related to development projects in the pipeline – continued to expand and led to a record deficit amounting to over CFAF 400 bn or about 9% of estimated 1986/7 GDP. This was financed by a hefty increase in domestic debt (commercial arrears mainly) and by Central Bank advances[21].

The austerity budget for FY 1987/8 reduced development outlays by as much as 58% from the previous year's level and operating expenditure by 13% – including cuts in the wage bill, subsidies and other transfers[22]. The brunt of these economies was to be borne by the transport and service sectors. Indeed, this was to be the first instalment of a four-year stabilisation programme whose objectives were: i) to keep current public expenditure within budgetary receipts; ii) to bring the budget deficit down to 6.5% of GDP; iii) to reduce total public debt service to 25% of budget revenue by 1991/2.

These targets were to be achieved by the following measures: tighter budgetary discipline (including sanctions) and closer monitoring; the immediate suspension of non-budgeted expenditure and the proscription of additional domestic and foreign arrears; improved vetting of new development projects and expediting performance reviews of all public sector enterprises. No measures, however, were announced to cope with the serious problem of insolvency of the domestic banking system. In prosperous years government finances supported the banks' liquidity out of budget surpluses and the savings of a few efficient parastatals. These deposits (of unstated duration) in the commercial banks camouflaged the latter's *technical* insolvency, stemming from the accumulation of non-performing assets – loans extended for poorly evaluated projects. In 1986 the value of bad debts was six times that of corresponding provisions and at least four times the commercial banks' capitalisation[23]. Nothing was done after 1986 to lighten the direct tax borne by the banks, earmarked for the public holding company (SNI) and for the small industries' credit guarantee agency (FOGAPE). Nor was lending made more profitable by waiving the tax component of the banks' already narrow statutory margins. Likewise, taxes on most deposit instruments – whose effect was to reduce real rates of interest – remained intact.

Heavy bank withdrawals by private companies and individuals in 1987 accentuated the banks' lack of liquidity and the expected (seasonal) reconstitution of private bank deposits failed to occur at the year's end. The positive (CFAF 43 bn) 1985 credit balance of the commercial banks switched to a CFAF 8 bn deficit by the end of the following year and increased rapidly in 1987. As of September of that year payments of private and public sector arrears – amounting to about CFAF 200 bn – were suspended; the repatriation of external assets (begun in 1986) dwindled, obliging the banks to increase their external indebtedness to meet current claims. With the private sector in a state of 'suspended animation' and the public sector no longer the propelling force, a generalised economic crisis set in. In the second half of 1987 import volume was some 18% below that of the previous year.

The ensuing downward spiral was characterised by a 30% fall in total domestic demand, an 8% reduction in the volume of money (M_2), and by the draw-down of two-thirds of all external assets. Even Cameroon's perennial credit position in France's Operations Account switched in January 1987 to a deficit that rose progressively. The Treasury's withdrawal of some CFAF 100 bn from commercial banks during 1987, in the face of a 13% expansion of domestic credit, sharpened the banks' liquidity problem and their external borrowing doubled in value. The building and construction sector was the worst to suffer with a 75% fall in activity in 1987. New car and truck sales contracted by between 40 and 50%. The volume of retail trade shrank by 40% and even the historically buoyant output of the breweries slumped.

The 1987/8 Budget cuts of 13% in current and 26% in development expenditures still left a deficit amounting to over CFAF 400 bn, the financing of which would raise public debt by about one-half[24]. It was in such circumstances that France was approached for debt rescheduling, and negotiations began with the IMF and the World Bank on assistance in support of the adjustment measures initiated in 1988. These included higher domestic prices on petroleum products, beer and soft drinks (estimated to bring in CFAF 30 bn) as well as a modest rise in the Central Bank's discount rates, but all of which still left the Treasury with a deficit of CFAF 210 bn for the year 1987/8. The results of the negotiations became public soon after the presidential and legislative elections of April 1988. The main proposal was a massive injection of external resources and debt reschedulings through the London and Paris Clubs, coupled with far-reaching institutional reforms, the privatisation of many public enterprises and the dissolution of some 'basket cases'[25].

As export earnings declined during 1986, the government elaborated an interim, four-year, stabilisation programme aimed at restoring internal and external equilibrium and reconstituting budgetary savings. Current expenditure was to be limited to budgetary receipts, the budget deficit cut by three-quarters and the ratio of public debt service, including arrears, to one-quarter of budget revenue. In line with this programme, the 1987/8 budget was cut by CFAF 412 bn, involving both operating and capital expenditure. However, these measures – in isolation – could not be counted upon to re-invigorate the economy and certainly not to bring about the deep structural changes that were called for as a result of declining oil revenues. They did, however, demonstrate the government's readiness to undertake radical measures in the general direction of policy recommendations urged upon it by the donor community.

INDUSTRIAL ACTIVITIES IN THE FACE OF RECESSION

What were the sectoral effects of the financial and economic crisis? Did manufacturing show any resilience to the slump by shifting sales to external markets? Had import substitution deepened in recent years and the processing of local primary products made further headway? These are some of the questions addressed in this section, which concludes with a critical look at the assumptions underlying the draft master plan for industrial development to the year 2000 (DPI).

The enviable rate of GDP growth during the 1979–85 period was propelled by petroleum extraction and primary refining, the other two dynamic sectors being manufacturing – with an average annual growth of 15.3% – and building-cum-public works (14.6%) (see Tables 5.A6 and 5.A7). The strong performance of these three sectors more than offset the contraction (– 15% in volume) of agricultural output as a result of the 1983 drought and its aftermath[26]. In the three years preceding the onset of the recession, the largest gains were recorded in the manufacture of beverages, cigarettes, sugar, soap and building materials (see Table 5.A9).

The last full year covered by the official index of industrial production (1974/5 = 100) was FY 1985/6 when growth of only 4.4% was recorded. 70% of industrial sub-sectors recorded some expansion; the remaining 30% contracted, the severest falls being recorded in industrial fishing (− 57%); grain and oilseed milling (− 33.5%); textiles and clothing (− 16.7%); chemicals and rubber (− 15.5%); forestry and woodworking (− 12.4%).

As no official industrial statistics covering the more recent period were available at the time of writing, evidence of the recession's sub-sectoral effects during 1986 and 1987 must be deduced from three particular sources. First, indirect indices, covering the consumption by the manufacturing sector of electricity, gas and packaging materials during 1987, and the volume of cargo handled in the country's main port – Douala. Second, reports on their overall activity to the industrial association SYNDUSTRICAM by a representative sample of 104 member enterprises and, third, from volume trends in external trade data.

In general, the figures from these sources suggest only a moderate decline in manufacturing activity during calendar years 1986 and 1987. They point to the sector's relative resilience to a steadily deteriorating macroeconomic environment, which is largely ascribable to the government's deficit financing and the commercial banks' continuing expansion of credit to the private sector.

There was no apparent change in the trend of power supply to the sector between 1986 and 1987. The consumption of industrial gas in 1987 showed only a marginal decline from the previous year's levels; that of *plastic* containers and packaging – a fall of 20% year-on-year, but there was a more pronounced fall in the volume of paper-board packaging used.

For the first nine months of 1987 total pre-tax turnover of the 104 sample firms was only 13.5% below that for the corresponding 1986 period; their wage bill was a mere 7.5% lower, and employment about 6% less. However, their total export sales were 21.5% lower – the fall mainly due to *a 47% shrinkage in their exports to neighbouring, preferential UDEAC markets* which were likewise in recession.

As mentioned earlier, the sector which suffered most in 1987 was building and construction (− 80%). In manufacturing, the broadly-defined chemicals sub-sector (plastics, rubber, petroleum refining) registered a 30.5% fall in activity, followed by food processing (− 23%) base metals processing (− 21%), and consumer semi-durables (− 17%).

. Data on external trade were not available beyond calendar year 1986. They show that exports of all non-primary goods (but inclusive of logs and of primary aluminium) were only 3% lower than in 1985. Among exported semi-manufactures, the tonnage of worked timber products (sawn wood, railway ties, veneers, building timber) was 46% of the previous year's level and that of aluminium ingots and scrap 82%, but ginned cotton tonnage was more than double the 1985 figure. The volume of manufactured aluminium exports, principally to neighbouring African markets, was also lower in 1986 – by 32.5% relative to the previous year when the London Metal Exchange (LME) average price of the metal was almost one-fifth higher. Cotton textile sales abroad were some 15% lower in quantity and in value. The exports of other manufactured goods during the last three years for which data were available are set out in Table 5.14:

Table 5.14 *Exports of principal manufactured goods, 1984-6 (metric tonnes & CFAF m.)*

	1984		1985		1986	
	Quantity	Value	Quantity	Value	Quantity	Value
Roasted coffee	1,291	836	1,233	918	2,649	1,815
Hydraulic cement a	3,277	176	18,333	437	6,148	262
Perfume, cosmetics	1,727	1,917	2,700	2,890	2,377	2,996
Paints	287	212	381	278	318	241
Refined sugar a	3,308	473	144	33	19,017	948
Clothing & access.	29	110	128	116	33	95
Soaps	3,754	1,361	3,471	1,421	5,323	2,224
Leather travel goods	76	165	66	180	83	228
Beer	2,648	1,281	4,292	2,282	5,989	2,174
Shoes & parts	134	207	209	407	81	168
Matches	649	407	779	687	1,334	1,244
Linen, table & bed	219	777	222	811	150	526
Batteries	8,529	5,805	10,409	7,457	12,580	9,504

Source: Ministry of Planning & Regional Development and GICAM.

Note: a Much of the cement and sugar were re-exports.

All the major foreign-exchange earning manufactures maintained or enlarged their market shares during the start of the recession. The support provided by exports was substantial, particularly as regards the production of batteries, soaps, matches, perfumes and cosmetics. The recession only began to make itself felt on the level of imports towards the end of 1986. Thus, for the year as a whole, the volume and value of imports expanded by 23.6 and 16.1% respectively, financed by growing public and private indebtedness. Imports of raw materials and industrial semi-manufactures rose by 58% in volume, followed by similar increases in the quantities of such intermediates as fuels, lubricants and agricultural raw materials, for example malt for brewing. But substantial contraction occurred in consumer durables (− 21%) and industrial machinery and materials (− 10%).

Some insight into the state of import substitution during the period 1982/3–1986/7 is provided by considering changes in the *structure* of imports. Import data are in value terms only for the twelve months 1986/7 and their structure by end use is compared to that in 1982/3 in Table 5.15.

Table 5.15 *Structure of imports by end use 1982/3–86/7 (%)*

	1982/3	1986/7
FINISHED GOODS		
Food & agric. products	5.7	9.9
Consumer semi-durables	12.0	14.8
INTERMEDIATE GOODS		
Animal, vegetable, mineral	6.0	4.5
Semi-manufactures	20.8	15.2
Other industrial inputs	24.6	25.4
CAPITAL GOODS		
Transportation equipment	9.3	10.9
Machinery and tools	20.2	18.7
FUELS & LUBRICANTS	1.4	0.6
TOTAL IMPORTS	100.0	100.0
Current Value (CFAF m.)	429.4	497.4

Source: Ministry of Planning and Regional Development.

The first striking fact evident from Table 5.15 is that, given the inflation in import prices, the real volume of imports in 1986/7 was considerably smaller (at least by 20%) than in 1982/3. The second is the substantial reductions in the relative shares of intermediate semi-manufactures and of fuels and lubricants in total imports, suggesting that import substitution in these two categories continued in recent years, propelled to a large extent by buoyant demand for Cameroonian manufactures in neighbouring African markets. The sizeable rise in the relative share of foodstuffs and consumer semi-durables, on the other hand, points to insufficient industrial complementarity between domestic and neighbouring markets to justify the creation of *new* import-substituting capacities.

Economic and industrial prospects

PROJECTIONS AND FORECASTS
We begin this section with a review of the demand and price assumptions underlying the macroeconomic scenario used by World Bank staff in support of their prescriptions of adjustment and that elaborated by UNIDO consultants to trace the macro-effects of the new industrial projects they identified as economically efficient and which could form the core of a medium-term industrial programme.

The main variables determining the outcome of the macroeconomic projections are Cameroon's petroleum-related net foreign-exchange earnings, the extraction rate of the remaining reserves of petroleum and its expected world market price. In the World Bank's

Economic Memorandum of 1987, the results of projecting alternative *rates of depletion and oil prices* on Cameroon's balance of payments underlie a base scenario involving no new policy reforms and one incorporating a well-publicised set of market-based policy measures inspired by seminal studies of Third World protectionism by Balassa and associates[27] and also by the conclusions of Elliot Berg and his colleagues regarding marketing systems in sub-Saharan Africa[28]. The alternative oil price forecasts and Cameroon's estimated production and oil exports are reproduced in Table 5.A10[29].

Given the large contribution (17%) of oil-related activities to 1984/5 GDP and to total revenue (50%), the drop in oil extraction was bound to aggravate the post-1986 recession. The projections demonstrate that, even if the adjustment measures recommended by the Bank are implemented with despatch, *oil-inclusive* GDP would not expand at more than 1.3% a year in the period 1987–1991 and at 4.1% to 1992. Without any adjustment, the oil-constrained projections result in stagnation. In the absence of information on the sectoral effects of the more 'optimistic' Bank scenario, the historical growth relationship between GDP and the manufacturing sector is instructive.

During the oil-boom period MVA/GDP *elasticity* came to just under 2. Hence, in the conditions of *falling* oil output that will characterise the future, MVA is likely to expand, on average, at *less* than 2.6 and 8.2% a year during the two sub-periods over which GDP is projected by the Bank. This 'optimistically dismal' projection is *catastrophic* when translated into per capita terms and related to the need to create 2m. new jobs by the year 2000. The Bank's projections are intended to demonstrate, on the one hand, the structural plight of the Cameroonian economy and, on the other hand, that even adequate incentives and smoother functioning market mechanisms will not generate its past dynamism before the next millennium. Subsumed in the demonstration is the belief that non-oil exports of goods and services can be made to expand at very healthy rates (accelerating from 6.4 to 8.1% a year) and that the economy's average import elasticity can remain substantially *below unity* as income growth accelerates. These fundamental assumptions require further discussion.

Export growth rates deemed feasible for Cameroon by the World Bank are reproduced in Table 5.16, along with the medium-term forecasts of world demand for the same products published in the Bank's October 1986 *Price Prospects for Major Primary Commodities* (Report No. 814/86).

Table 5.16 *Target export growth rates assumed as feasible & world demand growth forecasts (%)*

Product	1985 share in non-oil exports	'Feasible' volume growth rates		World demand growth 1985–2000
		1987–91	1992–6	
Cocoa	17.7	4.3	3.7	1.7
Coffee	18.3	5.0	3.5	1.3
Other agric. prod.	6.8	5.0	5.4	–
Rubber		–	–	2.2
Tobacco		–	–	1.7
Tropic. wood		–	–	1.4
Aluminium	4.2	2.0	2.0	1.6
Manufactured goods	8.4	14.9	14.4	–
Minerals	0.6	10.0	70.0	–
Non-factor serv.	38.0	6.0	6.6	–

Source: World Bank, *Economic Memorandum, (1987:73) and (1986b)*. October 1986.

Where comparisons are possible, the proposed target rates imply that it should be within Cameroonian exporters' capacities to broaden their market shares in the short term, and to diversify outlets to a very significant extent. Not only is it questionable that such gains can be made in the face of a sluggish world demand for primary commodities and of periodic gluts, but also highly unlikely that quality improvements in Cameroon's manufactures, coupled with effective marketing techniques, can be brought to levels already attained by many Asian (and even some industrialised African) competitors. The impression remains that the 'feasible' adjustment scenario recommended by the Bank not only encompasses errors of composition, but is also over-optimistic about achieving radical and rapid changes in traditionally easy-going African commercial practices – in the wake of economic liberalisation.

One example of a major inconsistency within Bank documents lies in the 'feasible' growth rates of 4.3 and 3.7% set out for Cameroon's cocoa over the next ten years in its Cameroon document and the following forecast made in 1986 by its Commodity Studies and Projections Division:

> Cocoa production in *Cameroon* remained stable at around 120,000 tons from 1980 to 1982; it fell to 106,000 tons in 1984 before recovering to 120,000 tons in 1985. . . . .With moderate replanting, Cameroon could maintain (sic) current production growth and produce around 130,000 tons by 1995 and reach 160,000 tons by the year 2000. . . . Since a major rehabilitation program has not yet been seriously undertaken, the current forecasts for Cameroon cocoa production are based on the behaviour of the past 20 years. Thus production will decline (sic) at an annual rate of 1.6% from 1985 to 2000, mainly because of the age of the present population of cocoa trees.

Another fundamental point that needs to be raised in relation to the Bank's adjustment package concerns the likelihood of maintaining *any* economic growth at all in import-dependent Cameroon in the face of a *protracted reduction* in the volume of imports and a falling rate of marginal investment. Yet these possibilities would appear to be implicit in the very low import/GDP elasticity[30] and the *negative* growth rate of investment (-2.7% in 1987-91) in the 'feasible' adjustment scenario summarised in Table 5.17. Also perplexing is the Bank's sanguine view of the future trend of Cameroon's terms of trade – which are assumed in the adjustment scenario to improve between 1987 and 1996 – when in the past quarter of a century changes in sub-Saharan countries' terms of trade were negative save for the 1973-80 period[31].

Table 5.17 *World Bank's 'feasible' adjustment projections 1979-85, 1987-91, 1992-6 (% and coefficients)*

	Average annual growth rates		
	1979-85	1987-91	1992-6
Non-oil GDP	7.9	4.0	5.2
Total GDP [a]	10.2	1.3	4.1
Exports (goods & nfs)	12.8	-6.0	5.0
Non-oil exports	4.0	6.4	8.1
Imports (goods & nfs)	4.3	0.6	5.6
Consumption	7.4	5.3	5.0
Investment	9.9	-2.7	3.5

	Coefficient		
	1982-5	1987-91	1992-6
Import/Non-oil GDP elasticity	0.24	0.15	1.08

	Index (1984 = 100)				
	1987	1989	1991	1994	1996
Terms of trade	63.3	74.1	83.7	98.9	105.2

Source: As for Table 5.16.

Note: [a] = GDP adjusted for terms of trade.

In the light of these questions, it needs to be asked how much credence can be placed on the adjustment scenario's claims of Cameroon being able to achieve an acceptable level of unemployment by the year 2000. According to the Bank, two million new jobs will be created over a 14-year span. Table 5.18 provides the sectoral breakdown.

The effects of the 1987/8 budget cuts on the Cameroon economy were taken into account by UNIDO's consultants assigned in mid-1987 to assist the Ministry of Planning and Regional Development with the finalisation of a medium-term industrialisation plan. Their alternative *short-term* GDP growth estimates (using the World Bank's assumptions regarding the rate of oil extraction and its world price) for the 1986/7-1990/1 period were 1.3 and 2% a year, on average, that is, consistent with the Bank's 'adjustment' scenario. Their

Table 5.18 *Projected employment growth, 1986–91*

Sectors	1986 Employment ('000)[a]	'Feasible' growth rates Value Add. (percent comp.)	'Feasible' growth rates Employment (percent comp.)	2001 Employment ('000)
Agriculture & Forestry	2,800	3.8	2.2	3,875
Indus., Constr., Services	830	6.3	5.0	1,725
Government	150	2.1	1.3	180
TOTAL	3,780	5.3	2.9	5,780

Source: World Bank, *Economic Memorandum* (1987).

Note: [a] World Bank estimates based on 1984 data.

macro-framework for testing the longer-term impact on the economy of the industrial projects identified as economically efficient, was built on the 11-sector general equilibrium model used by the Ministry of Planning[32].

The trend GDP growth rates (without adjustments) yielded by the model for the *medium-term* 1988/9–2000 period (2.1 and 2.9%) are well below the 3.2% rate of increase of population. The consultants' proposed programme of industrial investments (amounting to over CFAF 600bn at 1986 prices) and *supporting policies* were estimated to raise the level of real GDP by about one-fifth and *average* GDP growth to 2.9% per annum in the pessimistic oil price scenario, and to 3.8% in the optimistic one. The proposed industrial investment, however, was bound to produce a current account deficit of between CFAF 234 and 476bn in the terminal year, that would need to be financed by *external* savings. A brief sketch of the methodology used to arrive at their recommendations follows[33].

The base year for producing alternative scenarios for the year 2000 was 1984/5 – the last one for which (provisional) national accounts were available. The assumptions underlying the figures for the years 1985/6 and 1986/7 were based on the consultants' observations in the field, plus US price indices as proxies for world dollar prices for exports and imports. By 1988/9 they assumed that the recession in Cameroon would peter out, with investment and public consumption resuming their *1980–85* trend rate (when oil extraction was reaching peak levels). Non-oil price projections for the years after 1987/8 were taken to be neutral (that is, that the terms of trade would not deteriorate further) and the CFAF/US dollar rate, at 350, was taken as reflecting an assumed 'long-term equilibrium rate of 7 French francs to the dollar'. Technical progress coefficients, applied to the intermediate products sector – which includes oil – and to the non-factor services sector – which includes unrecorded oil revenues – were adjusted for the effects of alternative rates of oil depletion and oil prices. Both the less and the more optimistic growth scenarios produced by the model yielded growth rates for the economy significantly lower than those achieved during the Fifth Plan period 1980–85, even after the inclusion of the proposed industrial package (see Table 5.A11). In contrast to the World Bank's 'Gung-ho' assumptions regarding 'feasible' export growth to the year 2000, the UNIDO consultants' industrialisation scenarios incorporated more credible average rates of 3 and 4.7% respectively. Likewise, their implicit import/GDP elasticities – of 1.14 and 0.97 – are more convincing than those selected by the Bank.

The UNIDO consultants readily acknowledged the shortcomings (because of time constraints) of the projection model they were obliged to use for simulating the Cameroon economy, the chief ones being[34]: the model's mathematical determinism, which precluded the incorporation of structural change over time; its 'classical' domestic market-clearing assumption; and its excessive aggregation, particularly in respect of intermediate products – inhibiting the analysis of inter-industry flows.

Before examining the industrial profile that resulted from the consultants' analyses, it is worth pausing to take a brief look at the methodology they used. They first identified the productive sub-sectors that conform best to Cameroon's comparative advantage and then tested the corresponding manufacturing activities – realistically scaled to demand – for economic and financial profitability. This approach generated a mass of new data, conveniently collated, for the Ministry of Planning which will be invaluable to analysts and businessmen. These include an up-dated analysis of the nominal and effective protection received in Cameroon by 49 major products, their calculated domestic resource costs (DRCs) and revealed comparative advantage, as well as their mutual purchases/sales in the form of an inter-industry sub-matrix. The distribution of the 49 product sample, applying the DRC criterion, is shown in Table 5.19.

Table 5.19 *Efficiency of resource use by 54 import-competing activities. (Distribution according to Domestic Resource Costs)*

DRC categories	Sectors and sub-sectors involved
A. Very Efficient (Av. DRCs 0.76–1.60)	Agriculture, fishing, forestry, woodworking, (oil refining)
B. Relatively Efficient (Av. DRCs 1.60–2.30)	Agro-industries, base metal working, leather, rubber, paper & furniture
C. Inefficient (Av. DRCs >3.0 or negative)	Textiles, chemicals & plastics, machinery, building materials.

Source: UNIDO consultants' data in the Ministry of Planning and Regional Development.

Key findings of the UNIDO consultants' analysis confirmed and/or complemented those in Phase I of the present study. The more important ones are as follows:

- Manufacturing activities that were intensive consumers of domestic primary products were among the most efficient in terms of their international prices.
- The actual protection received by every import-competing economic activity was less than the apparent one.
- The average rate of nominal protection in 1986/7 was around 70% and the variance was small.
- Tariff escalation followed the level of processing (value added incorporated in goods). Because of it and of import licensing, a large number of import-competing activities enjoyed extremely high – and some even absolute – protection.
- The dispersion of DRC values was very great, with just over one-third suggesting good to moderate efficiency and one-third, relative or absolute inefficiency of resource use.

To be capable of making best use of the country's resource endowment and of pursuing its comparative advantage, it is recommended that the authorities should develop, as soon as practicable, a *reliable domestic data base* of manufacturing industries and keep these abreast of the experience of comparable economies.

The new industrial projects recommended for implementation over the next decade or so by the UNIDO consultants are set out in Table 5.20 where they are grouped by broad ISIC categories, along with the corresponding values of their internal rates of return at 'world' prices (IRR) and their DRCs. In addition, the consultants recommended that new feasibility studies be carried out *in the short term* of additional abattoirs, a latex processing plant, the manufacture of building materials based on local inputs, and the manufacture of car batteries. The non-inclusion of additional textile manufacturing capacity in the proposed package is at odds with recommendations of a later market-research study conducted for the government. It found the domestic market to be expanding at a rate warranting investment in the production of cotton thread, fibres, T-shirts and underwear. The regional export potential for Cameroon textiles was also found to be promising, by virtue of the very high yields obtained by cotton farmers in North Cameroon[35].

For still later implementation they recommended, *inter alia*, that the following promising industrial activities be subjected to technical appraisal: the manufacture of snacks out of plantain chips; the extraction of pyrethrin and dextrine from cassava starch; the processing of locally grown medicinal plants; the manufacture of industrial sodium from natural salt deposits; and additional cement capacity.

The orientation of this recommended 'package' towards the processing of domestic resources ensures that inter-industry flows will widen and increase in number without exacerbating the economy's import-dependence. Although it contains nothing markedly different from the typical profile of industries found in middle-income African countries, its modest scope and pragmatism make it far more convincing and should therefore attract the attention of investors at home and abroad. But what is the likelihood of the plan actually

Table 5.20 *Proposed new industrial projects and their profitability*

Branch	Project	IRR	DRC	Invest. (FCFA bn)
05	Forestry: Logging complex	–	–	29.6
	Charcoal manufacture	>100	–	1.7
06	Oil Extraction:			
	Fluid Catalytic Converter	25–33	0.2–3	39.3
08	Agricultural Processing			
	Palm oil refinery	13	1.15	2.1
	Soya oil mills (2)	19–21	0.4–5	1.6
	Malting factory	25	0.33	3.5
	Industrial Alcohol	11	0.60	0.4
	Tomato concentrate	19	0.60	0.5
	Pineapple processing	11	0.60	1.1
	Soluble coffee	5–12	–	2.1
14	Woodworking:			
	Drying & Sawing mills (2)	32–38	0.42–4	6.1
	Timber shaping mills (2)	>60	<0.30	1.9
	Plywood & board manufacture	44	0.41	4.1
	Chipboard factory	25	0.51	2.8
	Integrated timber manufacture	>50	0.28	11.6
16	Chemicals, Pharmaceuticals:			
	Fertiliser, packaging	>100	–	>1.5
	Adhesives factory	34	0.58	1.9
	Caustic soda & chloride	–	–	14.5
	Pharmaceuticals	20	1.06	1.3
162	Gas Liquefaction:			
	from petroleum	6–12	0.36–1.0	4.8
	natural gas	2–15	–	253.8
191	Aluminium processing:			
	Foundry	11.4	0.82	175.0
192	Steel-making (in 3 phases):			
	Electric Arc Foundry	4–20	<1.06	47.0
20	Mechan. & Electrical machinery			
	Nuts & Bolts factory	37	0.40	0.5
	Exhaust pipe factory	26	0.62	<0.1

Source: UNIDO Consultants' data in the Ministry of Planning and Regional Development.

being executed? Part of the answer to this question lies in analysing whether the various institutional problems facing the country will be addressed and whether the infrastructural bottlenecks will be removed. As solutions to these issues are likely to be *essential* for economic recovery in general, and for vigorous industrial growth in particular, they need to be considered in more detail.

IMPROVING THE DOMESTIC ECONOMIC ENVIRONMENT
For the whole period since independence, successive administrations have been trying to reconcile their professed faith in the allocative efficiency of market forces – to the extent that they operate in the sub-Saharan context – with the political imperative of protecting domestic producers and consumers from external perturbations. In the event, there has been a build-up of cumbersome administrative intervention (often politically motivated and technically faulty) and an absence of transparency in policy implementation. This has generated frustration and distrust of all things public on the part of private operators in the economy's 'modern' sector, as well as the virtual drying-up of new direct foreign investment.

The institutional and administrative impediments to Cameroon's economic development have been analysed periodically by the World Bank and by bilateral aid agencies[36], but systematically tackling them was conveniently postponed during the heady years of the oil boom. However, with economic recession setting in, their ill-effects became more glaring, while rapidly falling revenue obliged the government to curtail outlays and to rely more on private initiative as a motive economic force. In this context, policy options have become fewer and less debatable.

Correcting the widening external and internal imbalances was an obvious priority. The option of currency devaluation was put aside – at least for the foreseeable future – following the April 1988 decision of Franc Zone members not to alter the historic link of the CFAF to the French franc. With the CFAF due to remain relatively over-valued[37], recourse will perforce have to be made to offsetting policy instruments involving adjustments in the following areas:

- the country-specific element of the UDEAC common external tariff and the replacement of *quantitative import restrictions* and *specific* duties/export taxes by *ad valorem* custom duties;
- the overall fiscal regime, including the 1984 Investment Code's incentive structure;
- price and wage-setting mechanisms;
- the development and enforcement of norms and standards;
- technological support to producers;
- collection and dissemination of market information.

Enough analytical data exist for measures to be taken immediately in most of these areas. Thus, in revising the inefficient protective structure, the Cameroonian authorities are sure to be guided by the latest findings of the UNIDO consultants and those in the World Bank's earlier studies. This exercise brooks no delay because, as things stand, there is a strong anti-export, pro-capital-intensive (hence import-dependent) bias in the combined effects of tariffs, taxes and exemptions[38].

A global approach to improved resource allocation will require reconsideration of the nature and duration of the incentives provided by the 1984 Investment Code. More emphasis will have to be placed on economic profitability as a qualifying criterion. Similarly, good use can be made of the last fiscal analysis carried out by the staff of the World Bank (1986a) as well as the more recent *Economic Memorandum* (1987). These pointed to the urgent need to recapitalise the commercial banks, adjust the rediscount and interest-rate structure, reduce taxes on borrowing and credit, and develop a real capital market by creating new financial instruments.

The public sector rehabilitation exercise carried out in the first half of 1988 scrutinised in detail the past operations of such promotional bodies as FONADER, for agricultural, and CAPME, for small and medium enterprises in the light of an earlier decision to replace them with more effective credit institutions. Within the same framework, the effectiveness of the National Centre for Foreign Trade was evaluated with the purpose of strengthening the part it is expected to play in the post-oil era. In price-setting and controls over commercial margins, a timid step was already taken towards the end of 1987 to streamline the processing of company requests for price adjustments. The basic system, however, remained unaltered (except for decontrolling the prices of cosmetics, cigarettes, wooden or metal household articles and handicrafts[39]). Train and bus fares, as well as rates for public utilities, had remained unaltered for several years, swelling the operating deficits of the parastatals concerned.

The analytical spade-work undertaken in early 1988 by Cameroonian technicians and their consultants, in support of negotiations with the IMF and the World Bank for adjustment assistance and financial relief, overlooked no economic constraint nor policy blunder. The studies prepared for the Ministerial Commission on the rehabilitation of the public sector – to lay the ground for administrative and institutional reforms – in fact covered all aspects and sectors of the economy[40]. Not only was each and every public and parastatal enterprise subjected to an external audit and an impartial assessment of its historic performance, but the environmental situation – in which it could thrive – was also analysed. Hence all the juridical, institutional and administrative impediments to efficient enterprise management were identified and corrective action remitted to the political bodies for endorsement.

By the Spring of 1988 the Cameroon economy was thus being advised to steer a new course which had been reconnoitred with greater care than in the past. The seriousness with which the preparatory work was done is an indication of the earnest political will to look reality squarely in the face and to eliminate the more notorious impediments to growth.

STRENGTHENING THE MANUFACTURING SECTOR

Cameroon's comparative advantage lies in the manufacture of goods based on domestic raw materials, apart from imported alumina that can be processed at low cost using cheap hydro-electric power. Thus, with the proximate exhaustion of proven oil reserves, government action in the near term to promote economic growth needs first to focus on broadening the supply base and range of agricultural and forestry products that will reach consumers at competitive prices.

Domestic and foreign savings necessary for the achievement of this objective would be more easily mobilised were policy implementation – by the mighty *Office National de Commercialisation des Produits de Base (ONCPB)* – on pricing, collecting, storing and final disposal of major cash crops more adequately publicised. For instance, there would appear to be no known justification for the fact that, over the last five years, average prices paid to growers of Robusta and Arabica coffee by the ONCPB remained at about 40% of the cif export price. Transparency of decision-taking in that body would go a long way to infusing dynamism among the smaller producers and would give them guidance in product specialisation, particularly as regards the exporting option.

Ignorance is another major constraint. Although fieldwork assessments for the current analysis could not be fully comprehensive, it was confirmed that among *small* farmers in Central province there remained widespread ignorance of the demand for products other than a few traditional cash crops and local staples. Similarly, no wealthy or leading businessmen appeared to have been informed of the World Bank's view that, of the cash crops grown in Cameroon, rubber offered the best long-term prospect. These examples point to an obvious shortcoming in the use and dissemination of basic information that calls for corrective action.

At the root of many production and marketing problems shared by *light industries* – such as those processing agricultural products – lie an inadequate capital base, low cash flows and difficult access to medium-and long-term credit. It is to be hoped that this problem will be mitigated by the intermediation of the new *Banque Commerciale et Industrielle* and by giving the existing development bank more purposeful directives.

Much remains to be done in maximising the contribution that timber resources can make to Cameroon's prosperity. According to a recent survey, Cameroon has the potential of becoming 'Africa's largest producer and exporter of forest products in the next century' if action is mounted by government in pursuit of a balanced strategy of timber extraction and renewal[41]. This would involve:

- improving access to the dense tropical forests in the South and South East and reducing the rate structure for surface transport, port handling and loading of timber;
- extending industrial plantations of selected domestic species;
- encouraging *small* private sawmills to locate adjacent to reforestation centres and to be equipped with drying kilns and machinery for pre-shaping timber to common industrial requirements;
- providing fiscal incentives to exporters of *sawn wood*;
- promoting the use of timber in housing and rationalising its use as a fuel;
- altering the current practice of taxing logging concessions according to surface area granted, rather than as a function of the volume effectively extracted and processed on site.

There is also growth potential in the processing of hides and skins and in leather manufacture[42]. The import content of domestically produced shoes can be brought down substantially if local inputs become more price-competitive. Given the right incentives, privately run ranches-cum-fattening yards and abattoirs in traditional herding areas could help improve cattle off-take and the quality of the industrial by-products, notwithstanding the recent failure of the existing hide factory.

The textile sector is beset with problems that are common to several other sub-Saharan countries: low financial profitability with chronic over-capacity which even high protective barriers and outright prohibitions are incapable of preventing because of the magnitude of 'unrecorded' imports. As one major consequence, the Cameroonian vertically-integrated and (over)-diversified textile manufacturers consume a mere 13% of marketed cotton fibre. The value in 1986 of imported thread, yarn and cloth was more than four times that of exported textiles and clothing. Frontier (illegal cross-border) trade in Africa is traditionally intensive and difficult to control, so that protection can never be hermetic – to the benefit of consumers. But what might be attempted, particularly in Francophone West Africa where the Confédération Française pour le Développement Textile participates in all stages of textile production and sales, is to arrive at longer production runs through some informal market-sharing arrangement, thus lowering unit cost. This should be all the more feasible within the framework of existing regional bodies such as the UDEAC, one of whose aims is the co-ordination of industrial programmes.

Trade flows between primary agricultural and forestry activities, on the one hand, and manufacturing, on the other – aggregated as they are in the Cameroonian input-output tables – point to several promising import-substituting opportunities in the not too distant future. They cover intermediate inputs that could be produced from local raw materials, such as: urea-based resin for consolidating plywood and block board; additional types of packing and packaging materials based on domestic lignite and hard fibres; dyestuffs for use in textile manufacture and tanning; basic chemicals derived from palm and kernel oil, maize, sugar, cassava, wood, natural rubber and soda.

In 1984/5, agro-industry already contributed 70% of total manufacturing value added (see Table 5.A13) and will remain its mainstay until the mining of the known reserves of bauxite, iron ore and off-shore natural gas (unassociated with petroleum extraction) is fully developed. As this is bound to take a number of years, there is a good case for having a specialised body responsible for co-ordinating support for agro-industry in areas of technical training, research and adaptation of technology. It could also vet agro-industrial project proposals and help set quality norms that meet international standards[43].

Current estimates of accessible bauxite reserves suggest a possible recovery of about 350 m. metric tonnes of alumina but only after heavy outlays on transport infrastructure and with continuing availability of relatively inexpensive electricity. Total prime costs of production would have to be kept low for the end-products to be internationally competitive. The existing capacity for processing Guinean alumina could be utilised more fully by a vigorously pursued 'buy local' policy, coupled with quality enforcement and a small (less than 15%) premium for locally fabricated aluminium products in public – and external aid – tenders. Furthermore, UDEAC markets already provide fair prospects for aluminium goods that are priced competitively[44].

Given the outlook for continuing over-supply of steel products on world markets, raising the investment needed to mine and process Cameroon's iron ore becomes highly problematic. Import substitution in steel can become feasible in the not too distant future as more UDEAC countries establish rolling mills and thus complement Cameroon's estimated 1990 demand of some 120,000 metric tonnes. However, the profitable operation in Cameroon of even the appropriately-scaled, electric arc (scrap iron) smelter evaluated by UNIDO consultants, would require substantial (40%) protection against imports.

Although there are reportedly rich reserves of natural gas in addition to that associated with petroleum, they are located off-shore and their exploitation would require investments exceeding CFAF 200 bn in value and a sale price of LNG much higher than the current one. In such conditions, the undertaking is not one for the foreseeable future.

In the mechanical and electrical machinery sub-sector, the approximately 70 SMEs concerned were operating at low capacity levels in 1987 as deliveries to other domestic industries shrank, without a sufficiently offsetting rise in UDEAC exports. Given the bleak prospects for *rapid* economic recovery, the only promising *new* venture identified by the UNIDO consultants for this sub-sector involved the manufacture of vehicle exhausts and small hardware. They also drew attention to the obsolescence of many existing installations and to the insufficient concern with product quality and the supply of engineering personnel. Doubtless, were strict industrial norms and maintenance standards to become enforced in Cameroon, demand for the sub-sector's products would receive a welcome fillip. There is also a patent need for collating and disseminating product-level data on consumption trends in neighbouring markets – a task that should receive priority consideration by a revitalised National Trade Promotion Centre[45].

No new profitable ventures in the pharmaceuticals/cosmetics, chemicals and plastics sub-sectors have been identified for the near term. However, within a longer time frame, the processing of local medicinal herbs and the manufacture of PVC (polyvinyl chloride) may become economically feasible.

This review of additional manufacturing activities that are most likely to come on stream during the next 5–10 years, hardly constitute a locomotive force able to raise output at the high rate obtaining before the onset of recession. They even call for scepticism – if not disbelief that MVA growth in Cameroon would *average out at some 8% per annum*, which is the subsumed feasible rate in the World Bank's scenario based on market mechanisms receiving freer play and broad institutional reforms being carried out.

Concluding discussion

The overall impression that is left after a close look at Cameroon's experience with diversifying its resource-rich economy, is one of disorientation and under-utilisation of available policy instruments, much of it due to inadequate basic data poorly processed, and to an over-accommodating application of economic ground rules.

Since world economic growth began to decelerate at the start of the 1980s, Cameroon has been in the doldrums, as reflected in negligible levels of new productive investment and additions to industrial employment. After three years of quasi-stagnation in real industrial output, 1984/5 was marked by a 10% drop in the output of SYNDUSTRICAM's member-companies. The terminal year of the fifth development plan saw private investment under-shoot its target level by one-third. Indeed, of the 29 industrial projects encompassed by the plan, only one had been implemented. The expansion of total credit to the economy in the same year came to only 5.9% in nominal terms – far below the rate of inflation and of this 74% was in short-term advances, 24.9% in medium, and a mere 1.1% in long-term loans to industry. FOGAPE's lending capacity to SMEs was negligible.

Yet the country's resource endowment was being enhanced by confirmation of non-associated gas reserves adequate to feed two processing plants to manufacture methanol and ammoniacal urea for fertilisers. Rubber prospects were improving as new plantations began to mature and to promise a tripling of the 1983/4 latex removals by 1990. The output of university graduates was expanding strongly and local businessmen put no less than 40 industrial projects up for approval by the statutory body concerned. And still growth performance remained disappointing.

The latest five-year development plan, 1986–1991, does identify the many shortcomings of the recent past but, as far as the manufacturing sector is concerned, proposes essentially 'more of the same'. Several obvious policy gaps have been left unaddressed, including the following essential moves:

- to exact the fulfilment by enterprises benefitting from the Investment Code of their counterpart obligations;
- urgently to facilitate access to medium-and long-term credit, especially by SMEs;
- to discourage imports by differentiating commercial margins in favour of local products;
- to limit the scope of existing price controls to 'sensitive' products (i.e. those requiring prior authorisation for import) or those destined for mass consumption;
- as in Senegal, for instance, to have a representative body pass on the need for the importation of goods ostensibly in short supply;
- to set a firm time limit for the settlement of claims on the public sector;
- to take the lead in developing industrial complementarity within UDEAC.

Neglect of these will not help Cameroon to shake off its lethargy. Within the context of bleak prospects, what are its chances of mobilising non-productive domestic savings and attracting foreign venture capital, technology and marketing knowhow? Can it persuade the owners of petrodollars to invest in tropical hardwoods, fruits and vegetables?

In conclusion, some policy measures can be advanced that might complement those already in train or merely envisaged:

i) Efforts must be focused on lowering costs of production through more intimate sub-regional co-ordination of procurement and the expansion of productive capacities. Competitive import substitution by members of UDEAC must be discouraged. Industrial complementarity could be facilitated by sanctioning market-sharing arrangements between existing firms. Externally aided projects could be untied by donors to stimulate the use of local or UDEAC inputs. Line ministries could be instructed to 'buy local' without necessarily requiring European quality standards to be satisfied.

ii) Yields in agriculture, forestry and fishing must be raised and raw material supplies to the manufacturing sector assured, both in respect of quantity and of quality.

iii) The Cameroon Development Bank should be instructed to be more supportive of manufacturers' credit and technical assistance needs, as well as to provide the SMEs with adequate subsidised credit and technical aid through CAPME and FOGAPE.

iv) The divestment option already put forward by the SNI should be followed through to mop up as much as possible the private savings otherwise flowing into services or being invested abroad.

v) A review of the CFAF's parity should be undertaken so as to take full account of the evolving structure of external trade and payments, to ensure that there are no reasonable grounds for a devaluation.

Finally, mention must be made of a discordant note struck while preparations were in hand to liberalise the economy by reducing government's tutelage over it. At the beginning of 1988, Presidential decree No. 88/111 announced the establishment of a *Caisse de Péréquation* for rice, sugar and edible oils. Its Executive is to be responsible for setting the domestic farm-gate and consumer prices for the products concerned, plus import quotas and control of the collection of levies on competing imports by the Customs – all with the effect of protecting inefficient domestic producers[46]. Of late, state-fixed prices for these staples have been close to double those obtaining on over-saturated world markets and have naturally attracted massive 'unrecorded' imports that cut deeply into local producers' sales receipts. Since parastatals accounted for between 60 and 70% of domestic output of these commodities, the government was obliged to underwrite their borrowing or to increase direct subsidies, to the extent its own diminishing resources allowed. It is difficult to see how, in the circumstances prevailing at present, fraudulent imports can be radically reduced so that levies on licensed imports of these staples suffice to finance the rehabilitation of domestic production.

With the inception of comprehensive reforms backed by financial support (safety nets) from multilateral and bilateral sources, and with private initiative enjoying more elbow room and a bigger say in economic decision-making than in the past, the basic requisites for making better use of Cameroon's rich endowment will have been met. The industrial master plan to the year 2000 (DPI) will become public, indicating the manufacturing opportunities that government is willing to sanction, along with supporting macroeconomic measures. Even at the risk of echoing some of the policy prescriptions that are bound to accompany external assistance, this chapter will end with some suggested priorities for action.

Foreign capital with its technology and marketing facilities will have to be attracted to Cameroon in competition with other developing countries blessed with similar resources. Hence particular attention will have to be paid to the total package of incentives, so that average rates of profitability can be attainable under proper management. In the first instance, the fiscal and tariff regime will have to be adjusted after due consultations with representatives of all the sectors concerned, either through a symposium, or through public hearings by a commission of enquiry[47].

Much more transparency will have to be injected into decision-taking by the authorities and such *glasnost* be made a permanent feature of the re-defined economic ground rules. The views expressed by private enterprise associations during *regular consultations* with ministerial department heads should receive the same publicity as those of the government. Confidence between the private and public sectors will thus be strengthened and data – so crucial for planning and forecasting industrial development – should become more readily available.

Data on production and trade must be computerised and analysed at regular, frequent, intervals. A monthly *Statistical Gazette* should be printed, giving basic data on trade, domestic and foreign prices for the major products, interest rates on different types of credit, employment, etc. Top priority should be accorded to completing the checking and processing of the 1986 industrial census. The analysis should contain significant performance ratios and elasticities of factor use. In this respect, Cameroon has a long way to go in catching up with the 'state of the art' in the more industrialised SSA countries, such as Zimbabwe and Kenya.

Fiscal and material incentives to national and joint ventures with foreign partners should be time-bound and accompanied by strictly enforced counterpart obligations to satisfy product quality and environmental standards, to progressively raise local content of output, and to reinvest a negotiated share of pre-tax profits.

If these few priority measures were acted upon, they could expedite the process of further industrialisation in Cameroon.

Notes

1. The average 1979–83 ratio of collected customs revenue to the total value of imports came to less than 30%, whereas the nominal import tariff levels yielded a potential average of collectable trade revenue of 54% ad valorem; hence the importance for the Budget of the incentives contained in the country's Investment Code.
2. Duties for basic foods range from 7.5 to 20%, while those for consumer goods and 'luxuries' extend to 30%. On raw materials, intermediate products and capital goods rates vary between 2.5 and 20%, with a few carrying a 30% duty. The complementary import tax adds on between 5 and 25% more on competing mass consumption imports from non-UDEAC sources. But for the output of a series of 'infant' activities the complementary tax goes up to 90%. A variable 'unloading tax' is charged per unit weight as well as veterinary, photo-sanitary, chemical and mineral 'inspection' fees. Specifically listed imports carry an additional 10% turnover tax.
3. Other controlled import categories are: listed 'sensitive' products and those requiring prior authorisation; other products, directly competing with local manufactures, covered by import quotas established as a percentage of domestic purchases – the 'twinning' regime; the importation of used clothing, colza oil, hurricane lamps and large vehicles is prohibited. Uncontrolled goods are subject to licensing when valued at over CFAF 500,000, but the document is issued freely.
4. By the World Bank, UNIDO, *SEDES EDIAFRIQUE TIERS MONDE* and the EIU, to name those most widely available.
5. Dutch disease is the term used to denote the coexistence, within the traded goods sector, of booming and lagging sub-sectors, resulting in the relative decline of manufacturing i.e. de-industrialisation. The earnings from petroleum exports have not been publicised on a regular basis and have been kept in a non-budgetary account. According to African news magazines, oil revenue made up about 60% of total foreign-exchange earnings in 1986/7.
6. During the 1960s MVA grew at about 12% a year in real terms. This rate was regained during the 1976–82 period after a slowdown (under 4% a year) between 1971 and 1976. The World Bank's 1984 Country Economic Memorandum on Cameroon gives its overall manufacturing performance as equal to that of Côte d'Ivoire. After 1982, manufacturing output growth again slumped by about 3% per annum. The share of manufactures (70% of which were semi-processed goods) in total commodity exports fell from 22% in 1975/6 to a mere 6% in 1981/2.
7. The information in this and following paragraphs is illustrative, being based on discussions with representatives of industry and commerce and not with enterprise management.
8. SNI, *Rapports d'Activités, les Exercices 1981–2 et 1984–5.*
9. Several interesting country case-studies on the limited extent of import substitution in pharmaceuticals in developing countries have been published by UNCTAD in co-operation with WHO over the last 10 years. They highlight the oligopolistic structure of the world market for these products as well as the relatively high cost of their *primary* manufacture. Hence in most developing countries to date, the sub-sector's activities are limited to blending imported ingredients, coating, packing and packaging. The major exception is in the preparation of final products using domestically grown medicinal herbs.
10. For purposes of comparison, the single Saudi Arabian Al Jubail petrochemical complex produced 680,000 tonnes of polymers annually.
11. The average annual price of aluminium ingots quoted on the London Metal Exchange (cash basis) was as follows:

	1975	1980	1984	1985	1986
£ sterling/metric ton	430.6	756.2	933.1	814.2	784.2

Source: UNCTAD, *Monthly Commodity Price Bulletin*, various.

12. Industries accorded UDEAC 'regional' status are not quota-bound. The *taxe unique* on output is levied at source in lieu of all charges on imported inputs, all indirect taxes on intermediate consumption, and all excise taxes on the finished product. The privilege has no time limit. The preferential margin the *taxe unique* confers on 'regional' industries varies among UDEAC member states.
13. With 1975/6 = 100, the price index for foodstuffs in 1983/4, as estimated by GICAM, stood at 250, whereas that for bread came to only 164.
14. UNIDO, 'Cameroon', *Industrial Development Review* series, Oct. 1986. The principal tool of the performance analysis is the regression of the observed relationship between the growth rate of value

added in a sub-sector (independent variable) and the increase in VA per employee (dependent variable), and a normative one developed by Verdoorn.

15. As pointed out in the World Bank's Country Memorandum of June 1984, (p. 15):
    'The slow growth of manufactured exports and the decline in the share in industrial output of industries processing domestic raw materials, contrasted with rapid growth of manufactured imports. . . . .run counter to the expected path of a country relatively rich in natural resources and labour. . . . .'.

16. A DRC value of less than unity for an activity indicates that a unit of foreign exchange can be earned or saved through it with *less* than the equivalent value (at free trade prices) of the domestic resource consumed by the activity. But when the DRC is calculated for a single year, it may not be representative of an industry's *average* efficiency. Similarly, individual DRCs cannot be extrapolated to entire subsectors as indicators of efficiency. See World Bank, *Industrial Development and Policy in Cameroon*, September 1980, vol. 1.

17. Proven oil reserves were estimated at 103 m. tonnes in 1978 and extraction peaked at around 9 m. tonnes in 1985. No significant discoveries have been made since then. Petroleum extraction and primary refining contributed in 1985 over 17% of GDP and made up about 45% of total public revenue. Net foreign exchange earned (and retained) from this activity came to some 35% of total export earnings. In dollar terms per capita income in Cameroon improved from under US$500 in 1978 to about US$800 in 1985 and the savings ratio from 19 to 34% of GDP. (World Bank, *Economic Memorandum*, February 1987, No. 6395-CM.) It is estimated that by the early 1990s oil output will merely cover the country's domestic requirements.

18. Cameroon is not a member of OPEC. The price of its crude follows that of North Sea Brent.

19. The US dollar/CFAF rate evolved as follows:

Average	1983/4	1984/5	1985/6	1986/7
CFAF/US$	409.5	471.1	386.6	318.4

20. According to World Bank estimates, government subsidies to public sector enterprises in 1984 amounted to some CFAF 150 bn and represented about 50% of Cameroon's income from petroleum. *Ibid.*

21. *Budget receipts and out-turn, 1982/3–87/8*, (CFAF bn)

	1982/3	1983/4	1984/5	1985/6	1986/7	1987/8
Total receipts	695	723	790	903	648	n.a.
Budget surplus/Deficit	+90	−2	−98	−104	−413	−211[a]

Note: [a] = estimate
Source: Interview information.

22. Government subsidies to public enterprises included a variety of different forms of financial assistance, including future claims on them. In 1984 the total amount of public transfers to enterprises is said to have come to about CFAF 150 bn, representing one-half of government's oil earnings or 18% of total budgeted outlays. In the preceding year such transfers amounted to about CFAF 90 bn, of which 20 bn were direct subsidies, 15 bn in equity participation, 9.5 bn to repay publicly guaranteed debt and 8 bn on the repurchase of third party claims. Much of these debts were contracted by CAMSUCO and the now-liquidated CELLUCAM.

23. World Bank, *Cameroon: Financial Sector Report*, (1986a).

24. Cameroon's public debt at the end of 1986 was estimated by the World Bank at the equivalent of US$3.2 bn, the service of which came to $299 m. and rose to $353 m. in 1987. But these figures are commonly considered as underestimates because of unrecorded government borrowing from oil companies operating in Cameroon. The outstanding interest on all debts could well be in the neighbourhood of US$1 bn.

25. By February 1989, some $150 m. had been loaned by the IMF and France's Caisse Centrale de Coopération. The much larger (around $200 m.) structural adjustment loan of the World Bank was agreed in June 1989 (Ed.).

26. The national accounts and indices of industrial and agricultural production are not very reliable. Estimates of growth rates based on terminal years should therefore be viewed with caution. The strength of this caveat lies in the very low *implicit* import elasticity of the manufacturing sector (0.15) for the 1979–85 period, putting in question the official growth rate for the sector – and hence for total GDP. The earlier analysis brought out the economy's relatively high import-dependence, which argues for an import elasticity much closer to unity for the manufacturing sector. (This point is also made in the World Bank's *Economic Memorandum* of February 1987.)

27. B. Balassa and Associates, *The Structure of Protection in Developing Countries*, Baltimore, Johns Hopkins University Press, 1971.

28. These are reflected in, for instance, World Bank, *Accelerated Development in sub-Saharan Africa: An Agenda For Action*, Washington, World Bank, 1981.

29. The economically recoverable oil reserves – at 1986 world prices – were estimated to be 40 m. metric tonnes, rising to 50 m. tonnes should prices improve as of 1989 to the equivalent of 1984 US$20 per barrel and remain at that level. The export forecasts optimistically assume that variable costs of production can remain unchanged in real terms, even as secondary recuperation acquires greater importance.

30. In support of the low import/GDP elasticity assumed to be feasible under the adjustment scenario, the Bank's *Economic Memorandum* (Table 18) sets out the calculated sectoral import elasticities for the high growth years 1979–85. The only value close to unity was for consumer semi-durables, with other merchandise import elasticities ranging from 0.08 for food and beverages – a likely value given Cameroon's near self-sufficiency in food and significant exports of beer – as well as a surprisingly low elasticity of 0.20 for capital goods. However, Cameroon's trade data are notoriously fragile and unrecorded trade flows very substantial. The longer-term relation between GDP growth and imports in Cameroon should, in the author's opinion and based on observations in other Sub-Saharan countries, lie close to the 1.14 value for total imports, calculated by the Bank staff for the 3 years 1979–81.

31. See Table 10 in World Bank (1986b).

32. The Cameroon model is based on methodology developed by Dervis, de Melo and Robinson at the World Bank and applies a neoclassical, market-clearing framework – incorporating structural rigidities – to base year (1984/5) national accounts data. (Minplan internal document, *Travaux de MM Oyono, Mbong Mbong, Saha, sur le TES Camerounais de 1979/80 pour la preparation du VIe Plan*.) The model simulates the operation of a market economy and yields, for a given time-horizon, equilibrium prices of goods, services and factors of production. The model's constrained matching of total demand and supply does not allow for the accommodation of short-term disturbances, such as cyclical unemployment or inflationary surges.

Sectoral output is derived from Cobb-Douglas functions incorporating 3 categories of manpower and sectoral capital stock. The domestic and foreign markets are treated as distinct, with respective prices linked but non-identical. Thus, internal price changes are not automatically transferred to exports. Imported and domestically produced goods are not considered as perfect substitutes and hence face distinct elasticities of demand.

33. Based on a private communication to the author and interview information.

34. A technical appendix to their report contains recommendations to the planning authorities for improving their particular model.

35. According to the May 1988 issue of *African Business*, as much as 566 kg per hectare is obtained, compared to a world average of 514 kg per ha. and 329 kg per ha. for the whole of Africa.

36. The more burdensome shortcomings related to the inefficiency of the public and parastatal sectors, over-centralisation of decision-making, political and personal nepotism, political interference with the management of publicly controlled enterprises, anti-export bias of the protective fiscal and customs regimes, loose financial and monetary controls over public expenditure and borrowing.

37. Most studies of Franc Zone African economies agree on the overvaluation of the CFAF – in the 10–20% range relative to the major currencies – if judged merely by differences in inflation rates. The UNIDO consultants assumed the lower value, after calculating the shadow rate of exchange (SER) as follows:

$$SER = M + Tm + X + Sx + Tx/M + X$$

where

M = import value
Tm = tariffs and charges on imports
X = export value
Sx = export subsidies
Tx = export duties

38. In a representative sample of 54 products/groups, the index of trade distortion (B_j), which expresses the relative incentive to sell on the domestic rather than on external markets – calculated by UNIDO consultants – was in all cases well above unity. The formula they used is

$$B_j = (eH_j(net) + 1)/(eX_j(net) + 1)$$

where the expressions in the argument are net effective rates of protection on sales in home and export markets respectively. In almost one-half of the sample the distortion was infinite because value added at 'world' prices in the manufacture of these products/groups was negative.

39. Prices continued to be regulated by the provisions of a 1972 ordinance whereby ex-factory prices could be set at 12% above cost, to which a commercial margin could be added at the wholesale level, ranging from 15% for consumer staples to 55% for luxury goods and special items. A minimum retailing margin was also prescribed for every product. This tended to encourage traders to stock and promote higher-priced products, with a relatively high import content. Periodic requests for price adjustments to keep pace with inflation have had to be justified with some 10 different documents, all submitted in 15 copies!

40. The average share of publicly-owned or controlled (>25% of assets) enterprises in GDP during the

1983 period came to 7.6%; one-half of them were in the services sector. Those in manufacturing enjoyed virtual monopoly status, since competing imports were prohibited save in cases of patent shortages (see Table 5.A13).

41. Report of the UNDP/FAO project CMR/86/003 (the provisional version).
42. The estimated animal population in Cameroon for 1986/7 came to 4,361,000 cattle; 5,276,000 goats and sheep; 1,178,000 pigs. In calendar year 1986, recorded exports of raw and processed hides amounted to a mere 719 m. tonnes, of which the latter made up 11%.
43. UNIDO consultants recommended the establishment of a Centre with approximately the same mandate in their report to the Ministry of Planning and Regional Development.
44. These factors underlie the UNIDO Consultants' recommendations to expand, in the short run, the existing aluminium foundry and rolling mill and then to add extrusion and flow-moulding installations.
45. In the course of preparatory work in early 1988 on administrative reforms, serious consideration was given to making the existing Centre much less dependent on public subvention and government control, with close links to associations of private traders and producers.
46. Thus, CAMSUCO – a parastatal producing about 55% of all domestic sugar – did so with the relatively low yield of 5.14 m.t./ha. of cane in 1986/7. Because of its outmoded refining plant, the industrial sugar it manufactured was of mediocre quality (interview information). The ex-factory price of palm and kernel oil in the same year was about three times the CFAF world price (220: 77 CFAF per kg).
47. An example is provided by the work of the Zambian Tariff Commission of Enquiry, which held extensive hearings in the course of 1985, on the eve of the introduction of foreign-exchange auctioning, import liberalisation and price de-control. As pointed out in Chapter 9, the hearings generated substantive and wide-ranging debate on the major economic issues of the day.

References and Bibliography

Banque Camerounaise de Développement (BCD) (1987), *Rapport d'Activités, Exercices 1983–1984 et 1985–1986*, Yaoundé.
Banque des Etats de l'Afrique Centrale (various years), *Etudes et Statistiques*.
Centre National d'Assistance aux Petites et Moyennes Entreprises (CAPME) (1985), *Evaluation de l'Assistance du CAPME, 1982/3 à 1984/5*, Douala, October.
—— (1987) *Rapport d'Activité Intermédiaire de l'Exercice 1986/1987*, March.
Economist Intelligence Unit (EIU) (various years), *Country Report, Cameroon, CAR, Chad; Country Profile*, London, EIU.
Government of Cameroon, Ministry of Commerce and Industry (1984 and 1986), *Programme Général des Exchanges*, (pre-publication text).
—— Ministry of the Plan and Regional Development (1984), *Le Tes Camerounais de 1979/80 pour la Préparation du VIe Plan* (internal document).
—— (1986/7), *Note Annuelle Statistique 1987*, (pre-publication text).
Groupement Interprofessionel pour l'Etude et la Coordination des Intérets Economiques au Cameroun (GICAM) (1986 and 1987), *L'Economie Camerounaise, Bilans des Exercices 1982-1983, 1984-1985*, Yaoundé.
République du Cameroun, Ministère du Plan et de l'Aménagement du Territoire, Direction de la Statistique et de la Comptabilité Nationale (1985), *Comptes Nationaux du Cameroun (version SCN)*, Yaoundé, May.
—— *Tableau Entrees – Sorties, 1979/80*, Yaoundé.
—— (1986), *Note Annuelle de Statistique, 1984/5*, Yaoundé.
Société pour le Développement Economique et Social (SEDES) (1986), *Industrialisation des Pays d'Afrique Sub-Saharienne, Le Cas du Cameroun*, Paris, April.
Société Nationale d'Investissement (SNI) (1983 and 1986), Direction Generale, *Rapports d'Activités, Exercices 1981/2, 1984/5*, Yaoundé, June.
SYNDUSTRICAM (1987), *Rapport d'Activités 1985/6 and 1987*, Yaoundé.
United Nations Conference on Trade and Development (UNCTAD) (various years), *Handbook of International Trade and Development Statistics, Supplements*, Geneva.
—— (various years), *Monthly Commodity Price Bulletin*, Geneva.
United Nations Development Programme (UNDP) (1987), *Déscriptif du Projet CMR/87/015/01/12*.
United Nations Industrial Development Organisation (UNIDO), *Projet, Plan Directeur d'Industrialisation, (phase II)*, DPR/83/001, various sub-sectoral studies.
—— (1986a), *Country Profile – Cameroon*, IDDA/CMR/86, Vienna, June.
—— (1986b), *Cameroon*, Industrial Development Review Series, Vienna, October.
—— (1987a), *A Statistical Review of Economic and Industrial Performance*, "United Republic of Cameroon", Vienna, January.
—— (1987b), *Assistance dans L'Elaboration d'un Plan Directeur Industriel au Cameroun*, reports by Consultants (Maxwell Stamp Associates), Vienna/Yaoundé, September.

United States Agency for International Development (USAID) (1983), *AID Evaluation Special Study No. 16,* 'The Tortoise Walk, Public Policy and Private Activity in the Economic Development of Cameroon', Washington DC, March.

World Bank (1980), *Industrial Development and Policy in Cameroon,* (three volumes), Washington DC, World Bank, September.

—— (1984), *Country Economic Memorandum,* Washington DC, World Bank, June.

—— (1986a) *Cameroon: Financial Sector Report,* (No. 6028–CM), Washington DC, World Bank, June.

—— (1986b), *Price Prospects for Major Primary Commodities,* (No. 814/86), Washington DC, World Bank, October.

—— (1986c), *Cameroon – Industrial Sector Policies and Planning,* Washington DC, World Bank.

—— (1987), *Economic Memorandum* (No. 8395–CM), Washington DC, World Bank, February.

Statistical Appendix

Table 5.A1 *GDP: structure and growth, 1970–84 (constant 1980 US$ 10^9 and %)*

	GDP		Contribution of Value Added by:				
	Value growth		Agric.	Manuf.	Constr.	Trade	Trans/Stor.
1970	5.0)		27	11	3	21	6
	)	3.5					
1975	5.9)		28	10	4	15	7
	)	7.5					
1980	8.5)		27	10	6	13	6
	)	6.5					
1984	10.9)		25	10	6	13	6
			Services	GFCF	Exports	Imports (−)	
1970			17	22	20	24	
1975			20	21	21	23	
1980			21	25	22	26	
1984			21	23	17	25	

Source: UNIDO, Statistics and Survey Unit, 1987.

Table 5.A2 *Population and labour force, 1965–85 (million and %)*

	Population		Total Labour Force	
	Number	Growth rate	Number	Growth rate
1965	6.1	2.1	3.1	1.3
1970	6.7	2.3	3.4	1.5
1975	7.6	2.5	3.6	1.6
1980	8.6	2.7	3.9	1.7
1985	9.9	2.8	. .	. .

Source: Ibid.

Table 5.A3 *Manufacturing Value Added (MVA) in current producer values, growth rates (1975–85) at constant 1980 prices*

	a. MVA in CFAF 10^9		b. growth rate (%)
Subsector	1975	1985	1975–1982
Food processing	3.4	42.7	5.0
Beverages	10.4	119.4	15.2[a]
Textiles	4.8	25.1	n.a.
Apparel	1.2	8.5	6.3
Leather products	0.5	5.2	13.9
Footwear	1.8	11.1	13.9
Wood products	0.5	6.0	6.5[a]

Table 5.A3 *Cont'd*

	a. MVA in CFAF 10⁹		b. growth rate (%)
Subsector	1975	1985	1975–1982
Furniture (non artis)	neg.	0.8	6.5[a]
Paper and products	0.2	4.3	n.a.
Printing & publish.	0.4	5.2	n.a.
Ind. Chemicals	0.6	5.8	− 0.8
Other chemicals	3.3	17.6	7.8
Rubber products	neg.	2.0	n.a.
Plastic products	0.9	8.1	n.a.
Ceramic ware	0.6	4.3	2.5
Glass products	0.5	3.3	2.5
Non-metallic min.	1.3	8.8	2.5
Iron & steel	0.8	20.4	n.a.
Non-ferrous metals	2.0	15.1	4.1[a]
Fabricated metal	0.2	n.a.	5.7[b]
Non-elec. machinery	2.6	19.1	5.7[b]
Electrical machin.	0.7	5.2	− 2.7
Transport equip.	0.3	2.4	3.5
Other manufactures	0.3	10.0	n.a.
TOTAL	41.8	383.0	5.0[c]

Source: UNIDO, Statistics and Survey Unit, 1987, tables 4 and 8.

Notes: Petroleum not included for lack of data.
[a] 1975–83
[b] 1975–80
[c] 1975–84

Table 5.A4 *CFAF/US$ average par/market rates 1960–88*

1960	1965	1970	1975	1980	1985	1986	1987	1988
246.85	246.85	277.71	214.31	211.28	449.26	346.30	300.54	297.8

Source: IMF, *International Financial Statistics*, 1989.

Table 5.A5 *GDP by industrial origin, real annual growth 1979–85 and current values 1984/5, 1985/6*

	% (comp.) 1979–85	CFAF bn	
		1984/5	1985/6
Agric., Fisheries & Forestry	5.3	785.3	790.4
Oil Extraction & Quarrying	54.9	654.3	629.7
Manufacturing incl. oil refining	15.3	448.5	422.4
Electricity, Gas, Water	9.5	46.7	37.7
Building & Public Works	14.6	220.7	227.6
Trade, Restaurants, Hotels	7.0	414.9	564.9
Transport & Communications	4.8	169.6	230.7
Public Administration	7.4	245.0	248.8
Other services incl. Banking	9.0	495.9	512.6
Import Duties & Charges	3.9	197.1	174.4
GROSS DOMESTIC PRODUCT (market pr.)	10.2	3,838.1[a]	4,527.5
Memo item: Non-oil GDP	7.9	3,209.2	n.a.

Source: Ministry of Planning and Regional Development, *Note Annuelle Statistique* and World Bank, *Economic Memorandum*, Feb. 1987.

Note: [a] = Adjusted

Table 5.A6 *Sectoral contribution to GDP 1979/80 and 1984/5 (%)*

	1979/80	1984/5
Agriculture, Fisheries, Forestry	28.7	20.6
Petroleum extraction and Quarrying	7.5	16.4
Manufacturing incl. oil refining	8.8	11.0
Electricity, Gas, Water	1.2	1.0
Building & Public Works	6.0	5.9
Trade, Hotels, Restaurants	14.6	14.7
Transport & Communications	6.0	6.0
Public Administration	8.5	6.5
Other services incl. Banking	13.3	13.4
Customs duties & charges	5.4	4.5
GROSS DOMESTIC PRODUCT (market pr.)	100.0	100.0
of which non-oil GDP	92.5	83.6

Source: Ibid.

Table 5.A7 *Origin and use of resources, 1983/4 and 1984/5 (at constant 1979/80 prices, CFAF bn and %)*

	1983/4	1984/5
Gross Domestic Product	2,010.9	2,184.6
Terms of Trade Effect	24.6	11.0
Gross Domestic Income	2,035.5	2,195.6
Resource Gap	− 166.9	− 242.6
Imports (goods & n.f. services)	447.35	434.5
Exports (goods & n.f. services)	589.65	666.2
Capacity to import	614.3	677.1
Available Resources	1,868.1	1,953.0
of which:		
Private consumption	63%	62%
Public consumption	10%	10%
Gross fixed investment	26%	27%

Source: World Bank, 1987: Table 2.5.

Table 5.A8 *Export products: production, exports and prices, 1982/3–1986/7 (metric tonnes, US$ and CFAF)*

	1982/3	1983/4	1984/5	1985/6	1986/7
PETROLEUM					
Prodn. ('000 mt)	n.a.	6,812	8,835	8,977	8,589
Exports ('000 mt)	4,940	5,312	7,335	7,477	7,089
Price/barrel US$	( )	28.5	26.8	21.1	14.3
Price/barrel CFAF	( )	11,683	12,621	8,150	4,563
COCOA					
Prodn. ('000 mt)	106.3	109.0	120.9	118.8	123.1
Exports ('000 mt)	108.2	90.4	102.0	94.5	98.6
Producer price/kg CFAF	330	370	410	420	420
World price/kg CFAF	776	1,024	1,102	846	652
ARABICA COFFEE					
Prodn. ('000 mt)	24.9	16.8	18.9	19.3	22.9
Exports ('000 mt)	22.0	28.0	19.7	24.3	9.1
Producer price/kg CFAF	370	410	450	475	475
World price/kg CFAF	1,020	1,269	1,434	1,662	1,011
ROBUSTA COFFEE					
Prodn. ('000 mt)	105.4	46.9	118.9	76.8	120.1
Exports ('000 mt)	92.2	103.6	74.0	93.7	65.4
Producer price/kg CFAF	350	390	430	440	440
World price/kg CFAF	952	1,223	1,138	1,179	827
COTTON					
Prodn. ('000 mt)	72.4	94.6	97.5	115.5	122.8
Exports ('000 mt)	27.3	22.5	31.4	33.5	33.7
Producer price/kg CFAF	100	111	124	135	135
World price/kg CFAF	548	726	693	452	348
TOBACCO					
Prodn. ('000 mt)	1.6	1.8	2.5	2.1	2.2
Exports ('000 mt)	1.2	1.2	1.3	1.4	1.2
Producer price/kg CFAF	434	492	493	585	588
RUBBER					
Prodn. ('000 mt)	16.2	16.4	17.7	14.5	17.4
Exports ('000 mt)	13.6	12.8	19.1	15.9	15.5

Source: Ministry of Planning and Regional Development and the Cameroon Tobacco Company.

Note: World prices as reported and calculated by the ONCPB.

Table 5.A9 *Index of industrial production (1974/5 = 100)*

Subsector	1983/4	1984/5	1985/6	Change '86/'85
Industrial agric.	199	223	274	+23%
Industrial fishing	61	55	23	−57%
Forestry	194	227	199	−12%
Grain & oilseed mill.	240	208	138	−34%
Agric. processing	197	229	222	−3%
Bakeries	150	146	155	+6%
Other food industr.	1,724	1,875	2,225	+19%
Beverages & Tobacco	251	302	332	+10%
Textiles & clothing	173	182	151	−17%
Leather & shoemaking	96	91	113	+24%
Woodworking	135	153	184	+20%
Paper manufacture	242	272	269	+3%
Industrial chemicals	234	259	255	−1%
Rubber & plastics	201	223	285	+28%
Metallurgy	199	153	157	+2%
Mechanical Engin.	212	173	162	−6%
Transport equipt.	133	170	192	+13%
Other manufactures	668	562	637	+13%
Public utilities	197	214	221	+3%
Overall index	216	239	249	+4%

Source: *Note Annuelle Statistique*, 1987.

Table 5.A10 *World Bank's petroleum price and production forecasts 1985–86 (US$ and metric tonnes)*

	1986	1987	1989	1991	1994	1996
"PESSIMISTIC" SCENARIO[a]						
Price per barrel:						
in constant 1984 US$	19.9	13.6	15.8	16.1	17.5	18.6
in current US$	20.6	15.2	20.3	23.0	28.3	32.4
			in millions of tonnes			
Output of crude oil	8.85	8.25	5.50	3.60	1.80	1.00
Crude oil exports	7.68	7.00	4.08	2.00	–	–
"OPTIMISTIC" SCENARIO[b]						
Price per barrel:						
in constant 1984 US$	19.9	16.9	20.0	20.0	20.0	20.0
in current US$	20.6	19.1	25.7	28.6	32.2	34.9
			in millions of tonnes			
Output of crude oil	8.85	8.25	6.50	4.60	3.20	2.30
Crude oil exports	7.68	7.00	5.08	2.99	1.24	0.06

Source: World Bank, 1987: Table 24.

Notes: [a] = April 1986 estimate
[b] = January 1987 estimate.

Table 5.A11 *Industrial scenarios' average growth rates 1988/9–99/2000 (%)*

	Less Optimistic	More Optimistic
GDP (at factor cost)	3.64	4.82
Total Consumption	2.61	4.15
Exports (goods & services)	3.02	4.74
Imports (goods & services)	4.16	4.69
Import/GDP elasticity	1.14	0.97

Source: Interview data.

Table 5.A12 *Sectoral structure of effective protection, 1986/7 (%)*

Relative degree	Sub-Sectors	Average rate
LOW PROTECTION	Agriculture & Fisheries	0.72[a]
	Forestry & sawing	32.83[b]
	Petroleum products	n.a.
MODERATE TO HIGH	Furniture & paper prod.	296.34[a]
	Leather & rubber products	216.98[a]
	Base metal products	> 175.00
	Textiles	> 300.00
VERY HIGH TO	Agro-industrial products	Infinite[c]
INFINITE	Chemicals & plastics	Infinite[c]
	Mechanical/electr. mach.	Infinite[c]
	Building materials	Infinite

Source: Ministry of Planning and Regional Development.

Notes: [a] = Simple average; [b] = median; [c] = mode.

6 Côte d'Ivoire

ROGER C. RIDDELL

Introduction

Towards the end of the 1970s after nearly two decades of independence, Côte d'Ivoire[1] was heralded as one of the major success stories of African development – indeed the World Bank, among others, spoke of the 'Ivorian miracle'[2]. It would appear, too, that manufacturing played a major role in that 'miracle'. Between 1965 and 1980, GDP grew at the impressive average annual rate of 6.8%; yet the growth rate of the manufacturing sector was over 30% higher at 9.1% and well over twice the growth rate of the dominant agricultural sector. Of perhaps even more importance, manufactured exports expanded rapidly from the late 1960s to the late 1970s, accounting, by 1980, for a remarkable 35–40% of total output and the highest recorded value of manufactured exports from all countries of the sub-Saharan Africa (SSA) region (World Bank (1988: 224) and UNIDO (1986: 57)).

This early and indeed lengthy period of sustained growth and expansion, however, was not to last. Visible signs of trouble appeared as far back as the early 1970s, although the first major recession occurred only in 1976 and 1977[3]. Over these two years, the economy contracted by over 8%, even if this particular downturn was quickly eclipsed by a dramatic expansion – GDP rose on average by over 15% in each of the following three years. In the event, the recovery was short-lived and in the 1980s the record of aggregate economic performance would appear to have tarnished the country's reputation as a model for economic development. In the eight years to 1988, overall GDP growth has been negative with the economy contracting by an estimated 4% in 1987 and 1988.

Manufacturing, for its part, has fared equally poorly. During the 1980s there has been scarcely any rise in aggregate Manufacturing Value Added (MVA), even if, in the early years especially, this was the result of often violent annual fluctuations from high growth to substantial contraction rather than of persistent stagnation of the sector[4]. As for manufactured exports, when fluctuations in exchange rates are taken into account, trends indicate that these have contracted over the 1980s.

But, as the analysis of this chapter suggests, the problems of manufacturing are more deep-seated than a mere slowdown of the leading aggregates would suggest. In practice the sector remains fragile, linked into and vulnerable to changes in the externally-oriented agricultural sub-sector and built upon a type of foreign involvement which has inhibited the deepening of the sector and the emergence of a pole of growth distinct from the dominant export-oriented agricultural sector. Thus time-series data, highlighting prolonged expansion of manufacturing and a dramatic rise in manufactured exports, give a distorted view of a deep and permanent process of industrialisation at work in the early post-independence period. As a result, policies which in general terms advocate 'more of the same' are likely to perpetuate rather than address these deep-seated structural problems created by past industrialisation. With the benefit of hindsight, the 'miracle' – at least insofar as it refers to manufacturing industry – appears to be more of a mirage than an answer to achieving sustainable development.

For the future, the economy faces some major problems. Poor prospects for the dominant agricultural or agriculturally-based exports of cocoa, coffee and wood products, a substantial foreign debt burden, growing domestic unemployment and major problems of public finance together provide an inauspicious context for sustained and sustainable growth and development for the 1990s. Both these broader macro-constraints and the likelihood that export-led agricultural development will not provide a lasting solution to more structural development problems suggest that it will become increasingly necessary to look afresh at the manufacturing sector and the more substantial role it might well be required to take. Yet there remains a very real danger, unless the past record of manufacturing development is critically analysed and its fundamental weaknesses highlighted, that neither the more limited role for manufacturing currently envisaged by the policy-makers nor the more substantial role it might play will be achieved. If this happens, the economy is likely to be even more vulnerable and exposed in the mid-1990s than it has increasingly become since at least the early 1970s.

Analysing the evolution and the future role of manufacturing in Côte d'Ivoire is important for another reason. It provides the opportunity to examine critically the consequences of implementing macro-policies which, in many major respects, are not only strikingly similar to those being advocated by the World Bank and the International Monetary Fund for other countries in contemporary SSA but which represent probably the most detailed and elaborate example of such efforts in the entire African continent: an export-oriented development strategy fuelled by private, and in particular, foreign investment, with manufacturing expansion based predominantly on the further processing of leading primary products with little assistance (in the 1960s especially in the case of Côte d'Ivoire) from either high external tariffs or quantitative import restrictions. As will be discussed more fully below, the results to date of such policies in Côte d'Ivoire have been far from satisfactory, while the discussion of future policies instill little optimism that the fundamental problems of the sector will be successfully resolved. Indeed it could be argued that it has been in part because of the implementation of these policies that the country's manufacturing base exhibits major structural weaknesses today.

The rest of this chapter is divided into three further sections. The next section describes the evolution of manufacturing from Independence to the late 1980s and discusses the changing policy context. The third section outlines the major macroeconomic constraints facing the country in the late 1980s and those likely to persist into the next decade. Within this particular context, the final section discusses the prospects for manufacturing growth over the next few years, including critical analysis of the quantitative targets and policy prescriptions now being debated as well as highlighting some of the key factors which would need to be addressed if the structure of the sector is to be reformed.

The manufacturing sector post-independence

AN INITIAL LOOK AT THE EVOLUTION OF THE SECTOR

A quick overview can be obtained by tracing the time-series data of the key indicators of performance. Yet, as with the other country case-studies, great care has to be taken when using these statistics. Three particular problems need to be highlighted in relation to Côte d'Ivoire. First, there are no reliable official time-series data available in constant prices for the particularly interesting[5] pre-1972 and post-1984 periods; this probably goes some way to explaining the frequently very different figures provided for the historical values of MVA, even from the same agency[6]. Second, there is an increasing divergence between MVA at market price and at factor cost, arising largely because of the increasing importance of taxes on petroleum refining from the mid-1960s[7]. Finally, and relatedly, the definitions of what constitutes manufacturing differ in relation to different sources used within Côte d'Ivoire. In particular, data originating in the Ministry of Planning (frequently used in UNIDO time-series tables) diverge increasingly from those from the Ministry of Finance and used, for example, in World Bank tables in country-specific studies, although not (to add further confusion) in the Bank's *World Tables* and *World Development Report*. A major reason for these differences is the lack of consistency in relation to petroleum refining, with World Bank country-specific studies including this in manufacturing and at least country-based UNIDO studies and other World Bank sources including it in electricity, gas and water[8].

In spite of these problems, an analysis of the figures which are available shows a number of clear trends. Taken as a whole, World Bank data indicate that the 26 years to 1986 have been a period of sustained expansion in manufacturing: on average MVA has risen by over 7.5% a year[9]. With GDP growth averaging a little over 4% a year and agricultural growth a far lower 2.5%, manufacturing has not only become an increasingly important productive sector – accounting for some 10–14% of GDP by the end of the 1980s compared with only 4% at Independence[10] – but it has become relatively more important vis-à-vis the still-dominant agricultural sector. As shown in the Bank-sourced data reproduced in Table 6.1, in each successive period since Independence in 1960, manufacturing growth rates have been higher than those in both the agricultural sector and the economy as a whole.

Table 6.1 *Trends in growth rates, 1960–86*

	1965–80	1980–86	1965–73	1973–84
Gross Domestic Product	6.8	− 0.3	7.1	3.7
Manufacturing Value added	9.1	0.9ᵃ	8.9	5.0
Value Added in Agriculture	3.3	0.9	3.7	3.3

Source: World Bank, *World Development Reports, 1986 to 1988.*

Note: ᵃ estimate see Note for Figure 6.2.

Furthermore, the record of manufactured exports over the period appears also to reveal three important trends. The first is the absolute and progressive rise in manufactured exports measured in the local currency, the CFA (Communauté Financière Africaine) franc[11]. As shown in Appendix Table 6.A3, these increased eight-fold in the early 1960s, doubled between 1965 and 1973, doubled again over the next two years as well as from 1975 to 1980 and, finally, doubled from 1980 to 1984. The second positive trend is the large and in general growing share of manufactures in total exports; Figure 6.1 indicates a steady rise in this ratio to the late 1960s, followed by a more volatile period but which has resulted in the ratio of manufactured to total exports at still around 35% by the mid-1980s. Third, and also shown in Figure 6.1, has been the very high (in comparison with other SSA countries) share of exports in total manufacturing production.

A range of additional positive indicators are apparent from other aggregate trends of performance in the post-Independence period. Total industrial employment[12] has risen from

Figure 6.1 *Trends in ratios of manufactured to total exports and manufactured exports to total manufactured output*

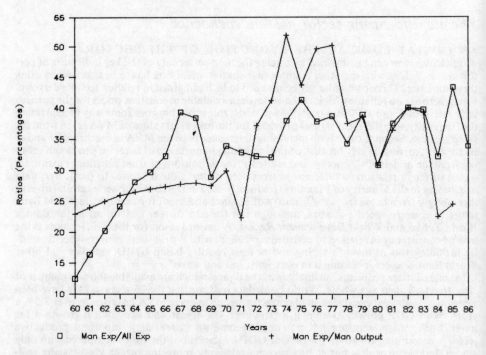

Source: World Bank (1975) and (1987) and UNIDO (1986) and Data-Bank, October 1988.

Notes: Figures for 1960–72 from World Bank (1975) with data from 1961 to 1964, 1966 to 1967 and 1969 extrapolated from data for 1960, 1965, 1968 and 1970 respectively. Post 1962 data are the average of UNIDO and World Bank data, the figures being very different from the two sources.

13,000 in 1960, to 36, 310 in 1970, 71,400 in 1980 and to 94,060 by 1986. As a share of total modern sector employment, manufacturing accounted for over 17% by the late 1980s compared with 13% at the start of the 1970s. Cumulative industrial investment, which stood at CFAF 22m. in 1960, had risen to CFAF 701 m. by 1980 and expanded to CFAF 1,756m. by 1986. Importantly, too, both investment per employee and labour productivity have shown significant gains: investment per worker rising from CFAF 1.7m. in 1960 to CFAF 9.8m. in 1980 and to CFAF 18.7m. by 1986, and labour productivity rising from CFAF 1m. in 1960 to CFAF 3.9m. by 1980 and up again to 5.8m. by 1986 (Ministère de l'Industrie, 1988).

Finally, Côte d'Ivoire appears to have succeeded – where so many African countries have failed – in attracting (in African terms) significant inflows of foreign capital into its manufacturing sector. In the period 1965–84, net private inflows recorded on the capital account of the balance of payments amounted to $1,160 m., or almost $60 m. a year. This is broken down as follows: an average of over $100 m. a year in the period 1973–83 and $25 m. a year in 1980–86[13]. In spite of this large foreign inflow, some data would appear to suggest that Côte d'Ivoire has had some success from the early-1970s onwards in increasing the share of Ivorian capital in manufacturing. In 1971, a World Bank survey (1975: Table Annex 8.A6) maintained that 90% of manufacturing was owned by foreigners; yet by 1980, 61% was apparently Ivorian owned and by 1986 the Ivorian share had seemingly risen to 81%[14]. It needs to be stressed, however, that these figures are contradicted by other data, as is apparent from Table 6.7 below. Wide diversity in ownership data arises both because of the omission of significant parts of manufacturing, such as the important informal sector and most Lebanese-owned enterprises, and because a number of the handful of foreign companies which dominate agro-processing have moved to create 'Ivorian' holdings – as Unilever did in 1981.

Combining all these positive attributes would suggest that Côte d'Ivoire has succeeded in producing a manufacturing base strong and diversified and well able to face the more hostile external environment of the 1990s. Such a conclusion, although the conventional view, remains profoundly misleading. As the next section shows, the sector is extremely fragile and highly dependent, in part as a result of the way in which the incentive structure, directly and indirectly related to manufacturing, has evolved in the post-Independence period.

A SECOND LOOK: WEAKNESSES EXPOSED

Declining growth rates.   The secular expansion of the manufacturing sector conceals a dramatic slowdown in growth since the 1960s and, at least over the past decade, a very volatile pattern of annual changes in growth rates. As the data in Table 6.1 suggest, and as clearly shown in Figure 6.2, the rate of growth of manufacturing slowed appreciably from the 1960s to the 1970s and slowed further in the early years of the 1980s. Manufacturing value added (MVA) contracted in 1987 and 1988 and in early 1989 this dismal performance was expected to continue for the remainder of the decade[15]. In constant prices, MVA peaked in 1980; by 1988, in spite of some growth in some of the previous years, MVA had still not reached the level achieved at the end of the 1970s. The secular trend in value added from 1963 to 1988 is shown in Appendix Figure 6.A1.

Trends in manufacturing export performance also look far less impressive when measured in constant US dollars. According to World Bank data, for instance, from 1965 to 1984 the percentage share of manufactures in total exports actually fell – from 39 to 36% – and only rose marginally (from 24 to 25%) if one excludes oil and petroleum product exports. The details are shown in Table 6.A3. Additionally, as shown in Figure 6.1, in current price terms, the rising trend of manufactured to total exports came to a halt as long ago as the late 1960s, while the ratio of manufactured exports to manufactured output has moved progressively downwards since the early 1970s. As for the contribution of manufacturing to total national production, Figure 6.3 reveals that the rise in this particular ratio occurred solely in the 1960s; thereafter, it has remained fairly static – indeed it it has progressively, albeit only marginally, tended to *fall*.

Size and industrial concentration.   Although the data for the size and number of industrial enterprises are both sketchy and contradictory, it is apparent that manufacturing industry consists predominantly of a tiny number of, in national terms, vast enterprises, many of them foreign-owned or in large part foreign-controlled. We look here briefly at the geographical concentration of industry and the dominant contribution to production by a very small number of large firms.

The concentration problem can be quickly told. In 1986, Côte d'Ivoire had a population of

Figure 6.2 *Trends in real MVA growth, 1960–88*

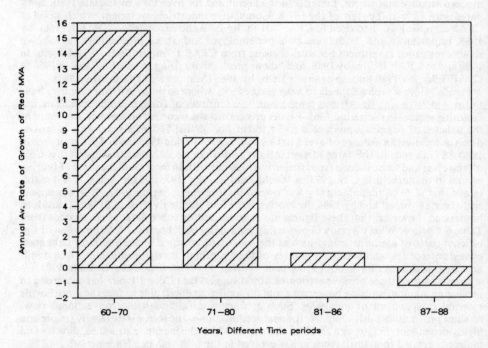

Years, Different Time periods

Source: UNIDO (1986), UNIDO data-base October 1988, World Bank (1975 and 1988) and (for 1987 and 1988) Economy and Finance Ministry, 1988 Annual Report.

Note: Up to 1980 data are averages of UNIDO and World Bank data; from 1981 to 1984 the figures are the averages of two different sets of UNIDO figures and the final figures from 1986 to 1988 are from UNIDO (for 1986) and estimates from the Economy and Finance Ministry for the latter two years.

around 10 million and, in African terms, a high level of urbanisation: an estimated 45% live in the main towns and cities, less than half of them in the capital, Abidjan. Yet Abidjan accounts for a little over half the industrial labour force and some two-thirds of all registered manufacturing establishments, and is responsible for some three-quarters of all recorded MVA. In spite of efforts to decentralise industry, especially in more recent years, there has been little change in these indicators of concentration at least since the early 1970s (World Bank, 1975: 8–9 and UNIDO, 1986: 31)[16].

To provide an accurate assessment of the breakdown of industry by size of establishment is difficult, as it is far from clear how many industrial enterprises there are. Data provided by the semi-official Chambre d'Industrie suggest that there were 727 individual industrial enterprises in 1982 increasing to 750 by 1984. For its part, the Ministère de l'Industrie suggests that there were 492 industrial enterprises in 1982 rising to 528 by 1984 (UNIDO, 1986: 32 and Minstère de l'Industrie, 1988). Yet, according to the Secrétariat au Plan et à l'Industrie, in 1980 there were closer to 18,000 enterprises (see République Francaise, Ministère de La Coopération, 1986: 79). Part of the reason for these huge differences relates to the extent to which the details of particularly small-scale and informal sector manufacturing establishments are captured in the official statistics.

Ministère de l'Industrie data provide a three-way classification of industries: large-scale (defined as undertakings with a turnover of more than CFAF 200 m. a year), small and medium-sized enterprises (those whose turnover ranges from CFAF 40 m. to 200 m.) and what are termed 'artisanal and informal sector' enterprises, defined as those with a turnover of less than CFAF 40 m. a year. According to the Ministry's statistics, in 1986 there was an almost equal division between the numbers within each grouping, with both the number and proportion of artisanal and informal sector enterprises expanding rapidly in the 1980s. When, however, these enterprises are broken down by contribution to employment, investment and turnover, it is clear that it is the large-scale enterprises which dominate[17]. As can be

Figure 6.3   *The share of manufacturing and agriculture in gross domestic product 1960–86*

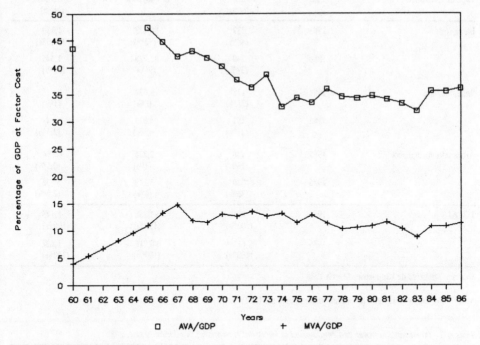

Source: World Bank (1975) and (1987).

Note: The 1984–86 figures for the MVA/GDP ratio are the author's estimates, based on data from the UNIDO data-base as of October 1988.

seen from Table 6.2, these account for over 90% of total industrial employment and 95% of total industrial investment.

Yet not even these figures capture the full extent of industrial concentration. In 1983, 72% of all value added and a similar proportion of exports originated in just 48 enterprises, less than 10% of the (lower estimated) total, with the leading 10 enterprises alone responsible for 47% of MVA for the whole of manufacturing[18]. In 1982, as shown in Table 6.3, just 4 enterprises (less than 1%) were responsible for 67% of all industrial investment, 11 enterprises (2.5%) for 41% of turnover and 9 enterprises (1%) for 30% of industrial employment. Clearly the performance of these dozen or so enterprises makes a major difference to trends in manufacturing in Côte d'Ivoire.

Sub-sectoral fragility.   More profound weaknesses are revealed when some sub-sectoral trends of the sector's evolution are examined. Although different sources produce differences in the time-series trends, it is quite apparent that the expansion has led to little substantial structural change within the manufacturing sector as a whole. As in the early 1960s, so today, Côte d'Ivoire remains dominated by the production of consumer goods, which still accounts for well over 60% (and perhaps as much as 70%) of total MVA. As a share of total MVA, intermediate and capital goods production has remained fairly static over the whole period. Of note, too, the data suggest that some of the diversification in production which had taken place to the mid-1970s has been reversed over the more recent decade and a half. The trends by broad sub-sectoral classification (in constant prices) are shown in Figure 6.4, with changes from 1960 to 1986 at current prices reproduced in Table 6.A4.

The trends in MVA by an 8 sub-sectoral division are shown in Figures 6.A2 and 6.A3. Of particular importance are the changes within the consumer goods branches. While textiles and clothing production have increased steadily in real terms, their share of total production has declined dramatically (from 31% of total MVA in 1960 to 10% by 1986). Similarly, there has been only a marginal increase in wood production over nearly 30 years, the share in total

Table 6.2 *Selected industrial indicators by size of establishment 1981–6, CFAF bn*

Type of Enterprise	Year	Number of Enterprises	Employment	Investment (gross)
Large-scale	1981	237 (48%)	86,438 (92%)	1,130 (98.5%)
	1986[a]	240 (39%)	82,728 (91%)	1,545 (95%)
Small/medium	1981	118 (25%)	5,624 (6%)	11 (1%)
	1986	151 (25%)	4,815 (5%)	41 (2.5%)
Artisanal/informal sector	1981	138 (28%)	2,226 (2%)	4 (0.5%)
	1986	220 (36%)	3,173 (4%)	36 (2.5%)
TOTALS	1981	493 (100%)	94,288 (100%)	1,145 (100%)
	1986	611 (100%)	90,716 (100%)	1,622 (100%)

Source: Ministère de l'Industrie, March 1988.

Note: [a] For employment and investment these figures are for 1985.

Table 6.3 *Investment, turnover and employment in industrial enterprises[a] in relation to size, 1982*

Enterprises No.	%	Total Investment CFAF bn	%	Enterprises No.	%	Total turnover CFAF bn	%	Enterprises No.	%	Total Employment '000	%
1	–	312.4	29	3	–	243.8	23	3	–	11.6	17
3	–	403.0	38	8	1	191.0	18	6	1	8.7	13
4	–	59.7	6	13	2	173.2	16	14	2	10.2	15
719 (remainder)	99	298.9	27	703	97	458.2	43	704	97	47.9	55
Totals:											
727	100	1,074.0	100	727	100	1,066.2	100	727	100	68.4	100

Source: Chambre d'Industrie, Abidjan, *L'Industrie ivoirienne en 1972* and *Centrale des Bilans* (1983) reproduced in UNIDO (1986:32 and 76).

Note: [a] These figures probably overestimate the degree of industrial concentration as they almost certainly include the major electrical energy company, EECI, responsible, in 1983, for 21% of total 'industrial' value added. Excluding EECI, however, and in terms of value added, the following five firms contributed nearly 60% of total industrial value added in 1973: CIDT (cotton); SITAB (tobacco); PALMINDUSTRIE (vegetable oil); BLOHORN-HSL (vegetable oil) and SODESUCRE (sugar).

manufacturing having halved from 10 to 5% of total MVA. On the other hand, food processing and beverages and tobacco production have expanded rapidly and consistently over the period and on their own these groups now account for almost half of all MVA, up from 28% in 1960. What this trend suggests is that the impression given in Figure 6.3, of the growing importance of manufacturing vis-à-vis agriculture, is exaggerated: the growth of manufacturing has been due predominantly to the processing of agricultural produce, not to any lessening of the linkage between the two sectors, nor the establishment of a manufacturing sector more independent from the export of a handful of agro-processed products.

As for the long-term trends of intermediate and capital goods production, Figure 6.A3 shows a steady rise in real value to the early 1970s followed by a volatile period to the end of

Figure 6.4 *Sub-sectoral breakdown of MVA by broad classification, 1963–88 at fixed (1980) prices*

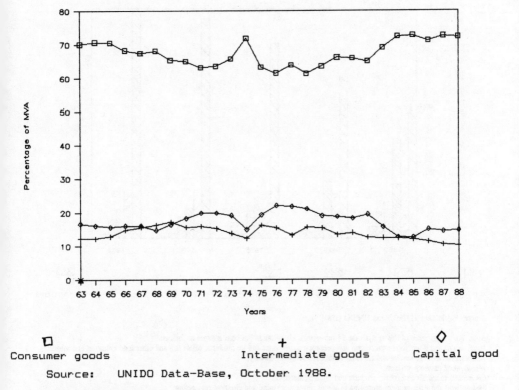

Consumer goods   Intermediate goods   Capital good

Source: UNIDO Data-Base, October 1988.

Source: UNIDO Data-Base, October 1988.

the 1970s and, finally, for all these sub-sectors, a marked decline in production from the 1980s onwards.

A far from strong export base.   The sub-sectoral analysis of manufactured exports confirms this picture of structural fragility. Figure 6.5 shows two clear and worrying trends. First that manufactured exports were far more diversified in the mid-1960s than in the early 1980s, second, the quite remarkable rise in the share of food-related manufactures in total exports, even if preliminary data for later years suggest some success in reversing this trend[19]. Wood, transport, chemical and metal exports have all suffered a proportionate decline in their share of total manufactured exports, at least since 1970, and, in the case of wood and metal exports, even earlier. Thus wood exports accounted for over 30% of total manufactured exports in 1965 but for less than 10% by 1982, metal exports for more than 10% of the total in 1965, but for less than 2% by the early 1980s, with transport equipment falling from just over 3% in the 1960s to a negligible amount by the early 1980s. As for food-related exports, these rose from just under 40% of the total in 1965 to nearly 70% by the early 1980s.

When trends in manufactured exports in fixed US dollar terms are analysed – see Figure 6.A4 – they reveal even more worrying trends. The only manufactured exports which have increased in real terms since the early 1970s are textiles, clothing, shoes and leather goods. In contrast, wood-related exports reached only three-quarters of their 1965 value by 1984, while 'other' exports (non-consumer good exports) lost over half their real value from 1965 to 1970 and have never really recovered since.

The expansion of manufactured exports has been substantially assisted by access to captive regional markets, initially among the French-speaking territories of West Africa under CEAO (the West Africa Economic Community), and latterly in the expanded market of

Figure 6.5 *Trends in manufactured exports by sub-sectoral grouping 1965–82, Current CFAF bn*

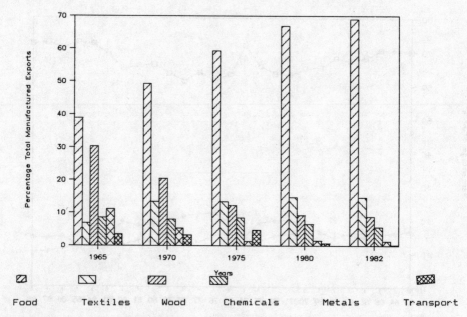

Source: World Bank (1975:32) and UNIDO (1986:57).

Note: For the purposes of this analysis the 14 sub-sectoral classification has been grouped as follows:
Food: grains and flour, food preservation and preparation, beverages and ice products, edible fats and other food industries and tobacco;
Textiles and clothing: textiles and clothing, leather and footwear industry;
Wood: wood industry products;
Chemicals: chemicals and rubber products and building materials;
Metals: iron and steel, primary processing of metals, other mechanical and electrical engineering;
Transport: transport equipment.

ECOWAS – the Economic Community of West African States[20]. Côte d'Ivoire was fortunate to be among the first French-speaking territories of West Africa to establish a substantial industrial base. Given the level of contacts between the countries, it quickly became a natural supplier of manufactured goods to these far less developed economies, the transport advantages and a favourable tariff structure vis-à-vis France and the non-CEAO countries in particular providing a natural market advantage and the ability to export at higher than internationally competitive prices[21]. As a result, Côte d'Ivoire's manufactured exports have been biased heavily in favour of these markets.

In the 1970s and 1980s, however, as trade has expanded between both French and English-speaking countries of West Africa and as other countries of the region have developed their own industries, the market for the simpler consumer goods exports which have dominated manufactured exports from Côte d'Ivoire have met with increased competition[22]. Yet the countries of West Africa continue to be its major market for non-food manufactured exports. Indeed the data, incomplete though they are, suggest that over the period 1971–83 the regional market has become a more significant outlet: in 1971, 24% of all industrial exports went to French-speaking African countries and 29% to Africa, but by 1983 the share appeared to be closer to 36%[23]. Excluding food-processed exports, UNIDO data indicate that around 42% of manufactured exports went to African countries. But when the narrower definition of manufactured exports is taken (SITC 5–8, less 68 non-ferrous metals and 332, petroleum products), UNIDO data for 1983 reveal that 68% of all these exports went to developing countries, most being within the West African region[24]. If in the future manufactures are to have a higher profile in national exports, as is the objective of the government and its advisers, it will be necessary to expand exports substantially beyond the traditional West African market.

Weak inter-linkages.   Yet other indicators of fragility come from an analysis of the inter-linkages between the different sub-sectors of the economy and the degree and extent of dependence upon imports for the supply of intermediate inputs. Recent and relatively comprehensive figures (of input/output data) showing these linkages are from the year 1980[25]. These reveal that an extremely high proportion of purchases of material inputs into manufacturing (some 54–58%) were imported. As shown in Table 6.4, the ratio of imported to total inputs was below 15% for only one industrial sub-sector, wood products and, remarkably, was almost 70% for the leather and footwear sub-sectors. For the food industry, the ratio exceeded 30% for two out of the three sub-sectors. More recent data for 1985 for the food sub-sectors give an overall import to total purchase ratio of 25%, ranging from 82% for fish preparations, 48% for cereals (substantially higher than that recorded in 1980) and a low of 2% for fruit and vegetable processing[26]. For textiles, too, almost 40% of inputs were imported. For the sub-sectors producing more complex products, the degree of import dependence was even more pronounced. Thus for the chemical, rubber, transport equipment and machinery and electrical-product sub-sectors combined, imported inputs constituted 75% of total purchases.

Comparing the 1980 data with similar, but not identical, input/output data for 1974, reproduced in Table 6.A5, enables some judgements to be made about import dependence links over a more extended period. The figures indicate that they changed little during the intervening period, one notable exception being the reduced dependence on imports of the textiles (textile/clothing) sub-sector[27].

Table 6.4   *Interlinkages and imports by industrial sub-sector CFAF bn, 1980 current prices*

Sub-sector	Total Purchases	Total Imported	Total from Agriculture	Total from Other Manufacturing sub-sectors
Grain Proc.	63.5	20.7 (33%)	20.7 (33%)	15.5 (24%)
Canned Foods	116.7	27.2 (23%)	69.0 (59%)	14.7 (13%)
Other Foods	129.2	52.8 (41%)	21.4 (16%)	37.8 (29%)
Textiles	112.3	42.8 (38%)	12.2 (11%)	42.3 (38%)
Leather/Shoes	13.2	9.1 (69%)		3.4 (26%)
Wood Industry	37.1	4.5 (12%)	11.0 (30%)	12.0 (32%)
Petroleum Prod.	166.7	47.8 (29%)		100.3 (60%)
Chemicals/rubber	148.0	95.4 (65%)	5.0 (5%)	38.4 (26%)
Non-Metallic	47.9	28.0 (59%)		16.6 (35%)
Transport Equip.	155.4	108.1 (70%)		40.5 (26%)
Machinery/Electrical	229.8	194.9 (12%)		28.6
Other Industries	96.1	78.2 (81%)	0.1	14.3 (15%)
TOTAL	1,315.9	709.5 (54%)	139.4 (11%)	364.4 (28%)
Total less Petroleum Products	1,149.2	661.7 (58%)	139.4 (12%)	264.1 (23%)

Source: Ministry of Planning, *Les Comptes de la Nation 1980.*

The major interlinkages between sectors, especially the links with the agricultural sector, are summarised in Tables 6.4 and 6.5 for 1980, and in Tables 6.A5 and 6.A6 for 1974. These figures reveal a number of important structural features. First, the share of agricultural output utilised as inputs to manufacturing appears to have remained fairly static and at a very low level of around 12% of total purchases by manufacturing[28]. Thus, as the sector has evolved, it has *not* tended to become any less dependent upon the performance of the agricultural sector. Equally, there has been no increase in the share of manufacturing products destined as inputs into the agricultural sector – the ratio remaining at a very low 3 to 3.5% in the two periods under examination. Finally, there has been no overall increase in linkages *within* manufacturing, either across sub-sectors or within particular sub-sectors. As the data in Tables 6.4 and 6.A5 show, the proportion of purchases of inputs originating from the manufacturing sector has remained around the 22% level.

Equally disturbing are the contrasting trends shown between Tables 6.5 and 6.A6 in relation to purchases of manufacturing products as inputs for further manufacture. The figures reveal a substantial fall – from some 37% of total manufactured sales in 1974 to only 16% by 1980[29]. The only sub-sectoral increase has been that of textiles (textiles/clothing), the proportion here rising from 35 to 38%. Excluding petroleum processing, textiles is the sub-sector which has by far the greatest degree of intra-industrial linkage. For all other sub-sectors, a higher proportion of inputs would appear to come from abroad than from within manufacturing. Remarkably, too, this would appear to include manufacturing sub-sectors devoted to food production, where in both 1974 and again in 1980, a greater proportion of inputs were imported than were obtained from other parts of manufacturing.

Table 6.5 *Destination of sales of produce of manufacturing sub-sectors, CFAF bn, Current Prices, 1980*

Sub-sector	Total Sales	Going to Manufacturing	%	Going to Agriculture	%
Grain Proc.	87.1	11.9	14	7.2	8
Canned Foods	164.2	2.4	2	–	–
Other Foods	224.2	28.0	13	3.4	2
Textiles	144.3	30.9	21	1.3	1
Leather/Shoes	20.6	0.5	2	–	–
Wood Industry	56.8	7.4	13	–	–
Petroleum Prod.	240.1	31.8	13	12.0	5
Chemicals/rubber	206.0	53.9	26	20.3	10
Non-Metallic	63.7	15.1	24	0.7	1
Transport Equip.	210.4	41.6	20	5.1	2
Machinery/Electric	313.5	35.1	11	15.8	5
Other Industries	125.9	43.5	34	1.7	1
TOTAL	1,856.8	302.1	16	57.5	3
TOTAL less petroleum	1,616.1	270.3	16	45.5	3

Source: Ibid.

A related feature of the economy's evolution – but one which is not shown in the performance of what is manufactured – is the high proportion of food products which have been and still are imported rather than manufactured. At the end of the 1960s, the country was self-sufficient in most basic foodstuffs, but thereafter rising levels of, predominantly, rice, wheat and livestock imports have radically altered the balance. By 1985, for instance, over 50% of meat consumption was obtained from imports[30], while cereal imports amounted to $95 m. In that year, total food imports amounted to $337 m., 15% of total imports. Since then the situation has worsened in a number of respects. For instance, in the first half of 1986, food accounted for 19% of all imports. The country is self-sufficient only in yams, cassava, maize and plantains[31]. The substantial deficiencies in domestic food production, and thus also in the processing and manufacture of basic foodstuffs, are clearly indicated in Table 6.6 which shows the ratio of imports to consumption for a range of common products.

Table 6.6 *Ratio of imports to consumption for selected food products, 1985*

Less than 50%		More than 50%	
Fruit and vegetables	1.6	Beverages	50.6
Cocoa products	2.1	Milk	54.4
Beef	26.0	Tobacco products,	78.1
Sugar	27.0	Food preparations	62.8
Cereals	48.3	Fish preparations	81.1

Source: Ministère de l'Industrie (1988).

The costs of foreign involvement. We return now to the issue of the role of foreign investment in the evolution of manufacturing and the benefits derived from the injection of such funds. Further investigation reveals that there have been some major costs, as well as benefits, from this particular relationship which raise important policy questions about the way foreign investment has been and should be promoted.

Given the marked influence of foreign investment within manufacturing, it would seem reasonable to attribute a part of the structural weaknesses of the sector – the high level of manufacturing growth associated with the processing of agricultural produce, the low level of other inter-linkages and the dominance of consumer goods manufacture – to the way foreigners have been invited to invest in the Ivorian economy. The point, however, can be put more forcefully: the package of incentives offered to foreign investors has had a major impact in the way the sector's structure has evolved.

Of central importance was the 1959 Investment Code which was drafted before independence but remained in force until 1984, when it was only marginally adapted[32]. This provided, among other things, for the exemption from import duties of machinery and equipment and some intermediate goods, together with lucrative fiscal incentives, such as tax-free profits for the first five years of operation and the exemption from tax of reinvested profits for four years following reinvestment. In addition, once industries were granted 'priority agreement' status, this resulted in fixing the rate of tax to be paid for the subsequent 25 years to that prevailing at the time of the investment. These priority agreements were by no means rare, for by 1971 60 firms (almost all French) and accounting for two-thirds of total MVA, had benefitted. In addition to the incentives provided by the investment code, an almost open-door policy with regard to finance from domestic banking houses has ensured that there has been minimal constraint on the expansion of foreign enterprises through lack of access to credit.

In the 1970s, these incentives were reinforced by rising external tariffs and domestic price regulations which helped to protect domestic industries, maintain high levels of profits and, in general, prevent exposure of firms to both international and greater domestic competition. For a number of products manufactured in Côte d'Ivoire, competing imports were banned entirely. As will be discussed more fully below, one result was that by the mid-1980s much of Ivorian industry had become increasingly uncompetitive internationally, including major plants owned and operated by foreign investors in, for instance, the transport equipment, agricultural chemical, textile and shoe and leather fields.

Some of the main effects of the incentive system were to put a major brake upon the manufacture of intermediate products and machinery, to discourage import substitution beyond the level of mainly simple consumer goods, and to frustrate progress towards intra-industry inter-linkages. This is because the greatest incentives were provided in the areas of further processing of primary products, while it was short-term profits rather than investment for industrial deepening which were encouraged.

There is little doubt, too, that the dominant position of foreign investors has influenced both investment and technology decisions within the sector. In part because of relatively high levels of capital intensity, the capital costs of industrial investments have been far greater than those in many other developing countries and sometimes higher than similar investments in Europe[33]. It has also been suggested that there have been substantial losses to the economy resulting from importing inappropriate or defective machinery; for instance in the agro-industrial field alone, losses could have been as high as $50 m. in the mid-1980s (*Marchés Tropicaux et Méditerranéens* (27 December 1985: –75)[34].

Ivorian inexperience in the area of machinery purchase has been accentuated by the

economy's high and continuing level of dependence on foreign labour to fill a high proportion of posts at the technical and managerial levels and to set up and operate the plants owned
by foreigners[33]. Figures published in 1988 (for the year 1984) revealed that Ivorians
constituted only 51% of senior personnel in industry, while of all other non-qualified
employees 15% were non-Ivorian (Ministère de L'Industrie, 1988)[36]. This compares with
data for 1969 which shows that Ivorians held 56.5% of salaried posts (World Bank
1975: 13)[37]. The 1988 figures also reveal wide variations in the use of foreign labour by
industrial sub-sector: for senior posts, Ivorians were in the majority in only 6 out of the 16
industrial sub-sectors; in half the sub-sectors they constituted less than 40% (details in
Table 6.A7).

The ease with which foreign skilled workers could be hired has not only inhibited the
training of more nationals but, together with the shallow nature of industry in Côte d'Ivoire,
has frustrated the development of a cadre of local engineers and of associated skills, now
increasingly recognised as crucial for the expansion and deepening of the manufacturing
sector (see Lall, 1988). Among problems arising from over-dependence on foreign skills have
been large numbers of machinery stoppages due to skill inadequacy, the lack of ability to
adapt and repair imported machinery often built for non-African conditions, and the low
level of stocks of key spare parts – all of which were highlighted by the government in its 1988
review of industry.

Dependence on foreign labour has also reinforced the relatively higher wage structure of
such workers which itself has played a role in bolstering the country's skewed income
distribution[38] not only through the comparatively high salaries paid to foreigners –
sometimes for the same job as is done by Ivorians (see Alfthan, 1982: 47) – but also by
providing an unsustainably high benchmark for judging the level of salaries paid to or
expected by more skilled Ivorian workers. One consequence has been to stimulate the
demand for and production of luxury rather than more basic manufactures, although in
practice the more important effect would have been to sustain high and rising levels of luxury
imports of consumer goods[39].

Available wage statistics, although only indicating some of the more direct costs involved,
reveal the influence that even a small proportion of foreign workers have had on overall
wages and hence on the pattern of domestic demand. In 1977, non-African employees
constituted 2.6% of the industrial labour force but received 26% of the total wages, with
average wages 18 times higher than non-Ivorian African wages (Alfthan (1982: 45)).

The direct effects on the balance of payments are even more grave. Large numbers of
highly-paid foreigners, in manufacturing and other sectors such as education, have resulted
in significant financial outflows, especially in the form of remittance payments. When this
outflow is combined with the, frequently inter-related, net outflow of foreign companies'
profits, dividends paid to foreign shareholders, management fees and royalties, then the
beneficial effect of foreign private capital inflows on the overall balance of payments
(highlighted above) is put into a completely different light[40]. In the early 1970s, for instance,
although the domestic savings ratio was around 22%, sufficient to finance domestic investment, almost one quarter of these savings were diverted out of the country in the form of
wage transfers and dividends (UNIDO, 1986: 4).

As Figure 6.6 graphically shows, in every year from 1965 to 1984, the outflow of profits,
dividends and remittances exceeded the inflow of private capital, quite dramatically in the
post-1975 period. Indeed in the more recent 1975–84 period, it totalled CFAF 1,202 bn, 16%
of total export earnings and 4 times the *total* net inflow of private capital in the period
1965–84.

The top line of Figure 6.6 also shows that, even without the rising outflow of remittance
payments, the net effect of private capital inflows when counterbalanced by profit and
dividend outflow only assisted the balance of payments in 8 years out of 20 from 1965 to
1984. Over the entire period, there was a net outflow of CFAF 1,350 bn (World Bank 1987,
Volume IV: 10)[41].

Clearly if foreign investors are making a profit then profit and dividend outflow is going to
be high, and such an outcome is by no means unexpected. What is particularly worrying in
the case of Côte d'Ivoire, however, and given the other adverse effects noted above, is the
extent of the economy's vulnerability to foreign investor confidence; any halt in the inflow of
new investment capital is going to lead to a dramatic rise in net private outflow, as occurred in
the late 1970s and again after 1983.

The final foreign investment issue which needs to be discussed is the apparent rise in the

Figure 6.6 *Direct balance of payments effects of profit, dividend and remittance outflow and net private capital inflow CFAF bn (Current prices) 1965–84*

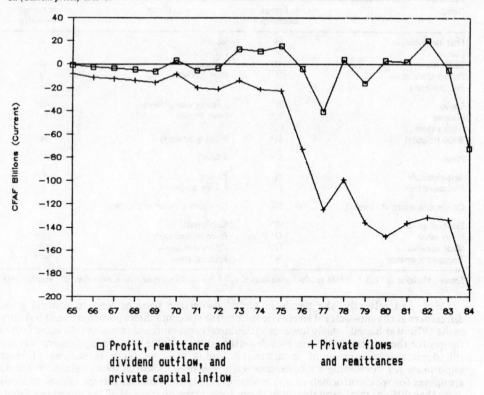

□ Profit, remittance and
   dividend outflow, and
   private capital inflow

+ Private flows
  and remittances

Source: World Bank (1987), Volume IV:10.

share of Ivorian capital in manufacturing. As noted above, some figures suggest that, in strong contrast to the early 1970s, and as a result of deliberate government policy, aggregate fixed investment in manufacturing is now largely Ivorian-owned. For instance, government data for 1986 show that of total industrial capital of CFAF 425 bn, 81% was Ivorian, 71% state and 10% private, while only 19% was foreign. While the trend has certainly been *towards* the further Ivorisation of manufacturing, three relevant points need to be made.

First, with notable exceptions, such as in 1977 and 1983, there has been no actual fall in the total amounts of foreign investment, the rising share of Ivorian capital being due almost entirely to the more rapid increase in local capital interests in manufacturing. In current terms, private foreign investment in manufacturing rose by over 10% a year from 1976 to 1982 and by 5% from 1983 to 1985 (UNIDO, 1986: 26 and Ministère de l'Industrie, 1988). Even in the post-1985 era, foreigners have continued to invest in manufacturing in Côte d'Ivoire. To quote three recent examples: the $17 m. expansion programme of FILTISAC (Filatures, Tissages, Sacs Côte d'Ivoire) which began in November 1987; the $6.6 m. investment of CIPHARM (Côte d'Ivoire Pharmaceutique) commissioned in May 1988 as the first pharmaceutical manufacturer in the country, and the announcement in mid-1988 that a US investor would be setting up a mini steel mill in the country.

Second, trends in authorised capital in Côte d'Ivoire tend to overestimate the contribution of different types of capital to value added. Thus, whereas the Ivorian share of corporate stock rose from 36 to 53% of the total from 1973 to 1979, the share of private capital in manufacturing value added rose from 29 to 53% (ECA, 1982: 5). Furthermore, of the top 20 industrial enterprises in 1983 in terms of value added – and responsible for 47% of total value added in that year – half were majority foreign-owned (see note 18 for some company details).

Table 6.7 *Foreign share of capital by industrial sub-group, 1985*

Group	% Foreign ownership	Group	% Foreign ownership
Fruit and vegetable	29	Sugar	0
Cereals	94	Coffee/cocoa	52
Edible oils	7	Tobacco	60
Food preparations	74	Meat products	52
Fish processing	69		
Cotton	35	Spinning/weaving/dye	42*
Clothing	91*	Other Textiles	61*
Leather/shoes	92*		
Wood (primary)	61*	Wood (secondary)	56*
Paper	51*	Printing	68*
Agro-chemicals	69	Plastics	67*
Pharmaceuticals	37*	Rubber products	31
Construction materials (simpler)	53	Construction materials (complex)	86
Electrical goods	95*	Simple metal	81*
Heavy metal	42*	Precision mechanics	100*
Metal manufacture	77*	Electrical motors	100*
Transport equipment	98*	Electrical goods	67*

Source: Ministère de l'Industrie 1988 and for figures marked with * *Marchés Tropicaux et Méditerranéens*, 27 December 1985.

Third, and relatedly, the trends in global ownership patterns tend to conceal great differences at the sub-sectoral level. The shift by the state into direct participation in industry in the 1970s was biased heavily towards agricultural processing industries. As the latest (1985) figures for the ownership pattern by sub-sectors show – Table 6.7 – foreign enterprises are still dominant in a range of industries, including most of those considered of most importance for developing a more independent dynamic industrial base. Indeed, of the 32 groupings for which information on ownership is readily available, foreign capital controls more than 50% of total capital in 24 of them, some three-quarters of all the groupings listed, including 5 out of 8 groupings within the food industry.

THE POLICY FRAMEWORK
This section sketches out the major changes in the incentive framework, including changes in policy, with regard to the manufacturing sector since the early 1960s. For the purposes of this discussion and following the approach of the Ministère de l'Industrie, the post-independence period can be classified as follows:

    1960–80   the period of growth:
                    1960–70 – the start-up phase;
                    1970–80 – the period of expansion;
    1981–84   the period of recession;
    post-1985   the period of the new industrial policy.

In the first decade post-Independence, the most rapid expansion of manufacturing and probably the greatest structural change within the sector occurred within a context of few controls and attractive incentives for private investment. That they were mostly foreign and, in the first instance, predominantly French investors was due both to historical links and to the almost complete lack of substantial private Ivorian capital outside the agricultural sector.

The achievements of this period, in broad terms, were consistent with the objectives of the first Plan: to substitute domestic production for major imported consumer products and to raise the value added of domestic resources. A range of new industries were established (or, in the case of nascent industries, substantially expanded), including plastics, cement, radio and motor assembly, textiles, wood processing, metal transformation, perfume and petroleum refining. There was, too, a notable expansion of a range of food processing industries which led to exports of butter, instant coffee, cocoa, canned fish and pineapples, as well as cigarettes and furniture.

It would be mistaken, however, to believe that the state played only a passive role even in this early period, providing merely the framework for expansion exclusively by the private sector. In the year of Independence, 1960, some 10% of manufacturing capital was state-owned and even in the early period expanded its direct involvement in the sector. For instance between 1960 and 1967, the following enterprises were set up: SAT (coffee) SOFITIS (sisal sacks), HATIKVAH (wood), SONACO (paper) and SAFICA (paper) all 100% state[42].

By 1971, however, the state still had a direct share in only 10% of the manufacturing base. A desire to expand the industrial processing and export of agricultural products in particular, together with the high profitability of many foreign firms (see World Bank, 1975: 28), provided the domestic pressure necessary to initiate the substantial change in policy towards greater direct state involvement. What is more, this policy objective was boosted significantly by the increase in revenues derived from the state stabilisation fund which, since 1966, had controlled the prices of the leading agricultural export crops – cocoa, coffee, copra, cotton, palm products, rice and cashew nuts.

As a result, during the 1970s, major state investments took place in the fields of sugar, palm oil, cocoa and cotton processing. When the critical post-1977 period arrived – critical because of the slump in cocoa and coffee prices – the juggernaut of direct state investment in industry scarcely slowed down; what changed was the source of funds. Investment from domestic agricultural revenue was increasingly replaced by borrowings from financial institutions, dominated by foreign loan finance. By 1981, for the first time, over 50% of manufacturing was state-owned, up from the 10% level of a decade earlier.

Other developments taking place at this time also played a crucial role. Increased wages, rising inflation, dependence upon foreign expertise and imported plant and machinery all provided the context for an industrial sector increasingly fearful of international competition. This led to pressures from private sector manufacturers for increased protection against imports which, as it occurred just when the state was embarking on its own programme of expansion into industry (and therefore, when it was most favourably disposed to infant-industry arguments), met with limited resistance from the government.

The results were seen on a number of fronts. First, beginning in 1973 the Customs Code was substantially revised to raise the level of tariffs across a wide range of domestic manufactures[43]. Second, in 1975, the system of import licensing was extended. Third, a number of competitive imports were subject to prior import agreement – which had the effect of restricting their entry. Finally, a (smaller) number of competitive imports were banned altogether. The number of products subject to import licensing rose from 86 in 1976 to 427 by 1982, dominated by textiles and clothing but also including fertiliser and petroleum products. Those imports restricted under prior import agreement were predominantly in the shoe and leather, fruit canning and transport equipment industries. In 1975, some 25 imports were banned altogether including textiles, clothing, footwear and (a few) mechanical and engineering products[44].

Policies introduced or under discussion in the 1980s have been very different in perspective and objective from the expansive 1960s and 1970s. The first half of the decade was dominated by broad macroeconomic changes in policy focused particularly on the series of (three) structural adjustment programmes inaugurated in 1981[45]. Given the severity of the overall economic crisis affecting Côte d'Ivoire, little direct attention was given in this period to altering policies targeted specifically at the manufacturing sector[46]. The principal aim was to address the twin problems of balance of payments and public-sector deficits, the principal means selected being deflationary measures, cuts in public-sector spending, particularly investment expenditure, and reductions in state subsidies[47]. The main effects were to induce a severe contraction in both manufacturing production and investment, leading, too, to a substantial fall in manufacturing employment[48].

Little attempt was made at this stage to address the more specific problems of manufacturing resulting, in part, from the policy regime of the previous two decades, such as its structural weaknesses, widespread inefficiencies in the recently expanded public sector enterprises, or the problems associated with the rising tide of protectionism. Indeed, some problems, such as low levels of capacity utilisation, were clearly exacerbated by the workings of the SAL programmes. Thus the policy objectives for manufacturing encapsulated in the 1981–5 Five-Year Plan were largely eclipsed by the structural adjustment programmes.

It is important, however, to note that the Plan did make reference, in its list of objectives, to the need to promote further inter-industry integration and to enhance industrial competitiveness so as to satisfy the needs of the domestic market, as well as to expand into external markets. Nonetheless, some direct measures affecting manufacturing were introduced during this period, even if they were the result of broader policy initiatives. Thus in 1984, wages in parastatal companies were cut by up to one third and the process of privatisation (of the 140 state and parastatal enterprises) was officially launched – at least on paper. In addition, from 1981 onwards, initiatives were taken to improve the efficiency of the various state and parastatal enterprises, including the introduction of performance targets for basic financial data and key indicators of management efficiency and the widespread use of a programme of management audits[49].

It would be an error, however, to view the 1980–85 period as one of inactivity in relation to the manufacturing sector. Indeed changes begun in the post-1985 period were due in no small measure to the discussions and detailed analysis especially between the government and the World Bank, and, latterly, the government and UNIDO, during the execution of the 1981–5 structural adjustment programmes (see Duruflé, 1989).

The Ministère de l'Industrie has understandably termed the post-1985 era the 'period of new industrial policy'. In 1985 Côte d'Ivoire agreed to adopt a series of policy changes, substantially influenced by the World Bank's proposals for economic reform and liberalisation contained in its four-volume 1987 publication, *The Côte d'Ivoire in Transition: From Structural Adjustment To Self-Sustained Growth*. The centre-piece of the manufacturing-focused initiatives of the overall reform programme was the incentive structure and tariff reform. The broad objectives were the following: to reduce tariffs substantially to an industry-wide average of 40% by the year 1990; to abolish all quantitative restrictions on competitive imports and to replace these, for a short five-year period, with a temporary import tax; to introduce an across-the-board export subsidy which would have the effect of neutralising the 40% export bias against exporters; to oversee the abandonment of the service tax (TPS)[50]; and, finally to revise the 1959 Investment Code.

The implementation of practically all these measures has been subject to some considerable delay. Nonetheless the reform process got under way in April 1985 with the introduction of the first phase of the tariff reduction programme, covering some 60% of manufacturing value added, and embracing all sub-sectors except fertilisers, pesticides, equipment goods and transport equipment. For some sub-sectors, however, such as chemicals and plastics, where the new regime would have meant a sharp drop in the effective tariff rate, the 'reduction' was accompanied by what was termed a 'temporary import surcharge', which it was planned would fall progressively to zero over a five-year period to 1990.

Given the manner and (slow) speed with which the tariff reductions have been introduced, one would not have expected any immediate and radical changes in the structure of manufacturing to have followed. In August 1987, however, the whole exercise suffered a major reversal when import tariffs were *raised* instead of *lowered*. The average increase was about 30%, the effect of which was to increase the level of effective protection to around 52%, up from around 30%. Ironically, given its adverse attitude to the earlier progressive increase in tariff levels, this perverse move had the approval of the IMF for the reason that the slide in the export price of cocoa and coffee and the concomitant fall in the revenue of the agricultural stabilisation fund (CSSPPA[51]) required the government to raise the overall level of revenue (Chamley, 1988: 24). In November 1987, however, and somewhat unexpectedly, the government agreed in principle to apply the five-year tariff reduction to the entire manufacturing sector and not simply to the 60% of the sector previously covered.

By the end of 1988, the overall practical consequences of these changes appeared to have been only minimal[52]. One major adverse, and rather unexpected, effect, however, has been the significant rise in international trade in smuggled goods, particularly of those most affected by the tariff reductions. For instance, tariffs on imported cloth were reduced from 50 to 30% in the five-year phased programme, and already, by mid-1988, there had been reports of a significant increase in smuggled cloth from Nigeria. More dramatically, Bata, the company historically responsible for over 50% of shoes manufactured in Côte d'Ivoire, had by mid-1987 trimmed its workforce by one seventh because of its inability to compete with illegal imports (*African Economic Digest*, 5 May 1987).

A second major element in the policy reform programme was to have been the adoption of a significant export subsidy scheme, introduced in large measure in the hope of boosting manufacturing (and particularly non-traditional) exports. Industries initially covered included chemicals, cardboard and mechanical and electrical goods. The subsidy was to cover a subset of goods affected by the tariff reform (about 54% of value added) and applied at a rate of 20% of domestic value added. Intended to be introduced in 1984, and then in 1985, the first payments were made only in August 1986, but were then suspended (temporarily) in late 1987 because of a shortage of funds[53]. By the end of 1988, the programme had still not been completely implemented.

Reports from industrialists throughout 1988 indicated both high levels of dissatisfaction with the operation of the scheme – for instance, delays in payments of up to 10 months were not uncommon in early 1988 (*African Economic Digest*, 5 February 1988). It was also argued that the measures had had little effect on the competitiveness of non-traditional manufactured exports. This did not prevent the government agreeing, in November 1987, to extend the scheme to the whole of the manufacturing sector, even though it had still not altered the rate of the subsidy in line with the August 1987 rise in tariffs.

The final change to affect the manufacturing sector directly was the introduction of the 'new' Investment Code which received government approval in mid-1985. As already mentioned, this differs only marginally from the original 1959 Code: it provides greater incentives to small and medium-sized enterprises and to those investing outside Abidjan. As it has been introduced within the context of increasing macro-problems and concomitant low levels of overall investment, it is not surprising that its impact on investment levels has been minimal.

In general, it would not be too harsh to conclude that, up to the end of 1988, the post-1985 period of the New Industrial Policy was characterised more by government agreement to initiate change, much of it quite radical, rather than by the sustained implementation of such policies. Part of the reason for the divergence between policy agreement and action has lain in the increasingly serious problems experienced by the economy as a whole in the post-1987 period, which have tended to eclipse sectoral initiatives. Yet it should also be added that there has been tension between government and, particularly, the World Bank over both the pace and direction of change and also between government and industrialists, in particular over the policy of tariff reduction.

Two things happened during the course of 1988, however, which suggest that the government is serious in its intention to address the fundamental problems of manufacturing in the immediate future. First, in March 1988 it adopted its new and detailed industrial development strategy, *Schéma Directeur du Développement Industriel de la Côte d'Ivoire* – to be described more fully below. Second in September 1988 Cabinet and ministerial changes led to the merging of the ministries of planning and industry into a single super-ministry[54].

TRENDS IN THE RELATIVE COMPETITIVENESS OF IVORIAN INDUSTRY

The World Bank, UNIDO and the government have all argued in recent years that the manufacturing sector in Côte d'Ivoire, or a significant part of it, is internationally uncompetitive. What is of far more interest, however, is to examine the change in the *relative competitiveness* of the sector over time. This issue is important as the agreement to alter – indeed lower – the general level of external tariffs appears largely to be based on the assumption that such a policy will play a major part in stimulating the competitiveness of those industries or sub-sectors which are currently uncompetitive, or in encouraging the expansion of those which are competitive and discouraging the expansion of those which are not. What is surprising is that there has been little discussion of the truth of this assumption.

One way of judging is to take a backward look at the evolution of industry. During the 1970s (and indeed, if minimally, from an earlier date), there was a general rise in tariff levels and an increase in protectionism. A crucial question to ask is whether, and if so to what extent, this was associated with a *decrease* in the relative international competitiveness of manufacturing in Côte d'Ivoire. While the data remain partial what are available suggest that, for a *majority* of sub-sectors and for a not inconsiderable number of individual enterprises, the rise in tariff levels was associated with an *increase* in international competitiveness. Such historical data raise extremely serious questions about the unproven but widely-held assumption that a reduction in tariffs will *predominantly on its own* lead to the desired increase in international competitiveness.

This conclusion is reached after examining the data on the Domestic Resource Costs (DRCs) as applied and as available. A DRC value of less than unity indicates that a firm, industry or sub-sector is competitive, a score of more than unity that, at the time specified, it

Table 6.8 *Domestic resource cost (DRC) estimates by sub-sector, enterprise and year*

Product/Enterprise	DRC scores for the following years					
	1971	1975	1979	1981	1985[a]	1985[b]
Flour, grain milling		3.33				
Canned, prepared food		0.94				
Beer, soft drinks		0.43				
Edible oil, soap		2.08				
Milk products		1.16				
Tobacco products		0.85				
Cocoa processing					0.41	–
Coffee processing					1.15	1.50
Food, beverages, tobacco				0.4–1.2		
Textiles/clothing		2.31				
Spinning, weaving, dyeing					2.13	–
Other textiles					2.14	–
Textiles, apparel and leather				2.1		
Footwear		3.16				
Lubricants		0.96				
Chemicals		2.05		0.8–1.0	0.84	
Rubber products		1.52				
Plastics					0.98	
Cement		0.92				
Transport equipment		0.99				
Metal products		2.15				
Board and paper		0.55				
Total all sectors		1.34				
individual enterprises in:						
Spinning, weaving, dyeing and printing[d]						
GONFREVILLE	2.83		1.32		1.21	1.61
UTEXI			1.10		1.13	1.28
UNIWAX	− 2.33		− 19.14		− 2.12	− 0.64
SOTEXI	− 7.66		− 1.33		− 1.27	− 0.54
ICODI	− 2.27		0.99		1.96	6.91
SOCITAS	5.09		1.45[c]		3.26	− 12.79
Other textile products:						
SIVOITEX			1.67[c]		5.10	− 19.83
FILTISAC	16.33		22.74		4.67	119.28
FIBAKO	1.06		0.89		1.18	2.18
SOFITIS	1.66		0.35		3.11	− 8.00

Source: World Bank (1987, Vol. III:221), Lall (1987), den Tuinder (1978:243) and Noel and Pursell (1982).

Notes: [a] Corden composition calculation.

[b] Equilibrium prices calculation.

[c] figures for 1978 and not 1979.

[d] of the four estimates used by Noël and Pursell the one used here is termed "basic DRCE", using the actual rate of return on foreign equity and at current rather than full capacity levels.

is not internationally competitive[55]. Table 6.8 reproduces the DRC scores available from 1971 to 1985. Although there are clearly major gaps in the time series data, a number of conclusions can be drawn.

First, there is no indication of sub-sectoral DRCs rising over time; the figures for chemicals show a clear progressive *fall* in each time period, while a fall is also suggested for both textiles and food products. Second, in relation to the DRC scores for particular firms in the textile sub-sector, the figures suggest, if anything, a lowering of the figures for the majority of firms in each of the time periods considered, suggesting an *increase* in competitiveness. In aggregate, the data provide the following pattern of results: comparing 1971 and 1979, of 8 enterprises 5 had lower DRCs in 1979 than in 1973 and only 3 had higher ones; comparing 1979 with 1985, of 9 enterprises, 5 had lower DRCs and 4 higher ones, while finally, considering scores from 1971 to 1985, out of 10 enterprises, 6 had lower DRCs and 4 had higher ones.

The third conclusion is that DRC scores have tended to vary quite markedly both from sub-sector to sub-sector, and from firm to firm, and that the range of DRC measures within sub-sectors is extremely large.

While it is not suggested that a rise in tariffs or an increase in other protective measures has been a *cause* of increased competitiveness of certain industries and sub-sectors, important policy-related conclusions can and need to be drawn from this discussion. The first is that factors *other than the overall tariff and incentive structure* and the other protective measures gradually introduced in Côte d'Ivoire play a role – often, clearly, a crucial role – in determining the relative efficiency of different enterprises. They were thus probably of critical importance in explaining the change in competitiveness of industry. These factors could include changes in management, engineering and other skills, changes in technological application or use, changes in demand, changes in competitiveness in other parts of the region or world, changes in financial arrangements and in domestic pricing policies, etc. The policy implication is that, if the historical evidence has any validity for the future, then concentrating on altering tariffs and other protective measures provides no guarantee that international competitiveness will be enhanced unless and until these other elements and their impact on economic and foreign-exchange usage efficiency are analysed and their relative importance vis-à-vis other factors assessed.

In addition, as the data in Table 6.8 clearly indicate, DRC measures can and do change over time, often quite substantially. The implication is that long-term strategies for industry ought not to be determined exclusively or (probably) predominantly by such snapshot indicators of performance. In part, this is little more than a restatement of the familiar infant-industry argument that protection is justified in the short term in the expectation that, over the medium to longer term, productive and technical efficiencies will increase and average production costs will fall. It is, what is more, a policy approach which the World Bank has advocated in the past as a basis for industrial development in Côte d'Ivoire (den Tuinder 1978: 244):

> Although average domestic resource costs in manufacturing are high compared with most agricultural activities in the Ivory Coast, this does not mean that Ivorian industrial development should not be pursued any further. For one thing, over the longer term industry is bound to become more important in the Ivorian economy as arable land becomes more limited. Moreover, industry offers greater possibilities than does agriculture for external economies in the form of technological training of labour. It should be possible, by appropriate policies, to increase production with the resources presently devoted to industry, given the need to improve efficiency and to expand in directions which are socially profitable.

The macroeconomic context for the future of manufacturing

Prospects for the sustained expansion and deepening of the manufacturing sector in Côte d'Ivoire and, as desired by both the government and the World Bank, for its increased role as an earner of foreign exchange in the 1990s will depend not only upon its inherited structure and the effectiveness of policies targeted directly at its growth and development, but also upon external events and trends both national and international. Some of these more important factors include the role of agriculture and agricultural exports, foreign debt and general balance-of-payments problems, public finance and levels of imports and investment.

For all the words of optimism that have been written about economic development in Côte d'Ivoire, by the end of 1988 the economy was in a state of major crisis and prospects for favourable international and domestic conditions to support sustained growth and expansion appeared bleak. In its penultimate country report on Côte d'Ivoire for 1988, the London-based Economist Intelligence Unit warned that 'the whole economy could seize up for lack of funds to run it' (EIU, *Country Report* 1988, No. 3: 3). A little later in its *World Outlook 1989*, the EIU reinforced its gloomy short-term assessment thus (1989: 145–6):

> After two years of negative growth caused by the continuing slump in commodity export earnings, the outlook for 1989 looks grim. . . The manufacturing sector seems set to remain a major victim of recession, which has reduced consumer purchasing power and encouraged a greater reliance on the cheaper informal market. With profits declining, the fragile industrial fabric will be increasingly threatened by disinvestment.

What is more, there is no doubt that the economic crisis is far worse than even recent macroeconomic trends would indicate because of the extremely favourable way in which the international institutions, donors and private creditors have supported the economy, both by injecting new funds and by agreeing to roll over substantial amounts of international debt. In the period 1981-8 the IMF, the World Bank and the French CCCE have on their own pledged to provide probably not far short of $2 bn in a succession of financing arrangements, an amount equivalent to over 12% of the 1981-8 total import bill[56], while external debt rescheduling arrangements for commercial and official debts have been ratified in four out of five years from 1984: in 1984, 1985, 1986 and again in 1988[57].

Perhaps the most fundamental structural difficulties relate, on the one hand, to the economy's openness and high level of dependence upon agriculture as a source of foreign exchange and state revenue earning and, on the other, to the poor prospects for agricultural exports. Some figures highlight these weaknesses. The vulnerability to external influences is illustrated by the fact that at the end of the 1980s exports amounted to nearly half of GDP, while imports were valued at between 28 and 35% of GDP[58]. In spite of the expansion in manufacturing over the past three decades, the economy remains highly dependent upon agriculture to earn its foreign exchange: over 70% of total export earnings (over 80% of non-oil exports) are derived from agriculture, if one includes those products which are subject to some further processing and more commonly classified as manufacturing exports. State revenues from agriculture, in the form of stabilisation fund (CSSPPA) surpluses, have formed a critically important part of government revenue - accounting for over 5% of GDP and over 16% of total government revenue in the first seven years of the 1980s[59].

POOR PROSPECTS FOR LEADING EXPORTS
Prospects for traditional exports in the next few years are extremely bleak, *inter alia* because of forecasts of low commodity prices and the lower than expected growth of production.

Almost 70% of export earnings come from just three products: cocoa, coffee and wood and timber. Of these, almost one third come from coffee exports. Recent trends and best judgements about coffee prospects over the next few years give an extremely depressing picture in terms of both production levels and prices.

The national stock of coffee bushes is ageing and production has fallen during the 1980s by some 5% to around 245,000 tons by the 1986/7 season and by a further one-third to 186,700 tonnes in the 1987/8 season (*African Economic Digest*, 11 November 1988). The government began an intensive crop regeneration programme in 1986 but its ability to raise output levels will depend critically upon world prices and quotas; and at the end of 1988 the future looked extremely gloomy. Côte d'Ivoire's coffee quota[60] for 1988/9 stood at 219,600 tons, a 10% fall over two years and, following agreement reached in September 1988, was to fall by a further 101,400 bags for the 1989/90 season. Côte d'Ivoire, like other African producers, stands to lose further if, as widely predicted in early 1989, the international coffee agreement is abandoned.

In the post-1986 period in particular, export earnings from coffee have fallen disastrously: from US$709 m. in 1986 to less than US$400 m. in 1987 and with a further 16% fall in the first five months of 1988, in spite of a 19% increase in the quantity of coffee sold[61]. The November 1988 price of 114 cents a pound was, in current terms, lower than the average 10-year price from 1976 and 1985. As for the future, World Bank projections made at the end of 1986 forecast a 1990 price for arabica 11% lower than that in 1985 with no change expected up to the mid-1990s (World Bank 1986, Vol. II: 1-22). Not only will robusta prices be even lower than those for arabica coffee beans but the September 1988 agreement of the International Coffee Organisation (ICO) to separate robusta and arabica producers will mean that robusta producers, like Côte d'Ivoire[62], will be relatively disadvantaged in a future which is likely to see a continued substantial oversupply and the further discounting of the official price[63]. With the likely end of the international coffee agreement by the end of 1989, a 'collapse in robusta prices' is expected (*Financial Times*, 11 April 1989, quoting EIU *World Commodity Forecasts*).

The future for wood-product exports is even bleaker. The export of logs and sawn timber was valued at $270 m. in 1986, 6% of total exports and equivalent to over 90% of total manufactured exports. Yet the past decades have seen such a massive over-exploitation of the country's forests that what constituted over 15 million hectares of exploitable timber at the turn of the century and 9 million at Independence had been reduced, by 1987, to just one million hectares. At that time, annual forest depletion was running at around 300,000 hectares a year. It is thus apparent that the rapid decline in wood and log exports – which were responsible for 12% of total exports and exceeded total manufacturing exports in 1981 – is set to accelerate even faster in the coming decade[64].

Other more minor crops will be dealt with briefly. Cotton production has increased rapidly in the 1980s to leave Côte d'Ivoire, by 1987, the third largest producer of cotton in Africa (after Sudan and Egypt). Raw cotton exports were worth $79 m. in 1986. While expansion of this crop is proceeding, world demand is set to slow to 2.3% a year and world prices to fall by over 5% at current prices to 1993 (Morris, 1988).

Substantial investment in palm oil has taken place in recent years, and in the mid-1980s it was the (over-ambitious) intention of the government to make the country the world's largest producer of palm oil[65]. Production has expanded steadily in the 1980s, rising from 155,000 tons in 1981 to 195,000 tons by 1986. While this expansion was justified in the early years of the decade – world consumption was rising by 9% a year and prices doubled from the mid-1970s to the mid-1980s, peaking at $728 a ton in 1984 – the rapid expansion of productive capacity worldwide together with an expected severe drop in the rate of increase in demand have led to a scaling-down of the ambitious expansion programme and a more realistic assessment of the potential for this particular crop. World consumption is expected to rise by only 4.2% a year from 1985 to 2000, while prices in real terms are expected to fall by 9% from 1985 to 1995 and by a further 7% to the year 2000 (World Bank, 1986, Vol. II: 212–257). By April 1989, the world price had fallen to around $400 a ton, substantially lower than the World Bank's 1986 forecasts. As a result of all these different factors, there is little likelihood that palm oil export earnings will constitute a significantly increased share of total export earnings in the next five years.

THE CENTRALITY OF COCOA AND ITS PROBLEMS

Of most – indeed of central – importance to both export earnings and government revenue, however, is the fate of cocoa. In the first half of the 1980s, cocoa alone accounted for 26% of export earnings, rising to 34% by 1986 and 40% by 1987. By the end of the 1980s, Côte d'Ivoire was the world's major exporter of cocoa, accounting for 30% of world production of raw cocoa, up from 23% at the start of the decade.

At first glance, future prospects look good. Production levels have risen steadily: from 470,000 tons in 1981, to 590,000 tons by 1986, 665,000 in 1987/8, and an industry forecast of from 700,000 to 750,000 tons in the 1989/90 season[66]. For the future, it certainly appears that significant expansion could be sustained even if not at the post 1986 rate, especially with improved techniques raising yields. Indeed, mid-1980s studies by the World Bank suggesting that one million tons could be produced by the year 2000 (a production target the government had been committed to for some time) look by no means out of reach. In April 1988, however, the Minister of Agriculture announced that the government was abandoning this target (*African Economic Digest*, 15 April 1988). The decision not to increase the area devoted to cocoa production does not necessarily mean that production levels will not continue to rise over the next few years, especially because of the increased attention being given to raising yields and improving bean quality. These upward trends in production raise more serious questions related to prices, however.

Since the heady days of 1977 when the price of cocoa (Ghana/London) reached 213 cents a pound, it has fallen steadily and consistently with few rallies, reaching a 13-year low in September 1988. In 1985, the price stood at 108 cents a pound, falling progressively to 85 cents by November 1988. And prices continued to fall throughout 1989. By March 1989, the latest failure of talks at the International Cocoa Organisation (ICCO) left little hope that non-market forces could effectively raise prices in the short term.

In the long term, price trends will be determined largely by changes in demand and supply. World Bank forecasts suggest only a minimal increase in demand at the world level of around 1% a year, even though at the end of 1988 (November) consumption was estimated to have risen by 4.9% in 1987–8, with a forecast rise of a further 4.4% in 1988–9. It is, however, the supply side of the equation which is of most concern. World supply has exceeded demand for five consecutive years and is set to continue to do so, while closing stocks have almost trebled in five years, from 424,000 tons in 1984/5 to an estimated 1,319,000 by 1989/90. Supply exceeded demand by 147,000 tonnes in 1987/8 and in March 1989 the surplus was forecast by a leading London trader, Gill and Duffus, to expand to 199,000 tonnes for the year 1988/9, while a month later the Economist Intelligence Unit forecast a 203,000 tonne glut (*African Economic Digest*, 13 March and 17 April 1989). World stockpiles were estimated in September 1988 to be between 743,000 and 835,000 tonnes (*African Economic Digest*, 4 November 1988: 16, *Financial Times*, 20 September 1988).

Clearly these factors provide increased downward pressure on long-term prices and more gloomy prospects for the producers. The Bank's higher price forecast (which is a scenario based on accelerated production – as has been occurring) is for real prices to fall by 1995 by 13% below their 1985 level (World Bank, 1987, Volume II: 23–48). They may well fall further if production plans by other leading producers come to fruition. In this regard, particular attention needs to be focused on Indonesia and Malaysia, neither of which are members of the ICCO. Malaysia, for instance, is planning to continue its rapid expansion and to take an even larger world share (*Financial Times, Malaysia Supplement*, 14 November 1988, p. 19)[67].

These long-term and bearish trends have in part been concealed by recent interventionist actions by the Ivorian authorities. Distressed at the progressive fall in world prices, they started, in January 1988, to withhold cocoa from the world market in the hope of bidding up the price. Superficially, and in the short term, that policy appeared to achieve some success, as by mid-1988 over 50,000 tons had been sold at a price some 20% higher than the London price, while towards the end of the year it became clear that a massive 400,000 tonnes had been purchased at a subsidised price by the French commodity broker, *Sucres et Denrées*[68]. But the longer-term effects of such actions on export earnings are unlikely to be of lasting value, especially if the trends in the early months of 1988 are to be projected forward. In the first five months of 1988, cocoa exports stood at only $220 m. compared with $453 m. in the first five months of 1987. On an annual basis this would lead to a 25% reduction in total export earnings. Not only will the Ivorians eventually have to unload their crop onto the world market, thereby accelerating the fall in the world price, but by the end of 1988 traditional major buyers had already begun looking for alternative sources, such as Malaysia[69].

The apparently perverse actions of the Ivorian authorities can in part be explained by a closer look at the domestic pricing structure of cocoa within the context of state financial revenues. The single most important explanation for the rapid expansion of Ivorian production has been the attractive price provided by the sole and guaranteed buyer, the CSSPPA – in 1988 and for 1989 fixed (by the government) at CFAF 400 per kg. In stark contrast, 1988 costs of the CSSPPA came to about CFAF 700 per kg, whereas the world price was around CFAF 450 per kg. In view of this increasing price/cost dislocation, the World Bank and other advisers had been recommending a cut in the official price in an attempt both to lower the rate of expansion of output and to help raise the world price. Estimates suggest that a halving of the producer price, on mid-1988 cost estimates, would be required to have a substantial price effect worldwide. Yet the political impossibility in the 1988/9 season of reducing the price by anything more than 10% has been widely recognised. In the event, the government failed even to do this and kept the price at the CFAF 400 level.

Finally, the impact of the cocoa subsidy on government finances reveals yet another dimension of the importance and complexity of cocoa in the national economy. In 1987, for the first time in its history, the CSSPPA suffered a trading loss estimated at CFAF 44 bn – equivalent to about 1.7% of GDP. Because of the CSSPPA's traditional role as a major source of state revenue, this contributed to the budget deficit that year which was equivalent to about 7% of GDP[70]. For 1988, assuming a crop of 680,000 tons and with the price fixed at CFAF 400 per kg, the CSSPPA would be expected to lose about CFAF 150 bn, accelerating still further the rise in the budget deficit[71]. The accumulated deficit of the CSSPPA was officially estimated to be CFAF 290 bn at the end of the 1987/8 season on 30 September 1988 (*African Economic Digest*, 16 December 1988). At the end of 1988, World Bank estimates were for a budget deficit of up to CFAF 350 bn, giving an estimated budget deficit/GDP ratio near to 12–15% (*African Economic Digest*, 11 November 1988).

A budget deficit/GDP ratio of this magnitude would be similar to that recorded in the early 1980s when the first structural adjustment programme was introduced – with the major objective of reducing the deficit to around the 2–3% level. At the end of the 1980s, however, the situation had far more disturbing implications because previously the CSSPPA was in surplus. Figure 6.7 shows the recent and forecast adverse trends in the budget deficit and the CSSPPA's revenue position as a proportion of GDP. It is in this context that the prospects for future industrialisation will have to be judged.

Figure 6.7 *Budget deficit and CSSPPA surplus as % of GDP, Two-Year Averages, 1980–89*

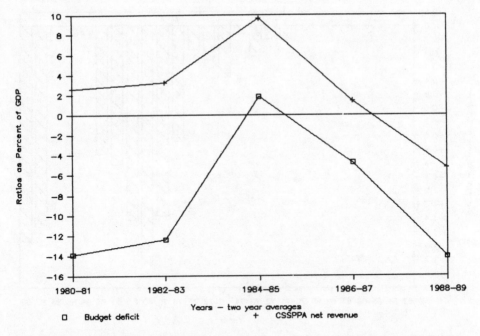

Years – two year averages
□ Budget deficit   + CSSPPA net revenue

Source: World Bank (1987), Chamley (1988), Schiller (1988), Economist Intelligence Unit (1988 and 1989), *African Economic Digest* 5 February 1988, 3 June 1988, 11 November 1988, 6 January 1989.

Note: Based on GDP estimated growth rate of − 1.5 per cent for 1988 and zero for 1989.

OTHER MACROECONOMIC INDICATORS

Poor prospects for traditional exports and a high and rising budget deficit need to be placed in a broader context. Figure 6.8 shows trends in the current account of the balance of payments to 1988: a small deficit in the early 1970s gave way at the end of the decade to a severe deficit, corrected in the mid-1980s but which worsened again in the more recent 1987–8 period[72].

For the current account of the balance of payments to strengthen over the next few years, improvements in four indicators in particular need to be examined. On the credit side, export earnings and foreign investment inflows would need to rise. But, as discussed above, neither of these is likely to occur in quantities sufficient to address the problem. Alternatively, imports would need to be cut and/or outflows drastically reduced. On the import front, while the cutting of more luxury imports could certainly help, the short-term improvements could be only marginal. The economy is already suffering from shortages of imports shown, in part, by the progressive fall in the merchandise import to GDP ratio from the mid-1970s onwards: from some 27% in 1974 to 16% by 1988. In real terms, imports (cif) were 15% lower in 1986 than they were in 1977–80. Further squeezes are likely to have a severe adverse effect on aggregate growth as well as more directly on the manufacturing sector, given the high import dependence of manufacturing inputs, as recent historical evidence reveals. Between 1980 and 1984, GDP fell by 15%, imports fell by 45% in real terms; between 1980 and 1983, MVA fell by 19% while imports of manufacturing fell, in current price terms, by 44% (World Bank (1988: 115)[73].

Besides profits and dividends (already discussed) the other major external debits are related to the high outflow of remittances and the servicing of the large external debt. The major elements of the remittance outflow are related to management contracts and the repatriation of

Figure 6.8 *Current account of the balance of payments 1963–88 US$ m.*

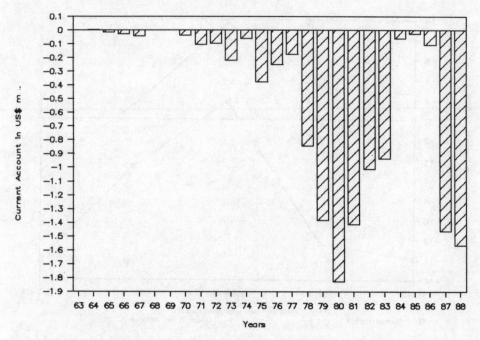

Source: World Bank (1987), EIU (1988 and 1989) and *African Economic Digest* (various issues).

Note: 1988 figures are estimates available in the first half of 1989.

salaries of non-Ivorians. In part the outflow could be lowered if greater use were made of Ivorians in more skilled posts and in the teaching profession, but it would take considerable time to achieve this. Some progress has already been made, but a number of problems remain. One is the degree to which foreign-controlled companies would be willing to extend the process of Ivorisation of senior posts. Another is that in spite of the comparatively low enrolment rates ·in secondary education – only 20% of the relevant age group are in secondary education and only 3% in tertiary – over 20% of central government expenditure is allocated to education. This is the third highest ratio in sub-Saharan Africa, above Ghana (24%) and Zimbabwe whose experience here is unique[74]. The government faces a dilemma here: it will not be easy both to trim its public expenditure programme and satisfactorily to address the continual problem of skill shortages by expanding its secondary (and thus more expensive) school system.

This leaves us, finally, with the outflow of debt repayments. If debt obligations are to be honoured, the future looks particularly bleak to the mid-1990s and almost certainly beyond. Côte d'Ivoire was the only country in Africa to be included in the 'Baker Fifteen'[75] and to be allowed multi-year rescheduling arrangements. Its external public debt at the end of 1986 stood at 0.9 bn, of which $787 m. (7%) was short-term; total outstanding disbursed public debt amounted to $6.5 bn, some 73% of GDP[76]. In that year, total debt-service payments amounted to $785 m., a debt-service ratio of 24%[77]. The most rapid build-up of external debt occurred in the second half of the 1970s when, from 1976 to ·1979, it increased at the extremely rapid rate of 47% a year; in the first seven years of the 1980s total debt rose by an average of almost 11% a year, with public outstanding and disbursed external debt growing by an average of just over 7% a year.

This increase in total external debt was reflected, at least until recently, in the rapid expansion of annual debt servicing, which more than doubled from $398 m. in 1978 to a peak of $964 m. in 1982. Thereafter, largely as a result of rescheduling arrangements, repayments fell to $638 m. in 1984 rising to $684 m. in 1985 and $785 m. by 1986. As a percentage of total export earnings, repayments rose from 17% in 1978 to reach a peak of 42% by 1982, falling back to 21% by 1985 and 24% by 1986[78].

Of most policy interest, however, are future repayments (and possible new obligations) and the restrictions that these will put upon future growth and options for structural change. Even before the most recent rescheduling agreements, the World Bank's major 1987 study suggested that, with favourable domestic policies and international trends (the base case scenario), Côte d'Ivoire's annual debt repayments would have to remain well above their 1982 peak from 1988 to 1993, and that only after 1991 could the debt-service ratio possibly fall below the 20% level. In its more pessimistic 'reference case' scenario, however, repayments were projected to amount to more than $1,240 m. a year at least until 1994, equivalent to almost 30% *above* the 1982 peak (World Bank, 1987, Vol. IV: 30–61).

The 'base case' scenario suggested that debt repayments would total $1,311 m. in 1987 and $1,476 m. in 1988 (see Table 6.9). If these amounts *had* been paid, then, given the country's actual and forecast export performance, Côte d'Ivoire's debt-service ratios would have been 51 and 66% respectively. It was because the country simply could not afford to repay its debt obligations at such high rates that the 1987/8 reschedulings took place and, in the second half of 1988, that even these rescheduling arrangements were abandoned as unworkable, with the country coming within a knife-edge of a formal declaration of default.

It would be sheer speculation to attempt to predict what debt commitments Côte d'Ivoire *will* honour in the coming years. Nonetheless what is certain is that unless it chooses to renege on its commitments – a most unlikely scenario given the support from both the international agencies and the French, including the French banking system – annual repayments will continue to be extremely high for at least the next ten years, even without any new external borrowing. At minimum, annual repayments of over $1,000 m. will need to be paid at least to the mid-1990s: total debt-service payments for 1989 were officially estimated to be $1,735 m. in January(*African Economic Digest*, 30 January 1989). But if, as in the post-1983 period, repayments over the short term continue to fall well below those required, then these high annual repayments will quite quickly stretch to the year 2000. Thus, especially with the far from bullish outlook for traditional exports discussed above, it is highly unlikely that the debt-service ratio could fall permanently below the 25–30% level before the mid-1990s.

The way in which external debt repayment projections have continually been revised upwards in recent years and the expected fall-off in repayments are well illustrated in Table 6.9.

The Bank's *World Debt Tables* for 1984–5 projected that, by 1991, total debt repayments would be more than halved from $1,121 m. in 1984 to $451 m. By the next year, however, the projected 1991 repayment figure had jumped by 52%, followed by a further 48% rise in the next year, 36% in the following year, and, a year later, by yet another rise of 3%. Thus over a four-year period, the repayment figure for 1991 had increased by $1,540 m. to $1,911 m., more than four times the original figure. In contrast, over this period total debt had risen by only 32%, short-term debt by less than 1%. Given the country's continual failure since 1983 to meet projected annual debt repayments – most recently in 1988 when failure to meet the new (lower) repayment commitments occurred almost within weeks of the signing of a new rescheduling agreement – it is highly likely that a similar upward movement in repayments for the years 1994 and beyond will occur. Annual repayment obligations in the second half of the 1990s are thus practically certain to be of the order of $1,500 m. and above.

A final policy area which has received increased attention in recent years is the exchange rate. At present, and since 1948, the CFA franc has had free and unlimited parity with the French franc at a fixed parity. This arrangement has certainly had major advantages for Côte d'Ivoire, providing financial stability, helping to promote external trade, boosting foreign investment, providing all the benefits of financial backing of France in obtaining external financing and, latterly, in assisting with debt rescheduling agreements. Nonetheless, three major disadvantages have arisen. First, the CFA franc became increasingly over-valued in the 1970s and the post-1985 period. Second, the nominal exchange rate cannot be used as an independent macroeconomic tool in economic policies; relatedly, the economy has to cope not only with the effects of its own external relations but is also directly affected by changes in the French economy, and most particularly by devaluations of the French franc. Third, the statutes of agreement limit government access to domestic credit and therefore inhibit independent monetary policy.

It is not within the framework of the present chapter to enter the debates on whether the

Table 6.9 *Projections of annual external debt repayments Interest and Principal, 1984–9 $m.*

Year	Actual Repayments	Projected Future Repayments					1987 Country Study	
		1984–5 Debt Tables	'85–86 Debt Tables	'86–87 Debt Tables	'87–88 Debt Tables	'88–89 Debt Tables	Base Case Scenario	Reference Case Scenario
1980	874							
1981	921							
1982	964							
1983	798							
1984	638	112						
1985	648	1,099	1,349					
1986	785	1,083	1,287	1,544				
1987		987	1,258	1,470	1,143		1,311	1,313
1988		899	1,234	1,497	1,311	1,457	1,476	1,488
1989		795	1,116	1,443	1,498	1,721	1,507	1,547
1990		916	906	1,231	1,533	1,812	1,376	1,470
1991		451	688	1,020	1,383	1,911	1,251	1,423
1992			489	835	1,213	1,704	1,147	1,400
1993				564	925	1,443	1,016	1,331
1994					731	1,139	907	1,272
1995						1,024	862	1,247
1996						813		
1997						700		

Source: World Bank (1984–9), *World Debt Tables*, and World Bank (1987: Vol. IV, 31–62).

Note: Total debt service payments include official and private creditors and suppliers credits.

links with the French franc should be severed or altered[79], but to highlight one or two features as they relate more explicitly to the manufacturing sector. The apparent exchange-rate inflexibility can be overcome by other policy tools. Thus the high price of some Ivorian manufactures, and hence their international uncompetitiveness, has been mitigated to some extent by the introduction of the export subsidy scheme. This has a double benefit for manufacturing because, given the high proportion of imported inputs, it helps to keep down domestic prices and to lower the foreign-exchange costs of production. Conversely, a devaluation would increase the costs of imported inputs and provide upward pressure on domestic prices.

Other disadvantages from substantial devaluations have been assessed from policy simulations carried out in relation to the general equilibrium model of Côte d'Ivoire. These indicate (see Michel and Noël, 1984) that the structural problems of the sector, outlined above, would be accentuated. Thus the links between manufacturing and agriculture would tend to be strengthened by increasing the competitiveness of processed foods and textile products, while the more complex engineering industries and those producing for the domestic market would contract sharply. An additional effect, at least in the short term, would be a slowdown in GDP with additional adverse effects on those industries producing for the domestic market. But if, as could happen, exports of the major agriculturally–linked products did not expand markedly as a result of the exchange-rate changes (due to inelasticities in world demand) the effects would be even more damaging.

There is, however, no clear indication that steps will be taken in the near term to change the nature of the link with the French franc. Detailed discussion of the implications remain speculative, therefore.

The manufacturing sector to the mid-1990s

SCENARIOS, PROJECTIONS, FORECASTS AND PLANS
The first government forecasts of the growth of the sector beyond 1988 were in the 1981–5 development plan – indicating an annual GDP growth rate of 5.7% for the period 1980–85

and 7.4% for 1985–90. For manufacturing industry, the projected annual growth rates were 7.2% for 1980–85 and 8.6% for 1985–90. As for structural changes, the intention was to expand the heavy/capital goods sub-sectors faster than both the consumer and intermediate sub-sectors, increasing their share of total value added from 22% in 1980 to almost 30% by 1990. This change, however, was not to be reflected in the structure of industrial exports. While it was expected that these would rise from 30% of total exports in 1980 to 39% by 1990, the increase was to come predominantly from processing industries: the share of non-processed industrial exports was set to fall from 6% of the total in 1980 to 5% by 1990 (Ministère du Plan et de l'Industrie, 1982: 52, 91–3 and 398).

Not only have these projections substantially been overtaken by more recent events – they were conceived before the series of structural adjustment programmes of the early 1980s and before the more recent problems of the economy – but they have also been superseded by the more rigorous scenarios provided by the World Bank and published in 1987. In its four-volume publication, *The Ivory Coast in Transition: From Structural Adjustment to Self-Sustained Growth*, the Bank offers two scenarios to the mid-1990s: the first, the 'base case', dependent upon following through a series of prescriptions advocated by the Bank, the second, the 'reference case', based on no substantial changes in domestic policy. Not surprisingly, the base case scenario produces far higher growth rates for almost all virtuous performance indicators.

The 1986–95 period is divided into two: 1986–90, the transition phase, 1990–95, the self-sustained growth phase. The objectives in the first are 'to consolidate the structural adjustment process concurrent with a moderate rate of growth of GDP led by an expansion of exports'. During the second, 'the momentum gained as a result of the expansion of exports and of the increase in private savings and investment would, in conjunction with the productivity gains induced by the liberalization of the system of incentives, unleash the growth potential of the economy and lead to sustained growth of per capita income' (World Bank 1987, Vol I: 5).

The different growth rates and leading economic indicators under the two different scenarios and for the two periods are shown in Table 6.10. For the base case scenario in the transition phase, GDP is expected to grow at 3% a year but the growth rate of the industrial sector is expected to be far higher at 5.1%. Indeed, in the words of the Bank, in this period the economy's growth performance 'should essentially be led by the industrial sector' (Vol. I: 9).

Table 6.10 *Leading economic and industrial indicators, 1986–95 World Bank base and reference case scenarios*

	1986–90		1990–95	
	Base Case	Reference Case	Base Case	Reference Case
Annual Rate of Change:				
GDP	3.0	2.0	5.0	3.2
Industry	5.1	3.8	6.5	3.2
Agriculture	2.1	0.7	3.8	2.6
Total exports	2.6	0.7	5.5	2.8
Manufacturing exports	5.6	1.4	7.2	2.7
Industrial employment	10.8	8.7	9.1	12.9
Relationship at end of period				
Industry as % GDP	16.94	16.48	18.21	16.17
Coffee & cocoa as % of all exports	46	51	44	50
Manufacturing as % of all exports	33	29	38	31
Debt service (US$m.)	1,265	1,359	862	1,247
Debt service ratio	30	36	11	20
Average over period				
Current Account Balance (CFAF bn)	− 34.8	− 98.4	83.3	− 104.2
CSSPPA average receipts (CFAF bn)	193.1	213.0	115.7	292.8
CSSPPA revenue as % of GDP	5.2	6.0	2.1	5.9

Source: World Bank (1987), Vol. IV: 30–61.

In the second phase under the base case scenario, both the growth rates of GDP and of the industrial sector are to be even higher (at 5 and 6.5% respectively), although in this period the difference between the two is expected to narrow, (Vol. I: 12):

> This performance should result essentially from an increase in the rate of growth of industrial and agriculture value added in response to the lagged impact of the incentives reforms introduced during the transition phase on the growth of the tree crop sector and to the more immediate impact of increased export incentives on the growth of other diversification crops and industrial value added.

Overall, the more rapid rate of growth of industry vis-à-vis agriculture is expected to lead to industry's taking a larger share of GDP. It is clear, too, from the data provided, that the structure of manufacturing is also expected to change: the rate of growth of manufactured exports is to be higher than that of manufacturing production, leading, as shown in Table 6.10, to the share of manufactures in total exports rising – to 34% by 1990 and to 38% by 1995. Finally, the even higher rates of growth of manufacturing employment under this scenario suggest that, in the process of future expansion, the sector is to become increasingly labour-intensive.

Not surprisingly, under the Bank's reference scenario most of the relevant indicators for both industry and for the overall economy are substantially lower and, importantly, in the second phase, manufacturing exports are expected to rise at a lower rate than aggregate exports. The share of manufacturing in total production is projected, however, to be only marginally lower by 1995 than in the base case scenario while, strangely, industrial employment is expected to increase at a *faster* rate than under the base case scenario.

To achieve the more optimistic base case scenario targets, a range of policy changes are advocated and assumptions made by the Bank, in relation to the international economy, the domestic economy as a whole and (of interest to us here) the manufacturing sector in particular. For the external environment the following assumptions are made (Vol. I: 29 and Vol. III: 63–5). World prices of leading exports are expected to rise annually as follows: coffee by 6.3%; cocoa by 4.2%; timber by 7.9% and vegetable oils by 5.3%. The overall terms of trade are expected to deteriorate slightly by a cumulative 4.3% to 1990. Total new financial inflows are expected to amount to just over US$500 m. a year, of which concessional flows would constitute one fifth and Bank structural adjustment, project and sector lending would constitute 65%. It is also assumed that there would be no future debt rescheduling. The exchange rate is assumed to be equivalent to CFAF400/US$ in 1986, rising to CFAF375/US$ by 1988 and to CFAF345/US$ by 1990.

For the domestic economy, three broad and fundamental restructuring objectives are advocated: first, the liberalisation of the overall incentive system needs to be continued; second, the public/private sector mix needs to be altered significantly in favour of the private sector; and third, the rapid amortisation of the country's external public debt needs to be maintained both to increase domestic savings and to renew access to further commercial borrowing in the future (Vol. I: 11).

Within this context, three critical policy assumptions are made for the transition phase. First, there needs to be strict control of domestic credit, allowing credit increases to the private sector only to expand in line with international inflation. Second, public sector spending (consumption and investment) is to be controlled within strict (low) limits, transfers to public sector enterprises are to be cut to 0.7% of GDP by 1990 from 5% in 1985, and their operating surpluses are to rise to 2.8% of GDP in 1990 from 1.3% in 1985. Finally, all the industrial incentive reforms agreed under the third structural adjustment programme, begun in 1986, are to be in place and to extend throughout the economy by 1990. Particular mention is made of the tariff and export subsidy scheme and the necessity of removing all quantitative import restrictions (Vol. I: 8–9).

What distinguishes the self-sustained growth phase from the transition phase under the Bank's base case scenario is not so much any radical departure in macroeconomic policies already in place during the transition phase as, hopefully, substantial expansion of the whole economy resulting from the implementation of those policies. Little easing up on the constraints imposed in the latter half of the 1980s is envisaged. Tight money and tariff reform should lead to a progressive change in relative prices in favour of tradables and thus lead to a more rapid expansion of exports. On the demand side, tight credit to government and public enterprises should lead to an expansion in private investment, which should also encourage the inflow of foreign private investment. Overall, it is expected that the private sector would become the principal engine of growth of the economy in the 1990s. Once this engine is moving, then a certain lifting of constraints and controls is to be permitted. In particular, credit restrictions to the private sector should be gradually eased, public sector spending could expand at a rate comparable to the rate of increase of GDP and the export subsidy could rise by 5 percentage points to encourage an even more rapid expansion of exports (Vol. I: 9–12).

Much of the policy package applicable to manufacturing is embraced by the policy changes outlined earlier. Nonetheless it is important for subsequent discussion to draw specific attention to the four elements of the package applicable to manufacturing (Vol. I: 33):

a. a comprehensive tariff reform, with the objective of harmonising effective protection around a target level of 40% across-the-board;
b. the abolition of quantitative restrictions and of 'valeurs mercuriales', and their replacement by temporary import surtaxes that gradually decline over a period of five years;
c. the establishment of an across-the-board export subsidy scheme designed to neutralise the bias against exports induced by tariff protection; and
d. the revision of the Investment Code, in particular the abolition of tariff exemptions on the purchase of intermediate inputs by priority firms, and the revision of certain fiscal measures pertaining to industry, in particular the extension of the value-added tax system to the first processing of agricultural raw materials.

All these measures are to be completed by 1990. Thereafter, it is proposed that the government could reduce the rate of net effective protection to a target level of unity across-the-board[80].

According to the Bank, the overall strategy is open to two major risks (Vol. I: 13–14 and Vol. II: 45–7). First, it is highly dependent on expanded receipts for coffee and cocoa, especially during the transition period – coffee exports are projected to rise from US$594 m. in 1986 to US$686 m. in 1990, cocoa exports from US$1,069 m. to US$1,492 m. over the same period, an overall increase of 28% and of over US$100 m. each year for both crops combined. Second, the strategy implies a further decline in per capita urban income by 2.6% a year from 1986 to 1990 and by a further 0.4% a year to 1995, resulting in an absolute fall of 18% from 1984 to 1995.

In a key paragraph, however, the Bank argues why it sees the proposals it is advocating as the only alternative for the future expansion of the economy and of the changed role for manufacturing (Vol. I: 14).

> Despite these risks, the adoption of an outward-oriented development strategy appears to be the only viable option open to the Government for achieving sustained improvements in the living standards of the population over the medium and long term. By contrast, the adoption of an inward-oriented strategy would progressively reduce the competitiveness of the production apparatus and result in lower factor productivity growth rates and an overall weakening of the longer term growth potential of the economy. In this context, any attempt to foster GDP growth through demand stimulation policies, for example through an expansion of the public sector investment program, in the face of reduced dynamism in the productive sectors, would inevitably lead to unsustainable internal and external resource gaps. Finally, the adoption of an inward-oriented strategy would lead to over-protection in industry and increased discrimination against agriculture in the system of incentives, thereby encouraging migration away from the country-side and further exacerbating downward pressures on per capita income in the urban areas.

The Bank, however, has not been the only international institution to involve itself directly in policies towards the industrial sector. In March 1988, following assistance from UNIDO and a number of professional organisations, the Ministry of Industry published a four-volume study detailing a strategic plan for the future of industry (largely manufacturing) entitled *Schéma Directeur du Développement Industriel de la Côte d'Ivoire* (Ministère de l'Industrie, 1988). In brief, it provides a range of not-too-specific objectives, priorities and proposals to propel industry into the 1990s, while providing a wealth of sub-sectoral detail[81] listing opportunities and the potential for expansion as well as, in some cases, detailing measures to be taken to achieve the stated objectives.

In many ways the *Schéma Directeur* is a strange document. To begin with, and in contrast with the Bank's study, it makes no attempt to project or forecast the pattern of industrial development or even to give much indication of the structural changes expected to occur within any particular time-frame. At the industry-wide level, its objectives are very vague and even at the sub-sectoral level – where proposals for expansion are given – there is no indication of when either the new investment levels or the expanded employment opportunities are expected to be achieved. Indeed, the document explicitly states that it is impossible to determine in advance when the objectives can be achieved[82]. Importantly, too, very little is said about the specific policies which need to be maintained, promoted or changed in order to achieve the stated objectives. In part this is because (as is explicitly acknowledged) the *Schéma Directeur* has been produced more as an 'instrument of dialogue between the private and public sectors' (Vol. I: 178). Also of interest (again, somewhat surprisingly), the *Schéma* makes only indirect mention of the Bank's own four-volume report and fails altogether to comment upon the Bank's base case scenario proposals. Nonetheless, the explicit policies advocated by the Bank under its own (base case) structural adjustment programme – especially in relation to tariffs, quantitative restrictions and fiscal incentives – appear to have the approval of the *Schéma Directeur*.

Table 6.11 *A pragmatic judgement of sub-sectoral opportunities for achieving the major objectives of the Schéma Directeur*

	Further processing, raising value added	Further export opportunities	Regional development opportunities	Small & medium scale industry opportunities	Opportunities for further ivorisation
a. *Sub-sectors in which expansion of industrial opportunities predominate*					
Cereals	xx	x	xx	xx	xx
Coffee/cocoa	xxx	xxx	xx		x
Oils	xxx	xx	xxx		xx
Tobacco	xx	xx	xxx		xx
Food preparations	xx	xx	xx	xx	xx
Meat	xxx	xx	xx	xx	xx
Fish	xx	xxx		x	x
Cotton	xxx	xx	xx	x	xx
Petroleum products	xxx	xx	x		xxx
Agricultural chemicals	x	xx			x
Plastics		x		xx	x
Rubber	xxx	xx	xxx	x	xxx
2ndry Transf. wood	xxx	xxx	xxx	x	x
Repair and maintenance			xx	xxx	xx
Fibre packaging		x	xx		x
Paper packaging	xxx	x	x		x
Metal packaging		x			x
Plastic packaging		x		xx	x
b. *Sub-sectors in which industrial restructuring predominates*					
Fruit and vegetables	xxx	xx	xxx	xx	xx
Sugar cane	xxx		xxx	x	xxx
1ry Transf. wood	xxx	x	xxx	x	x
3ry Transf. wood	xxx	xx	xxx	xx	xx
Cement and related products		xx	xx	x	xx
Assembly and sub-contracting				x	x
c. *Sub-sectors in which new industrial promotion predominates*					
Root-crops	xxx	x	xx	xx	xx
Paper	xxx	x	xxx		xx
Pharmaceuticals	x	x			x
1ry Transf. of metals	x			x	xx
Agricultural machinery	x				xx
Glass containers	xxx	x	xx		xx

Source: Ministère de l'Industrie (1988, Vol. I:41–42).

Note: Trans = transformation.

Under the *Schéma*, the major objectives for industry are set out under five themes: the further processing of primary and particularly agricultural products; providing a great contribution to foreign exchange and payments, both through further import substitution and expanded exports; the deepening of the industrial structure; accelerating the process of Ivorisation in relation both to capital and employment; and, finally, the promotion of industry on a regional basis and through medium and small-scale enterprises. Mention is made, too (but also at a very general level) of the policy environment needed to support and promote the country's industrial future. Four principal areas named are industrial promotion, assistance for industrial restructuring and for small and medium-scale industry promotion and, finally, the setting up of a centre for technological development and product quality standards.

Some sense of the way in which these rather vague objectives are to be fleshed out in practice can be gleaned from the list of the sub-sectors of industry where the best opportunities are presented. These sub-sectors themselves are broken down into three groups: those were the principal concern is industrial expansion, those where the predominant concern is industrial restructuring and, finally, those where the primary concern is with promoting new industries. The details are reproduced in Table 6.11.

Most change is expected to result from the expansion of existing sub-sectors (albeit with the introduction of some new products), with restructuring and new industry promotion coming together but well behind in third place. The greatest opportunities in relation to raising value added and expanding manufactured exports are expected to lie in those sub-sectors producing simpler goods based predominantly on the processing of primary products with, additionally, some export potential in the rubber and agricultural chemical sub-sectors.

Of the CFAF 423 bn to be spent on investment, 37% is expected to occur in the foodstuffs sub-sector and a further 25% in the cotton industry. The only other substantial investments are in agricultural chemicals (CFAF 70 bn) primary and secondary transformation of wood products (CFAF 41 bn) and assembly and sub-contracting (CFAF 30 bn). The processing and consumer-oriented sub-sectors are also the ones where the greatest potential for expanded regional development would appear to exist, although overall the prospects do not appear to be all that good. Similarly, there would appear to be little potential for further ivorisation except in petroleum products, rubber and sugar processing. Few dramatic opportunities for the development of small and medium-sized industries are indicated, with the exception of repair and maintenance services. Of interest, too, for the three industries where new industrial development potential is indicated – root crops, paper and glass containers – the opportunities for export expansion appear to be minimal.

ASSESSMENT, PROBLEMS AND GAPS

Given the nature of the *Schéma Directeur*, its recent adoption by the government and its lack of statistical scenarios, projections or forecasts, it is not possible to judge whether its particular objectives will be attained, and if so, over what period of time. Similarly, as it was published in 1982 and based on data largely up to the end of the 1970s, the projections up to 1990 contained in the *Plan Quinquennial de Développement Économique, Social et Cultural 1981-1985* are now largely of only historical interest and will not be discussed here further. Thus initial comment in this section will focus upon the scenarios, policies and proposals put forward by the World Bank. There is no doubt that these are of extreme practical importance, as many of the main policy proposals outlined in the base case scenario have already been agreed and have begun to be implemented.

The first point to make about the World Bank's base case scenario is that its quantitative targets are wildly optimistic. Neither its scenarios for annual GDP growth of 3% to 1990 and 5% to 1995 nor, importantly for the present discussion, those for the annual growth of industry of 5.1% to 1990 and of 6.5% to 1995, are likely to be achieved.

A major reason for the need substantially to downgrade the Bank's base case scenarios is the fact that by 1988 most of the central and key indicators had turned out to be dramatically at variance with – and far worse than – those used by the Bank. These include export earnings, commodity prices, balance-of-payments data, debt repayments, government deficits and CSSPPA receipts. The degree of error of most of these figures is shown quite clearly in Table 6.12. The one notable omission is a figure for debt servicing. The Bank's base case judged that this would be $1,507 m. for 1989 following payments totalling $4,068 m. for 1986, 1987 and 1988. In practice less than one half of the 1986 and 1987 payments were made;

Table 6.12 *Comparison of World Bank's base case scenario and recent estimates of key economic indicators*

Indicator	World Bank's base case	Final quarter 1988 Estimates	Percentage difference
Annual GDP growth 1986, 1987 and 1988 combined	9.68	1.2[a]	− 88
Balance of payments current account, 1988 $m.	− 94	− 987[b]	950
Exports of coffee and cocoa, 1987 $m.	1,786	135[c]	− 24
1988 $m.	1,918	852[c]	− 56
CSSPPA net revenue 1987/88, $m.	204	− 223 to − 255	− 199 to − 255
Government receipts, net, 1988 CFAF m.	992	638[d]	− 36
Government expenditure, 1988 CFAF m.	863	1,041[d]	21
Budget surplus/deficit $m.	37.6	− 789 to − 1,151	− 2,198 to − 3,161

Source: World Bank (1987), Vol. IV:31–67, various issues of the EIU (1988 and 1989) and *African Economic Digest*.

Notes: [a] EIU (1989:145).
[b] World Bank estimates, quoted in *African Economic Digest*, 12 November 1988.
[c] 1987 figures from EIU (1988:3); 1988 estimates based on first five months estimates, *African Economic Digest*, 4 November 1988.
[d] World Bank mid-year estimates, *African Economic Digest*, 3 June 1988.

in 1988, the government budgeted to repay about $652 m. but these plans were abandoned in mid-year. In February 1989, estimates suggested that $1,735 m. principal and interest payments were due for 1989, some 15% over the World Bank's projected figure (*African Economic Digest*, 3 June 1988 and 30 January 1989)[83].

What these figures combined suggest is that, even if further agreements with the Bank and the IMF are reached and new funds not dissimilar to those previously provided from these sources are forthcoming (as has continued to happen during the 1980s), and even if the French banks continue to support their Ivorian counterparts and to inject new funds into the economy, the resource gap and funding problems have grown so large since the mid-1980s that not even the 'normal' rescheduling and financial package arrangements will be able to put the economy onto a secure economic footing until well into the 1990s. Thus a judgement of probably greater importance is that there would appear to be little realistic prospect that any form of *self-sustained growth and expansion* of either the economy as a whole, or of the manufacturing sector in particular, will be possible up to the mid-1990s.

Defenders of the Bank's perspective might argue that the failures of the base case scenario to match what happened even in the very early period of the decade to 1995 are understandable for both external and internal reasons. For instance, externally, the drop in the prices of major export crops, especially of coffee, were entirely unexpected when the scenarios were drawn up in the mid-1980s. On the internal front, the slowness with which, for instance, the tariff reduction programme has proceeded, together with the failure of the government to resolve the financing problems of the CSSPPA and to reduce public sector spending in line with the parameters outlined by the Bank, add weight to the view that it was not so much poor policy as a failure to carry out that policy which has been to blame. This, it is argued, accounts for the country entering the 1990s in such a weak position and with such poor prospects for sustainable growth expansion in the near term.

While there is some validity in these comments, they provide nothing like an adequate answer. What is worrying is not so much that the numbers were wrong – forecasting even a year ahead is a hazardous game – but, as clearly shown in Table 6.12, that they were out by so large a margin, in some cases by many hundreds of percentage points[84]. It is no easy task for a country to embark on a programme of quite substantial, and therefore high risk, economic structural reform; for so many of the key external assumptions to be so wide of the mark raises serious questions about the proposals being made. At minimum, it puts in question the

Bank's strongly held view that there was no real alternative to its approach and that other scenarios would produce worse results.

More worrying still, however, is that this type of criticism does not appear to have been unique to the post-1985 period: there has been a history of high expectation and poor delivery for probably the entire duration of each of the structural adjustment programmes from the early 1980s onwards. Indeed, it could be argued (at least with the benefit of hindsight) that the programmes advocated by the Bank, and supported by hundreds of million of dollars of new external funds, have acted as a means of *avoiding* radical structural change and of maintaining intact the very structures which have been a principal cause of the Côte d'Ivoire's major problems.

Thus the Bank's programmes and policy options have all rested firmly on the gravely erroneous assumption that most export earnings would, could, and should be derived in the near future from agriculturally-linked exports (and from coffee and cocoa in particular) and that these would be high enough to support, firstly, the restructuring programme and, then, a longer period of sustained growth. Interestingly, this interpretation of the failure of the adjustment programmes to address substantially the key structural problems of the economy, with which Campbell (1985: 303) concurs, has not been absent from analysis and debate conducted within the perspectives of the World Bank itself. Thus, Chamley (analysing the 1980s for the Bank) wrote in mid-1998 (1988: 12, 17, 18 and 22):

> The SAP recognized the main imbalances and policies that were required to address these issues. However, the seriousness of the situation of Côte d'Ivoire was seriously under-estimated because the fall of cocoa and coffee prices was still not considered to be permanent, and the recent discovery of oil had raised expectations too high . . .
> The purpose of the second SAL was to strengthen the structural adjustment process that had been supported by SAL I. This continuation had been anticipated from the beginning of the SAP. A second SAL was particularly necessary because of the worsening of the situation in Côte d'Ivoire . . . the program had one shortcoming. It did not succeed in the implementation of a set of proper incentives for the diversification of the economy . . .
> (SAL III) The situation has in fact worsened with further decreases of the commodity prices that took place in the beginning of 1988 and the prospects for a price recovery in the near future are not good . . . (Yet) the pressure seemed to be off. As before, this lack of pressure may have produced some complacency and may not be foreign to the long lag between the initialization of the SAL and its effectiveness.

A related set of questions is raised by a 1988 paper published by the World Institute for Development Economics Research of the United Nations University (WIDER) as part of a global study on stabilisation and adjustment programmes. Here Hiey (1988: 1) argues that orthodox absorption-reducing policies combined with trade liberalisation have led and are likely to continue to lead to stagflation in Côte d'Ivoire; in contrast, it is argued, a more heterodox and interventionist policy package would probably have more beneficial results for the Ivorian economy. One scenario put forward would include, for instance, an increase in average tariff rates and the reduction of some import quotas. Simulations suggest that this would result in a *greater* reduction of the fiscal deficit and a more substantial *improvement* in the external account than the World Bank's liberalisation approach. Not only does Hiey's analysis of the 1981–4 period support this view but his simulations point to the conclusion that the more heterodox approach would be likely to leave the economy stronger by the year 1990 and beyond. The main thrust of his approach, which, incidentally, appears to address some of the issues which Chamley hints have been avoided by the Bank's programmes, is summarised thus (1988: 37–8):

> The Ivory Coast will remain structurally vulnerable to external shocks as long as its income remains so dependent upon commodity exports with erratically fluctuating prices. Even the best adjustment policies cannot suppress the negative impact of adverse move-ments in the terms of trade. One remedy is clearly the diversification of the productive structure oriented toward a deepening of the domestic market . . .
> The problem is not whether or not to sever the economy from the external market; as long as we import intermediate inputs, machinery and equipment, we must export . . .
> As soon as the internal market deepens, as a consequence of productivity gains in food production, which provides employment for the majority of the population, the interrela-tionship between agriculture and industry will tighten . . . The farther the integration of

industry and agriculture goes the larger the internal market. These are the kind of policies that can gradually reduce, though not eliminate, the vulnerability of the economy to external shocks and put it on the path to self-sustaining growth.

These comments bring us directly back to the future of industry in general and of manufacturing in particular. It is clear that the approaches of the Bank and its critics (Hiey, Campbell and Duruflé) for the future of manufacturing in the 1990s differ sharply.

The Bank advocates a process of manufacturing sector expansion and structural change taking place in the context of, and very much determined by, further liberalisation. This would result, especially, in a rise in exports of processed agricultural products, a substantial increase in overall manufactured exports and a rise in the share of manufactures in total exports. For his part, Hiey sees a form of manufacturing expansion determined more by domestic interventionist policies, stimulated in particular by rises in rural incomes through expanded food crop production, which forges greater interlinkages between industry and agriculture but which go well beyond the past pattern of linkage, dominated by the processing of export crops.

There is little doubt that the adverse and all-pervasive macroeconomic context of the economy in the early 1990s will have both direct and indirect effects on manufacturing. Poor export prospects leading to lower than expected demand for agricultural products, large debt-servicing commitments and the need to trim state expenditures will adversely affect domestic demand and inhibit the supply of imported inputs. In addition, the poor overall economic climate and the need to cut back on public investment programmes will adversely affect both inflows of new foreign investment capital and levels of domestic investment in both the public and private sectors. Both factors are likely to reinforce domestic saving constraints, thereby continuing to provide a brake on manufacturing investment in the coming years. As a result, the scenario outlined under the World Bank's base case will fall well short of its projected bullish expectations (World Bank, 1987, Vol. I: 9). The more likely scenario is one of hesitant, and on average much lower levels of, growth of MVA to the mid-1990s with little prospect that the growth rates of the 1960s and 1970s will be repeated.

Such a conclusion by no means ends our discussion of the future of the sector. It is still crucially important to ask what are the prospects for structural change. Two types of question need to be considered in this respect. The first is the extent to which the changes advocated or implicit in the Bank's proposals are likely to be achieved. The second is to raise the more fundamental question about the appropriateness of this type of evolution of manufacturing for the future development of Côte d'Ivoire.

A series of factors raise doubts about whether the type of changes implicit in the Bank's view of the structural changes within manufacturing and the wider economy will be achieved over the next few years. A major one relates to the implementation of the tariff and quota reform programme and the prospects for continuing a policy that has already confronted major problems[85]. A number of considerations point to even greater difficulties in continuing to implement the tariff reduction and related proposals in the future. One is that the revenue-raising problems which led to the August 1987 policy reversal have persisted and at the end of 1988 did not look near to resolution. At the same time, pressures on the expenditure side of public finance have become increasingly more acute than foreseen in the Bank's base case scenario (see Table 6.12). In addition, the easiest phase of tariff reduction – over which there were considerable delays – has already taken place. When further reductions are implemented, political resistance from groups who will be adversely affected (for instance through factory closures) will be at its height. Finally, the incidence of the smuggling of imported goods, customs evasions and transfer pricing among private sector undertakings has risen substantially since the reform programme began in 1985, challenging the effectiveness of these policies in achieving the objectives intended. In short, given the record to date, the prospects of the government achieving the 1990s goals by that date look remote, while the tentative proposal to reduce the rate of effective protection to unity by the year 1995 looks little more than a pipe-dream.

But there are other questions which need to be asked about the ability of the reforms to achieve their objectives. One concerns the consequence of scaling down the share of the public sector in manufacturing production and replacing it with the private sector. According to its advocates, this policy is supposed to provide the motor for a substantial increase in overall investment (domestic and foreign) in manufacturing. A series of factors raise serious doubts about this assumption. To begin with, the process of privatisation has moved extremely slowly in Côte d'Ivoire since it began in the early 1980s, slowing substantially in the post-November 1987 period. Given the recent adverse performance of the economy and poor near-term prospects, there is little optimism that external investors will be willing to raise their profile in Côte d'Ivoire in either the short or medium term. What is more, not only is the indigenous private sector far too small to be in a position to make a major impact on the overall ownership pattern of the manufacturing sector – through buying into state and parastatal concerns[86] – but it is by no means certain that the interests within the ruling elite which engineered and obtained benefits from the massive increase in direct state involvement in industry, especially during the 1970s, would stand idly by and allow these interests to be dissipated[87]. Finally, even if such a policy were embarked upon with any degree of seriousness, there are many who consider it would produce dramatically perverse results. Thus UNIDO is quoted as arguing that too rapid a shift to private sector ownership of manufacturing would be a major investment disincentive and would act not simply as a deterrent to increase private sector investment but also as a stimulant to further disinvestment (*African Economic Digest*, 5 February 1988).

Questions also need to be raised in relation to the expected expansion of manufactured exports. Even were the export subsidy scheme to be in place and operating smoothly[88], there are major misgivings that the rapid expansion of manufactured exports and the rise in the share of manufactured to total exports (see Table 6.10) will not be achieved. One reason is that the expansion of processed agricultural exports is based on over-optimistic scenarios about world demand for these products and the ability of the primary product-linked subsectors of manufacturing rapidly to expand production and to maintain (or in many cases improve) the quality of their products. A second concern is that the rapid expansion of wood-related manufactured exports is also unlikely to happen particularly because of the rapid rundown of domestic timber supplies and the slowness with which the forest regeneration programme has been implemented. As for the hope that non-traditional manufactured exports would expand rapidly in the 1990s, it appears to be the judgement of the *Schéma Directeur* (see Table 6.11) that this is an area of manufacturing where further export opportunities are *least* likely to arise.

It is difficult, therefore, to avoid the conclusion that substantial structural change is very unlikely within the parameters outlined by the World Bank. When economic expansion does take place, it is most likely to result in export-oriented agriculture and industry continuing to move closer together, with only small numbers of more discrete developments occurring in other sub-sectors of manufacturing. What is more, if the objectives of the Bank's base case scenario were to be achieved, these types of structural changes would be likely to be reinforced as a result of a predicted sharp decline in sub-sectors linked with investment (construction and engineering) and a more rapid expansion of sub-sectors involved in food processing and textiles (Michel and Noël, 1984: 113). Such a future would be one tinged with déjà vu: perpetuating into the future the post-1977 era, which so singularly failed to remove either the overall dependence of the economy on a handful of export crops or the dependence of the manufacturing sector upon primary processing. In other words, the Bank's 'remedies' for industrial expansion are not remedies at all.

Are there any alternatives? We can begin to answer this question with a rather simple observation. If there is one thing particularly striking about the debates on the future of industry in Côte d'Ivoire and the fundamental problems and weaknesses of manufacturing outlined in this chapter, it is the lack of any substantial inter-relation between the two: the Bank's strategies for the future of manufacturing, in particular, do not appear to address the sector's most fundamental weaknesses. If industry is to be a key actor in the development of the economy in the 1990s a good starting-point would seem to be to examine how these critical problems and weaknesses might best be solved.

In relation to the structure of manufacturing five weaknesses have been highlighted: subsectoral fragility, weak interlinkages, a far from strong export-base, the costs of foreign involvement, and the problems of concentration and size. Turning these problems into the principal objectives of policy discussion suggests that what Côte d'Ivoire needs now more than ever before is a manufacturing sector with the following characteristics:

- a more balanced sub-sectoral and regional composition with less dependence upon processing of primary products destined for the (increasingly fragile) export market;

- a far greater degree of inter-linkage both within its different sub-sectors and to other sectors of the economy, but, especially, the development of forward linkages to agriculture of those sub-sectors supplying inputs used by agriculture;
- a higher level and increased range of non-traditional manufactured exports produced increasingly (but by no means exclusively) for non-West African markets with at the same time an expanded domestic and regional market.

Only if manufacturing advances along these lines will there be any realistic hope of creating an industrial sector increasingly independent of export-based agriculture and therefore less susceptible to the vagaries of international market forces – in other words, a sector whose growth is determined more by an expansion of domestic demand for basic consumer goods and whose exports cover a far wider range of products. The question is how best these policy objectives can be achieved. It is certainly encouraging to note that among the objectives of the *Schéma Directeur* are the following: further import substitution, deepening of the industrial structure, accelerating the process of Ivorisation and promotion of industry on a regional basis[89]. The problem, as mentioned above, is that there appear to be few policy guidelines drawn up to encourage their rapid achievement. While this is not the place to attempt to provide such guidelines, it might be useful to end this chapter with a few comments drawn from the post-colonial history of industrialisation in Côte d'Ivoire.

Three points from the previous discussion need to be brought together. First, the present structure of manufacturing in Côte d'Ivoire has been created as a result of, on the one hand, an extremely liberal attitude to foreign capital, and on the other, state-induced investment concentrated predominantly on further processing of primary products. Second, the analysis provided little evidence to suggest that when tariffs and controls increased, manufacturing became dramatically less competitive. Third, high levels of dependence upon foreign skilled personnel have led to sizeable and increasing outflows of remittances, while the failure to continue to attract new foreign investment inflows has meant that, with the large stock of foreign capital already present, the outflow of profits and dividends has become an additional and severe strain on the balance of payments.

What implications can one draw from these factors for future policy? One is surely that 'more of the same', or attempts to return to the even more liberal period of the 1960s, are unlikely to lead to the deepening of the manufacturing sector and the development of further inter-linkages. To address these weaknesses, what appears to be needed is an incentive system which encourages the establishment of new industries, which will deepen the process of import substitution, and which will provide, *inter alia*, a greater proportion of domestic inputs to agriculture than has been achieved to date. For this to succeed, it would clearly be necessary, and for some time, to protect new and emergent industries through tariffs and/or quantitative controls. Increased protection in these areas should itself provide an added incentive for new foreign investment (as it did in the past), although the involvement of the public sector should by no means be ruled out[90].

A significant inflow of new foreign investment would clearly assist the balance of payments, but the advantages would be likely to be broader than this. If the protective measures necessary to attract investors were to be of a specific duration (after which quantitative restrictions were to be removed and tariffs gradually reduced), this would encourage foreigners to invest in plants large enough to manufacture for export as well as for the domestic market. Thus over time – and there would seem to be no *a priori* reason why the time could not vary from investment to investment – the objective of deepening the industrial structure would be married with that of expanding the range and importance of non-traditional exports. An additional advantage of new foreign involvement is that those firms with the research and development capacity and marketing expertise to bring in, utilise and adapt the technologies required to penetrate new and to expand existing export markets, are likely to be attracted.

The issue of skills training is also one of central importance. Experience elsewhere[91] suggests not only that industrial deepening is unlikely to occur when an agriculturally-dependent economy faces the volatility of the international economy unprotected, but also that it is unlikely to take place unless a widespread pool of domestic skills in management, engineering and a range of lower level technical skills exists. While Côte d'Ivoire has come some way along the road of foreign skill replacement, it clearly still needs to expand significantly the training (formal and on-the-job) of Ivorians, as well as to marry better the formal and informal training programmes and the overall reward system[92]. Thus, in spite of the budget constraints which will persist at least to the 1990s, high priority needs to be given to the expansion and better integration of skills development training at the secondary, tertiary and practical levels[93]. In addition, steps need to be taken to change the reward system so as to encourage the expansion of the more informal apprenticeship system. These measures could be assisted or accelerated by requiring (with due tax and related incentives) foreign companies (both existing and new investors) to introduce a system of local skills training. Domestic training would also play a positive role in addressing the problems of size and industrial concentration. If an expanded stock of skills were to be linked to financial packages to assist the establishment of small and medium-sized industries outside Abidjan, then a more substantial expansion of these enterprises, initially in the areas of more simple consumer goods, repair and assembly, would be likely to occur[94]. If these are located within the rural areas and linked to greater incentives for food production – along the lines proposed by both Hiey (1988) and Alfthan (1982) – then this should also help to address, though not by any means solve, the problem of smuggling and illegal importation of consumer goods.

All this sounds seductively simple. Clearly, there are many other and more complex macroeconomic issues which need to be resolved if such an alternative strategy were to be attempted, while the political feasibility of such an approach also needs to be addressed. Enough has probably been said, however, to make the simple point that an approach in many ways different from that proposed by the World Bank in its influential policy documents merits further debate and analysis. Indeed, such a debate is worth pursuing if only because it attempts to address head-on the structural weaknesses which have faced the Côte d'Ivoire's manufacturing sector for so long but which, if the record is to be believed, appear to have been so studiously avoided in the post-Independence period.

Notes

1. The government has decreed that the official name of the country in both the French and English languages shall be Côte d'Ivoire. This is the convention now used by the United Nations and the World Bank and it will be followed in this chapter.
2. In 1978, the World Bank published a book on the economic performance of the Côte d'Ivoire subtitled 'The Challenge of Success', Den Tuinder (1978). Its performance has continued to be termed a success up to at least 1987 – see, for instance Riboud (1987: v).
3. Three indicators of the more serious problems to come which were apparent in the early 1970s were the slowing down of industrial growth rates below the growth of GDP, a slowdown of agricultural growth rates and deterioration in the current account of the balance of payments. For detailed discussion of these points see Duruflé et al. (1986).
4. UNIDO data record MVA growth of 16.7% in 1980 followed by three years of contraction of from 6 to over 11%, while World Bank data record growth rates of MVA of 26% in 1980 and 27% in 1984 contrasted with a contraction of 13% in 1982 and no growth in 1986. More details concerning these differences will be given in the following section.
5. Interesting because this was the period of the most rapid expansion and diversification of the sector, as explained below.
6. The following data, both of World Bank origin, for MVA at current factor cost for selected years between 1965 to 1972, illustrate this problem. Figures in the left-hand column are from the 1975 Industrial sector report, those in the right-hand column from the 1986 macro-study. Both are in CFAF bn. Differences range from 136% in 1965 to over 30% in 1972.

Year	MVA (1975 published data)	MVA (1986 published data)
1965	11.8	27.9
1970	27.6	41.4
1971	33.1	45.1
1972	39.2	51.7

UNIDO figures from different sources within the organisation also differ, again often markedly. In the next table, the figures in the first column give the rate of growth of MVA provided in UNIDO's 1986 country study, those in the second from the general statistical data base of UNIDO, both in fixed local currency terms, MVA at factor cost:

Year	Rate of growth of MVA (1986 country report)	Rate of growth of MVA (late 1988 data-base)
1981	− 6.1	− 9.9
1982	− 9.9	6.64
1983	− 11.5	− 3.87
1984	8.5	− 0.23

It is also important to note that the figures published by the World Bank in contemporary documents also differ substantially. For instance, *World Development Report* and *World Tables* consistently record far higher figures for MVA in Côte d'Ivoire than do the country-specific studies. This is in part due to the fact that the former figures include petroleum refining. It does not, however, provide a complete explanation as the table below, with data in CFAF bn, illustrates.

Year	MVA (World Tables)	MVA (Country Reports)	Oil/petroleum
1980	195.6	193.2	15.4
1981	201.0	219.0	37.9
1982	263.5	207.1	63.9
1983	301.6	188.4	113.9
1984	334.2	232.2	62.8

7. At current prices, the growth rate of MVA between 1965 and 1972 was 21% at market prices and 18.7% at factor cost; at constant prices the figures were 16.9 and 14.7% respectively. (World Bank 1975: Annex Table 6.A1.)
8. The differences for the period 1970–83 are shown below. They not only affect the total value attributed to MVA but also the contribution manufacturing is assumed to be making to the whole economy.

Year	MVA Current CFAF bn	MVA/GDP %	MVA Current CFAF bn	MVA/GDP %
	UNIDO figures		World Bank figures	
1970	55	13.2	41.4	13.0
1980	260	11.7	193.2	10.6
1983	288	10.9	188.4	8.7

Source: UNIDO (1986) and World Bank (1987).

9. UNIDO data give an annual average growth rate of 7.9% for the period 1963–88. (UNIDO data-base, October 1988.)
10. Notwithstanding the trends recorded in Note 7 above. The World Bank's *World Development Report* gives a consistently higher figure. In its 1988 Report, the MVA/GDP ratio given is 16% for 1986, falling from 17% for the years 1985 and 1984, and 13% for 1983. The 1986 comprehensive country-based study, published in 1987, however, gives the ratio as 8.7% for 1983. UNIDO data (1986) give 10.9% for the same year. Unpublished data from early 1988 originating from the Ministère de l'Industrie in Côte d'Ivoire give the ratio as 11% for 1980 and 13% for 1985.
11. See Appendix Table 6.A1 for the exchange rate of the CFA franc and the dollar over the post-independence period.
12. Although industry is a broader grouping than manufacturing, and hence these figures exaggerate some of the trends within the manufacturing sector, the rates of change are close enough to those of manufacturing to be used here. The share of manufacturing in total industrial production over the period has been as follows:

Year	Manufacturing output as % of total industrial output
1960	85
1965	92
1970	94
1975	93
1980	93
1986	90

Source: Ministère de l'Industrie, 1988.

13. World Bank figures from World Bank, 1987, vol. IV, Table 1.10, and 1980–86 from *Investment of Transnational Corporations in Africa*, addendum to Report of the Secretary General to the General Assembly of the United Nations, A/43/500Add. 2, 15 August 1988, pp. 5–6. According to this study, Côte d'Ivoire recorded the highest inflow of private direct investment of all non-oil exporting African countries (36 countries in the continent of Africa) in the period 1975–80.

14. In 1986, out of total capital of CFAF 425 bn, the Ivorian share amounted to 344 bn and the foreign share to 81 bn. (Figures from *Marchés Tropicaux et Méditerranéens*, 27 December 1985, pp. 70–71 and 10 June 1988, p. 1481.)

15. 'The first few months of 1989 will bring more arduous negotiations with all creditors. The manufacturing sector seems set to remain a major victim of the recession which has reduced consumer purchasing power and encouraged a greater reliance on the cheaper informal market. With profits declining, the fragile industrial fabric will be increasingly threatened by disinvestment.' (EIU, 1989: 146.)

16. In 1975 Abidjan's share of total industrial employees was 49.8%, rising to a peak of 52.9% in 1978 and falling back to 51.3% by 1982. (Chambre de Commerce et d'Industrie de Côte d'Ivoire, quoted in Ministère de la Coopération, France, 1986: 82.)

17. The very different, even if dated, figures from the Secretariat d'Etat au Plan et à l'Industrie are as follows for 1980:

Types of enterprise	Number of Enterprises	per cent	Number of Employees	per cent
Large-scale	210	1	64,000	20
Small/medium-scale	219	1	5,700	2
Transitional sector (other small/medium-scale)	1,800	10	18,000	6
Artisans and local informal sector	15,700	87	67,000	21
Informal sector			159,000	51
TOTALS	17,980	100	313,700	100

18. These were the following:

Enterprise	Ownership % foreign	Turnover 1983/4 CFAF bn	Value Added 1983 CFAF bn	Total Employment 1983/4
CIDT (cotton)	45% French	43.6	26.8	3,327
SITAB (tobacco)	60% foreign	32.3	16.5	890
PalmIndustrie (palm oil)	100% Ivorian	26.5	12.8	14,510
HSL-Blohorn (vegetable oil)	100% UK	42.7	12.4	1,300
Sodesucre (sugar)	100% Ivorian	21.2	11.9	4,875
Solibra (beverages)	79% foreign	19.0	9.4	1,900
Gonfreville (textiles)	34% French	19.4	7.4	3,000
Capral (coffee processing)	62% Swiss	17.7	6.2	396
Cotivo (textiles)	7% foreign	10.2	4.7	1,600
Utexi (textiles)	80% Dutch	6.5	4.4	1,238

Source: UNIDO (1986), Ministère de la Coopération, France, 1986 and *Marchés Tropicaux et Méditerranéens*, 27 December 1985.

19. 1988 Data from the Ministère de l'Industrie give the following trends in industrial exports 1981–5 in CFAF bn:

Year	Agro-Industrial Exports	Per-cent	Non-agro-industrial exports	per-cent
1981	141	70	61	30
1982	160	68	75	32
1983	193	66	100	34
1984	269	67	131	33
1985	266	58	191	42

20. The CEAO countries, in addition to Côte d'Ivoire, are Benin, Burkina Faso, Mali, Niger, Mauritania and Senegal and the ECOWAS countries Benin, Cape Verde, Gambia, Ghana, Guinea, Guinea Bissau, Liberia, Nigeria, Sierre Leone and Togo. The CEAO was formed in June 1972, ECOWAS in May 1975. As for the importance of these two regional groupings to the expansion of trade, the position is well summarised by Atsain in Zartman and Delgado (1984: 188):

> While CEAO institutions have come to perform quite satisfactorily, progress in implementing the ECOWAS treaty is limited mainly to a set of decisions reached in political enthusiasm, the application of which remains hypothetical.

21. The population of Côte d'Ivoire stood at 10.1 m. in 1986, those of the other countries of the CEAO at 30 m. In 1965 the GDP of Côte d'Ivoire was $760 m., that of the other five countries of the CEAO combined almost three times as large at $2,060 m.
22. One example is the local subsidiary of the US company EverReady which in 1987 exported 40% of its batteries to the CEAO region but which has reported increasing difficulties in raising or even maintaining the level of exports (*African Economic Digest*, 24 January 1987).
23. The data on regional manufactured exports are more unreliable than other trade or macroeconomic data. The following table reveals the evidence of regional manufactured exports from Côte d'Ivoire from a number of sources.

Manufactured exports[a] in CFAF m. (Current) (Percentages in brackets)					
Year	Manufactured exports to CEAO		Manufactured Exports to ECOWAS		Total Manufactured Exports	
	ALL	Less Food	ALL	Less Food	ALL	Less Food
1971[b]	7.2		7.9		30.4	
	(24)		(26)		(100)	
1975[c]	7.6	6.8	9.9	8.7	88.7	36.2
	(7)	(19)	(10)	(24)	(100)	(100)
1979[c]	15.6	11.2	22.0	14.6	171.1	58.9
	(9)	(19)	(13)	(25)	(100)	(100)
1983[d]			66.9	538.5	1,813.6	1,290.2
			(42)	(36)	(100)	(100)

Source: World Bank (1975: 34–35), UNIDO (1986: 57–62) and Atsain in Zartman and Delgado (1984: 204–207).

Notes: [a] For the purposes of this calculation the exports of petroleum products were excluded.
[b] World Bank for industrial exports rather than exclusively manufacturing exports.
[c] Atsain.
[d] UNIDO data for 'developing countries'.

24. The dominance of developing country (largely West African) markets can be seen from the following UNIDO (1986) data for trade in 1983:

SITC Category	Total Exports $m.	% going to developing countries
Miscellaneous food prep.	16.9	98
Tobacco manufactures	3.1	71
Oils and perfumes	11.8	80
Fertilisers	17.0	100
Plastic materials	4.4	100
Other chemicals	6.8	97
Wood and cork products	23.8	42
Textile yarn, fabrics	44.7	56
Non-metallic minerals	15.6	99
Iron and steel	5.3	88
Non-ferrous metals	7.1	61
Non-electric machinery	20.0	59
Transport equipment	21.1	56
Footwear	5.0	100

25. Although the figures will therefore be somewhat dated, it should be remembered that (according to the UNIDO data-base) real MVA was higher in 1980 than in any other subsequent year to 1988, therefore making them more relevant to policy discussion than might initially be thought.

26. For 1985, data provided in 1988 by the Ministère de l'Industrie are as follows:

Food sub-division	Total Inputs	Total Imported Inputs	Percent imported
		CFAF m.	
Fruit and vegetables	5,400	86.4	1.6
Sugar	5,850	1,580	27
Cereals	29,400	14,112	48
Coffee/cocoa	72,600	1,524	· 2.1
Oils	47,100	3,049	4.2
Tobacco	10,700	8,346	78
Food preparations	13,300	8,379	63
Meat	5,160	500	9.7
Fish products	17,000	13,906	81.8
TOTALS	206,510	51,482	24.9

27. According to the World Bank's 1975 industrial study of Côte d'Ivoire, in the early 1970s about 20% of intermediate inputs came from Ivorian industry and 80% were imported (1975: 6).

28. Figures reproduced by Alfthan (1982: 31) suggest that the 20% figure applied in 1974. His figures, going back to 1961, show that the proportion of inputs originating from the 'primary sector' (therefore broader than just agriculture) constituted 19% of total intermediate consumption in both 1961 and 1966, but increased to 23% by 1976.

29. Alfthan's figures (1982: 31) suggest that the 1974 figure may have been exceptional: he records the proportion of intermediate inputs originating from the secondary sector as 25% in 1961, 37% in 1974 and down to 25% again by 1976.

30. In 1984 the ratio of production to consumption for different meat products was as follows: beef, 26%; sheep and goats, 45%; pork, 92% and poultry 88%, giving an overall weighted average of 48% (Source: Ministère de l'Industrie, 1988).

31. It is not being argued here that Côte d'Ivoire – or, indeed, any other country – *needs* to be self-sufficient in food production. Indeed, in the case of Côte d'Ivoire food imports, including livestock on-the-hoof, are obtained predominantly from the West African region, a structural feature which in general is positive as it encourages inter-regional trade. What are worrying, however, are both the rapid fall in self-sufficiency and dependence for imports on a source of (regional) supply that is by no means secure, together with the very large amounts of money which have had to be devoted to food imports in the context of growing foreign-exchange shortages.

32. Notable changes in the November 1984 Investment Code include the abolition of customs duties on imported raw materials, the granting of tax credits for creating jobs for nationals, additional incentives for small and medium-sized industries and additional incentives for firms locating outside Abidjan.

33. The semi-official report on Ivorian Industry in *Marchés Tropicaux et Méditerranéens* (27 December 1985: 74–75) reports cases of investment costs in Côte d'Ivoire being three times as high as similar projects in Europe.

34. These points, and others, are developed in a case-study of the impact of multinational corporations on the Côte d'Ivoire economy, written by Masini and colleagues. They conclude thus (Masini et al., 1979:'55):

> The tendencies we have (found in our analysis) . . . indicate that a high foreign capital participation in the sector reflects very substantial import coefficients, which limits industrial integration and the development of employment and of the internal market. But the higher the foreign participation and the import coefficients, the higher is the capital intensity and the lower the productivity of capital. This will also restrict the creation of jobs and the growth of the domestic market.
>
> In these circumstances, it can be said that the scope of the Ivory Coast domestic market is both the cause and the effect of the behaviour of foreign firms: the cause because it inhibits the establishment of factories which to earn a profit must produce on a large scale, especially in the case of basic industries and capital goods; and the effect because by importing a large part of their inputs foreign firms reduce the internal demand and by using capital-intensive techniques they restrict the creation of jobs.

35. As the 1986 report on Ivorian industry produced by the French Ministry of Co-operation puts it (Ministère de la Coopération, France, 1986: 106):

> La circulation captive de la technologie à l'intérieur de l'espace intégré de la firme s'est accompagnée d'une dépendance profonde vis-à-vis de l'étranger sans acquisition véritable par une capacité de réproduction locale.

36. This is certainly an improvement (a 12% absolute increase) on the 1979 figures which showed that Ivorians constituted only 34% of senior personnel. However, these figures include both 'direction' and 'cadres supérieurs'. The 1979 figures show that when only the senior 'direction' posts are considered, Ivorians constituted less than 20% ('Bilan national de l'emploi en Côte d'Ivoire, May 1982, Ministère des Relations Extérieures, quoted in Ministère De La Cooperation, France 1986: 106.)

37. As the *Financial Times* of 15 July 1987 commented: 'The President has never hidden his desire to use foreign expertise to accelerate his country's economic development. It has some 40,000 out of 300,000 French citizens on the African continent'.

38. In 1985–6, 19% of the population earned 60% of the income (*West Africa*, 8 August 1988, quoting World Bank analysis of income distribution).

39. As the *Financial Times* wrote on 24 June 1987, in spite of the financial crisis in Côte d'Ivoire, 'there will still be French champagne on the shelves of the supermarkets'.

40. To the extent that the presence of foreigners also stimulated the demand for imported luxury consumer goods, the overall effect on the balance of payments would have been even more adverse.

41. The figure is derived from summing three elements; private capital on the capital account and other investment income and workers' remittances on the current account of the balance of payments.

42. It should, perhaps, be pointed out that manufacturing by no means 'started' at Independence. A number of establishments, including some in the public sector, originate as far back as the 1940s, 1930s and even the 1920s. For instance the textile firm GONFREVILLE began in 1921, the state-owned fruit conserving enterprise SALCI in 1947 and the wood factory SCAF in 1920. Of interest, too, none of these were set up in Abidjan.

43. The change in tariffs from 1973 to the early 1980s is well summarised by the World Bank (World Bank, 1987, Vol. III: 164):

> Taking regular tariffs as a reference, Effective Tariff Protection (ETP) coefficients increased in 12 out of the 19 sub-sectors under analysis. Increases were particularly marked in the case of edible oils and fats (from 1.01 to 1.83), other food processing (from 0.64 to 1.85), spinning, weaving and dyeing (from 1.28 to 2.26), other textile products (from 1.60 to 2.65), vehicles (from 0.93 to 1.25) and simple machinery (from 0.99 to 1.37). By contrast, ETP coefficients declined in food canning, coffee processing, leather, chemicals, plastics and machinery. In 1980, ETP rates exceeded the 100% level in the case of food canning (112%), coffee processing (355%), spinning, weaving and dyeing (126%), and other textile products (164%). They exceeded 50% in the case of edible oils and fats (83%), and other food processing (85%), while remaining in the 30 to 40% range in the other sub-sectors.

44. It would be mistaken, however, to believe that moves towards greater protection were exclusively a post-1970 phenomenon. Import licensing and even outright prohibition occurred, albeit (in retrospect) on a smaller scale, throughout the 1960s.

45. A brief chronology of relations with external funders since the early 1980s is given here:

> Côte d'Ivoire's recent adjustment programmes began in the autumn of 1980 when a joint World Bank/IMF mission began discussion with the Ivorian authorities which led to the elaboration of a Structural Adjustment Programme supported by the Extended Financing Facility (EFF) of the Fund and the Structural Adjustment Lending (SAL) of the Bank.
>
> SAL I ran from 1981 to 1983 with the IMF taking the lead and the Bank concentrating on micro-issues but not directly concerned with industrial questions.
>
> SAL II, 1984–6, had the broad objective of restoring internal and external equilibria with the same thrust of programme reforms as SAL I.
>
> Initialling of SAL III began in February 1985 with the negotiations completed after the end of the recovery of 1986.
>
> The second tranche ($150 m.) of the SAL III loan ($250 m.) was delayed towards the end of 1987 because of the failure of the government to meet target dates on key issues such as the introduction of the export subsidy scheme (see below).
>
> In March 1988, the IMF agreed the release of $241 m. of fresh funds under its Compensatory Financing Facility (CFF), while in May 1988 a commercial debt agreement was signed, rescheduling some 90% of all commercial debt accrued since 1983.
>
> A month later, however, the government missed its first private debt repayments. By August 1988, the whole IMF programme was 'under review' following the government's inability to finance repayments to the Fund and a month later both the Fund and the Bank were continuing to withhold disbursements pending 'further discussion' with the authorities.
>
> To the contributions of the Fund and the Bank must be added that of the French Caisse Centrale

de Coopération Economique (CCCE), whose new commitments from 1980 to 1984 rose to 2,662 m. francs. Its importance is well summarised by Campbell (1989a):

> the Caisse Centrale de Co-opération Economique . . . although it does not apply its own adjustment proposals has worked closely with the World Bank, notably in the area of the reform of public enterprises. If one excluded facilities resulting from rescheduling loans, it is significant to note that the CCCE contribution was greater than that of the other organisations over the period 1980–1985 and represented 44% of total foreign funding and 68% of adjustment funding.

46. Chamley summarises the major macro-problems facing the economy in 1981 as follows (1988: 5–6):

- the deficits of the government budget and the current account (12 and 17%, respectively) illustrated the link between internal and external balance;
- the ratio of foreign debt to GDP had reached 35%;
- there was no centralised budgetary process. Government expenditures were out of control . . .
- the competitiveness of the economy had badly deteriorated, and real growth on non-cocoa exports had declined during the second half of the seventies. During the period 1980–1981, i.e. after the end of the boom, the terms of trade fell by another 20%.

47. 25 to 35% of the subsidies on cotton to local processing firms and 1984–5 fertiliser subsidies to cotton farmers were abolished and consumer prices for bread, rice and palm oil were raised to world prices. It is not possible or necessary to go into all the details of these programmes here. For further discussion see World Bank (1987), Chamley (1988) and Hiey (1988).

48. Though levels of investment fell substantially, from, for instance, CFAF 83 m. in 1981 to CFAF 47 m. in 1983 at current prices (excluding the petroleum sub-sector). In fixed (1975) prices gross fixed investment for the economy as a whole fell annually as follows (Ouattara, 1986: 1086): 1979, −9.6%; 1980, −8%; 1981, −21.4%; 1982, −13.3%; 1983, −20.2%; 1984, −7.1%.

49. Similar initiatives were taken in Zambia in relation to the INDECO group of companies. For a discussion of the successes achieved in this regard see Chapter 9.

50. This is the 'taxe des prestations et des services', a levy imposed on pre-tax bank transactions which by common agreement acts as a major disincentive to investment. In 1986 the levy was 25%; by early 1988 the government had reluctantly been persuaded to reduce this to 15%, still the highest rate for such a tax in the region.

51. The CSSPPA is the abbreviation commonly used for the Caisse de Stabilisation et de Soutien des Prix des Productions Agricoles – the stabilisation fund. Confusingly, the fund is also abbreviated to CAISTAB, indeed this is the form most commonly used in Côte d'Ivoire itself, including the official publication describing its functions which is called *CAISTAB, Ivory Coast Stabilisation Fund, Caisse de Stabilisation et De Soutien Des Prix Des Productions Agricoles*. Originally there were separate funds for cocoa and coffee but these were merged in 1962; in 1964 the presently constituted fund was established whose remit now also embraces other products, such as oil seeds and cotton. To add to the confusion, World Bank documents frequently refer to the fund as the CAISSTAB, rather than the CAISTAB.

52. One exception appears to have been in textiles where, for instance, one of the largest manufacturers in the country, R. GONFREVILLE, has expressed concern about imports of cloth from Asia competing with local products (*African Economic Digest*, 24 April 1987).

It is expected, however, that if a progressive and across-the-board reduction in tariffs were to take place, the viability of a number of industries would be threatened. In this regard, Renault stated in 1987 that its vehicle assembly plant would have to close as did SIVENG, the manufacturer of fertilisers.

53. The funds were to have come from an increase in customs revenue which itself has been adversely affected both by the increase in smuggling and in the growing practice of under-invoicing of traded goods.

54. From October 1988 this ministry was to be headed by the former Minister of Planning, Oumar Diarra, the former Minister of Industry, Bernard Ehui, being demoted to the portfolio of Youth and Sports.

55. DRC values are a widely-used measure of short-run comparative advantage, representing the value of domestic resources (net of subsidies and other domestically-initiated distortions) expended in saving or earning a unit of foreign exchange, usually valued in domestic currency at the shadow exchange rate. For a general discussion of DRCs see Balassa (1971). For African-related and Côte d'Ivoire-specific discussions, see Noël and Pursell (1982), Pearson, Nelson and Stryker (1976), Shepherd and Popiel (1977), Stryker, Pursell and Monson (1975) and Jansen (1983). Subsequent to her 1983 work in Zimbabwe, Jansen has been involved in work for the World Bank deriving DRCs in both Zambia and in Kenya.

56. IMF funds provided have been: SDR 48.5 m. in the 1981–4 period, SDR 82.75 m. in 1984–5, SDR 66.2 m. in 1985–6, $100 m. in 1986–8 and the approval of the release of $241 m. in March 1988 under the Compensatory Financing Facility (CFF), of which $113 m. could be drawn down immediately. World Bank funds under three structural adjustment loans have been for $150 m. in 1981–3,

$250.7 m. in 1983–5 and $250 m. in 1986–8. CCCE contributions 1981–5 represented, on their own, some 44% of total external funding (see Campbell, 1989a and Duruflé, 1986).

57. In February 1985 a London Club (commercial banks) agreement was ratified to reschedule 100% of principal due in 1984 ($230 m.) and 90% of that due in 1985 ($220 m.). A further agreement was ratified in November 1986 for a multi-year rescheduling: 80% of principal due in 1986, 70% of that due in 1987, 60% of that due in 1988 and 50% of that due in 1989, repayable over nine years with two and a half years grace period with the first repayments due in December 1988. Agreements to reschedule the Paris Club official debt were reached in May 1984, June 1985 and June 1986. Financial support also included a commercial bank package of $106 m. made in February 1985 for seven and a half years with three years' grace. In April 1988 yet another commercial debt agreement was signed and sealed allowing a rescheduling of 90% of all commercial debt outstanding since 1983, accounting for about 30% of total external debt estimated at that time at around $8.6 bn, payment to be extended over 15 years with a five-year grace period and the provision of $151 m. in new money. This was also abandoned and by March 1989 the London Club had postponed yet another attempt to resolve the country's commercial debt obligations. (IEAS, 1988 and *African Economic Digest*, 6 May, 1988 and 6 March 1989).

58. Exports fob, imports cif, see World Bank sources.

59. At the time of the (short-lived) commodity boom in the late 1970s, the revenue of the CSSPPA amounted to an astounding 17% of GDP.

60. Determined by the International Coffee Organisation (ICO) of which Côte d'Ivoire is a member.

61. 1987 figures based on a figure of US$323 m. for the first eleven months of the year (EIU, 1988, 3: 15). 1988 figures are from the forecasting department of the Economy and Finance Ministry (*African Economic Digest*, 4 November, 1988).

62. Robusta accounts for 98% of coffee grown in Côte d'Ivoire.

63. The 1987/8 season was a good one for Brazil, leading to world production of 109.3 m. bags and an off-take of just 88 m. bags. In the following, 1988/9 season, Brazil had a poor crop but this made little or no difference to the world price because of the large level of stocks already carried. In the final quarter of 1988, with the world price at around 11 cents a pound, reports of discounts of up to 40% of the official price were being reported.

64. FAO presented a draft plan to the government in mid-1988 for a slowdown of the rapid depletion of the country's forests. The five-year programme, aimed at replanting 90,000 hectares and rehabilitating a further 150,000, would cost an estimated CFAF 60 bn. Yet even at this pace, total forest resources would be fully exploited by the middle of the 1990s while in 1988, 'the year of the Ivorian Forest', optimistic government plans were only for 25,000 hectares to be replanted – less than 10% of recent exploitation rates.

65. In 1985, Côte d'Ivoire's production stood at 165,000 tons, just 2.2% of world production; Malaysian production stood that year at 4.13 m. tons, 55% of world production.

66. Some traders at the end of 1988 put the 1988/9 forecast as high as 800,000 tons. In 1982/3 drought and serious fires cut production to 366,000 tons but, in the event, this was short-lived.

67. In 1975, Malaysia produced 17,000 tonnes; by 1987 this had risen to 185,000 tonnes of which 157,000 tonnes were exported (*Financial Times*, 14 November 1988).

68. In November, French officials denied any intention of subsidising a planned 200,000 tonne purchase of Ivorian cocoa by *Sucres et Denrées*. However, consideration was being given to the provision of an 'exceptional loan' to help finance cocoa purchases with the Banque Centrale des Etats de l'Afrique de l' Ouest (BCEAO).

69. It was also being suggested in late 1988 that holding back sales to the world market might lead to substantial wastage. Thus Gill and Duffus commented in their November 1988 *Cocoa Market Report* (1988: 3): 'Current circumstances in Côte d'Ivoire mean that it is quite possible that a part of the crop will remain unsold and some of the main crop now being harvested may never leave the farms'.

70. While the accounts of the CSSPPA are not dependent totally upon cocoa, it is the domestic cocoa price vis-à-vis the world price which is the major influence.

71. It would be erroneous to think that the deficit of the CSSPPA is due entirely to the problem of cocoa pricing; indeed one estimate in December 1988 was that cocoa would only be responsible for about one-third of the deficit for 1988 (*Financial Times*, 2 December 1988).

72. For a more thorough and systematic analysis of recent trends in the balance of payments see Ouattara (1986) and Chamley (1988).

73. According to Ouattara's figures (1986: 1090), in constant dollar terms the imports of machinery fell progressively from $625 m. in 1978 to $292 m. by 1982.

74. All education figures quoted here are from the 1988 edition of the World Bank's *World Development Report*.

75. The 15 countries selected in 1985 by the US Treasury Secretary, James Baker, for particular attention because of their high debt profile.

76. Côte d'Ivoire's total debt was thus the second largest in sub-Saharan African in 1986, following Nigeria which had a total debt of $21.9 bn. It had the third largest public and publicly guaranteed debt, after Nigeria, $21.5 bn and Sudan, $7.1 bn.

77. Debt-service ratio: total debt-service payments divided by total exports.
78. Figures on external debt discussed here are taken from the World Bank's *World Debt Tables* series and from World Bank (1987), export figures from the Bank's *World Tables 1987*.
79. For more detailed discussion of these issues see Krumm (1987), World Bank (1987) and Michel and Noël (1984), Devarajan, Jakobeit, and de Melo (1986) and Devarajan and de Melo (1987).
80. For more detail on the specific proposals see World Bank, 1987, (Vol. II: 175ff).
81. Annex II of the report, *Présentation Sectorielle*, consists of over 200 pages covering each industrial sub-sector in turn.
82. 'Le Schéma Directeur du développement industriel n'est pas un document figé, énonçant des objectifs chiffrées à réaliser, pendant une certaine période de temps déterminable à l'avance' (Ministère de l'Industrie, 1988, Volume 1: 177).
83. Clearly this estimate is not based on the payment of all past obligations which have not been met, for, as indicated in Table 6.9, the World Bank's 1988–9 debt tables give a figure for 1989 of $1,812 m. assuming payments in 1987 and 1988 of over $3 bn which were not made.
84. This point holds true particularly in relation to domestic policy proposals and quantitative targets both because the Bank ought to be in a good position to judge the extent to which domestic policy proposals are likely to be implemented, and also, in this case, because the government by and large agreed to implement the proposals put forward by the Bank, albeit at a somewhat slower pace than outlined in the base case figures.
85. See pp. 168–71 above.
86. In 1985, out of total capital of CFAF 408 bn in industry, CFAF 290 bn (71%) consisted of Ivorian state interests and only CFAF 41 bn (10%) was private Ivorian capital.
87. Between 1971 and 1981 Ivorian state capital in industry rose by CFAF 97 bn, private Ivorian capital by CFAF 24 bn (UNIDO, 1986: 26 and World Bank, 1975: Annex Table 6.A6). As the *African Economic Digest* of 30 January 1989 commented: 'The slackening pace of privatisation reflects official concern about the need to ensure divestments are in the national economic interest.'
88. As already noted there have been major problems with the scheme since its inception, in part resulting from general financing problems of central government which do not appear to be near early resolution.
89. The articulation of most of these objectives provides an indication of substantial differences in viewpoint between the Bank and the government.
90. There is merit in the argument that if the government commits public funds to new industrial projects this will encourage foreign investors to believe that it is genuinely concerned to promote this dimension of industrial expansion, providing, of course, that these industries are run efficiently. There is no reason either why there should not be a state/private sector partnership in the development of new industries, nor why the state should necessarily have to continue running industries that it decided to initiate.
91. See, for example, Chapter 10 on Zimbabwe.
92. For a discussion of these latter points see, for instance, Grootaert (1987).
93. Notwithstanding the fact that during the recent recession there appeared to have been an oversupply of graduates from formal Vocational and Technical Education (VTE) institutions. In part, this has been due to the rigidity of the labour market.
94. The problem of wage differentials, however, would also have to be addressed. Earnings of poorly educated workers in Abidjan are over 40% higher than those in other cities (see Grootaert, 1987: 111).

Statistical Appendix

Table 6.A1 *Exchange rate CFAF against the US$, market rate, period average*

	Franc per dollar
1969	259.71
1970	277.71
1971	277.13
1972	252.48
1973	222.89
1974	240.70
1975	214.31
1976	238.95
1977	245.68
1978	225.66
1979	212.72
1980	211.28
1981	271.73
1982	328.61
1983	381.06
1984	436.96
1985	449.26
1986	346.30
1987	300.54
1988	297.85

Source: International Monetary Fund, *International Financial Statistics, February 1989 and 1987 Yearbook*, Washington DC, IMF, 1988 and 1989.

Note: CFA stands for Communauté Financière Africaine - it used to stand for Franc des Colonies Française d'Afrique. The CFA franc is pegged to the French franc at the fixed rate of CFAF 1 = FFr 0.002. From 1959 to 1969 the rate was CFAF 246.85 = US$1.

Table 6.A2 *Manufacturing value added, agricultural value added and GDP: CFAF bn at current and 1984 prices, 1965–86*

Years	World Bank Data for:					
	MVA	AVA	GDP	MVA	AVA	GDP
		at current prices			at fixed 1984 prices	
1965	20.6	89.3	188.2	53.5	485.5	847.6
1966	27.9	94.2	210.5	72.0	497.7	915.2
1967	32.5	92.6	220.4	89.0	496.0	949.3
1968	30.9	112.8	262.1	80.4	577.9	1,091.8
1969	32.7	118.8	284.4	83.0	580.1	1,137.0
1970	41.4	128.2	318.4	102.3	604.9	1,219.0
1971	45.1	134.7	357.1	115.8	651.4	1,399.7
1972	51.7	138.9	382.4	133.1	655.0	1,477.0
1973	56.8	173.6	448.9	131.4	695.4	1,532.0
1974	75.6	188.2	574.5	146.4	621.7	1,597.7
1975	78.4	235.7	684.7	149.5	680.1	1,811.8
1976	104.8	272.7	814.2	183.7	721.1	1,781.8
1977	117.6	373.5	1,037.7	172.0	689.7	1,662.6
1978	137.0	461.4	1,334.2	184.4	755.3	2,019.8
1979	158.1	513.5	1,496.5	200.0	758.3	2,114.0
1980	193.2	621.2	1,787.5	251.7	856.3	2,472.7
1981	219.0	646.8	1,897.3	273.1	874.4	2,539.5
1982	207.1	670.7	2,011.1	236.0	862.2	2,406.5
1983	188.4	686.2	2,148.4	203.5	767.0	2,322.3
1984	232.2	767.9	2,155.9	232.2	767.9	2,155.9
1985	398.5*	833.5	2,434.9	384.5*	804.2*	2,261.5*
1986	375.0*	916.9	2,536.0	352.5*	861.8*	2,383.6*
1987				350.0		2,319.3*
1988				344.0		2,284.4

Source: World Bank (1986a: Vol. IV, Tables 1.1 and 1.3) and World Bank (1988:112–113).

Notes: * Estimates, based on real growth rates as provided in World Bank (1988) and EIU (1989).

Table 6.A3 *Trends in manufactured and total exports, 1960–84*

Year	Manufactured exports in current CFAF bn	Total exports in current CFAF bn	Percent	Manufactured exports in fixed US$ m. (1984)[a]	Total exports in fixed US$ m. (1984)	%
1960	3.9	45.5	8.6			
1961–4						
1965	24.4	80.5	16.0	278.3	1,152.4	24.1
1966				306.2	1,191.7	25.7
1967	31.2	91.8	19.0	343.1	1,187.1	28.9
1968				452.3	1,536.1	28.9
1969	24.4	120.5	20.2	268.7	1,327.7	20.2
1970	27.1	132.3	20.0	253.9	1,350.7	18.8
1971	23.6	126.3	20.0	195.4	1,389.3	14.1
1972	33.2	141.4	24.0	261.2	1,645.4	15.9
1973	46.8	183.2	25.5	353.0	1,681.7	21.0
1974	114.1	310.6	36.7	636.2	2,103.4	30.2
1975	109.1	275.4	39.6	597.3	2,256.6	26.5
1976	125.3	426.1	29.4	590.1	2,204.7	26.7
1977	165.3	610.5	27.1	722.3	2,250.0	32.1
1978	173.1	592.5	29.2	720.2	2,568.8	28.0
1979	198.6	603.6	32.9	755.7	2,540.6	29.7
1980	210.4	636.5	33.1	680.3	2,710.4	25.1
1981	314.6	743.0	42.3	883.0	2,812.3	31.4
1982	388.9	806.0	48.2	826.7	2,581.6	32.0
1983	369.7	797.0	46.4	710.7	2,191.0	32.4
1984	449.4	1,218.0	36.9	720.5	2,787.5	25.8

Source: World Bank (1975) and (1986).

Notes: [a] Fixed price figures of manufactured exports exclude exports of oil and petroleum products.

Figure 6.A1 *Value added in manufacturing, 1963–88 in CFAF bn at fixed (1980) prices*

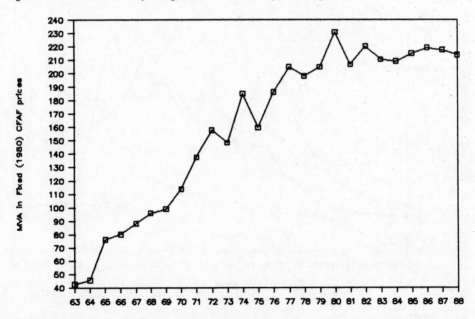

Source: UNIDO Data-Base, October 1988 and *African Economic Digest*, 6 January 1989.

Notes: The data from which this figure is derived are based on estimates and forecasts for the post-1986 period. The value added in petroleum refining has been omitted.

Figures 6.A2 and 6.A3 *Trends in manufacturing value added by sub-sectoral grouping 1963–88 at fixed (1980) prices*

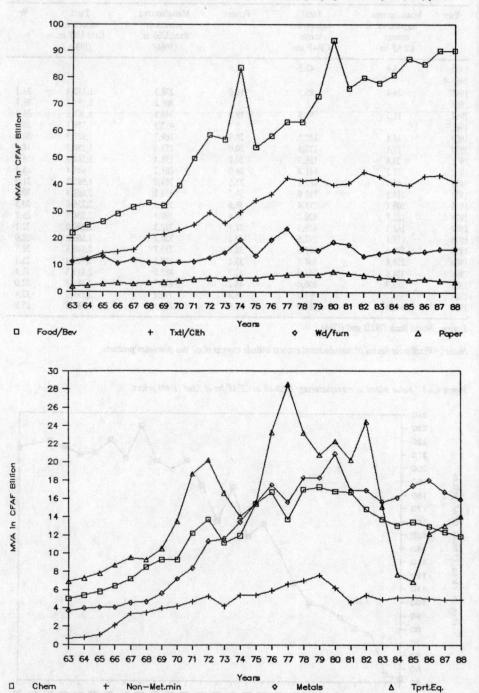

Source: UNIDO Data-Base, October 1988.

Note: Data exclude petroleum refining.

Table 6.A4 *Manufacturing value added by sub-sector 1960–86, CFAF m. current prices*

Sub-sector	1960 Value Added	%	1970 Value Added	%	1980 Value Added	%	1986 Value Added	%
Grains & Flour	470	4.7	4,020	9.0	14,180	6.1	47,032	15.0
Canned Foods	191	1.9	3,557	7.9	25,131	10.8	39,910	12.7
Beverages	706	7.0	2,066	4.6	15,897	6.9	16,664	5.3
Edible fats	974	9.7	2,341	5.2	17,206	7.4	171,421	5.5
Other Food/Tobacco	501	5.0	2,687	6.0	20.971	9.1	30.194	9.6
Textile & Clothing	2,756	27.5	8.905	19.9	37,537	16.2	26,434	8.4
Footwear/Leather	322	3.2	1,042	2.3	2,167	0.9	5,290	1.7
Wood Products	1,024	10.2	4,187	9.3	18,518	8.0	14,723	4.7
Chemicals	82	0.8	2,570	5.7	15,979	6.9	29,460	9.4
Rubber	15	0.1	481	1.1	917	0.4	813	33.3
Non-Metallic Minerals	370	3.7	1,349	3.0	6,210	2.7	8,214	2.6
Basic Metals/Steel	91	0.9	511	1.1	516	0.2	479	0.1
Transport Equipment	656	6.5	2,782	6.2	22,113	9.5	36,998	11.8
Other engineering	656	6.5	2,782	6.2	22,113	9.5	27,336	8.7
Miscellaneous	788	7.8	2,367	5.3	11,910	5.1	13,960	4.4
TOTALS	**10,027**	**100**	**44,836**	**100**	**231,569**	**100**	**313,022**	**100**

Source: Ministère de l'Industrie, March 1988.

Figure 6.A4 *Manufactured exports by broad sub-sector 1965–84 in fixed (1984) US$*

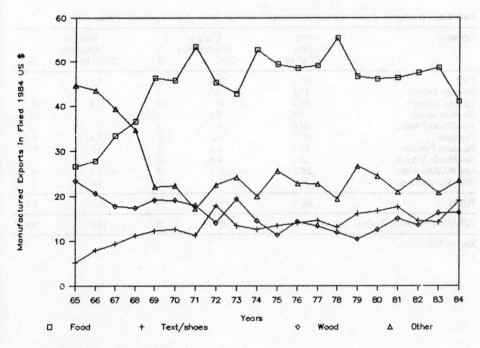

Source: World Bank (1987, Vol. IV, Table 1.8).

Table 6.A5 *Interlinkages and imports by industrial sub-sector CFAF bn, 1974, current prices*

Sub-Sector	Total Purchases	Total Imported	Total from Agriculture	Total from Manufacturing
Food	115.4	40.3 (35%)	45.1 (39%)	23.7 (20%)
Beverages/Tobacco	15.6	11.7 (75%)	0.1 (1%)	3.1 (20%)
Textiles/Clothing	41.2	20.5 (50%)	3.6 (9%)	14.4 (35%)
Footwear/Leather	4.8	3.1 (65%)	–	1.4 (29%)
Wood/Paper/Printing	18.1	0.9 (5%)	6.1 (34%)	7.3 (40%)
Chemicals	54.0	36.4 (67%)	2.9 (5%)	12.9 (24%)
Petroleum Products	33.5	4.0 (12%)	–	2.3 (7%)
Non-Metallic Minerals	15.8	10.1 (64%)	–	5.1 (32%)
Base Metal/Machinery	147.2	116.1 (79%)	–	27.4 (19%)
Other Manufacturing	23.9	18.5 (77%)	–	4.8 (20%)
TOTAL	469.5	251.6 (54%)	57.8 (12%)	102.4 (22%)
TOTAL less Petroleum	436.0	247.6 (57%)	57.8 (12%)	100.1 (22%)

Source: Ministère du Plan, *Comptes de la Nation, 1974*, reproduced in United Nations, *Statistical Information Bulletin for Africa*, No. 18, E/ECA/SIB/18, Addis Ababa, 1984.

Table 6.A6 *Destination of sales of produce of manufacturing sub-sectors CFAF bn, Current Prices, 1974*

Sub-sector	Total Sales CFAF bn	Going to Manufacturing CFAF bn	%	Going to Agriculture CFAF bn	%
Food	165.1	16.8	10	2.9	2
Beverages/Tobacco	27.8	0.7	3	–	–
Textiles/Clothing	69.2	10.3	15	0.3	0
Footwear/Leather	8.0	0.1	1	–	–
Wood/Paper/Printing	28.0	4.3	15	–	–
Chemicals	71.7	14.7	20	5.8	8
Petroleum Products	61.2	4.8	8	5.7	9
Non-Metallic Minerals	21.1	4.9	23	–	–
Base Metal/Machinery	200.5	37.0	18	8.3	4
Other Manufacturing	27.4	8.3	30	0.8	3
TOTAL	680.0	250.2	37	24.1	3.5
TOTAL less Petroleum Products	618.8	245.4	39	18.4	3.0

Source: Ibid.

Table 6.A7 *Country of origin of industrial employees by sub-sector 1984, '000s*

Sub-sector	Senior levels and management	% Ivorian	Skilled workers	% Ivorian	Unskilled workers and apprentices	% Ivorian
6	188	40.4	886	81.1	2,703	51.2
7	187	66.3	1,311	77.3	4,236	23.7
8	89	34.8	866	73.4	1,826	83.1
9	339	69.9	1,993	82.3	3,188	63.9
10	338	70.1	4,158	96.2	9,975	91.7
11	268	47.7	2,683	82.3	7,584	95.6
12	54	20.3	238	89.9	555	80.2
13	251	3.0	1,723	63.5	6,769	53.6
14	218	94.4	584	98.1	254	94.5
15	184	37.5	1,196	82.5	1,725	86.4
16	15	33.3	57	70.1	166	80.1
17	38	34.2	202	70.8	558	64.0
18	14	78.5	75	93.3	55	80.0
19	175	21.7	1,446	80.2	1,272	72.0
20	238	34.4	1,741	80.3	2,263	72.7
21	249	52.6	883	81.4	1,484	75.5
TOTAL	2,845	50.9	20,044	84.6	44,583	75.6

Source: Ministère de l'Industrie, March 1988.

Note: Sub-sectoral classification is as follows:

6. Grains and flour.
7. Canned and prepared food.
8. Beverages.
9. Edible oils and fats.
10. Other food products
11. Textiles and clothing.
12. Leather and shoes.
13. Wood, timber products.
14. Petroleum products.
15. Chemicals.
16. Rubber products.
17. Construction materials.
18. Steel and metals.
19. Vehicles, transport.
20. Other mechanical and electrical industries.
21. Miscellaneous industries.
22. Electricity and water.

References and Bibliography

ACP and EEC Expert Group (1988), *Investment in the A.C.P. States and Related Financial Flows*, Vols. 1 and 2, Brussels, Nairobi and Nice.

African Economic Digest (1988), *Côte d'Ivoire*, Special Report, 5 February.

Alfthan, T. (1982), *Industrialisation, Employment and Basic Needs: The Case of The Ivory Coast*, Geneva, International Labour Office, World Employment Programme Research, Working Paper No. 2-32/WP 40, July.

Alschuler, L.R. (1980), *Multinationals and The Development of Periphery Capitalism in The Ivory Coast 1960-1975*, Ottawa, International Development Studies Group, University of Ottawa, Discussion Paper No. 808, October.

—— (1988), *Multinationals and Maldevelopment: alternative development strategies in Argentina, the Ivory Coast and Korea*, Basingstoke, Macmillan.

Atsain, A. (1984), 'Regional Economic Integration and Foreign Policy' in Zartman and Delgado.

Balassa, B. (1971), *The Structure of Protection in Developing Countries*, Baltimore, Johns Hopkins University Press.

Blackburn, P. (1985), 'Ivory Coast: An AED Business Feature', *African Economic Digest*, 30 November.

Bourke, G. (1988), 'The Cocoa Conundrum', *African Report* (New York) September-October.

Budoc, R.L. (1987), *Les PME-PMI et le sous-développement: problèmes et stratégies financières possible en AFRIQUE Le cas de la Côte d'Ivoire*, Paris, Publisud.

Campbell, B.K. (1985), 'The Fiscal Crisis of the State: The Case of the Ivory Coast' in Bernstein, H. and Campbell B.K. (eds), *Contradictions of Accumulation in Africa*, London, Sage Publications, Sage Series on African Modernization and Development Vol. 10.

—— (1989a), 'Indebtedness and Adjustment Lending in the Ivory Coast: Certain Social and Political Dimensions' in Campbell (1989b).

—— (ed.) (1989b), *Political Dimensions of the International Debt Crisis*, London, Macmillan.

—— and Loxley, J. (eds) (1989), *Structural Adjustment in Africa*, London, Macmillan.

Chamley, C. (1988), 'Structural Adjustment in Côte d'Ivoire', Washington DC, World Bank, May, (mimeo).

Devarajan, S., Jakobeit, C. and de Melo, J. (1986), *Growth and Adjustment in an African Monetary Union: The CFA Franc Zone*, Washington DC, World Bank, CPD Discussion Paper No, 1986–30, May.

—— and de Melo, J. (1987), 'Adjustment with a Fixed Exchange Rate: Cameroon, Côte d'Ivoire and Senegal', *The World Bank Economic Review*, Vol. 1, No. 3, May.

Diejomaoh, V.P. and Iyoha, M.A. (1980, *Industrialization in the Economic Community of West African States (ECOWAS)*, Ibadan, Heinemann for the West African Economic Association.

Duruflé, G. *et al*. (1986), *Déséquilibres structurels et programmes d'adjustement en Côte d'Ivoire*, Paris, Ministère de la Coopération.

—— (1989), 'Structural Disequilibria and Adjustment Policies in the Ivory Coast' in Campbell and Loxley.

Economist Intelligence Unit (1982–8), *Côte d'Ivoire Country Report*, London, EIU.

—— (1987–8), *Ivory Coast Country Profile*, London, EIU.

—— (1989), *World Outlook 1989*, London, EIU.

Gbetibouo, M. and Delgado, C.L. (1984), 'Lessons and Constraints of Export Crop-Led Growth: Cocoa in Ivory Coast', in Zartman and Delgado.

Gern, J-P. and Faivre, P. (1986), *Côte d'Ivoire: Développement et Crise*, Neuchâtel, Faculté de Droit et des Sciences économiques, Université de Neuchatel.

Gill and Duffus (1988), *Cocoa Market Report No. 332*, London, Gill and Duffus Group, November.

Grooteart, C. (1987), *Vocational and Technical Education in Côte d'Ivoire: An Economic Assessment*, Warwick, Development Economics Research Centre, University of Warwick, Discussion Paper 87, June.

Hiey, J.P. (1988), *Stabilization and Adjustment Policies and Programmes Country Study 16 Ivory Coast*, Helsinki, World Institute for Development Economics Research (WIDER).

Jansen, D. (1983), 'Zimbabwe, Government Policy and the Manufacturing Sector', Larkspur, California, Study Prepared for the Ministry of Industry and Energy Development, Harare, April (mimeo).

Krumm, K.L. (1987), 'Adjustment in the Franc Zone: Focus on The Real Exchange Rate', Washington DC, Trade and Adjustment Division, Country Study Department, World Bank, November (mimeo).

Lall, S. (1987), 'Long-Term Perspectives on sub-Saharan Africa: Background Paper, Industry', Washington DC, World Bank (mimeo).

Lee, E. (1980), 'Export-Led Rural Development in Ivory Coast', *Development and Change*, Vol. 11, No. 4, October.

Marchés Tropicaux et Méditerranéens (1985), 'Ivorian Industry The Strategy of its Development', Vol. 41, No. 2094, 27 December.

Marcussen, H.S. (1983), 'The Ivory Coast Facing the Economic Crisis' in Carlsson, H. (ed.) *Recession in Africa*, Uppsala, Scandinavian Institute of African Studies.

Masini, J., Ikonicoff, M., Jedlicki, C. and Lanzaroti, M. (1979), *Multinationals and Development in Black Africa: A Case Study in the Ivory Coast*, Farnborough, Saxon House in association with the European Centre for Study and Information on Multinational Corporations.

Michel, G. and Noël, M. (1984), *Short Term Responses to Trade and Incentive Policies in the Ivory Coast*, Washington DC, World Bank Staff Working Paper No. 647.

Monson, T.D. and Pursell, G.G. (1979), 'The Use of DRCs to Evaluate Indigenization Programs: The Case of the Ivory Coast', *Journal of Development Economics*, Vol. 6.

Morris, D. (1988), *Cotton to 1993: Fighting For The Fibre Market*, London, Economist Intelligence Unit.

Mytelka, L. (1984), 'Foreign Business and Economic Development' in Zartman and Delgrado (1984).

Noël, M. and Pursell, G. (1982), 'Effective Protection and Economic Performance in Selected Branches in the Ivory Coast: Textiles and Clothing', Washington DC, World Bank, January (mimeo).

O.S. Consultants (1985), *The Private Sector in the Economy of the Ivory Coast*, Washington DC, International Finance Corporation, July.

Ouattara, A.E. (1986), 'The Balance of Payments Adjustment Process in Developing Countries: the Experience of the Ivory Coast', *World Development*, Vol. 14, No. 8.

Pearson, S.R., Nelson, G.C. and Strycker, J.D. (1976), 'Incentives and Comparative Advantage in Ghanaian Industry and Agriculture', Washington DC, World Bank, (mimeo).

République Francaise, Ministère de la Coopération (1986), *Industrialisation Des Pays D'Afrique Sub-Saharienne: Les Cas De La Côte d'Ivoire*, Paris, Société pour le Développement Economique at Social (SEDES), June.

République de Côte d'Ivoire, Ministère de l'Industrie (1987), *Investing in Côte d'Ivoire The Investor's Guide*, Abidjan, Ministère de l'Industrie.

——, Ministère de l'Industrie (1988), *Schéma Directeur de Développement Industriel de la Côte d'Ivoire* (four volumes), Abidjan, Ministère de l'Industrie.

——, Ministère du Plan et de l'Industrie (1982), *Plan Quinquennial de Développement Économique, Social et Cultural 1981-1985*, (Vols 1 and 2), Abidjan.

Riboud, M. (1987), *The Ivory Coast 1960 to 1986*, San Francisco, International Center for Economic Growth, Country Studies No. 4.

Ridler, N.B. (1985), 'Comparative Advantage as a Development Model: Ivory Coast', *The Journal of Modern African Studies*, Vol. 23, No. 3, September.

Schiller, C. (1988), *The Fiscal Role of Price Stabilization Funds: The Case of Côte d'Ivoire*, IMF Working Paper 88/26, Washington DC, International Monetary Fund, Fiscal Affairs Department, March.

Shepherd, G. and Popiel, P.A. (1977), 'Incentives and Comparative Advantage in Cameroon Industry', Washington DC, World Bank (mimeo).

Stevens, C. and Weston, A. (1984), 'Trade Diversification: Has Lomé Helped?', in Stevens, C., (ed.), *EEC and The Third World: A Survey (4): Renegotiating Lomé*, London, Hodder and Stoughton.

Stryker, D., Pursell, G. and Monson, T. (1975), 'Incentives and Resource Costs in the Ivory Coast', Washington DC, World Bank (mimeo).

Teal, F. (1986), 'The Foreign Exchange Regime and Growth: A Comparison of Ghana and the Ivory Coast', *African Affairs*, Vol. 85, No. 339, April.

Torp, J.E. (1979), *The Textile Industry in France and in The Ivory Coast*, Roskilde Denmark, Institute of Geography, Socio-Economic Analysis and Computer Science, Research Report No. 2.

Tuinder, D.A. den (1978), *Ivory Coast: The Challenge of Success*, Baltimore, Johns Hopkins University Press for the World Bank.

United Nations Industrial Development Organisation (UNIDO) (1986), *Industrial Development Review Series Côte d'Ivoire*, Vienna, Regional and Country Studies Branch, UNIDO, October.

United Nations Economic and Social Council, Economic Commission for Africa (1982) *The Impact of The Activities of Transnational Corporations on The Balance of Payments of The Ivory Coast A Technical Paper*, Addis Ababa, ECA/UNCTC Joint Unit on Transnational Corporations, ST/ECA/UNCTC/6, January.

World Bank (1975), *Current Status and Prospects of the Industrial Sector in the Ivory Coast*, Washington DC, World Bank, February.

—— (1981), *Finance in the Development of the Ivory Coast*, Washington DC, World Bank, December.

—— (1982-1988), *World Development Report*, Oxford, Oxford University Press.

—— (1986), *Price Prospects for Major Primary Commodities* (5 Volumes), Washington DC, World Bank, October.

—— (1987), *The Côte d'Ivoire in Transition: From Structural Adjustment To Self-Sustained Growth*, (4 vols) Washington DC, World Bank, 9 March.

—— (1988), *World Tables 1987*, Washington DC World Bank.

Zartman, I.W. and Delgado, C. (1984) *The Political Economy of Ivory Coast*, New York, Praeger.

7 Kenya[1]

The Manufacturing Sector to the mid-1980s[2]
JENNIFER SHARPLEY & STEPHEN LEWIS

Overview

KENYA'S DEVELOPMENT RECORD
International Perspectives. Kenya has attracted a good deal of interest in development because of its generally above-average performance, its position as a relatively industrialised country within sub-Saharan Africa and its reputation as a country which has depended relatively heavily on private enterprise. The World Bank's 1987 *World Development Report*

Table 7.1 *Kenya in comparative perspective*

	Kenya		Low income other than India and China		Sub-Saharan Africa	
Annual growth rate of GNP per capita, 1965–85	1.9		0.4		1.0	
1985 GNP per capita in US$	290		200		400	
Annual growth rate:	*1965–80*	*80–85*	*1965–80*	*80–85*	*1965–80*	*80–85*
GDP	6.4	3.1	3.2	2.8	5.3	−0.7
Inflation	7.3	10.0	11.4	18.9	12.7	16.7
Agricultural GDP	4.9	2.8	2.0	1.9	1.9	0.9
Manufacturing GDP	10.5	3.8	5.3	5.5	9.8	3.5
Government Consumption	10.4	−0.3	3.2	2.3	8.0	0.7
Gross Domestic Investment	7.1	−8.9	3.2	−2.1	4.4	0.3
Exports	0	−3.9	0.2	0.1	9.6	−5.0
Imports	1.7	−9.0	0.3	−0.5	9.8	−9.4
Percentages:	*1965*	*1985*	*1965*	*1985*	*1965*	*1985*
Agriculture/GDP	35	31	41	36	39	34
Industry/GDP	18	20	17	19	19	27
Manufacturing/GDP	11	13	10	12	10	10
Government Consumption/GDP	15	18	11	12	11	12
Investment/GDP	14	19	15	15	16	13
Domestic Saving/GDP	15	16	15	6	18	13
Exports of Goods and Non-Factor Services/GDP	31	25	19	14	25	21
Share of Merchandise Exports to Developing Economies	29	48	29	32	19	17
Share of Manufactured Exports to Developing Countries	75	91	37	27	44	40
Debt Service as Share of Exports	5.8	25.5	8.4	18.4	5.3	21.5
% of Labour Force in Industry	5	7	8	10	8	9

Source: World Bank, *World Development Report*, 1987.

characterises it as 'moderately inward-looking'[2] in terms of its trade policies in both the 1963–73 and 1973–85 periods analysed in the *Report*.

As the data in Table 7.1 indicate, the record from 1965 to 1985 compares favourably with that of other low-income countries (excluding India and China) and with sub-Saharan Africa (SSA). In terms of economic structure, it has had a higher share of manufacturing in GDP, and the improvement in both its investment ratio and its ratio of domestic saving to GDP between 1965 and 1985 was also relatively high. Kenya is a comparatively open economy, with the share of exports of goods and non-factor services in GDP higher than average for low-income countries and SSA. Of particular interest to our examination of the manufacturing sector, the share of manufactured exports destined for developing countries is much higher in Kenya than in other countries, as is its general share of merchandise exports. This reflects its relative importance as a regional manufacturing centre, a characteristic originating from the colonial period.

Finally, in several other respects Kenya's economic record is perhaps less encouraging. Its export performance in aggregate does not compare favourably with other low-income countries, and the fall in exports as a share of GDP was of similar proportions to that for SSA. The share of government consumption in GDP is substantially higher in Kenya, and its debt-service ratio increased more than in the rest of SSA and considerably more than in other low-income countries over the 20 years 1965–85.

Aggregate Domestic Performance. The period 1964–84 has been grouped into four sub-periods: 1964–70; 1970–75; 1975–80 and 1980–84. These periods were *not* selected at random: there were important differences in policy, external shocks, and aggregate performance between them. Briefly, performance in virtually all dimensions was best during the first period; the first balance-of-payments problems arose during the second period, culminating in the first 'oil shock' of 1974; the late 1970s saw a mixture of initially improved terms of trade and later substantial external borrowing which eased the foreign-exchange constraints of the late 1970s; and the 1980s, following the second oil price shock and the world recession, was a period of crisis and relatively poor performance.

Table 7.2 *Key economic indicators*

	1970	1975	1980	1984
1. *Major Aggregates*				
Population (million)	11.2	13.4	16.7	19.5
Real GDP(1976 prices £m)	960	1,248	1,606	1,811
Real imports (1976 prices £m)	439	392	487	299
Foreign exchange reserves as % of annual retained imports				
percentage	57.7	9.8	13.4	2.0
weeks equivalent cover	30.0	5.1	7.0	1.1
Debt service ratio as % of exports of goods and services	5.8	3.9	12.3	21.4
	1964–70 average	1970–75 average	1975–80 average	1980–84 average
2. *Sectoral Growth Rates* % increase in real GDP (1976 prices) over previous year.				
Agriculture	5.0	5.1	4.5	2.6
Manufacturing	7.5	7.3	7.2	4.0
Retail	4.7	4.7	3.0	1.2
Government	9.9	9.0	5.7	4.4
Total	6.7	5.6	5.0	3.2
3. *Sectoral Shares of Real GDP %*				
Agriculture	44.2	41.3	40.8	38.6
Manufacturing	10.4	11.3	12.3	13.2
Retail	12.9	11.7	10.6	9.9
Government	11.6	13.1	14.2	14.7
Total	100	100	100	100

Table 7.2 *contd*

	1964–70 average	1970–75 average	1975–80 average	1980–84 average
4. *Growth in Wage Employment and Population*				
% increase over previous year				
Manufacturing employment	6.4	5.9	5.8	2.1
Total persons employed	1.9	4.6	3.4	2.9
Population (million)	3.3	3.5	3.8	3.9
5. *Inflation*				
% increase over previous year				
GDP deflator	1.1	8.3	11.1	9.8
Lower income cost of living index	1.9	9.7	14.1	13.3
6. *International Terms of Trade*				
Index (1976 = 100)				
Barter terms of trade	126	107	101	78
Income terms of trade	83	96	99	72
7. *Real Imports and Exports per capita*				
(1976 prices £m.)				
Visible imports	33.6	38.0	30.0	19.8
Exports good and services	34.7	39.5	32.6	25.2
8. *Use of Resources*				
% total GDP factor cost – current				
Exports (+)	33.3	33.0	34.4	30.7
Imports (−)	−31.6	−36.5	−39.7	−37.3
Net import surplus (−)	0.7	−4.4	−6.7	−6.7
Gross investment	19.7	25.9	27.6	28.8
Domestic savings	20.4	21.5	20.9	22.1
External savings	−0.7	4.4	6.7	6.7
9. *Out-turn of Government Revenue and Expenditure*				
% total GDP factor cost				
Recurrent revenue	18.1	22.7	26.0	27.5
Total expenditure	23.1	29.4	34.3	39.1
Fiscal deficit	5.1	6.6	8.3	11.6
10. *Domestic Credit*				
% total domestic credit				
Public sector	8.1[a]	21.6	29.3	35.6
Private sector	91.9[a]	78.4	70.7	64.5
Total domestic deficit	100[a]	100	100	100
11. *Real Domestic Credit*				
% increase over previous year (1976 prices)				
Public sector	n.a.	67.6	13.8	14.8
Private sector	n.a.	12.6	9.2	1.8
Total domestic credit	n.a.	18.4	9.6	5.1

Source: *Economic Survey*, *Statistical Abstract*; Central Bank of Kenya *Annual Report*; IMF, *International Financial Statistics*.

Note: [a] 1968–70.

As can be seen in Table 7.2 and Figures 7.1 and 7.2, there has been a deceleration of GDP growth, particularly in the 1980s. The ratio of investment to GDP rose from under 20% in the late 1960s to over 25% in the 1970s and reached more than 30% in the early 1980s before the crisis hit hard in macroeconomic terms. Saving rates initially rose from the 1960s into the early 1970s but by the most recent period they were no higher than they had been a decade earlier. The widening gap between saving and investment is mirrored in three other major

Figure 7.1 *Investment and saving as % of GDP at factor cost*

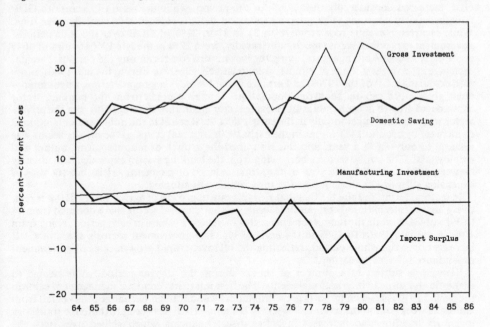

Source: *Statistical Abstract*; 'Use of Total Resources'.

Figure 7.2 *Government revenue and expenditure as % of GDP at factor cost*

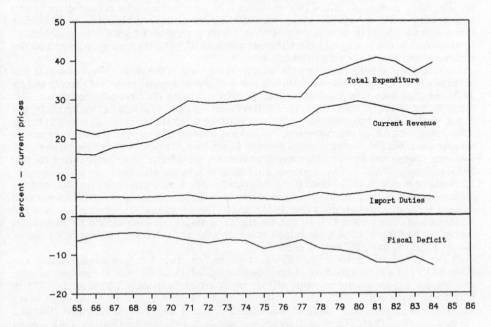

Source: *Statistical Abstract*; 'Out-turn of Revenue and Expenditure'.

aggregates: import and export ratios and the government budget. The share of imports in GDP increased considerably over much of the period, while the ratio of exports to GDP remained fairly constant. The government fiscal deficit widened substantially over time. While recurrent revenue rose from 18 to 22 to 25 to 27% of GDP over the four periods, government expenditures rose much more rapidly, from 22% in the late 1960s to almost 40% in the early 1980s. And, again reflecting the various differences among the periods, foreign-exchange reserves as a share of imports were relatively generous during the late 1960s, more modest during most of the 1970s, and meagre in the 1980s. In aggregate terms, wage employment grew more rapidly than did population. Domestic credit from the banking sector showed real growth in both public and private sector credit through the 1970s, but the private sector was squeezed substantially in the early 1980s. Real credit to the public sector continued to increase by around 14% a year in the early 1980s, but real credit to the private sector was reduced to only 1.8% a year, and this restrained the growth of manufacturing output and employment. The public sector's borrowing from the banking system expanded dramatically between 1980 and 1982 (the year of the worst balance-of-payments crisis) but the rate of expansion subsided as the stabilisation programme was adopted.

In sectoral terms, despite the fact that Kenya's rate of growth of agricultural GDP was relatively high in international comparative terms, the agricultural sector share declined from 44 to 39% of GDP while the manufacturing sector increased its share in each period, rising from 10% in the late 1960s to 13% in the early 1980s. The government sector's share of GDP increased over the whole period, reflecting the relatively rapid growth rates of government expenditure referred to earlier.

Kenya was subject to a number of shocks during the 20-year period, some related to domestic and some to international events. The first jolt to its economic management came in the period 1970–71, when imports grew dramatically and foreign-exchange reserves fell from almost 30 weeks of import cover to 7 weeks. The 'mini-crisis' has been attributed to transitory inventory building and increases in deficit fiscal financing which spilled over onto the demand for imports (King, 1979). The authorities responded by the first major use of import controls for macroeconomic management purposes, and the practice was maintained throughout the rest of the years under study. The two oil price shocks of 1974 and 1979 hit Kenya very hard. In the early years, Kenya was heavily dependent on imported oil as a source of energy in virtually all sectors of the economy. Kenya has an oil refinery and in fact exports considerable amounts of refined petroleum products to other countries in the region, as well as providing a major refuelling stop for international airlines in Nairobi and bunkering operations for shipping at Mombasa. Even so, with petroleum imports averaging 10% of total imports in the years just before the oil price hike of 1974, the aggregate impact on the balance of payments was very substantial.

Kenya enjoyed a huge improvement in its terms of trade in the years 1976–8 as coffee and tea prices boomed internationally. During this period real imports increased sharply and by 1978 had risen to a level equal with that in 1974 following the first oil price shock. The management of the economy during the coffee boom is a matter for another major study, but in our view the failure to undertake some restructuring of incentives in the economy at a time when foreign-exchange reserves were plentiful was a major missed opportunity in economic management. Finally, Kenya's initial partners in the East African Community, Uganda and Tanzania, began import substitution against Kenyan manufacturing exports during the late 1960s and early 1970s. Rising economic difficulties in Uganda after the coup which brought Idi Amin to power in 1971 raised further difficulties for Kenya's recorded exports, and the ultimate demise of the East African Community in 1976 meant that it lost privileged access to a major market for its manufactures. In the mid-1970s, for example, exports to Uganda and Tanzania had been around 15% of its total export earnings, and from around 1973 onwards, smuggling and unrecorded transactions accounted for an increasing amount of its manufactured exports to neighbouring countries.

At the end of the coffee boom, Kenya continued to expand its government sector and financed this to a large extent by external borrowing. Much of this was at commercial rates and from short-term sources, with private credit rising from only US$89 m. in 1975 to US$955 m. at the end of 1980. The debt-service ratio was quite modest for many years, being less than 6% in 1970 and falling to 3.9% in 1975; but it then rose to 12.3% in 1980 and reached 21.4% in 1984. The most dramatic increase occurred between 1980 and 1982 – when it rose from 12.3 to 21.5%. Combined with the effects of the second oil shock and weak markets for exports, this pushed Kenya into a major balance-of-payments crisis in the early 1980s which reached its worst point following the attempted coup in August 1982.

Kenya clearly showed a deceleration of economic growth despite the fact that, until the crisis and adjustment period of the early 1980s, it maintained a steady, or even rising, ratio of investment to GDP. By definition, these two trends represent an increase in the capital costs of achieving increased output, or a decline in the productivity of new investment. While there were large swings in incremental capital productivity during the two decades, there was a clear upward trend in the incremental capital output ratio, and the only substantial decrease came in the period of the coffee-tea price boom in the mid-1970s, which both produced large increases in agricultural GDP and relaxed the foreign-exchange constraint on other industries, allowing relatively large increases in output and value added per unit of capital investment. The increased incremental capital costs of added output suggest a need to pay greater attention to the efficiency with which investment was used – particularly in light of the fact that domestic saving was not rising. As will be seen, efficiency of resource use was decreasing, not increasing.

Manufacturing Sector Overview. As shown in Table 7.2, the growth of GDP in manufacturing was greater than that in agriculture and overall GDP throughout the 20-year period under review[3]. Until 1982, employment growth in manufacturing was significantly higher than in other sectors of the economy, but not as rapid as the growth of real manufacturing GDP, a result that is fairly common in most countries, and might be taken as an indicator of increased productivity of labour in the manufacturing sector. The sector absorbed a substantially larger share of domestic investment than the agricultural sector, except in the late 1960s. In fact, the share of manufacturing in total investment has been consistently higher than its share in GDP.

While policy towards manufacturing is dealt with in detail below, it is important to note here, before discussing the patterns of manufacturing growth in the four periods, that there has always been some ambivalence, particularly some discrepancy between stated policy and actual measures undertaken, on the extent to which Kenya wished to pursue a policy which involved the promotion of manufactured exports or a policy of relatively highly protected import substitution. Statements of policy in a series of sessional papers beginning in the early 1970s and continuing through the early 1980s spoke in terms of the need to reduce protection to domestic sectors in order to encourage efficiency and reduce the burden on other sectors of the economy. Measures adopted include the introduction of an Export Compensation Scheme in 1974 to assist manufacturing exporters with cash subsidies intended to offset the protective effects of tariffs on inputs and the cascading effects of domestic excise and sales taxes which might not be otherwise rebated. Of greater significance in practice, however, was the consistent rise in the average level of scheduled tariffs after 1971 when import licensing became an important element both of macroeconomic management and of the system of protection for domestic manufacturing industries.

While protection was given to foreign-owned firms, locally owned firms and parastatal enterprises, the rate of effective protection for foreign private firms, and especially parastatal enterprises, was considerably higher than for local firms.

Patterns and sources of manufacturing growth

Kenya presents some unique opportunities for observation and analysis of the pattern and causes of industrial growth because of the relatively consistent way in which statistics have been collected for the entire post-independence period. Imports and exports are both classified according to ISIC classifications so that one can match output both with competing imports and with exports from the same sectors of origin. In addition, imports are analysed by 'end use' (private final demand, government demand, and intermediate demand) and the import duties paid on each category of imports are reported as well.[4] As a result, it is possible to construct annual figures for 20 years for ten standard industry sectors showing the total supply (imports plus domestic production) in each industry, export demand, and, by subtraction, domestic demand (both intermediate and final). Year-to-year fluctuations in final demand due to inventory changes or changes in stock levels will obviously affect such things as the ratio of imports to total supply, but over long periods such fluctuations will be evened out.

Three sets of fairly aggregative statistics can be compiled for each industry sub-sector and for manufacturing as a whole. One of these is the ratio of output to total supply, or, its complement, imports as a ratio to total supply. This gives an indication sector by sector of the relative importance of imports and competing domestic output. One would expect that the process of import substitution in most industries would produce a rising ratio of output, or a falling ratio of imports, to total supply. How rapidly these ratios changed, and in which industries, would be determined in turn by investment patterns, comparative advantage, and patterns of industrial incentives.

Another measure of importance is the ratio of exports to total supply (or the ratio of exports to output). This would give some indication of the extent to which expansion of output in the industry came from the expansion of export markets relative to the domestic market.

The third aggregate statistic of some interest is the ratio of value added to gross output in each sub-sector. While 'import substitution' might take place because of an increasing ratio of domestic output to total supply in any given industry, it could also take place through a rising ratio of domestic value added to total output within any given sub-sector.[5]

The normal pattern of import substitution is one in which there is some protection in the domestic market, which allows a firm to compete with international goods at prices above the international level (at the existing exchange rate). In 'successful' import substitution, domestic costs of production decrease over time (for any of a number of reasons), and the ratio of domestic to international prices falls. Eventually some industries, at least, will be competitive enough in their cost structure to export. This suggests that a normal pattern of industrial growth would find first import substitution and then exports as important sources of growth for an industry over time. During the import-substitution phase there might be increases in the ratio of domestic to international prices, but as one moved towards a period when exports were important, one would expect a decline in domestic relative to international prices. Naturally, there could be, and have been, a number of variations on this theme: some of the more successful exporting countries have maintained relatively high prices of goods in domestic markets while either inducing or forcing exports from the same industry as a condition of the industry receiving continued protection in the domestic market. A short summary of the empirical literature examining 'successful' import substitution and export expansion in Japan, South Korea and Turkey can be found in Chenery et al. (1986, pp. 301-7).

Unfortunately, detailed price indices to explore some of these possible developments do not exist in Kenya. Nonetheless, we have been able to produce a number of estimates of tariffs and protection which give some indication of what has been happening to the process of industrial growth in Kenyan manufacturing.

Several of the principal findings of our analysis of growth in the manufacturing sector can be seen visually in Figures 7.3, 7.4a and 7.4b which show the importance of manufacturing output relative to total supply of manufactured output plus imports; the relative importance

Figure 7.3 *Manufacturing exports and imports (% of output and total supply)*

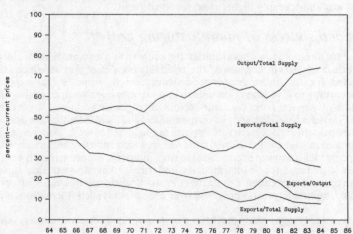

Source: Statistical Abstract

Figure 7.4a *Manufacturing value added: % of output (all & major groups)*

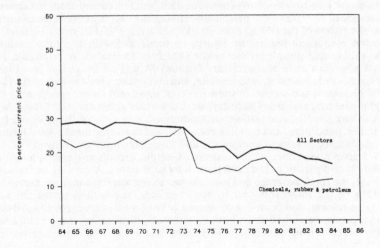

Source: Ibid.

Figure 7.4b *Manufacturing value added: % of output (major groups)*

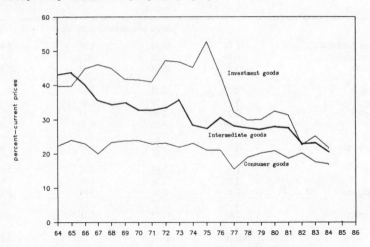

Source: Ibid.

of exports in output and in total supply of manufactured goods; and the ratio of value added to output in the manufacturing sector as a whole. It is quite clear that the trend in 'import substitution' reflected by the rising share of domestic production in total supply of manufactures from just over 50% in the mid-1960s to nearly 75% by the mid-1980s, is a dominant feature of the entire sector. On the other hand, the importance of exports in the manufacturing sector declined dramatically, from over 20% of total supply and nearly 40% of the value of manufacturing output in 1964 to less than 8% of total supply and just over 10% of manufacturing output by 1984. The decline in the relative importance of exports is clear both before and after the demise of the East African Community and the economic difficulties in Uganda, following the 1971 coup. The other major feature is the declining ratio of value added to output in manufacturing as a whole. As will be shown later, the general features exhibited for the manufacturing sector (rising ratios of production and total supply, falling shares of output which are exported, and declining ratios of value added to output) are not due to the dominance of one or two sub-sectors but are shared generally throughout the manufacturing sector as a whole.

For the purposes of analysing the *sources of growth in manufacturing output*, we have divided the sector into 10 sub-sectors for which data could be compiled for the entire 20-year period. Because of the size of the petroleum refining sub-sector in the value of output, and because of the effects of the two oil price shocks which might distort overall results, we have also reported manufacturing sector figures in total, and with the total excluding the chemicals, rubber and petroleum sub-sector (which is dominated by petroleum refining). Further, we have (in a somewhat arbitrary fashion) divided the ten sectors into four groups which we have called consumer, intermediate, and investment goods as well as the chemicals, rubber and petroleum sub-sector. In some respects, one might more appropriately call these groups light, medium, and heavy industry, since consumer goods consist of food, beverages, tobacco, clothing, textiles, and leather; while intermediate goods consist of wood, furniture, paper, printing, publishing, and building materials; and the 'investment goods' include metal products, machinery, transport equipment, and miscellaneous manufactures.

Table 7.3 gives a summary of the sources of output growth in manufacturing over the period 1964–84 and partitions the total growth by sub-sectors. A number of features are of interest. First, the food, beverage and tobacco sub-sector was the dominant factor in overall growth (42% of the total) followed by the chemicals, rubber and petroleum sub-sector (principally petroleum, and contributing almost 24% of total output growth). All other sub-sectors made a relatively small contribution, with only the clothing, textiles and leather and the metal products sub-sectors contributing more than 6% of total output growth.

Table 7.3 *Sources of growth in manufacturing output, 1964–84 (current prices)*

	Output Growth	Growth Domestic Demand	Export Growth	Import Substitution
Sector		percent of increase in total output		
Food beverages & tobacco	42.28	34.50	1.30	6.48
Clothing textiles leather	6.80	2.24	0.14	4.41
consumer goods	49.07	36.74	1.44	10.89
Wood & furniture	2.10	1.61	0.07	0.42
Paper printing publishing	5.04	3.26	0.11	1.68
Building materials	3.26	2.45	0.53	0.28
intermediate	10.40	7.32	0.70	2.38
Chemicals rubber petroleum	23.71	13.94	2.77	7.01
Metal products	6.73	3.68	0.07	2.98
Machinery	3.89	1.86	0.00	2.03
Transport equipment	5.46	4.94	0.00	0.53
Miscellaneous	0.74	0.25	0.04	0.46
investment goods	16.81	10.72	0.11	5.99
TOTAL	100.00	68.72	5.01	26.27

Source: Statistical Abstract, Economic Survey.

Another feature is the dominance of the growth of domestic demand in 'explaining' the growth of manufacturing output. More than two-thirds of output growth was due to domestic demand, and more than one-third came as a result of increased domestic demand for food, beverages and tobacco products. Import substitution provided just over one-quarter of the sources of domestic output growth, with the two most important contributing sub-sectors being chemicals, rubber and petroleum and, again, food, beverages and tobacco. Finally– and of major significance for macro-management – is the fact that export growth contributed only 5% to total growth of manufacturing output between 1964 and 1984.

Tables 7.4a, 7.4b, 7.4c and 7.4d summarise the relative contributions of the ten different sub-sectors. The rising importance of food, beverages and tobacco is evident through the whole period. The effects on the petroleum sub-sector following the two oil shocks are shown by the increases in the share of chemicals, rubber and petroleum refining in the 1970–75 and

1980–84 periods. The contribution of some of the more import-intensive sub-sectors (metal products; machinery; transport equipment; clothing, textiles and leather) moved inversely in relation to the contribution of chemicals, rubber and petroleum, partly for statistical reasons and partly because those import-intensive sectors were affected more sharply by the foreign-exchange constraints in the early 1970s and early 1980s.

There are a number of differences between the four periods in terms of the relative contribution of the different 'sources' of output growth. In all four periods, however, the growth of domestic demand was the dominant source, ranging between 73 and 95% of the total.

Table 7.4a *Sources of growth in manufacturing output: 1964–70 (current prices)*

	Output Growth	Growth Domestic Demand	Export Growth	Import Substitution
Sector		percent of increase in total output		
Food beverages & tobacco	29.74	23.59	1.03	5.13
Clothing textiles leather	13.33	6.67	0.00	6.67
consumer goods	43.08	30.26	1.03	11.79
Wood & furniture	5.13	4.10	1.03	0.00
Paper printing publishing	8.21	6.15	1.03	1.03
Building materials	6.15	5.13	1.03	0.00
intermediate goods	19.49	15.38	3.08	1.03
Chemicals rubber petroleum	15.38	10.26	5.13	0.00
Metal products	7.18	6.15	0.00	1.03
Machinery	8.21	4.10	0.00	4.10
Transport equipment	5.13	9.23	0.00	−4.10
Miscellaneous	1.54	0.72	0.10	0.72
investment goods	22.05	20.21	0.10	1.74
TOTAL	100.00	76.10	9.33	14.56

Source: Ibid.

Table 7.4b *Sources of growth in manufacturing output: 1970–75 (current prices)*

	Output Growth	Growth Domestic Demand	Export Growth	Import Substitution
Sector		percent of increase in total output		
Food beverages & tobacco	34.45	29.75	1.79	2.19
Clothing textiles leather	7.83	4.47	0.00	3.36
consumer goods	42.28	34.23	1.79	6.26
Wood & furniture	2.68	2.01	0.00	0.67
Paper printing publishing	6.49	4.47	0.45	1.57
Building materials	3.13	2.46	0.67	0.00
intermediate goods	12.30	8.95	1.12	2.24
Chemicals rubber petroleum	31.32	19.69	5.15	6.49
Metal products	6.17	3.80	0.22	2.68
Machinery	2.01	2.91	0.00	−0.89
Transport equipment	2.01	2.46	0.00	−0.45
Miscellaneous	3.36	1.12	0.00	2.24
investment goods	14.09	10.29	0.22	3.58
TOTAL	100.00	73.15	8.28	18.57

Source: Ibid.

Table 7.4c *Sources of growth in manufacturing output: 1975–80 (current prices)*

	Output Growth	Growth Domestic Demand	Export Growth	Import Substitution
Sector	percent of increase in total output			
Food beverages & tobacco	39.97	35.90	2.38	1.68
Clothing textiles leather	8.98	5.89	0.42	2.66
consumer goods	48.95	41.80	2.81	4.35
Wood & furniture	2.81	2.52	0.21	0.07
Paper printing publishing	4.35	3.93	0.14	0.28
Building materials	2.10	2.52	0.42	− 0.84
intermediate goods	9.26	8.98	0.77	− 0.49
Chemicals rubber petroleum	19.35	22.16	9.12	− 11.92
Metal products	8.27	9.54	0.28	− 1.54
Machinery	4.91	4.21	0.00	0.70
Transport equipment	9.96	4.21	0.00	2.52
Miscellaneous	− 0.70	0.98	0.14	− 1.82
investment goods	22.44	22.16	0.42	− 0.14
TOTAL	100.00	95.09	13.11	− 8.20

Source: Ibid.

Table 7.4d *Sources of growth in manufacturing output: 1980–84 (current prices)*

	Output Growth	Growth Domestic Demand	Export Growth	Import Substitution
Sector	percent of increase in total output			
Food beverages & tobacco	46.24	45.18	1.00	0.06
Clothing textiles leather	5.20	3.57	0.50	1.13
consumer goods	51.44	48.75	1.50	1.19
Wood & furniture	1.44	1.38	0.00	0.06
Paper printing publishing	4.76	3.63	− 0.06	1.19
Building materials	3.57	2.07	0.44	1.07
intermediate goods	9.77	7.08	0.38	2.32
Chemicals rubber petroleum	24.06	9.77	− 0.25	14.54
Metal products	6.02	3.70	0.06	2.26
Machinery	3.70	1.63	0.00	2.07
Transport equipment	4.45	2.63	0.00	1.82
Miscellaneous	0.56	0.13	0.06	0.38
investment goods	14.72	8.08	0.13	6.52
TOTAL	100.00	73.68	1.75	24.56

Source: Ibid.

Import substitution accounted for only about 15% of manufacturing growth in the late 1960s and was a *negative* contribution in the late 1970s, reflecting in both periods a relatively rapid rise in aggregate imports. Its share was highest in the early 1980s, and reflects in large part the stringency of import licensing and the generally depressed macroeconomic conditions.

The principal disappointing feature is the poor export performance throughout the whole period, particularly if one excludes petroleum exports. However, as already mentioned, from the mid-1970s onwards an increasing amount of Kenya's exports to neighbouring countries were unrecorded. For all sub-sectors, excluding chemicals, rubber and petroleum, export growth *never* exceeded 5% of manufacturing growth; and in the two periods of import stringency (1970–75 and 1980–84) the contributions of export growth were only 4.6 and 2.6% of total output growth, respectively.

There are substantial differences among sub-sectors in the relative importance attached to the three 'sources' of output growth, and disaggregation gives a somewhat different picture of what was happening to the manufacturing sector. Because of the dominance of food, beverages and tobacco in total manufacturing output, the very low rate of import substitution in that sub-sector (15% of total growth) is the major factor bringing down the overall contribution of import substitution to manufacturing growth. Textiles, clothing and leather show the highest share of import substitution as a source of growth (almost 65% over the entire 20 years), followed by miscellaneous manufactures (62%), machinery (52%), metal products (44%), paper, printing and publishing (33%), and chemicals, rubber and petroleum (30%).

On the other hand disaggregation by sub-sector does not improve the picture for exports; indeed, it raises more concern. The principal contributors to exports as a source of manufacturing growth are refined petroleum products (where there is little smuggling) and building materials, which is basically cement production, and which enjoyed a major cost advantage in providing the Middle East and the Indian Ocean basin with bulk cement from Mombasa. Other than these two sub-sectors, only miscellaneous manufacturing had more than 4% of its output growth accounted for by exports over the full 20-year period.

Examination of the *sources of growth of manufacturing value added* over the same periods, and using the same framework of analysis, yields somewhat similar results but a new set of issues regarding the changing ratio of value added to output.

Before examining the partitioning of value added growth, however, we might look in Table 7.5 at the growth rates of different manufacturing sub-sectors in 'real' terms. Unfortunately, there are no deflators available for the individual sub-sectors within manufacturing, so we have had to deflate all of them by the manufacturing GDP deflator. This undoubtedly misses some important differentials in relative prices (in particular the change in petroleum prices in 1974 and 1979), but it does give some rough indications of relative growth rates among industries and particularly over time. The real growth of MVA averaged 8% a year over the 20-year period, with the most rapid increases occurring in consumer goods (clothing, textiles and leather; and food, beverages and tobacco), wood and furniture, and chemicals, rubber and petroleum. Real growth was much slower in the second decade than in the first, especially for intermediate goods, investment goods, and chemicals, petroleum and rubber. As

Table 7.5 *Real growth of MVA in constant (1976) prices*

	1964–70	1970–75	1975–80	1980–84	1964–84
Sector		average annual percentage increase			
Food beverages & tobacco	5.53	13.82	6.87	8.93	9.20
Clothing textiles leather	14.17	10.40	9.13	2.75	9.63
consumer goods	9.00	12.85	7.09	7.28	9.60
Wood & furniture	12.10	13.19	3.53	2.69	9.31
Paper printing publishing	6.59	10.38	4.04	4.34	6.91
Building materials	10.37	9.70	− 2.65	2.86	5.15
intermediate goods	8.80	10.23	1.58	2.72	6.38
Chemicals rubber petroleum	6.41	15.25	2.53	3.84	9.13
Metal products	15.80	15.54	2.30	− 1.20	7.90
Machinery	14.99	9.36	9.07	7.74	8.78
Transport equipment	4.76	5.36	13.42	7.72	5.44
Miscellaneous	19.95	7.71	1.26	9.78	8.56
investment goods	10.70	9.20	7.44	4.42	6.62
TOTAL	8.89	11.68	4.94	4.96	8.00

Source: Ibid.

Table 7.6 *Sources of growth in MVA 1964–84 (current prices)*

Sector	Growth Value Added	Growth Domestic Demand	Export Growth	Growth Import Substit'n	Residual
	percent of increase in total Value Added				
Food beverages & tobacco	41.52	51.15	1.91	9.59	− 21.13
Clothing textiles leather	10.31	1.89	0.11	3.73	4.59
consumer goods	51.83	53.04	2.02	13.32	− 16.55
Wood & furniture	3.71	3.49	0.13	0.94	− 0.86
Paper printing publishing	5.99	8.95	0.29	4.67	− 7.92
Building materials	3.05	7.40	1.58	0.83	− 6.76
intermediate goods	12.75	19.84	2.00	6.45	− 15.54
Chemicals rubber petroleum	17.27	20.78	4.13	10.45	− 18.08
Metal products	4.94	6.06	0.13	4.89	− 6.14
Machinery	5.68	8.80	0.00	9.57	− 12.68
Transport equipment	6.28	11.24	0.00	1.21	− 6.17
Miscellaneous	1.25	1.27	0.18	2.33	− 2.52
investment goods	18.15	27.36	0.31	17.99	− 27.52
TOTAL	100.00	121.02	8.45	48.21	− 77.68

Source: Ibid.

previously indicated, it would appear that the relative growth rates among sub-sectors were somewhat more even during the late 1960s, and were more differentiated in the second decade as the growth of MVA slowed down and even became negative in some sub-sectors (building materials, and metal products).

Table 7.6 gives a summary of the share of value added growth in manufacturing accounted for by each of the different sub-sectors over the 20-year period and in each sub-period. Again, the dominance of food, beverages and tobacco is evident. Moreover, the importance of the sugar sub-sector (or more generally, bakery, sugar, and confectionery) is evident. It accounts for between a quarter and over half of the growth of value added in the food processing industries and 19% of the increase in MVA for food, beverages and tobacco as a whole and, therefore, much of the outcome is a reflection of what has happened in the sugar industry. Nonetheless, the continued and even increased dominance of the consumer goods industries in the growth of overall value added (39% of value added growth in the first period, rising to 59% in the early 1980s) suggests a degree of concentration of manufacturing activity that is quite considerable.

As indicated earlier, the second most important sub-sector over the whole period was chemicals, rubber and petroleum, which is dominated by petroleum refining. This sub-sector provided over 20% of value added growth in the 1970s in the two periods containing the oil price shocks.

As noted previously, some of the industries which are heavily dependent on imported inputs (clothing, textiles and leather, paper, printing and publishing, metal products, machinery, and transport equipment) showed relatively larger contributions to the growth of MVA during the 1975–80 period when there was a general relaxation of import controls on intermediate goods. These same sub-sectors contributed substantially less in the early 1980s when there was increased import stringency, and particularly large falls in value added were exhibited in metal products, machinery and transport equipment.

We encountered a major problem in analysing the growth of value added by 'source'. The reason is the large negative value of the residual, reflecting a decline in the ratio of value added to gross output for manufacturing as a whole and in virtually every sector of manufacturing industry. The relative size of the residual compared with other sources was extremely large. Looking again at Table 7.6, we see the change in the value added ratio was *minus* 78% of the growth of value added. Other analyses which have used this method (e.g. Lewis and Soligo, 1965) found relatively small amounts of growth attributable to changes in the value added ratio, some positive and some negative. However, Kenya exhibits large negative contributions in virtually every sector in every period between 1964 and 1984. Indeed, so large are these negative numbers that it is extremely difficult to interpret the remainder of the partitioning exercise. In effect, what these numbers suggest is that, while value added was growing due to the growth of domestic demand, import substitution and exports within each sub-sector, it was declining because within each industry the ratio of value added to output was falling. Below, we explore further what the implications of these changes might be.

Meanwhile, we can make some comments about the relative importance of domestic demand, exports and import substitution in contributing to value added growth. As was the case in output growth, exports explain a relatively small amount of total value added growth over the total period 1964–84, and *half* of the export contribution came in the chemicals, rubber and petroleum sub-sector, which was almost wholly due to refined petroleum products. In most sub-sectors, import substitution was less important than domestic demand growth, and overall was only about one-third as important in explaining the growth of MVA. Again, only in clothing, textiles and leathers was import substitution of substantially greater importance than domestic demand growth.

The analysis of different time periods (for details see Lewis and Sharpley, 1988) yields results similar to those found in the discussion of output growth. Import substitution is relatively more important as a source of value added growth in the early 1970s and the early 1980s, the two periods of relative import stringency. Overall, it made a negative contribution during the late 1970s when imports were relatively freely available. In all cases, however, the petroleum sub-sector is a dominant factor in those periods. Further, the *negative* contribution of declining value added ratios is also of the highest importance during the periods of import stringency. We come back to this in our discussion of the implications of these findings.

In summary, the analysis and partitioning of the sources of growth of both output and value added in manufacturing yields a number of interesting and some troubling results. First, the growth of domestic demand is by far the most dominant factor. Import substitution, defined in terms of the changing percentage of domestic production in total supply, contributed only about a quarter of the total growth in manufacturing output.

Second, the high concentration of manufactured growth in food, beverages, and tobacco, and particularly in the sugar sub-sector, raises some questions about the breadth of industrialisation. The dominance of consumer goods would have been even higher if those produced in other sub-sectors were to be included, for example soaps in the chemical industry, radios and TVs in the electrical machinery industry, consumer ceramics and glass products in the building materials sector, etc. This suggests that the breadth and depth of industrialisation is not as great as a superficial analysis of the size of Kenya's manufacturing sector would indicate.

Third, a cause for concern is the small contribution of exports, and particularly their declining importance as a share of manufacturing output throughout the entire period.

Fourth, the negative residual or large decline in the ratio of value added to gross output in virtually every sub-sector in every sub-period of the analysis suggests that some of the 'import substitution' reflected in the increasing ratio of domestic output to competing imports may be offset by a declining contribution of domestic value added within those import-substituting industries. We return to this implication below.

All the above conclusions and implications suggest that the manufacturing sector in Kenya may not have been providing a firm basis for diversification of the economy and self-sustaining growth. However, in order to pursue that judgment it is important to turn to the question of the policy regime under which manufacturing was operating and the extent to which economic magnitudes measured at domestic prices reflect what was happening when variables are measured at something closer to their opportunity costs.

Policies towards manufacturing

THE MACROECONOMIC FRAMEWORK

One of the characteristics of Kenya's development from 1964 to 1984 was a rapidly expanding public sector. The budget deficit grew dramatically over the entire period, financed in part by domestic and in part by external borrowing, with the proportions varying considerably over time. Kenya pursued a relatively 'orthodox' fiscal policy during the years prior to its first balance-of-payments squeeze in 1971, and also followed relatively orthodox policies during the adjustment to the first oil shock. It was not until the late 1970s that, following the coffee boom in which government revenues did *not* expand to absorb the windfalls going to coffee and tea producers, budgetary policy started to rely excessively on borrowing from commercial sources abroad and from the domestic banking system. During the late 1970s, as already mentioned, considerable external debt was acquired, so that the expansionary fiscal policy was financed by large balance-of-payments capital inflows. It was after the second oil shock in 1979 that the rate of increase of public sector borrowing from the domestic banking system increased dramatically. The rapid expansion of public credit and the increasing costs of financing external debt produced the foreign-exchange reserve crisis of 1982, and all these events necessitated the stabilisation and structural adjustment programmes which were begun in 1983 and 1984.

The changes in budgetary and monetary policy discussed above generated differences in the four different periods under review in the foreign-exchange position. In turn, the relative stringency of the foreign-exchange constraint determined government attitudes on other policies toward the manufacturing sector. Thus, while there were few direct effects of general macroeconomic policy on the manufacturing sector, there were considerable effects which operated indirectly through the impact of macro policies on the balance of payments, foreign-exchange reserves, and the direction of trade policy.

The performance of the manufacturing sector and the incentive to invest in different types of industries can also be affected by the relative wage rates in different sectors of the economy and their changes over time. Figure 7.5 shows the movements of average real earnings in manufacturing over the 20-year period deflated by two alternative price indices: the lower income cost of living index, which would give an index of real earnings from the point of view of employees; and the manufacturing GDP deflator, which would give an index of the real wage from the point of view of the manufacturing sector. Real wages, however measured, rose substantially during the 1964–70 period. From the employee's point of view, average earnings increased by over 40%, while from the employer's point of view they rose in real terms by almost 35%. However, after 1970 real wages from the employee's viewpoint fell in

Figure 7.5 *Average real earnings in manufacturing (various deflators)*

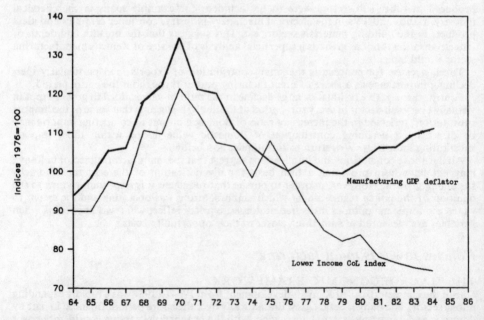

Source: Statistical Abstract.

virtually every year, so that by 1984 average earnings deflated by the lower income cost of living index were 20% lower than in 1964. On the other hand, the real wage as seen by the manufacturers declined from 1970 to 1974, but then rose again by the early 1980s. A good deal of the incentive effects of changing wages depends on what is happening simultaneously to changes in the exchange rate, a subject to which we turn in the next section. It may be relevant here to note that two of the most important export sub-sectors are exceptionally capital-intensive: petroleum refining and cement. Conversely, textiles which have been an important source of export growth in many other low-wage countries, have not been a major source of export growth in Kenya. Therefore, the very substantial increase in the real wage up to 1970 might suggest that wage policy has had some adverse effects on the structure of Kenyan manufacturing despite the fact that real wages from the employee's viewpoint had fallen considerably between 1970 and 1984.

In sectoral terms, as can be seen from Figure 7.6, the barter terms of trade for the agricultural sector slowly declined between 1964 and 1975, as the prices received for crops and livestock fell behind the rising costs of manufactured consumer goods and purchased agricultural inputs. However, the volume of marketed production expanded quickly during the first decade (when the level of manufacturing protection was relatively modest) and the income terms of trade for agriculture improved by more than 4% a year. The boom in coffee and tea prices in 1976–7 saw a dramatic improvement in the agricultural terms of trade, but this was short-lived, and in the crisis and adjustment period 1980–84, the prices paid for manufactured consumer goods and inputs rose more than twice as quickly as those for agricultural production, and the income terms of trade stagnated. The rising level of manufacturing protection encouraged the allocation of resources to manufacturing at the expense of agriculture, and by the 1980s the subsidies absorbed by manufacturing were large relative to the size of agricultural GDP, as will be seen later.

The last general policy that might be mentioned is that of price control. Ceiling prices on a wide range of goods are established by the Price Controller in the Treasury. In practice the price control authorities adopted a policy of permitting companies to meet cost increases, particularly those due to increased import costs, so that there was little incentive for firms to keep down their costs so long as they could document reasons for increases. The prevalence

Figure 7.6 *Agricultural terms of trade, 1964–86*

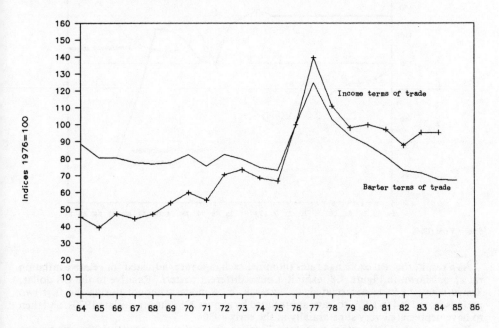

Source: Sharpley (1986).

of quantitative restrictions on imports, referred to below, meant that there was little discipline from competing imports in setting prices. It also meant that domestic firms using domestically produced import substitutes did not have the option of buying lower priced or higher quality inputs in international markets, and this also had the effect of pushing up their cost structure. Finally, if a firm did succeed in lowering its unit costs, or if it had the *potential* to lower unit costs by exporting at a price which was above marginal but below average cost, the Price Controller was likely to insist on a reduction in the domestic market price. This practice decreased the incentives for firms to move into exports since any potential profit to be gained by exporting was likely to be removed by reductions in domestic market prices. Because of Kenya's relatively open economy, even the apparently domestically-oriented policy of price control had an impact in terms of its interaction with the elements of foreign trade policy. To that subject we now turn.

TRADE POLICY

Five separate elements of trade policy will be examined here in turn: exchange-rate policy, tariffs, the import licensing scheme, the Export Compensation Scheme and domestic indirect taxes.

Exchange Rate Policy.   Figures 7.7 and 7.8 show graphically several elements of the pattern of exchange-rate adjustments over the 20-year period. In Figure 7.7, the *nominal* exchange rate between the Kenya shilling and both the US dollar and the SDR are shown, as well as the movement of relative inflation rates in Kenya and a basket of industrial countries. If one looks only at the behaviour of the nominal exchange rate in relation to the dollar, Kenya would appear to have had stability during the first period of our analysis, devaluation during the second, revaluation during the third, and a very substantial devaluation in the 1980s. However, Kenyan inflation was less than that in the rest of the world during the first period and, despite some acceleration, the index of Kenyan relative to world prices did not reach its 1964 level until the mid-1970s. From the mid-1970s onward, Kenya's inflation rate was above that of the principal SDR trading countries.

Figure 7.7   *Nominal exchange rate and relative inflation*

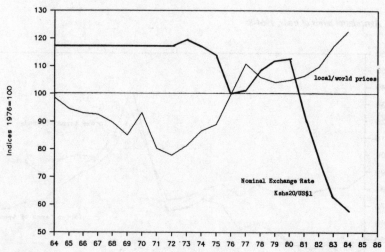

Source: Wood (1986).

As a result, the real exchange rates (nominal exchange rates adjusted for relative inflation rates), as shown in Figure 7.8, exhibit a quite different pattern. Relative to the US dollar, Kenya seems to have depreciated, on average, by a modest amount during the first two periods from 1964 to 1975, to have appreciated by almost 20% during the late 1970s, and then to have depreciated very substantially in the early 1980s.

Relative to the SDR, rather than the US dollar, the *real* exchange rate depreciated much

Figure 7.8 *Real exchange rate K Shs/US$, K Shs/SDR*

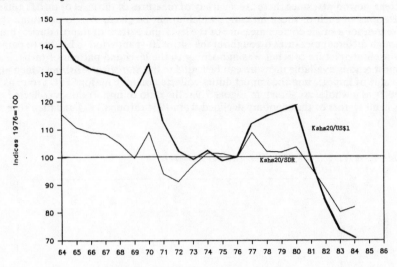

Source: Ibid.

more during the first decade after independence, appreciated only moderately (given the errors in measurement, probably imperceptibly) over the late 1970s, and depreciated by about 20% in the early 1980s.

Overall, our examination indicates that the Kenya shilling was not 'over-valued' by a substantial amount, particularly given the fact that in the immediate post-independence period there were virtually no import licensing controls on current account payments. The worst picture one can paint is of an appreciation of the Kenya shilling relative to the US dollar in real terms of approximately a third between 1972 and 1980, though the appreciation was more than corrected between 1980 and 1982. And in the mid-1980s, it was common to hear in Nairobi, both from government officials and from those representing bilateral and multi-lateral aid agencies, that the Kenya shilling was not 'over-valued'. However, the appreciation of the 'effective' exchange rate was considerably greater than that suggested by the movement in the real exchange rate. (The real effective exchange rate is the nominal exchange rate adjusted for changes in the relative rates of inflation along with changes in the levels of tariff protection and import controls).

We shall come back shortly to the exchange rate and incentive package, but it is important to note here that the meaning of the term 'over-valuation' is ambiguous and always needs to be defined with reference to some standard. It is possible that the Kenya shilling was not 'over-valued' in much of this period *if* one defines over-valuation as a situation in which there is excess demand for foreign exchange at the existing exchange rate *and other policies*. As indicated in the earlier discussion of the macroeconomic situation, the late 1970s saw a substantial widening of the current account deficit of the balance of payments financed by official and commercial capital inflows. Further, as will be seen below, the entire period from 1964 to 1984, and particularly since the mid-1970s, was one in which average tariff levels rose steadily and, in many cases, dramatically. Thus, the demand for foreign exchange for imports was being substantially dampened by the rise in tariffs. Finally, in the years 1982–4 the stabilisation programme had the effect of substantially reducing economic activity in a number of sectors, thus decreasing the demand for foreign exchange at the cost of reduced output. Thus, while there may have been relatively little excess demand for foreign exchange at the rates prevailing in the mid-1980s, it would be inappropriate to refer to this as a situation in which the effective exchange rate was not 'over-valued'. The exchange-rate-tariff-import-licensing-domestic credit package should be chosen not only with short-term balance-of-payments considerations in mind but also in terms of its effects on longer-term economic development and structural change.

Tariffs and Tariff Policy.   The subject of tariff policy has been approached from a number of different viewpoints, since there are a variety of measures of the level of tariffs and several interpretations of each of those measures which might be given. We do not think that one should search for a single correct measure of the level and pattern of import duties, but we do have enough different measures throughout the entire 20-year period to be able to paint a reasonably accurate picture of what was happening to the level and pattern of tariffs.

The most readily available measure can be found in the *Statistical Abstract* which gives the annual value of imports and the import duties collected on each major SITC group as well as for imports as a whole. As shown in Figure 7.9a, the ratio of import duties collected to total imports in all sectors of the economy declined from 1964 through 1974 and then rose slightly

Figure 7.9a *Pattern of import duties (all sectors excluding petroleum)*

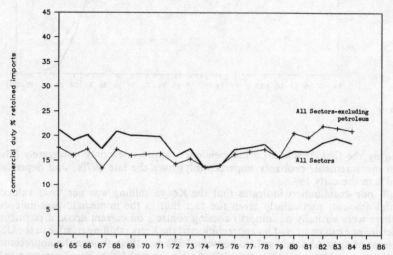

Source: Statistical Abstract.

Figure 7.9b *Pattern of import duties (consumer, intermediate and investment goods)*

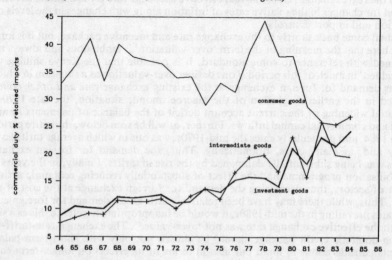

Source: Ibid.

in the late 1970s and early 1980s, though average import duties in the late 1960s were higher than in the early 1980s. This situation is reversed if one excludes the petroleum sub-sector, in which case the average tariff rises from about 16.3% in the late 1960s to about 21% in the early 1980s, having again fallen in the mid-1970s.

A somewhat different pattern emerges as one looks at import duties by individual sub-sectors and industry groups shown in Figure 7.9b. For some which are largely consumer goods (clothing, textiles, leather and footwear, food, beverages and tobacco) the average tariff rates when weighted by actual imports are much lower in the early 1980s than in the late 1960s. However, for many others (chemicals and rubber excluding petroleum; building materials; wood, cork and furniture; paper, printing and publishing; metal products; machinery; and to a lesser extent transport equipment) there is a consistent upward movement in the average import duty collected within each industrial sub-sector. Thus, even considering the pattern of tariff rates weighted by actual imports, one can see an increase in tariffs levied on imported intermediate and investment goods. The relative stability of total tariff revenue collected from imports as a whole is due to the changing composition of imports.

A second indication of what was happening to the pattern of tariffs and imports can be seen in Figures 7.10a and 7.10b. Figure 7.10a shows the results of an exercise in which we adjusted import tariff revenues each year for the increased rates of duty announced in the budget speech of that year. This gives a crude counter-factual indication of what the level of import tariff collections might have been had *scheduled tariff rates* under the Customs and Excise Act *remained unchanged* from year to year. What is quite clear is the substantial decline in the level of adjusted tariff revenue through virtually the whole 20-year period. Year by year, the Minister of Finance was attempting to recapture revenue by raising import duties that had been lost due to the shifting composition of actual imports away from higher duty items towards lower duty items. This clearly reflects the effect of import substitution in particular industries, where highly taxed imports of final products are replaced by imports of intermediate and capital goods at lower rates of duty, with fabrication taking place in Kenya but with a lower contribution to government revenue. To a large extent, then, the changing imports and the decline in the adjusted level of import duties was a result of the initial pattern of tariffs which produced incentives for import substitution of high duty items using low duty intermediate inputs.[6]

Figure 7.10a *Import duties, actual and adjusted (tariff rates unchanged, 1963/64 base year)*

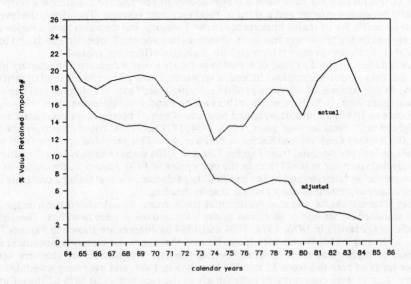

Source: Shah (1986); *Statistical Abstract*.

Figure 7.10b *Import duties, actual and adjusted (composition of imports unchanged, 1963/64 base year)*

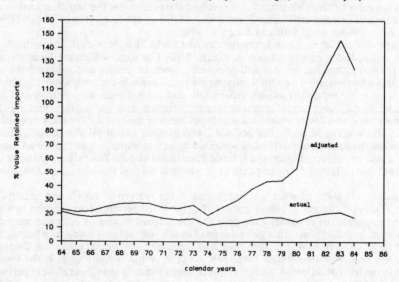

Source: Ibid.

As shown in Figure 7.10b, the obverse of the declining rate of adjusted tariff revenue imports is a substantial increase in what the rate of import duty might have been had the *composition of imports remained the same* and had the import duties risen at the rates established in each succeeding budget. Given the very large changes in rates over this period of time, a 'counter-factual' calculation of what the average rate of duty would have been at the 1964 composition of imports would be quite unrealistic, since it would generate implied average tariff rates averaging over 100%. Nonetheless, the exercise demonstrates quite clearly both the substantial shift in the composition of imports away from high duty toward low duty items as well as the substantial increase in the rates of duty on individual items.

The last point to be made about the budgetary approach to the examination of tariff levels is that tariffs on imports have been a major source of revenue for the Kenya government, normally between a quarter and a third of total recurrent revenue. Therefore, the level and pattern of tariffs are of major importance to the Treasury, but they also have a major effect on incentives facing producers and users of various categories of imported goods and import substitutes. Both the revenue effects and the incentive effects are critical.

Import duties weighted by level of actual imports are a useful measure of budgetary importance, but they give an incomplete, indeed, a very inaccurate, picture of the level of tariff protection. At the extreme, of course, a prohibitively high tariff rate will eliminate all imports of that particular item. In such cases, since there are no imports of the commodity, the weight of prohibitive tariffs in an import-weighted measure is zero. Therefore, we calculated average unweighted tariff rates for four years: 1970, 1974, 1978 and 1984, based on entries scheduled under the relevant Customs and Excise or Finance Acts. This provided one year from within each of our four periods, and from Figures 7.9a and 7.10a we have already seen that there was relatively little increase in tariff rates in the years prior to 1970. However, the choice of years was pragmatic and determined by the availability of documents containing a complete list of all tariff rates organised under standard chapter headings.

Using information for the non-preferential trade areas, we calculated the average tariff and its standard deviation for all entries under 100 standard chapter headings. The distribution of average tariffs in 1970, 1974, 1978 and 1984 by chapter are shown in Figures 7.11a, 7.11b, 7.11c and 7.11d, from which it can be seen that there was clearly a movement in the direction of higher and more uniform average tariffs. The number of chapters with an average tariff of zero fell from 13 in 1970 to only 5 in 1984, and over time scheduled tariff rates by chapter were concentrated increasingly in the range of 35 to 50% of the cif import value.

Figure 7.11a *Average unweighted tariffs - 1970 (Customs and Excise Chapters 00 to 90)*

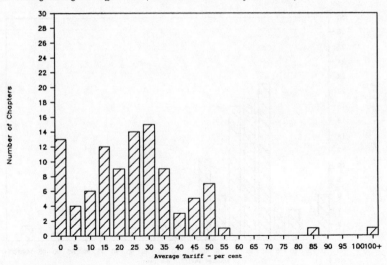

Source: Kenya Customs Tariffs Act (1970).

Figure 7.11b *Average unweighted tariffs - 1974 (Customs and Excise Chapters 00 to 90)*

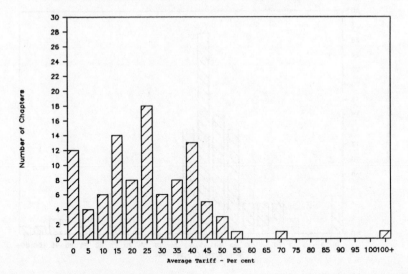

Source: East African Community, Customs and Excise Tariffs (1974).

Details for individual chapters were aggregated into major sectors, loosely corresponding to the ISIC classification used when analysing the 'sources' of manufacturing growth. These results, which are summarised in Tables 7.7 and 7.8, are broadly consistent with the patterns arrived at from the other two exercises, with the most substantial increases in average unweighted tariffs coming as they did in the late 1970s and early 1980s. Table 7.7 shows there were around 1,400 scheduled entries in 1970 and 1974, but in 1978 and 1984 this figure doubled, with most of the additional tariff entries to be found under chemicals and rubber, and particularly, textiles and clothing.

Figure 7.11c *Average unweighted tariffs – 1978 (Customs and Excise Chapters 00 to 90)*

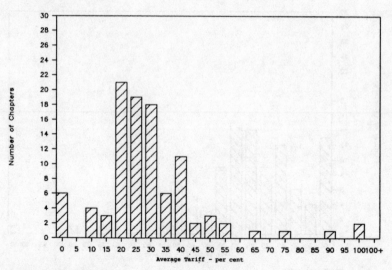

Source: Kenya Customs and Excise Act (1978).

Figure 7.11d *Average unweighted tariffs – 1984 (Customs and Excise Chapters 00 to 90)*

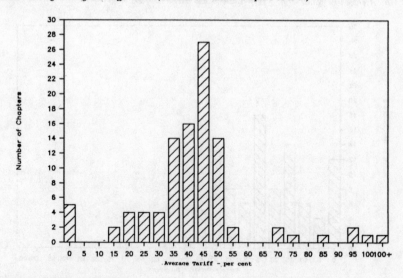

Source: Kenya Import Licensing Schedules (1984).

As shown in Table 7.8, there was a rise in the average unweighted tariff from 21% in 1970 to 22% in 1974 and then a large increase to 30% in 1978 and 41% in 1984. The same pattern, broadly speaking, emerges if one looks at the averages for different sub-sectors, e.g. chemicals and rubber; building materials; paper and printing; metal products; and machinery. Overall, the standard deviation decreased as tariffs tended to become more uniform, but the pattern varied among the different sectors. Between 1974 and 1984, it decreased substantially for food preparations, chemicals, rubber and petroleum; building materials, but increased for textiles; clothing; wood and paper products; machinery and transport equipment.

Table 7.7 *Number of scheduled tariff entries by major sectors*

Major Sectors	1970	1974	1978	1984
	percentage distribution			
Agriculture	1.13	1.03	0.74	0.95
Food beverages & tobacco	14.27	14.00	12.19	13.54
Food Preparation	12.43	12.07	10.82	11.97
Bakery cereal products	2.12	1.93	1.44	1.50
Sugar & confectionery	0.35	0.48	0.35	0.33
Oilseeds animal fats oils	2.40	2.28	2.31	2.41
Beverages & tobacco	1.84	1.93	1.37	1.61
Textiles clothing leather footwear	10.10	10.41	20.53	16.23
Textiles & clothing	8.47	8.90	18.28	13.50
Leather & footwear	1.62	1.2	2.24	2.74
Wood cork & furniture	5.08	4.97	3.47	3.79
Paper printing & publishing	3.46	3.38	2.98	3.21
Building materials clay & glass	9.32	8.28	5.04	5.29
Chemicals rubber & petroleum	15.40	16.41	20.21	20.90
Petroleum	1.98	2.41	1.68	1.75
Chemicals & rubber	13.42	14.00	18.53	19.15
Metal products incl. Basic Metals	14.34	13.38	10.37	10.94
Machinery & transport equip.	16.38	18.07	17.55	17.58
Machinery	11.79	13.10	13.87	13.90
Transport Equipment	4.59	4.97	3.71	3.68
Miscellaneous manufactures	11.86	11.31	7.57	7.88
Grand total – percentage	100.00	100.00	100.00	100.00
Grand total – number of entries	1,416	1,450	2,855	2,741

Source: Kenya – Import Licensing Schedules, 1984;
Kenya – The Customs & Excise Act 1978 – First Schedule;
East African Community – East African Customs & Excise Tariffs July 1974;
Kenya – Customs Tariffs Act 1970 – First Schedule.

One feature not adequately captured by these measures is the 'cascading' of tariffs within the same standard chapter between items with relatively less and those with relatively more processing. This is a problem in such categories as, for example, textiles or metal products, where the same tariff chapter heading, or the same ISIC groups, contain both intermediate inputs and final output. We shall return to this issue.

A fourth approach was to make use of three studies, by Reimer (1970), Phelps and Wasow (1972), and by the World Bank (1987a). The first two were made using data for the 1960s and the last for 1985. All three were concerned with measuring both nominal protection (the extent to which domestic prices exceed world market prices for comparable commodities), and effective protection (the extent to which the value added in domestic prices exceeds 'value added at world prices'), which is calculated as the difference between domestic output at world prices and material inputs at world prices, i.e., adjusted for the difference between world and domestic market prices. Effective protection calculations are used by different authors for different purposes. We use a rather straightforward interpretation here: effective protection can measure the share of the *measured value added* in an industry that is accounted for by protection to that industry (the difference between 'value added at domestic prices', and 'value added at world prices'). Phelps and Wasow were the only authors among

Table 7.8 *Average unweighted schedule tariff rates by major sector*

Major Sectors	1970	1974	1978	1984
		percentage[a]		
Agriculture	13.13	14.00	11.43	16.92
Food beverages & tobacco	36.04	31.35	25.31	39.79
Food Preparation	32.08	28.41	25.36	39.04
Bakery cereal products	32.08	33.52	28.23	37.20
Sugar & confectionery	46.70	29.00	39.80	27.78
Oilseeds animal fats oils	17.72	16.06	20.61	35.45
Beverages & tobacco	118.33	82.11	90.09	111.75
Beverages	82.17	66.36	99.64	90.84
Tobacco	238.88	139.83	67.91	155.60
Textiles clothing leather footwear	29.44	32.33	53.82	60.65
Textiles & clothing	29.87	32.44	56.66	64.92
Leather & footwear	27.20	31.66	30.72	39.60
Wood cork & furniture	22.25	23.43	28.15	44.71
Paper printing & publishing	17.60	18.79	24.12	38.07
Building materials clay & glass	13.55	16.37	23.47	38.03
Chemicals rubber & petroleum	18.38	18.42	20.75	33.39
Petroleum	19.45	14.26	15.65	18.00
Chemicals & rubber	18.22	19.13	21.21	34.80
Metal products incl. Basic Metals	12.34	12.91	19.46	34.82
Machinery & transport equip.	15.37	17.03	20.90	34.89
Machinery	16.18	17.51	20.28	33.79
Transport Equipment	13.31	15.74	23.05	39.01
Miscellaneous manufactures	20.67	21.64	25.07	35.00
Grand total – all entries	21.58	21.83	29.50	41.02
Grand total – standard deviation	28.74	24.1	24.1	27.14

(a) Tariff rates are those for: Fiscal Entry; outside-EAC; non-PTA.

Source: Kenya – Import Licensing Schedules, 1984;
Kenya – The Customs & Excise Act 1978 – First Schedule;
East African Community – East African Customs & Excise Tariffs July 1974;
Kenya – Customs Tariffs Act 1970 – First Schedule.

the three studies who used this particular interpretation, and we have converted the other measures of effective protection in Reimer and the World Bank to the same concept.[7]

In all three studies of Kenya, as has been true of studies of effective protection in other countries, there is a positive relationship between nominal and effective rates of protection. In general the higher the nominal rate, the higher the effective rate, reflecting the fact that most tariff structures, certainly in Kenya, are 'cascaded' so that the tariffs on intermediate inputs raise the costs to protected industries by less than the tariffs on their output raise the final selling prices of their goods. Figures 7.12a, 7.12b and 7.12c provide scatter diagrams and regression lines for all three studies, indicating the positive relationship that is present. Furthermore, for industries with relatively low rates of nominal protection, tariffs on their intermediate inputs may generate negative effective protection whereby these industries are discriminated against by the tariff system. There are a number of such cases in all three studies of effective protection in Kenya, and the industries concerned are predominantly those with strong linkages to the agricultural sector, such as animal feeds, meat and fish processing, bakery and grain mill products, confectionery, leather, sawmilling and wood. Of course, if one partitioned industries into their export component and domestic market components, the export component in all cases would involve negative effective protection, or discrimination against manufactured exports.

The advantage of using effective protection calculations is that one is able to weight the tariff levels by the importance of the products produced domestically, rather than by imports or simply using unweighted averages. This gives an estimate of the level of tariff in effect weighted by domestic output or value added. In their study, Phelps and Wasow found the average rate of effective protection in 1968 expressed as the share of value added due to, or accounted for by, protection was 31%. The World Bank study concluded that the effective rate of protection in 1985, based on the branches of manufacturing that it examined in 45

Figure 7.12a *Nominal and effective protection 1967 (Reimer estimates)*

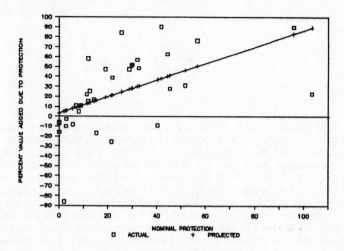

Source: Reimer (1970).

Figure 7.12b *Nominal and effective protection 1968 (Phelps and Wasow estimates)*

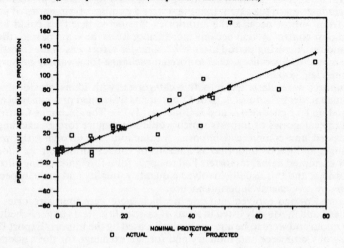

Source: Phelps and Wasow (1972).

Figure 7.12c *Nominal and effective protection 1985 (World Bank estimates)*

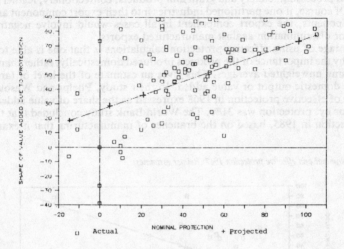

Source: IBRD (1987a).

firms, was 51% of value added, and it attempted to obtain a representative sample weighted for the whole manufacturing sector. Among the foreign-owned, local private and parastatal .enterprises included in the World Bank sample, there were considerable differences in the rate of effective protection. Expressed as a share of value added, the average rate of effective protection ranged from 35% for local private firms to 57% for foreign firms, and averaged 65% of value added for parastatal enterprises. The increases in the effective rates of protection from the late 1960s to the mid-1980s reflected by these two studies are completely consistent with the other measures of change in the protective system reported above. Alternatively put, the results already reported of unweighted tariff rates roughly doubling between 1970 and 1984, are reflected in similar increases in the rates of effective protection to import-substituting activities in Kenya. Of course, this has a counterpart in the increased discrimination against export activities over the same period.

Import Licensing.   Import licensing began to become important in Kenya in 1971, and grew in significance throughout the 1970s and 1980s. In both decades, import licensing was used both for general balance-of-payments control purposes and for specific protection measures for individual industries, to the extent that there were a number of categories of goods which were banned from import because the authorities considered that they could be produced locally. The import control system became more elaborate as the years passed, though in the stabilisation and restructuring period after 1982, a major effort was made to rationalise the licensing system and to liberalise access to foreign exchange for a variety of purposes, particularly intermediate goods.

In 1971, imports were classified into five categories, with items previously subject to licensing included under Schedules A, B or C, and items which had previously been imported freely contained under Schedules D and E (MacRae, 1979). The Exchange Control Circular also specified the categories of imports which would not require foreign exchange licences, and these included non-commercial imports, transactions not involving the provision of foreign exchange, and goods imported as a means of capital formation on a loan account basis. For non-exempted items, importers had to apply for a foreign-exchange licence before placing firm orders, and this usually involved a quantity, quality and price inspection by the Inspection Agency or General Superintendence.

By 1984 the system had evolved into one in which there were four categories of imports under Schedules 1 and 2, roughly listed in terms of essentiality. Items under Schedule 1A were not subject to quota and were to be automatically licensed by the Import/Export Department of the Ministry of Commerce and Industry and foreign exchange for these goods was to be readily approved by the Central Bank. For items falling under Schedule 1B, importers were granted annual allotments against which they were to be free to import any item or combination of items, within the shilling amount of their allotment. Importers had to apply for these allotments, and preference was to be given to manufacturers whose products qualified under the Export Compensation Scheme. Items under Schedule 2A-special (2AS) were subject to two qualifications, namely that licences were granted only with the approval of the designated government ministry; and licences for some items (such as oil, fertilisers and food grains) were given only to authorised importers. Finally, the most highly restricted category was Schedule 2B and these items required the assignment of specific quotas to eligible importers. The '2B' list reflected the increasing use of import licensing as a protective device, and in 1984 included over 800 items (see Table 7.9), almost all of which represented goods currently being produced in Kenya. Indeed, if one wanted to get a good feel of the individual products that are produced in Kenya, the simplest way would be to read through the list of items assigned to import Schedule 2B. Even after the liberalisation of imports began in 1983, the '2B' items received extremely low allocations of foreign exchange (6.4% of imports in 1983/4 and 3.3% in 1984/5).

The quantitative restrictions on imports interact, of course, with the tariff system. Both restrict imports, one by raising the price and the other by decreasing the quantity directly. Quantitative limitations make it possible for domestic prices to exceed duty-paid import prices and, therefore, for domestic producers to charge prices greater than those implied by tariff levels. On the other hand, competition in domestic markets, particularly when enforced or accompanied by price control measures on specific products, can result in domestic market prices below the level that would be implied by protective tariffs. Phelps and Wasow (1972) and the World Bank (1987a) found instances of both kinds: 'water in the tariffs' (i.e. domestic prices lower than tariff-implied prices) and 'additional protection' (i.e. quantitative restrictions permitting domestic market prices higher than those implied by tariff rates and world prices).

To get some further indication of 'cascading' tariffs as well as the impact of import licensing, we analysed the 1984 scheduled tariffs also by import licensing schedule for all items listed under the same 100 chapter headings. The results were then aggregated by sector, and details are reported in summary form in Tables 7.9 and 7.10. The cascading effect of

Table 7.9 *Number of import licensing schedule entries, 1984 (by major sectors)*

Major Sectors	Schedule 1A	Schedule 1B	Schedule 2A 2AS	Schedule 2B
	percent entries under each Schedule			
Agriculture	0.25	0.63	4.40	1.68
Food beverages & tobacco	5.99	6.78	46.15	22.24
Textiles clothing leather footwear	7.62	8.66	6.59	35.34
Clothing & textiles	6.99	4.49	3.30	31.49
Leather & footwear	0.25	3.86	0.00	3.49
Wood cork furniture & paper printing & publishing	2.00	8.77	1.10	10.22
Building materials clay & glass	7.74	4.70	0.00	4.57
Chemicals rubber & petroleum	49.19	8.98	37.36	5.77
Metal products incl. Basic Metals	9.74	17.12	0.00	6.97
Machinery & transport equipment	15.36	32.46	7.69	4.93
Miscellaneous manufactures	2.12	12.63	0.00	8.53
Grand total – all entries	100.00	100.00	100.00	100.00
Grand total – number of entries	801	958	91	832

Source: Kenya – Imports Licensing Schedules, 1984.

Table 7.10 *Average unweighted scheduled tariff rates, 1984 (by import licensing schedules and major sectors)*

Major Sectors	Schedule 1A	Schedule 1B	Schedule 2A 2AS	Schedule 2B
		percent (a)		
Agriculture	17.5	35	0	13.93
Food beverages & tobacco	36.25	39.92	35.36	46.22
Textiles clothing leather footwear	38.02	40.93	20.5	73.51
Clothing & textiles	38.13	40.12	30	76.7
Leather & footwear	40	42.7	0	39.03
Wood cork furniture & paper printing & publishing	38.13	35.83	0	50.59
Building materials clay & glass	33.71	38.22	0	44.87
Chemicals rubber & petroleum	31.82	42.51	8.41	50.73
Metal products incl. Basic Metals	27.24	35.46	0	43.19
Machinery & transport equipment	22.07	37.33	37.86	53.41
Miscellaneous manufactures	34.34	0	42.39	0
Grand total – all entries	30.73	37.7	23.36	55.54
– standard deviation	12.78	16.05	18.73	24.98

(a) Fiscal entry; non-PTA and outside EAC.

Source: Kenya – Imports Licensing Schedules, 1984.

tariffs as well as the likely differential effects of import licensing are demonstrated quite vividly by the figures in Table 7.10. This is because items on schedules 1A, 1B and 2AS tend to be either capital goods or intermediate products. Therefore, for a group such as metal products, where both intermediate inputs of steel re-rolling and final products appear in the same industry, the tariffs on 2B items which averaged 43% are likely to be final products produced domestically, while those on 1A items averaged only 27% and are likely to be imported intermediate inputs. To the extent that these 1A items are representative of the input costs in the industry, this implies a substantial cascading of tariffs on metal products, as well as a very high rate of effective protection. Since the metal products industry had a value added to gross output ratio of only 12.2% the differential between input and output tariffs would imply an effective rate of protection in the industry of nearly 160% or in excess of 60% of the value added in the industry due to, or accounted for by, protection. Thus, the information in Table 7.10 underscores that the import licensing system tended to work in the same direction as the tariff system in providing effective rates of protection to manufacturing industries that were in excess of the nominal rates of tariff on the goods.

A further effect of quantitative restrictions on imports was the adverse effect on export industries. Some of the earliest import substitution in the intermediate goods sector took place in the packaging industry. Before the introduction of import licensing, export industries that needed particular qualities and types of packaging in order to compete successfully in international markets were able to do so provided they were willing to pay higher prices including the tariffs on the intermediate goods. Indeed, during that period, there was still provision for the rebate of tariffs paid on inputs used in the production of exports. However, once import licensing was introduced, the authorities could prohibit domestic exporters from purchasing packaging materials in the world market and insist on their using domestically produced goods. As a result, in a number of cases manufacturers alleged that they were unable to compete in international markets, not because their product was inadequate in terms of price or quality, but because their packaging and shipping did not meet international standards – another side-effect of the quantitative restrictions on imports when used as a form of protection to domestic industry.

Export Compensation. Recognising the potential disincentive effects of the tariff and domestic indirect tax system on the competitive position of exports of manufactured goods, the government introduced an Export Compensation Scheme in 1984. Administered by the Customs and Excise Department, this was designed to provide exporters of manufactured goods with a 10% payment in cash to compensate them for the increased costs arising from the protective effects of tariffs and other indirect taxes which would lower their competitiveness in international markets. At the same time, the practice of providing duty draw-backs and rebates on imported inputs used in the production of exported goods was discontinued. This was aimed primarily at domestic production of imported intermediate goods. In 1982, the basic rate of export compensation was maintained at 10% and an incremental scheme was announced. Following these relatively confusing changes, in 1984 the basic rate was raised from 10 to 20% of the fob value, and the incremental scheme was later abolished.

While the concept of export compensation was an important potential contributor to rationalised incentives within the manufacturing sector, in practice the system did not provide automatic compensation, and only a small number of firms benefited. In 1984, there were long delays in payment of up to 40 weeks, even among large industries that devoted manpower specifically to collecting export compensation, and total payments amounted to only Ksh.10 m. or 4% of manufactured exports. In practice, therefore, the scheme acted more as a windfall for those few mainly foreign firms who were able to receive it, rather than as a basic incentive to encourage exports. Meanwhile, the continued rise in average tariff rates put Kenyan manufacturers at an increasing disadvantage when competing in international markets.

Domestic Indirect Taxes. Kenya made use of two sets of domestic indirect taxes during the period under study. The first was excise taxes, which tend to be levied at specific rates and cover a number of important consumer products – mainly petrol, tobacco products, beer, alcohol and sugar. The practice has been to adjust tariff rates and excise tax rates simultaneously in various budgets so that excise tax changes do not have effects on the level of protection received by domestic industries.

In 1972, the first sales tax was introduced. It was a straightforward, single-stage, manufacturer/importer level sales tax assessed at a single basic rate. As time went by, the government introduced increasing amounts of differentiation so that by 1984 there were several rates, some as high as 45% for refrigerators; 50% for toiletries; 70% for televisions and radios; and over 100% for passenger vehicles and buses. Since the tax was levied on both imports and domestic production at similar rates, it should have had no protective effect, nor any effect on the incentives facing exporters, since they were entitled to sell free of the sales tax. However, in practice administration of the sales tax has never been as efficient and comprehensive as income tax or customs and excise duties. As a result, there have been consistent allegations that domestic manufacturers substantially underpay their sales tax liabilities, which has the effect of increasing the amount of protection they receive (since competing imports pay the full sales tax and Kenyan manufacturers can sell at a comparable price to competing imports). Further, in order to be certain that sales tax was paid at least on the value of the intermediate goods used, the government began collecting sales tax on imported intermediates, even if they were going to be used in the production of sales-taxable goods, with the firm able to claim a refund of the sales tax on intermediates when it produced sales-taxable goods for the domestic market. Unfortunately, this had the added effect of providing cost increases for industries that were producing for export, since they had to pay sales tax on their imported intermediate goods but could not claim the refund until they had exported those goods in processed forms, and then would face long delays before receiving export compensation. Thus, while, by and large, the sales tax was neutral in its trade policy effects, because of its administration it had a number of unintended incentive effects providing further protection for import substitutes and further discouragement for exports.

Concluding Comments. From the analysis of trade policy over the entire 20-year period under study, a fairly clear-cut picture emerges with the possible exception of some ambiguity regarding the degrees of 'over-valuation' of the real effective exchange rate. Regardless of the measure one chooses, it is clear that the average rate of tariffs increased substantially between the late 1960s and the early 1980s. In sub-sectors such as textiles and clothing, transport equipment, and machinery, the standard deviation also increased as higher tariffs on intermediate and capital goods were accompanied by even greater increases in tariffs on final consumer goods. As a result, the incentive structure moved in favour of producing consumer goods for the domestic market, using imported intermediate goods. The changes in the import licensing system reinforced this set of incentives, as additional protection was provided by quantitative restrictions on imports of goods already produced in Kenya, and these restrictions tended to fall more heavily on imported consumer goods than on imported intermediate goods and capital items. The increase in the level of scheduled tariff rates had a corresponding effect in increasing the average rates of effective protection in manufacturing, so that while in the late 1960s less than 30% of MVA seemed to be attributable to protection, by the mid-1980s more than half of all MVA was due to protection.

At the same time as these changes were taking place in the incentives for protecting domestic industry, the shifts in tariff structure and quantitative restrictions were having a comparable effect in discriminating against exports. The Export Compensation Scheme, which was intended to deal with the effects of tariff rationalisation and of the increase in intermediate goods tariffs, did not function as intended, with the result that incentives turned against manufactured exports (as well as against agricultural exports). And the effects of the import licensing system on the quality of various intermediate inputs used by export industries, particularly packaging materials, had a further adverse effect on the incentives for exporting industries.

The changes in the real effective exchange rate have to be interpreted in the light of other policies, such as trade policy, external commercial borrowing and domestic credit expansion over the 20-year period. Thus, while it might appear, with the likely exception of the late 1970s, that Kenya tended towards only a modest overvaluation of the Kenya shilling, such a statement must be read against three other important pieces of information. First, the tariff and import control systems kept the demand for foreign exchange substantially below what it would have been had, for example, comparable revenue been raised by the use of a neutral sales tax rather than by a protective tariff. The fact that the levels of tariffs increased substantially over the whole period suggests that the demand for foreign exchange was being increasingly restricted by tariff policy. Second, especially during the late 1970s, macroeconomic policy allowed the increased demand for foreign exchange to be financed by capital inflows of both concessionary and commercial finance. Thus, increased domestic demand did not result in as much pressure on foreign-exchange reserves as might have occurred otherwise, because of the policy of external borrowing. Finally, in the mid-1980s, the demand for foreign exchange was further affected by the highly restrictive monetary and fiscal policy adopted after the 1982 crisis. In response to these restrictive stabilisation policies, international agencies, both bilateral and multilateral, provided increased balance-of-payments support, which further eased the pressure on the exchange rate.

Thus, it would appear that the principal direction of policy in Kenya over the 20 years under study was to shift incentives steadily in favour of production for the domestic market, behind increasingly high rates of protection from both tariffs and quantitative restrictions. The lower duties on intermediate goods, combined with the easier access to import licensing for intermediates, encouraged import-intensive import-substituting industries. As a result of these factors, Kenyan manufacturing became more dependent on imports and increasingly dependent on subsidies from other sectors of the economy or from capital inflows from abroad, and exports both of agricultural products and manufactured goods were discriminated against over the entire 20-year period. It is against this background of policy that we now turn to an interpretation of Kenya's industrialisation performance since 1964.

Interpreting Kenya's industrialisation

GROWTH PATTERNS AND POLICY EFFECTS
Our analysis suggests that Kenya's industrial growth can be understood as a response to differing macroeconomic and also trade policies in four periods: (i) the late 1960s with low protection, low inflation, and relatively orthodox macroeconomic policies; (ii) the early 1970s including reaction to the first oil shock, in which macroeconomic policies were not markedly expansionary and import licensing took hold as a major feature of balance-of-payments control and protection to manufacturing industry; (iii) the late 1970s when the coffee and tea price boom, and later substantial increases in external debt, permitted a relatively rapid expansion of imported intermediate goods. At the same time, tariffs were rising substantially, import controls continued to be used for protection purposes, and there was some appreciation in the value of the Kenya shilling compared with its trading partners. And

(iv) the early 1980s, which began with the effects of the second oil shock, and encompassed a major balance-of-payments crisis in 1982 followed by the beginning of stabilisation and adjustment programmes by 1984.

Industrial growth over this entire period was primarily driven by the growth of domestic demand for manufactured goods. Import substitution, defined as a rising share of domestic production in total supply of manufactures, accounted for around a quarter of total industrial growth, when measured in output terms, but at the same time there was a substantial drop in the ratio of value added to gross output in virtually every manufacturing industry throughout the 20-year period. Finally, recorded exports were a relatively small source of manufacturing growth, and were accounted for mainly by two capital-intensive sectors: petroleum refining and cement. Unrecorded exports to Uganda, Tanzania and other neighbouring countries increased from the mid-1970s onwards.

Throughout the period under study, the level of import tariffs was increasing and, since 1971, the general trend in the use of import licensing for both protection and balance-of-payments control purposes provided additional increases in protection to local markets. No matter how one measures the increase in tariffs, the average tariff level in nominal terms at least doubled (whether measured on an unweighted basis, or on a basis which takes account of the changing composition of imports, or on the basis of weights more closely approximating domestic producing sectors), and estimates of the effective rate of protection suggest that while about 30% of value added in manufacturing was attributable to subsidies from protection in the 1960s, over 50% of MVA was due to protection by the mid-1980s.

Overall, imported intermediate inputs (plus duty) represented nearly 30% of the gross output of the manufacturing sector, according to estimates from the 1976 Input/Output Table of Kenya (Table 7.11). Among the manufacturing sub-sectors with the highest import use (including duty) were petroleum (87%), transport equipment (61%), clothing (36%) and the broad group metal products, machinery and miscellaneous manufactures (34%). Food preparation and bakery had by far the lowest import content (8%), and other groups with strong agricultural linkages, such as leather and footwear, wood products, and paper were also relatively low in their use of imported inputs in 1976. More recent estimates, for 1983/4, further illustrate the relatively low import content of Kenya's agro-industrial output (Sharpley, 1988).

A characteristic of several industries which grew rapidly during the 20 years was their relative import intensity combined with cascading tariff structures in which the rates of duty on imported goods were considerably lower than the rates of protection given to the output sold in the domestic market. Such industries were clothing, textiles, steel re-rolling, and the assembly of consumer durables.

In addition to the generally import-using nature of Kenya's industrial growth, the falling ratio of recorded exports to output of the manufacturing sector meant that, even if rates of protection to each individual domestic sector had remained constant over the period, the average rate of protection to value added and output as a whole would have risen, since the unprotected share of output going to exports decreased substantially. Rather than promoting import processing that resulted in greater foreign-exchange earnings through exports, the manufacturing sector was involved in an exercise in which it used increasing amounts of imports to produce increasingly protected import substitutes for the domestic market.

THE DECLINING VALUE ADDED RATIO

One of the most puzzling features of the patterns of manufacturing growth revealed in the previous section was the near-universal decline in the ratio of value added to output. There are a number of possible explanations for this phenomenon and, therefore, a number of possible policy implications. We concentrate here on the one which is most plausible, namely the declining value added ratios which suggest that Kenya's approach to import substitution has not been 'successful'.[8]

A declining value added ratio means an increase in the ratio of purchased inputs to gross output, and both were measured in domestic prices. But if the value added ratios were to be calculated at international trade prices, then the decline would be even greater. Similarly, if the measurement of import substitution was done at domestic market prices, and measured using international trade prices, this would show that even less import substitution had taken place. In both cases, this is because adjusting imports to cif world prices calls for the elimination of actual tariff collections, which as we have seen did not rise very much relative to cif import values; and adjusting domestic production to world prices requires the elimination of all nominal protection, which did increase substantially over time because scheduled tariff rates were rising and because the import licensing system was more restrictive in the second decade than in the first. Further, for the major industrial groups, effective protection was greater than nominal protection, and the effective rates of protection also increased over the period.

Manufacturing growth in Kenya has involved investment in a succession of industries dependent on imported inputs, and whose profitability necessitates increasing rates of effective protection, or subsidy, from other sectors of the economy, almost always in terms of cascaded tariff rates, in order to be viable. The declining value added ratios are indicative not of a sector which is increasingly viable but of one which is increasingly dependent.

Another piece of evidence which supports this relatively pessimistic interpretation concerns the behaviour of exports. If the declining value added ratios were indicative of declining costs and increasing competitiveness, then we would expect to see rising ratios of exports output – or, at the very least, we would expect the share of output exported to remain constant. Unfortunately, the reverse is the case in virtually every industry group. The declining shares of exports in output are consistent with the view that the competitive position of the industries deteriorated as rates of domestic protection rose. Or, to take a less damaging view, the increases in tariffs on intermediate goods which are inputs into export industries have not been offset by increased productivity in those industries, so their costs have been raised and they have been unable to compete in export markets as effectively as they had done in the earlier years.[9]

THE MACROECONOMIC EFFECTS
OF THE PATTERN OF INDUSTRIALISATION

It is clear from the evidence cited above that Kenya's industrialisation has been increasingly inward-looking over the period 1964–84; that the rates of protection to domestic manufacturing industries have increased quite substantially; that discrimination against exports has increased; that the apparent amount of import substitution greatly overstates the import saving that took place due to manufacturing growth; and that, despite an early start in exporting to the other countries in the region (not just in the former East African Community), the manufacturing sector became less and less export-oriented. It absorbed some 13% of domestic capital formation throughout almost the entire period, receiving a larger share than monetary agriculture ever since the late 1960s. What can we conclude about the consequences of this pattern of manufacturing growth and, in particular, of its impact on the other sectors of the economy producing tradable goods and services (agriculture and tourism), and on the balance of payments?

Domestic protection, while appearing to discriminate against foreign producers, in fact must result in discrimination against other sectors of the domestic economy.[10] Protection involves paying domestic factors of production larger sums than the value of foreign exchange they save. The difference must be made up either by another domestic sector which receives lower factor payments than its foreign-exchange earning or saving or by a deterioration in the current account of the balance of payments. Thus, the subsidy to protected manufacturing industries could come either from export sectors, principally agriculture, tourism and some sub-sectors of manufacturing, or it could be provided by an increase in foreign capital inflows which would make it possible for *all* domestic sectors to receive payments greater than their net foreign-exchange earning or saving. Both these mechanisms seem to have been at work in subsidising the manufacturing sector in Kenya over the years 1964–84, though the relative importance of different sources has varied from period to period.

A few illustrative calculations indicate the quantitative significance of this, both for the agricultural sector, the principal alternative source of foreign exchange, and for the balance of payments. Table 7.11 illustrates the relative importance of protection to the manufacturing sector both over the whole 20-year period and for two sub-periods. Here we have adjusted MVA, and the growth of real manufacturing GDP, for the subsidy inherent in the effective protection rates calculated earlier.[11] In Table 7.11 we have calculated for three periods the *increased* subsidy going to the manufacturing sector because of protection and expressed it as a share of two other magnitudes: the increase in agricultural GDP over the same period and the increase in real imports. Despite the fact that the manufacturing sector makes up only about 13% of total GDP, its impact on other tradable goods-producing

Table 7.11 *The importance of protection to manufacturing*

	1970–80	1970–84	1964–84
	Increase over the period in (Km. in constant prices)		
1. Manufacturing real GDP at domestic prices	109.0	142.0	178.0
2. Manufacturing real GDP at world prices	25.1	49.8	72.9
3. Estimated subsidy to manufacturing GDP[a] (1 minus 2)	83.9	92.2	105.1
4. Agricultural real GDP at domestic prices	207.0	278.0	376.0
5. Real imports at domestic prices	350.0	230.0	349.0
		percentage	
6. Subsidy to manufacturing GDP as % of agricultural GDP (3 divided by 4)	40.5	33.2	28.0
7. Subsidy to manufacturing GDP as % of real imports (3 divided by 5)	24.0	40.1	30.5

[a] Effective protection as a share of MVA was taken as 32% in 1970, based on Phelps and Wasow (1972), and as 51% in 1984, based on World Bank (1987a). The interpolated rate for 1980 was estimated at 45% of MVA.

sectors and on the balance of payments is extremely large. For example, over the whole period of the study, the increasing subsidy required by the manufacturing sector was equivalent to 28% of the total increase in agricultural GDP, and to more than 30% of the increase in imports. Expressed in a different fashion, in order to provide the increasing subsidy to manufacturing required by the patterns of growth and protection, *either* 28% of agriculture's increased GDP had to be diverted to subsidising industry *or* new capital inflows would have had to finance 30% of the increased imports over the period, or some combination of these two phenomena would have to have taken place.

In the 1970–84 period, after protection started growing most rapidly, the increased subsidy required by manufacturing was nearly a third of the increased agricultural GDP, and over 40% of the increased imports. Unless agriculture could be increasingly 'taxed' to subsidise manufacturing industry, the balance of payments would be bound to deteriorate, as the real import saving of import substitution in manufacturing was *considerably* less than the apparent import substitution.

What these calculations suggest is that a substantial share of the macroeconomic deterioration of Kenya's economy in the late 1970s and early 1980s is directly attributable to the nature of its manufacturing growth. So long as the agricultural sector both increased rapidly in value added and could be 'taxed' to provide the necessary subsidies to industry at an increasing rate, it was possible for manufacturing to grow without having an adverse effect on the balance of payments. The most obvious period was during the coffee boom of the late 1970s. However, as the coffee boom collapsed, the growth of the manufacturing sector became dependent on subsidies from another source: capital inflow from abroad.

The intimate connection between the incentive structure facing manufacturing industry, as a major factor in the production and use of tradable goods, and the macroeconomic performance of the economy, seems to be vividly illustrated by Kenya's experience. The pattern of manufacturing industry and increasing protection was built up over a period of 20 years in which policies moved in the same general direction. The consequences of those policies necessitated a major stabilisation and structural adjustment programme in the mid-1980s. We turn next to the implications of our findings for macroeconomic and trade policy in the future.

POLICY AND ADJUSTMENT IN MANUFACTURING

In some respects Kenya in the mid-1980s was in a serious mess, while in other respects one could be quite hopeful. The problems, as already described, were a manufacturing sector that had been increasingly protected, using cascaded tariffs and import-licensing restrictions which discouraged the efficient use of resources, and making some investments profitable at domestic prices when there was very little likelihood that they would be competitive at international prices. Import intensity and protection had combined to put serious constraints on growth: increased manufacturing output in most sectors involved increased imported inputs but relatively little in the way of genuine import substitution. On the other hand, Kenya has had experience with exports from a number of industrial sub-sectors; and it is well placed regionally and has good communication links. It would appear that there are considerable opportunities for changing the structure of incentives in ways that would be expansionary in their impact on manufacturing and would improve its efficiency, thus contributing to the growth of output and reducing the drain that manufacturing currently represents on the rest of the economy and on the balance of payments.

The key elements in a package of restructuring the economy, in particular the incentives and constraints facing the manufacturing sector, involve changes in the pricing of foreign exchange, including both tariffs and the exchange rate. The exchange rate for the Kenya shilling has been defended or maintained by a combination of restrictive domestic macroeconomic policies (which have starved the private sector of credit and depressed aggregate demand) and a tariff structure (and import-licensing system) which has depressed the demand for foreign exchange in the aggregate while encouraging its use in producing protected import substitutes.[12]

A restructuring of incentives is needed to encourage exporters of manufactured goods by reducing the heavy penalty they now face. This means a compensated devaluation or continued depreciation of the Kenya shilling *while at the same time reducing tariffs* for almost all categories of imports. An initial depreciation in the currency of 5% , accompanied by a reduction in tariffs by 5% for all tariffs in excess of, say, 20%, would have a substantial effect on relative incentives to produce for the Kenyan and international markets without any discernible effect on inflation from a cost-push viewpoint. Following the adoption of stabilisation measures in 1982, in macroeconomic terms, aggregate demand has been depressed by government budgetary adjustments, which have had a multiplier effect on the economy. Continued budgetary restraint should be matched with some relaxation of monetary policy, particularly to support the private sector; but a compensated devaluation would have an expansionary effect on many sectors and, due to the reduction in tariffs, would improve the profitability both of import substituting and export industries.

The above may sound orthodox; but it is less so than it may at first appear. One real issue is to maintain a high enough level of aggregate demand, focused on increased exports, so that economic displacements that may occur due to tariff restructuring (particularly in industries heavily dependent on differential tariff rates, such as the assembly industries, steel re-rolling, and some sub-sectors of textiles) will be offset by increased output and employment in other sectors (those which now export marginally, are acquainted with regional markets, and are constrained in part by price competitiveness). The proposed restructuring of incentives would increase the share of exports in manufacturing output and GDP accounted for by protection and, therefore, reduce the relative drain on other tradable-producing sectors or on the balance of payments more generally. Measures which increase the profitability of selling in export markets while simultaneously reducing (not eliminating) the protection in the domestic market would provide a carrot-and-stick to manufacturing enterprises. Losses, or just lower margins, in domestic market sales can be offset by increased sales in export markets at the new set of prices that would come from such reforms.

Some sub-sectors responded to the devaluations of the early 1980s in precisely this fashion; indeed, some (such as paper) which broke into export markets were those which many observers had assumed were simply uncompetitive in international markets. The adjusted exchange rate substantially changed the competitive position. The sectors which would be most helped by the kind of exchange rate and tariff reform package suggested are those which are most heavily dependent on domestic inputs; and those which are heavily import-dependent would face increases in the cif prices of imported intermediate goods. This would push incentives further in a direction which would be extremely useful; it would be especially helpful to industries involved in processing agricultural goods for export.

It would be possible to provide *some* of the suggested incentive package without adjusting tariff levels or the exchange rate, if the authorities were willing and able to adopt more complex sets of incentives facing individual enterprises. Foreign-exchange retention schemes, whereby exporters retained for their own use some fraction of any export earnings, would have some of the incentive effects of the kind suggested. Or firms might be required to achieve export targets in order to be eligible for import-licensing allocations (or even to retain the protection that they have from tariffs and import controls on competing imports). While these kinds of alternatives are, in principle, similar in some of their effects to the compensated devaluation approach we would favour, they have the drawbacks of administrative complexity and the potential for abuse in implementation.

The tariff-restructuring exercise might have some adverse revenue consequences for the government in the short run (though in domestic currency terms devaluations would increase the base for all *ad valorem* taxes). If the manufacturing sector is able to respond to the incentive package as quickly as we believe it can, then there would be growth of GDP, of domestic consumption and of imports financed from new export earnings; in all cases, the tax base would increase. Finally, it would be desirable from several standpoints to improve collection and administration of sales tax on domestic firms. It may even be desirable to increase some rates of sales tax further to retain relatively high prices for some consumer goods without providing so much protection for local producers.

Our reading of the difficulties faced suggests that there is great reluctance to make any changes in relative incentives, particularly a reduction in the levels of protection that would result in layoffs or plant closures. The problem is, however, that in the absence of a restructuring, the only way to keep the economy in balance is through relatively restrictive macroeconomic policies. Manufacturing can grow in the present incentive structure *only* when growth of agriculture, or improved international terms of trade, or increased capital inflows, generate the increased subsidy necessary for a protected manufacturing sector to expand. Until, and unless, there is a fundamental shift in the pattern of incentives and protection, there can be no return to the growth rates of the 1960s and 1970s. The size of the manufacturing sector, and the size of the subsidy it now requires on an on-going basis, are simply too large for the rest of the economy to support in macroeconomic terms. If Kenyan manufacturing does not become a more efficient earner or saver of foreign exchange, permitting a reduction in the average rate of effective protection, it will remain a drain on, not a contributor to, the possibilities for economic growth.

Moving to the next phase?[1]
PETER COUGHLIN

Introduction

The gradual deepening of Kenya's industrial base is placing the nation at an historical juncture. The old policies and political-economic alliances are hindering, instead of accelerating, the nation's industrialisation. Though its industrial base has gone much beyond shallow import substitution in many industries, in others, the process has barely begun. Increasingly, Kenya needs to manufacture locally the components and material inputs used in making consumer goods and durables, implements and light machinery for agriculture, and industrial and agricultural chemicals. Cultivating inter-industry linkages and systematically improving local technological capabilities are urgently required. The focus of industrialisation strategy and policy also needs to become increasingly regional. But the growth and evolution of domestic political forces and their internal and external alliances do not correspond well to the new economic base.

As a result, much needed policy changes and industrial restructuring are ignored or postponed. The system buys time. Budget deficits and external debt soar, and external creditors use these weaknesses to push policies – though sometimes appropriate – often opposite to what the new epoch requires. Meanwhile, a significant shift has occurred; the nation has become a massive exporter of capital. These leakages have large macroeconomic implications dampening overall growth. Moreover, the government hesitates to invest in industry; and so do private investors.

Hamstrung by conflicting vested interests, the government's policies toward local manufacturing have been only partly supportive, and their implementation, very inconsistent. The initial import-substitution phase nurtured vested interests – previously proponents but now opponents of deeper industrialisation. These, together with bureaucratic and political allies, would oppose many of the policies now needed to break out of the slow-growth syndrome in manufacturing. The dilemma is acute: How to proceed to the next phase?

An industrial overview

After independence, Kenya had a temporary geo-political advantage. With independence wars in southern Africa, ostensibly socialist regimes in Tanzania, Uganda and Somalia, and, later, civil war in Uganda, Kenya's stable, pro-capitalist government and rapidly growing economy were an oasis for international agencies and multinational corporations (MNCs). Many started regional headquarters in Nairobi. After Zimbabwe became independent, politically stable, and economically healthy, it became a rival centre for MNCs, and some even moved their headquarters from Nairobi to Harare.

The post-independence period saw the Kenyanisation of most positions for low and middle-level technicians and managers as well as an increasing, though still insufficient, number of skilled African technicians and high-level managers. In 1968, 26% of the top-level managers and administrators in manufacturing firms were Kenyans; by 1975, 52% were Kenyans; and by 1982, 59% (Kim, 1985: 23). Many workers have also acquired the habit of industrial discipline. Moreover, Kenyan private and governmental capital investments in manufacturing have grown more rapidly than foreign investments. In 1966, foreigners controlled 60% of the issued capital in large manufacturing firms; by 1976, they only controlled 43.7% (Kaplinsky, 1982: 209–11). The period also witnessed the encouraging appearance of a few large African industrialists – though still far too few.

Though confronting difficulties and growing slowly in the 1980s – on average, by 4.7% a year between 1979 and 1988 – Kenya's manufacturing sector has achieved considerable successes since independence.[13] Since the terms of trade for agriculture were not allowed to deteriorate significantly, farmers have continued to produce and export enough to maintain food independence and earn foreign exchange (Jabara, 1985).[14] This, in turn, allowed the country to import the inputs needed to fuel industrial expansion.

Researchers were wrong when, in recent years, they still simplistically depicted Kenyan industries as pursuing only elemental types of import substitution. For example, Kaplinsky (1982: 198) asserted, 'There is little evidence of any profound change in the economic structure'. While true in some industries, this view ignores numerous significant accomplishments. Whole new industries have developed, e.g., plastics processing, power alcohol, pharmaceuticals, steel rolling and galvanising, electrical cables, welding rods, oil-seeds expelling, paper, vehicle assembly, industrial gases, rubber, ceramics, batteries, refractory bricks, and oil recycling. Others have blossomed from a few small establishments into industries with many employees and a wide range of products (e.g., in textiles and garment manufacturing, food processing, leather tanning, and footwear). Complementarity between industries has increased with considerable forward and backward linkages between suppliers and users in some industries, e.g. textiles, steel, food processing, printing and packaging. Moreover, after initial difficulties, many firms became efficient producers of quality goods. In some industries (textiles, pharmaceuticals, and plastics processing) a dynamism – usually impelled by competition – is noticeable: firms are investing and striving to improve the quality and diversity of their products.

Though the manufacturing sector is growing, 'a major weakness of Kenya's industrial development . . . [is the] extreme paucity of modern small-scale manufacturing establishments' (World Bank, 1987a: 210). Formal firms with up to 49 employees only contributed 17% of MVA in 1972, and 7% in 1980.

> Despite channelling over US$50 m. to this subsector by various development banks (KIE, KCFC, SEFCO, IDB), there has been a net addition of only 100 firms in a decade (World Bank, 1987a: 210).

In 1985, informal manufacturers (small firms with no postal address) had 37,300 workers; all manufacturing firms employed 159,000. Only 15% of all informal enterprises are in manufacturing; most are in commerce and services (Republic of Kenya, 1989b: 164).

Focusing on supply-side constraints, the government has tried to promote small and informal enterprises through providing training, extension services, capital, and infrastructure. Promoting demand for the informal sector's products and services has been ignored. The customers' low income and demand being the biggest constraint on growth of informal economic activities, more efforts are needed to improve the incomes of people who are the informal sector's customers. Policies to redistribute incomes to the poor (e.g., by squeezing the merchants' profit margins by allowing factories to sell directly to retailers and to establish direct factory outlets) or to increase jobs through better choices of process and product technologies would stimulate demand for products and services from informal businesses (Coughlin, 1988a: 295–6; 1988b: 143–68).

Despite some backward integration, Kenya's manufacturing sector has significant over-investment in some industries side-by-side major gaps in others. For example, the country manufactures little machinery, no pharmaceutical active ingredients, and no electronic components; it has an underdeveloped chemical industry, even for non-petroleum-based chemicals; and it has virtually no high-precision metal engineering capabilities. Meanwhile, much redundant investment has poured into pharmaceutical compounding and packaging; steel-sheet galvanising; steel rolling; vehicle assembly; low-precision foundries and mechanical engineering firms; and the manufacture of paints, glass bottles, and steel and polyvinylchloride pipes. Wasted investment is revealed in very low rates of capacity utilisation in some industries (e.g., pharmaceuticals, 21%; transport vehicles, 23%; mechanical engineering, 34%; steel rolling, 22%) though the rates of capacity utilisation were quite high in some other industries, e.g., textiles, 82% in 1986; paper, 91% in 1987 (Coughlin, 1986a: 278; Muraya, 1988).[15]

Excess capacity in different industries developed due to a combination of one or more of the following:

- defensive over-investment by firms squeezed by local monopolists supplying their inputs, e.g., steel rods and cold-rolled coils, and glass bottles (Coughlin, 1985a, 1986b);
- outrageously high effective rates of protection exceeding 100%, e.g., for nails, screws, and steel pipes (Coughlin, 1985a);

- fiscal discrimination against certain exports and some types of import-substitution products, e.g., pumps, refractory bricks, agricultural implements (Coughlin, 1985b; Kerre, 1985; Begumisa, 1982);
- inappropriate products, e.g., corrugated galvanised sheets instead of clay tiles, and tetrahedral cartons instead of plastic sachets for packaging milk as done in Zimbabwe (Coughlin, 1988b: 157–68).
- inability to achieve economies of scale due to the existence of numerous makes and models, e.g., pumps and transport vehicles (Begumisa, 1982; Murage, 1983; Masai, 1986; Obere, 1987);
- inability to escape low-level production traps even when Kenya's market size for specific products had passed the threshold whereby efficient local production became feasible economically, e.g., agricultural implements (Kerre, 1985);
- lack of co-ordination between the government's large development banks and their failure systematically to identify and channel funds to priority sectors (Ikiara 1988: 266–7); and
- near absence of any policy of sectoral preferences by the government, except for fiscal incentives for rural industrialisation.[16]

Several firms collapsed in the late 1980s due to extreme pressures from imports. Thus although the country had a shortage of mill-white sugar in 1986, permits were issued to import both mill-white and canners' quality refined sugar. As a direct result, Kenya's completely new and only sugar refinery – costing KSh 100 m. financed by the World Bank – was shut. Partly as a consequence, its mother company, Miwani Sugar Mills, suffered severe liquidity strains and collapsed in 1988. Similarly, (Henley, 1989: 20):

> notwithstanding the anguished cries of the 1,300 workers laid off by East African Baggage [sic] and Cordage and its sister company Kensack Kenya Limited [which were] unable to sell . . . bags, the Ministry of Commerce continued to license importation of several large consignments of gunny bags on behalf of various well connected individuals.

Local production of screwdrivers and cutlery also ceased due to premature competition from imports; and the local companies producing pencils and ceramics are in serious distress.

As import substitution progressed in the post-independence period, the composition of imports switched. Consumer goods became less important; capital goods, more. Thus in 1965, consumer goods accounted for 20.1% of all retained imports; the average for 1985 and 1986 was 10.8%. Capital goods accounted for 13.8% of all retained imports in 1965, but averaged 25.5% for 1985 and 1986. Though their nature changed, imports of intermediate inputs comprised a steady 57% to 60% of imports throughout this period. But the quantum index of manufactured exports – excluding machinery, equipment, and mineral fuels – declined in the latter part of the 1970s from a peak of 135.2 in 1976 to 110.8 in 1980, 77 in 1985, and 98 in 1987. In 1988, it jumped to 130 – still below its prior level.[17]

These statistics present the essence of the dilemma facing manufacturing in Kenya: manufactured exports are not growing quickly, and, alarmingly, their prospects are not very good. Industrialised countries have become increasingly protectionist against industrial and processed imports from developing countries (World Bank, 1985: 37–42; 1986: 111–19; 1987b: 133–53). Moreover, 'the advantage of inexpensive labour . . . could even be wiped out by new forms of protectionism in the North, by technological break-throughs or by a combination of both' (UNIDO, 1986: 139). Though Kenya must try to penetrate these markets more, it should not hinge its industrialisation strategy on sharp and sustained expansion of manufactured exports to the North. Thus increasingly, foreign exchange earned by other sectors – mainly agriculture and tourism – must be used to fuel industrial growth, unless the rate of import substitution accelerates or regional markets open further.

Though the exact proportions vary according to the period analysed, past industrial growth was largely driven by increases in domestic demand and import substitution, not by industrial exports.[18] For motivation, manufacturers got large income transfers from other sectors. Sharpley and Lewis (1988: 75) estimated that between 1970 and 1984,

> after protection [i.e., tariffs and non-tariff barriers] started growing most rapidly, the increased subsidy required by manufacturing was nearly a third of the increased agricultural GDP, and over 40% of the increased imports.

These subsidies are so large that it is difficult to conceive that their rate could be increased to spur investments to deepen the industrial base. Rather than increasing the overall subsidies going to manufacturing, the problem is how to shift the incentives backward to the producers of raw materials and components.[19]

As Kenya's market size increased, new possibilities for import substitution appeared. Preliminary evidence suggests, moreover, that if the market were consolidated to capture economies of scale – not cut up by numerous makes, models and producers – many products could be made in Kenya efficiently. For example the markets for pumps, cutlery, handtools, polyvinylchloride, polyethylene, flat glass, precision grey iron castings, many agricultural implements, and some pharmaceutical active ingredients have each passed the minimum size justifying one, efficient small plant (Begumisa, 1982; Coughlin, 1986b; GOSTOL, 1983; Kerre, 1985; Owino, 1985; Mwangi, 1984). The country could also switch from using mostly corrugated galvanized steel roofing (*mabati*) – requiring much foreign exchange and creating few jobs – to clay tiles, thereby creating many jobs in small decentralised factories using little foreign exchange (Coughlin, 1985c and 1988: 149–57).[20]

Kenya's mercantile attitude toward trade with nearby African states has hampered the expansion of trade with them. Together with ideological and political differences, Kenya's selling much and buying little so strained the East African Community that it collapsed in the mid 1970s. Even today, largely due to its stronger economy, Kenya only imports one shilling of merchandise from countries in the Preferential Trade Agreement (PTA) for every five shillings of goods it exports to them (Republic of Kenya, 1988a: 87). This ratio was worse; in 1984, it was nearly 1:8. This imbalance causes Kenya's neighbours to be disillusioned about the benefits from trade within the PTA. As a result, they are slow to remove bureaucratic and policy impediments to regional trade. For example, at least as of mid 1988, Tanzania did not pay export compensation for transactions denominated in the PTA unit of account though, as agreed, these should be netted out or paid in foreign exchange every two months.

Besides forming the PTA, the Kenya Government has done little to encourage imports from PTA countries. For example, though Zimbabwe manufactures railway bogeys – everything but the bearings – Kenya has never ordered any.[21] Also, though the Kenya textile industry often suffers from severe shortages of cotton, the Cotton and Lint Seed Board has been reluctant to import from Tanzania. Smugglers import Tanzanian cotton but in very insufficient quantities. As a result, Kenyan factories have increasingly shifted to weaving polyester blends that ultimately rely on imported polyester chips (Coughlin, 1986a). Or again, despite a severe shortage of oil seeds in Kenya and a surfeit in Tanzania in 1985, little was traded due to foreign-exchange and import-licence restrictions on both sides. Tanzania also manufactures electrical motors, small generators, and cutlery; Kenya does not. Still, Kenya has not tried to divert that trade to its neighbour.

Kenya does not have a speedy way to approve near-zero foreign-exchange transactions for private countertrade within the region or elsewhere. Nor has the formation of two-way trading houses been encouraged. Consequently, Kenya loses many opportunities to export due to its unwillingness to reciprocate by making the procedures for importing from its neighbours easier (Mwau and Coughlin, 1986).

Problems of external trade

Though officially the net inflow of investment minus the repatriation of investment income was only marginally negative between 1968 and 1979 (averaging -0.3% of GDP between 1968 and 1974, and -0.5% between 1975 and 1979), a rapid fall occurred afterwards. Kenya officially became a large net exporter of capital and investment income.[22] Net long-term capital inflows plummeted, and outflows of international investment income soared. The combined net averaged -3.3% of GDP between 1980 and 1988, and reached a shocking -4.8% in 1988 (Table 7.12). Even net capital inflows turned negative in 1988!

Extensive evidence, though anecdotal or for specific industries, suggests that much money also escapes the country through transfer pricing on imports and exports. In the industries studied, transfer pricing ranged from 5% to 25% of fob prices. For example, Kaplinsky (1978: 1) found that steel imports were overinvoiced by 5.9%, and pineapple exports were underinvoiced by 25%, wattle by 17%, and tea by about 3%. For tea, a major Kenyan export, Kaplinsky (1978: 12) found:

> Comparing identical leaf cuttings and tea grades, it appears that relative to the price obtained for Kenya Tea Development Authority estate tea:
> * Brooke Bond plantations' prices were 2.3% lower.
> * African Highland Produce prices were 2.7% lower.
> * Eastern Products tea prices were 5.2% lower.

Table 7.12 *Private long-term capital movements and international investment income flows, 1980–87 (K£m.)*

	1980[a]	1981[b]	1982[b]	1983[b]	1984[b]	1985[c]	1986[d]	1987[d]	1988[d]
A. Private long-term capital movements									
Inflows		22.0	16.2	14.9	12.1	19.0	29.3	35.3	− 15.3
Outflows		20.7	22.1	18.5	5.3	15.2	4.0	25.3	2.0
Net	55.4	1.3	− 5.9	− 3.6	6.8	3.8	25.2	10.0	− 17.3
B. International investment income									
Inflows		16.9	20.0	24.5	32.7	35.5	29.8	30.6	7.0
Outflows		106.4	109.7	139.9	171.8	204.2	222.9	262.8	304.6
Net	75.5	81.5	89.7	115.4	139.1	168.8	193.0	232.3	297.6
C. Total (A–B)	− 20.1	− 80.2	− 95.6	− 119.0	− 132.3	− 165.0	− 168.2	− 222.3	− 314.9
D. Total net outflows (C) as percent of GDP at factor prices	0.9	3.1	3.2	3.6	3.5	3.8	3.3	3.9	4.8
E. Mid-year average US$/K£ exch. rate	2.685	2.240	1.739	1.508	1.353	1.247	1.238	1.229	1.139
F. US dollar equivalent (C × E)	− 54.0	− 179.6	− 166.2	− 179.5	− 179.0	− 205.8	− 208.2	− 273.2	− 358.7

Sources: [a] Republic of Kenya (1984a); [b] Republic of Kenya (1987); [c] Republic of Kenya (1988); [d] Republic of Kenya (1989a).

Note: Totals may not add exactly due to rounding.

My own more recent research of company invoices corroborated Kaplinsky's conclusion about steel. A major firm in Kenya was importing hot-rolled steel coils invoiced for US$315 tonnes fob from Japan while these were being sold for US$272/t to the United States and, discriminatorily, for US$227 tonnes if sold to South-East Asia (*Metal Bulletin*, 19 December 1985). The cif cost of a different size and quality of hot-rolled coils imported by five companies between 1 October and 19 November 1985 varied 20.1% between the most and least expensive. There were even significant variations – between 7.5 and 15.4% – in fob prices from the same country. Though suspecting transfer pricing, at minimum, one may conclude that the companies were not shopping around for the cheapest sources. Either way, the cost is high. A consistent failure to get fully competitive prices would cost Kenya more than US$2 m. on imports of roughly 100,000 tonnes a year of steel plate and coils.

The overpricing ratio for MNC pharmaceutical subsidiaries in Kenya was 102% and for local companies, 40% (Owino, 1985). Overpricing of individual purchases ranged between 10 and 60% for polyester chips used to make yarn (Coughlin, 1986). In plastics processing, one production manager for a MNC subsidiary estimated that transfer pricing in that industry probably averaged about 25% and could not be less than 15%. Reportedly, the suppliers of plastic pellets and polyvinylchloride compounds would 'give you quantity discounts and also transfer them to your account outside . . . Even if you don't ask, the supplier will tell you how to do it'.[23]

Earlier, the ILO (1972: 454–5) found considerable evidence of transfer pricing and concluded:

> From our discussions in Kenya with officials and industrialists we think that an overinvoicing ratio of 5% is low. In other words, overinvoicing of intermediate goods probably more than doubles the real outflow of surplus from the manufacturing sector as compared with the outflow of profits and dividends.

This conclusion is most likely still valid. Kenya still has no local apparatus to screen the prices of even its high-value, fairly homogeneous imports. Moreover, Ramirez-Rojas (1986: 36) reported that foreign bank deposits by Kenyan residents and state enterprises equalled US$830 m. in 1984 largely reflecting the desire of many to get money out of the country in violation of Kenyan law.

Assuming that transfer pricing averaged at least 5% on imports and exports, then an additional US$130 m. would be flowing out annually; if 10%, then double that. Thus, the net capital and income flowing out of Kenya due to official plus illegal transfers could easily have been between US$500 m. and US$650 m. in 1988, i.e., 6.7% to 8.7% of the nation's GDP. On top of this, the external debt service payments equalled 4.3% of the GDP in 1988. These leakages have serious macroeconomic implications. They restrain economic growth and both reflect and reinforce the reluctance of foreign companies to invest in Kenya.

MNCs and the role of the retreating state

The World Bank has been urging the government to privatise commercial parastatals, whether profitable or not, and to slash the levels of protection for manufacturing, instead of switching the emphasis toward cultivating better domestic and regional inter-industry linkages. The *Development Plan 1989–1993*, published in May 1989, fully endorsed this thrust (Republic of Kenya, 1989: 145-9). The government promised to lower tariffs and 'drastically reduce its direct involvement in industrial and commercial activities', committing itself 'to the policy of broad-based liberalisation' (ibid.: 146, 148 and 153). But the strategic decision largely to refrain from investing in joint ventures – even with reputable firms – overlooks that since the early 1970s, MNCs worldwide have sought government participation in their investments in developing countries.

Perceiving the government's reluctance to invest in new joint ventures, its inability to provide strong incentives for investment in new industrial branches, and the improbability that traditional exports will propel fast growth in domestic demand – hitherto a prime motive for industrial growth – MNCs have adopted a wait-and-see attitude toward investment in Kenya (Vaitsos 1989). The 1982 attempted coup and consequent disruptions severely shook the confidence of MNCs, Kenya Asians, and other investors and motivated more capital flight as revealed by the increased gap between official and black-market exchange rates.[24] Policy turn-arounds – such as the abrupt suspension of export compensation for three months in 1983, the hasty and disruptive appearance and disappearance of the five-day week in 1986, and the still ill-defined dictum of April 1989 that manufacturers must use licensed wholesalers (apparently even if none had been used before) – also cause investors to be uncertain about the stability of the policy environment.[25] By January 1989, the *Africa Research Bulletin* (31 January 1989, p. 9382) reported:

> US banks now regard Kenya as a high-risk country where investments must yield immediate returns. Kenya still attracts UK interests, but British investors have been liquidating some of their investments and are now looking towards the larger market in Tanzania.

Various MNCs have withdrawn or sold portions of their investments in recent years, e.g., Firestone, Barclays Bank, Bank of America, First National Bank of Chicago, American Life Insurance Co., MacKenzie Dalgety, Leyland. Concomitantly, foreign-equity inflows increasingly favour services, not industry (Table 7.13). Apparently, MNCs can no longer be relied upon as prime movers for industrialisation in Kenya. They will follow, not lead the pace of the domestic economy (Vaitsos, 1989).

In line with the World Bank's advocacy of a reduced role for the state, the government declared in 1985 that investments of *more* than KSh 5 m. would *not* require approval by the then Ministry of Commerce and Industry. This was done to remove some of the obstacles to investment in Kenya and to eliminate the associated corruption. But the government thereby forsook one of its most potent tools for steering investment from low into high-priority industries (Coughlin, 1988a: 290).

Reliance upon broad macroeconomic instruments and changes in the level and structure of tariffs may be insufficient precisely during the epoch when a developing country's market is

Table 7.13 *Annual average foreign equity inflows (current US$m.)*

Receiving sector	1974-8	1979-84	1984-7
Services	3.19	15.69	27.66
Manufacturing	44.89	39.88	28.34
Total	48.08	55.57	55.00

Source: Central Bank of Kenya as reported by Vaitsos, 1989:6.

gradually becoming large enough to enable one or two firms to achieve economies of scale in producing a previously imported item. For example, Kerre (1985) revealed that local firms could produce three types of agricultural implements at less than the cost of imported implements *if* the firms supplied the entire Kenyan market. Their long-term average costs at that higher output would be less than the costs of imports. But the firms have been unwilling to embark on an aggressive low-price strategy to secure that market. Hence, they continue to produce at low levels of output. Indeed, the largest local manufacturer, Ideal Casements, collapsed in early 1988. Being small by international standards, these firms are risk-adverse. They cannot endure losses for several years in order to capture the local market before realising profits. This presents a dilemma: How to escape from the low-level production trap?

The government needs to be able to recognise the potential of local manufacturers and be ready to help them to capture the local market. But if government merely uses high tariffs to achieve this, it runs the risk of encouraging the inefficient chaos of many producers, makes and models in a small market. The inability to fine-tune tariffs to encourage just one or two producers for an item whose local demand has only recently passed the threshold justifying efficient local production points to the critical role of investment licensing as a supplement to tariff policy. Industrial licensing is most useful for industries with large economies of scale (e.g., glass, steel, certain chemicals) or where quality control and improved efficiency in repair services and spare-parts distribution are significant, especially if the products are standardised and the spare parts interchangeable. Licensing is not needed for most industries, e.g., furniture, printing, food processing, mechanical engineering.

Though the planning machinery is still in place, in practice the government has all but abandoned industry-specific planning within the manufacturing sector. For example, the 1984–1988 Plan promised to set up the following factories during the plan period: a paper mill based on bamboo, a pulp mill, a second tyre plant, a sheet-glass factory, a tinning plant, a hot-strip steel rolling mill, and a phosphate and ammonium-nitrate fertiliser plant (Republic of Kenya, 1989b: 202–4). *Not one was implemented*! The current 1989–93 Plan gave up promising specific projects; it merely states, 'the government will take firm measures in the form of various incentives designed to promote the development of core industries' such as telecommunications, information processing, capital goods (specifically machine tools and dies), and pharmaceutical, chemical, bio-technical, and other local-resource-based industries (ibid.: 162–3). The absence of real industry-specific planning was glaringly evidenced in the Plan's projection of manufacturing output and its 10 sub-sectors. Each sub-sector was mechanically projected to grow by 38.2% between 1987 and 1993.

The central government's retreat to even less involvement in productive activity and its increasing reluctance to adopt industry-specific policies is the opposite of what is required in the present epoch. For example, all the reasons listed above for the appearance of massive excess capacity in many industries show the need for considerable state intervention and industry-specific planning in the future.

In addition, the decentralisation of most of the Central Tender Board's responsibilities to the 41 districts (including Nairobi) spoiled the possibility of using centralised purchasing deliberately to promote local manufacturing for many products, though it may help promote small rural industries. So far, however, most of these local tenders go to middlemen or to well established enterprises, not to informal enterprises.

Previously, when offering a bid to the Central Tender Board, local manufacturers often had a competitive edge over imports since they could supply goods in bulk at an ex-factory price without trade mark-ups. Now they have to sell their products in small lots to diverse governmental organs at a higher price, including trade and transport margins. Moreover, imported goods often have an advantage since the small lots purchased by district governments do not allow local firms to benefit from economies of scale. Inadvertently the policy promotes both corruption and increased import dependence.

A limited derogation of purchasing power for items that could truly be produced in the districts, not just supplied by middlemen, would have been better (Ikiara, 1988: 239–40; Coughlin, 1988a: 291–2). The government could use its purchasing power systematically to encourage local industries to develop new products and technological abilities. Instead, government all but abandoned yet another major tool for promoting industrialisation: procurement policy.

The role of the banks

If the state continues to retreat and MNCs are reluctant to invest in Kenya, from where will the impetus for industrialisation come? In Germany and Russia last century, 'the role of the retreating government was taken over by the banks' (Gerschenkron, 1962: 22). But when examining the three largest development finance banks in Kenya, Ikiara (1988a: 227) concluded that they shared the following investment patterns:

- large investment in low-priority industries or low-priority enterprises with a particular industry;
- lack of clear priority in their investment programmes; and
- over-investment in industries already suffering from excess capacity, e.g., in the textile industry.

The development banks have lacked an industrialisation strategy. They have usually waited passively for proposals to be brought to them for consideration. Their investments have not increasingly targeted investment for production of intermediate goods or capital equipment. 'Perhaps the most striking features of the government's joint-venture equity portfolio [largely held by development banks] are its heterogeneity and the absence of disinvestment' (Henley, 1989: 25). The commercial banks are not dynamic proponents of industrialisation either. Mostly, they lend manufacturers short-term working capital – e.g., for purchases of imported inputs – not long-term money for major capital investments. Evidently, the banks are just not ready to become aggressive financiers organising and pushing the pace of industrialisation in Kenya.

Similar to Gerschenkron's (1962: 19–20) observation that disastrously low business morals made banks in nineteenth century Russia refrain from long-term lending and, hence, increased the importance of the state's role, Henley (1989: 30) observes:

> Where the possibilities of enforcement of rights is dependent on an uncertain and slow judicial process, bonds of personal loyalty and obligation may seem to offer a more effective guarantee of performance. They flourish where the outcomes of the formal system are less acceptable or unpredictable. In short, opaque policies and administrative procedures nurture clientelism. For new entrants, the undocumented and constantly changing complexities of the informal system for 'getting things done' provide substantial barriers to entry. It takes time, persistence and considerable resources to learn survival techniques.

This may yield some insight into the commercial banks' aversion to long-term lending for manufacturing in Kenya. If so, changes in moral standards and the predictability of the just application of law may seriously retard investment and, hence, the nation's industrialisation. Yet for this to explain, even partly, the increasing foreign-exchange outflows and decreasing *foreign* investment in Kenya, it must be shown that the practices cited are worsening or, due to changing circumstances, their effects are assessed more adversely than before by multinational investors. Though this is a plausible hypothesis, the evidence has not been systematically examined to validate it. Still, the thesis merits serious consideration and further research.

The political basis of economic policy

The social-economic basis of the Kenyan state partly explains its narrow, short-term and often inconsistently supportive approach to industrialisation: the bulk of the nation's politicians and senior bureaucrats do not have major economic interests in manufacturing. Rather, their investments are in farming, transport, services, small trading, and real estate. Some also get very rich through access to import licences. Their short-term interests favour keeping imports cheap, not fostering local manufacturing industries.

Unlike many developing countries, Kenya does not have a political party or group within a party closely allied with the nation's manufacturers. Kenyan manufacturing is mostly controlled by parastatals, MNCs, and Kenyans of Asian origin. Due to the nation's racist colonial history, Kenyans of Asian origin maintain a low profile politically. Thus, their influence on government policy and their relationships with politicians are highly problematic.

Since independence, Asians have been on the periphery of Kenya's political system except as sponsors of certain politicians as their power brokers within the system. Such power brokerage, however, frequently involves bypassing established rules and getting decisions made as favours and not as official procedures. Hence, Asian businessmen who cannot do this, and who are undercut by their fellow Asians or by MNCs, cannot get their business[es] going. The result has been that Kenyan compradors in power position have been successful brokers for MNC subsidiaries and have left enterprising Asians cooling their feet in the corridors of power while their factories lie idle (Anyang' Nyong'o, 1988: 41).

Though this is true for many manufacturers, a few are very well connected. Moreover, the Kenya Association of Manufacturers, the Kenya Federation of Employers, and the Kenya Chamber of Commerce are lobby groups with significant, though not always prevailing, influence. Their interests and hence their efforts often conflict. Then their organisations become immobilised, and rival industrialists bombard the government, lobbying and sending memoranda.[26] Since few local industrialists have big multiple investments in diverse industries, the medley of short-term interests dominate, thwarting agreement about sectoral issues and the attainment of a dynamic, comprehensive long-term perspective stressing the need to develop backward linkages.[27]

This is an historical problem: since the domestic large industrial bourgeoisie hardly exists and is mostly non-African, it cannot be a *dominant* political force. Hence, assorted pressures from an array of influential groups – merchants, farmers, industrialists, bureaucrats, and foreign interests – work upon the government, each with some success. This and the partial dichotomy between the owners of manufacturing enterprises and the political circles largely explain why it has been so difficult for the government to delineate and consistently implement a strategy to greatly accelerate development of a national industrial base with strong inter-industry linkages.

The current recipients of industrial subsidies – due to high tariffs, bans on competitive imports, and low tariffs on imported inputs – would, moreover, oppose shifting the subsidies backward to favour local production of the inputs they now import. Nurtured by two and a half decades of policies favouring import-substitution industries – often monopolies – highly dependent upon imported inputs, a veritable army of lobbyists and wheeler-dealers stalk the halls and backrooms of political and bureaucratic power. Though individually quite rational, their crisscrossing interests are extremely contradictory from the viewpoint of industrialisation. Sometimes, even the same manufacturer ardently advocates stronger protection for his industry while urgently soliciting import licences and reduced protection for his inputs even if these can be produced locally.

Though not marshalled, cumulatively these industrial lobbyists together with the more consistently motivated merchandise-import houses are a large political force who, shortsightedly, often oppose deeper industrialisation and the medium-term sacrifices required to build a regional basis for industrialisation. Thus the very way Kenya promoted import substitution – with little encouragement for the manufacture of producer goods and capital equipment – bred powerful political forces later opposing deeper industrialisation.

Buying time, the government continues borrowing at home and abroad, even to finance part of its *recurrent* budget.[28]

With an external debt of about US$4 bn and foreign-exchange reserves to cover only 40 days' imports, Kenya is plagued with a debt-service ratio of between 36% to 39% . . . Businessmen are wary of what the future may hold (*Africa Research Bulletin*, 31 January 1989: 9382).

If the pace of borrowing continues, the result is predictable: increasingly severe austerity measures dictated by the World Bank and International Monetary Fund. These medium-term prospects scare investors.

Conclusions

If Kenya fails to adopt new strategy and policies, it will be locked into sluggish growth dependent primarily upon the slow-growing and highly volatile demand for its traditional exports: coffee, tea, and pineapples. MNCs and the markets of the North cannot be relied upon as the *main* engines for industrialisation. The MNCs are hesitant about investing in Kenya, and undue export optimism is no substitute for an industrialisation strategy.

Despite opposition, tariff incentives must be shifted backward to encourage local production of components and material inputs and the creation and development of industries able to radiate technological improvements throughout manufacturing. Industry-specific policies and planning are needed to channel investment to fill the big gaps in Kenya's industrial structure and to steer investment away from low-priority industries. But government, disillusioned by several large failures in manufacturing and pressured by the World Bank, is retreating from direct involvement in manufacturing and relying increasingly upon macroeconomic policies alone.

Kenya needs to export more, but most of its industrial exports are within Africa. Yet to promote exports within the region, Kenya must reject its mercantile approach toward regional trade. To sell more, it must buy more from the PTA states and institutionalise policies promoting imports from them e.g., by setting up two-way trading houses and a swift 'green channel' for private and state-arranged countertrade. Regional specialisation needs to be reassessed in detail and promoted for some industries. This requires creating confidence in the long-run benefits from developing an interdependent regional market and economic system, and the willingness to make short-term sacrifices to persuade sceptical neighbours to drop impediments to increased integration and trade.

Vision and a strong political will are required to overcome the short-term interests of merchants and even some industrialists who, together with their bureaucratic and political allies, oppose specific measures to deepen the industrial base and promote regional integration. Unless this happens, the nation will plod ahead, only gradually increasing its industrial base though population pressures on the land become extreme. And slowly, social and political pressures will accumulate for a démarche.

Notes

1. The first part of this chapter was written by Stephen Lewis and Jennifer Sharpley, the second part by Peter Coughlin. The respective authors are not responsible for nor necessarily subscribe to the views of the parts they did not themselves write.
2. For a fuller discussion of the first four parts of this chapter see Lewis and Sharpley (1988).
3. We should point out that there are a variety of statistical problems connected with assessing the performance of the manufacturing sector, some of which are noted in later sections. The quantity index of manufacturing, for example, shows more rapid rates of increase than does the growth of real GDP in the national accounts, largely, we believe, due to differences in coverage of the two measures. In our detailed analysis of manufacturing value added we have used data from the *Statistical Abstract* on the Gross Product of 'All Firms and Establishments, 1972–84' and 'Large Scale Firms and Establishments – Manufacturing and Repairs 1964–84'. For the years 1972–84 in which the two series overlap, the gross product of Large Scale Firms was expressed as a share of the gross product of All Firms at the sub-sector level, and the ratios were found to be extremely stable prior to 1982. These ratios were averaged for the period 1972–82 for each sub-sector and the average used to estimate the gross product of All Firms in the years 1962–71. Price deflators are not available for individual sub-sectors of manufacturing and so we used the deflator for manufacturing GDP. In fact, deflating the gross product of All Firms by the GDP deflator for the manufacturing sector produced higher real growth rates in the period since 1972 than those reported in the national accounts for manufacturing GDP.
4. There are, however, a number of problems of classification, particularly regarding crude and refined petroleum in 1979 and 1980.
5. With a large number of different industries and activities contained in any one industrial sub-sector, changes in the ratio of value added to gross output might also be a reflection of the changing relative importance of different industries with different value added ratios within the industrial group.
6. Using the annual adjustments that we made to import duty collection for changes in duty rates, one can calculate the 'buoyancy' and the 'elasticity' of import duty revenue with respect to imports as a base. The buoyancy (percentage change in revenue divided by percentage change in base) of tariffs was 0.95, giving the impression that imports were a relatively elastic source of tax revenue. However, using the adjusted revenue figures, i.e., removing the effect of increases in the rates each year, produces an elasticity of only 0.32 over the whole period. The apparent buoyancy of import taxes as a source of revenue was due, in the main, to increases in tax rates, not to the automatic elasticity of the system.

7. If T = the effective rate of protection expressed as the percent by which domestic value added exceeds value added at world prices, and U = the percentage of value added at world prices that is accounted for by protection, then U = T/T + 1. E.g., an industry which has an effective rate of protection T = 100% is an industry in which 50% of its value added is accounted for by protection (U = 1.0/ (1.0+1) = 0.50.

More formally, if V_i is value added in industry, i, O_i is gross output at market prices, O_{ji} is the intermediate delivery from industry j to industry i, all at domestic prices, then:

$$V_i = O_i - \Sigma O_{ji}$$

in the absence of indirect taxes on output. On the assumption that tariffs and other indirect taxes are the only difference between world and domestic prices, one could compute value added at world prices by deflating all domestic flows by the appropriate tariff rate applicable to that good. If $\hat{V}_i$ is value added at 'world prices' and t_i and t_j are the nominal tariffs on products of industries i and j respectively, then:

$$\hat{V} = \frac{O_i}{1 + t_i} - \sum_j \frac{O_{ji}}{1 + t_j}$$

If we defined T_i as the effective rate of protection, or the protection to value added in industry i, or the percentage by which actual value added exceeds that which would hold under 'free trade', then:

$$V_i = (1 + T_i) V_i$$

$$T_i = \frac{V_i}{\hat{V}_i} - 1$$

U_i is defined as the percentage of actual value added that is 'due to' the tariff protection, or

$$U_i = \frac{V_i - \hat{V}_i}{V_i} = 1 - \frac{\hat{V}_i}{V_i}$$

The relationship between the two measures is:

$$U_i = \frac{T_i}{T_i + 1}$$

$$T_i = \frac{U_i}{1 - U_i}$$

(See Lewis, 1971: 35).

8. Other explanations are possible but they do not fit the facts of Kenya's experience. For example, the most policy-neutral explanation is that, as industrial growth proceeds, industries become more interdependent (in effect, filling in the cells of an input-output matrix); any activity measured over a period of time shows a systematic change in the degree of specialisation; more and more specialisation within the sub-sectors of an activity raises the ratio of gross output, and of intermediate purchases, to value added in the industry. A proper definition of activities, and an appropriate level of disaggregation, would eliminate the apparent fall in the value added ratio. There is no policy implication from the observed facts.

Another explanation consistent with a falling ratio of value added to gross output would be that the level of protection to each activity was falling, either because of rising tariffs on inputs which raise intermediate purchases or falling prices of output which lower gross output at domestic prices (in each case relative to value added). The declining ratios of value added to gross output would be a promising development, a sign of rising productivity and lower costs (or reduced excess profits) from protection and an indication that the growth of 'real' output in the economy was greater than the measured growth. Unfortunately, in Kenya's case protection rates have been consistently rising, so this explanation is not plausible.

9. We note that the share of exports in output is sufficiently small for virtually all industry groups except petroleum refining for the effect of rising intermediate goods tariffs in squeezing value added margins in export markets not to have a quantitatively significant effect on the overall ratios of value added to output.

10. The only exception would be if the country faces less than elastic supply of imports or demand for exports, in which case there might be some sharing of the cost of protection to a domestic sector between other domestic producers and foreign suppliers through a change in the external terms of trade. This is highly unlikely in Kenya's case.

11. We have had to interpolate a rate of effective protection for 1980, which we have estimated at 45% of value added in manufacturing. This rate is based on a combination of (i) the rise in import duty rates as indicated in annual budget speeches, and (ii) the increased stringency of import licensing for protection purposes during the entire period after 1971. We note, however, that the basic mechanism

and message of this set of calculations is unaffected by the use of 1980 figures, though we do believe that some aspects of the mechanism we are illustrating can be usefully shown by including the 1980 figures.

12. Note that this drain is *not* a simple calculation of foreign exchange used or foreign exchange earned, which has sometimes been used to express the net foreign-exchange position of various sectors. The drain comes because domestic value added, or factor payments, in import-substituting industries greatly exceed the real net foreign-exchange saving in those activities, and the difference must be made up either by another tradable-producing sector (agriculture or tourism) or by a deterioration in the current account of the balance of payments.

13. Parts of this section are adapted from Coughlin (1988a: 276–7).

14. Jabara (1985) estimated that the real income index for smallholders in Kenya increased from 133.5 during 1975–6 to 204.2 during 1982–3. Thereafter, the agricultural terms-of-trade index slowly declined from 100.0 in 1982 to 98.9 in 1988:

Price and terms of trade indices for agriculture 1982–8

	1982	1983	1984	1985	1986	1987	1988
Agric. output prices	100.0	113.6	130.0	136.8	149.0	150.3	168.7
Prices paid:							
Purchased inputs	100.0	104.2	125.1	120.7	123.2	129.6	145.5
Consumer goods purchased in areas	100.0	113.8	134.0	154.8	159.9	167.8	178.6
Weighted average of prices paid	100.0	111.4	131.8	146.3	150.7	158.8	170.5
Agric. terms of trade	100.0	102.0	98.6	93.5	98.9	94.79	98.9

Source: Republic of Kenya (1988 and 1989a).

The dire consequences for industry when agriculture is mismanaged are illustrated in Tanzania. There, real producer prices for all crops fell by 33.4% between 1969/70 and 1979/80 (Skarstein and Wangwe, 1986: 235). Consequently, production, especially for export, fell, thus depriving manufacturing of foreign exchange needed to buy inputs. As Skarstein and Wangwe (1986: 271) argue, 'the decline in marketed agricultural production, especially the production of export crops, is the single most important factor bringing about the grave stagnation of the industrial sector since the mid 1970s'.

15. The World Bank (1987a: vol. 2, 49) estimated that the manufacturing firms it surveyed used 79% of their installed capacity. Nowhere, however, did the report explain how these figures were derived. Its estimates sharply conflicted with those by the Industrial Research Project (IRP) of the University of Nairobi, obtained from extensive surveys, often of nearly all the firms in an industrial sub-sector, as in the case of steel, textiles, pharmaceuticals, and plastic processing. For each industry, the IRP used the manufacturers' own estimates of the reasonably obtainable maximum physical output (sugar, steel, cement) or production time (as in the case of mechanical engineering)). Highlighting these differences is important as different perceptions about the true rates of capacity usage in Kenyan manufacturing can yield markedly different interpretations about the efficacy of macroeconomic policies affecting investment and the desirability of using stronger tools for planning industrial development and steering investment into priority industries and away from industries with much redundant capacity.

16. For a more detailed discussion of the policy deficiencies, see Coughlin (1988a).

17. Calculated by adjusting earlier official indices to the 1982 base year (Republic of Kenya, 1980, 1984a and 1989a). Though machinery and transport equipment and miscellaneous manufactured exports were excluded, these comprised only 3% of total manufactured exports in 1987. Mineral fuels were excluded for special reasons. Kenya imports all its crude petroleum and refines it for domestic use and sale to foreign ships and airplanes. The refinery does not have a naphtha cracking plant. Thus, a portion of the imported crude petroleum is re-exported for cracking elsewhere. If these exports were subtracted from total manufactured exports, exports of finished petroleum products would equal 13.6% of the remaining manufactured exports.

18. See the sources of growth analysis in the first part of this chapter.

19. Lewis and Sharpley (see p. 240) favour 'a compensated devaluation or continued depreciation of the Kenya shilling *while at the same time reducing tariffs* for almost all categories of imports' in order to 'encourage exporters'. I differ. This would be insufficient to stimulate investment to produce currently imported components and materials locally. The tariffs need to be reduced and be *adjusted internally* to motivate industrial deepening.

20. The World Bank (1987a: vol. 1, 5) argues 'Opportunities for further import substitution are running out except in subsectors in which Kenya is not likely to have a comparative advantage in the near future'. Or again: 'Import substitution possibilities dried up'. (1987a: Vol. 1, 10). Though its report

studied many existing industries in depth, it did not evaluate *even one* potential new industry or product line. Its conclusion corresponds to the predilections of the Bank's team, not to investigative results.

21. By contrast, in 1988, Uganda purchased 600 wagons in a countertrade deal for $25 m. financed by Zimbabwean banks.

22. Though Vaitsos (1989) placed this reversal in the mid-1970s, official data reveal a sharp break with past patterns, starting in 1980.

23. Confidential interview in June 1983. This and other evidence of transfer pricing in the plastics processing industry were also reported in Mwangi (1984: 130).

24. I am grateful to G.K. Ikiara for insights into the influence of local and regional political changes.

25. This sudden pronouncement in April 1989 met stiff, though diplomatic, resistance from the Kenya Association of Manufacturers. If enforced for industries that sell directly to retailers or other factories with no need for a wholesaler, the rule would increase the cost of locally produced items, making them less competitive against imports. The few additional non-productive jobs created in distribution could easily be more than offset by job losses in manufacturing due to increased imports. At present, it is still unclear whether this rule will ever be enforced, and, if so, how.

26. The steel industry with a chain of forward and backward economic linkages was plagued by bitter conflict between purchasers and suppliers throughout the years 1984–7. The government requested the Kenya Association of Manufacturers (KAM) to help reach a solution. Its committee for the steel industry held many meetings in futile search for a modus operandi. 'KAMs leadership knew that an accommodation needed to be worked to be able to support the local manufacturers. But the manufacturers' claims and counterclaims about quality, price, and technical abilities were so vehement and contradictory that the issues were obfuscated. The willingness to seek an agreement was absent and the interests appeared diametrically opposed' (Coughlin, 1985a: 96).

27. In a study of 20 MNC subsidiaries, Gershenberg (1983: 21) reported, 'In no case did we find firms undertaking to assist in the development of local suppliers'. He concluded, 'Subsidiaries of multinationals, while not opposed to utilising local sources, neither seek out local suppliers nor do they contribute to the development of local sourcing' (p. 31). In a survey of the textile industry, Langdon (1981: 50) was yet more emphatic: 'the evidence does suggest that in developing technological capacity, as in employment expansion and linkage initiatives, the record of the private domestic firms is superior' to foreign subsidiaries.

28. The 1981/82 fiscal year was a turning point. Before then the central government's current account always showed a surplus which was transferred to fund development projects. Thereafter it began to run a deficit averaging 2.0% of the nation's GDP and climbing to 3.6% in 1988/89, though borrowing to finance recurrent costs is precarious. External debt has also been climbing; it equalled 13.8% of GDP in 1975, 24.7% in 1980, and 41.5% in 1988.

References and Bibliography

Anyang' Nyong'o, P. (1988), 'The Possibilities and Historical Limitations of Import-substitution Industrialization in Kenya' in Coughlin and Ikiara.

Begumisa, G. (1982), 'Machine Goods and Spare-parts Industries: A case study of the water pumps industry in Kenya', MA research paper, Economics Department, University of Nairobi.

Central Bank of Kenya, *Economic and Financial Review*.

—— *Annual Report*.

Chenery, H. (1960), 'Patterns of Industrial Growth', *American Economic Review*, Vol. 50, September.

—— Robinson, S. and Syrquin, M. (1986), *Industrialization and Growth: a Comparative Study*, Washington DC, Oxford University Press for World Bank.

Coughlin, P. (1985a), 'The Kenyan Steel and Steel-Related Industries: A programme for domestic reliance and export promotion', Monograph, Industrial Research Project, Economics Department, University of Nairobi.

—— (1985b), 'Converting Crisis To Boom for Kenyan Foundries and Metal Engineering Industries: technical possibilities versus political and bureaucratic obstacles', *African Development*, Vol. 10, No. 4. (An earlier version of this article appeared as IDS (Nairobi) Working Paper No. 398, 1983.)

—— (1985c), 'Tile versus Steel Roofing: what's appropriate for Kenya?' Discussion Paper, Industrial Research Project, Economics Department, University of Nairobi.

—— (1986a), 'The Gradual Maturation of an Import-Substitution Industry: the textile industry in Kenya', Report for the World Bank, Nairobi, (mimeo).

—— (1986b), 'Monopoly, Economies of Scale and Excess Capacity in the Kenyan Glass Industry', Discussion Paper, Industrial Research Project, Economics Department, University of Nairobi.

—— (1988a), 'Toward a New Industrialization Strategy in Kenya' in Coughlin and Ikiara.

—— (1988b) 'Development Policy and Inappropriate Product Technology: the Kenyan case' in Coughlin and Ikiara.

—— and Ikiara, G.K. (eds) (1988), *Industrialization in Kenya: in search of a strategy*, Nairobi, Heinemann and London, James Currey.

Fransman M. (ed.) (1982), *Industry and Accumulation in Africa*, London, Heinemann.

Gerschenkron, A. (1979), *Economic Backwardness in Historical Perspective: A Book of Essays*, Cambridge, Mass., Harvard University Press.

Gershenberg, I. (1983), 'Multinational enterprises, the transfer of managerial know-how, technology choice, and employment effects: A case study of Kenya', International Labour Office, Multinational Enterprises Programme, Working Paper No. 28.

GOSTOL (Yugoslav engineering consultants) (1983), 'Feasibility Study for a Precision Grey Iron Foundry in Kenya: preliminary report' Section 1, Report for the Industrial Promotion Department, Kenyan Ministry of Commerce and Industry.

Gulhati, R. and Sekhar, U. (1982), 'Industrial Strategy for Late Starters: the experience of Kenya, Tanzania, and Zambia', *World Development*, Vol. 10, No. 11, November,

Henley, J. (1989), 'The State and Foreign Investor Behaviour in Kenya: capitalism in a mercantilist state', Department of Business Studies, University of Edinburgh, (mimeo).

Ikiara, G.K. (1988), 'The Role of Government Institutions in Kenya's Industrialization' in Coughlin and Ikiara.

ILO (International Labour Organisation) (1972) *Employment, Incomes and Equality: A Strategy for Increasing Productive Employment in Kenya*. Geneva, ILO.

Jabara, C.L. (1985) 'Agricultural Pricing Policy in Kenya', *World Development*, Vol. 13, No. 5, May.

Kaplinsky, R. (1982), 'Capital Accumulation in the Periphery: Kenya' in Fransman.

—— (1978), 'Report on foreign exchange leakages with particular reference to transfer pricing', Vienna, UNIDO (mimeo).

Kerre, H.O. (1985), 'The Manufacture and Importation of Handtools and Cutlery in Kenya', MA Research Paper, Economics Department, University of Nairobi.

Kim, C.H. (1985), 'The Concept and Social Position of 'Managerial Elite' in Contemporary Kenya: with special reference to Africanization', IDS, University of Nairobi, Working Paper No. 431.

King, J.R. (1979), *Stabilization Policy in an African Setting: Kenya 1963-73*, London, Heinemann.

Langdon, S. (1981), 'Industrial dependence and export manufacturing in Kenya', Paper for the International Seminar on Alternative Futures for Africa, Dalhousie University, Halifax, Nova Scotia, May.

Lewis, S.R. (1965), 'Domestic Resources and Fiscal Policy in Pakistan's Second and Third Plans', *Pakistan Development Review*, Autumn.

—— (1969), 'Domestic Saving and Foreign Assistance when Foreign Exchange is Undervalued', *Research Memorandum* No. 34, Centre for Development Economics, Williams College, Mass.

—— (1971), *Economic Policy and Industrial Policy in Pakistan*, London, Allen and Unwin.

—— (1972), 'The Effects of Protection on the Growth Rate and on the Need for External Assistance', *Research Memorandum* No. 49, Centre for Development Economics, Williams College, Mass.

—— and Sharpley J. (1988), *Kenya's Industrialisation 1964-84*, Discussion Paper No. 242, Institute of Development Studies at the University of Sussex.

—— and Soligo R. (1965), 'Growth and Structural Change in Pakistan's Manufacturing Industry, 1954-64', *Pakistan Development Review*, Spring, reprinted as Yale University Economic Growth Centre Paper No. 99, 1967.

Little, T., Scitovsky, T. and Scott, M. (1971), *Industry and Trade in Some Developing Countries: A Comparative Study*, Paris, Oxford University Press and OECD Development Centre.

MacRae, D.S. (1979), 'The Import Licensing System in Kenya', *Journal of Modern African Studies*, Vol. 17, No. 1.

Masai, S.W. (1986) 'Approaches to Promoting an Efficient Transport Vehicles Industry in Kenya', Discussion Paper, Economics Department, University of Nairobi.

Mitra, A.K. (1980) 'Report of the Field Mission in Kenya, Uganda, Tanzania, Zambia and Mauritius for upgrading foundry, forging, heat treatment, machine shop, tool room, and identification of the manufacture of selected agricultural machining capital goods and spareparts', UN, Economic Commission for Africa, Joint ECA/UNIDO Division, Addis Ababa.

Murage, Z. (1983), 'The Vehicle Assembly Industry in Kenya: an economic evaluation', MA Research Paper, Economics Department, University of Nairobi.

Muraya, M.A. (1988), 'The Demand and Supply of Paper in Kenya: an econometric analysis', MA Research Paper, Economics Department, University of Nairobi.

Mwangi, H. (1984), 'The Plastics Processing Industry in Kenya', MA Research Paper, Economics Department, University of Nairobi.

Mwau, G. and Coughlin, P. (1986), 'Industrialization and Government Policy in Kenya: the case of electrical cable manufacturing', Discussion Paper, Industrial Research Project, Economics Department, University of Nairobi.

Obere, J.A. (1987) 'Auto-ancillary Industry in Kenya: the study of the manufacture of leaf springs, exhaust systems, filters, radiators, brake pads, and batteries', MA Research Paper, Economics Department, University of Nairobi.

Owino, P. (1985), 'The Kenyan Pharmaceutical Industry', MA Research Paper, Economics Department, University of Nairobi.

Phelps, M.G. and Wasow, B. (1972), 'Measuring Protection and its Effects on Kenya', *Working Paper* No. 37, Institute for Development Studies, University of Nairobi.

Prebisch, R. (1959) 'Commercial Policy in Underdeveloped Countries', *American Economic Review, Papers and Proceedings*, May.

Ramirez-Rojas, C.L. (1986), 'Monetary Substitution in Developing Countries', *Finance and Develop-ment*, June.

Reimer, R. (1970), 'Effective Rates of Protection in East Africa', *Staff Paper* No. 78, Institute for Development Studies, University of Nairobi.

Republic of Kenya (1975), 'Economic Prospects and Policies', *Sessional Paper* No. 1, Nairobi, Govern-ment Printer.

—— (1980), 'Economic Prospects and Policies', *Sessional Paper* No. 4, Nairobi, Government Printer.

—— (1981), *Statistical Abstract 1980*, Nairobi, Government Printer.

—— (1982), 'Development Prospects and Policies', *Sessional Paper* No. 1, Nairobi, Government Printer.

spsp(1984a), *Statistical Abstract 1984*, Nairobi, Government Printer.

—— (1984b), *Economic Survey 1984*, Nairobi, Government Printer.

—— (1986), 'Economic Management for Renewed Growth', *Sessional Paper* No. 1, Nairobi, Govern-ment Printer.

—— (1987), *Economic Survey 1987*, Nairobi, Government Printer.

—— (1988), *Economic Survey 1988*, Nairobi, Government Printer.

—— (1989a), *Economic Survey 1989*, Nairobi, Government Printer.

—— (1989b), *Development Plan 1989–1993*, Nairobi, Government Printer.

—— *Input/Output Tables for Kenya 1976*, Nairobi, Government Printer.

—— *Financial Statements* from the Fiscal Budget (mimeo).

—— *Budget Speeches* of the Minister of Finance when Presenting the Fiscal Budget, Nairobi, Govern-ment Printer.

—— *Import Licensing Schedules July 1984*, Nairobi, Government Printer.

—— *Customs and Excise Act 1978*, Nairobi, Government Printer.

—— *Customs Tariffs Act 1970*, Nairobi, Government Printer.

—— *Annual Trade Report*, Nairobi, Government Printer.

Shah, A. (1986), 'Elasticity and Buoyancy of the Central Government Taxes 1963/64 to 1976/77', Nairobi, Ministry of Finance (mimeo).

Sharpley, J. (1986), 'Economic Policies and Agricultural Performance: the Case of Kenya', *OECD Development Centre Papers*, Paris.

—— (1988), 'The Import Content of Kenyan Agriculture', *IDS Bulletin*, Vol. 19, No. 2, April.

Skarstein, R. and Wangwe, S. (eds) (1986), *Industrial Development in Tanzania: Some Critical Issues*, Uppsala and Dar es Salaam, Scandinavian Institute of African Studies and Tanzania Publishing House.

United Nations Industrial Development Organisation (UNIDO) (1986), *Industry and Development: Global Report 1986*, Vienna, UNIDO.

Vaitsos, C. (1989), 'The State and Foreign Business Interests in Kenya', University of Athens (mimeo).

Wood, A. (1987), 'Global Trends in Real Exchange Rates 1960–84', World Bank, International Economics Department, *Division Working Paper* No. 1988 1, October.

World Bank (1985), *World Development Report 1985*, Oxford, Oxford University Press.

—— (1986), *World Development Report 1986*, Oxford, Oxford University Press.

—— (1987a), *Kenya: Industrial Sector Policies for Investment and Export Growth*, Washington DC, World Bank.

—— (1987b), *World Development Report 1987*, Oxford, Oxford University Press.

—— (1987c), *Kenya: Industrial Sector Policies for Investment and Export Growth*, (2 volumes) Nairobi, World Bank.

8 Nigeria[1]

CHRISTOPHER STEVENS

Overview

The development of manufacturing in Nigeria has gone through three main phases. The first, up to the oil boom of the early 1970s, involved moderately rapid growth much of which was domestic resource-based and import-substituting. The second phase lasted for roughly a decade from the early 1970s to the early 1980s. Domestic demand increased very rapidly as the revenue from oil spread through the economy. Domestic manufacturing also grew very rapidly, but not as fast as consumption so that imports increased as well. Moreover, domestic manufacturing was based to a substantial degree on imported inputs. Hence, a continuation of this pattern of growth was dependent upon the maintenance of buoyant exports to finance imports and maintain a healthy trade balance. This prerequisite disappeared in the 1980s with the oil slump – the third phase. In this period, manufacturing was hit both by the sharp fall in consumer demand caused by the general austerity and by the drop in supply of imported inputs.

THE GROWTH OF THE ECONOMY AND OF MANUFACTURING

Discussion of manufacturing in Nigeria is seriously impaired as many relevant statistics are suspect. Nonetheless, it may be helpful to cite some aggregate figures to indicate what most would agree are some of the main features and trends. This section is based largely on World Bank data, not because they are considered superior to those from other sources but because they are comprehensive and there are advantages when relating trends in various aggregates to use data from a single source.

In 1966 Nigeria had an estimated current GNP per capita of US$70; two decades later, this had risen to an estimated US$640 (World Bank, 1987). Even in constant prices, GDP doubled over the period (Table 8.1). The main engine of this growth was the development and exploitation of oil and a very favourable movement in Nigeria's terms of trade during the 1970s resulting from the world oil price rise.

Table 8.1 *Selected economic indicators 1966–86*

	1966	1970	1974	1978	1982	1986
Current GDP at factor cost (Nm.)						
Total	3,247	7,013	18,298	33,375	51,125	66,220
Manufacturing	233	313	661	2,378	6,129	5,470
Constant GDP at factor cost (1980 Nm.)						
Total	19,306	26,661	40,260	43,292	42,562	38,119
Manufacturing	724	1,100	1,422	2,619	5,638	4,282
Manufacturing activity (1980 = 100)						
Employment	22.3	44.3	64.5	105.2	114.1	139[a]
Real earnings per employee	102.4	95.5	97.3	87.0	101.5	41.8[a]
Real output per employee	68.6	97.3	73.7	75.2	119.2	59.1[a]

Source: World Bank, *World Tables 1987*.

Note: [a] 1985.

Figure 8.1 *MVA and GDP In Fixed (1980) Naira Million*

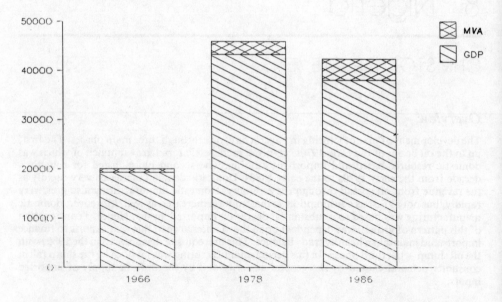

Source: World Bank (1987).

Manufacturing activity increased even faster than GDP. In the two decades, it grew in constant 1980 prices by almost 500%. As a result, its share of constant GDP rose from 4% in 1966 to 11% in 1984 (Table 8.2). The index of manufacturing employment increased more than six-fold during this time. In the 1970–81 period, annual Manufacturing Value Added (MVA) growth was significantly greater in Nigeria (at 6.7%) than in Africa as a whole (2.8%) or in the developing world (4%) (UNIDO, 1988: 5). As a result Nigeria accounted for somewhat under one-fifth of Africa's total MVA in 1982 (UNIDO, 1985: 4).

The growth appears even more impressive if the cut-off date is put back to 1982. This is because most of the gains were made during the 1970s when the oil sector was buoyant. During the 1980s, there has been a sharp reverse consequent upon the decline of oil exports and exacerbated by the dependence of manufacturing on imports. Real output and real earnings per employee slumped by one-half between 1982 and 1985, ending lower than they had been in 1966.

Towards the end of the 1980s, manufacturing accounted for only around one-tenth of GDP (Table 8.2) – although a post-1988 statistical series (still considered unreliable) almost halves these figures. MVA per capita in 1981 (at 1975 constant prices) was $48 in Nigeria, $46 in Africa, and $101 in all developing countries (UNIDO, 1988: 4 and 5). Moreover, there has been only limited diversification and deepening. The current structure of the sector has been described as mainly concentrated on 'easy' import substitution goods – the localisation of assembly and the final processing of relatively simple products. In 1985, MVA was equivalent to 45% of gross manufacturing output, only a small increase on the 43% recorded for 1975 (UNIDO, 1987a: Table 4).

Large-scale manufacturing is also heavily concentrated around the main urban centres: greater Lagos, Kano, Kaduna, Zaria, Port Harcourt, Enugu, and Aba. This is partly because most of the industries are market-oriented in their locations. It also reflects the highly localised incidence of supporting infrastructure required for manufacturing – power, water, rail access, etc. This concentration appears to be becoming more marked: Lagos' share of. industrial production is estimated to have risen from 38% in 1968 to 71% by 1976 (UNIDO, 1988: 33).

Table 8.2 *Structure of GDP at constant 1977/8 prices (%)*

	1977	1978	1979	1980	1981	1982	1983	1984	1985	1986
Agriculture	23.4	22.9	19.9	20.0	19.4	22.5	22.8	25.9	26.6	28.1
Oil & mining	25.3	24.2	28.3	24.5	18.0	16.1	16.5	18.9	19.8	18.4
Manufacturing	5.0	6.1	5.6	7.4	8.4	8.8	8.2	11.5	9.3	9.0
Infrastructure	13.2	14.0	14.0	14.9	16.4	15.2	14.1	10.7	8.8	8.9
Services	33.1	32.8	31.2	33.2	37.8	37.4	38.4	33.0	35.5	35.6
Total GDP (Nm.)	32,510	30,510	30,037	31,086	30,366	29,860	27,861	25,855	26,159	25,290
% Change in GDP	7.6	−6.2	−1.6	3.5	−2.3	−1.7	−6.7	−7.2	1.2	−3.3

Source: Central Bank of Nigeria, *Annual Report and Statement of Accounts, 1986*; Federal Office of Statistics, *Economic and Social Statistics Bulletin, 1985*.

PROBLEMS OF MANUFACTURING

Why did the rapid growth of the 1970s give way to the decline of the 1980s, with manufacturing operating at an estimated one-third of capacity by mid-decade? The answer is that the pattern of growth in the 1970s was unsustainable when foreign exchange became scarce. Criticism of this pattern centres on two claims: that manufacturing growth was slower than could have been achieved given the combination of oil wealth and a large internal market; and, even more important, that the pattern of development has been unsatisfactory since much of the increase in MVA derives from import-dependent, assembly-type operations that can survive only behind heavy protection, and from capital-intensive projects with few linkages to the rest of the economy.

These criticisms, which are considered in more detail below, need to be viewed within the broader context of the overall development of the Nigerian economy. To a large extent what has happened in manufacturing is the result of pressures generated elsewhere. Since 1973, the economy has been dominated by oil which has been a twin-edged influence, providing the government with the financial means to undertake activities denied to many other Black African states, and, together with the large population, resulting in substantial effective demand on the domestic market. Both have provided a certain stimulus to manufacturing. At the same time, however, the pressures generated by oil have had less beneficial effects.

The stimulus provided by oil is obvious. It has financed a very large public investment programme. It has contributed materially to political stability by providing the federal government with a substantial power of the purse over the 19 states. But there is another, gloomier, side of the picture. Imports have risen just as fast as exports, making the economy vulnerable to the periodic slumps experienced in oil exports. These cause balance-of-payments problems and, even more seriously, divert government attention away from long-term development to short-term crisis management. Imports have also undermined some sectors of domestic production. Agriculture presents a striking example: Nigeria has been transformed from a major agricultural exporter into a substantial importer.

A consequence has been its inability to move beyond the initial stages of a rather haphazard type of import substitution, and manufacturing has remained heavily dependent on imports. This has been partly the result of government policies, which have favoured production oriented towards domestic consumer demand rather than exports, and has depressed artificially the cost of imported inputs. But it is also independent of government policy. Nigeria's large domestic market grew very rapidly with the oil boom. It would have absorbed a very high proportion of domestic output even without the bias of government policies, and the speed of growth would have predisposed manufacturing to favour import-dependent solutions even without the artificially low price of imports.

The number of direct government interventions, for good or ill, has been fairly limited. In its industrial policy the government has been fairly orthodox and has eschewed direct involvement in large areas of manufacturing. There have, for example, been no widespread nationalisations. The principal area in which its policies have had a negative effect is in diverting funds and energies into highly capital-intensive, heavy industry which has relatively little spin-off into the rest of the economy and, in the case of steel, has resulted in high priced inputs into other areas of manufacturing. The indigenisation decrees, which have resulted in the Nigerianisation of ownership to a significant extent, also had the less desirable side-effect of diverting private funds away from investment into new capacity.

Where the government has had a negative effect on the manufacturing sector it has often been a case of 'sins of omission' rather than of 'commission'. For example, it has failed to protect the sector from the adverse consequences of its other policies (eg on exchange rates or wage levels) or to deal with problems in other sectors (eg the decline of agriculture) which have had an impact on manufacturing. Possibly the most pervasive policy prejudicial to manufacturing development has been its failure to manage oil (see below). Government actions have tended to accentuate rather than dampen the gyrations introduced into the economy by the volatile world oil market. As a result, periods of intense overheating of the economy have been followed by sharp recessions.

This stop-go behaviour has applied also to government investment. During the 1970s, there was a rush to extend infrastructure in order to ease bottlenecks that were undoubtedly a constraint on manufacturing. But, such was the pace of construction that costs rose, quality fell and less was achieved than might have been. Moreover, the beneficial impact of such investments has been limited because the period since the early 1980s has been one of acute depression for manufacturing as a direct result of foreign-exchange constraints. Hence, the sector has not been able to take full advantage of the new facilities.

Had government policies in these areas been different, growth might have been more substantial and diversification more rationally based and durable. Nonetheless, manufacturing would still have had to cope with pressures generated by the 'oil syndrome'. In particular, oil has an in-built inflationary impact on the rest of the economy that has pushed up labour costs and reduced the supply of labour to manufacturing. It has also led to a substantially overvalued exchange rate.

High production costs and the overvalued exchange rate have made domestic production vulnerable to import competition despite high nominal protection of many goods. The government's most common response to this has been to introduce quantitative controls that have had a differential impact on sub-sectors. It is claimed, for example by the World Bank, that greater protection has been provided to industries in which Nigeria does not have a comparative advantage than to those with better growth prospects. Finally, the pressures generated by oil have tended to make distribution much more profitable than manufacturing. The same is true for agriculture, which has declined with adverse consequences for agro-industry.

THE RECENT HISTORY OF OIL

Such has been the impact of the stop-go policies engendered by the oil market that it is important to bear in mind throughout this study the chronology of oil prices and production. Indeed, the ups and downs of oil provide a shorthand guide to the overall state of the economy. For this reason, Figure 8.2 presents the level of oil production since 1973 and an illustrative price index[2].

The first big price increase occurred in 1973 and export revenue almost doubled (in current Naira) over the previous year. In 1975, Nigeria experienced the first of a series of oil hiccoughs, each of which has been more severe than its predecessor, when production slipped causing the government short-term financial problems even though there was no fall in unit price. Following a brief recovery, there was another production trough in 1977/8 which was exacerbated by falling unit prices. Export revenue fell even in nominal terms and caused the government serious short-term financial problems. Revenue was buoyant again in 1979 and 1980 as production recovered and unit prices rose rapidly. But in 1981–2 production and revenue once again went into a steep slump.

In both 1977/8 and 1981/2, a contributory factor in the production slump was Nigeria's poor pricing strategy: unit prices were left too high for too long and customers switched to cheaper sources. In 1982, a new ingredient was added. Nigeria was viewed increasingly by both the OPEC hard-liners and the oil majors as the weak link in their 'war of nerves' and suffered a particularly severe drop in production as a result. In 1983, it unilaterally cut its unit price and production began to climb slowly but by early 1989 had never reached an annual average of 1.5 million barrels a day, let alone the 2.2–2.4 mbd. that was the government's target for the first half of the 1980s. In 1986, the unit price of exports fell to $16/barrel (against a 'high' of $40/b. in early 1981) but by 1987 it had recovered slightly to just under $19/b.

Figure 8.2 *Oil production and prices (Production: million barrels a day; Price index, 1980 = 100)*

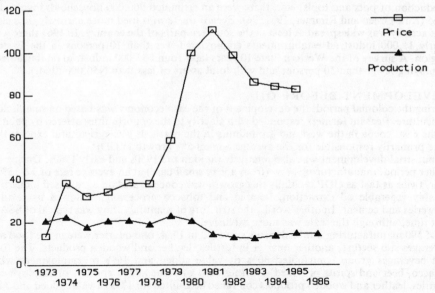

Source: International Monetary Fund, *International Financial Statistics*, (various editions).

The development of manufacturing

PROBLEMS OF METHODOLOGY

Nigeria presents an unhappy mixture of economic complexity, rapid growth, and inadequate data. Nigerian statistics may not be worse than those of most of its neighbours, but the economy is so much more complex that these deficiencies are more apparent. The result is that although opinions abound about the causes of the country's economic problems, very few can be substantiated conclusively with hard data. It has not been possible, for example, to obtain statistics on total consumption of most manufactured goods. Nor has any adequate time series been found giving figures for actual production.

Moreover, smuggling makes it impossible to identify the true level of imports. Take the case of textiles, which is the best documented agro-industry in Nigeria; well over half the flow of total textile imports has commonly been in the form of contraband. Hence, while there is a widespread view that import penetration has increased, it is possible to document this only on the basis of guesstimates[3].

Another methodological difficulty concerns the availability and use of recent data. Official figures are slow to emerge at the best of times and delays have tended to increase during the 1980s oil crisis. In some cases it is more helpful to work on data for the 1970s than for the more recent past because the earlier period may be more typical of the underlying trends in the economy.

In many African states it is difficult to separate what is 'the normal situation' from what is an exceptional period. Most economies of sub-Saharan African (SSA) in particular have experienced considerable volatility over the past 15 years. But, apart from special cases like Uganda, it is difficult to think of a country where the volatility has been so sharp as in Nigeria. In consequence, almost the whole of the 1980s can be considered 'abnormal' in the sense that manufacturing and other sectors were either given an unsustainable stimulus (in the early years) or subjected to extreme restrictions to recover from the effects of the earlier excesses.

A final problem relates to the informal sector, by definition not incorporated into official statistics but in Nigeria of major significance. The informal manufacturing sector was already well established by Independence. If the term 'manufacturing' is used in its broadest sense to include cottage industries in rural areas engaged in food processing, weaving, the production of pots and tools, etc., there were an estimated 900,000 households involved in 1965 (Kirk-Green and Rimmer, 1981: 94). Even if the term is used more narrowly, it is clear that activity was widespread at least in the southern parts of the country. In 1961 there were nearly 11,000 industrial establishments employing fewer than 10 persons in the Eastern Region. A survey of the Western State 10 years later found 35,000 industrial establishments employing fewer than 50 persons and with total assets of less than N50,000 (ibid.).

DEVELOPMENT BEFORE OIL

During the colonial period, the development of the cash economy was based on smallholder agriculture. Peasant farmers responded with alacrity to the opportunities offered by palm oil in the east, cocoa in the west and groundnuts in the north. It was agricultural exports that were primarily responsible for the average annual 5% growth in GDP.

Industrial development was also relatively rapid in the 1950s and early 1960s. During the earlier period, manufacturing grew (from a very small base) at an average rate of 12–15% a year, twice as fast as GDP. Initially this growth was concentrated on agro-based industries, notably vegetable oil extraction, tanning and tobacco processing, followed by textiles, breweries and cement. In other words, the structure of manufacturing was typical of SSA at that time, although the scale was more extensive.

Of 590 manufacturing establishments surveyed in 1964, one-quarter were in the food and beverages sub-sectors, another quarter in textiles, leather and wooden products. The food and beverages group contributed 30% of value added and 16% of employment while tobacco, beer and spirits provided a further 16% of value added and 6% of employment. Textiles, leather and wooden products combined accounted for 17% of value added and 34% of employment (Forrest, 1983: Tables 16.8 and 16.9).

The initial stimulus to the development of manufacturing was competition from non-traditional sources of imports. Until the 1950s, the market was supplied primarily by British-based manufacturers and traders. As the market expanded in the years following the Second World War, new sources of imports appeared, encouraging the traditional suppliers to establish local manufacturing plants in order to maintain their market share. These trends continued into independence, supported first by the colonial authorities and then by the independent government. The most important government support was tariff protection. In addition, income tax relief for 'pioneer industries', tariff concessions on imported raw materials, and tax capital allowances were made available, supplemented in the late 1950s and early 1960s by government contributions to the equity and loan capital of industrial ventures.

Although the focus was on import substitution, it would appear that little progress was made. Writing of the period to 1966, Kilby argued that when account was taken of the cost of capital goods and expatriates, 'import substitution has resulted in a slight increase in imports per unit of consumption' (Kilby, 1969: 29).

By the eve of the Biafran civil war, Nigeria was a relatively strong developing country economy but still primarily an agricultural one – the world's leading supplier of groundnuts, groundnut oil, palm kernels and palm oil, and second only to Ghana as a cocoa exporter. Taxes on agricultural exports, levied through monopoly marketing boards, were the main source of government revenue. Industry accounted for less than 5% of GDP, and was focused on substituting local manufacture for imports. Just emerging as a significant influence on exports and revenue was oil extracted from wells drilled in the east of the country.

The economy exhibited considerable resilience to the upheavals of the Biafran war. Much of the Eastern Region's industry was destroyed while wartime import and foreign-exchange controls caused some disruption elsewhere. Yet, unlike the concurrent Vietnam war, it was not fought on credit. Exports of cocoa and groundnuts provided revenue which, with careful rationing of foreign exchange, enabled the federal government to finance military expenditure almost entirely out of domestic resources. The loss of capacity in the east provided a fillip for manufacturing in the rest of the country.

Nigeria thus emerged from the war with an internal debt that was big but manageable, modest external debt, and an increased level of economic activity. Industrial output grew slowly but by 1973 domestic production had very largely replaced imports for a number of traditional light consumer goods. Ratios of domestic production to total supply were over 90% for cotton textiles, beer, soft drinks, soap and detergents, and roofing sheets and, over

80% for paints and footwear. Oil production quickly climbed from a 1968 low of 0.14 mbd to 1.08 mbd at the start of the 1970s. By 1973 it had reached the level of 2 mbd that has been roughly the official target ever since, except when OPEC production quotas have been in force.

THE OIL YEARS

Overall growth. GDP grew rapidly in the years following the 1973 oil price boom. In the first half of the 1970s, real GDP grew at 11.2% a year compared to its pre-civil war rate of 5.5% (1960–65). But the rate of growth then fell back, so that over the 1970s as a whole it averaged 7.5% (ACP/EEC, 1988: i). Since 1980, however, there has been a decline in real output: GDP is estimated to have fallen by an average of 2.6% a year from 1980 to 1988 (World Bank, 1987: 329 and EIU 1989a: 170).

During the 1970s and early 1980s this growth was accompanied by an impressive level of domestic savings. Investment grew rapidly – by 18% a year in the 1970s. However, the implicit Incremental Capital Output Ratio (ICOR) rose to about six compared with three in the 1960s, reflecting both an emphasis on heavy industry/infrastructure and cost escalation, estimated at about 20% a year over the decade (ACP/EEC, 1988: i).

The oil crisis of the 1980s has resulted in an acute hiatus in domestic savings and a sharp fall in investment. The share of gross investment in GDP fell from almost 30% in 1981 to 10% by 1986. When account is taken of depreciation, net investment must have been very small or even negative by the end of the period. This is largely because of the dramatic fall in the investable surplus accruing to the federal government, accentuated by the drying up of new foreign investment funds. In recent years, foreign direct investment has been running at only $350 m., annually, compared to an annual financing gap in excess of $4 bn [*Financial Times*,

Table 8.3 *Sources of growth in manufacturing output (at current prices)*

Sector/Period	Output Growth	Growth of Domestic Demand	Export Growth	Import Substitution
		Percentage of Increase in Total Output		
Consumer goods				
1963–73	57.65	31.30	5.16	21.24
1973–83	50.20	50.35	− 1.08	0.92
1963–83	46.00	37.57	− 0.01	8.40
Intermediate goods				
1963–73	11.86	9.10	0.05	2.40
1973–83	15.63	15.61	0.00	0.08
1963–83	13.27	11.19	− 0.01	2.08
Chemicals, rubber, petroleum				
1963–73	17.74	12.88	0.01	4.83
1973–83	4.27	2.61	0.11	1.55
1963–83	22.90	16.17	0.06	6.67
Investment goods				
1963–73	11.77	10.64	− 0.74	1.87
1973–83	29.90	20.17	0.00	9.14
1963–83	17.74	19.22	− 0.92	6.62
Miscellaneous				
1963–73	0.93	0.83	0.05	− 0.01
1973–83	0.03	− 0.02	0.02	0.03
1963–83	0.12	0.05	0.06	0.01
All manufactured goods				
1963–73	100.00	64.75	4.53	30.33
1973–83	100.00	88.72	− 0.95	12.32
1963–83	100.00	76.20	0.00	23.80

Source: Ohiorhenuan, 1988: Table 5.

7 March 1988]. This low level results both from the uncertain outlook of the economy following the oil crisis, and also partly from deliberate government policies[4].

Trends in manufacturing have mirrored those for GDP. During the 1970s, manufacturing growth was more rapid (as it had been in the pre-oil years) but the gap between the two rates narrowed over time. In the first half of the decade, MVA increased (in constant 1975 prices) by an annual average of 9.2%, compared with GDP growth of 7.4%. In the second half it grew by an average 13% compared with GDP growth of 6.6% (UNIDO, 1985). It continued to grow, albeit slowly, in 1981 and 1982 despite the fall in GDP, but then slumped by an estimated 13% in 1983 and continued its downward trend to 1986 when it is judged to have fallen by some 4%. The following two years, 1987 and 1988, saw a reversal with MVA estimated to have risen by just over 4% in 1987 and perhaps by as much as 8% in 1988[5]. This upturn, however, is not expected to be sustained.

Sources of growth. An attempt has been made by Ohiorhenuan to estimate the relative importance of three components of growth in manufacturing output: import substitution, domestic demand and export growth [Ohiorhenuan, 1988: 39–41]. His findings are summarised in Table 8.3[6]. Since these are in accord with what would be expected intuitively, it may be interesting to consider his results as perhaps the best indicator available of the relative magnitudes of the changes in these important variables.

Throughout the period 1963–83, domestic demand was the major source of growth in manufacturing. This dominance has been particularly marked since the onset of the oil boom. The role of exports as a source of growth has been negligible and has declined over the period. The contribution of import substitution was much smaller in the decade after 1973 than in that before. It contributed 30% of the growth for all manufactured goods in 1963–73 but only 12% in 1973–83. This is in line with the observation that demand grew so rapidly during the 1970s that it outstripped the increase in domestic production.

The United Nations Industrial Development Organisation (UNIDO) has also made estimates of the sources of growth (reproduced in Appendix Table 8.A1). These confirm the finding of Ohiorhenuan that domestic demand was overwhelmingly the most important source of growth. It accounted for an estimated 99.75% of total manufacturing growth in the 1970–79 period, and up to 211% in wearing apparel and 571% in pottery and china. For manufacturing as a whole, UNIDO estimates no significant change in import substitution over the period.

Sub-sectoral changes. Consumer goods industries retain a substantial share of MVA, accounting in 1984 for four-fifths of private sector MVA (Table 8.A2b). They are dominated by traditional concerns such as food, beverages and tobacco, textiles and clothing, leather goods and footwear, furniture and paper products. The combined share of these industries in total MVA in 1971–2 was 61%, and by 1984 it was still as high as 57%, despite diversification into activities such as plastic and glass products, soaps, detergents and cosmetics. These 'new' products began production in the late 1960s and continued to expand rapidly during the 1970s. They have tended to benefit from higher levels of protection than have the older, traditional consumer goods industries.

Although there has not been any substantial diversification or deepening of manufacturing, there have been significant changes in the relative importance of the sub-sectors. These provide some evidence of relative profitability and of the impact of government policies. In 1973, the top four industrial branches were food manufacturing, textiles, fabricated metals and petroleum refining. By 1980, the order had changed to transport equipment, food products, petroleum refining and beverages.

This shifting pattern is illustrated at the level of individual industries in Table 8.A3 which gives the government index of manufacturing production[7]. The index for total manufacturing increased by 121% between 1975 and 1983 with the following sub-sectoral changes: vehicle assembly increased by 544%, refined petroleum products by 382%, beer by 216%, and soap detergents by 146%. Sugar confectionery, radios and pharmaceuticals production fell, however. Of particular interest, given the comments made below about the impact of government policies, is the differential performance of cotton textiles and a group described as 'other textiles' – primarily synthetic goods. Production of cotton textiles stagnated, but output of synthetic textiles grew by 74%.

The fast growers can be observed from Table 8.4 in which the data from Table 8.A3 are rearranged in order of growth rate[8]. At first sight, the group of fast growers might appear to include a high proportion of industries processing domestic raw materials. But this would be

Table 8.4 *Manufacturing winners and losers (comparative ranking of industries according to growth rate of manufacturing index 1975–81)*

	Rate of growth (%)	
	1975–81	1981–6
Faster than average		
Refined petroleum products	360	
Vehicle assembly	277	− 68
Beer	238	− 3
Soap and detergents	235	− 59
Other petroleum products	218	
Slower than average		
Soft drinks	137	
Paint and allied products	108	
Other textiles	106	
Cotton textiles	62	− 69
Cement	47	68
Roofing sheets	39	
Footwear	33	
Cigarettes	13	
Radios, TV assembly	9	
Pharmaceuticals	− 14	
Sugar confectionery	+ 16	
Total Manufacturing	147	

Source: UNIDO, 1988: Table 2.1.

an incorrect interpretation. The most rapid growth has been in the industries largely dependent on imports. In the case of petroleum products most of those consumed in Nigeria during the period in question were refined in Venezuela using Nigerian and other crudes. Moreover, there must be some doubt as to the economic benefits of the rapid growth in consumption which was due, in part, to highly subsidised consumer prices[9]. In the case of vehicle assembly, the growth has been almost entirely on the basis of imported inputs. As for beer, as noted below, even though part of production uses domestic raw materials import penetration has increased rapidly.

These data on the sub-sectors can be aggregated to show the performance of distinctive industry groups. Particularly rapid growth was experienced by three main groups of enterprises: final assembly of consumer durables (such as motor vehicles); food and drink processing for final consumption (such as brewing and soft drinks); and construction-related (such as cement, roofing sheets and paints). By contrast, natural resource-based industries have performed particularly badly. Vegetable oil and tin metal production fell by 90% and 62% respectively between 1971 and 1980.

The slow growers. The relatively poor performance of intermediate goods, and the differential progress of the various sub-sectors, provide some evidence as to the nature of manufacturing development in Nigeria. The low average growth of chemicals, metal working, tyres and tubes, for example, is particularly noteworthy as cross-country evidence suggests that the first two tend to increase their share of manufacturing output as industrialisation proceeds. Their decline relative to other manufacturing during the 1970s illustrates the limited structural deepening of the sector. The tyres and tubes industry could have been expected to grow substantially given the very rapid expansion of vehicle assembly. In this case, the slow growth of indigenous products reflects the reliance on imported inputs.

Although the capital goods industries increased their share of private sector MVA between 1973/4 and 1984 from 1% to 21% (Table 8.A2b), growth was dominated by vehicle assembly and steel. During the 1970s, the government encouraged the establishment of several car and truck assembly plants, all of them almost entirely dependent upon imported inputs. It also began construction of a very capital-intensive steel industry.

Because of the relatively poor performance of intermediate and capital goods and the minimal amount of manufactured goods exported, growth in manufacturing has been dependent predominantly upon increases in domestic demand. This weakness has perhaps been less evident than in many other SSA states because of the very rapid growth of demand in Nigeria during the 1970s. But, as in other SSA states, manufacturing has been very badly hit by the fall in inputs resulting from foreign-exchange shortages. Clearly, the short-term future prospects require that the size of import-dependent capacity be related to the likely long-term availability of imported inputs.

Trade in manufactures: imports.   There has been a major growth in manufactured imports over the past 15 years (except when constrained by foreign-exchange shortages). It is unclear, however, how far there has been a general *increase* in import penetration (as opposed to a maintenance of previous relative levels at a much higher absolute value). In many cases domestic production was able to expand sufficiently rapidly during the 1970s to absorb the growth but this has not been the case in all sub-sectors [Kirk-Green and Rimmer, 1981: 96].

In spite of these particular data inadequacies, there is little doubt that imports have provided a growing share of total manufacturing inputs. Evidence for the increasing import dependence can be gleaned from statistics on the structure of trade. During the period 1973–81 the value of raw material imports for industrial processing rose by 820% (in current prices) compared to an increase of only 735% for capital goods imports (UNIDO, 1985: 27). It is judged that *at least* 60% of total raw materials consumed in manufacturing are currently imported: one estimate is that over two-thirds of the cost of industrial raw materials used in 1983 had to be paid for in foreign exchange (UNIDO, 1986).

Ohiorhenuan has made an ambitious attempt to identify the input structure of 12 industrial sub-sectors (Table 8.A4)[10]. His estimate is that in three-quarters of the sub-sectors, imported inputs form a higher proportion of total output value than do domestic intermediate inputs. Overall, he calculates that about one-third of gross output value is accounted for by imported inputs. About half the value of gross output is made up of primary inputs (domestic and imported) with wages and salaries accounting on average for about one-tenth, and operating surplus for about one-third of the total.

The share of imports varies widely between industries. The World Bank has made estimates for a small number of enterprises which indicate an import dependence ranging from 100% for Nigalex (a metal products manufacturer) and 90% for the Nigerian Bottling Company (soft drinks) and Aswami Textiles, to negligible imports for NTM (textiles), Vegetable Oils (Nigeria) Ltd., and Lacon (bricks).

Import penetration increased in brewing during the 1970s. Nigeria was virtually self-sufficient in beer in 1968, but by 1977 imports accounted for 41% of total domestic supply. In cement, too, the ratio of domestic production to total supply fell from over 80% in the mid-1960s to less than 60% by 1973 and to under 40% in 1975. The Third Plan (1975–80) proposed a major extension to capacity in the cement industry, with the aim of achieving self-sufficiency by 1985. However, production rose only very slowly as a result of inadequate power supplies, shortages of skilled manpower, and lack of spare parts (Government of Nigeria, 1979: 59). In the case of plastics, 97% of raw materials were imported in 1983, and for engineering-based manufacturing the proportion was 79%. The lowest import contents are found in the agro-linked sub-sectors, with a figure of 60% for the year 1983. Nonetheless because of the absolute size of this area of activity, nearly 40% of total raw material imports are absorbed by the agro-linked group.

Because of the prominence of import-based manufacturing, the sector is very vulnerable to disruption by oil-induced balance-of-trade problems. By 1985, for example, capacity utilisation had fallen to an estimated 30–40% of 1981 levels. The import of industrial inputs in 1984/5 was about half its 1982 level. By the late 1980s the situation had not markedly improved, although there was a more marked division between levels of capacity utilisation. Thus it has been estimated that overall capacity utilisation levels had risen to some 40% by 1988, but still ranged between 12 and 25% for industries most dependent upon imported inputs (*West Africa*, 16–22 January 1989).

The vehicle assembly industry has been especially vulnerable to the shortage of foreign exchange for imported inputs. Together with the squeeze on consumer disposable income cause by the crisis of the 1980s, the result has been a cut in capacity utilisation to about one-tenth (*Financial Times*, 7 March 1988). Two plants have been closed (Leyland and Fiat Iveco) and further rationalisation may be required. Interestingly, the plant operators have reacted to the crisis by refurbishing existing vehicles.

More generally, the results have been widespread lay-offs and plant shut-downs. No aggregate statistics are available on the extent of the retrenchment, still less on the share attributable directly to the import squeeze as opposed to other aspects of the recession, such as the fall in effective demand, or a reduced willingness by foreign parent companies to accept short-term operating losses in the hope of profits in the medium term. However, the Manufacturers' Association of Nigeria maintains that during the period 1984–6 some 200,000 workers, or 40% of the industrial labour force, were laid off, while in 1988, after an apparent rise in MVA of over 5% a further fall in employment of 2.8% occurred [*West Africa*, 16–22 January 1989]. No sub-sector, with the possible exception of drinks, appears to have been exempt from the decline in output[11]. The scale and speed of the lay-offs have been facilitated by the lack of any effective employment protection legislation covering the private sector which dominates manufacturing.

Some firms have been able to adjust to the difficulties, at least some of the time. In the early years of the recession, profit levels in some firms were reported actually to have increased despite the input supply problems. This was especially marked for drinks: pre-tax profits in Nigerian Breweries, for example, increased by 113% in 1983 on increased turnover. And other companies also increased profits even on slashed turnover. These apparent anomalies occurred partly because of sales from stock and because companies were able to use the retrenchment exercise to reduce over-manning and cut less profitable activities. And partly it was because the advantages of reduced competition from 'finished' imports outweighed the problems of imported input supplies.

The incidence of such successful 'adjustment' appears to have declined as the recession continued, if reported figures on, especially, large and quoted companies are any guide[12]. But industrialists argue that these figures paint too rosy a picture, a view confirmed by the continued decline from 1986 to 1988 in the pre-tax return on sales. Many industrial companies, it is claimed, are under-depreciating their plant and machinery. Hence, while the results are encouraging, much greater investment will be required if they are to be sustained in the medium term.

Trade in manufactures: exports.   In comparison with overall exports, manufactured exports are negligible: in all but the most detailed statistics, they are normally lumped into the residual 'other' category. In 1982, for example[13], manufactures and semi-manufactures accounted for just 0.2% of merchandise exports (Government of Nigeria, 1983: Table 74). Even this greatly overstates the export of 'manufactures' as understood in the present context, for almost *all* manufactured exports are accounted for by the well established first-stage processing of agricultural goods[14]. Excluding these products, all other 'manufactured and semi-manufactured' exports accounted for less than 0.06% of the total. Apart from cocoa products, the only goods that accounted for more than 5% of manufactured exports were leather (almost half), tin (almost one-quarter) and 'miscellaneous structures and parts' (8%) (UNIDO, 1987b).

It was not always so. Export-oriented agricultural processing formed a major part of early manufacturing: in 1958 export processing accounted for half of industrial production (Bailey, 1977). Such first-stage processing has declined with the drop in export crop production. Yet this decline is by no means confined to the period since oil. The share of export-processing industries in manufacturing had already fallen to 25% by 1967 (World Bank, 1974: 5).

There is little evidence at an economy-wide level that even nascent manufactured exports are likely to emerge in the short term. The preferential trade provisions of the Economic Community of West African States (ECOWAS), for example, are likely in practice in the short term to result in greater Nigerian imports from other West African states rather than greater exports from Nigeria to its neighbours. Even the (relatively) improved performance of manufacturing in 1987/8 compared with earlier years of the decade has failed to result in a significant increase in' exports. Export markets are developing for only a limited range of products – notably textiles and, to a very limited degree, beer, and then slowly.   ·

There have been a number of attempts to boost exports, of manufactures as well as other goods, including the creation of a Nigerian Export Promotion Council in 1977, favourable bank credit ceilings (see below) and, most recently, the establishment in 1988 of Nigerian Export Credit Guarantee and Insurance Corporation[15]. But Forrest has observed shrewdly (1983: 333):

The pressure for this policy at this particular stage of Nigeria's industrialization appears to come from the bureaucracy, academics and the conspicuous success of Brazilian trade

drives in Nigeria. It does not originate within industry which has experienced few constraints from the domestic market.

It follows that substantial manufactured exports are unlikely to occur until manufacturing
industry is able to satisfy a far greater proportion of domestic demand. This, in turn, is linked
to the issue of import dependence. At present, the level of both industrial activity and
domestic demand is heavily influenced by the state of the oil sector and the availability of
foreign exchange. When, as now, demand is weak it does not result in increased exports of
manufactures as a 'vent for surplus' since the level of production is also low. By the same
token, when production is high, so is domestic demand. In the medium term this link is likely
to be broken only by a shift in the structure of production so that output and output growth
become less dependent upon imported inputs. A future slowdown in consumer demand might
then lead to a search for export markets.

Investment patterns: the level of investment. Gross investment in manufacturing rose
substantially in the second half of the 1970s. In 1971–4 it had been in the region of
N500–550 m. (in 1975 prices), but by 1975–8 it had risen to an estimated N3.6 bn. However, it
has fallen sharply during the oil slump. It is estimated that gross domestic investment (GDI)
fell from 25% in 1982 to just over 10% by 1985, and that in real terms total gross domestic
capital formation fell by two-thirds in the same period (UNIDO, 1988: 8). By 1988, the ratio
is estimated to have fallen to around 8% (*Financial Times*, 6 March 1989). UNIDO has also
estimated that GFCF in manufacturing declined by 60% in 1983 and by a further 46% in 1984
(UNIDO, 1988: 29). Much of the investment in manufacturing has been domestic rather than
foreign, especially since the 1970s.

The savings ratio averaged 27.6% of GDP during 1976–80 although it then fell to 13.4% in
1980–85 (ACP/EEC, 1988: ii). The level of domestic saving might have been even greater had
it not been for large-scale capital flight. Ohiorhenuan has estimated that capital outflows in
the period 1970–78 averaged 12% of the value of imports (Ohiorhenuan, 1988: 82). Over the
period 1970–85 as a whole, the external sector's contribution to gross capital formation was
only 10% (ACP/EEC 1988: ii). But in the periods of oil crisis the share was very much larger.
The majority of foreign capital inflows in recent years have been of the 'forced investment'
variety due to exchange controls. Unremitted profits (62% of the net flow of foreign private
investment in 1984) and unpaid suppliers' and trade credits have been of particular
significance (ibid.: Table 2.6).

The greater part of the expansion which did occur was due to direct public investment,
especially by the federal government in a relatively small number of very capital-intensive
enterprises. Federal government expenditure contributed 60% to the 1975–8 total, and the
state governments also undertook substantial investment. The level of the government's
contribution has been heavily influenced by the state of the oil market; for this reason its
share has been smaller than average during the 1980s.

There was also an absolute growth (but relative decline) in private investment during the
1970s, averaging about N380 m. a year (at constant 1975 prices), almost all from the
corporate sector; individual savings contributed less than 1% (ACP/EEC, 1988: ii). Since
then the level of private investment has stagnated, if not declined, due to a number of factors.
Apart from the effects of indigenisation (see below) in diverting domestic and discouraging
foreign investment, these include the complex and time-consuming administrative
procedures and a general shift in incentives against manufacturing industry. It remains to be
seen whether the changes announced in 1989 and early 1990, such as the establishment of the
Industrial Development Co-ordinating Committee (IDCC) as a one-stop approval agency for
new investments, will materially address these problems.

Even during the 1970s, however, private investment was still small in relation to profits
derived from the sector. Table 8.5 presents information from a sample of over 200 firms on
the ratio of gross profits to value added, value added to output and investment to value
added. The average ratio of net capital expenditure to gross profits over the period 1973–7
was 34% (with a standard deviation of 14.3). As much of the investment during this period
was financed by bank loans it is reasonable to conclude that the reinvestment of profits has
been relatively low in Nigeria[16].

Table 8.5 appears to show a negative correlation between the rates of profits and investment. However, this impression may be misleading. It applies in particular to motor vehicles,
other manufactures and tyres/tubes. In the case of motor vehicle assembly, the period in
question was one in which large-scale investments were just coming on-stream. Hence, a low

Table 8.5 *Performance indicators for selected manufacturing establishments (%)*

	Gross profit/ Value added		Value added/ Output		Investment/ Value added
	1973–7	1980–83	1973–7	1980–83	1973–7
Vegetable oil	70.0	51.1	32.8	21.6	30.0
Textiles	63.0	48.5	40.4	40.6	30.4
Made-up-textile goods	65.0	52.7	40.6	15.0	47.0
Leather products	63.6	37.6	52.6	38.5	8.8
Saw milling	38.4	45.5	49.2	47.1	64.6
Other wood and cork products	77.7	66.6	57.2	54.5	42.5
Wooden furniture	63.2	51.8	44.7	39.8	43.5
Container and paper board	73.4	86.7	39.2	29.1	11.6
Paper products	76.2	83.5	37.0	41.4	31.6
Printing, publishing	58.0	75.6	57.6	48.0	105.2
Tyres and tubes	80.8	92.7	62.6	52.1	6.2
Cement	82.4	75.2	69.2	53.6	99.6
Concrete products	77.8	68.1	53.4	52.1	27.7
Iron, steel and non-ferrous metals	92.0	94.2	57.7	35.1	–
Motor vehicle assembly	85.7	89.3	25.5	44.7	11.7
Other manufactures	83.6	79.6	48.8	49.0	17.6

Source: UNIDO, 1985 and 1988.

level of reinvestment and a high level of profit-taking was to be expected. Similar considerations may apply to the vehicle-related industry, tyres/tubes. It is difficult to draw any conclusions for 'other manufactures' since this is a residual category.

Investment patterns: the direction of investment.   Private and public investors have tended to put their money into different sub-sectors. Private investment has gone where profits have been highest and has remained concentrated on the consumer goods industries which absorbed almost three-quarters of total manufacturing investment in 1975–8. Other popular sub-sectors were building materials, metal working, saw milling, chemicals and transport equipment.

Public investment, by contrast, has been made in the areas favoured by the government's development strategy, predominantly in the 'commanding heights' of intermediate and heavy goods industries, dominated by major capital-intensive projects in petrochemicals, petroleum products, iron and steel, pulp and paper, and cement. Thus, public sector investment has tended to lead into diversification into second-stage import-substituting industries, while the private sector has diversified from traditional consumer goods industries into other non-durable consumer goods, consumer durables, and, to a lesser extent, intermediate goods.

Employment.   According to government figures, total modern sector employment in manufacturing in 1985 was 681,000, or 24% of the total (ACP/EEC, 1988: Table 4.4). Unfortunately, such statistics provide only a very partial picture because they overlook the informal sector which is very extensive, very labour-intensive, and appears to include a substantial amount of manufacturing activity[17]. As a result, estimates of total employment in the sector (including informal manufacturing activities) vary widely[18].

Within the formal sector, consumer goods industries have been the largest employers, accounting for over 70% of the total manufacturing work force (Table 8.A5), the main ones being textiles/clothing plus food, beverages and tobacco.

A 1977 federal manpower survey estimated total urban formal sector wage employment at about 2 million (Government of Nigeria, 1979). About one third of these were employed by the government. Although the composition and extent of the informal manufacturing sector is ill understood, it has been estimated at roughly 5 million in the same year. Not only is it larger than the formal sector, but it also appears to be more closely associated with manufacturing. Manufacturing accounted for 14% of the formal sector total in 1977 but around 30% by 1988[19]. By contrast, a 1977 survey of the Lagos informal sector found that 40% of enterprises were involved in manufacturing, with tailoring and leather-work accounting for two-thirds of this employment [Fapohunda, 1978]. Most informal sector manufacturing is of a similar, labour-intensive nature, with one significant exception – printing accounted for some 7% of Lagos establishments and involved relatively expensive equipment.

Factors affecting the performance of manufacturing

Why has Nigerian manufacturing industry been unable to achieve sustainable growth given the advantages of the large domestic market and oil revenue? Many explanations have been put forward. Among the most widespread are that:

- government macroeconomic policy has hindered its development by encouraging excessive, wasteful consumption expenditure;
- government industrial policies have been misguided;
- exchange-rate and import policies have so distorted incentives that they have encouraged the growth of industries in which Nigeria does not have a comparative advantage and have hindered the growth of potential winners;
- there are inherent weaknesses in Nigerian management organisation which have been exacerbated by acute shortages of appropriate manpower.

Each of these explanations is examined in this section. For convenience they are grouped into two broad areas: those involving 'government policy' (that is, in which a change in government policy over a relatively narrow issue range might have produced significantly different results) and those that are more deep-seated which are grouped under the umbrella phrase – the effects of the 'oil syndrome'. The dividing line between the two is a narrow one. The overvalued exchange rate has been included in the 'oil syndrome', even though some might argue that this is inappropriate since it is amenable to change through government policy. The reason for including it in the woes of the oil syndrome is that the currency became so grossly overvalued because of the pressures generated by oil.

GOVERNMENT POLICY

The government stands accused of waste, mismanagement and corruption. Specific aspects of these charges relating directly to manufacturing are discussed below and not all are found to be proven. In one respect, however, the charges of mismanagement are undoubtedly well-founded. This concerns oil and the government's response to the problems that it has created.

Oil has been a source of considerable volatility for the economy. A reasonable government objective might have been to offset this to a certain degree but, in practice, policies have tended to exacerbate rather than cushion the effects of oil gyrations. This was particularly marked from the return to civilian rule in 1979 until the advent of the present government in 1985 – crucial years in the history of the oil markets[20]. The failure of governments to 'manage' oil has undoubtedly affected manufacturing, as it has all other sectors. The period since 1973 has seen a succession of oil peaks, when liquidity was very high, punctuated by sharp troughs. The government was slow to respond to the troughs and when it did act its controls were accompanied by much confusion. The exigencies of crisis management also diverted attention away from long-term development needs.

Macroeconomic policy and planning.   Nigeria is not one of the states in which government has attempted to intervene across the board in economic activities and to suppress or tightly control the private sector. In this respect the policies of independent Nigeria show considerable continuity with the colonial period. The colonial administration did not become directly involved in production on a significant scale. Its principal roles were the imposition of a Pax Britannica that provided a favourable environment for economic growth, the construction of infrastructure along which agricultural exports and manufactured imports could pass, and the nurturing of education and health care.

During the 1950s both the economy and the government's role grew. The development expenditures of the federal government increased fivefold. This trend accelerated after independence in 1960 and government experimented with direct involvement in manufacturing production (see below). But the economy still remained a basically free enterprise one.

Federal government policy in the 1970s was dominated by oil, the most obvious effect of which was on government revenue, which increased in current terms from a 1970–3 average of N1.15 bn to N13.8 bn by 1979–80, a 43% average annual rate of increase. It then slumped drastically in 1982–3 and has been stable around N11 bn since 1984. Even though the economy has a strong private sector, the scale of government spending has had a marked effect on the level and distribution of economic activity since 1973.

One frequent criticism is that this oil wealth was wasted on public consumption. This criticism has some validity but, in important respects, is somewhat wide of the mark. The problems have not been so much of excessive consumption as of volatile expenditure and poorly directed investment. Gyrations of the magnitude quoted above cause serious short-term problems of economic management which divert attention from long-term planning and play havoc with monetary policy. In 1977, for example, the government had to cut capital expenditure by 30% across the board, while in 1982 a similarly wide-ranging cut of 40% was instituted. It is easy to imagine the effects of such measures on, for example, the demand for cement or the implementation of power supply projects.

In aggregate terms, much of the government's revenue has been used for investment rather than consumption. The Third Plan was drafted just as the extent of oil wealth had become clear. The projected level of total investment was ten times higher than in the Second Plan – built on the assumption that finance was no longer a constraint. In the period of maximum government liquidity, between 1973–4 and 1978–9, public investment spending grew almost three times as rapidly as public consumption. The rate of investment (public and private) rose from 15% of GDP to over 30%.

Unfortunately the planners were grossly over-optimistic about the government's capacity to administer funds of such magnitude. Among the results were that by the mid-1970s the country's infrastructure was clogged up dramatically. Project implementation fell far behind schedule and costs rose so rapidly that expenditure broke through the planned limits. By the end of the Plan period it had become only too clear that money was a constraint after all – as were manpower and physical infrastructure. The Plan was also partly self-defeating since its spending programmes contributed to the cost increases[21].

All these problems have had a direct effect on manufacturing: infrastructural problems disrupted output and sharp policy changes because of cash-flow problems caused dislocation. Such problems have fed through into increased production costs. Many factories, for example, were able to work only fitfully, in time with sporadic electricity supplies, or had to invest in high-cost generation of their own power. At one stage, Peugeot had to truck its car kits across the Sahara because of blockages in the ports. Even simple exercises like telephoning a supplier or maintaining delivery vehicles were especially problematic during the boom periods and remain a problem even now.

Partly for these reasons, the high level of investment has not had the expected impact on production. Real output grew at less than 3% a year between the mid-1970s and early 1980s. Another explanation for this low growth is that the investment has been very capital-intensive and concentrated on traditional targets: physical infrastructure (especially transport and, to a smaller extent, heavy industry) and social infrastructure (particularly education facilities)[22]. Given the severe infrastructure and manpower constraints, these investments may have an indirectly beneficial impact on manufacturing, but there will be a time lag. The new physical infrastructure was coming on-stream just as the bottom fell out of the oil market and introduced a new set of constraints.

These problems have applied equally to the 25% of the Third Plan's capital expenditure that was devoted to manufacturing. Even those projects that were carefully selected and executed tended to have a long gestation period and a high capital-to-output ratio. Unlike the First and Second Plans (1962–8, 1970–75), which focused on light industry and assembly, the emphasis was shifted and most public investment was directed into heavy and intermediate industrial goods. These produce only modest increases in output in the short run and tend to have a high import content, which strains the balance of trade during the periodic oil slumps. In the longer term, much of this investment will tend to make Nigeria more rather than less vulnerable to the vagaries of the oil market, since it will increase claims on the recurrent budget.

The *Fourth Plan (1981–5)* claimed to have taken heed of these errors, even though it foresaw total public and private investment of N82 bn. It was, indeed, based upon revenue assumptions that appeared at the time to be fairly cautious: oil exports were to increase by only 1.6% over the 1980 level of 1.9 mbd. Unfortunately for the planners, their 'caution' turned out to be wildly over-optimistic as Nigeria suffered a series of slumps in demand for its oil. As a result the Fourth Plan was, in most respects, a 'dead letter'.

The introduction of the Fifth Plan was abandoned in October 1988. Since the Fourth Plan was drafted there have been three changes of government: one following civilian elections in 1983, and two as a result of military coups. No recent government has been able to indulge in the luxury of medium-term planning although a new plan is now in preparation. Short-term crisis management has been required instead to deal with the problems of an external debt that was not unduly great ($18.3 bn or 26% of GNP at the end of 1985) but whose repayments were heavily bunched and biased towards the short term.

In mid-1986 the government introduced a two-year *Structural Adjustment Programme (SAP)*. This included the introduction of a second-tier foreign-exchange market which led to a substantial devaluation of the Naira, the abolition of import licences, changes to import duties intended to reduce the protection of domestic industries and the import dependence of manufacturing, the abolition of export duties, deflationary demand management policies, deregulation of the banks, and a programme of privatisation for some parastatals. These measures were sufficient to win the approval of the IMF and the World Bank, bringing to an end several years of confusion and inadequate action over debt arrears that had been linked to policy disagreements with the IMF. The Naira depreciated by 44% in 1986 and 67% in 1987, bringing it nearer to what observers saw as a realistic level.

Under the SAP, total capital expenditure was planned to reach some N1.8 bn, of which 15% was earmarked for industry. Agriculture was the only sector with a higher allocation (19%). At the time of writing (in early 1989), the out-turn of actual expenditure was not known.

Industrial policy. The government's formal policy has been to use the oil wealth to develop the industrial and manufacturing base. This has been translated into four principal operational objectives:

- to develop supporting infrastructure;
- to encourage private capital into infant industries which it tries to protect from import competition;
- to take a lead in developing heavy industry;
- to encourage private capital into the other sub-sectors.

Successive governments have been fairly orthodox in pursuit of these objectives. They have shown little enthusiasm, for example, for establishing manufacturing enterprises wholly in *public ownership*, despite a proliferation of parastatals. During the 1960s the regional governments and development institutions established a number of wholly owned manufacturing enterprises in, for example, oil seed processing, soft drink bottling, boat building, rubber processing, glass manufacturing and brewing[23]. In the main the performance of these enterprises was 'deplorable, being distinguished by inefficiency, heavy financial losses, nepotism and corruption' (Kirk-Green and Rimmer, 1981: 100). Since the 1970s, however, the government has been concerned to ensure its direct involvement only in the 'commanding heights', together with a substantial Nigerian participation (public or private) in all large-scale economic enterprises.

Another 'sin' of which it has not been guilty (at least in relation to manufacturing) is over-severe taxation. In the case of agriculture very heavy taxation (levied indirectly through the marketing boards) had an undoubted adverse effect. But taxation of manufacturing enterprises has been light. Oil revenue has enabled the government to keep its fiscal demands on the private sector within strict limits[24].

The government has been quite successful in its *development of infrastructure*. Power remains a problem but a massive port and road building programme has eased transport congestion. Ironically, though, as noted above, the new infrastructural developments have not yet had the full impact that might have been expected because the economy has been operating well below capacity since much of it was completed.

The government has been just as active, but much less successful, in pursuit of the second objective – *protection from imports*.

Tariff, and especially quota restrictions on imports have proliferated, both in order to protect domestic industries and, during the oil slumps, to defend the balance of trade. But rampant smuggling has undermined the effect of such measures. Smuggling appears to have increased during the period of civilian rule.

Overall, in both its support for the private sector and as regards direct involvement, government industrial policy has been biased towards large-scale activity, with little attention being given in practice to small-and medium-scale sectors. Industrial employment and the spatial distribution of industrial activity have also been of little concern (see Forrest, 1983: 332).

Vintage plans to develop a *steel industry* dating back to the 1950s were dusted off in the 1970s when the government found that it had the wealth to turn its dreams into reality. In 1975, plans were announced for a blast furnace at Ajaokuta using domestic iron and coal, with an annual capacity of 1.5 m. tons, and two direct reduction plants. Since then, one of the plants has been shelved, and progress on the blast furnace has been little short of disastrous, with endless delays and escalating costs. By early 1989, the project had cost $3 bn with a further $1 bn required to complete the first phase. A confidential government report of 1984 stated that the whole venture was 'uneconomic and will incur recurrent losses to the end of the century' (reported in *Financial Times*, 1 March 1989). But the other direct reduction plant, using imported raw materials, was commissioned at Aladja in Bendel state in December 1981, and three rolling mills went into service, in 1983. As of 1985 there were 16 steel mills in Nigeria: 5 wholly owned by the federal government, 2 jointly owned by the federal government and domestic and foreign interests, and 3 wholly private sector (UNIDO, 1988: section 3.4).

The steel plants suffer from the twin problems that have afflicted Nigerian industry in the past: import dependence and infrastructural deficiencies. The Aladja plant has been operating at around one-fifth of capacity (of one million tons per annum) in recent years because of shortages of imported iron ore and power cuts. Similarly, the rolling mills are heavily import-dependent and have been operating at only about one-third of capacity. Added to this, the plant produces a very narrow product range heavily concentrated on inputs into currently depressed sub-sectors, such as vehicle assembly and construction. Capacity utilisation within the sub-sector as a whole was estimated in 1988 at about one-tenth (ibid.).

The first steps in the development of the *petrochemicals industry* were taken in 1982 when contracts were awarded for the first phase of a N1.25 bn plan. Three plants were to be attached to the Warri and Kaduna oil refineries to produce carbon black, high octane gasoline and synthetic detergent. By early 1989, phase I at the Kaduna and Ekpan plants had been operating for a little over a year and the larger Phase II operation was under way and expected to be on-stream by 1992. While these two phases will lead to considerable import substitution, a host of problems remain, ranging from lack of adequate capital finance and plant breakdowns to export markets and pricing and the ability to produce the precise products required by the domestic market[25].

The economic justification for these different mega-projects is highly questionable. They do little to stimulate other industries. Indeed, if they continue to lead to an increase in the domestic price of industrial inputs such as steel, they will act as a brake on downstream activities. The government has been faced, therefore, with the choice of either subsidising the prices of domestic output or protecting it from imports by tariff or non-tariff instruments, either of which would increase the cost of inputs to steel-using industries. The government's initial preference was for protection, only issuing import licences when domestic production had been absorbed.

One side-effect of this emphasis has been to reinforce the bias in favour of imported rather than indigenous *technology*. Despite various attempts to foster the transfer of technology, including the establishment of a National Science and Technology Development Agency, there has been very little adaptive technology. Forrest made an interesting comparison between the dominance of imported technology in present-day Nigeria and the situation obtaining in Biafra during the civil war. He pointed out that (1983: 338):

> under conditions of autarchy with no MNC presence in secessionist Biafra, adaptive innovation in the oil and weapons industry flourished. The power of the bureaucracy declined sharply and scientists and engineers enjoyed unprecedented status and freedom[26].

The government's attempts to stimulate other industries is largely indirect. By tax concessions, loan subsidies, directives to the banks and tinkering with the indigenisation decrees, it has tried to channel private investment to its favoured sub-sectors.

One favoured instrument is the regulation of *bank credit*. From 1970 onwards, the government has used various means to influence the sectoral distribution of lending, and since 1975 it has divided the economy into the 'more preferred' and the 'less preferred' sectors. This system has been refined over the years. Sectors have been broken into sub-sectors, and

Table 8.6 *Bank lending targets classified by purpose (%)*[a]

Category of Borrower	1980[b]	1981	1982	1983
A. *Commercial Banks*				
i) Preferred	75 (−4.2)	75 (−5.0)	75 (−5.7)	76 (−8.1)
Production	56 (+4.8)	56 (+3.4)	59 (+0.2)	61 (−2.9)
(Manufacturing)	36 (−5.2)	36 (−5.1)	36 (−5.5)	36 (−7.6)
(Construction)	10(+12.8)	10(+10.4)	13 (+7.6)	13 (+7.5)
Services	12 (−3.5)	12 (−2.8)	12 (−3.1)	12 (−3.3)
ii) Less Preferred	25 (+4.2)	25 (+5.0)	25 (+5.7)	24 (+8.1)
B. *Merchant Banks*				
i) Preferred	79(−10.6)	79(−13.2)	65(−14.5)	79(−21.3)
Production	69 (−3.6)	69 (−6.1)	62 (−7.1)	69(−14.0)
(Manufacturing)	41 (+0.9)	41 (+1.1)	41 (−6.3)	41 (−7.4)
(Construction)	20 (−3.3)	20 (−5.5)	16 (−4.1)	20 (−3.5)
Services	7 (−4.1)	7 (−4.1)	3 (−4.5)	7 (−4.4)
(ii) Less Preferred	21(+10.6)	21(+13.2)	35.5(+14.5)	21(+21.3)

Source: Central Bank of Nigeria, *Annual Reports*.

Notes: [a] Figures in brackets indicate extent to which actual lending deviated from the prescribed lending targets.
[b] April–December.

thresholds established for each unit which specify either the minimum proportion it must receive of total lending (in the case of the favourites) or the maximum proportion (for the others). Different thresholds are established for the commercial and the merchant banks.

In the light of the charge that manufacturing has suffered from misdirected government policies it is significant that government's preferences for the private sector are fairly orthodox. They favour agro-based industries and food processing, building materials, engineering and transport, scientific instruments, educational, telecommunications, electrical goods and electronics and household equipment. A comparison of targets and achievements illuminates the question whether or not private investors share the same priorities. The answer is that they do not. It may be assumed that the banks have attempted to massage the data on the application of loans the better to fulfil their targets. Even so, they have had difficulty in keeping to some of the targets.

Table 8.6 and Figure 8.3 show where there is a private sector demand for credit: in manufacturing, construction and commerce, only the first of which is in the government's 'preferred' category. In the period 1980–3, both the commercial and the merchant banks missed the government's targets[27]. Lending to manufacturing by the commercial banks fell below the threshold by roughly the same proportion as to the 'preferred' group as a whole. However, given that manufacturing had the highest minimum threshold by a wide margin it would appear that lending to the sector was fairly satisfactory. In the case of the merchant banks, lending to manufacturing was above target in the first two years under review and fell below target by much less than the total for the preferred sector as a whole in the second two years.

These differences between targets and achievements tend to support the observations of relative profitability already made and developed further below. They reinforce the view that construction and commerce have been among the most profitable activities and competed with manufacturing for funds and, by implication, entrepreneurial talent.

Other government instruments for influencing the level and pattern of investment in manufacturing include tax holidays, depreciation allowances, monopolistic concessions; preferences in government purchases, the construction of industrial estates, price controls and export incentives. Of particular importance are import controls but in practice, as noted below, their impact has often been contrary to that assumed under government policy.

Until 1984, the government operated an 'Approved User Status' (AUS) system for providing substantial concessions on normal import duty rates for certain raw materials,

Figure 8.3 *Bank lending 1984 (% share of actual lending)*

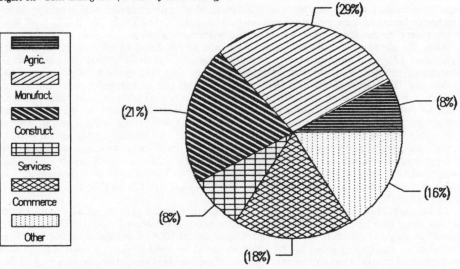

Source: Central Bank of Nigeria, *Annual Report*.

components and spare parts together with machinery and equipment where they would be used in manufacturing rather than for direct resale. This concession was highly sought after because of its financial importance. By 1980, it covered a broad range of goods and benefitted more than 200 companies. Most of the beneficiaries were large and medium-scale concerns, and to this extent government policy had the effect of favouring such companies at the expense of small-scale firms. Nearly 40% of the companies enjoying AUS status by the time it was abolished in 1984 were in the engineering sector, the bulk of them engaged in assembly-type operations and primarily in consumer goods production. More than 60% of AUS beneficiaries were located in Lagos (NISER, 1980 and World Bank, 1983a: 37). This conforms to the observation made above that the government does not have an active policy to spread the spatial distribution of industry.

Fiscal concessions on depreciation are biased in favour of investment in buildings and other structures rather than equipment and transport assets (World Bank, 1983a: 44), also in favour of investment in equipment with a long life span. Such biases do not appear to be dovetailed into policy for favouring certain types of manufacturing activity. There are also possibilities for tax holidays under the Pioneer Industry Status (PIS). However, in practice the scheme has been little used. In the two years up to the end of 1981 no applications for PIS had been made (ibid.: 47).

Indigenisation. Private investment to expand manufacturing capacity has made less impact than it might because capital was absorbed to a significant extent during the 1970s in acquiring existing assets instead of creating new ones. This was a result of the indigenisation exercise. Government indigenisation policies from the early 1970s to the mid-1980s have had 3 aims:

– to substitute Nigerian for foreign ownership of enterprises;
– to place part of the transferred equity with the government, ostensibly to prevent the concentration of shares in a few private hands;
– to substitute Nigerian for foreign staff.

The process was effected through decrees of 1972 and 1976 which set minimum levels of Nigerian ownership. Under the 1976 decree, enterprises were classified into three schedules with 100, 60 and 40% minimum levels of Nigerian ownership. The banks and the major expatriate trading companies were in schedule Two – 60% Nigerian-owned. The deadline for compliance was September 1976 for the banks and June 1977 for the rest. These short deadlines caused severe operational problems. More substantially, the resulting Stock Exchange bonanza drew private funds away from other investments that might have been more central to the government's industrial development strategy.

After the decrees were promulgated there was some shuffling of enterprises between schedules. The main aim has been to encourage foreign private investment into sub-sectors that the government wants to stimulate: for example, integrated agricultural production and processing. The crisis of the mid-1980s sharpened this partial reassessment of the role of foreign private investment. Nonetheless the overall effect of indigenisation has probably been to reduce foreign private investment, with the negative effects of the 1976 decree outweighing the incentives introduced more recently. Even before indigenisation, foreign ownership was on the decline. In 1963, non-Nigerian private capital accounted for 68% of total paid-up capital in manufacturing, and even in 1970 there were almost 400 wholly foreign-owned companies in the country. By 1975, the share of non-Nigerian capital had slipped to 42% (ACP/EEC, 1988: iii). Indigenisation has further reduced it substantially. In 1970, private foreign investment accounted for 40% of GDP, but by 1986 this had fallen to 20% (ibid.: iv).

In January 1989, the long-awaited new foreign investment provisions were announced, substantially liberalising the 1976 Nigerian Enterprises Promotion Decree (NEPD). There is now to be only one schedule – of enterprises reserved for 100% Nigerian ownership. Yet even the 40 or so enterprises listed in this category could be open to foreign investment if such participation brings in equity capital of not less than N20 m. One drawback, however, is that the provisions apply only to new investments. Few observers within industry believe that these (legal) changes will in isolation provide a major boost to foreign investment in manufacturing in the near term.

THE OIL SYNDROME

Manufacturing development has been constrained both indirectly and directly by the distortions engendered by oil. The periodic foreign-exchange crises have wrought havoc on import-dependent industries. The decline of agriculture has created supply problems for agro-industry and the overvalued exchange rate has both hindered manufactured exports and encouraged manufactured imports. Oil-induced migration to the towns has made it far more profitable for private investors to put their money into construction rather than manufacturing.

Inflation. There is an inherent inflationary tendency in Nigeria's oil economy which operates even if the government abides by balanced budgets. Over 80% of federal government revenue accrues as foreign exchange except during the oil slumps, and the import content of domestic expenditures is much less (possibly only 40%). Hence, unless the government deliberately underspends and lets its foreign-exchange reserves accumulate, expenditure on domestic resources will rise faster than supply (at least in the short term) and so will prices. The volatility of oil revenue has added another twist to the inflationary potential by encouraging big wage increases in times of plenty, and heavy government borrowing during the lean years[28].

The true rate of inflation is a matter of conjecture and, in any case, in a dual society like Nigeria's a great deal depends on the representative 'basket' of commodities used. The official inflation rate as recorded by the government's indices of consumer prices, which are unlikely to overestimate price increases, indicates a gradual deceleration from the mid-1970s to the early 1980s, but from a high base, and a subsequent rise in the period after 1986[29]. Inflation as high as 25% is judged to have occurred in 1988 and even higher rates for 1989 of 47% appear to have been recorded.

Attempts have been made to adjust changes in price levels for purchasing power parity (though both the price and exchange-rate data are highly dubious). The results of one such exercise, presented in Table 8.7, suggest that price movements have been relatively unfavourable for manufacturing and export agriculture, and favourable for food crops for domestic consumption, and for commerce.

Labour costs and labour supply. There is evidence that wage levels are higher in manufacturing than in some other sectors. All such evidence should be treated with extreme caution. But, with this caveat, Table 8.A6 compares wage levels in the private manufacturing,

Table 8.7 *Index of relative price movements for different sectors 1973-81*

	1973	1975	1977	1979	1981
Agriculture	100.0	175.9	228.8	282.2	332.8
(Food Crops)	(100.0)	(180.8)	(215.7)	(283.0)	(373.3)
(Export Crops)[a]	(100.0)	(94.7)	(235.3)	(216.0)	(157.2)
Manufacturing	100.0	196.8	199.6	213.0	210.8
Trade and Commerce	100.0	162.1	214.1	270.2	323.3
Government Services	100.0	114.4	133.7	256.0	291.6
Exchange Rate[b]	100.0	134.6	156.5	161.9	187.0

Source: World Bank, 1983b.

Note: [a] Export prices. Domestic prices higher in individual years through support programmes.
[b] Adjusted for purchasing power parity.

services, and construction sub-sectors as well as the public sector, showing that wages in private sector manufacturing were about one-eighth higher than in the public sector and one-sixth higher than in construction. The government has had an influence on wage levels in two ways. Most obviously, the fixing of minimum levels has a direct impact, although it is not clear how far they are observed in practice outside the largest firms. In addition, public sector wage rises have fed through to the private sector; in 1975, they jumped by nearly 90% following a review by the Udoji Commission, and thereafter private sector wages tended to 'catch up'. Then, at the turn of the decade, minimum wages were increased twice in two years from N72 to N125 per month by 1981.

These rises have had much more to do with excess demand than with trade union pressure. Unionisation is not widespread in private manufacturing. All officially recognised unions must belong to the Nigerian Labour Congress (NLC). Although it boasts a membership of 3m., all but 300,000 of these work in the public sector (McCulloch, 1985: 35).

To put Nigerian wage rates into perspective they can be compared with those in an internationally competitive, labour-intensive economy like that of Thailand. Nigerian production costs need to approach those of the successful emerging Newly Industrialising Countries (NICs) if domestic manufacturing is to become viable without heavy protection. The minimum wage in Thailand was equivalent to only about N35 per month at the end of 1979 using official exchange rates, compared to Nigeria's N72 and N125 two years later. Moreover, while the average manufacturing wage in Thailand tended to be only about 25% above the minimum, experienced Nigerian workers were able (at the time the calculation was made) to earn double the minimum with allowances and fringe benefits possibly adding another 60%.

These high nominal rates of pay have not been matched by high productivity. UNIDO reports estimates by Olaoye for the period 1962-80 indicating that total factor productivity fell during the 1970s (UNIDO, 1988: 19). Its own estimate for the period 1980-84 indicates a further fall from an index value of 100 in 1980 to 71 by 1984: value added fell to 87 and capital services declined slightly to 96 but the cost of labour shot up by 50%.

One estimate is reproduced in Table 8.A7. Although it covers only four industry groups, it suggests two points of interest. Wages have been absorbing an increasing proportion of value added even when real wage levels have been falling. Second, wages form a higher proportion of value added in the four sub-sectors identified than the overall average.

Manpower, especially skilled, is a critical constraint on growth in all areas. The government has long recognised this, which is not to say that it has always recognised its implications for the (in)feasibility of its initiatives. The progress reports on the Second and Third Plans singled out shortages of qualified manpower as a major reason for the failure to achieve targets. In 1977 the overall vacancy rate was 22%.

There are some indications that the overall capital intensity of manufacturing increased substantially during the 1970s. This was partly the consequence of public investment in the mega-projects mentioned above. It was also due to the increasing cost of plant and equipment because of the high costs of construction, power supply, and labour. One estimate is that the average cost of fixed assets per job in the modern sector was US15,000 (in 1977 replacement values) in 1978, with indications that the marginal cost has increased significantly since then

(World Bank, 1983a: 15). The manpower constraint may also have encouraged private sector firms to favour capital-intensive rather than labour-intensive modes of production. It has been estimated that the 'real cost of labour' to manufacturers rose by about 30% between 1972 and 1976.

During the periods of fast growth, costs were further inflated by rapid personnel turnover. A 1979 guide intended for foreign investors claimed that 'One company operating in Nigeria finds that the cost of labour is among the highest experienced by any of its worldwide operations' (*Business International*, 1979: 98), principally because of the high rate of turnover among both senior expatriate staff and indigenous workers – 30% for factory workers and 35% for those in the finance department. The problem was exacerbated during the periodic wage freezes imposed on the private sector, since changing jobs provided one of the easiest ways for a worker to raise his earnings. Real wages and labour turnover may have fallen as a consequence of the rapid increase in unemployment in the 1980s, but industrial efficiency is still impaired by poor infrastructure and unreliable power supplies.

The Fourth Plan foresaw massive recruitment of technical personnel, if necessary from abroad. Although legally registered expatriates account for less than 4% of modern sector employees they are heavily concentrated in a few job categories and so can have a significant impact on certain activities. Moreover, as the mass expulsion of perhaps 2m. illegal aliens in February 1983 emphasised, the phrase 'legally registered' is a major limitation on the data. These vacancies cannot be filled quickly. Too widespread a use of expatriates creates obvious political and social tensions and, equally important, there are types of work for which it is not helpful or practical to use temporary expatriates. Even where positions are filled by Nigerians the rapid expansion of the job market has spread experience very thinly: a 1977 survey of Nigerian managers found that 58% were under forty years old and 53% had no more than six years experience in a managerial position (Government of Nigeria, 1979).

The recession of the mid-1980s has eased the labour constraint (though since it has substituted an even more severe input constraint the beneficial effects are not yet clear). Labour surveys suggest that the unemployment rate trebled from 4% in 1979 to 12% in 1986, and Central Bank figures indicate a 50% increase in registered job seekers in 1986/7 (*Financial Times*, 7 March 1988). These data suggest an unemployment level in the region of 4 m. (assuming a total labour force of 34 m.).

Attitudes to management. A related, but distinct, explanation for Nigeria's poor manufacturing performance is based on the notion that the country's social attitudes are not well suited to current industrial requirements. It is argued that even successful Nigerian businesspeople prefer small-scale firms dominated by an individual entrepreneur. It follows that growth takes the form of a proliferation of small enterprises controlled by the same individual, rather than the deepening of a single establishment with more formalised chains of command. Such development does not favour the deepening of manufacturing into more complex operations; rather, it leads to concentration on finishing and processing operations.

The evidence adduced to support this line of argument starts with an analysis of firm size and of the background of individual businessmen (see Cockcroft, 1987 and McCulloch, 1985). It is certainly the case that Nigerian manufacturing enterprises tend to be small and privately owned. Over one-third of the 628 firms registered in 1972 were either sole proprietorships or partnerships: the majority employed less than 100 workers, and only 3% employed more than 1,000 (Adejugbe, 1979: 34 and 40). A survey by UNIDO in Kwara state revealed that most establishments had no backward, and few forward, linkages in the area: most were oriented towards final consumption (UNIDO, 1988: 35). Kilby's survey (1969) in the early 1960s of 298 businesses showed that almost two-thirds of entrepreneurs had only limited primary school education, while almost one-fifth had no education at all. Akeredolu-Ale argues that 'private indigenous entrepreneurs in Nigeria are still to cultivate the discipline of conserving more than they consume (and exhibit) a tendency to spread their thin investments over many ventures . . .' (quoted in Cockcroft, 1987: 34).

It is difficult, however, to assess these sorts of views. As Cockcroft himself recognises, psychology is not the only possible explanation for the small size of enterprises. In a situation of intense competition in a market limited by low purchasing power per head, opportunities may become exhausted fairly quickly so that it is perfectly rational for a businessman to develop several parallel companies rather than to develop forward and backward linkages from his initial enterprise.

Shortage of trained personnel is certainly a constraint in Nigeria but, on the other hand, there are also many talented people. A 1988 survey argued, for instance, that 'the visitor to Lagos cannot fail to be impressed by the quality of management in many private sector companies' (*Financial Times*, 7 March 1988). The main problem has been the speed of manufacturing growth which clearly outpaced decision-making capacity. This was due to the stimulus of oil (which government neglected to restrain).

The exchange rate.   Inflationary pressures have fed through directly onto the exchange rate. Until the structural adjustment programme (SAP), government policy (backed by vociferous public opinion) was strongly opposed to exchange-rate adjustments. Instead, the Naira was kept overvalued in order to dampen the impact of high domestic inflation.

In September 1986, a second-tier foreign-exchange market (SFEM) was introduced for all commercial transactions with the value of the Naira being set broadly in relation to market forces. During its first year of operation, the Naira was devalued by 66%. At the same time, import licensing was abolished. Any company that wished to import could do so, subject only to its commercial judgement of whether importing would be profitable at the new rate of exchange. In theory, therefore, it should have become evident which of the import-dependent companies and sub-sectors were more, and which were less, efficient.

In practice, however, there were problems in interpreting the outcome of the new system and, in any case, systematic data on its operations were not available at the time of writing. The principal problem is that the relative profitability of sub-sectors was still heavily influenced by import controls. Major cuts in tariffs were made at the same time as the SFEM was introduced (on the assumption that the devaluation provided adequate protection), but they have not borne equally on all activities. The Manufacturers' Association of Nigeria (MAN) complained in particular that tariffs on finished goods were lower than those on components, biasing their impact against domestic assembly industries.

The attempt to set a realistic rate for the Naira was undermined in 1988 by the excesses of the budget, which added to pressures of overvaluation. By the time of the 1989 budget, however, it seemed – on the surface at least – that the commitment had been renewed: it was announced that the two-tier exchange rate would be abandoned and that the new rate would 'primarily reflect the basic underlying forces of supply and demand for foreign exchange' (*Financial Times*, 3 January, 1989). By March, though, it was clear that these changes had not materialised; the Central Bank was continuing to intervene in the daily auctions and the black market rate varied by nearly 50% from the over-valued official rate.

The immediate effect of the liberalisation is likely to have been dampened by the shock of the Naira devaluation and by the restrictive monetary policy introduced under the SAP. The first may have encouraged initial caution among potential manufacturing importers, while the second may have limited their financial capacity to import. An added problem is that the recession has depressed consumer demand. One official estimate suggests that real urban incomes halved from 1980 to 1987, while overall per capita income which stood at $670 in 1979 is judged to have fallen to a mere $300 by 1988 (*Financial Times*, 13 November 1987 and 6 March 1989).

Moreover, it is not clear how far a more 'rational' exchange-rate policy would benefit industry in the short term because of the smuggling problem. In a situation of wide differentials between domestic and 'world' prices, the government's past preference for import restrictions obviously facilitated smuggling. The problem is exacerbated by the fact that some of Nigeria's neighbours are in the franc zone and are therefore able to trade in freely convertible currency. But the uncompetitiveness of many domestic industries in terms of quality as well as price, the sophisticated tastes and standards of urban consumers, and long-established trading traditions will make smuggling a continuing problem especially as the Naira returns to a competitive international rate.

Import policy.   The past overvaluation of the Naira has made an active import control policy vital to the survival of many Nigerian industries. High effective protection for manufacturing is not a new phenomenon; the World Bank has calculated that in 1968 the rates of effective protection were 120% for cotton textiles, 143% for metal goods, and over 200% for furniture, glass products and radio and television assembly (World Bank, 1974: 83). But its extent has increased. From 1979 until the SAP was introduced in 1986 the import regime was increasingly used to protect domestic industry rather than as a revenue source. Revenue from import duties had risen rapidly until 1977–8, but has since declined due to the shift in government policy.

A relatively low overall level of tariffs has been combined with much higher protection for specific industries. Despite a number of sharp changes of direction on individual commodities the general trend of tariff policy until the mid-1980s was for an increasing tightening in reaction to the growing shortage of foreign exchange. This trend was initially reversed in 1986 with the adoption of the SAP; as a result, the average rate of protection fell in October 1986 from 35 to 26%. On 1 January 1988, a comprehensive new tariff structure was announced to remain in operation for seven years but by the end of the year the average rate had returned to 32%. The 1989 budget included the announcement that the overall tariff structure would remain, but particular variations, both up and down, added to the general sense of confusion.[30].

During the 1970s nominal tariffs were set at around 5–10% for intermediate and capital goods, and 50% for non-food consumer goods. But because public sector imports were duty-free (until April 1982) actual tariffs tended to be lower; the weighted average level was particularly low in 1981 at around 13.5% and some manufacturing activities were favoured over others. For example, the average realized tariff for capital goods was 15% and for intermediate goods 18%; for food, by contrast, it was only 9% because of large-scale government imports of rice, wheat, sugar and other staples. A study for the World Bank in 1981, for the period 1979–80, found that while there was strong net effective protection for some industries (for instance 216% for assembly industries) there was negative protection for others (-14% for mineral and forest resource-based industries) (see Table 8.8)[31].

Tariffs have also provided more protection to the processing of imported inputs than of domestic raw materials, as illustrated in the bottom half of Table 8.8. The net effective rates of protection for import-based industries are significantly higher than for industries using domestic raw materials. These variations are reinforced by differences in on-tariff import controls, which have undoubtedly influenced investment patterns, probably in a direction other than that indicated by the government's overall industrial policy.

Sectoral distortions. *Agriculture* has been one of the most visible victims of the oil syndrome. This has had a direct adverse effect on parts of agro-industry (see below). The decline has been most marked (and of most relevance to manufacturing) in the case of export agriculture.

This decline is not just a post-oil phenomenon. Agricultural exports began to stagnate from 1962 onwards. Up to the early 1970s the pricing policies of the marketing boards together with industrial protection discriminated against agriculture. Since then it has been the distortions of the oil syndrome that have been responsible for the poor agricultural

Table 8.8 *Net effective rates of protection for selected industry groupings*[a] *(1979–80)*

	Net Effective Rate of Protection %
A. *BY INDUSTRIAL SUB-SECTORS*	
Agro–allied industries	14.7
Mineral and forest resource based industries	− 13.5
Industries producing construction materials	− 3.1
Metal working and engineering industries	50.8
Export oriented industries	− 15.1
Industries processing domestic raw materials	39.9
Industries processing imported raw materials	66.8
Assembly industries	215.8
B. *BY SOURCE OF INPUTS*	
Consumer goods industries[b]	124.9
– Processing mostly domestic raw materials	81.7
– Processing mostly imported raw materials	146.9
Intermediate and capital goods industries[b]	37.7
– Processing mostly domestic raw materials	16.4
– Processing mostly imported raw materials	65.6

Source: World Bank, 1983a.

Notes: [a] Based on an exchange-rate distortion of 35 per cent. Weights are based on sectoral shares of value added measured in world prices. A number of activities may come under more than one heading.
[b] Processing of mostly domestic raw materials or imported materials constituting 50% or more of total inputs.

performance. Now, only cocoa remains a significant export crop, topping the $500 m. mark in 1988. Palm produce never recovered from the civil war, while groundnuts were devastated first by drought in 1973 and then by rosette blight in 1975, with subsequent recovery retarded by the use of inferior planting materials[32].

If agriculture has been a major victim of the oil syndrome, a significant beneficiary has been the important *services* sector[33]. The importance of distribution has implications for manufacturing. In the first place, if Nigerian investors accurately perceive potential profit levels, it indicates that profit margins are highest in activities that are unlikely to fulfil the government's objective of using oil wealth to build up the production base. Most Nigerian entrepreneurs made their debut in commerce and services rather than in manufacturing (McCulloch, 1985: 34). Secondly, it provides further evidence to that obtained from casual observation indicating that distribution lines in Nigeria are extensive. More links in the distribution chain have the effect of pushing up the final price of manufactured goods which contributes to their uncompetitiveness with imports particularly in urban areas close to the import point of entry.

There are some fragmentary data to confirm that investors have accurately perceived differential profitability. They suggest that profit rates in manufacturing have remained far lower than in distribution. It is important to stress that what are being referred to here are relative profits. Absolute profits were very high in manufacturing, at least during the 1970s, as shown in Table 8.A8, which indicates a mean gross profit to value added ratio of around 0.80, compared with a UNIDO estimate for a representative group of 28 developing countries of 0.66 in 1978 (UNIDO, 1983: 242). UNIDO also provides data at a firm level. It shows that 'the largest industrial and commercial group' (presumably the Unilever subsidiary UAC) increased its operating profit by 346% during the period 1971–80 on increased sales of about 300% (UNIDO, 1985: 20). However, these profits do not necessarily apply only to manufacturing.

Private, including foreign, capital has responded to differential profit opportunities by beating a path to service industries and to construction. As of 1986, the contribution of private foreign capital was highest in the commercial sub-sector, minimal in agriculture, with manufacturing in between (ACP/EEC, 1988: iv).

Agro-industry – an example

A key feature of agro-industrial development in Nigeria is that there has been significant growth but this has been based on increasing levels of imported agro-inputs (see Table 8.4 and 8.A2). Moreover, Table 8.8 shows the estimated net effective rate of protection for agro-allied industries as 14.7%. The table also illustrates that 'agro-allied' does not equal 'domestic resource-based'; whereas industries processing domestic raw materials were accorded effective rates of protection of 40%, industries processing imported raw materials had protection that was half as high again at 67%.

Ohiorhenuan (1988: 4b) has demonstrated the negligible importance of agriculture and manufacturing as suppliers of inputs to each other. Only a small proportion of textile inputs, for example, are supplied from domestic resources. Similarly, beer production has increased rapidly but largely on the basis of imported raw materials. One of the reasons for this reliance on imported raw materials is the inability of the domestic agricultural sector to cope with the increased demand. Another is that government policy has not been sufficiently supportive. The problems of domestic resource-based industries are illustrated by textiles (see below) which is the most important agro-industry, accounting for some 22% of total MVA.

THE DECLINE OF AGRICULTURE
The development of agro-industry has also been adversely affected in recent years by the relative and in certain periods absolute decline of agriculture. Until the 1970s, Nigeria's wealth was agriculturally based. Even by 1975, agriculture still accounted for 64% of total gainful employment, and it undoubtedly remains the most important source. As noted earlier, Nigeria was the world's largest exporter of groundnuts and palm produce, and the second largest exporter of cocoa. In addition, cotton, rubber and timber were important exports. Shortages of basic foods were unknown until recently, and even during 1972–4 (in the aftermath of the civil war) Nigeria is reported to have fed many immigrants from the Sahel.

The decline of cocoa was masked in the mid-1970s by the very high world prices which more than compensated for falling volumes. But when prices began to tumble, so did export revenues which fell as a proportion of total export earnings from 7.7% in 1977 to a 1980 low of 2.2% (exactly one-tenth of their 1960 level). Even in 1983, when petroleum exports were at their lowest level of the decade, cocoa accounted for only 3.6% of total merchandise export revenue, and by 1985 (with petroleum still depressed) had fallen back to 2.6%.

A decline in agricultural exports is not necessarily a bad trend either for the sector or for domestic agro-industry. Given the preponderance of farms that grow both export and domestically-orientated crops, the fall in the former may simply reflect a response, say, to the growing domestic demand for food. Unfortunately, while trends in the performance of food crops are not without ambiguity, they certainly suggest poor overall growth rates. According to the FAO Index of Agricultural Production, output fell in the early 1970s and then rose slowly from 82 in 1974 to 114 by 1985. This is less than the population growth rate. Hence, even if production has not declined, the country's capacity to feed itself has. The FAO index of per capita agricultural production fell from 101 to 96 over the same period. This excess of demand over supply restricts the supply of inputs to food processing and other industries utilising agro-inputs.

Moreover, the growth in food imports is concentrated on a relatively small number of commodities. This indicates not only changes in consumer tastes but also domestic agriculture's inability to respond to these changes and, by implication, possibly other changes required to satisfy new agro-industrial demand patterns.

GOVERNMENT POLICY
Government has been accused of penalising agriculture and industries utilising domestic resources. There certainly appears to be a case of tariff bias against domestic resource-based industries (see above), but criticisms of the government's anti-agriculture policy have been overstated. They hinge on the claim that poor performance has been due to low producer prices. And there is little doubt that in the years before oil wealth, export agriculture was used as a milch cow. But in the 1970s, when the sharp agricultural decline occurred, pricing policy was different. Producer prices rose steeply and in many cases topped world market levels by a substantial margin – not only for export crops but also for some domestic food crops brought within the price-fixing net. Nevertheless, the attractions of agriculture declined relative to other economic activities. While export producer prices did not do badly against world prices, they compare less favourably with the consumer price index (which probably underestimates the rate of inflation) or with price trends in other sub-sectors (see Table 8.7)[34].

The government has recently paid more attention to domestic resource utilisation. One of its responses to the current foreign-exchange problems has been to set local manufacturing firms targets for increasing their utilisation of domestically produced raw materials. In 1985 it set the following five-year targets for minimum levels of local raw materials sourcing:

- soft drinks and breweries   100%
- agro-food industries   80%
- agricultural processing industries 70%
- petrochemicals   50%
- machine tools   50%
- chemicals   60%

As can be seen, these targets do not apply only to agro-industry, but the thresholds for this group are generally higher than for other manufacturing sub-sectors.

It is not yet clear whether companies are implementing the new proposals. On past form it seems highly likely that the deadlines will be extended and/or the thresholds lowered as domestic manufacturers plead increased competition from smuggled imports of final products.

THE TEXTILE INDUSTRY
The Nigerian textile industry is not only the largest agro-based sub-sector, accounting for almost one-third of formal sector manufacturing employment, but also the largest of its kind in West Africa. It deserves special attention in any review of Nigerian manufacturing both because of its size and because its recent history exemplifies well the problems of agro-industry.

The industry grew rapidly during the 1960s as a result of large-scale foreign investment attracted by high profit rates as a result of strong import protection. But by the mid-1980s it was in severe difficulties. This was partly because during the 1970s it had shifted its raw material supplies from domestic to foreign origin leading to increased vulnerability to the foreign-exchange squeeze, and also because of competition from imports.

Structure. There are some 100 'modern sector' textile establishments (in addition to a surviving cottage industry) with a total capacity of 400–600 m. metres of cloth. Of these, 37 are members of the Nigerian Textile Manufacturers Association (NTMA) and, between them, account for a large proportion of total capacity. There is a heavy concentration around Lagos and Kaduna which account for three-quarters of the spindles and looms (UNIDO, 1988: Table 3.3). The industry spans both spinning and weaving. Twenty-six firms are engaged in spinning, with most in the range of 25,000–55,000 spindles; a further 17 combine spinning with weaving, knitting or embroidering, and the remainder are mainly small-scale weaving companies. Despite the requirements of the Indigenisation Decree, which provides for a minimum 40% of Nigerian equity in spinning and 60% in other textile firms, strong foreign dominance remains with Nigerians acting as fronts. Indian and Hong Kong Chinese businessmen are particularly well represented, especially in the larger enterprises.

The industry suffers from low productivity and high profits which are not reinvested. Output per hour in spinning is estimated at about one-third the level in Italy, half that of Greece and about 40% that of Turkey. Wage costs per unit of output are high – twice as high as in Egypt, and four times higher than in Kenya. There are also supply constraints. Until the sharp fall in capacity utilisation in 1984–6, there was a severe shortage of installed spinning capacity, estimated at about 100,000 spindles in 1983.

Raw material supplies. Cotton has been produced commercially in Nigeria since pre-colonial times, but its large-scale production and export took off after the Second World War. Production was on a rising trend to 1977, albeit with large annual variations. From 1978 onwards, however, it fell rapidly. As a result, an industry that had developed using local raw materials turned to imports. In 1979, 30% of total supply was accounted for by domestic fibres and imports were non-existent (the balance of supply being made up of imports of yarn and man-made fibre); by 1984, only 14% was accounted for by domestic fibre and 29% by imports.

The reasons for the decline in cotton production are similar to those for the poor performance of agriculture as a whole described above. There has been sharp competition for farmers' interest from food crops, which have attracted much higher prices. Moreover, cotton production, being labour-intensive, has been adversely affected by the shortage and consequent high price of labour. In addition, the marketing board system had a particularly adverse effect on cotton between 1977 and 1986[35]. At the same time, the overvalued exchange rate made import prices artificially low. Production of woven fabrics fell from 655 m., metres in 1982 to 275 m. in 1985 and has not recovered since then.

This strategy made it very vulnerable to the foreign-exchange crisis of the 1980s, and this vulnerability was increased by the fact that non-fibre inputs (such as chemicals, dyes, machinery, spare parts) also have to be imported. As a result, the industry has had to operate at a fraction of capacity in recent years, although no systematic figures are available on the precise impact of the recession.

The problems have not been fully resolved either by the devaluation or by the abolition of the marketing board, but there is evidence of some recent progress. With the scrapping of the marketing boards in April 1986, the states have had a residual role as buyers of last resort, but the primary responsibility for marketing now lies with the private sector. Unfortunately, the first year of operation was marred by confusion. Nonetheless, there was a 300% increase in cotton production in the two years to the end of 1988, when some 50% of the raw materials processed in the textile mills was of local origin[36]. Seven new textile mills have been commissioned since the beginning of 1987 and capacity utilisation increased (from 38% in 1986 to 46% by mid-1988) (UNIDO, 1988: Section 3.2).

A new problem is now emerging. Equipment is becoming obsolescent and is unsuitable for the new cloths for which demand is growing fastest. The shortage of foreign exchange is a constraint on industry efforts to overcome this problem.

Import competition. This takes two forms: competition with domestic supply of inputs to Nigerian textile factories (see above), and competition from imported finished goods, analysis of which is complicated by the prevalence of smuggling.

Estimates vary on the level of imports (legitimate and smuggled) of finished fabrics. According to the Textile Manufacturers Association, more than half of domestic demand is supplied by smuggled imports. But according to the World Bank, the peak of competition from imports occurred in the mid-1970s. The Bank has calculated that in 1977,.for example, over one-fifth of total supply was accounted for by imports, both legitimate and imported; by 1983–5, however, the share of imports in total consumption had fallen substantially (Table 8.A9). The goods smuggled over the borders are produced elsewhere in Africa (notably Côte d'Ivoire and Cameroon) and in India, South Korea and the European Community. The situation appears to have improved since 1982, due to a combination of very high prices (reflecting the scarcity of foreign exchange on the black market), improved customs control and declining effective domestic demand.

Until the import ban of 1977, the industry suffered from negative protection. As noted in Table 8.8, nominal rates of protection of 10–40% are transformed into negative rates when adjusted for exchange-rate overvaluation.

Prospects for the medium term

The main issues for manufacturing prospects in the medium term concern:

– *foreign-exchange availability*: the issue here is whether the oil price will rise and the external debt renegotiations be resolved sufficiently to enable domestic demand-induced manufacturing expansion to be pursued hand in hand with further import substitution;
– *the role of government policies*: the questions here are how far the structural problems encountered in the 1970s were due to government policies (and hence are potentially reversible); and how far they were simply the consequence of the very rapid growth of demand fuelled by an export industry with few direct linkages to the rest of the economy (and hence are liable to reappear when/if oil exports rise again); and the likelihood that the government will persist with the kind of policies considered most likely to cope with such structural problems;
– *the impact of the oil crisis*: the extent to which the retrenchment of the 1980s has 'cured' the structural problems or simply added others to them.

Foreign exchange.   The pace of economic reform is closely linked to the inflow of foreign exchange either from oil exports or from investment/loans. The outlook is not good for an increase in oil prices in the medium term in spite of the price rises during the first quarter of 1989. The probability is that prices will tend to fall rather than rise as a result of OPEC's continuing over-production. This is despite the OPEC production limits agreed in November 1988 if, as is likely, the record of past agreements of this kind is repeated.

By early 1989, the government had failed to obtain a clean bill of health from the IMF, even though a $620 m. stand-by agreement was reached in February. Aid inflows have continued, however, including project loans from the World Bank and the pledging of some $300 m. by Japan and Britain in 1989. Moreover, there is evidence that a number of international credit agencies are planning to resume cover on exports to Nigeria. The US Eximbank has already done so and by late 1988 had agreed to extend medium-term loans, guarantees and insurance contracts worth up to $10 m. These monies have had some effect in easing foreign-exchange constraints, but problems remain. Nigeria's current account deficit remained at $1.1 bn in 1987 and although it was estimated to have fallen to $0.46 m. in 1989 is forecast to rise to $1 bn again by 1991.

These improvements all need to be put into broader context, however. Without a genuine reconciliation with the IMF (it was the government's hope in early 1989 that the IMF funds would not need to be drawn down), new loans and further rescheduling of old debts are unlikely. The need for further capital inflows is very great. In 1987 there was a gross inflow of only N1.2 bn (against expectations of N2.75 bn) resulting in a net outflow of N1.25 bn.

In the medium term there is some prospect of higher levels of foreign direct investment, or at least the government is now acting to induce a new inflow. It does not appear, however, that such an inflow is at all likely to resolve the balance-of-payments and foreign-exchange problems in the absence of an oil price rise and/or a resolution of the debt problem. The indigenisation decrees and the decline in economic prospects have taken their toll. In 1970, Nigeria accounted for over half of the total net foreign direct investment in Africa, but by 1985 its share had fallen to just over one-fifth (UNIDO, 1988: 4).

It is hoped that foreign investment will be increased by the government's privatisation plans. As part of the SAP, the federal government announced plans to eliminate its participation in some 90 parastatals in the commercial or manufacturing area. These include hotels and 'traditional' state enterprises such as the telephone and electricity utilities. Forty-nine enterprises are to be fully privatised – mainly hotels, food and timber companies, breweries, dairies, insurance companies and transport businesses. A further 38 will be partially privatised or 'commercialised', including all the banks and newspapers together with several major manufacturing parastatals – the steel mills (including Ajaokuta and Delta), oil marketing companies, vehicle assembly plants – as well as Nigeria Airways and the Nigeria Railway Corporation. However, as of late 1988 and as part of the policy changes associated with the SAP, the government was still reviewing, but had not entirely shelved, expansion plans for steel. It had, however, committed itself publicly to building a flat steel products plant at Ajaokuta.

This exercise should also ease the budget constraint. Only sketchy data exist on the financial operations of the parastatals, but they suggest that they have absorbed massive financial transfers from the government. Federal government loans to public corporations totalled N5.75 bn during 1980–86. In addition, there were large grants: in 1986 total government transfers reportedly amounted to N830 m., of which only N450 m. were in the form of loans (*Financial Times*, 7 March 1988).

Apart from its effect on financial flows, however, privatisation, by itself, may not achieve a significant improvement in the operating efficiency of these organisations (or reduce the problems of the manufacturing firms which depend on them). Three other major constraints also need to be addressed: major capital investment and reinvestment is required, new technological processes have to be (selectively) introduced, while management personnel, skills and processes need to be overhauled in many such organisations.

Government policies. The outlook for the medium term is closely linked to government policy. The SAP measures responded initially to a number of well-publicised criticisms of previous government policy, including the overvaluation of the Naira and the distortions caused by selective import licensing, both of which have had negative effects on the manufacturing sector. The addressing of these impediments under the SAP might be considered beneficial, therefore, for manufacturing.

But such is the scale of the short-term problems caused by the earlier mismanagement that the government's new policies have not yet removed all of the severe dislocations in the economy. Only if they are continued and extended for several more years will it become possible to observe manufacturing operating under anything that could be described as 'normal conditions'.

The SAP formally came to an end in July 1988 and by the first quarter of 1989 no firm, consistent and long-term programme had replaced it. The launch of a Fifth National Development Plan was abandoned in October 1988 to be replaced by a longer-term but even more uncertain planning framework. The government is walking a political tightrope between the need for continued austerity and the political dangers that this can provoke, epitomised in April 1988, for example, by widespread disorders following the increase in prices for petroleum products.

Not surprisingly, the government has difficulty in maintaining its course. Under the 1986 agreement with the IMF the fiscal deficit was targeted at 3% of GDP. In the event, the 1986 deficit was 10%, rising to some 16% in 1988, double the forecast at the start of the year. As a result, the IMF programme expired in 1987 without a successful review. The IMF requires a substantial reduction in the fiscal deficit ratio, accelerated depreciation of the Naira and the installation of its own monitoring teams in relevant ministries.

The reason for the difficulty in keeping to target is clear enough. The process of adjustment initiated under the SAP is painful. Real GDP is now lower than in the mid-1970s (see Table 8.1) and real per capita incomes have continued to fall.

Of direct concern to the future prospects for, and structure of, the manufacturing sector, the government's commitment to import liberalisation appears to have weakened under the onslaught of pressure from the industrial lobby. The substantial liberalisation introduced under the SAP has been partially rescinded. The new tariff structure sets a basic rate of 10% for capital equipment and a range of 10–30% for raw materials and intermediate goods; the rate on most consumer items was reduced to 30%. To ease the shock effect on domestic manufacturing, some items received additional temporary protection, due to last only for a year, in the form of countervailing duties, and there was a surcharge of as much as 170% on luxury items. The argument behind these tariff changes was that domestic industry was obtaining additional protection from the depreciation of the Naira and, in any case, was paying lower duties on imported inputs. Nonetheless, the manufacturers complained loudly and the government responded by retreating from its initial cuts. The general level of tariffs was increased, first in February 1987 and then in the 1988 budget.

On the positive side, there is already evidence of greater utilisation of domestic raw materials, encouraged by import bans and increased prices for imports resulting from devaluation, and, following from this, increased investment in their production. The import ban on malt, for example, has been forcing brewers to use maize and sorghum, leading to a sharp increase in the prices of these commodities which should, in turn, boost production.

Further devaluation of the Naira is likely in the short term. On the market for autonomous funds[37], the rate of exchange fell sharply in 1988 to N4.54 to the US dollar and to N7.8 by the end of 1989. This shift should provide further protection for domestic manufacturing, which will also benefit from changes in the rules for public sector imports. In the past, imports by government organisations were duty-free; this exemption has now been removed.

On the other hand, manufacturing faces sharply increasing input costs. Not only have petroleum product prices increased, but the National Electric Power Authority indicated in late 1988 that it might have to increase electricity prices by a staggering 600% as a result of new regulations requiring federal ministries and parastatals to meet their import requirements through the foreign-exchange market at the rates applying to the private sector. As a result of food shortages (following drought in the north) and higher wage settlements after the lifting, in 1988, of the wage freeze imposed during the SAP, inflation rose to nearly 50% in 1989, after averaging about 10% over 1980–86. There are also wide annual variations in output. Hence, unless the underlying structural and financing problems of the economy are resolved, the 1987–9 upturn noted above (like that of 1985) may prove to be a temporary blip rather than the first indication of an upward long-term trend in manufacturing output. Estimates (by the EIU) are for MVA to average only 2% in 1990 and 1991.

The differential ability of manufacturing sub-sectors to cope with the new conditions of austerity, differing levels of protection and more market-oriented exchange rates continued in the late 1980s. According to company reports for 1987/8, within the larger formal sector enterprises, paints, textiles, printing and soap/detergents manufacture all registered improved performance. Output in the paint industry rose by over 10%, while detergent production shot up by 175%. The sub-sectors that appear to have been adversely affected by the changes are cement (output down by 15%), electronic goods (production down by a quarter as a result of competition from imports) and motor vehicle assembly. Moreover, in spite of the changes noted above, the sector as a whole still remains heavily dependent upon imported inputs (see Table 8.9).

Impact of the oil crisis.   The positive effect of oil during the 1970s was to fuel a very rapid increase in effective demand. This resulted in a rise in domestic manufacturing production that was substantial by any standard. But the other side of the coin was that it contributed to rapid inflation, an increase in labour costs, and sectoral distortions that would have been difficult to control whatever the government policy. There is no reason to suppose that the economic changes resulting from the oil crisis have altered in any significant way the capacity

Table 8.9 *Sources of raw materials used in production by industrial branch, mid-1987*

Sub-sector of manufacturing	Imports as % of raw materials used
Food, beverages, tobacco	34.8
Wood and wood products	22.4
Non-metallic minerals	23.5
Textiles and wearing apparel	47.6
Chemicals and pharmaceuticals	55.8
Industrial plastic and rubber	79.4
Basic metal and fabricated metal products	50.3
Vehicles	78.2
Electrical machinery	80.7
Paper products	60.1

Source: UNIDO, 1988: Table 2.6.

of the economy to absorb a future oil boom. What the crisis may have done is to alter government attitudes to the management of oil so that, in future, public policy tends to offset rather than to exaggerate the negative effects of the oil syndrome.

In its failure to take account of domestic inflation in its exchange-rate policy, in its differential protection for import-based and domestic resource-based manufacturing, in its focus of capital expenditure on heavily capital-intensive industry, and in its failure to moderate the peaks and troughs of the oil industry, the government failed during the 1970s and early 1980s to manage the economy in the fashion most conducive to manufacturing and development. It is clear that in its attempts to grapple with the economic crisis of the mid-1980s the Babangida Government has radically altered the approach to many of these issues. These changes have been unpopular and, to a certain extent, are already being rescinded. It may be assumed that such recidivist tendencies will gain strength as the economy climbs out of its current trough. Nonetheless, future governments will be prepared to recognise the inherent dangers of oil-led growth in a way that their forebears were not.

So long as the Nigerian economy is dominated by oil it will remain vulnerable to the adverse features of the oil syndrome as well as benefitting from its positive effects upon demand creation. The negative features are likely to be most prominent if there is a sudden surge in oil revenue as there was in the mid- and late 1970s. By the same token, the government is more likely to be able to offset some of the negative consequences if oil recovers at a moderate, sustained pace from its present trough. The best outlook for manufacturing, therefore, would be for the immediate constraint of debt to be removed, for there to be a resumption of foreign-exchange flows sufficient to ease the blockages currently disrupting normal economic activity and for oil export earnings to rise moderately rapidly.

How likely is it that such a scenario will occur? As noted above, the outlook is clouded on all of the main variables. Neither the rescheduling of old debt nor the adequate flow of new funds is assured, and the medium-term outlook for oil is obscure. Without an adequate inflow of foreign exchange in the short term there must be a real danger that the government will be able to offer too few incentives to efficient industries to offset the political opprobrium resulting from the removal of privileges and protection to established firms.

Hence, of all the variables, the most important is the flow of foreign exchange in the immediate future. The government is most likely to maintain a set of policies conducive to manufacturing development if the foreign-exchange account avoids the extremes of either too little or too much. Unfortunately, there is little reason for optimism about the likelihood of these extremes being avoided. The worst outcome would be a continuation of the present foreign-exchange constraint in the short to medium term, followed by a major increase in oil production/price in the medium term consequent upon some unpredicted shock elsewhere in the global oil system.

Nonetheless, whatever assumptions are fulfilled, there would appear to be little hope that in the next few years the structure of manufacturing will change sufficiently to alter the present domestic focus. An export-oriented manufacturing sector in Nigeria is still a long way off.

Notes

1. The research for this chapter was substantially completed during the course of 1988. I am grateful to Roger Riddell for assistance in up-dating the text in the light of events taking place up to the first quarter of 1989.
2. Since actual prices have changed frequently (and not always in accordance with stated government policy) the price line in Figure 8.2 is based on the most relevant of the available IMF indices for petroleum – that for Libya (Es Sidra). The vertical axis is denominated in hundred thousand barrels per day for production and in units for the price index.
3. It has been estimated, for example, that 300,000 tonnes of wheat were smuggled into the country in 1987. This would be equivalent to 10 times the volume of domestically grown wheat. The same problem, but in the reverse direction, affects fertilisers. Government policy is designed to boost domestic agricultural production through the provision of a 70% subsidy on imported fertiliser to increase its utilisation. This is by far and away the largest item in the Ministry of Agriculture's budget. But smuggling out of the country and poor storage lead to losses each year put at about 50% of distributed fertiliser (*Financial Times*, 7 March 1988).
4. See below, for a description of the indigenisation policies of the 1970s.
5. These figures are from the 1989 budget speech and unofficial estimates. See *West Africa*, 16–22 January 1989 and *Financial Times*, 6 March 1989.

6. While his data are of considerable interest, Ohiorhenuan does not explain how he has overcome the major problems of data (non)-availability in undertaking this exercise. Hence, the figures should be used with some caution.
7. The table incorporates recalculated data for 1982–3 to make them comparable with the earlier years. But, because of lack of data on the precise coefficients to use, the figures for the last two years should be treated with caution. The base year of the index was changed from 1981.
8. Because of the methodological problems noted above, figures for the period to 1981 and from 1981 are presented separately.
9. The outlook for the future is for a growing share of petroleum products to be domestically refined but, as noted below, this is at the expense of very heavy capital investment with a high opportunity cost. It is difficult even to assess whether domestic refining is economically efficient since the trade in refined products is distorted by both import and price controls.
10. Once again, the source of his data is unclear and, given the general statistical problems noted above, the precise figures should be treated with some caution (Ohiorhenuan, 1988: 42).
11. As these figures presumably only refer to the formal sector, they almost certainly understate the full extent of employment contraction, given the size of the informal manufacturing sector.
12. An analysis of the figures of 13 major companies reporting for the first half of 1986, for example, revealed only three cases in which the profit/turnover ratio was higher in comparison with the same period a year previously (EIU, 1987: 11). But more recently profits appeared to be on the increase once again. This is arguably an indication that the crisis has bottomed out, supported by the published results of 61 Stock Exchange-listed companies which show both turnover and profits up in 1986–7 over the previous year. Both rose by more than 17%, compared with a 6% rise for turnover and 2% for profits in 1985–6.
13. The latest year for which detailed export statistics were available at the time of writing.
14. Some 0.19% of merchandise exports were in relation to cocoa butter, 0.03% in cocoa powder and 0.01% in cocoa cake.
15. Set up with authorised capital of N100 m. subscribed by the government and the Central Bank.
16. It is not clear why bank loans are favoured over the reinvestment of profits. Quite probably, this reflects an artificially low cost of borrowing either because interest rates are subsidised or because default is tolerated.
17. The exclusion of the informal sector also limits the utility of output data, but because the output of informal enterprises tends to be small, this is not so serious as the distortion to employment figures.
18. Thus a 1983 estimate by the World Bank that the informal and formal manufacturing sectors together accounted for about 10% of employment (World Bank, 1983: 8) can be compared with the 24% of formal sector employment cited above and figures given below for 1977 claiming employment shares of 14% percent for the formal and perhaps as much as 40% for the informal sectors.
19. According to the 1988 *Financial Times* survey of Nigeria.
20. The 1979 civilian elections were won by a government headed by Alhaji Shehu Shagari. It was unable to provide the quick, decisive action required by the sharp changes in the oil market. It was also characterised by large-scale and ostentatious corruption and by the chaotic build-up of unfunded debts. It won controversial elections in 1983 but was then overthrown when the army returned to power led by Major General Buhari. This military government was also unable to act with sufficient authority and in 1985 was replaced in a coup led by General Babangida. The Babangida government remains in power to the present day. It has at last begun seriously to tackle the economic problems arising from the oil crisis.
21. A government report on the 'Causes of excessively high cost of government contracts' found that the average cost of government contracts was 200% higher than in Kenya and 130% higher than in Algeria. And it attributed the high costs to the rapid increase in government spending: between 1973 and 1975, for example, the value of federal highway contracts increased tenfold.
22. A quarter of capital spending under the Third Plan was in transport, while education received 8%. Over half of the existing road network was widened, strengthened or improved, power output rose by 15% per annum, new port facilities were created, and universal primary education introduced.
23. In 1967 these accounted for 18% of the total paid-up capital in enumerated manufacturing, but for only 0.7% of the total value added (World Bank, 1974: 82).
24. The burden of tax in Nigeria is very low by international standards, particularly if the oil sector is excluded. The ratio of non-oil tax revenue to non-oil GDP is 6–7%. An IMF study of 47 developing countries recorded average levels of 15–16% (Tait, 1978). Company tax has grown less rapidly than either non-oil GDP or company profits despite a sharp increase in the number of companies paying tax. It should be noted, though, that low tax rates are not the only reason for this: enforcement is also a major problem.
25. For instance, only 3 out of the 5 hard grades of carbon black are produced, with the result that considerable quantities required by Dunlop and Michelin are still sourced from abroad.
26. He also argues that the concurrent implementation of several projects provides far fewer learning opportunities than a sequential process which might have applied had Nigeria not had the windfall oil revenue.
27. In the case of the commercial banks, lending to the 'preferred sectors' was between 4 and 8% below

the prescribed level, while for the merchant banks the deviation was greater at 11–21%. The activities most 'over target' were construction and credit, and financial institutions.

28. The 1981–2 oil slump, for example, was accompanied by massive public sector domestic borrowing. Bank lending (mainly by the Central Bank) to the government rose from N1.7 to N8.1 bn during the twelve months from May 1981, and was the main cause of a 75% surge in bank lending, most of it short-term.

29. After a surge of nearly 35% in 1975, the rate fell to 24% in 1976 and then by degrees to 10% in 1980. It bobbed up to 11% in 1981. In 1983 and 1984 it rose again to 23% and 40% but, according to official figures, dropped back to single figures in 1985 and remained there in 1986. Central Bank estimates indicate that it increased to 12% in 1987, and to an estimated 20% in 1988 (EIU, 1989: 170). The 1989 budget, however, gave the 1988 figure as 25%, while businessmen judge it to have been closer to 40%.

30. Tariffs were reduced, for instance, in regard to battery parts, hot rolled sheets for metal packaging and for plates printed and non-printed while cigarettes and particle board have been removed from the list of banned imports, albeit attracting import duties up to 200%. On the other hand, duty increases were announced for enamel ware, syringes and needles, bicycles and motor-cycles, while alkyl benzene, bentonite and barytes have all joined the list of banned products (*West Africa*, 16–22 January 1989). These measures need also to be seen in the context of the 1988 budget which introduced extra landing charges to be imposed on imports that have local substitutes. It also added to the list of banned imports aluminium sulphate, malt, barley and used tyres.

31. This analysis assumed that the Naira was overvalued by 35% and used this estimate to convert nominal rates of protection into net effective rates.

32. The conventional wisdom has it that agricultural decline is due to government neglect. There is a kernel of truth in this, but it does not tell the whole story. The government certainly has neglected agriculture relative to some other sectors despite various campaigns ('Operation Feed the Nation' and the 'Green Revolution') suggesting the contrary. But deliberate neglect has not been the sole, nor even the main, cause of decline. Nor would more active government intervention (within the bounds of political feasibility) necessarily have reversed the trend. Agricultural decline is a feature of the oil syndrome.

33. In the national accounts statistics, services accounted for some two-fifths of GDP at factor cost in 1981. This is high for Africa: in Kenya the figure is 31%. But where Nigeria stands out is in the relative importance of the sub-sectors. Government services are relatively modest, accounting for 5% of GDP in 1981 (as compared with 15% in Kenya). Nor are they growing at an alarming rate; in 6 of the years 1973–81 they grew more slowly than GDP. The major sub-sector is domestic trade, which makes up 24% of GDP. These statistics provide only a broad indication and should not be taken too literally. Most Nigerian statistics are based on 'very scanty information' (the Central Bank's words) but in few areas is the situation worse than it is for services. The result is that the sector is often treated as a residual item. Despite this caveat, the broad figures are of importance: services are big, and distributive trade accounts for over half of them.

34. The efforts to revive agriculture are fighting a trend for labour, especially young labour, to move to even more profitable activities. It is claimed that the average Nigerian farmer is aged over forty. These alternatives need not necessarily be in the towns: many farmers have employed hired labour in order to engage in more lucrative activities themselves. This process has undoubtedly been accelerated by the spread of primary education, which has both withdrawn children from the farm workforce and given them expectations that cannot be fulfilled by agriculture. The recession of the mid-1980s may help to soften the problem. The collapse of urban employment together with the increased local currency value of agricultural exports (following the Naira devaluation) appears to have prompted a partial return of labour to the rural areas. There is some evidence that the rural labour force may have grown by as much as one-quarter in recent years (*Financial Times*, 7 March, 1987).

35. In 1977, the marketing board system was subject to one of a series of reorganisations. Regional marketing boards responsible for a range of commodities were disbanded and replaced by a set of federal boards each responsible for only one commodity. The Nigerian Cotton Board appears to have been one of the more inefficient, and these problems were exacerbated by serious cash shortages which resulted in farmers being paid often below the official price and with promissory notes. In consequence, farmers changed their cropping pattern to give priority to food crops.

36. The rise in farmer prices has undoubtedly had an important influence on this growth in production. Prices were increased from N560 in 1983/4 and N700 in 1985/6 to N850 a tonne in 1987, and by early 1988 grade 1 cotton was selling at the farm gate for N1600–1800 a tonne. According to USDA figures, production increased from 10,000 tonnes in 1985 to 27,000 tonnes in 1987. The increased availability of labour has undoubtedly also played a part. In an effort to increase local supply, several textile firms are investing in cotton cultivation, and some have negotiated medium-term production contracts with growers.

37. That is, foreign currency purchases using export revenues from commodities other than oil and funds repatriated from abroad.

Statistical Appendix

Table 8.A1 *Source of growth in gross manufacturing output, 1970-79 (%)*

	Domestic demand	External demand	Import substitution	Statistical[a] discrepancy
Total manufacturing	99.75	0.25	− 0.00	1.44
Food products	166.96	0.10	− 67.06	9.54
Beverages	99.90	0.01	0.09	0.00
Tobacco	99.77	0.00	0.23	0.00
Textiles	92.53	− 0.31	7.78	0.80
Wearing apparel	211.19	3.83	115.03	0.00
Leather and fur products	99.06	30.31	− 29.38	14.85
Footwear	94.19	0.00	5.81	0.00
Wood and cork products	113.14	− 2.90	− 10.24	5.90
Furniture and fixtures	94.78	0.01	5.21	0.00
Paper and paper products	64.82	0.13	35.05	0.00
Printing and publishing	105.14	0.98	− 6.12	0.12
Industrial chemicals	48.21	0.10	51.69	0.03
Other chemical products	82.01	0.03	17.96	0.02
Petroleum refineries	84.76	6.64	8.60	0.07
Mix petroleum and coal products	108.86	0.07	− 8.93	0.21
Rubber products	156.13	0.00	− 56.13	0.01
Plastic products	92.33	0.00	7.68	0.00
Pottery china	570.47	0.48	− 470.96	0.00
Glass and glass products	92.16	0.05	7.80	0.00
Other non-metallic minerals	110.76	0.39	− 11.14	0.00
Iron and steel	0.00	0.00	100.00	0.00
Non-ferrous metals	162.93	− 25.09	− 37.84	74.61
Metal products excluding machinery	114.13	0.63	− 14.76	0.01
Non-electrical machinery	12.15	0.02	87.83	0.00
Electrical machinery	82.83	0.06	17.12	0.00
Transport equipment	11.34	0.00	88.66	0.00
Professional and scientific goods	− 468.10	− 0.14	568.24	− 0.19
Other	154.32	− 0.02	− 54.30	0.07

Source: UNIDO, 1988, Table 2.8.

[a] Statistical discrepancy in matching ISIC gross output data with SITC trade statistics.

Table 8.A2a *Distribution of MVA by industry groupings (1971/2 and 1977/8) (%)*

	1971/2[a]	1977/8[a]
CONSUMER GOODS	*70.30*	*65.70*
of which: Food, beverages and tobacco	35.7	26.5
Textiles and wearing apparel	18.0	14.6
Leather goods and footwear	0.7	1.2
Paper products and printing	4.5	5.2
Plastic and rubber products	2.3	3.3
Other non-durable goods	6.2	10.2
(including soaps and detergents, pottery and china, glass and glass products)		
Wood and metal furniture	2.1	3.8
Television and radio equipment	0.8	0.9
INTERMEDIATE GOODS	*29.0*	*25.8*
of which: Chemicals and paints	11.5	7.9
Leather tanning and finishing	0.4	0.4
Tyres and tubes	2.4	1.8
Sawmills and wood products	2.1	1.8
Building materials	3.7	4.9
Metal working industries	8.2	8.7
Miscellaneous	0.7	0.3

Table 8.A2a *contd*

	1971/2[a]	1977/8[a]
CAPITAL GOODS	0.7	8.5
of which: Machinery and equipment	0.2	3.5
Other electrical equipment	0.4	1.0
Transportation equipment	0.1	4.0

Source: World Bank, 1983: Table I.4.

[a] Data shown are 2-year calendar year averages based upon data in current prices.

Table 8.A2b *Distribution of MVA, 1981, 1983 and 1984 (%)*

Sub-sector of manufacturing	1981	1983	1984
Consumer, non-durable	*64.4*	*66.4*	*71.8*
Food, beverages and tobacco	27.9	27.2	32.1
Textiles, wearing apparel	8.7	10.5	15.2
Footwear and leather	0.7	0.8	2.5
Paper and products	3.5	3.7	5.2
Rubber and plastics	4.0	2.1	3.0
Pottery and china	0.9	0.4	0.6
Pharmaceuticals	9.2	6.5	8.4
Petroleum products	9.5	13.1	5.0
Durable consumer goods	*8.2*	*8.8*	*6.8*
Furniture	4.4	5.0	2.2
Non-electrical household goods	1.1	1.3	1.2
Radios and TV sets	1.0	0.4	1.4
General electrical household goods	–	–	–
Other consumer goods	1.7	2.0	2.2
Capital Goods	*36.0*	*24.8*	*21.3*
Basic metal products	–	–	1.6
Fabricated metal products	4.5	5.8	6.9
Machinery	0.01	0.1	0.0
Transport	19.6	14.4	4.6
Other capital goods	3.7	4.7	8.3

Source: UNIDO, 1988, Table 2.2.

Table 8.A4 *Input structure of manufacturing (input components as % of total output)*

Industrial sub-sector	Domestic inter-mediate inputs	Imported inputs	Wages & salaries	Operating surplus	Deprecia-tion	Indirect taxes	Subsidies (−)	Total*
7	23.64	25.31	9.11	37.39	3.03	2.15	0.31	100.0
8	20.21	16.24	7.24	48.03	5.90	2.79	0.41	100.0
9	18.40	30.03	14.08	28.94	4.91	1.93	0.28	100.0
10	22.92	31.80	12.00	29.50	2.21	1.83	0.27	100.0
11	25.19	22.30	10.01	36.24	4.47	2.11	0.31	100.0
12	10.17	48.39	12.63	24.59	2.43	2.10	0.31	100.0
13	10.48	48.16	6.93	30.90	1.47	2.41	0.35	100.0
14	18.92	37.42	13.46	25.56	3.18	1.70	0.25	100.0
15	21.61	20.50	16.31	34.89	3.57	3.66	0.53	100.0
16	10.57	41.59	11.10	32.75	2.37	1.90	0.28	100.0
17	11.82	51.80	3.94	27.70	1.47	3.77	0.55	100.0
18	21.38	24.54	13.49	35.81	3.00	2.08	0.30	100.0

Source: Ohiorehenuan, 1988.

* Totals may not sum exactly to 100 due to rounding.

Table 8.A3 *Index of manufacturing production 1975–83 (1972 = 100)*

	Weight	1975	1976	1977	1978	1979	1980	1981[a]	1982	1983[a]
Sugar confectionery	4.5	118.4	127.1	207.3	201.6	168.9	98.8	99.5	84.4	78.5
Soft drinks	5.6	224.9	322.1	303.5	332.3	433.5	514.0	533.3	655.3	565.8
Beer	28.2	178.5	191.0	185.6	285.2	310.8	604.8	605.3	619.9	654.2
Cigarettes	20.3	107.0	128.3	122.0	129.0	117.3	123.0	121.3	–	145.9
Cotton textiles	24.4	144.9	161.0	172.9	167.1	184.2	257.3	235.2	315.6	–
Other textiles	4.5	611.0	1,051.8	964.7	1,129.3	1,297.1	1,257.5	1,260.8	1,436.9	1,062.1
Footwear	1.6	122.6	110.0	123.5	119.3	128.8	161.8	162.6	327.2	20.4
Paint and allied products	1.8	151.7	180.2	241.8	280.3	274.6	315.3	315.0	316.7	190.8
Soap and detergents	12.6	177.9	228.1	328.4	362.5	325.5	449.2	596.0	591.6	437.0
Refined petroleum products	4.8	105.4	128.0	123.6	124.5	150.6	460.8	483.4	508.6	508.6
Other petroleum products			84.9	86.6	74.6	93.1	175.4	193.4	–	–
Pharmaceuticals	1.8	148.3	239.8	186.5	352.9	227.2	122.4	127.9	–	–
Cement	6.0	115.6	115.4	117.1	139.6	161.9	146.9	170.2	199.4	160.3
Roofing sheets	3.5	137.9	161.2	214.7	191.7	218.9	187.5	191.8	314.2	237.3
Vehicle assembly	0.7	302.2	698.6	1,097.3	992.7	1,138.9	2,808.2	1,139.1	3,601.8	1,947.2
Radios, record players, TV assembly	1.3	108.0	119.1	128.6	95.7	240.8	218.4	117.3	23.4	9.8
Total manufacturing	150.2	147.7	182.2	193.5	221.4	327.5	344.7	364.2	411.3	326.0

Source: Central Bank of Nigeria, *Annual Reports*.

[a] Estimated.

Table 8.A5 *Distribution of manufacturing employment by industry grouping*

	1971–2 No. of Employees	%	1977–8 No. of Employees	%
CONSUMER GOODS INDUSTRIES	*116,649*	*75*	*226,653*	*72*
of which: Food, beverages and tobacco	32,323	21	66,186	21
Textiles and wearing apparel	43,432	28	83,159	26
Leather goods and footwear	3,521	2	5,745	2
Paper products and printing	11,888	8	17,637	6
Wood and metal furniture	9,521	6	16,502	5
Plastic and rubber products	7,926	5	19,161	6
Other non-durable goods	7,170	5	16,544	5
Television and radio equipment	868	1	1,719	1
INTERMEDIATE GOODS INDUSTRIES	*37,868*	*24*	*72,885*	*23*
of which: Chemicals and paints	3,000	2	7,551	2
Leather tanning and finishing	929	1	1,391	0
Tyres and tubes	2,378	2	3,096	1
Sawmills and wood products	9,573	6	15,764	5
Building materials	6,240	4	16,114	5
Metal working industries	13,598	9	27,850	9
Miscellaneous	2,150	1	1,119	0
CAPITAL GOODS INDUSTRIES	*2,155*	*1*	*16,031*	*5*
of which: Machinery and equipment	507	0	5,139	2
Other electrical equipment	963	0	2,940	1
Transportation equipment	685	0	7,952	3
TOTAL	*156,672*	*100*	*315,569*	*100*

Source: World Bank derived from Federal Office of Statistics (Lagos): *Industrial Surveys*.

Table 8.A6 *A comparison of minimum wages in the public and private sector* (N per year)

	1979			1984		
	Minimum wage	Cash benefits	Total	Minimum wage	Cash benefits	Total
Public sector	846	428	1,274	1,500	428	1,928
Private sector	560	168	728	–	–	–
Manufacturing	–	–	–	1,560	610	2,170
Services	–	–	–	1,500	440	1,940
Construction	–	–	–	1,500	360	1,860
Public sector as % of private sector	–	–	175	–	–	–
Manufacturing	–	–	–	–	–	89
Services	–	–	–	–	–	99
Construction	–	–	–	–	–	104

Source: Khan, 1986.

Note: Information has been obtained for the private sector from the Wages and Productivity Unit of the Federal Ministry of Employment, Labour and Productivity which carried out surveys in 1979 and 1984. For the latter year the survey data are available for specific sectors.

Table 8.A7 *Wages, factor share of labour and labour productivity*

	Money wage (N per year)	Real wage (1975 prices)	Wage as % of Value Added (current price)	Value Added per worker (N per year)
Textiles				
1973	564	892	36	1,583
1974	702	930	31	2,265
1975	1,076	1,076	32	3,319
1976	1,186	954	48	2,469
1977	1,315	929	38	3,486
1978	1,495	849	39	3,797
1980	2,145	984	43	5,036
Vegetable oil milling				
1973	436	690	18	2,443
1974	308	408	11	2,849
1975	373	373	52	719
1976	524	422	45	1,176
1977	436	308	44	991
1978	728	414	46	1,595
1980	1,040	477	53	1,972
Saw milling				
1973	999	1,581	46	2,153
1974	660	874	50	1,322
1975	802	802	44	1,824
1976	1,022	822	121	845
1977	905	640	47	2,011
1980	1,605	737	38	4,172
Cement				
1973	1,045	1,653	14	7,377
1974	1,400	1,854	14	10,124
1975	1,103	1,103	28	4,001
1976	1,669	1,343	15	11,023
1977	1,293	914	17	7,680
1978	1,552	882	28	5,608
1980	2,128	977	41	5,243
All industries				
1973	727	1,150	20	3,582
1974	843	1,117	21	4,113
1975	1,026	1,026	21	4,853
1976	1,299	1,045	20	6,443
1977	1,356	958	23	5,814
1978	1,651	938	22	7,410
1980	2,279	1,046	19	11,899

Source: Khan, 1986.

Table 8.A8 *Some indicators of performance of the manufacturing sector 1970–78* [a]

Year	Gross profit N'000	Gross profit Wages	Gross profit Value added	Gross profit Employment N'000
1970	325,338	3.41	0.82	2,513
1971	353,116	3.95	0.80	2,427
1972	388,720	3.64	0.78	2,362
1973	463,852	3.90	0.83	2,780
1974	575,580	3.98	0.80	3,094
1975	934,555	3.73	0.79	3,820
1976	1,397,759	3.96	0.80	5,151
1977	1,443,384	3.28	0.77	4,492
1978	1,759,273	3.48	0.78	5,759
1979	–	–	–	–
1980	2,852,823	3.57	0.78	9,819
1981	–	2.29	0.70	–
1982	–	2.69	0.73	–
1983	–	3.88	0.79	–
1984	–	2.91	0.74	–

Source: World Bank, 1983; UNIDO, 1988, Table 2.4.

[a] Estimates are for the entire Nigerian manufacturing sector defined as ISIC 3000 less 3530.

References and Bibliography

ACP/EEC (1988) *Investment in the ACP States and Related Financial Flows*, Report by a group of ACP and EEC experts, May.

Adejugbe, A. (1979) 'Manufacturing' in F.A. Olaloku, *Structure of the Nigerian Economy*, London, Macmillan.

Ait, Alan A., Gratze, Wilfred L.M. and Eichengreen, Barry J. (1978) 'International comparisons of taxation for selected developing countries 1972–6', *IMF Staff Papers*, March.

Andrae, A. and Beckman, B. (1987) *Industry Goes Farming: The Nigerian Raw Material Crisis and the Case of Textiles and Cotton*, Research Report No. 80, Uppsala, Scandinavian Institute of African Studies.

Bailey, R. (1977) *Africa's Industrial Future*, Denver Col, Westview Press.

Business International (1979) *Nigeria: Africa's Economic Giant*, Geneva.

Cockcroft, L. (1987) *Miners and Millhands: Industrial Cul-de-sac*, Mimeo.

Decaux, B. (1979) 'The industrial sector in Nigeria', World Bank (mimeo).

Economist Intelligence Unit (EIU) (1987) Country Report, *Nigeria*, No. 1–1987.

—— (1989a) *World Outlook 1989*, London, EIU.

—— (1989b) *Nigeria to 1993*, Special Report No. 1134, London, EIU.

Fapohunda, O.J. (1978) 'Characteristics of the informal sector of Lagos', *Research Bulletin*, No. 78/01, Human Resources Unit, University of Lagos.

Forrest, T. (1983) 'Recent developments in Nigerian industrialisation', in M. Fransman (ed.) *Industry and Accumulation in Africa*. London, Heinemann.

Government of Nigeria (1979) *Study of Nigeria's Manpower Requirements 1977*, Lagos, Federal Ministry of Economic Development.

—— (1983) Central Bank of Nigeria, *Annual Report and Statement of Accounts for the year ended 31st December, 1983*.

Khan, A.R. (1986) *Wages and Employment in Nigeria*, CPD Discussion Paper 1986–15, Washington DC, World Bank (mimeo).

Kilby, P. (1969) *Industrialisation in an Open Economy: Nigeria 1945–1966*, Cambridge, Cambridge University Press.

Kirk-Green, Anthony and Rimmer Douglas (1981) *Nigeria since 1970: A Political and Economic Outline*, London, Hodder and Stoughton.

McCulloch III, William P. (1985) *The Private Sector in the Economy of Nigeria*. Prepared for International Finance Corporation, October.

NISER (1980) 'Study on Fiscal Measures'.

Ohiorhenuan, John F.E. (1988) 'The industrialisation of very late starters: historical experience, prospects and strategic options for Nigeria', Ibadan, April (mimeo).

Tims, W. (1974) *Nigeria: Options for Long Term Development*, Baltimore, Johns Hopkins University Press.

UNIDO (1983) *Industry in a Changing World*, New York.

—— (1985) *Nigeria*, Industrial Development Review Series, UNIDO/IS.557, Vienna, 9 September.

—— (1986), Draft report on the UNDP/UNIDO Mission to the Federal Republic of Nigeria from 7 to 18 April 1986 concerning Review of the Industrial Sector, Vienna, May.

—— (1987a), *Nigeria: A Statistical Review of Economic and Industrial Performance*, Statistics and Survey Unit, Division for Industrial Studies, 21 January.

—— (1987b), 'Industry Composition of Exports, 28 January.

—— (1988), *Nigeria: Industrial Restructuring Through Policy Reform*, Vienna, 21 December.

World Bank (1974), *Nigeria: Options for Long-Term Development*, Baltimore and London, Johns Hopkins University Press.

—— (1983a), *Nigeria: The Industrial Incentive System*, Report No. 4272-UNI, Washington DC.

—— (1983b), *Nigeria Macroeconomic Policies for Structural Change*, Report No. 4506-UNI, Washington DC, 15 August.

—— (1986), *Nigeria NIDB Textile Subsector Strategy*, Washington DC, (mimeo).

—— (1987), *World Tables*, Washington DC.

9 Zambia

IGOR KARMILOFF

Introduction

The post-Independence economic development of Zambia and the contribution made by manufacturing provide an example of both marked similarities and differences with other African countries which became independent in the early 1960s. There would appear to be five cogent reasons for considering the Zambian case in some detail.

First, and of most immediate contemporary interest, is the abrupt reversal of economic policy initiated in May 1987 after four years of progressive liberalisation of an economy that had been administered, since Independence in 1964, in the pursuit of the political goal of socialism with humanism. Under close supervision by the IMF and with substantial technical help from the World Bank, price controls and quantitative restrictions on imports were abolished, subsidies removed from all but one staple product, interest rates raised to yield positive real returns on savings, public sector employment compressed and, after several devaluations, the national currency (kwacha) left to float against the US dollar with its rate set through weekly auctions.

The very sharp devaluation of the kwacha produced by the float had given rise to a two-week suspension of auctions early in 1987 which was hesitantly agreed to by the IMF. It patently signalled the unpalatable nature of the prescribed medicine for a debt-ridden economy with a dwindling import capacity. But the Fund's conditionality remained unaltered, thereby setting the scene for President Kaunda's May Day announcement reinstating the former controls and foreign-exchange allocations. The Fund's Lusaka office was closed overnight and the Bank's technical staff drastically curtailed.

Yet no more than a month elapsed before the Fund's Area Chief, speaking at a high-level joint meeting of the Organisation of African Unity (OAU) and the Economic Commission for Africa (ECA) in Abuja (Nigeria), voiced a muted *mea culpa* for the Fund's perseverance in its belief that Zambia's difficulties would ease from an expected upturn in the price of its major export, copper, thus allowing the continuation of liberalisation with no sacrifice of welfare.

The second major reason for analysing the Zambian case is the stark illustration it provides of the acute hardships faced by a developing mono-product economy in adjusting to a hostile external environment. Well over 90% of Zambia's foreign exchange earnings have come from sales of copper, cobalt and zinc (92% in 1987). Production bottlenecks in Zambia, weak world prices and demand for non-ferrous metals – largely the result of the irreversible substitution of man-made products – the absence of foreign investment, diminishing aid flows in real terms, expensive commercial loans, have combined to aggravate the country's external sector constraint.

Third is the model way in which the Fund's and the Bank's precepts concerning management practices, cost accounting, cross-borrowing among parastatals, public wage restraint and the reduction in current outlays, were followed by Zambia. Public sector enterprises achieved commendable results in introducing a tight and up-to-date system of management reporting providing decision-makers with most of the information they usually require. To that extent Zambia is in advance of other SSA countries with large public sectors and which are unable to monitor their activities and steer their economies through troubled times.

Fourth, Zambia typifies the post-colonial experience of most SSA countries in acquiring foreign technology. Freshly installed politicians and administrators lacking technical support hastened to demonstrate to their electorate the structural changes that political independence allowed. The absence of reliable basic statistics precluded the preparation of sound feasibility studies. Turnkey factories were foisted on these countries, frequently too large for their requirements and export potential, and with technology ill-adapted to their factor and resource endowments. Import substitution was inefficient and found no dynamic outlets even in neighbouring countries. Regional trade lacked complementarities as countries engaged in easy import substitution, involving first-stage processing of commonly available raw materials, or end-of-process manufacturing and/or assembling. In this early period of accelerating industrialisation, little heed was paid to debt monitoring and hopes were pinned on an ever-expanding volume of foreign transfers.

Finally, one cannot but be impressed by the remarkable resilience of Zambia's social fabric, woven loosely from 73 tribes and with about as many dialects or languages, and which has withstood for well over a decade the burden of repeated reductions in real incomes and consumption.

To paraphrase a Nobel prize-winning poet, Joseph Brodsky, the quality of reality always lies in the search for a scapegoat. By the late 1980s, IMF-sponsored measures, backed by the World Bank, however widespread their acceptance in other Third World countries, had become the focal point of all past difficulties and frustrations in Zambia. New reforms to back up the policy turn-around have been slow to appear. Some discarded precepts may well have to be presented in repackaged form before light appears at the end of the tunnel in Zambia.

The remainder of this chapter is sub-divided as follows. It begins with an overview of the economy and the manufacturing sector from the time of Independence to the late 1980s, including a discussion of the liberalisation efforts of the mid-1980s and the period, post May 1987, when this experiment was abandoned. It is followed by an examination of relative successes and failures, and the overall performance of manufacturing activities, and then by analysis of factor productivity, levels of protection and efficiency in the use of domestic resources to earn foreign exchange. Attention is then focused on inter-industry linkages, with particular attention to those of the food processing sub-sector.

The New Economic Reform Programme (NERP) and broad macroeconomic issues are the subject of the next section, followed by discussion of the inter-connections between the NERP and industry. Forecasts of growth in the economy and in the manufacturing sector to 1993 from the Fourth National Development Plan (FNDP) are then described. The concluding sections address the scope for deepening import-substitution and widening raw materials processing, taking account of regional co-operation initiatives. They also incorporate a series of suggestions for opening up and exploiting fresh industrial opportunities, together with proposals for policy changes to strengthen the sector into the 1990s.

Economic Overview

STRUCTURAL CHANGE AND MANUFACTURING
Government intervention in the management of the economy has its roots in the colonial marketing monopoly of the major agricultural products. After independence in 1964, the concurrent boom in copper prices raised fiscal revenue to a record level of 25% of GDP, allowing heavy public expenditure on economic and social infrastructure, along with the nationalisation of public utilities and transport, and the acquisition of majority shares in mining and many manufacturing enterprises. Rhodesia's Unilateral Declaration of Independence in 1965 and Zambia's efforts to reduce its strong economic links with its dissident neighbour stimulated import substitution (I/S) but also ushered in tight trade and foreign-exchange controls.

State control was exercised through a pyramidal structure of public holding companies, with the Zambia Industrial and Mining Corporation (ZIMCO) at the apex, embracing all formal mining, most manufacturing and some service activities. Thanks to high tariff levels and strict import licensing, manufacturing output made rapid strides. State-controlled enterprises received additional support from cross-subsidisation as and when required.

Urban centres were the main beneficiaries of the early development strategy. Urban living standards improved markedly during the 1964–74 decade when the nation's gross output rose at an average annual 4% rate in real terms. But in 1974 the index of export unit values, dominated by copper prices, reached its zenith and began a decline, as shown in Tables 9.1 and 9.2.

The output of refined copper declined steeply from its 1976 peak of 713,000 metric tons to a low of 459,000 tonnes in 1986, rising slightly to 483,000 tonnes by 1987 (Government of Zambia, (GOZ), 1989: 172). During the 1970s, the effect of the fall in copper prices was to

Table 9.1 *Copper prices and derived ratios*

| Year/period | Current price | | Const. 1982 price | Copper terms of trade |
	$/MT	cents/lb	cents/lb	(1970–74 = 100)[a]
1965–9 av.	1,333	60	195	127
1974	2,059	93	155	101
1970–4 av.	1,482	67	154	100
1975–9 av.	1,459	66	83	54
1980–4 av.	1,675	76	74	51
1985	1,417	64	61	43
1986	1,373	62	(51)[b]	(40)
1987	1,806	81	(60)	(44)
1988	2,620	118		

Source: World Bank, *Commodity Trade and Price Trends*, various issues and International Monetary Fund, *International Financial Statistics*, various.

Notes: [a] Current price index deflated by the cif value index of industrial countries' exports to developing countries.
[b] Figures in brackets are author's estimates.

Table 9.2 *Commodity terms of trade and exchange rates 1970–85 (1980 = 100)*

	1970	'73	'75	'77	'79	'81	'83	'85
Export unit value	68	81	61	63	92	82	76	68
Import unit value	26	36	50	56	78	102	93	91
Terms of trade	263	223	122	113	119	81	82	75
Export purchasing power	299	242	124	124	136	81	69	46
US$/kwacha market exchange rate	1.4	1.5	1.6	1.3	1.3	1.1	0.8	0.4

Source: UNCTAD, *Handbook of Statistics, 1986*; IMF, *International Financial Statistics*, 1986.

reduce by over 40% the real value of commodity exports. In terms of the country's over-valued national currency[1], copper production costs soared above the world market price. By 1970, tax revenue from mining activities had dropped to insignificant levels and mining companies ceased paying out dividends. There were no offsetting developments. Industrial diversification was discouraged by the high exchange rate and the stringency of price and foreign-exchange controls. Capacity utilisation in the mainly inward-oriented manufacturing industries plummeted as the procurement of imported inputs became increasingly difficult, even with recourse to external borrowing and supplier credit.

The relative sectoral and branch performances during the years following 1970 were such as to raise the shares of services and of manufacturing within a stagnating volume of output. As shown in Tables 9.3 and 9.4, gross domestic investment's share in total output slid from 28% in 1970 to 24% in 1980 and to a mere 8% by 1988. Public and private expenditure on GDP followed a similar trend, but with the latter expanding at *double* the rate of the former.

These figures highlight the sharp deceleration after 1974 in the contribution of the manufacturing sector to GDP, until a partial recovery was sparked off in 1984 by a series of liberalisation measures. They also highlight the diminution over the twenty-year span in per capita real incomes as the population increased by well over one million.

The pattern of manufacturing sub-sectoral growth was generally uniform to the watershed year of 1974, led by chemicals, plastics and rubber (ISIC 35), followed by metal products and other manufacturing (ISIC 38–39), which together accounted for about 40% of total manufacturing output but were also part of the subsequent deceleration. Buoyant private and public consumption supported the textiles and clothing sub-sector (ISIC 32) in the face of the overall decline.

Behind these changes lay relative shifts in investment. Thus metal products and other manufacturing absorbed over 70% of fixed capital formation during the boom years and no less than 45% of all new investment during most of the 1975–85 decade. Fertilisers and fabricated metal products were the chief attraction. The latter branch, along with other manufacturing, was also the most resilient to decline in the years preceding liberalisation.

Table 9.3 *Growth and structure of GDP by type of expenditure and economic activity 1960–88 (%)*

Real average growth of GDP	1960–70	1970–80	1980–85	1986–8
	8.3	1.0	−0.3	1.9

A. *Expenditure:*	*1970*	*1980*	*1985*	*1987*
Govt final consumption	16	26	23	21
Private final consumption	39	55	62	70
Gross domestic investment	28	23	14	8
Exports	54	41	32	
(Less) Imports	(37)	(45)	(35)	

B. *Sectoral contribution:*	*1970*	*1980*	*1985*	*1988*
Agriculture	11	14	15	18
Manufacturing	10	19	21	22
Mining, quarrying, public utilities	37	33	15	12
Construction	7	4	3	3
Wholesale & retail trade	10	12	13	10
Transport & communications	4	6	5	5
Other services incl. govt.	20	27	28	30

Source: UNCTAD (1986); World Bank (1986) and GOZ (1989).

Table 9.4 *Sectoral growth of real GDP and of manufacturing sub-sectors (%)*

	1965–70	70–4	74–5	75–9	79–83	84–5	86–8
Contribution to GDP by:							
Agriculture	−2.1	2.5	4.3	0.5	1.8	1.8	4.3
Mining & quarrying	0.4	0.8	−9.8	−2.2	4.7	−8.0	0.9
Manufacturing	11.4	8.5	−11.9	0.8	3.1	6.2	4.2
Per capita real GDP	−1.3	0.7	−5.4	−4.2	−1.4	−2.0	−1.8
Manufacturing index (Weight)							
(1973 = 100)	(100)n.a.	7.8	−4.6	−2.3	1.1	8.5	8.1
Food, bever. tobac.	(31)..	4.3	−2.1	−3.4	0.4	−1.8	14.1
Textiles, clothing	(12)..	7.2	−0.1	5.7	−22.5	22.1	7.5
Wood & wood prod.	(4)..	9.3	−34.4	−4.2	−13.4	16.4	−13.9
Paper and paper prod.	(5)..	9.0	14.2	−4.5	−3.6	33.3	72.5
Chem. rubber, plastic	(19)..	13.6	−10.6	0.0	−4.5	−7.3	−9.4
Non-metallic miner.	(7)..	3.8	3.8	1.5	−3.2	72.7	−17.8
Basic metals[a]	(2)..	6.1	−34.3	4.0	−5.9	−4.0	−25.5
Metal prod. & other manufacturing	(20)..	10.3	−6.7	−13.2	3.5	15.7	−10.8

Source: CSO, *Monthly Digest of Statistics* (various issues); World Bank (1984) and GOZ (1989).

Note: [a] Excluding copper refining.

Zambia's manufacturing performance in the 1970–84 period was distressingly poor even in the context of developing Africa, as UNIDO data, reproduced in Table 9.5, illustrate. The only sector to exceed the African average in growth was agriculture.

The narrowing fiscal base, resulting from the drop in mining profits after 1975, led the authorities to finance current expenditure by heavy borrowing from the central bank, albeit the bank's credit policy remained generally restrictive for fear of exacerbating inflationary pressure. Deficit financing thus pre-empted credit required by the private sector, obliging it to turn to foreign lenders. But the deficit financing increased the money supply which, in the face of reduced import volume and declining domestic output, rendered price stabilisation illusory.

With government firmly in control of the economy's commanding heights and wielding powerful policy instruments, a reduction in the economy's economic, financial, and

Table 9.5 *African comparative growth rates, by sector at 1980 prices, (%)*

Sector	Period	Zambia	All developing Africa
Agriculture	a) 1970–80	3.1	0.1
	b) 1981–4	2.3	1.7
	c) 1970–84	2.1	0.4
Total industrial activity (MVA incl.)	a)	0.4	2.8
	b)	− 2.8	0.9
	c)	0.3	1.1
Manufacturing (MVA)	a)	0.4	5.3
	b)	− 4.4	2.1
	c)	0.5	5.0
Construction	a)	− 1.7	8.4
	b)	5.4	− 3.4
	c)	− 3.0	6.0
Wholesale & retail trade, hotels, etc.	a)	− 2.0	3.7
	b)	− 4.6	− 1.0
	c)	− 1.4	3.0
Transport, storage and communications	a)	2.0	6.7
	b)	− 1.4	0.8
	c)	0.7	5.7
Other services	a)	1.1	6.3
	b)	− 0.7	2.8
	c)	1.6	5.9
Per capita	a)	− 2.6	2.4
manufacturing	b)	− 7.5	− 0.9
value added (MVA)	c)	− 2.6	2.1

Source: UNIDO, Statistics and Survey Unit.

technological dependence on foreign sources might have been expected. But there is little evidence to show that this occurred.

GDP has historically exceeded national income (GNP) due to significant resource outflows in the form of investment income and expatriate salaries. These accounted for no less than one-sixth of domestic savings throughout the 1970s – funds which could have been channelled into local productive activities. Averaging some 135 m. annually, this resource transfer represented 3–4% of GDP. The *legal* resource outflow between 1975 and 1980 totalled K950 m., while the total value of new direct and indirect foreign investment in this period came to K875 m.! Some supporting data on the principal capital flows are provided in Table 9.6. In a parallel development, the share of non-concessional flows (including direct investment) in net financial receipts dropped precipitously, as shown in Table 9.7.

During the lean post-1975 period, Zambia's foreign partners were loath to engage in direct investment. As the mining companies' profits vanished, they and others sought government guarantees on external borrowing which, in effect, facilitated the outflow of company funds, *inter alia*, through intra-firm procurement.

Debt servicing became progressively more burdensome. The long-term debt-service ratio climbed sharply from a mere 5.5% of the value of exports in 1970 to 18.6% ten years later – considerably above the 13.6% average in 1980 for all middle-income developing countries. From 1975 onwards, the government fell behind in its repayment obligations, creating an arrears pipeline of K700 m. by 1983. Reschedulings followed, allowing the debt-service ratio to fall to 16.2% in 1984. In the meantime, heavy drawings on the IMF brought Zambia's non-negotiable debt to that agency to SDR 640 m. equal to four-fifths of the country's annual export earnings. Investment during the late 1970s rose and fell with the level of grants received by the government, plus IMF loans.

During this period about one-third of all parastatal investment was financed by foreign funds borrowed by central government. Since the mining sector was still perceived as the

Table 9.6 *Selected capital flows, Current Kwacha m. 1970, 1975, 1980, 1984*

	1970	1975	1980	1984
Principal inflows:				
Long-term private capital, net	− 98	155	− 99	− 32
Short-term private capital, net including parastat. equity	142	21	38	n.a.
Long-term Central Government borrowing	14	85	259	129
Grants to Central Government	4	3	26	23
Sub-total	62	265	224	120
Principal outflows:				
Investment income, net	62	80	95	371
Salaries & gratuities	35	45	48	36
Sub-total	97	125	143	407
Net movements	− 37	+ 141	+ 81	− 287

Source: CSO and Makgetla, 1984.

Table 9.7 *Net capital inflow, 1970–83*

	1970	1975	1980	1983
Total net flows ($m.) (a)	27.0	311.1	353.1	218.1
of which, non-concessional (b)	13.5	112.7	57.8	1.7
b) as % of a)	50	36	16	0.1

Source: UNCTAD, 1986: Table 5.5.

most promising one by the national authorities and foreign lenders and shareholders alike, concentration of investment in mining was perpetuated to the detriment of sectoral balance and industrial diversification. Structural change in the period 1973–1980 was insignificant, as can be judged from a rough breakdown of industrial output into: consumer goods (ISIC 31, 32, 39), intermediates (ISIC 33–7), and capital goods (ISIC 38). The share of the first category rose from 57% in 1973 to just over 60% in 1980, while the intermediates' share dropped from 28 to 25% and that of capital goods remained unchanged at 15%.

Investment in manufacturing, in real terms, stayed at about one-half of its 1975 level through the early 1980s. New investment stuck to traditional paths, failing to reduce external dependence in any substantial way or to promote self-reliance. Import substitution continued to focus on consumer goods[2]. Investment in the manufacture of agricultural implements was deterred by the lack of rural credit and adequate extension support. The parastatals continued to be guided by short-term market considerations, as determined by the structure of purchasing power and hence biased towards the production of non-essentials[3].

The ownership structure of manufacturing enterprises for the years 1973 and 1980 is set out in Table 9.8. The wholly state-owned units include statutory bodies and establishments of central and local government. Parastatal companies are those in which ZIMCO had majority shares, whether they were fully or partly owned. The private companies include a few in which ZIMCO had minority holdings. The important food, beverages and tobacco sub-sector was dominated by state-controlled firms throughout the years under review. It should be remembered that 45% of parastatals were jointly owned with foreign interests and that as late as 1982 the foreign equity share in more than one-half of these joint ventures exceeded 40%.

The share of privately owned enterprises in total manufacturing output shrank from 47% in 1973 to 42% seven years later. Private firms outweighed the publicily owned ones in the relatively small or at that time slow-moving sub-sectors, for example, paper and printing, basic metals and metal product fabrication, as well as in other manufacturing. However, these were to become the more dynamic activities during the years of liberalisation.

What effects did structural change have on income distribution? In the competition for dwindling resources peasants lost out to unionised industrial labour. Migration to cities became ever more massive: between 1969 and 1980 the urban share of the total population jumped from 29 to 43% and the rural/urban terms of trade deteriorated[4].

Table 9.8 *Ownership structure of manufacturing enterprise, 1973 and 1980 (% of all enterprises)*

ISIC No.	S/Sector 1973	Weight 1980	Wholly State 1973	Wholly State 1980	Parastatal 1973	Parastatal 1980	Private 1973	Private 1980
31	47	46	1.6	6.6	70.9	66.7	27.5	26.7
32	9	12	0.0	15.7	23.1	41.8	76.9	42.5
33	3	3	0.0	38.6	28.3	13.0	61.7	48.4
34	4	4	9.3	15.4	9.3	11.1	81.4	73.5
35	15	11	0.0	0.0	54.6	62.2	45.4	37.8
36	5	5	0.0	0.0	37.1	64.1	62.9	35.9
37	1	2	0.0	0.0	0.0	0.0	100.0	100.0
38	15	15	0.0	0.0	23.7	19.2	76.3	80.8
39	negligible		0.0	0.0	0.0	0.0	100.0	100.0
3	100[a]		1.1	6.8	50.6	50.7	47.2	42.5

Source: CSO, *Census of Industrial Production 1973, 1980* and author's calculations.

Note: [a] Totals do not add up to 100 because of rounding.

Whereas before the watershed year (1974) the rate of increase in the cost of living of low-income groups *trailed behind*, the *reverse* occurred in subsequent years and became pronounced after subsidies began to be removed in 1982. Indirect evidence suggests that the already skewed income distribution curve revealed by the 1976 household survey, became more so. Unemployment increased considerably as job openings in the formal sector grew at less than the natural population increment, and still less than the rate of urbanisation.

MOVES TO LIBERALISATION
The economy was in deep trouble by the start of the present decade, notwithstanding some IMF-oriented tinkering from 1976 onwards. The nine years separating the end of the copper boom and 1983, when the first radical reform measures began to be implemented, were marked by negative domestic savings, a drop in the investment/GDP ratio from 30 to 23%, and the continued outflow of resources in profits, salaries and interest, leaving national income at 88% of GDP.

The current account deficit grew under the pressure of defence expenditure in the face of armed conflict in neighbouring countries and lower revenue from external trade (see Table 9.20, below). Development budgets shrank; productive assets went without maintenance and repair, giving rise to net dis-savings. In 1982, the country's terms of trade index was at one-third of its 1974 level and the deficit on current account came to 20% of GDP. Gross external reserves represented only two months of normal imports, while external liabilities amounted to 4.5 bn.

Commercial credit began to be unavailable. By January 1983, the Central Bank ceased reimbursing capital on outstanding loans and sought the first of a series of re-schedulings through the London and Paris clubs. To make matters worse, several years of drought cut into supplies of food and of industrial crops. Price, exchange and trade controls were tightened and the parastatal sector became a net drain on public resources as profitability considerations were obliged to yield to the maintenance of employment and consumption levels. Excessive price controls on flour, sugar and beer made these firms operate at a considerable and frequently mounting loss. Only enterprises producing non-essential goods like textiles and capital goods succeeded in remaining solvent. For the well protected manufacturing enterprises in the state-controlled sector, financial efficiency was seen to depend on the ability to charge what, in effect, would have been monopolistic prices.

Following a 20% devaluation of the kwacha at the end of 1982, an IMF-sponsored stabilisation programme was initiated. Prices were decontrolled except for a few basic items. Agricultural prices were raised and wages and urban salaries restrained. The volume of imports over a single year was pared down by one-third, which brought the trade deficit down to 9% of GDP. Tax incentives were made available to exporters of non-traditional goods; imports involving no foreign exchange were freed and competition on the domestic market was enhanced by lower tariffs on a certain number of imports. In mid-1983, a flexible foreign-exchange system replaced administrative allocation, which brought the kwacha down a further 22% within a year and gave exports a much needed fillip.

Manufacturing was slow to respond to this package of measures and the index of industrial production rose by only 10% in 1985, namely, after the auctioning of foreign exchange had brought the kwacha down to about one quarter of its dollar value two years earlier. The initial period of liberalisation and economic revival – mainly in agriculture and services – saw industrialists and would-be investors unwilling to risk their capital because of uncertainty regarding the permanence of the reform measures which the politicians did nothing to dispel. The amount of foreign exchange that the flexible system made available to entrepreneurs was no greater than in pre-reform days. They were thereby unable to re-tool, expand or get more raw materials from abroad in order to raise capacity utilisation and lower their costs of production. The only enterprises which benefited from the new export incentives were those able to export from their then available capacity, hence at the expense of satisfying domestic requirements.

The 50% retention of export earnings allowance played a big part in shifting some purely import-substituting manufacturing into exports between 1984 and 1985. Aided by the falling kwacha, the *number* of exported manufactures, mainly to *neighbouring* markets, did increase, but the quantities involved were very small. Among new export products were lead oxides (to Tanzania and Malawi), varnishes, lacquers and paints (to SSA countries), chemical preparations (to South Africa), paper rolls and stationery (SSA and a little to the USA), raw cotton and fabrics (EEC and SSA), asbestos-cement pipes (SSA), dry batteries (Tanzania) and clothing (to SSA)[5].

One of the principal constraints on new market penetration was the inadequacy of quality controls in Zambia, as well as the non-application of international norms. Up to the mid-1980s, only 30 national standards existed in respect of all manufactures. Another major constraint which reduced Zambia's geographic exporting range, was the unreliability of surface transport, either along the long railway line to the perennially congested port of Dar es Salaam, or by truck and rail to Mozambican ports. Pilferage was high and delays made delivery schedules outside the SSA area hypothetical.

No new import-substituting activities of any size accompanied the rise in manufacturing output, but not for want of opportunities. The more obvious ones were cottonseed and sunflower seed crushing and refining, rock salt mining and processing, and the manufacture of toothpaste and petroleum jelly to replace purely repackaging operations.

The dollar value of *total* exports continued to drop, since the slight shifts in the commodity structure were outweighed by the slump in copper earnings. The country's cost structure tended to rise. Between the start of liberalisation and 1985, the wholesale price index of all non-copper products rose by almost 90%, which put an additional drag on the achievement of export competitiveness. It is indeed surprising that, under the conditions then obtaining, any export diversification took place at all.

Inflation was high and raised the cost of living of low-income households by 94% in the same period. Yet no major social upheavals took place, attesting to the resilience of the country's social fabric and to the stoic manner in which both the urban population and organised labour responded, under the country's political leadership, to growing economic hardship.

The year 1985 brought in its wake more market-inspired measures. Interest rates were raised to yield positive returns to savers, a foreign-exchange auction was installed, while import licensing along with quota restrictions were abolished. The customs tariff was made more uniform and protection levels reduced for import-intensive products with low value added. The average rates of nominal tariffs (in the 30–40% range) became moderate by SSA standards and the whole subject of protection and competitiveness was thrown open to public debate at the hearings of a Tariff Commission of Enquiry.

The Commission's recommendations, which the hearings generated, were indicative of the problems faced by the manufacturing sector. There was consensus in respect of an array of policy measures, for instance in relation to the need to maintain the 50% foreign-exchange retention allowance for non-traditional exports as well as the no-foreign-exchange facility involved, with only a small licence fee. In addition, there was agreement to provide small industries with credit on preferential terms; to raise duties on *potentially competing* manufactures; to have nil tariffs on raw materials not locally available; to broaden the buy-local campaign; to give a 15% preferential margin to local contractors in government tenders and use aid money to purchase local goods and services when available; to discourage aid-tying and barter transactions; to prolong the protection enjoyed by all ailing industries but, if corrective measures proved ineffective, to liquidate them; to have foreign holders of pipeline debt swap it for equity in Zambian joint ventures and to establish an exchange-rate guarantee scheme for non-traditional exports. In relation to *ancillary measures* there was agreement to maintain price decontrol and the exchange auction system in its Dutch version[6] with the bids publicised; to make profit incentives more uniform between sectors; and to encourage local manufacturers to contribute to a more effective Bureau of Standards.

The above desiderata reflected the preponderant views of the private manufacturers and, as such and importantly, reflect some of the major handicaps faced by the sector in the mid 1980s. Overall, the general assessment of the auction system and accompanying market-oriented measures by the vocal part of the private sector was positive. It left less room for corruption or favouritism. Capacity improvement became possible in plants whose owners found the wherewithal to acquire the expensive foreign currency. But small enterprises and farmers were left at a distinct disadvantage in the scramble for foreign currency[7].

THE END OF LIBERALISATION?

A crucial change in the government's management policy was announced by President Kaunda on 1 May 1987. The progressive liberalisation of the economy, that had been initiated under IMF auspices in 1983, was abruptly ended. The auctioning of foreign exchange was replaced by administrative allocations according to set criteria and at a pegged dollar rate; prices and wages were frozen and imports subjected to closer surveillance. Two months later the New Economic Reform Programme (NERP) was published, free of all IMF tutelage, aimed at stabilising the economy in a manner consonant with domestic political imperatives and, hopefully, with greater reliance on domestic savings than in earlier planning exercises. Implementation of the NERP, initially over an 18-month period, was expected to yield a modest increase in total output – a rate inadequate to boost the country's per capita income. The volume of foreign aid was expected to remain unchanged with bilateral flows playing a more important role[8]. Debt service was henceforth to be limited to 10% of foreign-exchange earnings, after deductions to cover the imports needed to operate vital public services, transport and the mining sector.

It should be recalled that Zambia's recent growth record has been very disappointing (see Table 9.9). For the period 1980–88 real GDP expanded by only 8% – the annual rate averaging around 1% – principally because realised investment came to about one-half of the level envisaged in the country's Third Plan and mineral-based export earnings permitted less than two-thirds of required inputs to be imported. Capacity utilisation dropped, as did formal sector employment – a fall of nearly 20,000 in the period as against a total population increment of around 1.5 million[9]. The stringent IMF-sponsored structural adjustment programme, encompassing decontrol of prices and interest rates, currency devaluation, elimination of fertiliser and maize subsidies, higher farm-gate prices and privatisation of agricultural marketing, was initiated in 1983. But it failed to reverse the declining trend in the two subsequent years, as shown in Table 9.9.

Table 9.9 *Selected indicators, 1980–88*

	1980	1982	1984	1985	1986	1987	1988
Population (million)	5.68	6.05	6.42	6.72	6.95	7.27	7.53
Formal sector employment ('000)	379.3	367.5	365.3	361.5	360.5	356.5	360.7
Real GDP index	100.0	103.2	100.8	102.4	103.0	105.3	108.1
Per capita index (1977 market prices)	100.0	96.9	89.2	86.6	84.2	82.9	82.1
Exports as % of GDP	41.4	27.6	36.6	38.7	45.6	45.4	36.7
Imports as % of GDP	45.4	36.5	32.8	38.2	45.7	42.1	36.2

Source: CSO, *National Accounts Statistics Bulletin*, No. 2, *Economic Report, 1987* and GOZ (1989).

Indeed, following the introduction of foreign-exchange auctioning, the dollar value of the kwacha fell almost tenfold and the rate of inflation accelerated sharply. The positive output response to higher agricultural prices was more than offset by a 117,000 tonne decline in processed copper production between 1980 and the beginning of 1988. During the same period, the manufacturing sector's severe import dependence remained unchanged. The index of industrial production *decreased*, on average, at 1.4% a year between 1980 and 1987 (first quarter) with no new investment going into secondary import-substituting activities.

It was thus not surprising that the country should change direction yet again, in mid-1989 with the introduction of a package of belt-tightening measures that received the blessing of the IMF, the World Bank and bilateral donors towards the end of the year. As ever, however, the question has to be asked: is this for real?

Manufacturing: problems and performance close-up

Industrialisation objectives were enunciated soon after Independence in two White Papers, and received wide publicity[10]. They echoed the conventional wisdom among the newly independent African states and were not tailored to Zambia's administrative and policy implementation capacity. Then in the Mulungushi Declaration of 1968 the government set itself the task of:

• decentralising industrial location away from the rail line;
• encouraging labour-intensive techniques of production and small-scale industries, utilising domestic products; and
• promoting import substitution of intermediate products and essential consumer goods.

These politically determined objectives were not realised during the next two decades, largely for want of *feasible strategies* for attaining them. Two fundamental issues were not explicitly addressed. First, how to develop an alternative source of financing new manufacturing investment, as opposed to the historical, copper-generated investment, and second, how to promote manufacturing activities that would be *net* earners of foreign exchange.

These lacunae had very negative effects on industrial growth and structural change in the aftermath of the copper boom. As late as the beginning of 1987, Central Bank reports contained no data on medium- and long-term loans to the different economic sub-sectors; no Industrial Development Bank was in existence. The Development Bank of Zambia's loan operations to the manufacturing sector amounted in 1985/6 to only K22.5m. Most of them involved the rehabilitation/extension of existing large enterprises, plus the establishment of a few small-scale ones. The share of manufacturing in total loan operations had shrunk from an average of 45% during the 1975–85 period to 35% in 1985/86.

THE DOMINANCE OF IMPORT SUBSTITUTION

Import substitution was incontestably the main driving force behind industrial growth until the beginning of the 1970s. The share of manufactured imports in the total consumption of manufactures dropped from 66% in 1965 to 46% in 1972. Import substitution accounted for 55% of the growth of manufacturing output in this period, while domestic demand accounted for 44% and exports for a mere 1% (Gulhati and Sekhar, 1982: Table 3). In subsequent years manufactures barely exceeded 2% of the value of total exports and domestic consumption/demand lacked dynamism, as per capita incomes declined and income distribution did not favour the development of mass markets.

There was relatively little policy impact on the spread of import substitution to intermediate goods. Between 1964 and 1981 the share of imports of these goods in gross manufacturing output *declined* from 26 to 23%. Indeed, the import dependence of manufacturing, as expressed by import coefficients from input/output data, even rose slightly between 1975 and 1980, as shown in Table 9.10. The chief cause was the start-up or capital deepening of heavy manufacturing industries (tyres, vehicle repair and assembly, fertilisers, plastics, cement, lime and bricks) during the 1975–80 period. However, industries that were more important in terms of value added and employment – food, beverages, tobacco, textiles, clothing, paper and printing – *increased* the share of local products in their intermediate consumption.

Inevitably, the extent of this import dependence within the context of a tight foreign-exchange constraint directly determined the level of capacity utilisation. Zambia was no exception to the severe underutilisation which characterised African industrialisation[11].

Unweighted branch averages for the 1972/3–1982/3 period, as extrapolated by the World Bank staff from their sample, suggest that, with the sole exception of textiles, clothing and leather, only about 50% of installed capacity was utilised. Variation between individual enterprises in the same branch was large. Some general improvement was noticeable towards

Table 9.10 *Import coefficients of manufacturing by branch, 1975 and 1980 (% of total intermediate consumption)*

	1975	1980
ISIC Branch		
311 + 312 Food manufacturing	12.1	6.5
313 + 314 Beverages & tobacco	10.8	6.3
32 Textiles, clothing, leather	63.0	31.3
33 Wood & wood products	18.5	16.3
34 Paper & printing	48.1	29.8
355 Rubber products	8.3	58.5
35-355 Chemicals	70.6	72.2
36 Non-metallic minerals	2.9	4.7
37 Basic metals	84.6	77.3
38 Metals & machinery	12.9	34.7
39 Other manufacturing	60.6	54.3
Weighted Average	34.5	35.3

Source: CSO's Input-Output tables and author's calculations.

the mid-1970s, with the average for manufacturing as a whole rising from 43 to 70% of capacity. But with the economic decline the figure dropped to 52% by 1983, with three-quarters of sampled enterprises participating in the deterioration (Steel and Evans, 1984: Table 15)[12].

Given the perennial foreign-exchange scarcity, an analysis was conducted in the University of Zambia of industrial sectors' interlinkages and of their net foreign-exchange absorption contribution (Sheshamani and Hasan, 1985). Only food manufacturing figured among the top third of the 29 branches ranked according to economy of foreign-exchange use, that is, the consumption of imported goods and services less export earnings. Three other branches, (producing mainly tyres, cement, lime and bricks, fabricated metal products and vehicle assembly) ranked high according to the forward linkage criterion, but poorly on backward linkage.

Were there compensating economic and social aspects in terms of employment and income generation, regional dispersion, labour and capital productivity? The concentration of formal employment along the line of rail in the Copperbelt province did drop slightly between 1973 and 1980 – from 50 to 46% – with Southern province the gainer. But there was relatively little change in the spatial concentration of firms so that, in 1980, just two provinces contained 84% of all industrial units.

Formal employment in manufacturing rose moderately from 38,200 in 1970 to 44,300 in 1975 and 50,440 by 1988, when it made up 15% of the formal sector labour force. This compares with the exception of a rise to 66,000 by 1984 under the Third National Development Plan (GOZ, 1989: 66). The total increment, to 1985 at least, related to Zambian nationals. By mid-1985, foreigners made up only 2.6% of manufacturing employment, that is, less than the national average (3.3%). The increases in formal employment were accounted for by publicly-owned or controlled enterprises, the private ones discarding some employees in the intervening years. The ratios of increments in employment to those in real manufacturing output suggest the absence of gains from economies of scale and very slight improvements in productivity, particularly when capital assets per worker rose rapidly in the years prior to 1975.

Manufacturing value added (MVA) in constant 1970 prices expanded during the 1965–70 period at a high annual average rate (13%), dropped sharply in 1974–5 and followed a declining trend thereafter to the mid-1980s. Some improvements in MVA per worker occurred in several sub-sectors – tobacco, textiles and clothing, wood and furniture, paper and printing and 'other manufacturing' (UNIDO, 1987). But in the 15 years to 1985, hardly any structural changes took place within the sector: the ordering of sub-sectors in terms of MVA at end years remained virtually unchanged (UNIDO, 1985: 8). Beverages (mainly brewing) and tobacco processing stayed in the lead throughout. Minor shifts occurred among the next four highest-ranking sub-sectors (textiles, metal products, chemicals, foods). Although the combined share of consumer goods in total output fell from just over 60% in 1970 to 56% in 1985, their production continued to dominate manufacturing output. In parallel, the combined share of capital goods (fabricated metal products) and intermediate goods (chemicals, rubber and plastics) rose from 25 to 28% of manufacturing GDP.

The year 1975 was the last one when customs tariffs determined the allocation of resources. Thereafter it was performed primarily by licences cum foreign-exchange allocations. In principle, these were issued only for goods which did not compete with local products or when these were in short supply, even at less than full capacity operation of the firms concerned. As with all administrative controls, authorisations were at times made available for extra-economic considerations. Under the regime, domestic producers, in principle, could enjoy absolute (open-ended) protection. Because importers of consumer goods received relatively few authorisations, local producers were fairly isolated from world prices and quality norms. Although the sale prices of local products required the approval of the Prices and Incomes Commission, a cost-plus formula was generally applied with no allowance for quality differences. As a consequence, local consumer goods manufacturers were able to attract proportionately more investible funds, perpetuating Zambia's historical bias against import substitution of intermediate and capital goods.

In a related development, the composition of imported manufactures changed, as shown in Table 9.11. The copper boom raised the shares in total imports of both consumer and capital goods. But the latter's share slumped heavily in the 'watershed' period and failed to recover subsequently.

Table 9.11 *Imports by end use, selected years, 1968–81 (%)*

	1968	1970	1975	1980	1981
Imports of					
1. Consumer goods	26	34	22	20	20
of which:					
food	..	8	5	5	..
other non-durables	..	13	9	8	..
durables	..	13	8	7	..
2. Intermediate products	48	44	56	55	57
3. Capital goods	26	22	22	25	23

Source: Steel and Evans, 1984: Table 12 and World Bank, 1984b.

The shifts in the composition of imports had unfavourable repercussions on fiscal revenues as ever more goods facing relatively low customs charges entered (or came in duty-free under the Investment Code). In addition, the continuing use of specific rates of duty rendered tariff revenue price-inelastic. As a result, while the unit value of imports in the early 1980s increased strongly, the customs revenue collected contracted by about 40%, until a correction in trade-related revenue set in after the revision of the Customs Act in 1983.

As to the degree of import substitution (I/S) achieved, this was analysed in a study which related changes during the 1964–80 period in domestic industrial output to increments in their total supply (Sheshamani, 1985b). For all such goods, the analysis showed that the derived import-substitution index (known as the Chenery-Desai coefficient)[13] rose by a mere 3%, largely because of the negative performance of mining and quarrying since 1975. The index for manufacturing proper, however, rose vigorously – not so much during the boom years, as in the grimmer ones that followed (see Table 9.12).

Beverages and tobacco, textiles and base metal products recorded acceleration in their rates of import substitution between the sub-periods 1970–74 and 1974–80. Since their contribution to MVA was preponderant, the whole of the sector's index of import substitution increased correspondingly from 0.14 to 0.37. No significant correlation was found between I/S indices of manufacturing production and of the volume of manufacturing exports during the 1970–80 period.

We have seen that most import substitution occurred in the consumer goods industries, but what were the chief propellants and hindrances? The system of protection since 1975 afforded domestic manufacturers full formal protection, overriding the price advantage over competing imports provided by customs tariffs. The licensing authorities had wide latitude in interpreting the criterion of the essentiality of imports – for the economy and consumers. But temporary interruptions in domestic supplies, aggravated by ignorance of the real levels of

Table 9.12 *Rates of import substitution in manufacturing 1970–80 (%)*

	1970–74	1974–80	1970–80
All products	0.00	− 0.07	− 0.04
All manufacturing,	0.14	0.37	0.33
of which:			
foods	1.61	0.81	0.57
beverages and tobacco	0.02	0.18	0.12
textiles and clothing	0.42	0.74	0.70
wood and products	0.56	0.50	0.54
paper and printing	0.89	0.13	0.64
chemicals, rubber, plastics	0.43	− 0.07	0.32
non-metallic minerals	2.27	0.25	0.40
base metal products	− 0.32	0.03	0.63
fabricated metal products	0.75	− 0.14	0.60
other manufacturing	0.00	− 0.07	− 0.04

Source: Sheshamani, 1985b.

stocks, often gave rise to the authorisation of significant quantities of competing imports to the detriment of domestic capacity utilisation.

The comprehensive protective regime did allow substantial differences to develop between domestic and cif border prices. In 1981, these ranged from 50 to 140% for a sample of manufactured products studied by World Bank staff and which included edible oils, detergents, metal furniture, structural metal products, plastic and jute bags, cotton cloth and suitings (Gulhati and Sekhar, 1981). It should be noted that several of these are from sub-sectors that were resilient to the economy's overall decline after 1975. But consumer welfare need not have borne the full weight of these price differentials in a landlocked country like Zambia, where frontiers are relatively porous and border traffic intense.

PRODUCTIVITY, COMPETITIVENESS AND EFFICIENCY
In the boom years, 1964–75, while manufacturing employment grew at over 10% a year, the index of output expanded at an even higher rate, as assets per workers rose strongly. In wood and furniture-making, capital intensification was very marked as the result of declining employment and a rapid increase in investment. In non-metallic mineral products, assets per worker increased by almost 75% over a four-year period and impressive rises in investment were achieved in paper products, chemicals, rubber and plastics, with smaller increments in foods, beverages and tobacco. For a sample of six sub-sectors for which elasticities were calculated by the Central Statistical Office, in three of them rising capital inputs 'explained' two-thirds or more of the output increment. Thereafter, most of the productivity trends were reversed. Although assets per workers continued to rise for several years in parastatal firms, the relative movements of factors and output in the whole sector suggest a drop in the productivity of both labour and capital.

A more precise measure of factor productivity is that of their combined effect on output, also taken to encompass the impact of technological change. A fall in the value of total factor productivity (TFP) is tantamount to an increase in the unit cost of production. Hence such an index is of particular relevance to the study of price competitiveness of a country with a heavily overvalued currency that impedes export diversification/expansion. World Bank computations of TFP changes in Zambia over the 1965–80 time span, along with those of factor/output ratios, are reproduced in Table 9.13.

For manufacturing as a whole, TFP declined over the 15-year period, although 3 relatively minor sub-sectors out of 17 (leather, rubber and mineral fuels) recorded some TFP gains. In the first five years, within the boom period, both TFP and MVA rose. In the following five years, MVA continued to rise but TFP began its long decline as output shrank. The proximate cause of the continuing TFP deterioration in the face of expansion in capital assets was difficulty in assimilating the technology embodied in new equipment. Again in respect of the whole sector over the 15-year span, only a marginal improvement took place in labour productivity, while that of capital fell. As increases in capital investment outpaced increments in output, the capital/labour ratio rose in most sub-sectors.

Manufactured exports. What then were the effects of the cost-raising developments on the

Table 9.13 *Changes in TFP and factor/output ratios 1965–80 (%)*

	TFP	Factor Ratios Capital/labour	Factor Ratios Output/labour	Output/labour
Sub-sector				
Food	−4.5	1.9	−6.0	−4.0
Beverages and tobacco	−0.1	5.0	−1.9	3.1
Textiles	−1.2	8.5	−5.8	2.7
Clothing	−7.4	19.8	−17.1	2.7
Leather products	8.4	−0.5	8.6	8.1
Wood & products	−0.6	16.6	−9.8	6.8
Furniture	−1.8	4.0	−3.5	1.0
Paper & products	−2.7	10.1	−9.7	0.4
Industrial chemicals	−5.8	18.9	−13.5	5.4
Other chemicals	−2.7	2.7	−3.8	−1.1
Petroleum & coal	4.0	−14.2	7.8	−6.4
Rubber products	1.0	−3.7	2.7	−1.6
Plastics	−13.8	17.6	−19.2	−1.6
Non-metallic minerals	−3.8	8.8	−7.1	1.7
Base metals	−9.2	3.8	−10.7	−6.9
Fabricated metals	−1.7	−0.6	−1.0	−1.5
Other manufactures	−5.7	12.9	−10.7	2.1
All Manufactures	−3.8	7.7	−6.8	0.9

Source: World Bank, 1984b: Table 2.5.

exports of manufactures (SITC classes 6–8, less 67 and 68) referred to in official documents as 'non-traditional' exports? As a very small supplier of such products on the world market, Zambia could in no way influence foreign demand and prices. The fiscal incentives and small export subsidies provided exporters with very small advantages. In 1982, for instance, the total value of the Export Subsidy Fund came to a mere K35,000 and went exclusively to two parastatal firms. The only tariff preferences received by Zambian exporters of manufactures in developed country markets were those under the General System of Preferences (GSP) and hence were common to all other developing countries, including the Newly Industrialising Countries (NICs).

The export value of Zambia's manufactures in 1979 came to about $10m., less than 1% of the country's commodity export earnings. Of this, over 95% were absorbed by neighbouring African markets, where they enjoyed a definite transport cost advantage large enough to offset the negative effects of the overvalued exchange rate and any quality differences or consumer bias. Three years later, the export structure showed little change and it was only by 1984 that some diversification became apparent, with the EEC and Asian markets beginning to acquire importance.

In 1979, there were eight export categories of any consequence, that is, with export values exceeding $0.5 m. Ranked by value these were: non-metallic mineral products (cement and lime); machinery and transport equipment (simple agricultural equipment and assembled vehicles); rubber products (tyres from imported latex); refined petroleum (using imported crude oil); sugar and molasses; chemicals and compounds (fertilisers and explosives); processed cotton; and, finally, electrical machinery and appliances (assembled). By 1982, only one product could be added to this list – natural abrasives. Unpublished trade data for 1984 show that varnishes and paints had replaced sugar and molasses, as the latter products were pre-empted by domestic demand. New additions to the list included paper products, knitted man-made fabrics, base metal goods such as rails and wire, plus small quantities of batteries and ready-made garments. This export structure is replicated in a dozen or so other African countries.

International competitiveness. Leaving aside the cost of new market penetration for Zambian manufacturers and abstracting from their problems in the acquisition of inputs, how did they manage to be competitive abroad during periods of shrinking purchasing power at home? In constant 1966 kwachas, the wholesale prices of Zambian manufactured goods almost quadrupled between 1974 and 1983, that is, rising at an average annual rate of about 16%, whereas the average unit prices of all manufactures imported by Zambia's neighbours (and by other non-oil-exporting developing countries) increased by only 9% per annum. Hence, in terms of domestic inflation alone, Zambian exportables were uncompetitive *prima facie* in foreign markets. This disadvantage was additional to those resulting from falling capacity utilisation and the unfavourable level of the value of the kwacha.

A plausible answer to the question is that the shrinking domestic market still allowed exporters to cover their variable costs, even if that required fewer provisions for amortisation and maintenance. Exports could be priced at marginal cost, passing on to the domestic consumer the difference between average and marginal costs – made possible by the insulation of the domestic market and the authorities' habit of sanctioning cost-plus pricing. In this regard, the investigations by the World Bank of the extent of effective protection (ERP) afforded value added in manufacturing in Zambia by its trade regime, as well as of the domestic resource cost (DRC) of earning foreign exchange, need to be considered.

The combined price-raising effect of tariffs cum licensing related to value added in an activity indicates the extent to which the activity is privileged and allowed to maintain an uncompetitive level of operation. The sample of 16 manufacturing firms, mentioned above, yielded ERP and DRC values for 1975 and 1981/2 that are listed in Table 9.14. These sample results are characterised by very great variance within product groups because of differences in the performance levels of individual enterprises. As is common in developing countries, the hierarchy of ERP levels follows that of nominal tariffs, with consumer goods receiving the highest protection and heavy intermediates and capital goods the lowest.

Table 9.14 *ERPs and coefficients of DRCs, 1975 and 1981/2 (16 firms)*

Type of manufacturing activity	ERPs 1975[a] (%)	DRCs 1981/2[b]
Consumer goods, of which		
food products	67.3	0.47
other non-durables	342.4	1.53
durables	472.9	2.58
Light intermediate goods	182.5	1.60
Heavy intermediate goods	29.8	3.02
Capital goods	59.7	1.45
All goods (unweighted)	160.6	n.a.

Source: World Bank (1984b: Tables 3.3 and 3.6).

Notes: [a] Expressed in ad valorem cif terms.
[b] Relative efficiency increases as values fall below unity.

The values in Table 9.14 indicate that, in the sample, capital goods manufacture was the least likely to attract investment on financial profitability considerations during the late 1970s, as it received about one-eighth of the social subsidy enjoyed by producers of consumer durables. The value added generated by the latter thanks to the protective regime was more than four times what would otherwise have been possible. Little wonder that consumer goods manufacture grew faster than other sub-sectors and that the extension of import substitution to intermediate and capital goods did not take place to any substantial degree.

An approximation to the international competitiveness of products is provided by another widely used measure: the ratio of the economic costs of domestic factors of production per unit value of output, all valued at free trade (international market) prices, the DRC[14]. For Zambia, the DRC calculations made by the World Bank in 1983 were based on a 24-firm sample – most of them parastatals, but which nevertheless accounted for one-fifth of total industrial output in 1981/2. As with the ERP ratios, intra-group variance was great, except for the two capital goods manufacturers. Thus the sub-sector averages listed in Table 9.14 are not necessarily representative of the whole of manufacturing in Zambia. But, *faute de mieux*, they are consistent with what has already been ascertained regarding productive efficiency and competitiveness.

As might be expected, food industries based on domestic raw materials have a higher comparative advantage than those producing consumer durables and heavy intermediates – both import-dependent. The relatively low DRC value for the two capital goods producers is explained by the low level of protection they received, which more than offset their high import dependency (low value added). As will be shown in the next section, domestic procurement of inputs by producers of heavy intermediates and consumer durables (six firms in the World Bank sample) was low and did not expand appreciably between 1975 and 1980.

LINKAGES AND FOOD MANUFACTURING

The prime objectives of Zambian planners during the past 15 years or so have been to increase the levels and quality of consumption, to create more jobs and to broaden import substitution to the production of intermediate and capital goods. These objectives were, of course, subject to minimising net foreign-exchange usage. The allocation of a shrinking amount of investible resources required difficult trade-offs and much scarce manpower was devoted to the collection of reliable data through family budget surveys, censuses and follow-up visits to respondents[15].

Zambia's input-output table for 1975 was subjected to statistical analysis in the University of Zambia in 1984. The results pointed not only to the economy's high import dependence, but also highlighted the planners' practical difficulty in selecting for priority treatment the sub-sectors which would unequivocally lead to the maximum attainment of proclaimed national objectives. The study also demonstrated the economy's structural bias, reflected, *inter alia*, in the high correlation between the intensity of inter-industry linkages and the potential for creating new jobs in the different sub-sectors (Sheshamani and Hasan, (1984).

According to these researchers, if Zambia's planners were to be guided solely by analytic indicators, they would recommend channelling public investment into services rather than, say, agriculture or construction. Table 9.15 sets out the ranking of manufacturing sub-sectors in respect of the intensity of their backward and forward linkages with the rest of the economy in 1975. The indices used are those associated with Diamond and Hazari[16].

Table 9.15 *Manufacturing sub-sectors ranked by their linkage effects, 1975*

Backward Linkages		Forward Linkages
1.	Non-metallic mineral products	4.
2.	Rubber products	3.
3.	Fabricated metal products	2.
4.	Beverages and tobacco	7.
5.	Food processing	8.
6.	Wood and wooden products	10.
7.	Textiles and apparel	6.
8.	Paper and paper products	9.
9.	Base metal products	1.
10.	Other manufacturing	11.
11.	Chemicals	5.

Source: Computed by the author from Annex Tables in Sheshamani and Hasan, 1985.

If one were to select for particular promotion the sub-sectors that ranked highest according to both linkage intensities, they turn out to be those with a relatively high import content of inputs and not in activities reflecting Zambia's comparative advantage. The planners' dilemma is further illustrated by the data in Table 9.16. The promotion of the most promising sub-sectors[17] in the generation of inter-industry linkages in 1975 would not have contributed most efficiently to the attainment of many of the other major development objectives.

A comparison of the 1975 and 1980 input-output tables brings out several new features, while confirming such earlier findings as rising import dependence. Thus, between the two benchmark years and for all the 29 sub-sectors together, the ratio of the intermediate consumption of domestic goods to gross output (supply) declined somewhat – from 24.4 to

Table 9.16 *Development objectives related to sub-sectors, 1975*

National objective	Top-ranking sub-sectors according to achievement potential
Maximising linkage effects	Rubber and fabricated metal products
Maximising consumption	Sub-sectors 1, 2, 4, 5, 12, 16, 17, 20, 23, 29
Maximising employment	Fabricated metal products, wholesale and retail trade
Economising on foreign exchange	Sub-sectors 2, 5, plus five service sectors, mining, beverages and tobacco

Source: As for Table 9.15.

22.7%. For the whole of manufacturing, the proportion of purchases from domestic sources to total output also dropped, but even less markedly (from 65.5% in 1975 to 64.6% five years later). But there was strong linkage growth between the productive sector of the economy as a whole and its service sector, giving rise to a higher overall level of intra-sectoral trade in 1980 per unit increment in final demand (supply) than in 1975.

For the food-processing sub-sector, several developments call for further comment. The proportion of imports in the sub-sector's total purchases fell by about 50% between 1975 and 1980. The number of sub-sectors purchasing processed foods as inputs increased by 2, while the number supplying inputs to the food industry fell by 6. But the volumes involved in the two benchmark years differed substantially and the net result was the intensification of trade between food manufacturing and the rest of the economy. Exports of processed food represented only 1% of the sub-sector's output in 1980, while it made up 1.5% five years earlier.

The chief characteristics of the food sub-sector are set out in Table 9.17. Its structure changed somewhat during the 1970s with a sharp curtailment in the number of dairying establishments as expatriate farmers departed. The number of grain mills and bakeries rose in line with urban demand, the new taste for bread as a staple and the availability of cereals at subsidised prices. In 1973, direct subsidies to the mills equalled the amount due in direct taxes on their output. After direct subsidising ended, their value added became negative.

Table 9.17 *Characteristics of the food-processing sub-sector. (A) = 1973 (B) = 1980*

ISIC sub-sector		Number of firms		Employment '000s		Value Added Km.	
		A	B	A	B	A	B
311/2	Food processing	105	111	11.3	16.6	35.2	71.0
3111	Meat preparation	18	15	1.3	1.3	2.0	8.0
3112	Dairying	12	3	0.8	1.1	3.5	3.1
3113/4	Canning	7	6	0.4	0.2	1.1	0.7
3115	Edible oils/fats	3	2	0.4	negl.	2.1	0.2
3116	Grain milling	16	27	2.4	3.5	10.5	− 2.9
3117	Bakeries	38	47	1.9	2.5	4.8	25.2
3118	Sugar refining	3	3	4.2	7.3	9.9	31.7
3119	Confectionery	4	3	0.1	0.1	0.2	0.4
3121	Other foods	4	5	0.3	0.6	1.1	4.7

ISIC sub-sector		Direct Subsidies Km.		Indirect Taxes Km.		Net Profit Km.	
		A	B	A	B	A	B
311/2	Food processing	8.4	0.0	− 6.9	1.3	11.1	0.2
3111	Meat preparation	1.4	0.0	− 1.4	0.0	− 2.0	2.3
3112	Dairying	1.0	0.0	− 1.1	0.0	1.2	0.2
3113/4	Canning	0.0	0.0	0.0	0.0	0.2	− 1.1
3115	Edible oils/fats	0.5	0.0	− 0.5		0.9	0.1
3116	Grain milling	5.6	0.0	− 5.6	0.1	5.7	− 15.5
3117	Bakeries	0.0	0.0	0.0	0.5	1.5	6.8
3118	Sugar refining	0.0	0.0	1.4	0.7	2.9	5.5
3119	Confectionery	0.0	0.0	0.0	0.0	0.1	0.1
3121	Other foods	0.0	0.0	0.0	0.0	0.5	1.9

Source: Central Statistical Office, *Census of Industrial Production, 1973 and 1980*, Lusaka, CSO.

Meat processing and dairying also made no net contributions to public revenue in 1973 but began to pay profit taxes by 1980. The spectacular expansion of baking activities – a widely-shared African phenomenon – merits attention as well as the more than fourfold increase (in current kwachas) in the value added and profits of the still small 'other foods' sub-sector.

THE PARASTATALS
The pattern of manufacturing development has been crucially determined by the performance of the parastatals which account for about two-thirds of total industrial employment and value added.

The annual reports of parastatal holding companies give a positive evaluation of the effects of the liberalisation of trade and payments, the decontrol of prices and interest rates, as well as the auctioning of dollars, on their operations during 1986. Thus ZIMCO, accounting for 35% of formal employment and 55% of GNP in 1985, reported that:

- even the less import-dependent firms succeeded in getting enough foreign exchange through the auction to satisfy their *immediate* import requirements so that companies were able to by-pass the more expensive lines of supplier credit;
- more attention was paid to economies in production because of the high kwacha cost of foreign exchange;
- marketing and competitiveness in foreign markets attracted more attention;
- higher capacity utilisation was achieved by most, but not all, ZIMCO enterprises, allowing some improvements in labour and capital productivity.

Two major problems have been common to most parastatals in the last few years. With the rapid devaluation, the burden of external indebtedness *doubled* and the larger inflow of competing imports caused problems of disposal on the domestic market. Shortages of working capital, due to the accumulation of losses in the past, were widespread. In 1985/6 out of 37 Industrial Development Corporation (INDECO) companies, in only 20 was net working capital positive. This burden was not relieved by the reforms. Bank overdrafts for bidding at auctions were restricted so that indebted enterprises had difficulty in achieving success.

INDECO, for its part, ascribed the increase in non-traditional exports during 1985–6 by its subsidiary companies directly to the reforms. They were optimistic about being able to add new products to their exports if conditions were to remain unchanged. These included industrial fabrics, glass bottles, bicycles, galvanised hollowware, wheelbarrows, edible oils, detergents and canned pineapple. But the only new import-substituting activity that came on-stream during the period was the extraction of cooking oil from domestic oilseeds. And total manufacturing employment did not rise significantly above its 1984 level of 48,000.

ZIMCO recorded pre-tax profits in only three of the past five years, so that overall parastatal performance has not been very satisfactory. Although this is mainly due to the poor performance of mining enterprises, there were a number of loss-makers in manufacturing proper, including firms producing batteries and parts, food canning and pork products, saw-milling, ceramics and clay products, nitrogenous fertilisers and industrial acid. Had company assets been valued at replacement rather than historic cost, ZIMCO's out-turn would have been much worse.

Cost and product accounting was introduced by ZIMCO quite early in the reform period and was followed by the imposition on all the parastatals of *uniform* quarterly reports based on an exhaustive financial manual aimed at capturing all of the data essential for exercising efficient control. The result has been telling. Company books could be closed just two months after the end of the 1985/6 financial year. As soon as all manufacturing enterprises become computerised, they will be required to submit to ZIMCO via INDECO for vetting – on a *monthly* basis – balance sheets, profit and loss statements, value added, sources and uses of funds, financial ratios, capital expenditure and foreign-exchange transactions. Still tighter financial control will be placed on the less profitable companies. Such data and analyses of company performance should make corporate budgeting and planning feasible and allow the Party and government leadership to exercise both *ex ante* and *ex post* controls.

Within the INDECO holding of 37 manufacturing and service enterprises, 3 of the 9 loss-makers in 1982/3 achieved a turnaround by 1986 and one heavy loser – the nitrogenous fertiliser plant – was sold to a consortium which had been promised multinational assistance for rehabilitating the plant. INDECO's return on capital has risen to 13 from 9% in 1982/3 but overall operations have yet to yield net foreign-exchange earnings.

The reasons for the lack of profitability in parastatal manufacturing are historical and primarily due to many having been badly planned, located and equipped. Prior to 1975, company boards were too directly under the influence of politicians and were obliged to operate as quasi-social instruments. For instance, the fertiliser plant was the second *in the world* to use an expensive and delicate electrolytic reduction process based on coal; in other words, it has had to become the object of radical rehabilitation with World Bank participation. The over-sized design of the brick plant is traceable to a poor feasibility study which overestimated demand and came down in favour of a capital-intensive plant capable of producing 35 million high quality bricks annually, but which are not competitive with less sophisticated products preferred by local consumers. Motor cars assembled at a major plant cost, on average, $2,000 more than the border prices, so that annual throughput has seldom exceeded 100. The tyre manufacturing company was originally sanctioned on the explicit understanding that latex would be produced locally, but 15 years later continued to import its raw rubber.

Such situations need not recur as there is currently enough expertise in INDECO to monitor activities closely and to carry out the studies on which to base sound economic decisions. But since the return to administrative controls and regulations as of May 1987, can INDECO's momentum be maintained?

The new economic reform programme (NERP)

NERP AND MACROECONOMIC ISSUES
As noted above, May 1987 saw a fundamental change in economic management and policy with the inauguration of the NERP. Stabilisation was one of its principal policy objectives, to be effected by concerted measures to throttle the strong, predominantly demand-sided,

Figure 9.1 *Money supply and inflation rate changes, 1985-7 (Average monthly % growth)*

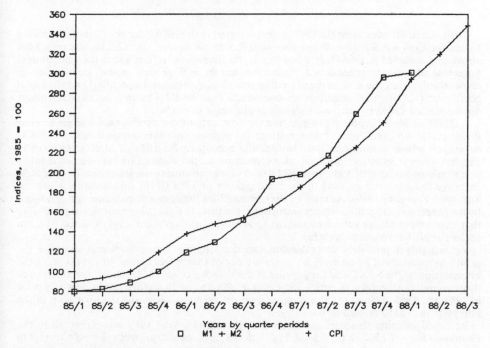

Source: IMF, *International Financial Statistics*, February 1989.

inflationary pressures that persistently negated efforts to improve per capita real incomes. Deficit financing through heavy domestic and foreign borrowing by the public sector was accompanied by a high (20%) average annual expansion in money supply (M_3) between 1980 and 1985, increasing to over 90% in 1986 and estimated at 60% the following year. The almost tenfold drop in the value of the Kwacha that followed the introduction of foreign-exchange auctioning put imports out of reach of a large number of enterprises and depressed their output. It also stimulated the illegal export of such domestic products as foodstuffs, provoking recurrent shortages and pushing up the price spiral (see Figure 9.1)[18].

The budgetary targets announced for 1988 encompassed a much lower (40%) expansion in M_3, a reduction of the budget deficit and tighter control over unbudgeted expenditure, more selective channelling of bank credit to parastatals and private enterprise, smaller subsidies for maize and less financial support for parastatals[19].

Another major area addressed by the NERP was the accentuating relative fall in the proportion of resources being devoted to investment. As a proportion of GDP, gross fixed capital formation (GFCF) has been shrinking steadily over the years to reach a low in 1987 of a mere 7.8% – pointing to the Achilles' heel of development planning in Zambia. The ensuing consumer bias of expenditure has accentuated since 1986, as shown in Table 9.18.

Table 9.18 *GDP by type of expenditure, 1984–7 in constant (1977) Km.*

	1984	1985	1986	1987
Private final consumption	1,114	1,237	1,194	1,467
Government final consumption	484	460	464	448
Change in stocks	30	62	217	74
Gross fixed capital formation	212	199	169	164
Exports less imports	154	63	36	36
Statistical discrepancy	18	24	2	–
Gross domestic product	2,012	2,045	2,056	2,106

Source: NCDP, 1988: Table I.10, and GOZ, 1989: 2 and 8.

The volume of investment (in 1987 prices) targeted in the NERP for the 18 months ending December 1988 was K3.3 bn. When pro-rated for the fiscal year, the K2.2 bn was only 14% above that achieved in 1986/7. In other words, the investment referred to in the 1988 Budget Speech as adequate to generate a 2.2% increase in real GDP presupposed a rate of inflation considerably below the level in the preceding year. It also subsumed a peculiarly small capital coefficient (ICOR), particularly when one recalls that the K1.4 bn in gross capital outlays during 1986/7 failed to generate a significant increase in output.

It therefore seems legitimate to question the adequacy of the interim plan's target level of investment. An additional consideration in support of this view is that ZIMCO holdings – whose subsidiaries have historically accounted for 60% of total investment in Zambia – based its estimates of capital expenditure on the assumption that domestic inflation would be half that of 1987, that is 27.5%. Yet the consumer price index rose by over 50% from the third quarter of 1987 to the third quarter of 1988 (IMF, *International Financial Statistics*, February 1989). As most of the commodities for domestic consumption produced by the parastatal and public sector enterprises are subject to tight price control, the possibility that they would realise sufficient savings to achieve the investment level expected of them under the NERP remains doubtful.

Yet in highly import-dependent Zambia, facing a perennial foreign-exchange shortage, the prime determinant of investment is the availability of that scarce commodity. Following the introduction of the NERP and the pegging of the Kwacha at 8 to the US dollar, production of the preponderant metal – copper – increased by 4% and, with a sharp rise in its world price in 1987 and 1988, helped to raise Zambia's export earnings above the level foreseen in the interim plan – $150 m. above that in 1986[20].

Recorded external financial assistance for the calendar year 1987 was estimated in the *Economic Report 1987* to total $483.5 m. – down by some $80 m. from the 1986 level. On this basis, foreign-exchange allocations after the abandonment of the auctioning system could be maintained at an average monthly level of $33 m. – much in line with the auction

Table 9.19   *Foreign-exchange allocations to ZIMCO parastatals. Financial years 1985/6, 1986/7 and 1987/8 (1st half) ($m.)*

Sector	FY 1985/6 Actual	FY 1986/7	FY 1987/8 (6 mos) Actual	Required
Mining	238.3	257.2	139.6	355.2
Manufacturing	67.9	69.9	47.1	132.5
Agriculture	0.4	1.5	2.3	2.7
Energy	170.2	89.6	56.0	147.7
Finance	5.2	8.2	7.8	9.7
Transport	33.3	41.2	19.4	88.1
Communications	9.3	8.5	0.2	11.4
Commerce	4.8	4.1	1.4	8.8
Hotels etc.	2.5	2.2	1.1	1.4
Real Estate & Constr.	0.1	0.1	0.6	1.1
Group Total	532.0	483.0	272.5	759.0

Source: NCDP, *Economic Report 1987*, table VI.4.

average in 1986. But it is important to note that these allocations fell far short of the foreign-exchange requirements of major enterprises for the following uses: improving on past under-utilisation of capacity for want of imported inputs, ensuring proper repair and maintenance, and implementing investment plans.

The order of magnitude of this shortfall is illustrated by the allocations received by the parastatals grouped within ZIMCO. Their foreign-exchange earnings in the first half of FY 1987/8 amounted to $423 m. but their total budgeted requirement of foreign currencies for the same period was $759 m. and the allocations they actually received came to only $273 m. or 36% of what was necessary for them to honour their own investment intentions fully. Although data are not available, private companies probably fared no better. Table 9.19 gives the sectoral breakdown of ZIMCO's allocations of foreign exchange for the three years to 1987/8.

BALANCE-OF-PAYMENTS POSITION

We conclude this broad overview of the economy with a presentation of recent trends in the balance of payments and some questions about the appropriate exchange rate for the Kwacha. The country's balance of payments position continues to be under severe strain (see Table 9.20).

In current Kwacha prices, the current account deficit has risen significantly since the mid-1980s; it is also higher in dollar terms: $216 m. in 1983 in relation to $249 m. in 1988. Furthermore, the decision taken in mid-1987 to limit debt-service payments to 10% of net export earnings means that annual flows fail to reflect total current obligations. The current

Table 9.20   *Current account of the balance of payments, 1980–8 (Km. and $m.)*

Year	Trade Balance Kwacha	$	Merchandise Imports Kwacha	$	Current Account Balance Kwacha	Current Account Deficit as % of GDP
1980	270.3	343	878.7	1,116	− 423	13.8
1981	− 60.1	− 69	926.4	1,065	− 645	18.5
1982	− 51.8	− 56	932.0	1,006	− 524	14.6
1983	308.9	247	895.2	716	− 271	8.1
1984	542.0	303	1,108.0	620	− 317	6.4
1985	708.7	262	1,703.8	630	− 429	6.1
1986	1,360.7	190	4,032.6	564	− 2,346	18.1
1987	1,486.4	163	5,572.2	629	− 1,340	6.8
1988	2,209.0	265	6,043.0	725	− 2,049	9.1

Source: GOZ, 1989:8 and 196–7; IMF, *International Financial Statistics*, February 1989.

Note: All figures from GOZ except for the last two columns for the years 1980–3, taken from the IMF.

account deficit expressed as a percentage of GDP fell to a low of around 6% in the mid-1980s but it has begun to rise since then. What is particularly worrying is the high deficit recorded in 1988 in spite of the rise in the price of copper. The long-term deterioration is well reflected in the dollar value of imports. As shown in Table 9.20, these fell to almost 50% of their 1980 value by 1984 and although rising by almost 20% in the subsequent four years were still, by 1988, 35% lower than in 1980.

The parity of the Kwacha at 8 to the US dollar was fixed on 1 May 1987, some 40% below the average rate struck at preceding auctions[21]. From the inception of the NERP, the authorities proclaimed their readiness to review the exchange rate in the light of circumstances and this was reiterated in 1988 and again in 1989. Indeed, as could have been expected, the rate which was fixed gave rise to considerable controversy and on a number of occasions traders in the private sector were formally invited to present evidence in support of a lower valuation of the Kwacha, indicating a lack of competitiveness of their products. In the event, not a single trader responded. Evidently there was a trade-off between a rate which allowed imports to be purchased relatively cheaply (when foreign exchange could be mobilised) and one that made exports more competitive abroad[22].

Under NEPR rules and arrangements, traders obtained imported goods against a span of exchange-rate premia. On the thriving black market in mid-1988, the US dollar fetched rates approximating the highest reached at auctions (above K20 in early 1988). By paying more than the official rate, traders could have needed imports transferred to them from firms to whom foreign exchange was allocated by the Foreign Exchange Management Committee (FEMAC), as *a posteriori* controls of licence use are not effective. Traders also managed to acquire foreign goods at premia from enterprises/persons importing essential inputs under the 'no foreign funds involved' facility. Hence the NEPR regime and control capabilities gave rise, in practice, to a variety of different exchange rates, which could eventually be formalised as export-promoting or protectionist measures.

NERP AND MANUFACTURING

The most important assumptions listed in the NERP for achieving growth rate expansion during the economic recovery programme were as follows: a normally distributed adequate rainfall, a world price of copper above £1,000 per tonne, the continued allocation of foreign exchange to industry at levels prevailing before the start of the NERP in mid-1987 and which would permit better use of existing capacities (NCDP, 1988: 48). They need to be seen in the context of major constraints applicable to Zambia but also regarded as endemic in sub-Saharan Africa: low domestic savings and investment, skill shortages, fraudulent trade flows, poor commercial and physical infrastructure (see Steel and Evans, 1984).

In the initial phase of the NERP there was no sign that the hoped-for allocations of foreign exchange to industrial enterprises could be maintained as before. A slump in overall inflows during the first 10 months of 1987 was compounded by a sharp drop in general balance-of-payments support[23], which had been a major prop of the auction system and had allowed a partial improvement in industrial output to develop during 1986, 1987 and into 1988 (see Table 9.21).

During the first months of the NERP, the manufacturing sector as a whole did not suffer unduly from cuts in foreign-exchange allocations. But at the sub-sectoral level some of the substantial reductions in output were attributable to unsuccessful requests for foreign exchange, as in the case of the base metals industries. The necessarily selective allocations – based on objective criteria[24] applied *in camera* by FEMAC – permitted several industries to meet pent-up domestic and regional demand for their products and thereby to record significant gains in output. This was the case for paper products, mechanical and electrical machinery and consumer durables – which boosted the sector's overall index of production significantly.

The parastatals enjoyed no revealed preference in the allocation system. During the first six months of the NERP, those grouped under ZIMCO received only 36% of their targeted foreign-exchange requirements: they had been able to acquire a higher percentage (64.3%) during the preceding auctioning regime. The parastatals that were least successful in the 1987 allocations were those in transport, communications, distribution and mining. Allocations to INDECO manufacturing enterprises came to 36% of their budgeted level, compared to 54.5% during the corresponding 1986 period (data from interviews).

Another crucial issue for the buoyancy of industry is the nature of domestic supply

Table 9.21 *Indices of industrial production, 1985–8 (1973 = 100)*

Year	Mining: All:	Food/Bev: Tobacco:	Textiles: Clothing:	Wood: Prods:	Manufacturing sub-sectors Paper: Prods:	Chem/Rubb: Plastics:	Non-Met: Mins:	Base Metals:
1984	77.0	90.6	160.7	45.1	77.8	93.0	79.9	97.1
1985	71.2	89.0	196.2	52.4	104.4	86.2	138.0	93.3
1986	67.9	90.2	162.8	51.5	131.5	83.8	101.2	83.7
1987	70.9	95.1	174.6	45.7	204.0	78.4	112.1	66.2
1988	72.8	115.7	200.9	37.2	322.2	68.1	83.2	41.0

Source: CSO, *Monthly Digest of Statistics* various and CSO worksheets and GOZ, 1989.

responses to the radical changes in Zambia's macro-policy and their effects on factor utilisation. In the period of a rapidly depreciating Kwacha and accompanying price and import liberalisation, the profitability of exporting non-traditional products (agricultural and manufactured goods) increased sharply. The supply response to higher producer prices was strong on the part of farmers. Assisted by favourable rains, the share of agriculture in GDP rose by some 2 percentage points in 1986. Manufacturing's response to market-oriented measures was somewhat weaker, however. Proximate causes included the influx of competing imports, sharply higher Kwacha costs of externally procured inputs and generalised illiquidity – all in the context of rapidly rising inflation.

As might have been expected, the re-imposition of tight price and import controls, along with a re-valued Kwacha, triggered off the reverse mechanism, with the causal effects again magnified by the weather. Drought in 1987, lack of spare parts and inadequate deliveries of fertilisers constrained agricultural output and the sector's share in GDP fell. Notwithstanding proclamations to the contrary[25], the agricultural sector was not visibly favoured by preferential allocations of foreign exchange.

Manufacturing activities were also affected by the disappointing agricultural performance but were less constrained by shortages of foreign exchange and foreign inputs[26]. Thus manufacturing's share in GDP rose to 21.2% in 1987 and to 22% in 1988 (GOZ, 1989: 11) – an all-time high. It also benefitted from the 'forced-draft' import substitution that the reinstated direct controls allowed, as with the import prohibition of concentrates and syrups. The local soft drink manufacturer adjusted rapidly to the use of domestic fruit derivatives and, with the collaboration of its foreign partner (and patent holder), put several new domestic brands on the market, including tonic water. However, it was the same direct controls which scared away a large multinational firm from injecting much-wanted capital investment into the food-processing sub-sector, soon after the introduction of the NERP[27].

Overall capacity utilisation in manufacturing is judged to have risen from 38% in 1987 to 42% by the end of 1988 (GOZ, 1989: 23). More detailed production data in early 1988 covered the first nine months of 1987 but were limited to parastatals. These showed better than budgeted out-turns for only 3 out of 18 products: mealie meal (+17%), copper rods (+16%) and cement (+6%). Eight products were produced in line with their respective planned volumes and substantial shortfalls were recorded for 7 others: textiles (−49%), cooking oil (−45%), batteries (−41%), soaps (−38%), detergents (−35%), sugar (−25%), stock feed (−23%) and bread (−19%). Several of the poorly performing enterprises were handicapped as much by the absence of local mechanical repair/replacement facilities, as by inadequate supplies of domestic raw materials and such intermediates as packaging materials.

Employment levels were slow to adjust to the shifts in economic policy. During both the liberalisation phase (1983–6) and the following year when controls were reimposed, overall change in the level of total formal sector employment was minimal although, as shown in Table 9.22, the national aggregate showed significant sub-sectoral variations, most notably a downward shift in both the construction and mining industries. This had adverse effects on the manufacturing sub-sectors supplying to those particular industries. The drop in

Table 9.22 *Year-on-year changes in sectoral employment, 1984–8 (%)*

Sector	1985/4	1986/5	1987/6	1988/7
Agriculture				
Forestry, fishing	−1.0	−2.7	+4.4	+1.1
Mining/quarrying	−2.0	−1.0	−1.8	−1.4
Manufacturing	+0.1	+0.8	+2.2	+1.0
Electricity & water	+3.0	+3.4	–	+1.4
Construction	−13.0	+9.0	−17.6	−8.8
Trade, hotels, catering	−6.7	+2.5	−3.7	−2.2
Transport and communications	+1.0	+0.7	+4.3	+1.4
Finance, insurance	+0.1	+0.1	+5.6	+1.7
Other services	+0.3	+2.9	+3.6	+0.7
Total annual change in formal employment	−1.0	−0.3	+0.3	−0.3

Source: NCDP, *Economic Report 1986* and *1987*, and GOZ, 1989:66.

agricultural wage labour in the face of rising output in the period 1984–6 was due principally to the better utilisation of capital equipment in the large commercial farms.

Little if any new investment took place during these eventful years. The rate of capacity utilisation in manufacturing improved marginally but *only* in privately owned firms. In contrast, capacity utilisation in parastatal manufacturing fell from an average of 45% in 1985 to 41% in 1986[28], reflecting vulnerability to competition from abroad and lack of adaptability to a changing domestic environment which years of costly protectionism had engendered in a good proportion of firms.

In the review of intersectoral linkage trends above, it was noted, not surprisingly, that strong linkages were clustered mainly around mineral extraction. Subsequent developments have altered this pattern somewhat. The substantial depreciation of the kwacha during the auction period increased the cost of imported heavy fuel to the extent of prompting mineral and manufacturing base metal primary processors to switch to domestic coal as their primary fuel. This positive import-substituting result of currency devaluation does not appear to have spread to other sectors and may be reversible. Yet it does point to a promising policy option for reinforcing Zambia's industrial fabric.

There are no firm indications that the export of manufactures and semi-manufactures as a whole expanded during the period of liberalisation[29]. As happened in 1984/5, however, some non-traditional products penetrated new competitive markets, albeit in relatively small volumes. For instance, leather gloves were exported to the USA; knitted fabric, terry cloth and trousers to the UK; garments to Sweden; clothing accessories to Japan; fabrics to Switzerland; and cotton linters to Romania. In the SSA region, substantial quantities of sawn wood, parquet flooring and fabrics were sold to Botswana; plastic piping, telephone equipment, explosives and cosmetics to Malawi; poultry feed, sugar, yarn and various fabrics, raincoats, insulated electric cables, gramophone records and accumulators to Tanzania; sugar and syrups, glass bottles and diamond drill bits, fabrics, piping and sanitary paper to Zaire; detonators and ammunition, paint thinners, synthetic yarn and fabrics to Zimbabwe; refined sugar and matchwood to Burundi.

The annual plan for 1987 targeted a 10–15% rise in the value of all non-mineral exports. Partial trade returns, covering only the first nine months of 1987, showed that their share (10%) marked a welcome shift in the direction of commodity diversification. A new export category, industrial chemicals, was scheduled by INDECO for sale in SSA markets in 1988.

The importance of neighbouring markets for Zambian manufactures has already been highlighted; the 1986 trade data lend added weight to that finding. Because of proximity and, more recently, because of tariff preferences within the framework of the PTA[30], these products enjoy advantages that are beginning to challenge the competitiveness of those of their chief rivals – the NICs and mainland China. Moreover, they have begun to receive institutional support from the Southern African Development Co-ordination Conference (SADCC). This takes the form of active encouragement of regional product specialisation and the co-ordination of import-substituting investment[31].

In 1987, an indicative (long-term) industrial development plan for the SADCC area was produced (by the Commonwealth Secretariat), based on a target average annual GDP growth rate of 4.1% (close to the World Bank's 4.3% rate in the high-growth scenario of the 1982 *World Development Report*). Both rates are based on the countries raising their investment ratios from their then-current rates of below 20% to *above* 30% of GDP, provided export earnings expand faster than GDP and their import content is radically reduced – as a result of regional co-operation. But the plan met with little acclaim among donors and must have appeared academic for a country like Zambia where the investment ratio was slumping towards the 8% level. By early 1988, just about one-fifth of the $1.2 bn required to fund the 63 SADCC-approved projects had been secured, more than half of it being absorbed by a Tanzanian pulp and paper mill (*African Economic Digest*, 29 January 1988).

Against this backdrop, we can now compare the level and structure of loans to the private sector by the Development Bank of Zambia (DBZ) prior to and following the reinstatement of administrative controls over the economy (see Table 9.23).

When inflation is taken into account, the levels of development loans to the private sector are seen not to have been affected by the radical change in economic management, but their focus did shift away from manufacturing towards quarrying and tourism (INDECO, *Annual Report and Accounts, 1987*). Most of the loans to manufacturing went towards the rehabilitation or expansion of existing private firms producing such items as sacking, tyre

Table 9.23   *Sectoral distribution of DBZ's loans*[a]*, 1985/6 and 1986/7*

Sector	1985/6			1986/7		
	Number of projects	Value Km.	%	Number of projects	Value Km.	%
Agriculture						
Agro-industry and forestry	18	23.8	38	18	25.8	34
Fishing	1	0.5	1	0	–	–
Manufacturing	18	22.5	35	6	17.2	23
Mining & quarrying	2	11.4	18	2	23.7	31
Tourism	6	3.8	6	3	9.1	12
Distribution	0	–	–	0	–	–
Transport and water haulage	4	1.1	2	0	–	–
TOTAL	46	63.0	100	29	75.8	100

Source: DBZ, *Annual Report*, 1986 and 1987.

Note: [a] Excluding small-scale and rural development loans.

retreads, starch and glucose, and engineering repairs, and covering inflation-bred cost overruns. The only new activity financed in the post-auction period was an edible oil mill. In contrast in the preceding year, DBZ financed nine medium-scale firms producing a goodly range of import substitutes.

The level of investment in the parastatal sector rose significantly in the last year of economic liberalism – from K753 m. in 1985/6 to K1,359 m. in 1986/7, and the return also improved, from under 15 to about 24%. Indeed, even in the face of tight liquidity, INDECO labelled 1986/7 as its 'Year of Achievement'. In terms of institutional change, a parastatal poultry complex was partially privatised and a large Asian company brought into partnership to straighten out the bicycle assembly plant. But three private grain milling companies were taken over. Investment in new manufacturing was modest – a veneer mill and a magnet wire firm were launched. The year also witnessed a turn-around in the six-year, loss-making performance of Nitrogen Chemicals (NCZ). Sales more than doubled in volume and capacity utilisation improved sharply, following major rehabilitation funded by the International Development Association (IDA) and the Kreditanstalt für Wiederaufbau[32].

There does appear to be some evidence to suggest that the rate of investment accelerated during the last year of liberal economic management. It will, however, be some time before national accounts data can confirm or deny this and still longer for the effects on investment of the reimposition of administrative controls to be more firmly established. What does seem clear from ZIMCO's investment plan 1987/8–1989/90 (as it stood before the publication of the group's Annual Report for 1988) is that uncertainty about the availability of foreign exchange makes a mockery of investment planning[33]. Thus INDECO's planned capital spending was seen to fall from $20.4m. in 1987/8 to a mere $6.2m. in 1989/90, dragging the share of manufacturing down from 14.7 to 3.3% of total parastatal investment[34]. The breakdown of this bearish programme is given in Table 9.24 by type of activity. Of the 21 manufacturing activities listed, for only 6 could any investment be planned in 1988/9 and for only 2 in 1989/90.

The chief foreign-exchange earners in the INDECO group of companies were expected to be base metal fabricators, sugar refineries and textile mills. New export products destined for PTA markets are geyser frames and hollow-ware. The ZIMCO group of companies has accounted for about 60% of total gross capital formation in Zambia for the last several years and was the main source of public sector savings. As a large proportion of its 1987/8–1989/90 intended investment is destined for replacement and rehabilitation of existing capacity, it need not necessarily result in a net addition to value added. As for investment by the private sector, only the approved investment licences for manufacturing during calendar 1987 are available. These were compiled by the newly-created Investment Co-ordinating Committee and amounted to some K193 m. ($24 m. at the official exchange rate). Approved licences, however, are no guarantee that the required foreign exchange will be forthcoming and bring the intended investment to early realisation.

It might be useful, finally in this section, in the light of the abrupt demise of economic liberalisation in May 1987, to cast a glance at the operational profile of a large *loss-making*

Table 9.24 *INDECO Group's investment plan, 1987/8–1989/90 (in US$m. as of Feb. 1988)*

Type of Manufacturing	Cumulated 3-year Investment
A. On-Going activities:	
Tyres	0.9
Real estate development	0.2
Glycerine distillation	2.7
Brewing	0.3
Industrial gas	2.2
Woodworking	0.6
Sugar refining	0.3
Sub-total	7.2
B. New projects	
Textiles	0.8
Maize milling	2.5
Mechanical engineering	1.5
Brewing	19.9
Coffee processing	0.1
Bread-making	0.2
Engineering	0.5
Paper bags	0.6
Brick-making	0.8
Steel rolling	0.6
Barley malt	0.3
Marble grinding	0.1
Electrical appliances	0.2
Cannery	0.2
Sub-total	28.3
GROUP TOTAL	34.0

Source: ZIMCO/INDECO interview data.

food manufacturing parastatal to highlight some of the major problems that have to be resolved under Zambia's renewed system of administered economic management.

The enterprise comprises four cereal mills and enjoys monopoly conditions of sale. In two of the factories the machinery is around 50 years old. For want of spare parts and repairs, milling coefficients are low and operating costs high. Before price decontrol, these costs could not be passed on to the consumer. Moreover, while the landed price of wheat rose by over 50%, the ex-factory price of flour had to be kept unchanged by administrative fiat. Losses were high and obliged the company to default on its payments to the cereal purchasing and importing agency in 1982. The following year was taken up with the preparation of a rehabilitation study and then three more years were spent on mobilising the necessary foreign finance – just when praise was being heaped on Zambia for its bold reforms by all donors – and ordering equipment.

Meanwhile the, by then, unencumbered enterprise raised the price of its flour, as agreed with the retailers, from K50.5 per 90 kg bag to K68 per bag, causing offtake to contract proportionately. In 1986, as the excess liquidity and auctioning of foreign exchange accelerated the price spiral, the retail price of flour had to be raised from K147.4 to K224 per bag. The price elasticity of consumer demand took its toll of flour sales, which dropped to less than half their pre-liberalisation level.

Behind these figures lies a radical switch in the main constraint on the enterprise: from the supply side, because of foreign-exchange unavailability, to the demand side as the national currency underwent a massive devaluation and dragged down urban consumer purchasing power – a trend reinforced by events in 1989.

The future of manufacturing development

THE FOURTH NATIONAL DEVELOPMENT PLAN, 1989–93[35]
The Fourth National Development Plan (FNDP) was published in early 1989. It is not seen as a document distinct and different from the NERP but rather, in the words of the President,

as 'the first medium-term programme in the implementation of the country's New Economic Recovery Programme that was launched on the 1st of May 1987' (GOZ, 1989: i). It has 24 separate objectives of which the most important in relation to future industrial development are the following (1989: 27–8):

- to achieve an overall growth rate of 3% in real terms over the Plan period;
- to mobilise and utilise external resources only as a supplement to domestic resources, strictly in line with the needs and priorities of the FNDP;
- to reduce inflation to below 20% by the end of the Plan period;
- to reduce the overall budget deficit to below 2% of GDP by 1993;
- to increase formal sector employment from 357,000 in 1987 to 400,000 by the end of the Plan period;
- to expand and diversify the country's export base, by encouraging non-traditional (non-copper) exports;
- to restructure production and consumption patterns in order to conserve foreign-exchange resources and to improve the country's balance-of-payments position;
- to strengthen the parastatal and private sectors by promoting their operational efficiency and productive capacities, and
- to increase the contribution of the private sector to economic growth to 45% of GDP.

For manufacturing industry in particular, the following objectives are to be noted. Capacity utilisation levels are to rise to above 70% of industrial averages by 1993 (1989: ii).

> The strategy will . . . take account of the current under-utilisation of productive capacity in productive sectors, the strong technological dependence that undermines efforts at increasing utilisation of local raw materials and the stress that has been exerted on social infrastructure . . . The strategy will thus seek to redress these problems by providing the necessary foreign-exchange resources to existing productive enterprises in the manu-facturing sector for importation of raw material inputs. Appropriate incentives will be worked out to encourage enterprises to restructure their plant technology to greater use of raw materials (1989: 29).

This restructuring is elaborated upon a little further in the document thus (1989: 26):

> The FNDP strategy takes into account the past development of manufacturing entities that have heavily depended on imported inputs in the manufacture of certain products under cover of the policy of import substitution. In this way, while the country has benefited from the local manufacture of such products, enormous amounts of foreign exchange have, on the other hand, been spent on supporting the raw material imports of such industries. The FNDP will thus accord higher priority to those industries producing goods using local raw materials intended to meet the same consumption needs or require-ments. Where possible, conversion programmes will be undertaken to take advantage of readily available local raw materials for the replacements of goods with a high import content.

Other strategies of the Plan for the sector include the following (1989: 193–194, 200):

- establishing small-scale industrial estates;
- encouraging the establishment of industries whose imports would be inputs specially geared for processing products for exports;
- increasing and encouraging long-term financing by the banks and other financial institu-tions;
- creating an industrial environment conducive to increased labour productivity;
- establishing a mechanism that will ensure the flow of information between research institu-tions and industry, large-scale industry and small-scale industry and between parastatal companies and private companies;
- reactivating and strengthening corporate planning at public and private enterprise levels as an integral part of national planning, and
- giving priority to exports of high quality manufactured goods as against the export of raw materials.

In this broad context, a range of more explicit financial targets are presented. Within the overall target growth rate of GDP of 3% a year, the manufacturing sector is forecast to grow

Table 9.25 *FNDP macroeconomic and financial year, 1989–93*

	1988	1989	1990	1991	1992	1993
GDP growth (%)	2.8	3.0	3.0	3.0	3.0	3.0
MVA growth (%)	2.3	2.3	2.7	3.1	3.5	3.8
MVA/GDP ratio (%)	22.1	22.1	22.2	22.3	22.4	22.3
Investment/GDP (%)		20.0	21.7	22.7	24.0	25.0
Export growth[a] (%)	2.4	− 1.6	6.4	2.2	2.5	4.0
Import growth (%)	8.5	9.7	6.0	2.8	3.1	4.2
Current account balance (Km.)	− 2,049	− 2,333	− 3,093	− 3,747	− 4,209	− 4,222
Manufacturing employment	50,440	51,358	52,077	52,806	53,546	54,295
Manufacturing[b] investment (Km.)	767.7[c]	1,380.0	1,422.6	1,483.5	1,576.2	1,629.8
Manufacturing/total investment	20.0	35.6	33.7	32.7	31.7	30.3

Source: GOZ, 1989:28–29, 38, 41 and 71.

Notes: [a] The Plan states that non-traditional exports are to increase from K590m. in 1987 (7%) to K1,800m. by 1993 (19%); this is two and a half times the forecast rate of increase of all exports.
[b] This is the figure for manufacturing and trade.
[c] Figure for 1987.

at an average annual rate of 3.1%, starting at 2.3% in 1989 and rising to 3.8% by the end of the Plan period. By 1992, the MVA/GDP ratio is expected to be still only about 22%. Employment growth in manufacturing is also expected to rise only slowly, at the lower annual rate of 1.4% throughout the period. Even for these modest rates of expansion to be achieved, it is clear that investment levels need to be boosted dramatically. According to the Plan, the investment/GDP ratio is to rise from 20% in 1989 to 25% by 1993. Some of the leading FNDP macroeconomic targets are shown in Table 9.25.

PROSPECTS FOR FOREIGN-EXCHANGE EARNINGS

In the near term, a major factor in the evolution of manufacturing will be the economy's ability to expand its foreign-exchange earnings, which in turn depends largely on the world price of base metals, predominantly copper, and on the country's ability to respond to price rises. What can be said about the near and medium-term foreign-exchange earning prospects? Abstracting from new mineral finds, the situation appears to offer, at best, hope for only a very moderate expansion, as is apparent from the following discussion of the demand outlook for Zambia's principal exports.

Copper.   The average grade of copper ore extracted in Zambia has been continually falling. The 20,000 tonne increase in production in 1987/8 was due primarily to the initiation by Zambia Consolidated Copper Mines (ZCCM) of its rehabilitation and rationalisation programme, whose medium-term results should merely halt the recent downward spiral of processed copper output. The expectations reflected in the NERP that production would attain 500,000 tonnes of finished copper soon after the commissioning of the Nchanga Concentrator and the Tailings Leach plant proved to be over-optimistic (see NCDP, 1988: 166). Thus, this high level should be taken as a maximum over the next five to ten years, particularly as the non-economic mines closed in 1986/7 were not re-opened when the world copper price rose sharply. Any increase in ore output implies a very heavy outlay, most of it in foreign exchange, on over-burden removal, extensive drainage and modern extraction techniques (ibid.: 173). This would be feasible only with additional external aid, either in the form of direct investment or through the less likely channel of concessional financing[36].

The attractiveness of putting substantial resources into an expansion of copper production does not appear great in the light of World Bank commodity forecasts and the expectations of private metals specialists. The intensity of copper use by OECD countries has been on the decline since the 1960s, reflecting structural shifts in output, raw materials substitution and input-saving innovations (miniaturisation). This downward trend is likely to continue in future years. Assuming robust medium-term growth of industrialised countries' GDP (3.3% a year), world consumption of copper is unlikely to expand at more than 1.7% a year during the rest of the century, even if one assumes that the current demand for copper by developing countries is sustained. Analysts concur in the belief that the London Metal Exchange price of copper – in constant dollar terms – is likely to increase only moderately during the 1990s

Figure 9.2 *Copper (wire-bars and cathodes) prices, actual and projected, 1980–2000 (US$/tonne)*

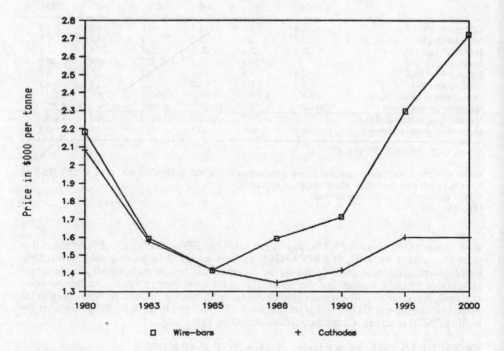

Source: World Bank, Economic Analysis and Projections Department, 1987.

from the average level of around $0.73/lb (expressed in 1985 dollars)[37]. Since manufacturing unit value (MUV) is expected to grow at a much faster rate, copper terms of trade should fall over the next 12 years. The values in Figure 9.2 illustrate this point.

Other metals. The principal by-product of copper production in Zambia is cobalt. Its output will therefore keep in step with that of copper and should be in the range of 3,500–4,000 tonnes per annum over the medium term. The world price of cobalt has been extremely volatile in recent years, oscillating for instance, from $9.50/lb in early 1986 to $4/lb four months later. However, the price-fixing arrangement between Zambia and Zaire in November of the same year has had a stabilising effect which might well be enhanced in the future, were other cobalt exporters to collaborate.

The outlook is extremely bleak with regard to Zambia's proven lead and zinc deposits which are rapidly nearing depletion. Relative to what these two metals earned Zambia in foreign exchange in 1987, the gap to be filled by other exports is roughly $17.5 m. In contrast, coal output is scheduled to expand, thanks to substantial rehabilitation of the single large colliery, and may reach the level of 750,000 million tonnes over the next few years. This could leave an exportable surplus of some 150,000 million tonnes to neighbouring countries. The medium-term price outlook is for a slow but steady rise (of $2–3 per tonne per annum) to the year 2000.

Other major exports. In the past these have included tobacco, maize and electricity but more recently also sugar and gemstones[38].

The foreign exchange earned by tobacco exports by the marketing board (NATCO) in 1987 came to $3.5 m. The major part of tobacco output comes from smallholder farmers who, under the proposals of the NERP, will receive a number of incentives for which budgetary provisions have been made. Targeted output for 1989 was estimated at 2,836 million tonnes and there is every reason to count on increasing exportable surpluses in future years. World consumption is projected by the World Bank to grow at 1.7% per annum over the next one and a half decades, mainly in developing countries. Zambia's Virginia and Burley leaf is of good quality and should continue to find ready markets. The medium-term price is forecast to reach $1,850 per tonne (expressed in 1985 dollars).

Gemstones are but one group of a great variety of sub-soil wealth in Zambia. Their extraction is dominated by wildcat digging and smuggling so that recorded values of exports are necessarily understatements. Efforts are being made to industrialise mining operations and to control marketing, particularly of high unit value stones like emeralds. The recorded 1987 production of gemstones came to 1,157 million tonnes with a market value of $11 m. Not only does this product group face ready outlets and strong demand prospects, but it also offers considerable potential in employment opportunities in cutting, polishing and jewellery making.

Zambia's hydroelectric potential is vast and electricity exports to Zimbabwe had risen to about $21 m. before that outlet disappeared as client installations became converted to coal fuel in 1987. This foreclosure was not anticipated by the public electricity company (ZESCO), which had to raise domestic power prices in consequence. Alternative export outlets will be difficult to develop and will require costly investment in transmission infrastructure.

Overall, therefore, foreign-exchange earning prospects of non-manufactured products are not very reassuring for the next 15 years unless there is considerably more processing and transformation carried out and new exportable surpluses generated.

THE POLICY CONTEXT

Need to improve the industrial data base. Zambia's physical and human endowments are varied and rich enough to sustain income growth in a well-managed and stable environment. Thus, the World Bank's 1986 *Country Economic Memorandum* argues that with strong external support an average annual GDP growth of 3.1% *would be attainable* during the following five to six year period[39]. Yet it should also be stressed that from the onset of economic liberalisation there has been no systematic work done in macro-planning and forecasting: the last macro-model was elaborated in 1985 and provided a current payments forecast for the Third Five-Year Plan. Limitations in underlying time-series data and their forecasting unreliability because of particular recent events precluded its subsequent development. Within the NCDP, an unpublished Kalecki-type model was reportedly recently tested on an *ad hoc* basis; however, scarce planning resources have largely been devoted to improving project evaluation. A third point is that the industrial monographs of the early 1980s (which were promising in their analytical scope) were abandoned – incomplete. In the late 1980s, no comprehensive data on private sector manufacturing were available to complement parastatal reporting through ZIMCO.

The inadequacy of primary data on industrial production, intermediate consumption and investment, was coupled with a severe shortage of trained personnel and hardware for electronic compilation, processing, dissemination and analysis within the Central Statistical Office, not to mention line ministries. Politically significant economic variables seemed to be produced on an emergency basis, as occasion demanded – as with the need to refer to capacity utilisation, import content or changes in the composition of imports in some important public addresses. Some of these lacunae should be filled through UNIDO's ongoing support to the Ministry of Industry and Commerce, whose Permanent Secretary is herself an experienced statistician. To that extent, criticism of data inadequacies may seem gratuitous, but for the additional weight they could impart to departmental claims on scarce public resources and external support.

Thus the very understandable preoccupation with reducing import dependence throughout the economy and intensifying inter-sectoral exchange should not distract attention from building up, as rapidly as possible, a comprehensive industrial *cum* foreign trade data base, and radically improving the current reporting system[40].

There is no doubt that the allocation of foreign exchange would be on a much firmer foundation were claimants' files to incorporate *objectively established* ratios not only of the intensity of factor use and financial profitability, but also of the efficiency with which fixed capital and foreign exchange are used. The actual allocations should be submitted to continuing statistical analysis at the sub-sectoral level and publicised quarterly.

In the commendable drive to expand non-traditional exports, export promotion should be conceived in the broadest sense. This would then lead to the gathering of more market information, and improvements in quality and product presentation[41]. The efficient operation of the requisite financial infrastructure – the new Export/Import Bank and the central bank's Export Credit Guarantee Scheme for small-scale industries – must be ensured, broadened in coverage and complemented with a currency-hedging facility. There are also important reasons for following the advice of both the World Bank and SADCC to put in place a revolving fund for export development and to keep abreast of the changing incentive structures of neighbouring countries, most especially Zimbabwe.

Every effort should be made by the Bank of Zambia, with the collaboration of ZCCM and, hopefully, major donors, to prepare and publish periodical forecasts of likely foreign-exchange availabilities. Such information would provide businessmen with a referential basis for programming output and sales, placing orders for inputs – which may take up to three months to arrive from, say, Europe – and enabling them to bid, with greater confidence than in the past, for domestic and regional tenders.

Facilitating export expansion.   Finance permitting, short-term credit to exporters of non-traditional products could be subsidised to facilitate market penetration and to assist in facing up to foreign competition[42]. In addition, the import duty drawback procedure should be streamlined and verification procedures made less burdensome for all concerned.

As it is unlikely that administrative controls over imports and foreign exchange will be removed entirely in the near future, a comprehensive study needs to be undertaken of the scope of *effective incentives* being offered to risk capital in different lines of production. Upon completion, a pragmatic approach would have to be followed in reconciling the social cost of transforming domestic and external savings into investment with, *inter alia*, revenue objectives and with lessening industry's stubborn dependence on imported inputs.

Turning to the physical links between landlocked Zambia and its external markets, it is interesting to note that neither progressive economic liberalisation nor the reimposition of administrative controls appears to have affected the transport sector's gradual decline. Its share in real GDP slipped from 5.8% in 1984 to 5.2% in 1987. The availability of aid finance varied as between particular modes of transport and infrastructural requirements. Thus, in line with international political decisions to help reduce the dependence of southern African economies on South Africa, from 1985 onwards multilateral and bilateral backing has been provided for rehabilitating and upgrading Zambia's northern and eastern transport corridors to ocean ports. This assistance prevented a sharp contraction in the *overall* level of transport services at the disposal of Zambian industry. Thus, the same volume of freight (4.6 million tonnes) was transported by rail in 1987 as in 1986. After ZCCM closed its liaison office in Johannesburg, rail traffic shifted somewhat in favour of the jointly operated Tanzania-Zambia rail line (TAZARA)[43]. But there were no reported improvements in the inadequate rolling stock, the high rates of rail accidents, theft, and in the severe speed limitations imposed over long stretches of rail[44].

Donors' commitment to assisting the diversion of commercial exchange away from South Africa, plus SADCC's complementary activity, augur well for gradually lowering the rail carriage component of the fob price of Zambian goods.

Unfortunately, this sanguine assessment does not extend to the other main transport mode – road haulage. The quality of Zambia's road network has deteriorated in the face of rapidly rising costs of upkeep, not to mention extension, and 'donor fatigue'[45]. The outlook for early improvement is bleak. In turn, the short lifetime of heavy vehicles in Zambia is not likely to be lengthened nor truck operators' outlays on repairs reduced in the foreseeable future.

Price regulations.   By 1989 price-regulating procedures needed to be overhauled and made transparent. Validation of inflation-induced price increases could be carried out *a posteriori*, particularly if coupled with stiff penalties for misrepresentation. While consumers' interests must remain paramount and protected against fraudulent or monopolistic price rigging, price setting need not be at the expense of 'normal' financial profitability, as it had been. In this respect, the practice of 'customising' trading margins according to the nature of the product – distinguished by its perishability, turnover, shelf-life etc. – did not appear to be economically optimal. Urgent consideration needed therefore to be given to its replacement by uniform prescriptions of distributional margins, discriminating against imports in general. Such an approach would tend to have trading activities reinforce other import-substituting incentives in a product-neutral manner and would simplify the existing price-setting procedure. Thus it was not surprising to hear that a wide range of price controls were lifted in mid-1989.

CONCLUDING OBSERVATIONS

Among the many challenges facing the Zambian authorities in promoting industrial development, raising the abysmally low (8%) investment/GDP ratio is clearly paramount. The problems created or accentuated by deteriorating terms of trade and falling mineral output did give rise to greater public concern for husbanding resources, improving management in parastatal enterprises and keeping the price of staples affordable for low-income groups. In so doing, new institutions and policy instruments have been put in place, even if some had by 1990 still to demonstrate their operational effectiveness. The time has come to use them in a *concerted* manner for mobilising and channelling risk capital – domestic and foreign – into manufacturing activities.

With interest rates newly fixed under the new system of controls, domestic savings will be largely determined by price and wage levels. Incomes have already reached all-time lows, thus in the short to medium term domestic investment will depend crucially on the inflow of net foreign savings. While the volume of concessionary aid should now steadily increase the level of the country's indebtedness is such as to discourage commercial long-term loans of any consequence. Hence it must pin its hopes on attracting direct foreign investment in all its forms, including possible debt/equity swaps arranged with the creditors. The 1986 Investment Act provides generous and well-balanced incentives and guarantees. The financial infrastructure has been bolstered by the Lima Agricultural Bank, the credit guarantee facility for small industry of the Development Bank of Zambia, and the embryonic Export/Import Bank. They deserve the support of the international community in their task of diversifying output and raising the economy onto a sustainable development path.

The approach followed by the young Small Industries Development Organisation (SIDO) would appear to merit extension and emulation. Basically it provides a fairly complete package of supporting services to would-be entrepreneurs, from the conception of an activity to its material realisation. It also entails the involvement of suppliers of inputs in the outcome of their clients' initiatives. Of course, much has still to be done in perfecting SIDO's operations, but its modest achievements are already commendable.

The Ministry of Commerce and Industry's Action Programme, July 1987 to December 1988, contains sectoral objective 4(iv) which calls for the provision of incentive packages for trade-oriented activities. Because of its importance to the future well-being of the economy, the furthering of this objective should have a high claim on public resources to mount a broadly-based promotional service for other than small-scale manufacturing activities. Assistance would have to be provided not only with project identification – as is done at present – but also with the following:

- the search for financial partners and assistance with negotiating contractual terms and conditions;
- the identification of technology most appropriate for Zambian factor endowment and of the cheapest and most dependable sources of all necessary inputs;
- monitoring the project's progress through the financing and banking stages;
- assistance in clearing administrative hurdles;
- ensuring that products merit Zambian quality labels;
- facilitating the disposal of output by identifying all possible marketing channels at home and abroad;
- promoting intra-product specialisation and product complementarities within the southern Africa region;
- in line with Action Programme objective 4(c), to provide business novices with problem-solving instruction in cost-accounting, pricing, labour relations, production and procurement planning, marketing and after-sales servicing.

On a more innovative plane, there would appear to be merit in using a task-force approach to pursue some obvious import-substituting opportunities that have been held in abeyance for years. These would include the processing of molasses into industrial alcohol, methane and other more complex derivatives of the sugar chain. Together with projects related to domestic production and export markets there are several economically viable ventures in manufacturing. These include the manufacture of insecticides and pesticides (provided the active ingredients can be produced locally), hardwood forest products for export, irrigation equipment, tanned leather and shoes, brass/bronze appliances, magnesium-fused phosphate fertiliser, electrical motors and transformers, glycerine from soap by-products, tyres for earth-moving equipment, and animal stock-feed. Many of these new industries would generate new linkages, while products could become competitive in foreign markets with careful attention paid to plant design and location.

The Department of Industry's voice clearly needs to be heard on several major fiscal measures impinging on investment, such as the undifferentiated treatment of capital equipment along with all other goods imported under the 'no funds involved' facility, and which have to pay a 5% *ad valorem* levy. As part of export promotional measures, it should strive to make the 50% retention facility for non-traditional exports *fast-disbursing and cumulative* (instead of allowing it to lapse three months after the export receipts are handed over to the central bank).

Furthermore, the requirement that the Kwacha equivalent of all foreign exchange requested be deposited in favour of FEMAC in commercial banks, needlessly cuts into firms' revolving capital, at a time of general illiquidity. The Ministry should support the suggestion of having only *successful applicants'* bank accounts debited and FEMAC credited accordingly.

It should also take a firm stand in support of the as yet unpublicised (but widely known) plans to privatise – in whole or in part – non-strategic parastatal manufacturing enterprises and services once they have been rehabilitated and made saleable. It could even aspire to playing the role of 'honest broker', in the ensuing process. As a corollary, the Department should put its full weight behind the idea of creating a Stock Exchange and capital market, again in demonstrating its natural vocation as *the mainstay of all manufacturing and trading activity* – without distinction as to ownership. It might also consider preparing a strong brief in favour of institutionalising *freehold* land ownership to stimulate investment that finds the present 99-year leasehold arrangement unattractive.

In addition to paying continued attention to new ways of promoting regional economic co-operation, the Ministry of Commerce and Industry should explore the opportunities offered by counter and barter trade in its various forms, with the object, say, of exchanging hard-to-dispose-of nitrogenous fertilisers for deficit phosphate-based ones.

But even if all these suggestions were to be implemented, the manufacturing sector in Zambia cannot be counted upon to absorb a large proportion of present and future job-seekers. Nor can it alone ensure another period of rapid expansion of value added in manufacturing. It could, however, help stop its stagnation and decline, provided more foreign capital with its knowhow and marketing channels is attracted to Zambia. A climate of confidence and co-operation between the public administration and the private sector is a *necessary condition* for this, and would ensure that, with time, the latter's saving propensity would rise at least to equal that of the parastatals.

Zambia's 'left-about-face' policies and 'go-it alone' stance never constituted a durable policy. Rather they need to be seen as a politically-determined tactical move which, fortunately for Zambia, coincided with a cyclical rise in the world price of non-ferrous metals. With the prospect of more flexible and less doctrinaire attitudes to the problems of SSA countries evolving in the multinational funding agencies, co-operative arrangements that are politically acceptable to Zambia should be within reach.

Notes

1. During the first 20 years of independence Zambia had fixed exchange rates: until 1970 the kwacha was pegged to the pound sterling, then in 1970–76 to the US dollar, in 1976–83 to the SDR, and from July 1983 to October 1985 to a basket of trade-weighted currencies. In the course of adjustments after 1974, three discrete devaluations were carried out: in 1976 by 20%, by 10% more in 1978 and by a further 20% in 1983. These proved inadequate to diversify and promote exports so as to offset the continuing fall in metal-related foreign-exchange earnings. Reserves were repeatedly drawn down to the value of a few weeks' imports as the government persisted in relying on incomes and exchange controls to contain imports, to insulate the kwacha from supply and demand pressures, and to borrow its way out of what was thought to be a passing depression. It eschewed a substantial once-off depreciation for several likely reasons: the difficulty of deciding on the adequacy of a large devaluation in terms of its net balance-of-payments effect; the unpalatability of admitting its inability to sustain the value of the national currency and of inviting inflation from abroad via higher prices of imported goods and services on which so many activities were highly dependent; the

perceived unreliability of a positive supply response by producers of exportable products, given the run-down state of their capital assets and other supply constraints: and the continued preoccupation with supporting the purchasing power of urban dwellers to the neglect of internal terms of trade.

For detailed discussions see Daniel (1985), Harvey (1987) and Lancaster and Williamson (1986).

2. The performance of a Zambian firm manufacturing flashlight batteries epitomises the problems endemic to industrial growth in the 1975–85 period. A summary of the case-study of the firm by K. Rajeswaran (1986) describes this well.

'The firm was selected as typifying the outcome of import substitution in Zambia during the 1970s. Its principal characteristics included the following:

- consumer-oriented with few possibilities for diversifying its product mix;
- relatively capital intensive and utilising complex and costly machinery;
- sited in a non-industrial environment, lacking commercial and commercial and physical infrastructure;
- designed for output volumes well in excess of the needs of the domestic market;
- dependent on the importation of the greater part of inputs and on the use of foreign managerial and technical knowhow;
- not price-competitive & requiring protection from imported products;

The plant was inaugurated in 1978 as a joint venture with a large Finnish firm (Oy Airam Ab) that enjoyed its Government's patronage and INDECO, holding two-thirds of the company's shares, valued at KO.9 million. The project had been conceived in the early 1970s but site preparation took two years longer than anticipated largely because of its sub-optimal location – close to local deposits of manganese ore used as an input, but in a rural environment with poor communications with the country's main commercial and industrial centres.

The installed capacity (44 million flashlight batteries) was more than double the peak level of such imports in the 1973 to 1977 period and about four times the average level of similar imports. The responsibility for project planning, procurement of equipment and machinery, installation, commissioning, maintenance, management and training lay with the Finnish partner in the project.

It took but 18 months for the plant's operation to become seriously disrupted by defective equipment, inadequate technical supervision and, more crucially, the shortage of foreign exchange to purchase adequate supplies of raw materials and spare parts. This constraint was eased by additional Finnish assistance but also led to the divestment by the foreign partner of its shares in 1982.

Capacity utilisation during the 1978 to 1983 period (averaging 20%) never exceeded 29%. Employment levels varied between 200 and 250 persons. Downtime averaged 16,000 man-hours per annum in the period 1981/82 to 1984/85, four-fifths (equally) due to machine breakdowns and to shortages of various inputs. Because of these constraints, labour productivity declined after 1982. Additionally, no batteries were exported. The Kwacha cost of inputs almost quadrupled between 1979 and 1983. The higher costs of production could not be passed on fully to final consumers, thus reducing the firm's profit margins. Foreign exchange allocations to the firm by the Bank of Zambia covered, on average, only one quarter of the firm's requirements, obliging it to rely ever more on expensive supplier credit. By 1984/85, its long term debt amounted to K7.3 million.'

3. Examples cited by Makgetla (1984) are: first, the expansion of polyester fabric manufacturing with a high import content, in preference to more intensive use of domestic cotton and, secondly, the costly investment in automated wrapping by the state-controlled bakeries to help them stand up to competition from artisanal bread makers. For a full discussion of the structure of ownership in the manufacturing (and mining) sectors see Saasa (1987).

4. The ILO's JASPA report on Zambia (1981) estimated a 20% deterioration in both the barter and the cash domestic terms of trade between 1969 and 1980.

5. Later, a new 100% surrender requirement of all export earnings to the Central Bank, instead of the 50% in force before the break with the IMF, raised an immediate outcry among exporters who had recently gained precarious footholds in foreign markets with so-called non-traditional exports (all but metal minerals). Several of them claimed that the revalued kwacha made them uncompetitive abroad and called for it to be 50% lower.

6. In the Dutch variant of the foreign-exchange auction the bidders have to pay the actual rates they offer, rather than the struck rate at which transactions are subsequently made.

7. For details see *Conference Proceedings* (Lusaka, 29 June – 3 July 1987) The Auctioning of Foreign Exchange, organised by the Economics Association of Zambia.

8. Zambia's net receipts of official development assistance (oda) from OECD sources amounted to US$464.5 m. in 1986 (at current prices) having risen at an annual average rate of 4.2% in *real terms* from their 1980 level. Additional flows in 1986 from other (non-OECD) sources came to US$94 m. (OECD, *Development Cooperation 1987 Report*, Paris, OECD, 1988.)

9. The rate of population growth has risen from 3.1% a year on average during 1970–83 (according to UN data) to an annual average of 3.6% for 1980–85, as reported by the Central Statistical Office and used in the NERP planning exercise. According to the 1989–93 development plan (GOZ, 1989: 52), the average rate for the period 1985–90 is estimated at 3.7% a year.

10. The first White Paper entitled 'Outline of the Government's Industrial Policy' was published by the

Government Printer in October 1964. It was revised by the Ministry of Commerce and Industry in January 1966.

11. In Zambia, data on capacity utilisation in manufacturing are very patchy. For the early period, World Bank analysts derived their branch estimates from small samples of individual enterprises, most of which were state-controlled. More recently the INDECO group of parastatals have begun to include capacity use in their annual reports. UNIDO has listed this information for the years 1981–2 in its *Industrial Development Review* series (IS/520), Feb. 1985.

12. The 1989–93 National Development Plan gives figures for 1987 and 1988, indicating that overall capacity utilisation in the manufacturing sector rose from 38% in 1987 to 42% in 1988. For 1987, rates varied from 19% for Zambezi Saw Mills to 78% for ROP (cooking oil), with half the firms named having rates lower than 50%. By 1988, the rate for Zambezi Saw Mills had risen to 27%, that of ROP to 87% with only 25% of firms recording rates of 50% or lower (GOZ, 1989: 23 and 24).

13. The rate of import substitution was derived by the application of the formula $(U_2 - U_1)/(Q_2 - Q_1)$ in which $U_1 = Q_1/S_1$, $U_2 = Q_2/S_2$, $Q =$ domestic output, $M =$ imports and $S = Q + M =$ total supply.

14. As the computation of DRCs requires access to enterprise accounts and firm knowledge of border prices (a particularly complex problem for landlocked countries), the World Bank's calculations of DRcs are, so far, the only known attempt to work out these numbers for Zambia, dating back to 1981. As all practical economists know, the major uncertainties in calculating DRCs derive from the difficulty of arriving at so-called free trade and shadow prices. In the SSA context, the use of proxies and approximations is the rule, plus abstraction from usually significant differences in quality between domestic and competing imports. Also there are practical difficulties of valuing non-tradeable inputs, regarding which opinion differs. But the initial stumbling-block is the poor quality of accounting data regarding intermediate consumption by the sampled enterprises, a matter commented on below.

Firms with the lowest DRCs are the most efficient at transforming domestic resources into foreign exchange. The high DRC values result from low levels of value added (at international prices) which, in terms of Zambian patterns already discussed, would apply either to the firms receiving high tariffs and import-licensing protection yet consuming large quantities of imported inputs entering at low rates of duty, or to generally inefficient enterprises, using vast quantities of domestic resources per unit of value added (at free trade prices).

15. Before 1975, several industry monographs were published but their coverage (80%) of the manufacturing sector stopped short of analysing a few small but dynamic sub-sectors (base and fabricated metal products, electrical machinery and 'other' manufacturing). Because of the nature of enterprise accounts, the studies could not separate out imported and domestic inputs in intermediate consumption of the firms.

16. For a discussion of the methodology used see various articles by J. Diamond in the *Oxford Bulletin of Economics*, Vol. 29, No. 2; *Applied Economics*, Vol. 7, No. 4, and *Kyklos*, Vol. 29, No. 4. See also B.R. Hazari's articles in the *Review of Economics and Statistics*, Vol. 52, No. 3, 1970 and G.J.D. Hewings' important article in *The Developing Economies*, Vol. XX, No. 2, 1982.

17. The definitions of the 29 sub-sectors used in the 1975 I/O Table were as follows:

Sector number	Definition
1	Agriculture, forestry and fishing
2	Metal mining
3	Quarrying
4	Food manufacturing
5	Beverages & Tobacco
6	Textiles and wearing apparel
7	Wood & wood products
8	Paper & printing etc.
9	Chemicals
10	Rubber products
11	Non-metallic mineral products
12	Basic metal products
13	Fabricated metal products
14	Other manufacturing
(15–29	All services)

18. Smuggling during 1987 was officially estimated to have escalated to 30% of all marketed essential commodities (NCDP, 1988: 13).

19. In the case of roller meal, the government subsidy came to almost double the consumer price. For breakfast meal the subsidy was 184% of the consumer price or two-thirds of total retail cost.

Although the cost of collecting and distributing maize by the National Agricultural Marketing Board (Namboard) was recognised as being too high – over 60% of the price paid to producers – the authorities steered clear of privatising any segment of maize (and fertiliser) marketing. In order to dampen the inflationary impact of the K2.7 bn budget deficit, only one-half was to be financed through bank borrowing, and about 12% was expected to be covered by external loans (presumably on non-commercial terms). Over one-third was to be financed out of counterpart funds, generated out of donor balance-of-payments support. *Budget Address*, by the Minister of Finance, January 1988 and NCDP (1988). However, maize prices were raised twice in 1989.

20. The output of minerals other than copper, however, declined: cobalt by 29%, lead by 26%, zinc by 19% and coal by about 12%. The differing US and Kwacha values of copper exports is shown by the following annual export data. Average copper exports rose from K1,467 m. a year in the period 1983–5 to K5,642 m. a year in 1986 and 1987, yet in US dollar values they fell from an annual average of $787 m. in 1983–5 to $687 m. in 1986 and 1987 (GOZ, 1989: 196).

21. Dramatic events subsequently ensued. In May 1989 the Kwacha was reduced to K10.25 to the US$, followed by a devaluation to K16 to the $ in June. In July the old Kwacha was replaced (at parity) with a new Kwacha.

22. The writer attended a symposium at the University of Zambia's School of Business and Economics with the Minister of Finance and of the NCDP as guest speaker. Surprisingly, no mention whatsoever was made in the ensuing debate of the Kwacha parity, in preference to disquisitions on relatively more marginal issues relating, for instance, to the structure of central government expenditure.

23. Foreign aid inflows covering the first few months of the NERP fell considerably short of the previous year's level. The negative consequences were compounded by a structural shift in these flows – away from general balance-of-payments support which figured so prominently in the auction period. Thus, foreign *capital assistance* in 1987 (at an annual rate based on 10 month data) came to 72% of that in 1986. The relative shares of technical assistance and commodity relief in total aid receipts approximately doubled from one year to the next (*Economic Report 1987*, Table v.i.). During calendar year 1987, however, a total of $15.8 m. is reported to have been received as direct foreign investment. (*Report of the Zambian Investment Co-ordinating Committee*, Appendix 1, Lusaka, January 1988).

24. The criteria that FEMAC were directed to apply in allocating foreign exchange and/or granting import licences (including 'no funds involved' authorisation) were as follows: (a) first, to those producing essential or basic goods for *domestic* consumption; (b) second, to producers of non-traditional exports. In both categories priority was to be given to enterprises capable of switching input procurement from external to domestic sources and to those involved in labour-intensive activities. No licences were to be issued for the importation of goods already available locally.

25. NCDP, *Economic Review 1986* and *Annual Plan 1987*, Lusaka, 1987.

26. Yet the rules governing the *application of criteria* by FEMAC issued by the Cabinet Office in May 1987 stated that the percentage distribution should give priority to sectors in the following order: agriculture; mining/quarrying; manufacturing; tourism; energy; transport/communications; building/construction; health/education; trading/personal services; banking/finance. The sectoral allocations of foreign exchange by FEMAC during the first nine months of 1987 were as follows: manufacturing, 54.4%; services, 14.1%; agriculture, 8.3%; mining, 7.6%; transport and communications, 6.2%; energy, 4.6%; trade, 3% and construction, 1.8%. The average allocation per FEMAC sitting came to $8.75 m. (Data from Deloitte, Haskins and Sells, *Update – Foreign Exchange*, Lusaka, September 1987).

27. The company concerned, *H.J. Heinz*, had negotiated in 1986 the purchase of 49% of the parastatal ROP Ltd which mainly manufactured cooking oil, detergents, soap and cosmetics. It had intended to expand ROP's operations with an initial investment of $1.5m. (*African Business*, September 1987, p. 41).

28. According to the World Bank's 1986 *Country Economic Memorandum*, (p. 42), just 5 inefficient INDECO firms were responsible for the drop in the average capacity utilisation of manufacturing parastatals after the introduction of the auction regime. Factor productivity in the parastatal sector was estimated to have risen by up to 15% in line with an increase in its value added and with the dismissal of labour.

29. Yet the NCDP's *Economic Review 1986* (p. 6) reads pessimistically as follows: 'Worse still, the non-traditional exports have not increased substantially in response to the auctioning of foreign exchange envisaged in the plan.'

30. The Preferential Trade Area (PTA) for Eastern and Central Africa groups 15 countries which have agreed a common list of products on which tariff and quantitative restrictions have been reduced for the group members. The list points to a considerable potential for sourcing imports regionally and, by June 1987, covered commodities with a traded value of $3.1 bn. It has also established a clearing facility as a first step towards a regional payments union and a PTA unit of account, the UAPTA, to entice its members away from paying for bilateral trade in hard currencies. Progress in this area, however, has been unsatisfactory as only 20% of total intra-PTA trade payments were being thus cleared at the end of 1987 (*African Business*, January 1988). One of the main problems in promoting

regional trade lies in the high import content of exportable manufactures. Thus, Zambian excess bottle-making capacity could not be utilised to help Zimbabwean beverage producers overcome a container bottleneck in meeting their 1987 orders.

31. See SADCC (1987). In 1987, the Council of Ministers of SADCC approved the recommendations of the 1986 SADCC trade study. These included, *inter alia*: the establishment of joint, product-specific commissions charged with preparing bilateral trade agreements encompassing countertrade, specialisation and matching of excess capacities in national plans. Proposals also covered the creation of national export pre-financing revolving funds and a regional export credit fund. The importance of raising the quality of export products has also received SADCC endorsement and Zambia was given the task of reporting on the feasibility of harmonising standards and certification systems throughout the PTA area.

32. But the firm still had 26% more labour during 1987 than full capacity operation warranted and the prime costs of its finished products were considerably above the cif cost of competing imports (*The Financial Gazette*, (Harare), 19 February 1988).

33. For financial year 1987/8, INDECO required about $106 m. of which 60% was earmarked for intermediate inputs and 13% for capital equipment. No more than one quarter of this foreign exchange was expected to become available under the 50% retention allowance for non-traditional exports; the rest was to have been covered by FEMAC allocations.

34. These *foreseeable* levels of investment were expected to produce increases in physical output in 1987/8 of: soaps (+ 71%); roasted coffee (+ 40%); wheat flour (+ 33%); beer and bread (+ 31%); detergents (+ 30%); plastic bags (+ 28%); intravenous fluid (+ 275%); copper rods, shapes and wire cables (+ 24%); textiles (+ 17%) and cement (+ 115%). Shortfalls were foreseen in the following: timber products (− 5%); stockfeeds (− 13%) and batteries (− 25%), caused mostly by foreign-exchange shortages.

35. The Fourth National Development Plan was released to the public in February 1989 after the research on this chapter had been substantially completed. Thus it should be noted that the rest of this chapter was written *prior* to its publication.

36. By the second quarter of its 1988/9 year (beginning April 1988), ZCCM were 17% below their target of 500,000 tonnes production for the year. By January 1989 estimates for the year varied from a high of 430,000 to a low of 370,000 tonnes (*Financial Times*, 13 January 1989).

37. With the coming on stream of the massive Escondida project in Chile from 1991, world production is set to rise by some 300,000 tonnes of copper concentrate. This is expected to have a significant downward shift in the world price of the metal. (See *Financial Times*, 11 May 1989.) London copper prices fell from £1,867 a tonne in November 1988 to £1,622 a tonne by May 1989.

38. Manufactured exports are considered separately below.

39. The reforms advocated by the Bank in that document were deemed capable of accelerating this rate to 4.5% a year.

40. In this regard, consideration might be given to *combining in a single return* the statutory obligation to submit financial information for fiscal purposes with that on production, intermediate consumption, employment and exports, as is done in Cameroon and probably in some other SSA countries as well.

41. There must be greater public awareness of what goes on in neighbouring markets by making maximum use of information gathered by the PTA and SADCC secretariats. The orderly expansion of regional trade should be pursued on the basis of emerging industrial complementarities at the product and process levels.

42. The establishment in early 1987 of the credit guarantee scheme for enterprises registered with the Small Industries Development Organisation (SIDO) was doubtless welcome. Yet the going interest rate (21%) has severely restricted the number of users (*African Business*, June 1987).

43. Railways carry the bulk of the country's freight. About 60% of all imports and 29% of exports were transported in 1986/7 by Zambia Railways south through South Africa, while some 30% of imports and 62% of exports were freighted by TAZARA to Dar Es Salaam (NCDP, *Economic Review, 1986*).

44. These resulted from years of inadequate maintenance and replacement. For instance, only a small proportion of wooden sleepers, laid originally in the early 1900s and whose *normal* life in Zambian conditions is 15 years, had thus far been replaced with concrete ones. As of 1987, every cargo train is provided with police escort and weighed at terminals and frontiers (*African Business*, June 1987).

45. During 1986/7 private road hauliers have been known to refuse to operate in areas where road conditions were particularly poor.

References and Bibliography

Bank of Zambia (1988), *Report and Statement of Accounts for the Year Ended 31st December, 1986*, Lusaka, Bank of Zambia.
—— *Quarterly Financial and Statistical Review*, and *Report and Statement of Accounts*, various, Lusaka.

Central Statistical Office, *Census of Industrial Production*, Lusaka, CSO, (various years).
—— (1975–7), *Industry Monographs*, Nos. 1–6, Lusaka, CSO.
—— (1977), *National Accounts Statistics Bulletin* No. 1, Lusaka, February.
——, *Monthly Digest of Statistics*, Lusaka, CSO, (various issues).
Daniel, P. (1985), 'Zambia: Structural Adjustment or Downward Spiral,' *IDS Bulletin*, Vol. 16, No. 3, July.
Development Bank of Zambia (1986), *Chairman's Statement and Annual Report*, Lusaka.
Economist Intelligence Unit, *Zambia, Country Report*, (various years) London, EIU.
Government of Zambia (GOZ), *Budget Address*, Lusaka Government Printer, (various years).
—— (1986), *Report of the Tariff Commission of Enquiry*. Lusaka, Government Printer, September.
—— (1987), *New Economic Recovery Programme and the President's Speech*. Lusaka, Government Printer, May.
—— (1989), *New Economic Recovery Programme: Fourth National Development Plan, 1989–1993*, Lusaka, National Commission for Development Planning, January.
Gulhati, R and Sekhar, V. (1981), *Industrial Strategy for Late Starters: The Experience of Kenya, Tanzania and Zambia*, World Bank Staff Working Paper No. 457, Washington, World Bank, May.
Harvey, C. (1987), 'Non-marginal Price Changes . . .' Paper submitted to the Economic Association of Zambia Conference on the Auction System, Lusaka, June (mimeo).
Industrial Development Corporation (INDECO) (1986), *Chairman's Statement and Review of Operations*, Lusaka.
—— (1987), *Annual Report and Accounts for the year ended 31 March, 1987*, Lusaka, INDECO.
International Labour Office (1981), *Basic Needs in an Economy Under Pressure: Recommendations of an ILO-JASPA Basic Needs Mission to Zambia*. Addis Ababa, ILO.
International Monetary Fund (IMF), *International Financial Statistics*, (various issues), Washington DC, IMF.
Karmiloff, I. (1988) *Industrialisation in Sub-Saharan Africa, Country Case Study, Zambia*, Working Paper No. 24, London, Overseas Development Institute.
Lancaster, C. and Williamson, J. (1986), *African Debt and Financing*, Special Report No. 5, Washington DC, Institute for International Economics.
Makgetla, N.S. (1984), 'Investment in the Third World: the Zambian experience' in *Proceedings of IDRC National Workshop*, Lusaka, April.
National Commission for Development Planning (NCDP) (1987a), *New Economic Recovery Programme (Progress report No. 1 on the Implementation of the Interim National Development Plan)*, Lusaka, NCDP.
—— (1987b), *Economic Review 1986 and Annual Plan 1987*, Lusaka, NCDP.
—— (1988), *Economic Report 1987*, Lusaka, NCDP.
Ncube, P.D. and Kaunga, E.C. (1984), 'An Overview of the Zambian Economy' in *Proceeding of IDRC National Workshop*, Lusaka, April.
Ncube, P.D. and Mwanamwina, I. (1984), '1975 Input-Output Table for the Zambian Economy' in *Proceedings of IDRC National Workshop*, Lusaka, April.
Ncube, P.D., Sakala, M. and Ndulo, M. (1987) 'The International Monetary Fund and the Zambian Economy' in K.J. Havnevik (ed.), *The IMF and the World Bank in Africa*, Uppsala, Scandinavian Institute of African Studies.
Organisation for Economic Cooperation and Development (1988), *Development Cooperation Report 1987*, Paris, OECD, December.
Rajeswaran, K. (1986), *Mansa Batteries*, Teco Research Project, Publication No. 7, IDS and Helsinki University, April.
Saasa, O.S. (1987), *Zambia's Policies Towards Foreign Investment*, Research Report No. 79. Uppsala, Scandinavian Institute of African Studies.
Sanderson, M. (1987), 'Why Zambia's Auction Failed', Paper presented to the Economic Association of Zambia Lusaka Conference on the Auction System, July (mimeo).
Seshamani, V. (1985a), 'The Manufacturing Sector of Zambia since Independence: An Analytical Profile', in *Proceedings of IDRC National Workshop*, Lusaka, April.
—— (1985b), 'Import Substitution and Export Promotion in the Manufacturing Sector of Zambia', in *Proceedings of IDRC National Workshop*, Lusaka, April.
—— and J.K. Hasan (1985), 'Key Sectors in the Zambian Economy: An Attempt at Empirical Identification', in Osei-Hwedie and Ndulu, M. (eds), *Issues in Zambian Development*. Boston, Omenana Press.
Small Industries Development Organisation, *Development of Small Scale Industries in Zambia*, Lusaka, SIDO, (undated).
Southern African Development Co-ordination Conference (1987), *Indicative Industrial Development Plan*, London Industrial Development Unit, Commonwealth Secretariat, September.
Steel, W.F. and Evans, J.W. (1984), *Industrialisation in Sub-Saharan Africa: Strategies Performance*. Washington DC, World Bank, Technical Paper No. 245.
United Nations Conference on Trade and Development (UNCTAD), *Handbook of International Trade and Development Statistics and Supplement*. Geneva, UNCTAD, various years.

United Nations Industrial Development Organisation (UNIDO) (1985), *Industrial Development Review Series: Zambia*, Vienna, UNIDO, February.
—— (1986), *Investor's Guide to Zambia*. Vienna, UNIDO.
—— (1987a), *Statistical Review of Economic and Industrial Performance: Zambia*. Vienna, UNIDO, January.
—— (1987b), *Industry and Development: Global Report 1987*. Vienna, UNIDO.
Van Der Hoeven, R. (1982), 'Zambia's Economic Dependence and the Satisfaction of Basic Needs', *International Labour Review*, Vol. 121, No. 2, Geneva.
World Bank (1984a), *Zambia: Issues and Options for Economic Development*, Washington DC, World Bank, (Country Economic Memorandum), April.
—— (1984b), *Zambia – Industrial Policy and Performance*. Washington DC, World Bank, August.
—— (1986), *Zambia: Economic Reforms and Development Prospects*. Washington DC, World Bank, (Country Economic Memorandum), November.
Zambia Industrial and Mining Corporation (ZIMCO) (1987a), *The Chairman's Statement and Director's Report*, Lusaka, ZIMCO.
—— (1987b), 'Country Report: Zambia', Paper submitted to the Regional African Workshop on Public Industrial Enterprises and their Environment, ISGP/UNIDO/IDDA, Algiers, June.
—— (1987c), *Annual Report for the year ended 31 March, 1987*. Lusaka, ZIMCO.

10 Zimbabwe

ROGER C. RIDDELL

Introduction

Zimbabwe's manufacturing sector has expanded over a time span of more than 60 years to become one of the most advanced and diversified in sub-Saharan Africa. Indeed, the sophistication of the economy and the pivotal place occupied by its manufacturing industry have led to the suggestion that, with favourable domestic policies and a supportive external environment, Zimbabwe could (perhaps with South Africa) be the first country in SSA to join the ranks of the handful of Newly Industrialising Countries (NICs), currently confined to Asia and Latin America.

Impressive though the expansion of the manufacturing base may have been down to the present day, a growing consensus is emerging from within the country and among external advisers that changes (probably quite far-reaching) are needed if the sector is to continue on its historical path and to play a greater role in generating jobs and foreign exchange for the economy as a whole. Indeed, as the country embarks on its second decade of Independence, some fundamental re-thinking of a range of macroeconomic policies is required if real incomes are to continue to rise and access to basic services is to be expanded. It is within this context that the role and place of manufacturing are becoming the central focus of attention in current policy debate. As the First National Development Plan (1986–90) puts it: 'Manufacturing industry is the key sector for changing the structure of the Zimbabwean economy and for achieving rapid and sustained overall economic growth and development' (GOZ, 1986: 30).

There are two main reasons for this. First, given the size and dominance of the sector, policies affecting manufacturing have and will continue to have a profound effect throughout the economy. Second, as Zimbabwe is suffering from what have now become acute foreign-exchange problems and as the mining and agricultural sectors will not be able to earn sufficient foreign exchange to meet national requirements over the next decade, it is apparent that the manufacturing sector – itself the major user of foreign exchange – will have to play a far greater role as a foreign-exchange earner than it has done in the recent past. Otherwise, long-term overall growth rates will be low or negative and, together with other sectors, manufacturing will be starved of essential foreign exchange. As a result, the sector will be increasingly likely to suffer from a downward spiral of low investment, low growth, little employment generation and fluctuating but low levels of exports – even if this long-term deterioration is also likely to be continually punctuated with short spurts of growth, especially when a good agricultural season coincides with a comparative easing of foreign-exchange shortages.

The first objective of this chapter is to attempt to explain both why and how manufacturing industry developed in Zimbabwe up to the present time and to isolate and evaluate the importance of the different constraints, opportunities, policies and practices which the sector faces. The second is to assess its likely future pattern of development by analysing and critically evaluating proposals for achieving sustained expansion well into the 1990s.

The chapter is divided into five parts. The next section gives an overview of the sector. This includes not only trends in macro-indicators but also an examination (based on case-study research) of the factors determining success and failure between different industrial firms at the micro-level. It also contains an analysis of the foodstuffs sub-sector and an examination of the important links between the manufacturing and agricultural sectors.[1] The next section, summarising the main macroeconomic constraints facing the economy, provides the essential backdrop for the subsequent description and critique of the main options for the future of manufacturing currently being proposed and debated. The chapter ends with a discussion of alternative approaches to Zimbabwe's industrial future and assesses these in relation, particularly, to those favoured by the World Bank.

Overview of the manufacturing sector

GROWTH OF THE MANUFACTURING SECTOR

Historical summary and current status. Although the origins of manufacturing in present-day Zimbabwe can be traced back to the early years of this century, it was in the 1930s that a significant manufacturing sector could be identified and that sub-sectoral diversification became important. In 1938, when the first industrial census was taken, not only had the iron and steel foundries and mills been built and the Rhodesian Iron and Steel Corporation established[2], but the country was exporting manufactured goods in *each* of the International Standard Industrial Classification (ISIC) sub-sectors[3].

By this time Zimbabwe's[4] manufacturing sector was already responsible for 10% of GDP, it employed 7% of the formal sector labour force and accounted for 8% of total export earnings. To put this into a contemporary perspective, SSA-wide data show that by 1984 in at least 70% of countries, the ratio of Manufacturing Value Added to GDP was less than 10%, in over 56% manufactured exports accounted for less than 10% of total national exports and in over 40% fewer than 10% of employees were working in the manufacturing sector[5]. What these comparisons highlight is the need to place an assessment of Zimbabwe's contemporary industrial status within the context of an extremely long history.

The current status of the sector and its importance to the overall economy can be seen from the following summary data. By the end of the 1980s, the sector was responsible for around 26% of GDP, and in 1985/6 net output was valued at over Z$2.5 bn ($1.5 bn)[6]. By 1987, it was the second largest employer of labour, with a total of some 175,000 people, 16% of the formal sector labour force. In 1985, exports of manufactured products totalled Z$726 m., almost 50% of total exports, falling, however, to Z$392 m., 25% of the total, if exports of cotton lint and ferro-alloys are excluded[7]. Over the period 1983–4, 18% of total gross fixed investment originated in the manufacturing sector, valued at Z$215 m. for each year.

The sector itself consists of some 1,260 separate units producing over 7,000 different products. 50% of all manufacturing takes place in the capital, Harare, with almost half of the remainder in the second largest city, Bulawayo. Table 10.1 provides recent data on the sub-sectoral breakdown. Although the importance of each sub-sector varies to some extent in terms of different characteristics, the overall dominance of sub-sector (9), metals and metal products, is clear. In addition, Table 10.1 indicates that over 50% of all manufacturing gross output, value added, employment, capital stock and exports originates in just three sub-sectors: foodstuffs (1), chemicals (7) and metal products (9)[8].

Revealing the current contribution of manufacturing to the wider economy and examining its major sub-sectoral characteristics remain only of limited use to policy debates because they explain little of the evolution of the sector, its links with the rest of the economy and its present strengths and weaknesses. A start to a better understanding of these issues can be gleaned from examining the overall performance of the sector over time.

The most important factor to record is that substantial and almost uninterrupted expansion has taken place in the 50 years since 1938, with an increasingly important role in the overall economy. In real terms, MVA doubled in the period 1938–44, doubled again by 1948 and again by 1955. By this time the MVA/GDP ratio had risen to 15%. Figures 10.1 and 10.2 show the steady expansion achieved over the following 35 to 40 years, with the exception of a short period in the mid to late 1970s when both real MVA and the MVA/GDP ratio fell and more recently in 1982–4 when the volume of production contracted. The most marked expansion – in terms of both real increases in value added and in the contribution of MVA to GDP – occurred during the first full nine years of the Unilateral Declaration of Independence (1966–75) and the first few years of Independence.

Not surprisingly, manufacturing expansion has been paralleled by a steady increase in employment in the sector. Total manufacturing employment, which stood at 17,500 in 1938, doubled to 35,000 by 1946 and doubled again to 70,000 by 1953. Thereafter it rose progressively to reach some 170,000 by the mid-1980s, with the most rapid expansion occurring in the period 1964/5–74/5. As a proportion of total formal sector employment, manufacturing employment stood at 12% in 1954/5 but *fell* to 10.5% by 1964/5; it then rose steadily to reach 16% by the mid-1980s.

The structure and ownership of the sector has an important bearing upon both its origins and its evolution. Although Zimbabwe is an African country, neither decisions related to the establishment of its manufacturing base nor to its expansion owe very much to its indigenous black people. Manufacturing has always been largely owned, managed and operated by

Table 10.1 *Summary characteristics of manufacturing by sub-sector mid-1980s*

Sub-sectoral division[a]	Number of Units[b]	Gross Output[b] Z$m.	Value Added[b] Z$m.	Number of Employees[b] '000s	Capital Stock[c] Z$m.	Exports (broad definition)[d] Z$m.	Exports (narrow definition)[d] Z$m.
1	152	951.6	276.7	26.2	573.1	33.4	33.1
2	53	492.5	393.2	13.0	341.2	3.5	3.5
3	67	478.9	202.2	21.2	362.9	73.5	12.2
4	148	226.7	121.0	19.9	119.9	10.5	10.5
5	98	102.2	51.3	10.5	83.6	10.5	8.8
6	114	205.3	110.4	9.0	189.3	3.5	3.5
7	126	553.9	229.4	13.7	507.4	16.7	15.7
8	58	105.3	59.8	6.6	243.2	6.7	5.2
9	408	654.4	308.5	34.9	1,218.9	160.3	64.6
10	46	145.9	83.2	6.2	86.0	3.5	3.5
11	94	44.3	19.8	2.6	30.8	14.0	14.0
Totals	1,364	3,961.1	1,855.4	163.8	3,756.3	333.9	174.6

Source: CSO, *Census of Production 1982/83, 1983/84 and 1984/85, Statement of External Trade 1982 and 1983*, and UNIDO, 1986b:64.

Notes: [a] The *current* Zimbabwean industrial classification and the one mostly used throughout this chapter (unless specific reference is otherwise made) divides manufacturing into 11 sub-sectors as follows: 1. foodstuffs, 2. beverages and tobacco, 3. textiles, 4. clothing and footwear, 5. wood and furniture, 6. paper and paper products, 7. chemical and pharmaceutical products, 8. non-metallic minerals, 9. metals and metal products, 10. transport equipment, 11. miscellaneous manufactured products. For the way in which the 33 sub-sectoral classification is grouped to produce the 11 sub-sectoral classification see UNIDO, 1986b:62–3.
[b] 1983 data.
[c] 1984/5 data.
[d] 1982/3 data.

Figure 10.1 *Ratio of MVA to GDP 1955–80*

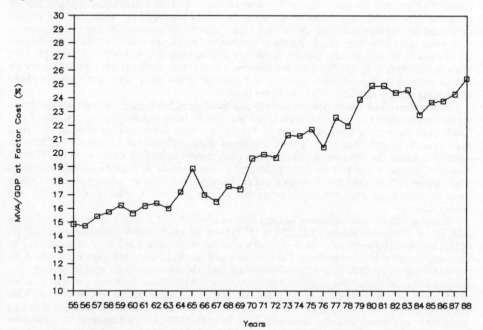

Source: CSO, *Monthly and Quarterly Digest of Statistics, National Accounts* and *The Census of Production* (various years), plus author's estimates for 1988 based on Ministry of Finance statements.

Figure 10.2   *Index of manufacturing production (1980 = 100)*

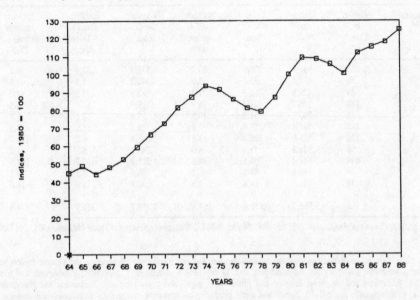

Source: As for Figure 10.1.

skilled personnel from the settler white community or else owned by foreign capital interests which made use of these settler skills. The local black population was used predominantly as unskilled labour up to the 1950s. Thereafter some openings were made for blacks to acquire skills, although these were scarcely reflected in wage levels, status or ability to achieve unimpeded upward job mobility until Independence. The 1981 National Manpower Survey recorded that, within the manufacturing sector, of all professional, technical and related personnel in employment, only 36% were black, and of all managerial and administrative personnel, only 24% were black. As the proportion of black personnel in the entire economy was 49 and 21% respectively, it is apparent that discrimination in senior posts was higher for manufacturing (GOZ, 1983a). The disproportion is dramatically seen when these figures are compared with the respective population distribution: in the early 1980s less than 3% of the total population was white, over 96% was black.

For decades, black entrepreneurs were in practice barred from establishing manufacturing enterprises outside the informal sector and because of both residential discrimination and harsh laws restricting the movement of blacks in urban areas, the small-scale informal manufacturing sector has been far less developed in Zimbabwe than in many other African countries. Since the removal of overt racial discrimination and all racial laws in 1979/80, however, scores of blacks have been promoted to senior posts in manufacturing companies while others (albeit still only a small number) have opened up their own operations. Many have advanced to top executive positions in the country's leading companies and corporations.

Official statistics and estimates suggest that in 1982, out of a total capital stock of some Z$3,756 m. in manufacturing, Z$2,250 m.(85%) was owned by private companies, Z$525 m. (14%) by central government or parastatals and the remaining Z$37 m. (less than 1%) by unincorporated private enterprise. On the foreign/domestic ownership mix, survey data for the mid-1980s (UNIDO, 1986b: 71–8) suggested that foreign companies were responsible for the ownership of some 48% of the sector's total assets. Since then, however – and in contrast to what has been happening in many other African countries in the last few years – the state has either directly or indirectly been *acquiring* either majority or part ownership of increasing numbers of key manufacturing concerns. Thus by early 1989, a Confederation of Zimbabwe Industries (CZI) survey suggested that only 25% of the capital assets of the sector were foreign-owned, 16% being government-owned and 50% by local private sector interests (Humphrey, 1989).

Table 10.2 *Origin of growth in gross output by sub-sector 1952–83 (%)*

Sub-sector	1952/3–83/3	1952/3–64/5	1964/5–78/9	1978/9–82/3
1	25.1	23.4	23.1	26.7
2	9.3	8.7	7.2	10.8
3	9.2	7.9	12.5	7.2
4	5.9	6.8	5.4	6.0
5	2.9	2.6	2.7	3.2
6	5.2	6.2	4.6	5.4
7	15.0	16.7	13.6	15.7
8	2.8	0.6	2.7	3.1
9	20.1	18.2	26.0	16.6
10	3.4	8.7	1.1	4.1
11	1.1	0.4	1.2	1.1

Source: Census of Production, 1953, 1962, 1979/80 and 1983/84, Statement of External Trade, 1950–52, 1965, 1975, 1976, 1978, 1979–83, CSO, Harare, 1954 to 1985.

Sources of industrial growth. Following similar methods to those adopted for the Botswanan and Kenyan chapters, the 'sources' of growth of Zimbabwe's manufacturing sector in the period 1952–83 have been calculated and decomposed into their three constituent elements – import substitution, domestic demand and export growth[9]. The results for the manufacturing sector as a whole are shown in Figures 10.3 and 10.4 and Table 10.2[10].

The first four more consumer-oriented sub-sectors accounted for an almost consistent 48–49% of total output growth. What distinguishes Zimbabwe's record from so many other SSA countries, however, is the consistently high proportion of total growth originating in the intermediate and capital goods sub-sectors. Sub-sector 9, metals and metal products, was not only the one contributing most to overall growth, after foodstuffs, but in the UDI period its rate *exceeded* that of foodstuffs. In addition, the importance of sub-sector 7, chemicals and pharmaceuticals, should be noted. In all, sub-sectors 3, 7 and 9 consistently contributed between 57 and 60% to total manufacturing output growth throughout the 30-year period.

With Figures 10.3 and 10.4, we begin to analyse the disaggregated 'sources' of growth. The overall picture confirms the conventional view of the Zimbabwean economy – a manufacturing sector characterised by an active policy of import substitution and (until post-1983) few policy initiatives geared towards expanding manufactured exports. Nonetheless, there are some important features, observable in the different historical periods – the period of the Federation of Rhodesia and Nyasaland (1953–63), the period of UDI (1965–79/80) and the post-Independence period – which need highlighting.

First, the major import-substitution thrust occurred *prior* to UDI, with the major source of manufacturing growth in the UDI period being domestic demand expansion. This result is of interest not only because the UDI period has always been known as the period of import substitution *par excellence* but also because, as shown in Figures 10.1 and 10.2, the first ten years of the UDI era was the period of the most rapid increase in real value added and in the MVA/GDP ratio.

A second notable feature indicated by the overall results – and one which, if an accurate reflection of what actually occurred, casts doubt, at least in part, upon the more free-market policy prescriptions for the sector – is that there is no marked difference in relative export performance during the more 'open' Federal period and the more 'closed' UDI period. There is, however, a striking contrast with the final period when the export growth component fell dramatically at the same time as domestic demand accounted for in excess of 100% of the increase in gross output[11]. This[12] confirms the hypothesis presented in the 1986 UNIDO report that, at least for non-traditional manufactured exports, there appears to be a trade-off between the domestic and export markets with the latter suffering when domestic demand rises (1986b: 267–306).

These results do, however, raise the more general question of the accuracy of 'sources of growth' analysis and the extent to which it does reflect adequately the dynamic changes which have taken place within manufacturing. In particular, it almost certainly underestimates the extent of import substitution because it regards a reduction in the import ratio as import substitution only in the year in which the relevant fall in imports is recorded. Thereafter the effect is not explicitly considered and the change in output is allocated either to domestic demand or export, as appropriate[13].

Figure 10.3   *'Sources' of growth of gross output by sub-sector, 1952–83*

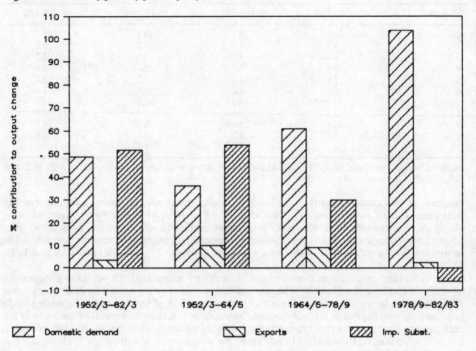

Source: *Census of Production, 1953, 1962, 1979/80 and 1983/84, Statement of External Trade, 1950–52, 1965, 1975, 1976, 1978, 1979–83*, CSO, Harare, 1954 to 1985.

Finally, it should be reiterated that this aspect of the 'sources of growth' analysis is designed to indicate *relative*, not absolute, changes in the different constituent sources of output. Thus although Figure 10.3 records import substitution as negative in the period 1978/9–82/3, this does *not* mean that there has been a reversal of import substitution in manufacturing over the post-Independence period: only a relative fall is indicated. Anyone familiar with Zimbabwean industry knows full well that continued import substitution has been a notable feature of many firms in recent years, running not infrequently into millions of dollars of import saving[14].

'Sources' of growth data for the whole sector over the past 30 years mask different patterns of performance within particular sub-sectors over different periods of time. Tables 10.3 and 10.4 summarise the data.

The pattern of greater relative import substitution occurring in the Federal rather than the UDI period, observed in the aggregate data, is repeated for *all* sub-sectors[15]: for sub-sectors 4, 5, 7, 8 and 9 the differences are extremely marked. During UDI there was also a significant fall in the relative growth of exports for the majority of sub-sectors, even though the overall contribution of exports did not fall substantially. The high relative rates of growth of exports and import substitution in the pre-UDI period tends to suggest that (for the relevant sub-sectors) import substitution and export growth were initially *combined* and perhaps inter-related rather than *sequential* activities[16]. The figures also show that for two sub-sectors – 3 and 9 – export growth was a more important source of growth during the 'protectionist' UDI than in the 'liberal' Federal period[17]. Part of the explanation lies in the rapid growth and export of cotton lint and ferro-alloy production[18]. But this does not provide an adequate explanation of either the maintenance of export growth in the foodstuffs sub-sector or the total growth of exports in sub-sector 9 – and the metals sub-sector also experienced a very significant rise in domestic demand as a source of growth in the UDI period. Finally in the most recent period, the predominant source of growth in all sub-sectors has been domestic

Figure 10.4 *'Sources' of growth, 1952/3–82/3 by sub-sector*

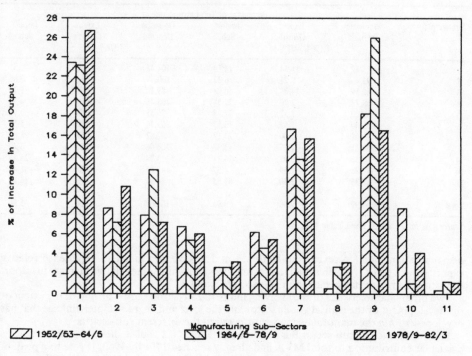

Note: For the calculation of these figures, detailed trade data were re-classified to conform with the industrial divisions of the census of industrial production.

Table 10.3 *'Sources' of growth in manufacturing output by sub-sector 1952/3–82/3 and 1952/3–64/5*

Sub-sectors	Percentage of Total growth due to:					
	Domestic Demand	Export Growth	Import Sub.	Domestic Demand	Export Growth	Import Sub.
	1952/3–82/3			1952/3–64/5		
1	79.50	2.52	17.98	74.10	12.61	13.28
2	88.61	0.08	11.31	78.32	11.52	10.16
3	19.66	4.95	75.39	33.20	1.13	65.67
4	41.62	1.08	57.30	13.71	18.84	67.64
5	40.48	3.45	56.06	2.94	18.29	78.77
6	45.61	0.87	53.52	45.13	7.59	47.28
7	34.56	0.71	64.73	28.99	6.40	64.60
8	69.59	2.89	27.52	0.00[a]	8.63	78.36
9	24.18	4.42	71.42	13.01	25.88	78.36
10	60.19	0.56	39.25	26.41	5.59	67.99
11	35.92	9.25	54.83	94.86	67.76	− 62.62
Total	48.70	3.50	51.70	36.06	10.17	53.76

Source: As for Figure 10.3.

Note: [a] Although this is the figure calculated from the raw data, it seems to be an unlikely result and may be due to change in sectoral definitions over time.

Table 10.4 *'Sources' of growth in manufacturing output by sub-sector 1964/5–78/9 and 1978/9–82/3*

Sub-sectors	Domestic Demand	Export Growth 1964/5–78/9	Import Sub.	Domestic Demand	Export Growth 1978/9–82/3	Import Sub.
			Percentage of Total growth due to:			
1	75.27	11.54	13.19	104.48	− 3.98	− 0.51
2	93.46	0.21	6.32	100.55	− 1.40	0.85
3	29.59	14.33	56.08	89.20	11.94	− 1.13
4	68.22	2.20	29.58	108.45	− 4.09	− 4.36
5	65.20	7.52	27.28	96.55	2.54	0.91
6	65.09	− 1.62	36.53	103.76	1.83	− 5.58
7	77.81	0.00	22.19	92.82	0.68	6.49
8	88.21	− 1.55	13.34	84.96	5.95	6.49
9	50.36	12.93	36.71	113.78	11.64	− 25.43
10	111.96	− 7.59	− 4.37	141.83	− 0.38	− 41.45
11	18.35	13.80	67.85	81.90	3.29	14.81
Total	60.99	9.08	29.93	103.60	2.30	− 5.90

Source: As for Figure 10.3 and Table 10.2.

demand expansion. However, sub-sectors 3 and 9 have continued to experience relative export growth (even if smaller than in previous periods) while some relative increase in import substitution growth has occurred in sub-sectors 7 and 8.

Two other characteristics of the evolving industrial structure should be noted: the extent of the development of the capital goods sector and the level and degree of inter-linkage that has developed *within* the manufacturing sector between the different sub-sectors[19].

The importance of sub-sector 9 is indicated in Table 10.1, but it should be added that its particular contribution to total MVA had already reached 17% by 1960. It rose to a peak of 32% in 1975 and has only recently fallen back to below 25% of total MVA. Its striking evolution is illustrated clearly in the 'sources of growth' data in Tables 10.3 and 10.4. This shows that over the whole period, over 70% of its growth originated in import substitution, not domestic demand, the most notable phase occurring immediately before the UDI period. Also of importance has been the long-term and *rising* significance of export expansion in overall growth.

The extent of intra-manufacturing linkages is shown in Table 10.5. Overall, 34% of inputs are obtained from within the manufacturing sector itself. For 6 of the 11 sub-sectors, the

Table 10.5 *Inputs into manufacturing obtained from within the manufacturing sector, 1975 and 1981/2*

Sub-sector	Total inputs Z$m.	of which imported Z$m.	%	Total from manufacturing Z$m.	%	% of manufacturing inputs from s/sector 9
1	214.0	19.2	9	52.9	25	12.8
2	40.5	4.1	10	17.5	43	11.7
3	92.0	32.2	35	46.9	51	10.4
4	52.5	13.1	25	33.7	64	4.2
5	20.8	8.3	40	9.4	45	18.8
6	37.9	19.7	52	14.2	38	10.4
7	102.7	60.9	59	27.5	27	16.9
8	23.5	7.0	30	7.8	33	57.3
9	183.4	86.3	47	57.1	31	82.3
10	32.2	26.4	82	5.3	16	48.5
11	6.3	3.8	60	0.5	8	51.4
TOTAL	805.8	281.0	35	272.8	34	31.0

Source: UNCTAD, 1980:354–5 and UNIDO, 1986b:153.

Note: 1. All data are for 1975 except the last column which are for 1981/82.

Figure 10.5 *Ratio of manufactured to total commodity exports, 1939–86*

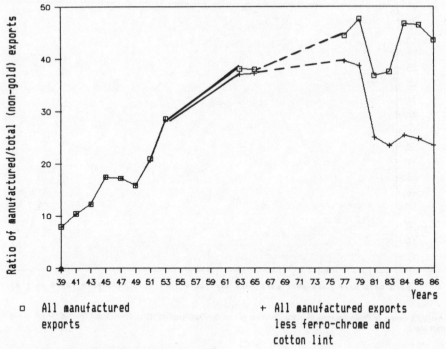

□ All manufactured
  exports

+ All manufactured exports
  less ferro-chrome and
  cotton lint

Source: As for Figure 10.6 and unpublished trade data, CSO (1987).

value of these inputs exceeds that of imported inputs, and for sub-sector 1, a greater value of inputs are obtained from manufacturing than from the agricultural sector of the economy. **Trends in manufactured exports.** At current prices, manufactured exports have expanded, at times rapidly, in the period up to the early 1980s, rising from Z$1.8 m. in 1938 to Z$28 m. by the start of the Federation, Z$98 m. by UDI in 1965, Z$307 m. just before Independence in 1979, to Z$741 m. by the end of 1986. This seeming secular rise is deceptive, however, for it conceals major structural changes apparent in different time periods. As a proportion of total commodity exports, the contribution of manufacturing did increase from 1938 to around 1975; however, as shown clearly in Figure 10.5, this increase progressively weakened over the period, and after the mid-1970s, was quite dramatically reversed[20]. After the first three full years of Independence, the proportion of manufacturing to total exports had fallen back to the pre-UDI levels recorded in 1963–5, although an equally dramatic recovery took place from 1984 to 1986. However, if the exports of cotton lint and ferro-alloys are deducted from both manufactured and total exports, then the post-Independence fall is even more severe, bringing the ratio down to just over 20%, back to the level of the early 1950s, with only marginal recovery in the final 1984–6 period.

An equally clear, though not identical, picture is evident from examining the relation over time of manufactured exports to the total gross output of the sector. As shown in Figure 10.6, by the early post-Independence period only some 10% was being exported compared with about 18% in the late 1970s and a peak level of around 26% at the start of UDI. The contrast between the Federal and UDI periods is striking: in the former, exports continued to rise as a proportion of total gross output but in the UDI period this ratio fell, and far more rapidly[21].

The data in Figures 10.5 and 10.6 are consistent with those in the 'sources of growth' analysis; however, they reveal far more clearly the substantial structural changes which have occurred in the sector as a whole. As could be expected, the aggregate data conceal substantial sub-sectoral variations, with the most dramatic shift occurring in relation to sub-sectors 1, 3, 4 and 9. Whereas in 1952/3, 43% of manufactured exports consisted of foodstuffs (1) and clothing and footwear (4), their joint contribution had fallen to 30% by 1964/5 and to a

Figure 10.6 *Ratio of exports to gross output, total manufacturing 1925/3–82/3*

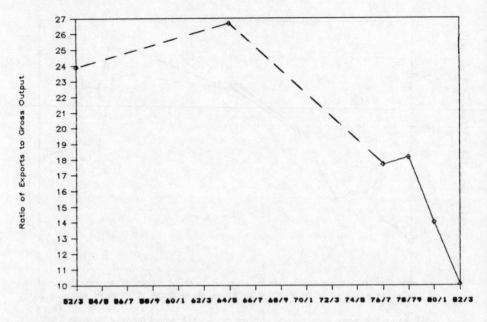

Source: CSO, *Census of Production* (various years), *Statement of External Trade* (various years), *Monthly and Quarterly Digest of Statistics*, (various years).

mere 13% by 1982/3. On the other hand, sub-sector 9 contributed only 11% to manufactured exports in 1952/3, but this had risen to over 45% by the early 1980s, with textiles (3) rising from 11 to 22% in the same time periods.

Perhaps even more dramatic have been the changes in the export to gross output ratios for the different sub-sectors over time (see Table 10.6). From the start of the UDI period down to the first years of Independence, a decreasing amount of gross output has been exported in each and every sub-sector. With the exception of 3 and 9, the ratio was less than 10% for every sub-sector, whereas it exceeded 14% for all at the start of UDI.

Disturbing though these developments have been, more recent evidence suggests that in the post-1983 period some more favourable changes have occurred. Although all data are not available to extend the trends of Figure 10.6 and Table 10.7, published trade statistics reveal that there were significant upswings in manufactured exports in 1984 and 1985, though the

Table 10.6 *Ratio of manufactured exports to gross output by sub-sector 1952/3–82/3*

Sub-sector	1952/3	1964/5	1976/7	1978/9	1980/1	1982/3
1	18.80	16.70	14.31	13.86	6.05	3.71
2	17.01	14.44	5.11	4.50	2.54	0.84
3	56.17	17.11	29.03	30.47	25.50	23.57
4	65.95	51.53	21.95	17.14	10.70	5.43
5	21.09	31.08	21.58	15.75	10.86	8.42
6	5.70	15.48	2.73	2.47	1.60	2.23
7	19.53	23.60	5.02	5.60	4.43	2.95
8	16.92	20.28	5.88	2.92	4.55	5.40
9	23.91	40.48	25.24	28.55	27.66	23.07
10	10.52	21.81	10.27	10.37	8.27	3.23
11	28.17	84.79	55.67	64.15	22.81	33.77
Total	24.07	25.41	16.66	17.24	13.25	9.51

Source: CSO, *Census of Production and Statement of External Trade* (various years).

Table 10.7 *Sub-sectoral changes in manufactured exports 1980/1–85/6, Z$m. (current)* [a]

Sub-sector	Manufactured Exports 1980/1 (two-year averages)	1985/6	% Change
1	33.9	95.7	182
2	4.5	3.3	− 27
3[b]	13.7	45.0	229
4	18.5	25.2	36
5	10.4	9.5	− 9
6	2.1	7.4	252
7	17.1	32.1	88
8	3.4	9.5	179
9[c]	29.3	44.0	50
10	5.7	14.4	153
11	8.2	31.9	289
TOTAL[d]	146.8	297.9	103

Source: CSO, *Statement of External Trade 1980 and 1981* and unpublished trade statistics, CSO.

Notes: [a] The statistical digest does not categorise exports by industrial sub-sector so judgments had to be made to classify them in this manner.
[b] Excluding exports of cotton lint.
[c] Excluding exports of ferro-alloys and steel.
[d] Total excluding the above-named items.

1986 figures were less encouraging. As can be seen from Table 10.7, some of the sub-sectoral increases were very significant, while beverages and tobacco (2) and wood and furniture products (5) performed exceptionally poorly. Overall, exports of manufactures excluding cotton lint, ferro-alloys and steel products have more than doubled over the past seven years, rising from Z$147 m. in 1980/1 to Z$318 m. in 1985/6. It is also important to highlight that, in spite of the value of exports of ferro-alloys, cotton lint and steel products doubling from Z$197 m. in 1980/1 to Z$412 m. in 1985/6, the proportion of 'other' manufactured exports rose, if minimally, from 42.7 to 43.6% of *all* manufactured exports.

Trends in manufactured imports. Manufactured imports fall into three groups: those that are purchased directly for final consumption (consumer and durable products); those that are to be used as inputs into production (including manufacturing); and plant and machinery used to expand the productive base of the economy. In general, as a country industrialises, manufactured imports tend to rise in value[22] but their composition will change. Over time one would expect a reduction in the proportion (and perhaps, though not necessarily, the total quantity) of more simple manufactured imports – many at the consumer end of the market – and an increase in the imports of more complex manufactured products, intermediate inputs and plant and machinery – in the case of Zimbabwe, those classified as products from sub-sectors 6, 7, 9 and 10.

In rather crude terms, this pattern is observable for Zimbabwe. In 1952/3, imports of simpler (mostly consumption) goods accounted for 36% of total manufactured imports, while more complex (intermediate and capital) goods accounted for 64%. By 1964/5 the simpler, mostly consumption, goods had fallen to 27% and by 1982/3 accounted for only 11% of total manufactured goods[23]. In contrast, 86% of all manufactured imports were by then more complex, mostly intermediate and capital products.

A further indicator of the process of industrial development would be provided by analysing the degree to which, over time, the origin of manufacturing inputs production changes. In general, one would expect that as a country industrialises, increasing amounts especially of intermediate and capital goods would be made domestically (with a decreasing foreign-exchange component in *their* production) rather than being imported directly. There are, regrettably, no reliable time-series data to analyse the respective proportions[24]. Data from the 1965 input/output model[25], supplemented by the 1980 UNCTAD update of these figures for 1975 and by crude estimates made in the 1986 UNIDO study[26] of the manufacturing sector (1986b: 41 and 70) for the period 1980–82 provide the best time series available. These are shown in Table 10.8.

With more accurate time-series data which do exist, it is possible to examine the relationship overall, and classified into industrial sub-sector groupings, between manufactured

Table 10.8 *Purchases by the manufacturing sector by imported and domestic origin*

Sub-sector	Percentage of Inputs Imported Directly[a]		
	1965	1975	1980–2 (average)
1	11.6	9.0	2.4
2	15.6	10.1	24.0
3	40.9	35.0	23.0
4	30.9	24.9	39.0
5	46.5	39.9	14.0
6	49.1	52.0	24.0
7	76.7	59.3	52.0
8	30.0	29.8	16.0
9	49.2	47.0	41.0
10	79.3	82.0	60.0
11	58.8	60.3	25.3
All	42.3	34.8	25.3

Source: Central Statistical Office, *National Accounts and Balance of Payments Statistics of Rhodesia, 1965*, Harare, CSO, UNCTAD (1980) Annex III and UNIDO (1986b:70).

Note: [a] The figures in this final column are based on a sample survey of manufacturers who were asked the origin *of their raw material* purchases, whereas the data in the first two columns are for total inputs, including purchases of capital equipment. Hence the 1980–2 data probably overestimate the reduction in direct import dependence.

imports and exports. Using these data a 'self-sufficiency index' has been constructed which is derived by expressing the ratio of exports over imports as a percentage. If the index value exceeds 100 then the country exports more of the goods than it imports in the groups defined, the greater the value in excess of 100 the larger the trade surplus and the lower the value less than 100 the larger the trade deficit. While there is, clearly, no 'correct' index level either for manufactured products as a whole or for different sub-sectors, a rising index over time would indicate a more favourable impact of manufactures on the balance of payments, while a falling index, and one consistently well below the critical level of 100, would indicate both absolute and increasing losses of foreign exchange.

Figure 10.7 records the aggregate index for all manufactures. Table 10.9 gives the various index levels by sub-sector. It suggests that they can be grouped into two sub-divisions. The first five sub-sectors have produced a self-sufficiency index value of over 100 almost continuously for the past 20 years, indicating that Zimbabwe exports more of the products of these sub-sectors than it imports, even if the values of the different indices fell substantially in the early post-Independence period. The reversed L-shape of Figure 10.7 is mirrored in the performance of the trade in items grouped under industrial sub-sector 9, with an extremely low level (less than 15) and a falling index level recorded for trade in items grouped under sub-sectors 6, 7 and 10.

Table 10.9 *Self-sufficiency index[a] of exports over imports by industrial sub-sector, 1952/3–82/3 (various years)*

Industrial Sub-sector	1952/3	1964/5	1978/9	1980/1	1982/3
1	85.9	143.0	2,042.3	319.9	382.6
2	131.6	250.0	407.1	236.8	147.4
3	15.5	13.2	150.3	87.9	113.0
4	49.6	171.1	596.3	248.0	101.8
5	16.9	102.5	331.8	173.3	197.8
6	4.5	30.0	21.1	7.3	14.7
7	7.1	32.8	13.1	9.7	7.9
8	31.0	57.6	13.0	25.4	35.5
9	5.7	39.3	70.4	54.8	41.0
10	2.9	15.3	7.1	4.1	1.6
All	15.3	41.4	70.0	42.8	33.3

Source: CSO, *Statement of External Trade* (various years).

Note: [a] The index is the ratio of products exported divided by products imported, grouped together by the census of production classification.

Figure 10.7 *Self-sufficiency index, manufacturing industry, 1952/3–82/3*

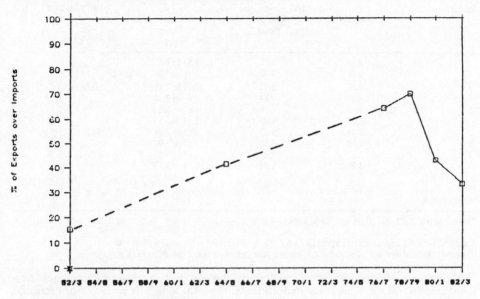

Source: CSO, *Statement of External Trade* (various years).

International comparisons of competitiveness.   While analysing rates of industrial growth, expansion and structural change and the relative differences in import substitution and exports over time provides some guide to the evolving health of the manufacturing sector, an increasingly-used method of ascertaining viability and strength is to calculate rates of protection for the sector as a whole, for sub-sectors and even down to the level of a particular industry or firm. Rates of effective protection provide a measure (at the time they are calculated) of the relative world or 'free' trade prices of goods manufactured domestically in contrast with the border prices of comparable goods; they thus give an indication of the degree of international competitiveness of the industry, firm or sub-sector being analysed. In this regard, an Effective Protection Coefficient (EPC) of less than unity implies that value added is lower than could be achieved with both inputs and outputs valued at international (border) prices. Likewise, the Domestic Resource Cost (DRC) measures the ratio of domestic costs at social prices to value added, also at social prices, giving a social profitability index. A DRC value of less than unity indicates that the firm, industry or sub-sector is producing a product or products which, even in the absence of government controls and domestic subsidies etc., would provide enough value added for the workforce to be remunerated and for a return on capital to be earned. Comparing EPCs and DRCs over time would thus show the changing pattern of industrial viability related to international competitiveness, and provide a good comparative indicator of the strength of industry. The measures are particularly useful in determining the extent to which industries or firms are able (at a given point of time) to export their products.

Measures of rates of protection have only recently been calculated for Zimbabwean industry; overall data are available for 1982, supplemented by some partial data for 1986. The 1986 calculations were done by a World Bank industrial sector mission[27]. *Inter alia*, its report indicates that the 1982 figures almost certainly underestimated Zimbabwe's degree of international competitiveness, dramatically so in some sub-sectors, such as steel (World Bank, 1987a: 69–72, 90).

The available data, reproduced in summary form in Table 10.10, show that in 1982, for four sub-sectors (accounting for 47% of MVA), the average DRC was less than unity and that for *every* sub-sector there were firms operating with DRCs substantially less than unity. The table highlights, first, that in 1982 Zimbabwean industry was, in general terms, in a far from weak internationally competitive position[28], and secondly, that behind the average sub-sectoral data lie an astonishingly wide array of different DRC scores.

Table 10.10 *International competitiveness of manufacturing industry, DRC calculations, 1982 and 1986*

Sub-sector	DRC Measures for 1982			DRCs for 1986
	General	With 25% Deval.	Range of Values Found	
1	0.88	0.70	0.53 to 1.65	
2	0.88	0.70	0.61 to 1.84	
3	1.28	1.02	0.75 to 2.45	0.89 to 1.14
4	1.05	0.84	0.89 to 2.20	
5	1.33	1.06	not available	
6	1.87	1.49	1.12 to 5.59	
7	0.94	0.75	0.38 to 2.44	0.28 to 0.91[a]
8	0.98	0.78	0.82 to 2.02	
9	2.41	1.93	0.40 to 5.49	0.58 (for steel)[b]
10	1.27	1.02	0.82 to 3.40	
Total Manufacturing	1.27	1.02		

Source: Jansen, 1983, Vol. II:84 and World Bank, 1987a.

Notes: [a] This was for fertiliser firms whose DRCs for 1982 were recorded in the range 0.65 to 1.00.
[b] The 1982 DRC for steel was calculated at 4.4; however, the method of calculation differed in the two studies.

Within the context of Zimbabwe's manufacturing history, these data (with their qualifications) lead to two important policy conclusions. First, the long UDI period of protectionist industrial policies does not appear to have led to the evolution of a highly uncompetitive manufacturing sector even though, as noted above, it did lead to a relative decline in changes in output derived from both import substitution activities and export growth[29]. Secondly, the wide *range* of DRC scores within different sub-sectors, and indeed within particular industries, indicates that for firms and industries to achieve international competitiveness involves far more than providing the 'correct' macroeconomic framework and incentive structure – an issue to be discussed further, below. Finally, however, it should also be borne in mind that the DRC calculations are themselves only *estimates* (the accuracy of which is itself unknown) based sometimes on questionable assumptions and guesses. Thus, as the 1987 World Bank study of Zimbabwean industry states, the DRC scores should be used with a great deal of caution (see Stoneman, 1989).

A further indicator of international competitiveness comes from available direction-of-export statistics. These not only reveal increased competitiveness achieved during the UDI period but also some significant shifts in export destinations. Whereas in the two-year period 1964–5, 92% of all Zimbabwe's manufactured exports[30] went to either South Africa or the Southern African Development Co-ordination Conference (SADCC) countries, in the period 1981–3, only 43% went to its southern neighbours.

In late 1987 comprehensive trade data by seven-digit classification for each country destination were made available for the years 1984, 1985 and 1986 enabling a far greater depth of analysis of manufacturing exports than has been possible for any year since 1964. In aggregate these confirm the UDI trends just mentioned. In 1984, only 41% of all manufactured exports went to countries in southern Africa, falling to 34% by 1986. If all exports of cotton lint, ferro-chrome and steel products are excluded, dependence on southern African markets increases significantly although a reduction – from 69% in 1984 to 61% in 1986 – is clearly observable over recent years. As the data in Tables 10.11 and 10.12 indicate, the most important changes in recent years have been the decrease in dependence upon South Africa as a destination for manufactured exports (estimated to be taking about 32% of total manufactured exports in 1980, with the exclusion of cotton lint[31]) and the significant rise – from 23% in 1984 to 34% in 1986 – in the share of non-traditional manufactured exports being sold to destinations outside Africa. For five manufacturing sub-sectors over 40% of all manufactured exports were sold outside Africa.

While these successes deserve due recognition, it is equally important to draw attention to some of the constraints impeding further export expansion. Clearly one major barrier is capital and machinery shortages which were highlighted in a survey conducted for the

Table 10.11 *Manufactured exports by area of destination, 1980, 1984 and 1986, Z$m.*

Market	Total Manufactured Exports				Total Manufactured Exports less cotton lint, ferro-chrome and steel			
	1984	%	1986	%	1984	%	1986	%
South Africa	137.4	23	101.7	14	82.3	30	65.1	20
SADCC	114.5	19	144.6	20	106.9	39	134.9	41
Other African	23.6	4	32.7	4	22.3	8	19.3	6
Non-African	318.6	54	462.0	62	63.3	23	112.9	34
Total	594.1	100	741.0	100	274.8	100	332.2	100

| | Total manufactured exports: | | | | | | | | | | |
| | Less cotton lint | | | | | | Less cotton lint and ferrochrome | | | | |
	1980	%	1984	%	1986	%	1980	%	1984	%	1986	%
South Africa	93.7	32	100.7	21	69.4	11	89.2	41	97.5	30	65.6	16
SADCC			114.5	24	144.6	24			114.5	35	144.4	36
Other African			23.6	5	32.7	5			23.3	7	32.4	8
Non African			240.0	50	363.8	60			88.8	27	158.1	40
Total	288.9	100	478.8	100	610.5	100	218.7	100	324.1	100	400.5	100

Source: 'Domestic Exports Valued FOR by Item/Country', CSO, Harare, 1988 (mimeo) and Riddell, 1981b.

Table 10.12 *Manufactured exports by industrial sub-sector and destination 1980, 1984 and 1986 % and Z$m.*

| Sub-sector | Percentage Exports by Respective Destination | | | | | | | | | Total Exports Z$m. | | |
| | South Africa | | | SADCC | | Other African | | Non-African | | | | |
	'80	'84	'86	'84	'86	'84	'86	'84	'86	1980	1984	1986
1	37	16	12	33	34	22	9	29	45	6.8	70.4	98.5
2	73	87	69	6	6	3	10	8	15	5.6	3.5	2.8
3	–	33	22	9	8	–	–	58	70	–	154.5	179.7
3[a]	58	36	14	37	38	–	1	27	46	10.7	39.2	49.2
4	93	55	36	12	15	1	1	32	48	15.4	20.5	28.9
5	86	60	43	30	41	5	4	5	12	8.8	11.8	9.1
6	56	7	14	80	76	1	3	12	7	1.2	8.6	6.7
7	26	8	9	78	77	2	4	12	10	1.8	31.2	30.6
8	15	54	4	40	75	5	3	1	18	0.6	10.0	11.5
9	–	14	6	11	11	2	5	73	78	–	248.3	324.3
9[b]	27	34	12	16	30	4	14	46	44	22.8	93.6	114.3
10	61	14	5	66	67	20	27	0	1	9.4	10.4	16.2
11	90	31	32	6	4	1	1	62	63	5.1	25.0	32.2

Source: As for Table 10.11.

Note: [a] Sub-sector 3 with cotton lint export data omitted.
[b] Sub-sector 9 with ferro-chrome exports omitted.

UNIDO study in 1985. These results show that whereas 90% of manufacturers maintained that they had adequate plant to manufacture goods for the domestic market, only 54% stated they had adequate plant to export to South Africa and only 30% for the overseas market (UNIDO, 1986b: 281–2)[32].

Seeking preliminary explanations. It is now time to step back from long-term macro-analysis and attempt to understand better not just what has happened but why it has happened. Marrying the secular expansion of Zimbabwe's manufacturing sector with political developments and observing (not surprisingly) that the growth of the sector has been closely linked to the pattern of GDP growth suggest that major political disruption and uncertainty have been both a cause of disruption in the progress of the manufacturing sector and a prelude to further growth. On three separate occasions – prior to the Federation, prior to UDI (including the disruptive period surrounding the ending of the Federation in 1963) and prior to Independence – industrial growth slowed and/or declined and then expanded, albeit most hesitatingly in the post-Independence period. While on each occasion the subsequent expansion was associated with a rise in aggregate growth, and so could be seen in part as demand-led, very different influences came into play in each of these periods.

The establishment of the Federation created a large and protected market for Zimbabwe's manufactured products: manufactured exports to Zambia and Malawi increased fivefold in the 10-year period of the Federation and by 1964/5 accounted for 19% of gross manufactured output compared with 11% in 1953. But an expanded domestic and a captive 'export' market were not the only factors favouring expansion. Increased settler immigration, especially in the late 1940s and early 1950s, brought a new injection of skills which, together with a rapidly modernised infrastructure and the already-established iron and steel works, added to the favourable environment. This, together with the political optimism of the Federation's early years and the absence of fears of private sector nationalisation or inhibitions to generous private company profit repatriation, provided the climate for a rapid inflow of foreign private (largely British-based) capital. There were other external factors providing a positive influence at this time, including the 1948 election victory by the National Party in South Africa which precipitated some capital flight northwards across the Limpopo, the severing of Indian ties with South Africa leading to the establishment of textile factories in Zimbabwe to supply the South African market indirectly, and the 1948 Customs Agreement with South Africa which was favourable to Zimbabwe's further industrial expansion, especially of consumer goods exports to the south[33]. In short, demand and supply factors were both extremely favourable.

In contrast, the start of the UDI era produced a series of potentially adverse factors for the health of the manufacturing sector. Economic sanctions not only led to the cessation of the lucrative trade with the former Federal territories; they also raised the costs of inputs and capital imports to the sector and reduced the competitiveness of those exports the country was able to sell. Sanctions also created an adverse climate for foreign investment and little substantial new foreign investment in manufacturing took place except from South African sources, while an extensive and more comprehensive price control system was introduced, reducing further incentives for domestic manufacturing expansion.

That rapid manufacturing expansion did take place, especially in the 1966–74 period, reveals that the adverse constraints, just listed, were either not of major influence or were eclipsed by other more favourable influences. These latter factors included the following: the introduction of a comprehensive system of foreign-exchange control which not only prevented the importation of manufactured products made domestically but provided foreign exchange for the manufacture of import substitutes; the freezing of foreign profits and dividends of non-South African companies, creating the 'incentive' to reinvest and diversify production; the diversification of commercial agricultural production which encouraged the expansion of food and cotton processing; and, finally, the introduction of export incentives to encourage export expansion and diversification. To this needs to be added the sense of unity and solidarity among the settler community which provided the drive and incentive to diversify, invest and engage in widespread sanctions-busting operations[34].

What, then, led to the post-1974 industrial contraction – the worst for 30 years – when the basic macro-framework of incentives established in the post-1965 period remained in place? There is little doubt that the war, which grew in intensity in the 1974–9 period, played a major part. Not only did it lead to a squeeze on non-defence and related expenditure but, more importantly for manufacturing, to the military call-up of white civilians for up to half the year which, with the spread of hostilities to more of the country, encouraged a rapid escalation in net white emigration. The result, combined with a series of poor agricultural seasons themselves exacerbated by the escalation of the rural war, was a fall in domestic purchasing power and an increase in skill shortages across the economy. This in turn occurred in conjunction with the international rise in oil prices – trebling Zimbabwe's oil bill in three years and increasing its share of total imports from 7 to 22% from 1973 to 1977 – which led to a drop in imports required by the manufacturing sector. The overall effects were a substantial drop in domestic demand for manufactures[35], a squeeze on imported intermediate and capital inputs and a substantial fall in manufacturing investment (after 1975) resulting in a rapid build-up of blocked but unused surplus profits of foreign companies.

These influences, however, need also to be seen in the longer-term context of the structural changes occurring within manufacturing particularly in relation to the balance of payments. The discussion on trends in manufactured exports (pp. 345ff.), revealed the increasing foreign-exchange dependence of manufacturing growth and the decreasing part played by manufactured exports in the economy from the 1950s right through to the mid-1970s. There can be little doubt that these changes led to the sector's increasing inability to respond to the overall and more rapid balance-of-payments constraints which confronted the economy after the mid-1970s. All these influences combined swamped the impact of the policies and incentives for manufacturing still in place from the mid-1960s, which had created the record levels of manufacturing expansion achieved in the first nine years of UDI.

Since 1979, growth has been renewed even if the annual pattern has been more volatile than in previous post-crisis periods and, in this instance, overall contraction occurred between 1982 and 1984. What factors have played a dominant role in manufacturing in this most recent period? Clearly the rapid ending of the war, the cessation of international sanctions, inflows of foreign aid and a dramatic rise in foreign borrowings, all leading to a substantial easing of the foreign-exchange constraint and a rapid growth in domestic demand, were major influences in raising both manufacturing growth levels and investment in the sector. Perhaps surprisingly, however, this rapid expansion took place with a still substantial emigration of skilled (white) personnel.

Also of major importance is the fact that with the ending of sanctions the renewed expansion of manufacturing exports simply did not occur during the early post-Independence (1980–3) period; indeed the fall in the ratio of exports to gross manufacturing output and in the proportion of manufactured to total exports is one of the most striking features of this period. Four factors seem to have influenced this particular development; first, the rapid rise in domestic demand for manufactured products; second, the increased shortage of foreign exchange required for exporting; third, the ignorance of exporters and potential exporters of how to conduct export business outside the hothouse atmosphere of sanctions-busting and close ties with former friend, but now largely hostile, South Africa; fourth, the initial removal of the pre-Independence export incentive for manufacturers. That these factors were influential is borne out by the post-1983 initiatives to revive and expand manufactured exports. The greatly enlarged export revolving fund, which provided guaranteed access to

Table 10.13 *Factors constraining industrial expansion, 1981–7*
Question: *What factors are currently affecting production?*

Constraint	% of respondents reporting output inhibited						
	1987[a]	1986	1985	1984	1983	1982	1981
Domestic Demand	27	31	32	69	73	48	57
Import quotas	83	76	66	55	65	67	56
Raw materials	73	62	46	42	45	45	36
Export demand	14	20	16	20	26	27	21
Skilled factory staff	14	18	9	17	27	37	48
Plant capacity	12	12	7	4	8	14	37
Working capital	3	7	7	15	12	9	5
Executive staff	4	5	6	3	7	11	7

Question: *What will limit capital expansion over next 12 months?*

Constraint	% of respondents reporting constraint					
	1987[b]	1987[c]	1987[d]	1986	1985	1984[e]
Inadequate return on proposed investment	36	45	42	38·	45	55
Shortage of internal finance	13	13	16	22	30	34
Inability to raise external finance	24	26	24	23	23	27
Cost of finance	12	17	16	14	22	25
Demand uncertainty	25	37	31	30	39	57
Lack of skilled staff	10	12	11	10	8	13
Other	28	29	35	31	22	17

Source: University of Zimbabwe, 'Business Opinion Survey' (1982–7); Confederation of Zimbabwe Industries, 'State of the Manufacturing Sector, Tri-annual Survey', August 1986 to July 1987.

Notes: [a] June, [b] November, [c] July, [d] March, [e] November.

foreign exchange, a package of new tax-reducing export incentives and substantial efforts to find new markets led to a 68% expansion in 'non-traditional' manufactured exports in 1984, a 33% increase in 1985 and continued expansion into 1987 and 1988[36].

Beyond these measures, however, perhaps the most striking feature of the post-Independence period has been the *continuity* in policy with the UDI period: price and foreign-exchange controls have remained firmly in place and the same system has operated in relation to new project and replacement capital investments requiring foreign exchange[37]. It is in this general context that manufacturing expansion has occurred and, more recently, that manufactured exports (albeit from a low base-point) have begun to expand once more.

We turn finally to the array of factors which *manufacturers themselves* consider to be the most important in constraining expansion of the sector. Table 10.13 reproduces the results from recent sector-wide surveys. While the replies reveal the importance of foreign exchange, domestic demand, price controls and skills constraints in restricting output and capital investment, the importance of each of these constraints has differed markedly from year to year.

If there is one lesson to be learnt from these results – and from the previous discussion – it is that the manufacturing sector is highly complex, being influenced by various factors in different ways and in different circumstances. Clearly, then, devising new policies for its sustained expansion is going to be a far from simple task.

Successes and failures at the micro-level

We now move to more detailed micro-data, using particularly some firm-level evidence gathered in mid-1987, to attempt to throw light on the main factors influencing performance, highlighting especially the ability of firms to *compete* both on the domestic and, more particularly, in the international market.

Manufacturers of agricultural implements.   We start with three private firms in a branch of sub-sector 9. Zimplow and Bulawayo Steel Products are the only two firms in the country manufacturing a range of hand-tools and animal-drawn implements, while Tinto Industries is by far the largest of the firms making machine-drawn implements, being responsible for some 80% of the domestic market[38]. There are eight main manufacturers of agricultural implements in Zimbabwe with a total turnover in 1985 of some Z$17 m., of which these three firms are responsible for over 90%.

Using the criterion of the 1982 DRC scores, it would appear that these firms would be judged among the most efficient in the country: the average DRC score for agricultural implement manufacturers was 0.91, ranging from a low of 0.40 to a high of only 1.12, the average falling to an extremely competitive 0.73 if account is taken of the overvalued dollar rate. What is more, in 1982 all three firms were exporting each with sales of over Z$100,000, while published results from Zimplow showed a post-tax profit/turnover ratio of 9% and from Tinto Industries of some 6%. Beyond 1982, developments appeared to confirm this bullish assessment: by the mid-1980s Tinto Industries was exporting products to the value of between Z$1 m. and Z$2 m. a year, Zimplow's exports trebled from 1982 to 1986, reaching an average of 24% of turnover in the 1984–6 period and by 1985 Bulawayo Steel Products was exporting 45% of production[39].

These data, however, at best give an extremely distorted and at worst a totally false picture of the longer-term viability of the firms in question. Zimplow and Bulawayo Steel Products argue that in the early 1980s they were in such serious difficulties that they could have folded, while from 1982 to 1983 Tinto Industries' profit of Z$826,000 turned into a loss of Z$11,000 and the company suffered serious financial difficulties over the next few years[40].

The chief difficulties facing Zimplow and Bulawayo Steel Products have revolved around three factors: the nature of their main products, their management, and the institutional policy environment. Both firms began[41] by making, and are still predominantly dependent upon supplying, the more simple range of implements and hand-tools for the domestic market. Their sales volumes therefore lie outside their control: when the country suffers from drought – as it did in 1982–4 and 1985–6 – domestic sales fall dramatically. On the supply side, because some 90% of raw materials (largely local steel) are supplied domestically, their dependence on import allocations is small[42]. Nonetheless, although production is fairly labour-intensive, certain pieces of machinery (presses and forges etc.) have had to be imported and both their age and the shortage of spares have had an increasingly adverse effect on productivity and product quality[43].

Until recently, however, none of these issues nor comparatively poor management challenged their viability; they have been able to maintain satisfactory (albeit not very high) profit levels without exerting much effort at expanding into the export market. Despite being the only two firms supplying the domestic market, a sufficiently 'competitive' environment existed to keep costs down and deter price-fixing collusion, while similar management and engineering capabilities led to 'adequate' levels of productivity and product quality on the factory floor. There was, however, no price or profit-related incentive for either firm radically to improve productivity. The overall setting was a price-control system which allowed price rises to be passed on to the domestic consumer in line with rises in costs of inputs in the normal cost-plus manner. There was little incentive to keep prices or costs down, to improve product quality, or to expand into the export field. Nonetheless, the fact that exporting (mostly to South Africa during the latter UDI years) did take place indicates that the institutional framework and the productive system did enable them to remain broadly internationally competitive (as confirmed by the DRC data). Over the longer term, however, the maintenance of this policy environment would almost certainly have done little more than lead to a widening between domestic and international prices, next to no improvement in product quality and if there was to be export trade it would have had to be financed increasingly from higher domestic prices.

Ironically, in practice it was neither the growing pressures from international agencies for greater liberalisation nor the dramatic cuts in foreign-exchange allocations (that adversely affected so many manufacturers in the mid-1980s) which uncovered the vulnerability and economic precariousness of the two firms. Rather it was altering the price-control mechanism (an essential part of the UDI institutional framework) which quite rapidly exposed the long-term weaknesses of both the firms and the policy environment under which they had operated for so many years.

After Independence the costs of inputs across the whole of the manufacturing sector began to rise more rapidly, due largely to increases in the minimum wage, the falling value of the Zimbabwe dollar, and other specific price increases, particularly for fuel, electricity and steel. At the same time the institutional price-control mechanism was tightened and extended so that for most of the leading products manufactured by both Zimplow and Bulawayo Steel Products specific price increase applications had not only to be made but were subject to Cabinet approval. This occurred at a time when the government was focusing its economic policies on two particular objectives: on the one hand, to keep down prices of goods purchased by low-income rural groups (including simple hand and agricultural implements) and, on the other hand, to check what it perceived as the excessively high profit levels of private companies[44]. The result was that from 1981 onwards, the government awarded price increases far lower both than those requested and than those required to accommodate the rise in input costs[45]. The immediate effects were clearly an erosion in profit levels[46]. What is of more interest from a policy perspective is the effect that this profit squeeze had on the companies: quite rapidly it exposed weaknesses and inefficiencies which led to the adoption of more cost-effective production methods.

Their immediate response to the profits squeeze and the drought-induced fall in domestic demand was vigorously to expand into the export market. This was successful inasmuch as export sales went up – Zimplow's exports doubled to Z$700,000 from 1982 to 1984, while Bulawayo Steel Products' exports rose from 25 to 50% of total production by 1985, including the export of Z$1 m. of goods to Zambia in 1985. However, from a cost point of view, the strategy would appear to have been foolhardy; in some instances products were exported at less than the marginal costs of production and in others the marginal costs were covered but, with domestic profit margins squeezed, the traditional subsidy of the domestic market had been cut substantially. It was in this context, with Zimplow returning substantial absolute losses and Bulawayo Steel Products, in the words of the Managing Director, 'gradually going under', that the management of both companies was replaced.

The changes within each firm were dramatic: factories were radically reorganised with production lines altered to a continuous flow system; more rapid throughput meant that stock levels could be reduced; staff training education was initiated to upgrade workers and identify particular tasks in the overall production process; new skilled staff were employed on the shop-floor, leading to higher quality products and improved designs of traditional lines. As a result, in the space of less than two years productivity levels were raised by as much as 25% with either no or only marginal increases in capital employed. In short, the squeezing of profit margins induced the most dramatic increases in efficiency that the firms had experienced in 15 to 20 years – an adjustment that would probably not have occurred (at least with such rapidity) in the absence of the government-induced domestic price squeeze and complementary export incentives.

Another positive outcome has been an expansion in product range; for instance, Bulawayo Steel Products in the last year or so have begun to manufacture forged wheel nuts, track rod ends for Nissan Sunny cars, specialised plant flanges and special types of studs. However, this beneficial outcome has been in part the result of an extremely negative price-control system. Legislation controls the prices of specific *products*, not the range of goods manufactured. Two directly controlled products are axes and picks which have traditionally been made by Bulawayo Steel Products. In spite of the very high domestic demand, especially among low-income rural households, the firm ceased making these in 1987 simply because at the legislated price they could not be made at a profit, thus achieving an outcome diametrically at variance with one of the main objectives for which price control was introduced and is maintained.

There is, then, little doubt that the institutionally-imposed profits squeeze has had significant adjustment results in terms of efficiency and cost-reductions. What is more, in 1986/7 both firms reported after-tax profits, even if of small amounts[47], while the prices of both exports and domestically-targeted products were far more competitive. Zimplow argued that if foreign-exchange and trade controls were lifted it would only fear competition (at zero-tariff rates) from Chinese-made hoes, whose quality is on a par with the Zimbabwean product.

To argue that more stringent price controls have shown certain measurable benefits for efficiency is, however, only part of the picture. In-house rationalisation and the need to diversify away from the dominance of the domestic market has also highlighted the need to up-grade some of the older machinery used in the production process. To reduce time lost through machine breakdowns, to further enhance product quality and to maintain labour productivity gains (which for Zimplow appears to be more immediately necessary) requires and will increasingly require the replacement of key pieces of machinery for which both capital and foreign exchange will be needed[48]. Clearly, then, once the substantial cost reductions from managerial and technical improvement have been achieved, there is a need for prices to be high enough for replacement and expansive capital investment to take place and for foreign-exchange levels to be sufficient for the necessary foreign purchase of these items.

Inadequacy of price as basis for policy implementation.   There are further lessons to be learnt from firm-level experience about the policy context for manufacturing. In particular, the evidence would tend to imply that an attempt to restructure the sector towards further export orientation through the main policy plank of removing controls and relying on the effects of international market and price forces would be open to greater dangers. This can be illustrated initially in relation to agricultural implement exporters.

In 1987, Zimplow and Bulawayo Steel Products exported to a range of African countries including the SADCC states, Uganda, Sudan and South Africa. Simply on the basis of price differentials, the figures indicate that Zimbabwe should not have been exporting to most of these markets because its prices (based on ex-factory costs) were generally higher than those of its competitors. To take one example, in 1987 India landed hoes in Uganda for Z$33 whereas the ex-factory price of Zimbabwean hoes was Z$42 – a differential in large part due to the 120% export incentive available to Indian manufacturers. Nevertheless, Zimbabwean products were still in demand and *were* being imported, for the following reasons: better delivery time, better quality product, better after-sales service and the fact that the Zimbabwean product is well known, tried and tested in these markets. Reversing the blind 'export at any price' policy of the last few years, Bulawayo Steel Products reported that in mid-1987 its export sales had gone up in volume terms while its prices had also been rising. There seemed, in addition, to be less concern than might have been expected about Brazilian hoes being imported by Mozambique at a cost 20–30% lower than Zimbabwean ones: Zimbabwean firms remained confident that the lower quality of the Brazilian product would soon end the Brazilian competition.

There is one, final, lesson to be learnt from the experience of Zimplow and Bulawayo Steel Products and it concerns *consistency*. The major physical input in the manufacture of agricultural implements is steel and Zimbabwe's ZISCO steel provides this basic component not only domestically but also regionally. At present, and consistent with practice stretching back over a number of years, ZISCO's pricing policy generally involves charging domestic customers a higher price than export customers. While this has the positive effect of encouraging immediate foreign-exchange maximisation, even if at the cost of raising the price to domestic consumers, an important indirect effect is to reduce the international competitiveness of export products made with the higher-priced ZISCO steel. In mid-1987, Zimplow and Bulawayo Steel Products had to purchase ZISCO steel at Z$550 a tonne. This same steel was exported to a rival company, Agrimol in Malawi, which produces implements of similar quality, at Z$150 a tonne – less than *one third of the price* to Zimbabwean purchasers. Clearly the more extensive differential pricing and the more integrated industry in Zimbabwe become, the greater will be both the impact of these sorts of anomalies and the ability to counter-balance them by administrative *fiat*.

Tinto Industries also provides two examples of the inadequacy of comparative price data as the basis for determining trade-related policy. The mid-1987 domestic prices of its mainstream machine-drawn products were estimated to have been between 10 and 15% higher than the landed cost of foreign-made alternatives. In spite of this substantial differential, Tinto Industries would have had few objections to import restrictions being lifted and Zimbabwean farmers given the choice of buying the imported rather than the domestically-produced product. The reason is that local farmers know well that the Zimbabwean product is of far higher quality and made for local conditions, engineered to plough to a greater depth and to handle rougher soils. On the other hand, this is a disincentive to expanding exports outside the central/southern African region, where (for example in West Africa) soils tend to be lighter and the less durable non-Zimbabwean product would be preferred even if it were priced less competitively.

Finally on the export front, these is an instance of the loss of a major market which had been acquired in spite of a substantial lack of price competitiveness. Until recently Tinto Industries had a major export market valued at some Z$2.5 m. in Tanzania, even though its products were priced 40% higher than the competition. However, in 1985/6 realising that, with the massive increase in domestic demand, it would not be able to fulfil both domestic and all its export orders, the firm decided to forgo the export side of its business in order to satisfy the (more lucrative) domestic market. As a result the Tanzanian market has now been lost to Brazil and it will take far more than an attempt to narrow price differentials to win it back again – reliability in delivery being one of the reasons for the Tanzanians being willing to purchase the higher-priced product.

Despite this incident, Tinto Industries do have the in-house research, development and engineering capacity to introduce, develop and adapt products for the regional as well as the domestic market. In 1987, however, the firm's ability to expand exports was severely constrained – not (in many of its potential markets) because of wide price differentials vis-à-vis its international competitors but rather because its potential customers simply did not have the necessary foreign exchange.

The inadequacy of using price signals as the major policy determinant in industrial restructuring is illustrated by discussions held with a wide range of industrialists across different sub-sectors. The first example concerns Hunyani, one of the two leading, and privately-owned, manufacturers of paper and paper products in the country[49]. According to the 1982 DRC calculations, Hunyani's principal manufacturing units were deemed uncompetitive and inefficient (DRCs for the industry averaged 2.40 and were as high as 5.93). However, recent analysis by the company indicates that, primarily as a result of labour rationalisation and capital investment, these figures have become totally inapplicable; over the five years to 1987, the number of man-units per tonne of product manufactured is estimated to have been halved, and could be brought down still further. It would therefore appear that the profits squeeze has had some positive side-effects in Hunyani's case.

An examination of Hunyani's exports further illustrates the weakness of international price comparisons as the major tool for determining external trade policies. South African paper manufacturers constitute the major competition within the region and the average 30% tariff needed to keep out imports of similar products was largely directed at South African imports. Nonetheless, South Africa is an export market for Hunyani's products in spite of a 10% tariff. The apparent anomaly arises because South African, like Zimbabwean, firms frequently operate a two-tier pricing system with their domestic sales helping to subsidise their exports. In the case of a range of paper products, Hunyani's exports are priced lower than the inflated domestic price prevailing in South Africa. In general, therefore, there are at least *two* price differentials one would need to know before judging whether Zimbabwean manufacturers were able to compete on the international market.

The second case concerns cigarettes. In 1987 Zimbabwean cigarettes were internationally competitive in terms of price: domestic prices were some 10% lower than border prices (net of excise duty, etc.). However, if import restrictions were lifted, Zimbabwean manufacturers would simply not be able to compete because of the power of international brand names. And of relevance to the debate about removing exchange controls, it would be quite possible for Zimbabwe's cigarette manufacturers to produce international brands for domestic consumption (they have the machinery and skills) but the patent holders would require international standards for packaging, filters, tips, paper and cellophane wrappings. This would necessitate importing these items, which for only one of the two major tobacco manufacturers, Rothmans, would have meant in 1987 laying out an additional Z$300,000 in foreign currency a *month*, or Z$3.6 m. a year.

Some concluding reflections. Contrary to much conventional opinion, the post-Independence period has been a time of quite substantial adjustment within the manufacturing sector – as the firm-level evidence discussed here reveals. While institutional controls have become *more* rather than *less* extensive during the 1980s (particularly in relation to the selling price of manufacturers), their effects have tended to make the sector *more* rather than *less* competitive: with tighter domestic price controls, manufactured exports have begun to expand again while, as the case-studies reveal, changes, especially in management practice, have led to some substantial increases in productivity and reductions in unit costs. Nor have these changes been painless; nearly 10% more firms were either liquidated or struck off the company register in the first five years after Independence than in the previous troubled five years[50]. What is more, there is little to suggest that the removal of controls and the *exclusive* use of the price mechanism would have led to a more rapid or more favourable process of adjustment.

To argue, however, that a generally favourable process of adjustment has taken place should by no means be taken as advocacy for a perpetuation of these policies in the future. There is no doubt that severe and growing foreign-exchange shortages and profit squeezes present policy-makers with fundamental decisions which need to be taken if sustained manufacturing growth is to continue and manufactured exports are to expand. And related to this, the choice has to be made as to whether manufacturing export growth should take place in the general context of attempts to narrow further the differences between international and domestic prices or of widening differentials and hence the domestic subsidisation of exports in the framework of extensive controls. These issues will be taken up below.

The foodstuffs sub-sector

General overview. Zimbabwe's foodstuffs sub-sector has expanded steadily, exhibiting little volatility and disruption, in contrast to most other sub-sectors or to the economy as a whole. This is largely because the origins of growth have lain predominantly, and increasingly, in the rise in domestic demand, and because this remained fairly inelastic.

Low and, as we shall see below, decreasing levels of export growth combined with a comparatively low level of import dependence for raw material inputs have insulated foodstuffs more than other industrial sub-sector from the vagaries of the international market or from the periodic shortages of foreign exchange[51]. This helps to explain the term trend in Figure 10.8, showing the ratio of the MVA of the foodstuffs sub-sector to total MVA over the extended period 1938–83. A number of features need to be highlighted. First, the most rapid falls in the ratio – during the periods 1947–56 and 1968–74, – coincide with the periods of most rapid growth of the manufacturing sector overall. Second, and obversely, the ratio tended to remain steady (1963–8, 1978–81) or to rise (1974–8, 1981–3) when the performance of the other sectors was static or when it contracted. Third, the severity of the poor overall 1981–3 performance of the sector is indicated, revealing that by 1983 the ratio had risen to 17% – a level it had not previously achieved since the late 1940s.

The indicators revealing perhaps the most significant changes in the foodstuffs sub-sector and in the food import dependence of the country as a whole are those for long-run food exports, gross output and manufactured food imports. The story is clearly told in Figures 10.9 and 10.10. In 1938/9, over 40% of all manufactured exports originated in the foodstuffs sub-sector. Then, as shown in Figure 10.9, this proportion fell consistently over the 25 years to the start of the UDI period. The top line, showing the ratio of all manufactured food exports to total manufactured exports, then rises slightly during the UDI period, highlighting the fact that export growth in the foodstuffs sub-sector remained significant in the UDI as in the Federal period.

Figure 10.8 *The ratio of MVA for the foodstuffs sub-sector to MVA for all manufacturing 1938–83*

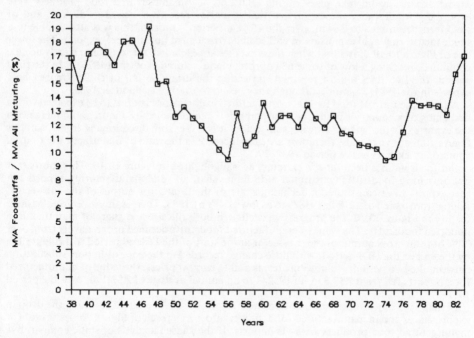

Source: As for Table 10.6, above.

Figure 10.9 *Food exports as a proportion of total manufactured exports 1938/9–82/3*

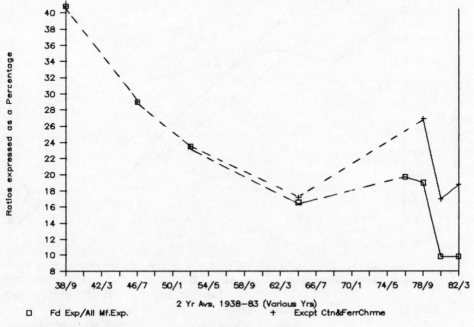

Source: As for Table 10.6, above.   *Note*: 1986/7 figures based on 1986 data.

The latter feature needs treating with some caution, however. While some substantial export expansion did take place during UDI and new manufactured food products were exported – for instance the exports of malted barley rose from zero to Z$2.8 m. and of stockfeeds from zero to Z$4 m. over the 15-year period – most of this was attributable to a single factor: the rapid expansion of chilled and frozen meat (mostly beef) exports. The lower line of Figure 10.10 shows that when *these* exports are excluded, the long-term steady decline continued, reaching a low of some 6% of total manufactured exports in 1976/7. In the final period, the two lines almost rejoined, reflecting the dramatic fall in chilled/frozen beef exports in the 1981/2 period, although they began to diverge again after 1983.

A fall in the ratio of food to total manufactured exports is, of course, to be expected with a deepening of a country's industrial base and if it is accompanied by a more rapid increase in the exports of other manufacturing sub-sectors it is a far from discouraging trend. And, as Figure 10.6 above reveals, there *was* a steady increase in the ratio of manufacturing to total commodity exports in the period 1939–79.

But the trend has been far *too* extreme, as is highlighted in Figure 10.10. This shows that not only have foodstuffs constituted a declining share of total manufacturing exports but that exports have constituted a declining share of the total gross output of the sub-sector, falling from a high of 22% in 1938/9 to as low as 4% by 1983. There is, however, one positive feature in Figure 10.10: the progressive decline in both the size and share of manufactured imported foodstuffs. The value of manufactured foodstuffs declined progressively from over 20% of total gross output of the sub-sector at the start of the Federal period to a minute 1% by the end of the UDI period, with little change recorded in the pace of import substitution between the two periods. In absolute terms and at *current* prices, the value of manufactured food imports fell from Z$7.8 m. in 1952/3 to an annual average of Z$7.1 m. over the period 1982–7.

Perhaps the most important question these trends raise is the extent to which the drop in export shares and in manufactured food imports arose as a result of higher domestic costs of manufactured food products vis-à-vis imports. If the Jansen analysis of static comparative

Figure 10.10 *External manufactured trade in footstuffs in relation to gross output of the foodstuffs sub-sector, 1938/9–82/3*

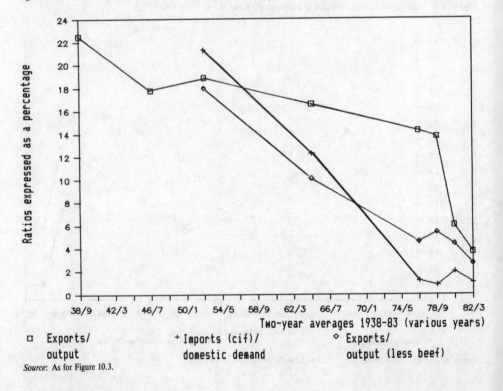

□ Exports/   + Imports (cif)/   ◇ Exports/
   output   domestic demand   output (less beef)

Source: As for Figure 10.3.

Table 10.14 *Comparative advantage indicators for foodstuffs sub-sector, 1982 data*

Branch of Sub-sector	Share of Value Added	DRC	DRC $/run	DRC Range (if given)
Slaught/process. of meat	33	0.69	0.55	
Grain, animal feeds	28	1.03	0.83	0.53 to 1.14
Bakery products	5	0.70	0.56	
Dairy products	14	1.11	0.89	
Sugar & confectionery products	10	0.83	0.66	0.72 to 1.95
Other food products	10	0.74	0.59	
ALL FOODSTUFFS	100	0.88	0.70	

Source: Jansen, 1983, I:48–67; II:84.

advantage, using 1982 data, is any guide, then the answer, as reproduced in Table 10.14, is that in general the sub-sector remained competitive with alternative imports, indicating that neither its expansion nor the reduction in its import dependence was achieved at the cost of substantial domestic subsidies paid for by higher domestic food prices vis-à-vis imported alternatives. More recently this conclusion has been confirmed by the World Bank's Industrial Sector Study of Zimbabwe which for mid-1986 prices found that food products in Harare were about 45% lower than in Washington DC.

But why, it needs to be asked, was export performance so miserable and what inhibited further export expansion? At a general level there would appear to have been a number of factors at work. First, the progressive expansion of domestic demand probably provided an increasingly sufficient market for the firms involved in food manufacturing, the high ratio of food exports to gross output in the late 1930s being explained in part by the small absolute numbers involved[52]. Thus the move away from exports by no means represented a loss of export demand but rather the switch in demand to an ever-growing, closer domestic market. It was partly for this reason that for at least three decades there has been very little 'tradition' of exporting among Zimbabwean food producers, in marked contrast, to manufacturers in the clothing, textile, tobacco, furniture and leather industries, for example.

Second, as most raw material inputs come from the agricultural sector and output tends to vary substantially from year to year because of differences in rainfall, there was little incentive to introduce plant of a capacity sufficient to cater for a substantial export market, expecially when international prices for such products have experienced long-term progressive declines. This factor is confirmed by the recent wide variations in the value added of three sub-groups of food manufacturing over the past 15 years: meat products, canning and preserving of fruit and vegetables and grain and animal foodstuffs. Third, while the food sub-sector was only minimally (and decreasingly) dependent upon access to foreign exchange for raw material inputs, there was a major and increasing foreign-exchange constraint in expanding its capital base; the first priority therefore went to providing capital to meet domestic demand. As food manufactures tend (disproportionately to many other manufactured goods) to be high bulk and low value products, margins are small and therefore a far higher throughput and even greater capital outlay are frequently needed to make exporting a viable proposition. Finally, not all products made for the domestic market were suitable for export, especially without incurring substantial capital costs investing in chilled and frozen containers to transport products to the larger markets beyond Africa.

To these longer-term explanations must be added those of more recent origin, discussed above. There is little doubt, for example, that the constraints of price control, increasingly severe foreign-exchange shortages, the lack of foreign exchange in neighbouring states, and the higher freight and insurance costs resulting from disruption to the Mozambique transport routes have had an equally severe effect on recent production levels in the foodstuffs sub-sector and on expanding manufactured food exports. Indeed, in the case of the sugar industry, Zimbabwe Sugar Refineries argues that the effect of insufficient domestic price increases has meant that the necessary investment to expand capacity even to meet future *domestic* demand has been in serious doubt for the last few years.

So much for the 'broad-brush' analysis of the foodstuffs sub-sector. Further insights can be gleaned by examining some company-based evidence.

Some firm-level evidence. Although there has been minimal new foreign investment in

Zimbabwe since 1980, the most significant investors have been companies with interests in the food business: Dandy (Denmark), setting up a new company to manufacture and export chewing gum; Heinz's major investment (in excess of US$15 m.) in Olivine Industries, also with a view to exporting, and the UK's Dalgety in a joint venture with the local conglomerate, Cairns Holdings (see Riddell, 1987b). The involvement of at least two of these foreign companies was based in large measure on their belief in the potential for manufactured food exports. This confirmed the view of a number of Zimbabwean companies that their fundamental weaknesses in expanding into export markets were the absence of modern technologies for food development, their outdated and inadequate research facilities and the high cost of reaching the most lucrative markets outside the African continent, rather than crude price and quality factors. This explains the willingness of local firms to form collaborative ventures with multinational corporations.

Canning industries illustrate well the range of problems and opportunities facing the foodstuffs sub-sector today. The experience of Super Canners, a family-owned factory in Bulawayo, both highlights the competitiveness of Zimbabwean industry and challenges the widespread view among manufacturers that firms are only able to expand substantially into the export field if they have a secure domestic market to fall back on. Not only did Super Canners export (1986 figures) some Z$15 m. of food products, consisting almost entirely of corned beef and making it the country's second largest food exporter to the Cold Storage Commission (CSC), but it exported its *entire* output and not to neighbouring countries within Africa but (at that time) solely to the United Kingdom.

Some recent developments illustrate the potential. While one of the main reasons for its location in Bulawayo was to be near to its main sources of raw materials – the CSC abattoir is situated across the road and Metal Box's canning factory was, until recently, located nearby – recent developments indicate that these factors are by no means fundamental to its competitiveness. Not only has the canning factory moved to Harare but its move led to quality problems and South African cans (some 20% more expensive) had for a time to be imported by Super Canners. But of even more cost significance, for three months in 1987/8, the CSC was not able to supply the basic ingredient, beef. As a result supplies were obtained from as far away as the Republic of Ireland, transported to Bulawayo for canning and returned to the UK to be sold. Although during this unique exercise little more than current running costs were covered, the scale of the operation indicates the potential for establishing competitive industry in Zimbabwe.

What made Super Canners competitive in the manufacture of a product where international competition was so fierce? According to management its success depended upon the following factors: good management that is versatile and flexible; good job security for the firm's employees and competitive wages leading to low labour turnover; access to the European market under the Lomé Convention; local supplies of beef and cans (usually); high quality of engineering capability within the firm, the ability to adapt a modern, highly-efficient plant consisting mostly of imported machinery to local conditions and to deal quickly with breakdowns, and, finally, continuity of high quality personnel able to maintain sales and, if necessary, to anticipate the need to find alternative markets.

The importance placed on all these different factors puts in sharp perspective the inadequacies of arguments that industry/export strategies depend excessively on 'getting prices right'. This is illustrated in particular by the more recent history of Super Canners. In 1981, the main market for its products was South Africa, made price competitive in part because of substantial capital investment and plant refurbishment which took place during the 1970s. Then suddenly and without prior notification, South Africa imposed a ninefold increase in its canned beef import tariff, raising the level of duty from 11c to Z$1.00 per kg[53]. The effect was to eliminate the major single market at a stroke. However, all was not lost and quite rapidly the firm was able to expand substantially into the UK market, absorbing the lost South African sales. Super Canners' ability to switch to the UK market, eventually for all its product, had its origins a good many *years* before South Africa's tariff-raising action. Anticipating political independence, the firm began to investigate the UK market as early as the mid-1970s and immediately after Independence obtained European Community veterinary approval for its factory. UK market sales are by no means permanently 'safe', however, especially from other exports under the Lomé Convention.

Without wishing to detract from the considerable achievement of Super Canners it must be pointed out that two substantial factors worked in its favour, both of which have assisted the lowering of unit costs. First, over the longer term the firm has benefited from the relatively low price of Zimbabwean beef compared with international prices. Second, while freight and insurance costs of shipping its product to Europe are comparatively low (estimated at only some 5% of the ex-factory price), its competitiveness is assisted by the large subsidies under which the National Railways of Zimbabwe (NRZ) have operated in recent years.

These benefits would, of course, apply to any firm in the canned meat business. It is therefore of more than passing interest to look briefly at the operations of Lemco[54], the largest producer of canned meat, vegetable and fruit products in Zimbabwe, because exports, mainly to regional markets, have traditionally played only a very minor part in its overall operations (accounting for between 5 and 15% of turnover). The root cause of *its* failure to expand into the export market would appear to have lain with the management[55]. Past policy appears to have been content to dominate the domestic market for canned beef. While this near-monopoly position did not lead to domestic prices becoming widely out of line with border prices, there is little to indicate that it aggressively sought to lower unit costs, at least to the extent of being able to penetrate the much larger European market or even to think much about expanding into the export field. A chain of factors have restricted such expansion. To export to the EEC requires EEC-registration of the canning factory, which would necessitate expanding and up-grading at a cost estimated at Z$1.5 m. a few years ago but no decision had been made on going ahead with this investment programme. To some extent Lemco has been in a far better position to export than Super Canners; it is part of a worldwide corporation with all the marketing expertise this brings and, domestically, it owns substantial cattle ranches located near its factory and so has direct access to the main raw material. On the other hand, there have been problems of water supply. The Super Canners story shows that within Zimbabwe there are the ingredients for highly efficient food manufacturing which is competitive worldwide; the story of Lemco shows that, especially with a captive and expanding domestic market *and* where domestic prices are not out of line with border prices, there is no guarantee that export potential will be exploited.

Apart from the somewhat anomalous case of temporarily importing beef from Europe to send back in cans, it does appear that there is a large untapped potential for expanding Zimbabwe's resource-based food manufactured exports. And this is well illustrated by the plans and actions of Cairns Holdings, seen, for instance, in its mid-1980s acquisition of the former family firm of Border Streams, one of some half-dozen privately-owned firms in the fruit and vegetable preserving/canning business in Zimbabwe. In spite of quite fierce competition in the domestic market (all companies argue that the market is 'over-traded') there has been little expansion of the industry as a whole into the export market: in 1983, exports of jams, including pulps, were valued at Z$3,000, of fruit juices at Z$22,000 and of processed vegetables at Z$2.7 m. This is in spite of Zimbabwe's ability to grow tropical and semi-tropical fruits and vegetables and the large and growing markets in the Middle East, the EC and Japan for such processed products which, in the case of the EC, could be imported under the concessional terms of the Lomé Convention.

Three key factors appear to have inhibited export expansion. First, the lack of a *reliable* supply of high quality products from the farming community; second, the age, quality and size of the processing/canning plants which were established for a smaller domestic market; and, third, a reluctance on the part of management to attempt to exploit these potential markets. Border Streams is of interest because it has attempted to address each of these constraints. While the takeover by Cairns was in part meant to provide more efficient production for the *domestic* market, the radical steps taken – moving the factory to Mutare, integrating the operation with its Tomango Foods operation in Mutare to increase throughput, and installing a wider range of more modern capital equipment – have provided the company with most of the technical ingredients necessary to produce high quality export products. A joint strategy with other companies, marketing under a joint label, was also under consideration. Although the raw material supply problems were by no means all solved in 1987, the expansion of irrigation facilities, increased pest control, a far greater realisation amongst farmers of the profit ability of diversification to this type of farming, and greater specialisation to a smaller range of products, all helped in overcoming this constraint. Finally, there is an increased awareness among management of the potential for export expansion, even if awareness has also grown of the international competition. Attention is being focused on a range of high value products, including asparagus, tropical fruit juices and jam pulps (guavas, mangoes, grenadillas) and, with tomatoes, canned trout.

That substantial progress has been made over the past few years to address the constraints inhibiting exports is borne out by recent trade statistics. In 1986, exports of jams were valued at Z$48,000, compared with Z$2,000 in 1983, while fruit juice exports were valued at Z$1.1 m. compared with Z$22,000 in the same years.

For these food manufacturers, however, and indeed for the whole of the manufacturing sector, other constraints have also existed. Foreign-exchange shortages for capital equipment and spares have not only inhibited exports but, more fundamentally, slowed down – and in some cases prevented – the process of adjustment and change needed to adapt plant and equipment to create or extend longer-term competitiveness. The food industry has been particularly affected by the periodic, and growing, shortage of cans and the variable quality of the cans which Metal Box has been manufacturing. Importantly, too, a noticeably slower pace of decision-making by government officials has become a major handicap to industrial efficiency and in particular to securing export orders precisely at a time when decision-making needs to *speed up* with the commitment to expand into the export market.

Agro-industrial linkages[56]

Agricultural inputs into manufacturing.   The data in Table 10.15 clearly show that over the past two decades or so the manufacturing sector has absorbed an increasing share of the output from agriculture – at constant prices, a sevenfold increase between 1965 and 1981/2. If only the output of commercial agriculture is considered, the relationship is even greater. That this increased linkage between the two sectors has been of importance to manufacturing is indicated by the fact that, as a proportion of total inputs purchased by manufacturing, those originating in the domestic agricultural sector doubled from 1965 to 1975 and rose by a further 50% by 1981/2.

Table 10.15 *Agricultural output and manufacturing inputs*

	1965	1975	1981/2
% of agricultural output used as input by manufacturing sector	12.8	31.1	43.9
% of *commercial* agricultural output used as input by the manufacturing sector	16.0	38.6	59.2
% of inputs used by manufacturing sector originating in the domestic agricultural sector	9.7	20.4	29.2

Source: National Accounts and Balance of Payments of Rhodesia 1965, Harare, CSO, 1966, Table 60; UNCTAD 1980: Annex III; for 1981, unpublished data provided by the CSO, Harare, in part reproduced in UNIDO, 1986b: 126–140; Annexes A to D; Census of Production 1983/84 and 1979/80, Harare, CSO.

Not surprisingly, most of these agricultural inputs are used in the foodstuffs and beverages and tobacco sub-sectors – accounting for 90% up to the early 1970s; however, more recently with the expansion of cotton production and cotton ginning facilities, the textiles sub-sector has increased its share dramatically, rising to 21% in 1981/2 and amounting to Z$96 m., compared with Z$310 m. used by foodstuffs, and over Z$21 m. by beverages and tobacco[57].

Although these figures suggest strongly that the manufacturing sector has continued to make greater use of the expanded production from agriculture, this is by no means the complete picture. From the point of view of maximising net foreign-exchange earnings, a more disturbing trend is discernible if agricultural export data are also examined. Although Figure 10.11 gives a positive view of both rising raw and processed agricultural exports in recent years, two particular features need to be highlighted: first, the proportion of processed to raw exports has changed little over time and, second, the absolute quantities of non-processed agricultural exports have risen very markedly – from Z$50 m. in 1966 to over Z$220 m. in 1979. What these figures indicate is a large and increasing loss of potential foreign exchange.

This is confirmed by the rising ratio of raw agricultural exports to gross agricultural output, which increased from just over 30% in 1966 to 50% in 1979, having peaked at 60% in the mid-1970s. While the increasing export orientation of the agricultural sector demonstrates greater absolute and relative foreign-exchange earning over *previous* periods, it also indicates an increasing potential loss through not maximising value added prior to exporting.

This is revealed, for instance, by some trade and output data for 1985. In that year, the value of coffee, tea, raw sugar, unmanufactured tobacco and cotton and cotton lint exports was Z$638 m. some 40% of total (non-gold) exports. However, less than 20% of the tea and

Figure 10.11 *Value of raw and processed agricultural exports, 1966–79*

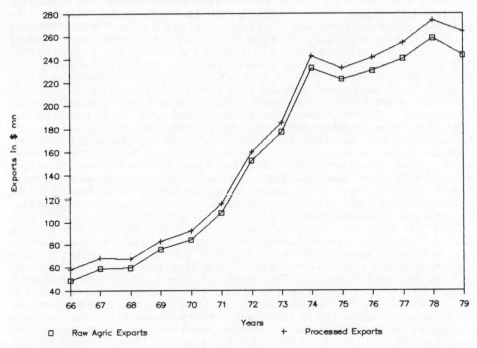

Source: Muir, 1981.

coffee produced and only some 2% of the tobacco was currently processed and manufactured; Z$52 m. was earned from the export of raw sugar at an average price of Z$264 a tonne while only Z$16 m. was earned from exporting refined sugar at a price of Z$421 a tonne; Z$150 m. of cotton exports contrast with only Z$30 m. earned from the export of textile products. Similarly for livestock products, excluding the more expensive cuts and those receiving premium EC prices under the Lomé Convention, expanding the export of canned meats would earn far more foreign exchange than concentrating on the export of chilled and frozen beef. For instance, Zimbabwe has recently been selling 'manufactured' meat to West Germany at Z$4 a kg. If this had been processed into canned meat it would have earned Z$7 a kg[58].

Manufacturing inputs into agriculture. The main indicators of this relationship are given in Table 10.16. As the data show, the agricultural sector is far more dependent upon manufacturing (accounting for some 45% of its total output) than manufacturing is upon agriculture, as less than 10% of its output is channelled into agriculture – even though the data suggest that this latter ratio has been rising significantly in recent years. Another striking feature of Table 10.16 in comparison with Table 10.15 is that whereas over time an increasing

Table 10.16 *The supply of material inputs to the agricultural sector*

	1965	1975	1981/82
% of inputs provided by the manufacturing sector[a]	42	43	48
% of inputs directly imported[b]	9	7.5	10.4
Inputs from manufacturing to agriculture as a percentage of total manufacturing output	3	6	7

Source: As for Table 10.15 and Muir (1981).

Notes: [a] The data for 1981/2 do not refer to capital purchases by the agricultural sector.
[b] The data in this row are broadly consistent with those of Muir for the period 1966–79.

proportion of agricultural produce has been utilised by manufacturing, the proportion of inputs from manufacturing used by agriculture appears to have increased only slowly from 1966 to 1981/2 – from 42 to 48%. Although Table 10.16 indicates little variation in the proportion of imported inputs used by agriculture (a slight rise is shown in the 1980s data) there has been a marked decline in the ratio of *imports* used by agriculture to *inputs* obtained from manufacturing (not shown in the table) from 22% in 1965 to 17% in 1975 and 10% by 1981/2. Inputs to agriculture originating from the manufacturing sector consist mainly of the following items: stockfeeds (31% of the total); fertilisers and crop chemicals (54%), machinery (11%) and transport equipment (3%), paper and packaging (1%)[59].

The data on trends in the relative shares of inputs sourced from imports and domestic industry are of limited value because they capture only the direct and final transactions, thus failing to encompass the indirect import component of domestically manufactured products. For instance, in the case of crop chemicals, almost all the domestically 'manufactured' products consist of simple formulation and packaging of imports, their import content being well in excess of 70% of their domestic selling price. A more complete (although still less than fully accurate) picture of this aspect of agro-industrial linkages can be obtained by looking in more detail at the supply of and demand for the key material inputs required by the agricultural sector. These would include the following: fertilisers, crop chemicals, agricultural tools and implements including tractors, and packaging materials.

Table 10.17 shows the total material input purchases made by the agricultural sector in 1984 sub-divided into the commercial and other (largely communal) sub-divisions of agriculture. In terms of value, fertilisers and stockfeeds dominate total supply purchases, accounting for 85% of total material inputs. Sub-dividing agriculture into two, however, produces some marked variations. The commercial sector purchased 83% of all input purchases in 1984, the remainder just 17%. Although this difference is clearly very great, it has narrowed considerably, especially since Independence; for instance in 1976, commercial agriculture accounted for 93% of total material input purchases. Communal/small-scale agriculture's purchases are dominated by fertiliser, with packaging materials (mostly grain bags) accounting for 12% of the total – and nearly half the national demand for such purchases. The relative differences in purchases of stockfeeds and fertilisers between the two sub-sectors has been due neither to the differences in livestock population nor to the area planted to particular crops but rather to the relative commercialisation of livestock production and intensity of crop production.

Table 10.17 *Purchase of material inputs by the agricultural sector 1984. Z$000s*

Item	Commercial	% Total	Communal & Small-Scale	% Total	Total all agric.	% each input
Fertilisers	107,916	72	42,420	28	150,336	46
Crop chemicals	30,043	97	682	3	30,725	10
Packaging materials	8,760	57	6,532	43	15,292	5
Stockfeeds/fodder	121,568	96	4,755	4	126,323	39
TOTALS	268,287	83	54,389	17	322,676	100

Source: Central Statistical Office, *Zimbabwe: Production Account of Agriculture, Forestry and Fishing, 1976–84*, Harare, Agricultural Statistics CSO, 1987 and unpublished data from CSO.

Maize has been far and away the largest absorber of fertiliser, accounting for 61% of all purchases, followed by 8% for winter cereals, 8% for tobacco and 6% for cotton in the late 1980s. With the greater absolute and also proportional increase in maize production in the communal areas and with domestic demand rising by between 3 and 4% a year, it is this part of agriculture which is likely to see the largest increase in demand for fertilisers over the coming decade[60].

Zimbabwe has had a long history of fertiliser manufacture, going back to the early 1920s when a superphosphate factory was opened in Harare. But the major developments occurred in the late 1960s/early 1970s when an ammonia plant, based on an electrolytic process, was established. There are currently four main fertiliser companies, two upstream plants producing ammonium nitrate and phosphate fertilisers and two plants which manufacture, package and distribute a broad range of fertiliser from local manufacture and from imports. Of the four broad groupings of product, Zimbabwe has been self-sufficient for 25 years in superphosphates (made from local raw materials) but has been totally import-dependent for potash (for which there are no local raw materials) and sulphur in recent years. As for nitrogenous fertilisers – accounting for greater tonnage consumption than the other three combined – the Sable plant has recently been able to produce about two-thirds of domestic requirements[61].

The Macroeconomic context of future industrialisation

FOREIGN-EXCHANGE CONSTRAINTS

Zimbabwe's economy is relatively open – exports plus imports (including non-factor services) have averaged 56% of national income over the last ten years. Thus in spite of its high degree of industrialisation, import levels are a critical determinant of aggregate growth levels, channelling essential intermediate inputs into agriculture, mining and manufacturing, as well as providing some 40% of the total value of investment spending. Given the present structure of the economy it is estimated (in the current development plan, GOZ, 1986) that for each 1% rise in GDP an increase in imports of 1.18% is needed. In its 1985 country memorandum, the World Bank put the figure higher at 1.43% for the latter part of the 1980s but two years later it raised the ratio further to 1.64% for the period 1988–90.

Not only is there a strong link between imports and aggregate growth rates but, under present and past policies, growth rates are being and have been constrained because of the government's control and compression of imports for which there continues to be strong domestic demand. In accordance with pre-Independence practice, a key objective of macroeconomic management has been to avoid running large current account deficits. The method of achieving this has primarily been to run a visible trade surplus (Zimbabwe has a substantial and rising invisible deficit), avoiding large external debt repayments and apportioning imports (through a rigorous system of quantitative allocations) in accordance with this policy. In the period 1980–82 the policy was briefly abandoned: imports were allowed to rise in excess of projected export earnings and this, together with rising non-service invisible payments, resulted in a substantial external debt (see below).

Between 1979 and 1982 the current account deficit increased sevenfold to Z$533 m. Since then it has been rapidly reduced until in 1986 a small surplus was again achieved, rising in 1987 and still positive in 1988. The details are shown in Figure 10.12 and Table 10.18.

Table 10.18 *The balance of payments, 1980–88 (Z$m.)*

	1980	1981	1982	1983	1984	1985	1986	1987	1988[a]
Exports	929	1,002	998	1,174	1,484	1,811	2,206	2,416	2,900
Imports	861	1,059	1,114	1,087	1,237	1,486	1,686	1,781	2,140
Trade balance	68	− 57	− 116	87	247	325	520	635	760
Services - earnings	91	83	116	131	157	160	237	252	
outflows	242	346	309	393	401	466	485	532	
Invest. income	85	75	83	93	101	112	111	77	
Invest. payments	119	171	245	314	257	386	404	429	
Transfers	− 40	− 23	− 62	− 59	− 52	16	54	79	
CUR. ACC. BALANCE	− 157	− 440	− 533	− 454	− 102	− 159	+ 13	+ 82	+ 110
Net Cap. Accnt.	− 44	134	343	286	233	280	138	119	− 85
Unrecorded flow	120	86	66	10	34	83	− 77	33	
Overall balance	− 81	− 220	− 124	− 158	+ 164	+ 204	+ 73	+ 234	+ 25

Source: Figures from Central Statistical Office, Harare, reproduced and up-dated from Hawkins (1989) and from Reserve Bank, *Quarterly Economic and Statistical Review*, Vol. 8, Nos 3 & 4, Table 6.2.

Note: [a] Estimate.

This success was achieved, however, at the cost of severe import contraction which itself led to depressed levels of aggregate growth and, given the manner in which the cuts in imports were achieved, a dramatic fall in investment levels. Between 1983 and 1986 the volume of capital goods imports fell by 34%; gross fixed capital formation as a proportion of GDP

Figure 10.12   *External trade and current account balance 1978–88 Z$bn*

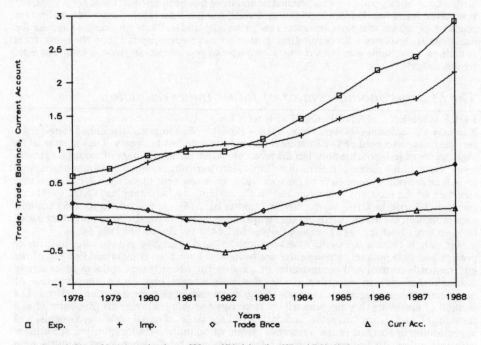

□   Exp.   +   Imp.   ◇   Trade Bnce   △   Curr Acc.

Source: *Quarterly Digest of Statistics*, various issues, CSO unpublished data (for 1987) and Table 10.18.

Note: 1988 figures are preliminary estimates.

contracted to an annual average of 12% (at fixed prices) in the years 1984–6 compared with 18% in the first three years of Independence and an average of 20% during the whole UDI period. As for imports of non-capital goods, largely fuel and intermediate inputs, these fell in volume terms by 22% from 1982 to 1986[62]. Overall, in 1987 imports (valued in SDRs) were only 53% of their 1981 value, while in volume terms they were, in 1986, some 6% lower than the level in 1973–6.

While import contraction appears to have been the immediate constraint upon overall growth, factors causing the authorities to reduce import allocations have been even more fundamental; first, the less than sufficient growth in export earnings, associated, secondly, with inadequate amounts of non-commercial external finance flowing into the economy to make up this shortfall and thirdly, and more generally, the failure to relate the level and degree of import demand for achieving high levels of sustained growth to the capacity of the economy to obtain sufficient non-debt-accruing foreign exchange.

A comparison of the Zimbabwe dollar values of external trade trends in Table 10.18 and Figure 10.12 with those in Figure 10.13 – which show trends in imports and exports valued in SDRs over the past 11 years – highlights the worrying external trade performance. Figure 10.13 reveals not only the substantially lower value of imports in 1987 compared with 1981 but also the dramatic contraction in real export earnings from 1981 to 1982 and the little subsequent change. Overall, from 1981 to 1987 real export earnings (valued in SDRs) fell by 23%[63].

Initially the post-Independence foreign exchange 'gap' was substantially filled by foreign aid, but this was soon supplemented by commercial borrowing[64]. The total external debt grew rapidly from Z$385 m.(US$572 m.) at Independence to Z$4,063 m. (US$2,421 m.) by the end of 1986. As a large proportion of this was short-term debt, high levels of repayments fell due almost at once. Debt-service payments rose nearly *sixtyfold* in the first seven years after Independence, from Z$10 m. in 1980 to Z$570 m. in 1986. By 1986, the debt-service ratio had risen to 30% and to some 34% by 1988. While it is set to fall (a figure of 25% was estimated for 1989 by the Governor of the Reserve Bank in May), annual repayments will average

Figure 10.13 *External trade in SDRs, 1976–87.*

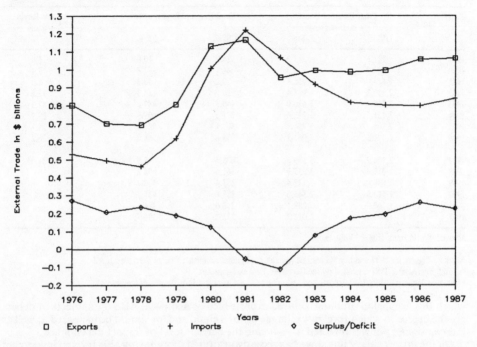

Source: Quarterly Digest of Statistics, September 1987 and IMF *International Financial Statistics*, 1986, unpublished CSO data and Hawkins (1989).

$273 m. over the period 1988–92 (Z$465 m. at the average 1987 exchange rate), 21% of the 1986 level of exports. The details are shown in Table 10.19. Clearly, increased export earnings over the next few years will be required not only to raise import levels necessary to achieve higher levels of aggregate growth but also to repay the substantial foreign debt commitments.

Zimbabwe has failed to attract substantial inflows of other forms of capital. For instance, the total gross inflow of private foreign investment from Independence to the end of 1986 probably amounted to less than $50 m., partly due to the generally poor climate for foreign investment flows but, in Zimbabwe's case, also influenced by restrictions on·the outflow of profit and dividends and on the financial assets of emigrants. While this has had a marked effect on the balance of payments in the short term – dividend and profit outflows fell from Z$188 m. in 1982 and 1983 to Z$18 m. in 1984 and 1985 – it has also created a pipeline of future foreign-exchange outflows as well as providing a deterrent to potential new investors[65]. The government declared that as from January 1988 import licences were to be extended to cover the freight and insurance costs of imports in the hope that the escalating rise in these outflows could be checked[66].

There is no doubt that Zimbabwe is facing a growing and increasingly grave foreign-exchange crisis – in spite of the fact that this tends *not* to be revealed in contemporary external trade and balance-of-payments statistics for reasons already explained. To the extent that the crisis *can* be eased (or solved) by policy intervention, this suggests that changes in policies affecting the earning and utilisation of foreign exchange must be made and in this regard, there is no dispute about the need tö expand export earnings. What is more, because of the poor worldwide climate for an expansion in volume and/or an increase in the price of Zimbabwe's mineral and agricultural exports, attention is now being focused on the rapid expansion of manufacturing exports as the best means of increasing aggregate foreign-exchange earnings over the next decade.

What is in dispute – indeed at the heart of controversy surrounding the future course of macroeconomic management of the economy and to be discussed below – is the manner in

Table 10.19 *External public debt profile, 1980–86*

Year	Total External Debt (+ undisbursed)		Total External Repayments		Debt-Service Ratio
	US$m.	Z$m.	US$m.	Z$m.	
1979	571.6	385.3	14.8	10.0	1.4
1980	782.7	493.5	44.1	27.8	3.1
1981	1,615.9	1,158.8	70.2	50.3	5.2
1982	2,130.3	1,958.4	139.6	128.3	13.2
1983	2,366.4	2,616.0	440.7	487.2	42.3
1984	2,151.5	3,232.4	271.5	407.9	28.1
1985	2,306.1	3,784.8	307.1	504.0	28.1
1986	2,421.2	4,063.1	338.6	568.2	26.2
1987[a]	2,134.2	3,589.6	403.4	678.5	31.5[c]
1988	1,877.4	3,157.9[b]	361.6	608.2	
1989	1,688.0	2,839.4	283.4	476.7	
1990	1,513.9	2,546.5	258.8	435.3	
1991	1,360.9	2,289.1	228.6	384.5	
1992	1,195.1	2,010.2	232.9	391.7	

Source: World Bank (1987b, Volume I).

Notes: [a] Figures for 1987 and beyond assume (unrealistically) that no further foreign debt is acquired.
[b] All Z$ figures after 1987 are based on the December 1987 exchange rate.
[c] Based on January to July 1987 exports and assuming proportionate trend for the rest of the year.

which this expansion of manufactured exports is to be achieved. Also the subjects of debate are the degree to which foreign-exchange inflows could and/or should be increased as well as interventionist policies directed at *reducing* the current level of import dependence.

On the inflow side, Zimbabwe has recently instituted more favourable foreign investment policies[67] and it could continue to borrow externally. Both policies have been advocated, by the World Bank for instance, but both carry risks and complementary costs. Higher levels of debt exposure can be justified only if these debts can be comfortably repaid by higher export earnings, while the liberalisation of foreign investment policies in the context of a poor climate for foreign private flows into Africa in general, and into the southern African region in particular, provides little optimism that *substantial* new levels of foreign private investment would flow in the short term[68].

Equally radical, but interventionist in nature, is the view that attempts should be made to reduce the current level of import dependence. In this approach, the main emphasis is placed on policies to raise the absolute incomes of the rural poor and narrow the gap between them and the richer 10% of the population, initially by engineering a reduction in real incomes of the elite. By thus altering the base of domestic demand, the import/growth ratio would be reduced at least over the short term, but for a period sufficient to restructure the economy towards a more rapid and sustained expansion of exports as the import/growth ratio again begins to rise.

GOVERNMENT FINANCE AND THE BUDGET DEFICIT

A number of interrelated trends in public finance since Independence are providing further constraints (see Table 10.20, below). First is the large and, in most years since 1980, growing budget deficit. At Independence this amounted to over 11% of GDP but was rapidly brought down to just over 4% by 1981/2. However, as shown in Figure 10.14, the ratio began to rise over the next five years to reach an estimated 9% in 1986/7 and totalling Z$766 m. For the financial year 1989/90, a record deficit of Z$1,100 m. amounting, also, to 9% of GDP, was forecast by the government.

Equally worrying, and also shown in Figure 10.14, has been the extremely low and, until recently, falling amount of central government expenditure allocated to capital projects. Indeed in real terms, this fell in each year from a peak of only 12% of total government expenditure in 1981/2 to 1985/6. These low and declining levels do not embrace all public capital expenditure. Indeed, one of the major gains of the post-Independence period has been the expanded capital development of the major infrastructural parastatal operations – the National Railways of Zimbabwe (NRZ), the Post and Telecommunications Corporation (PTC), the Cold Storage Commission (CSC), the Dairy Marketing Board (DMB) etc.

Figure 10.14 *Central government budget deficit and capital expenditure as a proportion of GDF 1978/9–88/9*

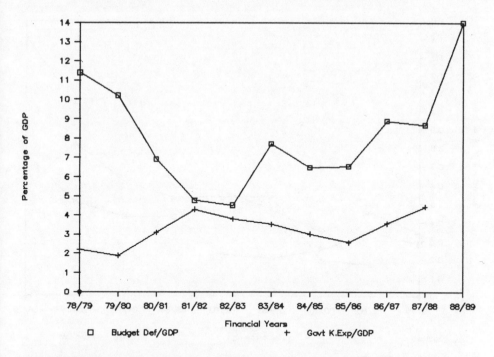

Source: *Quarterly Digest of Statistics*, various issues and, for 1986 and 1987, information supplied by the CSO, Harare. The 1988/89 figure for the budget deficit/GDP ratio is an estimate (see *Financial Times*, 25 May 1989).

Note: 1987 GDP estimated at 1% with 14% domestic inflation.

However, these developments have been costly both in relation to accumulated loans, the bulk of which are still outstanding, and to their high foreign-exchange component. Of total foreign loan obligations in mid-1987 (see Table 10.19) some 28% were liabilities of the parastatals[69]. Confidence would be higher if, in aggregate or even individually, they were running surpluses with which they could repay their past loans and finance steady future expansion. This, however, has not been the case: one of the major public finance problems has been the growing inability of the parastatals to operate without central government assistance[70]. Since Independence each of the nine major parastatal groupings has run an accumulated overall deficit of upwards of Z$100 m.[71], in the main, financed by central government. Their operating annual deficits rose from just under 5% of GDP at Independence to nearly 7% in 1986/7, amounting in that year to Z$582 m.[72]. Part of this has been met by the central government budget either directly or indirectly through subsidy and other transfer payments: these rose from 10% of total government expenditure in 1981/2 to 13% in 1986/7, amounting, in the latter financial year, to Z$500 m.

As shown in Figure 10.15, there have been even larger amounts of government borrowing to pay for the rising deficits and the rapid expansion in aggregate expenditure. While in the first few years after Independence rising expenditure was mirrored in rising – for a time even more rapidly – revenue (see Table 10.20), in recent years the gap between expenditure and revenue has widened. This trend is of particular concern because the scope for non-cyclical increases in revenue through the introduction of new taxation measures is *extremely* limited, as has recently been argued by the Commission of Inquiry into Taxation. Indeed the Commission's report revealed that the ratio of total tax revenue to GDP, at 27%, was on a par with that achieved in *industrial* economies and was far higher than the average 20% ratio for a selection of leading African countries and the 23% ratio for all upper-middle income countries (Chelliah 1986: 415).

The gap between central government revenue and expenditure widened from Z$350 m. in

Figure 10.15 *Central government budget deficit and total borrowing and parastatal deficits, Z$ bn, 1978/9–86/7*

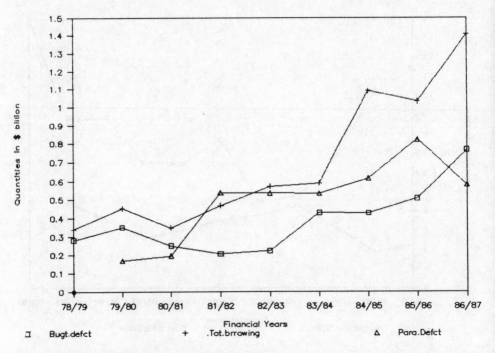

Source: As for Figure 10.14 and World Bank (1987b, Volume II:Annex II).

1980/81 to Z$1,406 m. in 1986/7, narrowing to a still extremely large Z$987 m. in 1987/8. It has been filled largely by a mixture of foreign and domestic borrowing. Between the three-year periods 1978/9–80/81 and 1984/5–86/7 foreign borrowing increased nearly sixfold, rising from 23% of total government borrowing in the first period to a massive 44% in the second. In the latter period, nearly Z$400 m. was in the form of foreign loans.[73]

While financing this substantial deficit through foreign borrowing clearly has serious implications for future foreign-exchange availability, the growing size of the overall borrowing requirement (see Table 10.20) means that there are also considerable costs to the economy from sourcing it domestically – drawing in financial assets for, largely, consumption expenditure that could have been used for raising levels of investment in the productive sectors of the economy. Indeed as Figure 10.16 illustrates, significant rises in the saving/GDP ratio in recent years have been associated with a dramatic fall in the invest-ment/GDP ratio and, if the estimates are accurate, dangerously low levels of net investment. But, in addition, the expenditure-revenue gap has also been bridged increasingly by what are termed 'overdraft facilities' drawn by government from the Reserve Bank. In the 1988 budget it was announced that this amount had doubled to Z$678 m., in spite of the government's stated wish to reduce this amount. In 1981/2, repayment of domestic borrowings amounted to Z$186 m., 11% of total revenue; by 1986/7 the figure has risen to Z$524 m., over 17% of total revenue collected in that year.

Clearly these trends cannot be sustained indefinitely, as the Minister of Finance has repeatedly told Parliament when presenting his annual budget. Zimbabwe is increasingly living beyond its means, and unless present trends are halted and reversed the constraints – domestic and foreign-exchange related – on raising aggregate investment will continue to challenge not only the future but the present viability of manufacturing industry.

While the *problems* are well understood there is far from unanimity concerning the course of action to *resolve* them. Disagreement has lain in the following areas: the extent and the speed with which policies should be implemented to reduce the budget deficit, to put the

Figure 10,16 *Saving and investment as proportion of GDP, 1980-86*

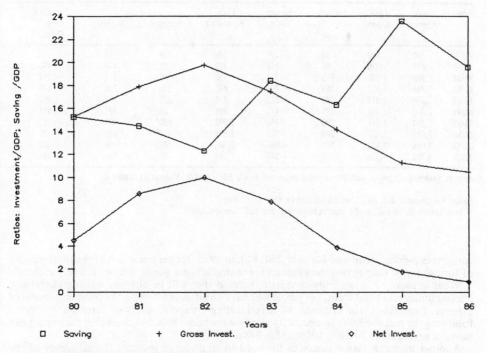

Source: As for Figure 10.15 and World Bank (1987b, Volume I:13).

Note: The net investment/GDP figures are a very crude estimate.

parastatals on a firmer financial footing, to reduce current expansion of recurrent government expenditure and to reverse public sector dis-saving. This dispute is important to the discussion of manufacturing because the manner in which the country's public finance problems are resolved – or the degree to which they are avoided – will have an effect, probably profound, on the future course of its industrial development.

Ironically, perhaps, there is no unanimity over the *degree* to which manufacturing industry will be affected – even if some broad generalisations can be made. For instance, if the current adverse public finance trends are reversed, the easing of the foreign-exchange constraint and the reduction in domestic borrowing will have a beneficial effect on manufacturing through raising the level of imports for general purpose allocation, increasing foreign exchange for investment, providing more domestic liquidity and, in general, boosting investor confidence in the productive sectors of the economy. These effects, however, provide only a partial picture. Overall, there are a range of other factors, some conflicting in their outcome, which also need to be incorporated into an overall assessment of the effects on manufacturing likely to result from measures implemented to address Zimbabwe's public finance problems.

For instance, domestic demand for a range of manufactured products has been stimulated by rising recurrent government expenditure, lower consumer prices for the subsidised products of the parastatals and lower input costs arising from the below-cost tariffs charged by the state transport system. Rising defence, education and health votes have had a substantial effect on the domestic demand for pharmaceuticals, foodstuffs, exercise and textbooks, furniture and school uniforms for example, while subsidised mealie meal, bread, milk, flour and beef prices have also helped to maintain a rapid expansion in domestic demand for foodstuffs. Clearly to the extent that these budget votes are trimmed and consumer prices rise as a direct result of raising the prices of goods and services provided by the parastatals, then manufacturing industry will be *adversely* affected. In addition, to the extent that curbing recurrent expenditure leads to a reduction in real incomes of public sector

Table 10.20 *Central government and parastatal finances, 1978/9–87/8, Z$m. (current prices)*

Year	Govt. Revenue	Govt. Expend	Govt. Cap. Exp.	Budget Defct.	Govt. Borrowing	of which:		Parastatal Overall Deficit [a]
						External	Domestic	
78/79	580	860	54	−279	340	129	211	
79/80	675	1,026	65	−351	453	97	356	−170
80/81	950	1,202	113	−252	350	40	310	−197
81/82	1,364	1,571	187	−206	470	256	214	−539
82/83	1,789	2,012	188	−222	574	232	342	−538
83/84	2,000	2,431	198	−431	591	86	505	−535
84/85	2,212	2,641	200	−428	1,092	632 [b]	460	−617
85/86	2,618	3,126	200	−507	1,035	410	625	−822
86/87	3,056	3,822	307	−766	1,406	502	904	−582
87/88	3,785	4,331	409	−546	947	81	906	−643

Source: Quarterly Digest of Statistics, various years and World Bank (1987b, Volume II: Annex II).

Notes: [a] Aggregated data for 12 parastatals and for local authorities.
[b] These include Z$408 million of 4 percent recycled bonds held "domestically".

employees (which accounted for over Z$1.1 bn in 1986/7, over one-third of the total earning of formal sector employees) the demand for manufactured goods will be similarly affected.

What is more, it is not only domestic demand that will be altered. Raising electricity, telecommunication and transport prices will have an adverse effect on the competitiveness of exports. Experience, for instance, of deteriorating competitiveness of ferro-alloy exports following the massive hikes in electricity prices in the mid-1980s, indicates that the impact can be quite severe (see UNIDO, 1986b: 185, 348).

Another important issue concerns the need to continue to improve the efficiency of the physical infrastructure. If a 'rationalisation' of the parastatals leads to a marked decline in their capital investment programmes then, again, the competitiveness of the manufacturing sector could well be adversely affected as would the profitability of those industries supplying capital and related equipment for these programmes.

A more direct effect is illustrated by the state-owned Zimbabwe Iron and Steel Corporation (ZISCO), the largest single manufacturing enterprise in the country. In the first seven years after Independence, ZISCO accumulated losses of Z$493 m. (at current prices). Almost all of these have been met by transfers from central government, amounting to an average of Z$84 m. each year in the four financial years to 1987/8, equivalent to over 1% of GDP and accounting for 16% of the budget deficit. While no contemporary commentator is currently advocating the closure of ZISCO[74], recent cost estimates suggest that at least Z$600 m. would be needed over a five-year period to 1992 to put it on a sound financial footing – implying that annual state subsidies will then no longer be needed, but only possible with significant hikes in domestic steel prices (World Bank, 1987b, Volume I: 112)[75]. If (most likely) this money were to come from the state sector, it would mean the addition of a further Z$70 m. a year to 1992 (at 1987 prices); if (less likely) it were to come from external loan finance, it would add further to the country's foreign debt obligations. Whichever way the re-vamping of ZISCO is financed, the effect will be to make it all the more difficult to put the remainder of the country's parastatals on a firm financial footing, implying substantially more radical adjustments in other areas of the economy[76].

OTHER MAJOR ISSUES

Unemployment.   Concern about unemployment has grown rapidly in the most recent post-Independence period. Indeed, in January 1988 the government announced a new and comprehensive plan to subsidise employment, encourage early retirement and cut expatriate staff. Some figures illustrate the scale of the problem. Between 1980 and 1985 formal sector employment rose from 1.010 m. to 1.060 m., all of it due to the rise in service employment (mostly public sector employment, including teachers); there was a net aggregate decline in productive employment. By 1987, it was estimated that some 550,000 potential employees were unemployed, giving a national unemployment rate of some 18%.

In the period 1987–91 it is estimated that there will be a net annual addition to the labour force of some 174,000, while the *most* optimistic growth projections would give an annual growth in formal sector employment of only 29,000[77]. As for the manufacturing sector, according to Volume II of the NDP, wage employment is 'expected to increase from 169,000 workers in 1985 to nearly 200,000 by 1990' (GOZ, 1988: 17). On these assumptions, by the early 1990s the unemployment rate will have risen to 30% and there will be (by 1991) almost the same number of formal sector employees as unemployed.

These trends and pressures are likely to have an important influence in determining the future direction of manufacturing which in mid-1986 employed 16% of the formal sector workforce but 3.5% fewer than in 1982. Given the extent to which official concern about unemployment has built up since 1986, in particular, policies and prescriptions for the manufacturing sector which lead to greater job creation are going to be looked upon far more sympathetically than in the past. Conversely, policy proposals with less expansive employment effects or, importantly, which carry higher risks of slow employment growth are likely to meet with substantial resistance.

Managing exogenous risk: drought and relations with South Africa. More radical critics of the governments record since Independence have accused it of maintaining colonial and other structures intact rather than taking the more risky course of initiating more substantial economic reform and structural change (see Astrow, 1983). The effects of drought and of the South African crisis are two important issues which need to be viewed in relation to the manner in which risk assessment is incorporated into macro-planning.

In neither the Transitional National Development Plan (1983–5) nor in the National Development Plan (1986–90) was account taken of the impact of drought on aggregate economic performance. Since Independence, however, Zimbabwe has been affected by a grouping of drought years and below-average rainfall among the worst on record. The effects on the main agricultural crops, on the cattle population and, indirectly through water rationing, upon manufacturing industry[78] have accounted for a fluctuation of one or two percentage points in annual growth rate between recent drought and normal rainfall seasons and an even greater differential between severe drought and 'good' rainfall seasons.

Especially since the NDP was being designed (post-1985), the view has become more widespread that these effects should be incorporated into future policy strategies. This is likely to lead to two results. First, planners are increasingly likely to make provision for lower growth arising from low rainfall in at least one year in five[79]. Second, it seems likely that greater consciousness of the fluctuations in annual agricultural performance will increase the reluctance of policy-makers to expose the economy to a new high risk path for manufacturing if alternative options are available.

The future of South Africa and, in particular, both the effects of events within South Africa and of South Africa's regional policy are also critical exogenous issues. While Zimbabwe has had limited success in the post-1985 period in reducing both its trade and transport links with South Africa (see Riddell, 1988b), South Africa remained by early 1988 both its leading trading partner and the country through which well over 50% of its trade had to pass[80]. To the extent that the growth rate of the South African economy remains at below historical levels and its belligerence towards the independent states of the region continues[81], Zimbabwe's external strategy will be increasingly determined by attempts to reduce these risks by attempting to reduce its economic dependence upon South Africa, and by resisting embarking on any economic strategy which exposes it further to external vulnerability which South Africa would be in a position to exploit.

The exchange rate. There is no doubt that alteration of the value of the Zimbabwe dollar (post-1972 but more significantly post-1982) has been a crucial tool of economic management in the recent past and will continue to be in the future. There is thus no dispute about the principle of direct intervention or management of exchange-rate policy. There has, however, been dispute over a range of issues, some of them – perhaps surprisingly – concerning matters of fact as well as about some of the more common areas of policy controversy relating particularly to the manner in which the different exchange rates should be determined and the level at which the value of the Zimbabwe dollar should be pitched vis-à-vis the currencies of its foreign trade and financial partners.

One of the central issues relates to the proposal, advocated most strongly by the World Bank in its November 1987 country report, that the effective exchange rate[82] be reduced by at least 20%, but possibly by up to 40% (World Bank 1987b, Volume I:41). This echoes the World Bank's 1987 Industry Report which argued that the 'modification of the exchange rate will be a crucial component of an overall package of policy adjustment' (World Bank

Figure 10.17 *The real effective exchange rate of the Zimbabwe dollar 1960–86*

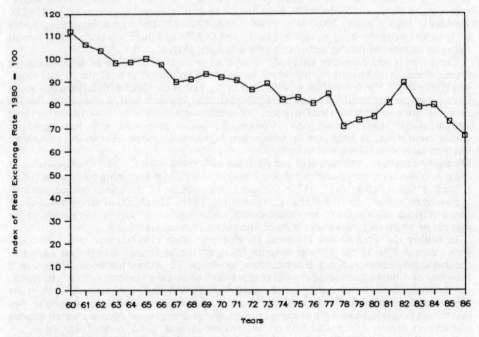

Source: For 1960 to 1980, Wood (1987), for 1980 to 1986, IMF data.

Note: The 1986 figure is for mid-year.

1987a: 77). Such a proposal immediately raises two questions: first, to what extent is the Zimbabwe dollar overvalued and, second, what would be the effect of a downward adjustment?

Figure 10.17 shows a long-term downward shift amounting to some 20% from 1965 (when extensive exchange controls were applied) to 1986 and a similar fall from the 1982 devaluation to 1986. While this trend would tend to confirm the view that the Zimbabwe dollar is significantly overvalued, a number of questions remain unanswered. First, on what basis should a particular year or group of years be chosen to judge the relative strength of the currency? For instance, if the period 1978–80 had been selected, the extent of 'overvaluation' would be far less. Secondly, different 'experts' have made widely differing assessments over the past five years about the extent, or otherwise, of the overvaluation of the Zimbabwe dollar. For instance, the World Bank-sponsored Jansen report on the manufacturing sector (published in April 1983) argued that it was not significantly overvalued in 1981 on the basis of purchasing power parity comparisons (1983, Vol. II: 83). Also on the basis of purchasing power parities over the 1975–84 period and taking account of the overvaluation of the US dollar, Kadhani and Green similarly judged that in 1984 the Zimbabwe dollar was 'not obviously over-valued or under-valued' (1985: 216). And perhaps of greatest interest given the downward trend shown in Figure 10.17, the World Bank's Country Economic Memorandum for 1985 argued in similar fashion that the exchange rate did not appear to be overvalued – even if it did advocate a gradual effective depreciation of the currency (1985: 67)[83]:

> Any attempt to quantify an appropriate exchange rate from the viewpoint of medium-term strategy is subject to uncertainty. But, in the view of this report, the current exchange rate is not severely distorted – as noted above, the short-run disequilibrium in the foreign exchange markets appears to be largely due to issues on the capital account, deriving from the transition period following Independence.

One of the reasons for these substantial differences in opinion is that there is no way of knowing precisely what the equilibrium rate of exchange is, given the many years that exchange controls have been operating. For instance, the World Bank's Industry Report points out that it is 'extremely difficult to assess how much excess demand there is because . . . the more telling signs of disequilibrium are not available. For this reason it is also difficult to estimate the level of the exchange rate that would bring the external accounts into equilibrium', arguing also that 'the excess demand for foreign exchange is not the result of a past real appreciation of the exchange rate due to differential inflation' (1987a: 37 and 38).

What is also of importance is the recognition (by the World Bank and the IMF, among others) that the Zimbabwean authorities *have* followed a policy of depreciating the currency to help maintain export competitiveness in conjunction with an increasing range of export and taxation incentives. Thus the main area of controversy relates to the *speed* with which the policy is being implemented. And here the argument in favour of more rapid depreciation appears to owe more to the assumed favourable impact on export expansion than to strong evidence pointing to a drastically overvalued currency[84]. It is quite clear that, although devaluation has helped and will help the expansion of manufactured exports (by making them more competitive internationally), there is nothing automatic about this. Indeed, a blind policy of currency depreciation is unlikely to have more than a marginal or only a long-term effect.

Clearly the effects of devaluation on imports also have to be considered. In the short to medium term there is an extremely high and price-inelastic demand for imports among manufacturers; further, demand will rise even more as investment in the sector expands again. Hence a rise in the value of imports following a devaluation of the Zimbabwe dollar will not lead to any short- to medium-term decline in the demand for such imports; it will merely raise the price of production, inducing a fall in demand for manufactured products produced for the generally more lucrative domestic market. It will also raise the price of producing exports, thereby reducing the overall effect of the currency depreciation – the final impact depending upon the import content of production in particular instances.

It is because of these various factors that the current, and in effect two-tier, exchange-rate system offers perhaps the best structure for the manufacturing sector. A slightly higher aggregate value of the Zimbabwean dollar in the context of the foreign-exchange control system helps to keep down the costs of imports, assisting the policy of reducing inflation and stimulating domestic demand. On the other hand, a slightly lower effective exchange rate for manufacturing exporters, brought about by the export incentive system and more favourable tax incentives, provides the same external cost advantage as perhaps some 10% overall depreciation of the currency[85].

One final observation.   In practice there is probably rather less disagreement over exchange-rate policy between Zimbabwe's banking and governmental authorities and the World Bank and the IMF than might appear from reading the reports of the international institutions and listening to their officials. In recent years, the authorities have engineered quite substantial depreciations quietly and without publicity, as illustrated by the quite significant movement between January and September 1988, when the Zimbabwe dollar lost 14% of its value against the US dollar, and further depreciation into 1990.

Proposals and projections for the future of manufacturing

THE MAIN FORECASTS AND INITIAL DOUBTS

Three major projections for the more immediate future have been made: two by the World Bank and one by the Government of Zimbabwe. The IMF has also estimated some growth rate scenarios. Table 10.21 summarises the main elements.

Before examining some of the assumptions in more detail a few general points need to be made. First, detailed analyses of the future performance of the manufacturing sector have been extremely sparse: Table 10.21 provides the most detailed available. They reveal major gaps – there are no detailed investment projections and no sub-sectoral breakdowns of projected rates of value-added, exports, employment or of domestic demand for different products. (Some attempts to fill these gaps were made in the earlier, and briefer, transitional development plan[86]). Nor has there been any attempt to address such critically important issues as levels of capacity utilisation or the extent to which domestic demand for manufactured goods would be met if the projected high to very high rates of manufactured export growth were to be achieved.

The extent and range of these gaps suggest that in practice there has been little in-depth analysis of the future evolution of the sector, the figures which have been produced being

Table 10.21 *Projections/forecasts for manufacturing sector growth 1988-95*

a) *1988-90*

	Actual 1980–86 Annual % chge.	Development plan 1986–90	World Bank October '85 Base case	World Bank October '85 Low case	IMF July 1987 Growth scenarios	IMF July 1987 Base	World Bank November '87 Reform case	World Bank November '87 Base case
GDP growth	3.12	5.1	4.6	3.3	4.9	3.1	4.4	2.0
MVA growth	2.41	6.5	5.0				4.3	3.0
Mf. exports	− 3.2	8.2	15.0[a]	6.5[a]			11.4	4.2[b]
Mf. emplymt.	1.84	3.0					2.1	0.9
Investment	2.62	>5.0						

b) *1991-5*

	Actual 1980–86 Annual % chge.	Development plan 1986–90	World Bank October '85 Base case	World Bank October '85 Low case			World Bank November '87 Reform case	World Bank November '87 Base case
GDP growth	3.12	5.1	5.5	3.6			4.1	1.8
MVA growth	2.41	6.5	6.5				4.8	1.6
Mf. exports	− 3.2	8.2	13.2[a]	6.5[a]			8.9	5.7[b]
Mf. emplymt.	1.84	3.0					4.2	1.9
Investment	2.62	>5.0						

Source: World Bank (1985 and 1987b) and IMF (1987).

Notes: [a] These figures exclude mineral-based exports.
[b] Not provided, but calculated from data given.

largely the fall-out from broader macro-wide model building, forecasts and projections. Not without relevance – indeed remarkable for its absence – the 1987 World Bank industrial sector study makes no judgement on either aggregate or sub-sectoral growth in the future nor on any of the crucial supply and demand factors relevant to such estimates, whether in relation to the policies proposed in the study or in relation to a 'no-change' scenario.

The second question raised is how seriously one should take the numbers. Clearly to the extent that the impact of different policy proposals will lead to different outcomes, one would expect projected figures based on alternative policies to differ. What is worrying, however, is the way in which the figures based on a *no change* scenario also differ, in many respects quite substantially. For instance, while changes in the external environment and different assumptions about the future course of the world economy clearly go some way towards explaining the 65% difference in GDP growth between the World Bank's 'low' and 'base' scenarios for 1985 and 1987 respectively, of more concern is the discrepancy between the IMF's view, in July 1987, that with no change in policies, GDP over the period 1988–90 would average 3.1% a year, while only four months later the World Bank produced a figure 35% lower. More serious still – because it relates to almost contemporary economic performance – is the wide margin of error found in the preliminary estimates made by both institutions about economic performance in 1987. In July 1987, the IMF was suggesting that GDP growth in 1987 would be − 1.9%; in November, the World Bank's figure was − 0.9%. In early 1989 it appeared that the actual figure was around + 0.3%.

Inaccuracies of such magnitude over relatively short-term periods raise further serious questions about the accuracy of the assumptions about the relationship between manufacturing and other sectors of the economy and the dynamics of the sector and its component parts, and of judgements about what will or will not happen if new policies are implemented or current policies are retained. For instance, in its November 1987 report, the World Bank was suggesting that there would be a 0.7% growth in MVA in 1987; the actual figure was 2.3% (*Stats-Flash*, No. 33, February 1988) – an error of 228%. The projected difference in the Bank's reform and base case scenarios for the 1988-90 period was itself only 2.4%[87]. For 1988, data for the first ten months of the year recorded a 5.2% volume increase when compared with the same period in 1987 (CSO, *Stats-Flash,* December 1988). If this were the growth rate for the year it would be almost 3 percentage points higher than the World Bank's base case (no-change) projection and even greater than its reform case target figure.

If one goes back to the more accurate figures of a few years previously, even wider discrepancies are found. Thus, the October 1985 World Bank report projected a rise of MVA for 1985 of 5% on the assumption of *changed* policies and an average rate of increase of MVA for the period 1985-7 of 4% a year. *Without* the adoption of policies advocated by the Bank, MVA growth in 1985 was 11.5%, and average growth of MVA in 1985-7 5% a year.

While these discrepancies lend weight to the suggestion that more favourable assumptions are made by the Bank in relation to the effect of its own preferred solutions and less favourable assumptions in relation to those policies which it dislikes, it has to be acknowledged that major misjudgments have also been made by those far more sympathetic to Zimbabwe government policies. For instance, in their 1985 paper[88], Kadhani and Green refer to a strategy under 'serious consideration' in 1983, namely that of eliminating the current account deficit of Z$440 m. by 1986 (1985: 236). This they vigorously attack as having implications ranging from being 'socially and politically unsustainable. . . (leading to) the exodus of skilled and managerial personnel to strikes', and to outcomes referred to as 'technically impossible' and 'totally unmanageable' (ibid.: 236–7). Yet, in practice, not only did the 1983 current account deficit prove to be slightly higher than they had assumed (Z$455 m.) but it *was* eliminated by 1986 without any of the dire consequences predicted. In aggregate terms, Kadhani and Green anticipated the outcome of such policies as a cumulative output fall from 1984 to 1990 of 10–12%; in practice there was a cumulative growth of GDP from 1984 to 1987 of 14% with the likely figure for 1988 GDP of around 6%.

A major part of the explanation for these consistent and widespread failures in forecasting would appear to lie in three factors: errors in the data upon which future trends are mapped, errors in the assumed ratios believed to exist between key variables, and, finally, the possibility that past relationships are not a good guide to the future. For example, Kadhani and Green made the key assumption that levels of capacity utilisation in the manufacturing sector averaged 95% in 1981, falling to 85% in 1983. Nowhere, however, is the basis for this assumption explained. In marked contrast, survey data from the 1986 UNIDO study of firms covering some 40% of total manufacturing production showed that in that year average levels of capacity utilisation (as defined by the different plants themselves) amounted to 69% and that the average highest level achieved (in 1981[89]) was no more than 81%. Furthermore, the UNIDO study found that with a less subjective assessment of full capacity, namely, machine-use time, the results differed markedly: for half the firms analysed, 'full capacity' is

Figure 10.18 *Index of manufacturing output over imported inputs required for the production process 1971–86 SDR and rand values.*

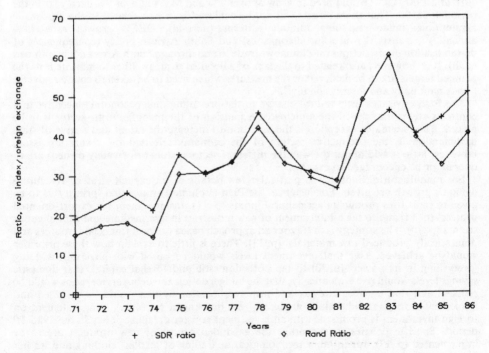

Source: The method by which these data were derived is explained in Note 91.

defined as working flat out for only one 8–9 hour shift period on a five-day week, that is for only 45 out of 168 hours per week (UNIDO, 1986b: 201 and 350).

Perhaps the most important technical relationship for both the economy as a whole and for the manufacturing sector in particular is that between imports and levels of output. For the economy as a whole, the widely differing assumptions have already been highlighted[90]. For the manufacturing sector, little work has been done even though projections/forecasts of future MVA growth clearly depend critically upon an accurate assessment of the relationship; for years, foreign-exchange shortages have constituted far and away the biggest constraint to expanding production and these are directly affected by overall import allocations.

For present purposes a crude attempt has been made to estimate long-term trends in the relationship. To the extent that its estimates are accurate, two clear conclusions can be drawn. First, the very large fluctuations evident from one year to the next. Although this is not a surprising result – because of the time delay between receiving an import allocation and the use of the imported input in the production process – its significance lies in the very large likely inaccuracies in forecasting future imported input/output relationships based on either one year or short-term data.

More substantially, however, the figures clearly show that over time there has been a marked and steady rise in the ratio of manufactured output over imported inputs (excluding investment); indeed over the period 1971–86 it has more than doubled (see Figure 10.18)[91]. What this upward trend suggests is that today less than half as many units of raw material inputs need to be imported to produce a given level of output as in the early 1970s. It should be noted, too, that this has occurred with a 60% rise in manufacturing output. In other words, the manufacturing sector does appear to have become an increasingly more efficient user of foreign exchange.

With these preliminary remarks, we now turn to the different assumptions upon which the future pattern and trends of growth in the manufacturing sector over the next few years have been based.

THE NATIONAL DEVELOPMENT PLAN

The NDP provides the most optimistic scenario but few details on how such targets are to be achieved. Given the actual performance of the economy and of the manufacturing sector in 1986 and 1987, GDP would need to grow at over 7% and MVA at over 9% each year in the period 1988–90. That these targets will *not* be achieved is in part related to the unrealistic assumptions made regarding rainfall patterns (normal), OECD growth rates (3% annually)[92], transport routes (no disruptions) and South African policy (consequences of destabilisation or restrictions on Zimbabwe trade to and through South Africa not mentioned at all). It is, however, also related to the lack of a detailed strategy either to indicate how the planned targets are to be achieved or the measures which need to be taken to counter adverse trends nationally and internationally[93].

The Plan envisages little radical change in the prevailing macroeconomic incentive and control systems into which the anticipated expansion of the manufacturing sector is to be placed. The one major exception is the intention to increase the extent and degree of state participation in the productive sectors of the economy. Beyond the ownership issue, however, little is said about the way the different sectors (state or privately-owned) are to operate or be encouraged to expand.

For manufacturing industry in particular few details of an explicit strategy for future dynamic growth are given. For instance, the Plan (Volume I) states that 'priority' is to be given to industries producing agricultural inputs (p. 11), to investment for export-oriented projects (p. 14) and to the establishment of new industries in intermediate and capital goods sectors (p. 30). The strategy is to 'favour an approach based on local financial resources and domestically produced raw materials' (p. 13). There is little to explain how these priorities would be achieved, save that investment levels would be raised with government doing 'everything in its power' (p. 30) to tap both domestic and foreign capital, that domestic savings levels would rise dramatically, that the budget deficit and debt-service ratios would be reduced and that an adequate tax and import allocation system would be designed and implemented to give additional stimulus to new investment (p. 14). A clear statement on foreign investment is promised, with an investment register detailing policy in the 1986–90 period. Specific policies to encourage the expanded export of new products are to be implemented (p. 17), for instance technological upgrading of textiles, clothing and leather plants, while the export of capital goods is also to be promoted (p. 30).

In the period up to mid-1988 very few of these policies had been set in motion except the provision of some additional taxation and export incentives and, in May, the publication of the second volume of the NDP. The incentive changes apply equally to all manufacturing firms; thus they do not favour particular sub-sectors as the Plan had indicated. Volume II of the Plan revised upwards the figure for total investment for the period 1988–90, by 44% to Z$7,148 m., with 70% of this coming from the public sector. Still no indication was given, however, of how the (now much larger) gap between intention and actual levels of investment would be filled while the investment register was still awaited[94]. In many of the key areas neither the targets have been fulfilled nor, in many cases, have the proposed instruments to achieve expansion been put into place.

It would appear, from the *absence* of more information in the NDP, that little detailed planning of the manufacturing sector's evolution has been carried out either in relation to sub-sectoral targets of output, investment, export orientation and employment generation or to specific policies at the macro, sectoral or sub-sectoral level required to achieve the objectives listed above. Volume II of the Plan lists five priority areas for investment: basic industrial products based on local raw materials, capital goods, consumer goods, manufacturing for export and manufacturing in growth points and industrial estates. It goes on to state that the criteria to be used in the selection of projects will be 'use of locally available natural resources, creation of employment opportunities, contribution to exports and import substitution' (GOZ, 1988: 24). Moreover, the Plan fails to address specifically a number of the critical constraints to expansion of manufacturing: price control, restrictive employment and wage legislation, low levels of domestic demand and, except peripherally, foreign-exchange shortages. In short, the Plan provides only the roughest guide to the future expansion of the manufacturing sector and next to no idea how the high target rates of growth and increased export earnings from the sector would be achieved.

THE WORLD BANK'S PERSPECTIVE[95]

From 1985 to 1987, the World Bank produced three major documents addressing the question of Zimbabwe's manufacturing future. The first and last are macroeconomic policy documents and thus place manufacturing within the broader context of the whole economy. The second is a specifically industrial sector study. Surprisingly, however, it fails to provide any detailed projections at either the sub-sectoral or even sectoral level. This is because its prescriptive sections are little more than a detailed elaboration of the specific set of macro-policies which, in the Bank's view, are required to achieve higher rates of growth, employment creation and export expansion than would be possible without them.

Briefly, the World Bank's view is that the only way Zimbabwe can achieve high rates of growth, and hence move towards the quantitative targets set in the NDP, is by altering key macroeconomic institutions and incentive structures. It is within this context that manufacturing industry, in the Bank's view, is expected to play a different role from that in the past, principally through greater export orientation and through becoming a leading earner of foreign exchange. A key failure is seen to be the extremely low and falling levels of investment of the productive sectors of the economy, including manufacturing. The only way that investment can rise again, according to the Bank, is for dramatic changes to be made in the foreign-exchange allocation system and the budget deficit. More specifically what are required are the following:

* a more competitive or 'modified' exchange rate;
* a radical – and quite rapid[96] – shift away from quantitative quota-based exchange controls to a market-determined 'allocation' of foreign exchange through trade liberalisation and the shift to a system based on (low) tariffs;
* a reduction in the public sector borrowing requirement to be achieved through the quite rapid elimination of government subsidies especially to parastatal organisations (accompanied by price increases) together with a reduction in recurrent state expenditure and a concomitant cutback in the budget deficit and rise in investment;
* a significant relaxation of the almost all-pervasive system of price control[97] and of current labour laws, especially those related to restrictions on firing unwanted labour, which will have the effect of raising profit levels and hence stimulating investment of private productive enterprises;
* a more liberal/welcoming attitude to foreign investment furthered by more explicit guidelines, a streamlining of the decision-making process and greater tax and investment incentives for such investors.

Two fundamental, interrelated and unproved assumptions lie behind these proposals. The first is that higher rates of medium- and longer-term growth and a desirable pattern of structural change can and would be achieved principally by altering the overall incentive structure. The second is that expansion and the desired structural change can *best* be achieved by the removal of non-market-based interventionist policies.

As already noted, none of the World Bank's documents spell out quantitatively the effects of such changes on the country's manufacturing sector beyond the derivation of some rather crude data on MVA, employment creation and aggregate exports[98]. But a number of adverse sub-sectoral effects of the proposals *are* acknowledged, as is the high-risk nature of embarking upon such a radically different strategy for the future. Some examples illustrate these points.

Perhaps the centre-piece of all the expected benefits to the manufacturing sector is the expansion of manufactured exports. But on what basis is this judgment made? The Bank's 1987 document appears to imply that non-exporting industries would in practice be worse-off, with those which have enjoyed high levels of protection actually 'suffering'.[99] In defence of its particular stance, the Bank makes two comments. First, that 'in the short to medium term, the European market is likely to be central to growth in manufactured exports, though clearly the PTA market would be expected to become of growing importance as the economies of its members expand'. Second, that (1987b, Vol. I: 70):

> In terms of individual products, the experience of other countries indicates that it is highly difficult to predict which manufacturing subsectors will enjoy rapid growth, but there is sufficient evidence on the responsiveness of Zimbabwe's manufacturing sector to be optimistic on its export prospects.

Strikingly, however, it fails to provide evidence to support such a bland conclusion. Another major question about the Bank's proposals is that they heighten concern about possible 'de-industrialisation'. The Bank refers, for instance, to concern about the closing of specific industries and a reduction in the government's capacity to plan industrial development (ibid.: 39). But, as with doubts about the achievement of export targets, it has no substantive answer to give. It merely repeats, yet again, its unsubstantiated assertion that in general all would turn out well in the end. Thus it writes that (ibid.: 39):

> these concerns are understandable . . . but it is the view of this report that the present system of quantitative allocations of foreign exchange will hinder and not support industrial restructuring. Trade liberalisation is viewed as an essential component of a package that will raise (not lower) industrial growth and lead to further deepening of the industrial structure.

The Bank's belief in the beneficial outcome of its policy proposals undoubtedly lies in its conviction that market-based policies work 'better' than interventionist solutions. There is *no* theoretical basis, however, for arguing that a *distorted* – or even a better functioning – market system would produce a better (more efficient) outcome than particular combinations of interventionism[100]. And in this regard it needs to be stressed that the strategy put forward by the World Bank is not designed to move Zimbabwe to a control-*less* economy but rather to one that is *less* controlled than at present. This is clear both from the ready acknowledgement in the Bank's discussion documents that some quite substantial tariffs should continue for the foreseeable future and from more specific comments, such as that there is a 'well-justified case for continued intervention' in the case of luxury imports where the *continuation* of the quota system is advocated (ibid.: 124). In this context it is also important to highlight that, in spite of harsh criticism – from the Bank and others – that the current system of quota-based foreign-exchange allocations is calcified and if based on real economy considerations on ones that were applicable ten and more years ago, it is simply untrue. There have been *continuous* alterations in the allocation of foreign exchange to different users in large part as a result of changes in relative demand.[101]

Yet another worrying aspect of the World Bank's most recent proposals lies in its acknowledgement of the *increasing* difficulty the country would have in achieving the objectives set out with the mechanisms it proposes. In advocating a strategy determined more than at present by external market forces and international price changes, it is clear that the economy would become more exposed and vulnerable to external changes beyond its control. In this context, the Bank writes thus (ibid.: 59):

Zimbabwe has a relatively open and vulnerable economy and its future economic prospects are closely linked to external developments through the impact on trading opportunities and capital flows. The current outlook is somewhat worse than was foreseen two years ago. It is also more uncertain.

A particular concern relates to the effects of greater exposure to South Africa, which would clearly provide South Africa with increased leverage over Zimbabwe. In commenting on this issue the final irony of the Bank's proposals is revealed. It states that in the event of action by South Africa leading to severe adverse effects on the economy[102], it may be necessary to reintroduce controls, including the current system of foreign-exchange rationing. Is this conclusion seen as reason for caution? Not at all. The Bank argues that with Zimbabwe's experience it is 'unusually well-equipped to do this quickly and efficiently' and with the old system re-established it would be well able 'to undertake *radical* adjustments in both its macroeconomic management and allocative policies' (ibid.: 125).

If the World Bank's latest (November 1987b) strategy *were* adopted and if Zimbabwe *did* succeed in achieving the Bank's objectives, it is worth highlighting some of the more worrying problems which would remain unresolved or become even more pressing. First, as already discussed, there would be a major loss of control of major aspects of the economy, making planning of the future direction more difficult and increasing external vulnerability. Second, the proposals include provision for additional foreign borrowing of up to US$900 m. to make up the shortfall in foreign-exchange requirements, since even the substantial price adjustments advocated would not lead to a high enough level of export earnings. This, of course, would have adverse implications for debt servicing just at the time when the country's dangerously high debt-service ratio would be falling. Third, the World Bank's own estimates suggest that their proposed 20% devaluation would induce a 6% fall in real wages while the price increases of the parastatals would be expected to add a further 2% to the cost of living of low-income groups. Fourth, while it is argued that its policies would make a more substantial impact on unemployment, it needs to be stressed that under the 'no-change' policies 83% of the increase in the labour force is not expected to be absorbed in formal sector employment, and under the policy reform case unemployment would still be at the very high level of 74%. It therefore needs to be asked whether the marginal changes predicted would be worth the extremely high level of risk involved[103].

THE IMF AND OTHERS

Inasmuch as the IMF has enunciated proposals for Zimbabwe's future development these have tended to be rather general and consistent with proposals made for most if not all other African countries; they have not addressed the more detailed issues of future development of the manufacturing sector. The few policy ideas expressed by the IMF are not too dissimilar to those advocated in the World Bank reports. For instance, the IMF sees the problems of public finance and of an 'overvalued' exchange rate as critical, while it advocates, more specifically, a simplification of investment procedures, an ending of all price controls as soon as possible and, for manufacturing specifically, a more outward orientation.

In strong contrast with these views Peter Robinson has outlined a set of proposals for overall development of the economy in which some suggestions about the future direction of the manufacturing sector are made[104]. His starting points are the high and rising level of unemployment, the low income levels for the poor (largely rural) population, and the highly skewed distribution of income. Not only does he believe that the NDP and the World Bank and IMF approaches would fail to solve these problems but also that they are incapable of doing so because they do not address the crucial issue of the structure of domestic demand. He agrees that one of the most fundamental constraints to future development is the shortage of foreign exchange but he believes that this should/can be solved, at least in part, as much by attempting to *reduce* the demand for imports as by attempting to maximise foreign-exchange earnings through policies aimed at increasing exports. In any case, he maintains that policies aimed principally at expanding exports – in the short to medium term – would necessarily conflict with the goals of maximising employment and raising the level of welfare gains for the poor majority.

In consequence, he proposes that a major element of future policy should be directed at reducing the high import content of investment and, in general, the high and (if the World Bank's figures are correct) sharply rising ratio of imports to growth. Two broad strategies are proposed: first, to stimulate the income-earning capacity of the poor and to provide productive employment to those currently under- and unemployed, especially in the rural areas; second, to hold down the real incomes of the richer income earners. The combined effects of these policies would be to reduce the share of imports required for both consumption and investment because, as he correctly argues, the less sophisticated the goods demanded, the lower would be their import content. On the negative side, he is against a massive devaluation of the currency. To address foreign-exchange shortages, he advocates both the rolling over/re-scheduling of current foreign debt commitments and great caution in contracting new commercial debt obligations[105].

Clearly such an approach has implications for manufacturing. If implemented successfully it would mean that domestic demand for basic and simpler consumer goods would rise, leading to demand-induced expansion of simpler foodstuffs, clothing, textiles and footwear, furniture and utensils, and less sophisticated electronic goods, such as radios, watches etc. as well as an increased demand for basic manufactured goods for mass transport, basic health service provision and education. Concomitantly, domestic demand for more sophisticated manufactured products would fall. While it would appear that such an approach would give manufacturing industry an important role, Robinson argues that, over the next few years, the country 'should not overexpose itself by an emphasis on industrialisation to the exclusion of other sectors' (1987: 76). He remains pessimistic about the projections of either the NDP or the World Bank in relation to future exports, including the ability to expand non-traditional manufactured exports either in the short or even the longer term, in the latter instance because of difficulties for a small country like Zimbabwe in maintaining its position in the prevailing technological revolution[106]. Nonetheless, and in spite of the rather unfortunate 'semi-autarchic' label Robinson gives to his particular strategy, it would be incorrect to dub his approach as anti-export. He advocates an expansion in exports even though he remains pessimistic about the annual increase in foreign exchange that can be expected to accrue in the next few years. His semi-autarchic phase is expected to last at least until the mid-1990s, after which development 'aimed at significant widening and deepening of the industrial sector should be initiated on a planned basis' (ibid.: 83).

There are clearly two major drawbacks to the Robinson proposals. The first is that, although the thrust of his approach has received sympathetic hearing both in government and academic circles, it does not (yet) have sufficient political support for it to be a serious contender in the future workings of either the economy in general or the manufacturing sector in particular. For better or worse, contemporary debate tends to be between the options outlined in the NDP and those being advocated by the World Bank. The second drawback is that, as the proposals are still only tentatively drawn up, many questions remain unanswered. What, for instance, would be involved precisely in raising the rural incomes of the poor and in engineering a radical shift in the pattern of income distribution? Is the strategy politically feasible? What would be the effect on the more affluent who would suffer disproportionately? Would the strategy lead to entrepreneurs committing themselves to the higher levels of investment required for sustained growth to proceed? What would be the potential, at least short-term, export losses arising from a likely exodus from the land of some of the wealthier farmers? How, within this perspective, would the major problems of the budget deficit and the drain to the exchequer of many of the parastatals be addressed? A number of these issues will be taken up in the following section.

Alternative approaches

Three factors stand out clearly from the preceding discussion. First, a comprehensive and detailed strategy on the future course of the manufacturing sector has not yet been produced; there is not even agreement on some of the key issues necessary for such a strategy to be agreed and implemented. Second, there is a growing (and now quite widespread) recognition that if the sector is to expand again as it did in the 1950s, late 1960s and early 1970s, a series of pressing industry-specific problems need to be addressed, as well as increasing agreement that there are major and growing problems of the wider economy, which impinge both directly and indirectly upon the present performance of manufacturing and its future prospects.

In this context, two crucial issues face policy-makers: how to raise the level of investment, and how to increase exports. To achieve both of these objectives, increased foreign exchange will be required which, together with the need to raise the level of public sector investment with increasingly limited sources of funds, means that the adverse trends in public finance will also have to be reversed. At least two key matters *have* to be resolved comparatively fast: a carefully worked out policy on investment (foreign/local, state/private) has to be agreed and published, and the present debilitating effects of contemporary price control legislation have to be removed[107]. Without this there is little likelihood of sustained expansion of manufacturing in the near term: solving them would have a profound effect on the decision of industrialists to raise investment levels across the sector.

The third factor which stands out from the analysis is that there is widespread agreement from within government, from the harshest critics of current or government-proposed policies and among industrialists that Zimbabwe's industrial base is strong and diversified and that the complex ingredients which have led to this (probably) unique position in Africa today are still present within the country. The crucial question for the future is precisely how these unique strengths can be harnessed to achieve the objectives desired. The radical pessimistic answer is simply that they cannot be achieved, because historically-rooted tensions and current disagreements represent such irreconcilable differences of class and power interests. As an alternative to this pessimism, thoughts on some different approaches are offered here as a tentative contribution to the debate.

THE INVESTMENT ISSUE

Quantifying the sector's investment needs.   It is surprising – and not a little worrying – that so little work has been done to quantify either sub-sectoral investment trends and requirements or even to estimate the aggregate investment required for the sector as a whole[108]. An initial, albeit partial, attempt to fill some of these crucial gaps – and as a result to sharpen the debate about investment and concomitant incentives – is made in the following paragraphs.

We begin with the (realistic) assumption that the reform-case scenario of the World Bank's 1987 *Strategy for Sustained Growth* offers an attainable future target. Under this scenario, MVA growth is expected to increase by 4.3% a year in the three years to 1990 and by 4.8% a year in the following four years to 1995. The question[109] is what would be the investment requirements for such a growth path.

On the basis of the best available estimates of the capital stock of the manufacturing sector, and assuming the projection forward of recent capital/output ratios[110], manufacturing investment would have to average a minimum of Z$584 m. a year (at current prices) in the period 1988–90, compared with an annual average of Z$185 m. (also at current prices) in the first half of the 1980s. In fixed (1982) price terms, to achieve the assumed growth targets, annual investment in manufacturing would need to rise by 65% in real terms in 1988–90 compared with 1980–84.

Although these figures undoubtedly represent a substantial rise in manufacturing investment over recent levels achieved, they are low in historical terms. A 4.3% annual growth rate of MVA from mid-1987 to 1990 would only require an expansion of the whole manufacturing sector of 2.8% a year *over and above the previous peaks reached*[111]. Over one-third of the required growth would be obtained from expanding output with current plant and equipment and moving back to rates of capacity utilisation previously achieved. For 5 out of the 11 manufacturing sub-sectors (responsible for 40% of all manufacturing output), the previous peaks in output would not have been reached by 1990 (assuming an annual increase in output of 4.3%) and for an additional 2 sub-sectors, growth rates lower than 4.3% would be sufficient[112]. For these 7 sub-sectors, therefore, the only investment required to sustain output expansion would be replacement investment. Indeed, in aggregate, to achieve an annual rate of growth of 4.3% to 1990, 49% of all required investment would be replacement[113].

Future investment requirements would change dramatically, however, if an annual growth rate of 4.8% is to be sustained in the subsequent period, 1991–5. *Real* investment levels would need to be 61% higher than those required for 1988–90 and a massive 166% higher than those achieved in the period 1980–84[114]. In this instance, only 35% of total investment would represent replacement requirements, and a full 65% would be required in the form of new investment.

An important and related policy issue concerns the amount of foreign exchange needed to purchase the investment goods required to achieve this projected output expansion. Using recent data[115], the foreign-exchange requirements for manufacturing investment each year from 1988 to 1990 would amount to Z$294 m. at current prices, some 16% of the *total* 1987 import bill and some 75% higher in real (Z$) terms than the foreign-exchange allocated annually in the period 1980–84. In the early 1990s, these foreign-exchange requirements would rise dramatically: in real terms, 72% higher than in 1988–90, an over three and a half times higher than in 1980–84[116].

In practice, the foreign-exchange requirements for manufacturing investment in both these periods would almost certainly be even higher than these figures[117]. This is because the current policy of progressive currency depreciation is likely to be retained. The implication is clear: if the manufacturing sector is to return to its historically high growth path, increasing quantities of foreign exchange will be required to sustain that expansion.

The attractiveness of planned investment growth.   The preceding discussion is based upon two assumptions: first, that capital/output ratios would remain the same in the future, and, second, that the projected expansion of the manufacturing sector would be uniform across the different sub-sectors. There are, however, no good reasons for believing that either assumption is correct. In particular, active policy intervention can be pursued to encourage changes in the capital/output ratio – a ratio which has been extremely volatile over the past 20 years in Zimbabwe[118] – and, most importantly, to induce the relatively greater expansion of some manufacturing sub-sectors than others. If this policy path is chosen some dramatic changes to the constraints inhibiting manufacturing growth would be likely to result.

The most effective tool available in Zimbabwe to alter the pattern of relative investment is the foreign-exchange allocation system. By allocating more foreign exchange to some sub-sectors than others, not only could the pattern of future manufacturing expansion be planned but it would be possible to make a *more* efficient use of scarce investment and foreign-exchange resources than would be likely if the control system is abandoned. Moreover, the objectives of restructuring future manufacturing expansion more directly in line with the government's other economic objectives would be achieved with greater certainty than under laissez-faire alternatives.

To illustrate the substantial effects of (and, in general, gains from) directing investment expansion into particular industrial sub-sectors, projections of a manufacturing expansion have been made which provide for the more rapid growth of some sub-sectors, but which produce the *same* aggregate growth rates for the sector as a whole as those in the World Bank's policy reform case – 4.3% annual growth in 1988–90 and 4.8% in 1991–5. More rapid annual growth (of 6%) in the simpler consumption-oriented sub-sectors (1–6) is assumed, and lower rates (of 2%) in the more complex, heavier sub-sectors (7–11).

Some of the more important results of this alternative scenario can be briefly summarised. In the period 1988–95 the same target growth rate for the manufacturing sector is achieved with only a 28% increase in real levels of investment over the levels of the 1980–84 period, compared with the 65% increase in the World Bank's policy reform case: in the alternative scenario case, annual investment levels would be 37% lower, in real terms, than in the policy reform case. In addition, as the illustrative alternative does not require such high levels of new investment as the policy reform case, the proportion of replacement to total investment is higher (59% as against 49%) while the foreign-exchange requirements are also considerably reduced – only 15% higher than those used in 1980–84 and 27% lower in real terms than in the World Bank's policy reform case[119]. The thrust of this latter outcome is of extreme importance to future planning. But there is more. Because sub-sectors 1–6 utilise less foreign exchange for raw material inputs than do sub-sectors 7–11, the alternative scenario also saves on non-investment foreign-exchange use. The illustrative example suggests that in the whole period up to 1995, for every Z$100 in foreign exchange used for raw material imports to manufacturing in the policy reform case, only Z$70 is needed for the alternative case, an additional foreign-exchange saving of 30%[120].

Moving on to the period 1991–5, in the illustrative alternative both lower levels of investment and lower amounts of foreign-exchange needed to purchase capital equipment abroad are required than in the policy reform case – even though, in this period, the differences between the two are not as dramatic as in 1988–90. The illustrative projections show that total annual investment (to achieve the same aggregate growth rates) would be 13% lower than in the policy reform case and that 14% less foreign-exchange would be required each year.[121]

The one major drawback to the illustrative alternative lies in the field of employment creation. In the whole period 1988–95, the gain in manufacturing employment in the World Bank's policy reform case is judged to be 58,000; in the alternative scenario it is 53,300, a shortfall of 8.8%. This adverse consequence needs to be weighed against a number of factors, however. First, because the alternative scenario utilises far fewer resources and, in particular, far less foreign exchange, the likelihood of its success must be higher than the policy reform case, which is more dependent upon optimistic export assumptions. Second, the employment effects of a particular growth path are themselves determined, in part at least, by interventionist policies designed to alter the capital/labour mix in the production process. Thus it can by no means be assumed that eight years hence a less capital-intensive investment path will not have been followed. Third, the foreign exchange 'freed' under the alternative scenario could be used in projects with additional employment-generating capability which, at minimum, would reduce the employment gap of the two growth-paths and might well lead to greater overall employment generation under the illustrative alternative.

Whatever the merits of the data and detailed assumptions upon which it is based, the alternative approach highlights a number of key policy issues for the future of the manufacturing sector. First, it explicitly addresses the problem of foreign-exchange shortages and indicates the quite considerable range of options open to policy-makers through careful interventionist policies which, it needs to be stressed, could well result in the *same* (and possibly higher) aggregate growth rates being achieved as in the policy reform case. Second, as the alternative approach provides for a more rapid expansion of sub-sectors 1–6, it is biased in favour of consumption-oriented (and simpler) expansion of the sector. This has direct relevance to the issue of domestic demand, for such a growth path would be more consistent (than a 'balanced' expansion path) with the broader macroeconomic strategy of income redistribution, as emphasised, for example, in the Robinson proposals (outlined above) but also as articulated by the government. Third, such a structural re-orientation is also consistent with the manner in which industrial expansion has already been occurring during the 1980s, assisted in this period by active government intervention.

These last two points need to be expanded further. Robinson proposes that policies be adopted which alter the inherited pattern of income distribution. There is evidence to suggest, however, that these policies are already being implemented and with some considerable success. Real incomes of peasant farmers have been rising, minimum wages have almost kept up with rising living costs while, in marked contrast, there has been significant erosion of the purchasing power of middle- and higher-income earners. A few figures illustrate these trends. The income generated by the sales of marketed agricultural produce from the populous rural areas has risen in real terms by 36% from Independence to the mid-1980s, leading to a rise in demand for less sophisticated manufactured goods[122]. A superficial analysis of wage trends would appear to suggest little change in the composition of domestic demand. For instance, the rise in minimum wages since Independence has just failed to keep pace with the rise in prices, and average (non-agricultural) formal sector wages at the end of 1986 were no higher than they were in 1980[123].

When, however, stagnation in average and minimum wages is taken in conjunction with the dramatic fall in disposable incomes for middle- and high-income earners, the proportionate shift in favour of lower-income groups is striking, as the following data illustrate. To achieve 1980 levels of consumption at the end of 1987, a married man with two children on an annual income of Z$840 in mid-1980 would have needed pre-tax earnings of Z$2,234 a year in 1987, a rise of 165%[124]. In contrast, a married man with two children with pre-tax earnings of Z$5,300 in 1980 would have needed pre-tax earnings of Z$20,500 to purchase the same goods seven years later, a rise of 287%. And even more dramatically, a married man with two children with a disposable income of Z$10,000 in 1980 would have needed pre-tax earnings of Z$47,000 in 1987, a rise of 343%, to achieve a comparable spending pattern. But as real earnings remained *stagnant* over this period and medium to high level salaries failed to keep up even with inflation, nothing like this rise in pre-tax earnings took place, indicating a substantial fall in disposable income[125].

Finally, although the data are by no means conclusive, the volume index of production from 1980 to mid-1987 suggests that faster expansion of the more basic consumer-based industries – foodstuffs, clothing and textiles – occurred at the expense of those sub-sectors geared either to more luxury consumption or to non-consumption production – drink and tobacco, metals, transport and furniture [126].

The precise choice of interventionist investment strategy clearly lies with the government. There is a wide range of alternatives open to it as suggested by the data in Table 10.22, which show the considerable variations within the different sub-sectors of labour and capital intensity and of use of foreign exchange for production and investment purposes. For example, if maximising output with lowest capital input is to be given highest priority, then the clothing industry should be expanded most rapidly, an option which also implies a relatively low foreign-exchange input for investment but a relatively higher one for raw

Table 10.22 *Employment, foreign exchange and capital usage indicators by manufacturing sub-sector based upon 1982/4 data*

s u b s e c t o r	Net output per Z$1000 capital employed	Number of jobs per Z$1m. of capital employed	Replacement		New Investment		
			Replacement investment required Z$m. 1984 @ 1982 prices	Foreign exchange cost of replacement investment @ 1982 prices Z$m.	Annual average new investment required for WB's PCR growth rates, '82 prices [a]	Foreign exchange costs of @ '82 prices	Imported raw materials needed for every Z$1000 of total raw materials purchased
	A	B	C	D	E	F	G
1	346	46	21.2	7.8	39.3	24.7	24
2	400	39	12.5	4.6	7.5	4.7	240
3	296	57	12.2	4.5	36.7	23.1	230
4	928	182	4.2	1.6	5.2	3.3	390
5	587	154	3.8	1.4	1.1	0.7	140
6	444	50	7.0	2.6	12.9	8.1	240
7	314	26	18.8	7.0	32.1	20.2	520
8	233	32	8.9	3.3	23.5	14.8	160
9	239	35	45.0	6.7	66.8	42.0	410
10	424	61	2.9	1.1	0	0	600
11	613	111	1.1	0.4	0	0	253
Total	332	47	137.7	0.9	225.1	141.8	253

Source: *Census of Production*, various years and UNIDO (1986b), especially chapters 3 and 12.

Note: [a] Assuming in this instance that the expected growth rates for manufacturing as a whole − 4.3 % a year to 1990 and 4.8 % a year to 1995 - are applied to each sub-sector.

material inputs. If job creation is to be the principal determinant of policy, then the expansion of the clothing industry would also be favoured.

In some instances, clear conflicts would arise between different government objectives. For instance, the low level of imported raw materials required by the food industry would suggest that a foreign-exchange constrained future should favour the expansion of this sub-sector; yet Table 10.22 indicates that the foreign-exchange requirement for capital expansion of this particular sub-sector is amongst the highest of all the sub-sectors. The important general point is that the government can work towards achieving an 'optimal' growth path by intervening to guide the relative pace of expansion of different sub-sectors, giving appropriate weight to maximising aggregate growth and employment creation within the overall context of the availability of foreign exchange[127].

Policies to enhance future investment.   The preceding discussion has indicated the potential benefits that could be reaped if Zimbabwe maintains a general policy of interventionism to guide the course and pattern of future manufacturing investment as against the uncertainties of the laissez-faire alternative. It would be incorrect, however, to equate support for such an approach with whole-hearted endorsement of all current interventionist policies. A series of changes in approach and execution would be required to achieve sustained expansion of the sector.

Perhaps the most important initial point to make is that the proposed *planned* interventionist approach can only succeed to the extent that active planning *does* take place. There has in practice been little since Independence[128]. Indeed it may well be - and there is no particular light that economic theory can throw on this question - that manufacturing *could* be worse-off under an unplanned interventionist regime than one run under more laissez-faire principles.

Thus the first pre-requisite is for the government, preferably in co-operation with representatives of manufacturing industry, to agree, at least in broad terms, on the achievable pace and changing 'shape' of industrial expansion in the short and medium term. The following should be given high priority: aggregate possible growth rates, differential growth rates of particular industries and industrial sub-sectors in relation to demand and supply and the subsequent ordering of priorities in foreign-exchange allocation, and the order in which major investments requiring substantial amounts of foreign exchange should be made.

Thereafter, it would be necessary for the government to allocate sufficient foreign exchange to manufacturing to enable it to achieve the targeted growth rates (in aggregate and by sub-sector)[129]. As, however, it is simply not possible to predict available amounts accurately (and in general because there are bound to be shortages in the foreseeable future), planners (and industrialists) will be faced with uncertainty over the precise level of foreign-exchange which will be available, one two, five or ten years hence. Clearly uncertainty over allocations cannot be eliminated entirely for an economy whose imports (quite correctly) need to be related to the ability to earn foreign exchange. It is possible, however, to find a middle way between the present system of almost complete uncertainty[130] and one based on the complete elimination of foreign-exchange allocations[131].

In rough outline, the present method of foreign-exchange allocation could be adapted as follows. While retaining a six-monthly cycle of allocation, the system would be extended to provide recipients with, initially, a broad band range (high and low) of the foreign exchange they would receive over the next two years, to be revised and up-dated on a rolling basis as each six-month period passed[132]. As far as possible the foreign exchange provided by foreign aid donors, most particularly from commodity aid programmes, would be incorporated into the forward planning process, with donors being encouraged to inform the Zimbabwean authorities of their aid commitments at minimum for the coming two years[133]. As at present, allocations would be divided up into four elements – raw materials (domestic and export), spares and capital investment – but two minor adaptations could be made. First, a larger emergency fund for all but new capital investment projects could be established and, second, greater emphasis than at present could be given to a publicly-known hierarchy of priorities. In this context, foreign-exchange allocations should be made first for inputs into the productive process, next for spares and replacements and finally for new investment.

There is one additional factor. Potential investors who require foreign-sourced raw materials to manufacture products in Zimbabwe are extremely reluctant to invest their funds in the country only to join the normal allocation system and be subject to such uncertainty on this key variable as to make it impossible to make reliable cost and profit projections. While this problem is addressed in part by the proposal to provide a minimum two-year high/low allocation band, it would probably still be insufficient to attract foreign investors. It is therefore proposed that for new foreign investors a high/low band of foreign-exchange allocation be provided (after relevant discussion and negotiation) for a minimum *five-year period* and, in this particular instance, that the government guarantees that the lower limit should not be breached[134].

Returning to the investment question more explicitly, providing foreign exchange for replacement and new capital investment is, of course, only one element in the fundamental objective of raising investment levels. It is also necessary for changes to be made in the current incentive system so that profit levels can rise to enable more than a minority of entrepreneurs in the private sector to be in a position to decide to commit funds. At the same time public sector managers should be provided with the necessary funds for investment.

The central policy mechanism for achieving the necessary changes is the all-pervasive price-control system, for there is little doubt that at present it is a major cause of low investment levels in the manufacturing sector. The crucial question, however, is the way it should be changed. The view of the IMF, the World Bank (sometimes with limited qualifications) and most industrialists is that the whole system should be abandoned as quickly as possible[135]. The main argument against such a course of action is that the dominant forms of manufacturing production in Zimbabwe are monopolistic and oligopolistic and not those of perfect, or even imperfect, competition; over 80% of all manufactured products are made by only a few producers and just over half by single manufacturers[136]. Even orthodox economic theory advocates controls to prevent 'super-profits' in such circumstances. Once it is accepted that the World Bank's preferred course of action of opening Zimbabwean industry to foreign competition should not be followed, then the question is how should price control be administered in an attempt both to provide incentives for investment and to protect consumers from excess profiteering?

There are three major problems with the current operation of the system: it is subject to inordinately long delays; in many cases of specifically controlled products the price granted is lower than that required to encourage investment; and, in those instances where prices are determined by a formula (the most common category of price control), the formula used is based on a historic cost-plus formula which increasingly fails to address the crucial problem of excess profits[137].

Possible solutions lie along the following lines. First, the basis needs to change to rate of return on investment, the exact level of which needs to be agreed by government and industrialists. Second, major areas of production where some semblance of 'competition' exists should be removed completely from price-control legislation. These would include, for instance, the clothing industry, parts of the furniture and paper industry and many parts of the engineering industry. Third, price awards should, in general, be granted automatically and not be subject to the present delay-prone system[138]. Finally, specific retail price control (based on the newly-proposed formula) should still be maintained for a very small number of key products dominant in the purchases of low-income groups, such as sugar, meat and cement, and produced by one or only a few manufacturers[139].

Streamlining the foreign-exchange and price-control systems are two major proposals which would receive quite a welcome from a government sympathetic to the need to boost incentives in order to achieve higher levels of investment[140]. Additional action, however, would be necessary. Thus, clarification is needed in relation both to the direct investment intentions of the government in manufacturing and, more generally, to the respective roles of the private and public sectors in the sector's evolution. In particular, answers are required to the following questions: which areas of manufacturing, if any, will be the subject of government involvement in the next five years and will that involvement be in the form of direct production or joint ventures etc? Which areas will be left open to private initiative in the next five years and which areas will be open to external as against Zimbabwean private capital interests? In addition, the government and industrial representatives need to agree on the areas where new private foreign investment is required and will be welcomed.

INCREASING THE COMPETITIVENESS OF THE SECTOR
There is a particular criticism of the present (and adapted) system of macro-interventionism, voiced especially by laissez-faire critics, which needs to be addressed explicitly. It is that the overall interventionist system is not only highly protectionist but also, as a result, perpetuates high-cost (inefficient) industrialisation, particularly since it fails to expose industries to international competition.

Two specific effects are said to result. First, domestic purchasers of consumer and intermediate goods are forced to pay higher prices for 'buying Zimbabwean' than they would in a less controlled economy where the option to buy cheaper imports existed. Second, because the system does not contain incentives sufficient to reduce production costs and increase efficiency, uncompetitive high-cost manufacturing enterprises are able to survive almost indefinitely, thereby accentuating distortions in the economy resulting in lower levels of economic growth.

The macro-evidence (discussed above) indicates not only that a substantial amount of Zimbabwean manufacturing *is* internationally competitive but that increased efficiency, for instance in relation to labour productivity and foreign-exchange usage, has been an important characteristic of the long-term development of the sector. Importantly, too, the micro-level evidence reveals the quite dramatic – if, apparently, unintentional – effect that the price control-induced profits squeeze has had on increasing productive efficiency over a very short period of time. Furthermore, the related expansion of non-traditional manu-factured exports in the post-1983 period (although not leading to a significant rise in the export/output ratio) does suggest that criticisms about the rigidities of the present incentive system may be seriously misplaced. At minimum, therefore, while the interventionist system has certainly not established a sector-wide internationally competitive manufacturing sector, the record is commendable: the system has been far from totally inflexible in its practical application and it has produced an industrial performance among the best in sub-Saharan Africa – from either interventionist or more market-oriented structures. What is more, not even the advocates of a more laissez-faire approach for the future have argued that Zimbabwean industry would have advanced and evolved to its current state and diversity in the context of a more open policy regime. Recent international evidence would tend to support the view that Zimbabwe's policies towards industry have prepared the ground well for future dynamic growth[141].

There is, however, substance in the argument that the system allows (and even with the adaptations proposed would continue to allow) uncompetitive firms to survive (and thrive) behind the system of protection which has operated at least since the UDI period.

Furthermore, and importantly, if the improvements in the operation of the price-control system proposed above were to be implemented, one of the major policy instruments that appears to have stimulated greater factor efficiencies and cost-savings recently would be severely blunted. Finally, it does not necessarily follow that because a particular incentive structure appears to have served the manufacturing sector reasonably well in the past it will remain useful or adequate in the future. These factors (together with the conclusions from the previous discussion) suggest that there is enough wrong with the present system for specific changes to be made.

In practice, future policy options would appear to lie between two extremes which, for the purposes of this discussion, can be labelled Choice A and Choice B. Choice A would consist of Zimbabwe abandoning its system of foreign-exchange control and allocation and allowing domestic purchasers the freedom to choose between domestic or imported goods, with the proviso (in the short term) that a system of differential tariffs be established or maintained as long as they are lowered over a relatively short space of time. Choice B would consist not of abandoning the present system but of adapting it in a way which maintains its advantages (such as its ability to guide the direction of manufacturing and industrial sub-sectors) while addressing current rigidities and disadvantages. Judging which option is preferable would involve analysing what the most likely effects would be of pursuing each of the alternatives. While, as discussed below, it is far from easy to do this because of a lack of knowledge of key variables, the nature of our ignorance and the importance of harmonising a wide range of policy objectives point in the direction of smooth adaptation of the present system rather than radical abandonment of it: in other words, change in the context of Choice B rather than Choice A.

The *only certain* thing one can say about the effects of the radical change in macro-policy associated with Choice A is that *a priori* one simply does not know what the consequences will be. Yet answers to a range of highly complex and extremely important questions need to be provided. For instance, will such a change lead to both a boost in investor confidence and the access to foreign exchange required for investment levels to rise significantly? How many firms will be forced to close down, what will happen to their work-forces and what will happen to their plant and equipment[142]? Will those firms which are internationally competitive necessarily wish to expand production and/or diversify? What will happen to prices and the pattern of domestic demand and the pattern and level of manufactured exports? What effect will the likely structural changes have on industrial inter-linkages? Are the transport, services and energy sectors capable of responding to perhaps major changes in domestic output and international trading patterns that could result from implementing such policies? Even without acknowledging the considerable successes of Zimbabwean industrialisation achieved in the context of widespread interventionism, it would still seem odd to embark on a policy where the answers to such critical questions cannot be found or accurately assessed.

Uncertainty would also appear to be the outcome of following the Choice B route. This is because the way in which the system should be adapted cannot at present be ascertained in detail for the reason that there is not enough known either about the precise nature of high-cost industrialisation or of the detailed costs and benefits of attempting to lower costs and increase efficiency. Whereas, however, the adherents of Choice A would advocate radical changes in macro-policy prior to the collection and analysis of these data, the Choice B option advocates the process of collection and analysis prior to any such measures being implemented.

The procedure for following through the Choice B option involves gathering a range of data as the basis for deciding the precise policy changes required. It is proposed, more specifically, that a comprehensive analysis of all manufacturing units in the country be carried out, with the active support of all industrialists, to ascertain initially the answers to the following questions: what is the difference between the domestic selling price of products made in Zimbabwe and the landed cost of imported substitutes, and, if domestic prices are higher, what are the causes of the higher domestic costs? Another question is whether, and if so to what degree, quality differences or other factors which override or alter the effects of price differences[143] are likely to affect the choice of purchasers in favour of domestic over foreign products. Finally, are these price differentials due to particular circumstances that may well be temporary in nature?[144]

Equipped with this information, two further tasks would need to be carried out. The first would be to examine if in particular industries some firms are internationally competitive while others are not, and to try to find out the reasons for such discrepancies[145]. The second would be to identify those industries where all, or the vast majority of, firms are internationally competitive and those where all or the vast majority are not.

What policy implications would follow the analysis of such information? There is clearly no need to change the incentive structure or policy environment for those firms or, if they exist, whole industries, which sell products at internationally competitive rates, for which higher domestic prices are assessed to be a temporary phenomenon, or where domestic consumers are nevertheless willing to continue purchasing products at prices higher than imported 'alternatives'. For the remainder, what should be done to address the distortions found?

Three different options present themselves: do nothing, close down the inefficient firms and import the products they manufacture, or initiate policies to enhance competitiveness. The range of possible causes of inefficiency suggest a variety of different policies to enhance efficiency. These could be at the firm level, at the level of a particular sub-sector or at the level of the manufacturing sector as a whole. At the firm or sub-sectoral level, direct interventionist policies could well be the most appropriate form of action to take; at the sector level it could be that alterations of the incentive structure to attempt to increase productive efficiency and lower unit costs of production (so as to reduce 'super-profit' accumulation) would be more appropriate[146].

There are a number of ways in which the current interventionist system could be altered to attempt to make it more efficient. One approach would be to make greater use of the foreign-exchange allocation system by allowing, and even encouraging, more efficient producers to take over allocations from less efficient producers where they can show that they can produce the products more cheaply[147]. It is not unlikely that such a policy would induce larger private firms to take over smaller ones.

It has already been proposed that an exercise should be undertaken to ascertain the tariff level required by industrialists to prevent the import of *any* product which is currently manufactured in Zimbabwe. There could, in addition, be advantages in implementing a policy which progressively reduced external tariffs for particular high-cost industries, in conjunction with allowing consumers to purchase alternative imports, if all the proposed alternatives discussed above had failed to make a significant impact on the inefficiency of those particular firms and/or industries. In cases where tariffs need to be exceptionally high (over 100%) to prevent imports, where attempts to address identified causes of inefficiency have failed, where detailed industry-level analysis has not been able to isolate particular causes of productive inefficiency that could be resolved by other tangible policies of intervention[148], and where the government has analysed the complex dynamic effects, and is willing to risk the consequences of plant closures, then there would be a case for drawing up a time-frame for the reduction of tariffs and the gradual and industry-specific choice of purchasing lower-priced imports in preference to the high-priced domestic manufactures. It should be noted, however, that the most likely outcome of implementing such a policy would be plant-closures rather than raising levels of efficiency[149].

It is not necessary to provide additional specific examples to summarise the general discussion. What it is important to highlight is that within the interventionist (Choice B) approach a range of policy choices is open to pinpoint the inefficiencies which exist in manufacturing industry and to attempt to resolve them. Not only are there three general options open to policy-makers in the case of firms and industries identified as inefficient – close them down, do nothing or attempt to increase their efficiency – but where (as would almost certainly be the initial response) the choice is made to attempt to increase efficiency, an array of different potential solutions would present themselves in different instances and over different time periods.

In the case of Choice A, however, this rich selection of policy choices would not be available. As a result, not only would it not be possible to guide and plan the future course and direction of manufacturing growth (or even to be sure whether the sector would grow) but the option of intervening to attempt to resolve the problem of inefficiencies through striving to increase competitiveness would also have been removed.

EXPANDING MANUFACTURED EXPORTS

The growth of manufactured exports should at minimum be large enough to raise again the sector's export/output ratio, reversing the downward trend which has prevailed since the early 1960s. Such an expansion is likely to become even more urgent in the next decade than it was in the previous one, both because the prospects for alternative agricultural and mineral-based exports are so poor[150] and because the manufacturing sector's own rising demand for foreign exchange would have to be met if expansion of the sector is to be sustained[151]. Two interrelated questions therefore need to be addressed: how best should the expansion of manufactured exports be promoted and how should the policy environment be altered to achieve the desired objectives?

There is no doubt that the imaginative package of export incentives introduced especially since 1983 has made a significant impact on the numbers of industrialists engaged in exporting, in the range of non-traditional products now exported and in the earnings of such exports. In broad terms, the package addressed three major problems inhibiting export expansion. It provided: access to foreign exchange needed to purchase imported inputs required for exports; encouragement, information and finance for export promotion (private and public sector) including the identification of and introduction to new export markets; and, finally, an exchange-rate policy of currency depreciation which, together with tax incentives, increased significantly the Zimbabwe dollar earnings of exporters[152].

Important though these interventionist policies have been, a number of problems still remained. One was that Zimbabwe's nearer and potentially most attractive international PTA and SADCC markets still provided the sector with only limited opportunities for expansion given their own foreign-exchange shortages. Related to this, various constraints were inhibiting expansion to the larger markets, especially in Europe and North America. These included higher transport and insurance costs, exacerbated by South African destabilisation policies, the small scale of many of the firms engaged in non-traditional export production, and the inadequacy of a considerable proportion of the plant and equipment to supply these non-African markets with high quality products packaged to their requirements.

Price considerations have constituted another range of constraints. One factor has been the dumping of competitive products by other countries on to third markets and the far greater incentives many of Zimbabwe's competitors have offered to their exporters. But perhaps the most important price issue relates to the fact that most manufacturers have been able to achieve higher returns from selling on the domestic market than on the export market; in extreme cases some firms have only been able to export on the back of domestic prices well in excess of potential imports.

Short-term 'solutions' to this problem have involved the squeezing of domestic margins through the price-control system, and expanded allocations of foreign exchange for exports in contrast to shrinking domestic market allocations. In addition, the November 1987 package of further export incentives allowed those firms which expanded their export levels over 1985/6 levels to use a bonus allocation of foreign exchange to purchase imported raw materials for production for the domestic market – a policy which, while it might well have raised the absolute level of exports, also reinforces the tendency to make use of higher domestic prices to support a firm's export drive[153]. Taken in isolation, these initiatives, are highly unlikely to lead rapidly to a significant expansion of manufactured exports. In particular, for many firms one of the effects of squeezing domestic profits has been a serious contraction of investment – unsustainable in the longer term – while the artifical separation of foreign exchange allocations into export and domestic market groupings has been open to rising levels of abuse as manufacturers have switched an increasing part of their production to the more lucrative domestic market, sourced with allocations meant for the export market.

Clearly if the problem of price differentials is to be adequately addressed, the only durable solution lies in making domestic industry more competitive so that adequate returns can be earned from exporting[154]. A number of proposals can be made in addition to those above. First, to the extent that interventionist policies succeed in increasing competitiveness, differences between domestic and export prices should continue to narrow. Second, as raising efficiency would be likely to lead to the establishment of larger rather than smaller manufacturing units, a greater proportion of total output should originate from firms requiring a permanent export market to achieve overall viability, thus resulting in the sector as a whole becoming increasingly internationally competitive. Third, as the projected and sizeable investment programme gets under way, in the context (hopefully) of a far more bullish climate than has prevailed over the recent past, both replacement and new plant and equipment would increasingly be purchased in the light of the establishment or creation of export competitiveness[155]. As a result, recent policy initiatives and those proposed here should go some considerable way towards changing the structure of manufacturing in the direction of the desired objectives.

To the extent, however, that this process of structural change does not occur *fast enough*, it may be necessary to examine additional short-term interventionist policies to complement those already in existence. For instance, particular care should be paid to the effects of easing the stringent price control system (proposed above) so as to ensure that higher returns on the domestic market lead, in practice, to higher investment levels and not to a reinforcement of the traditional domestic orientation of the bulk of the manufacturing sector. In this regard, consideration should be given either to raising the level of taxation of dividends and distributed profits or to providing more lucrative investment incentives.

In addition, it may be necessary over the short term to provide one more time-bound export incentive which further encourages manufacturers to re-orient their production to the export market. Specifically, the idea should be examined of providing manufacturers who have increased their exports from a base-date with a portion of their foreign-exchange bonus in a form which they are able to use as they wish and not, as at present, in relation to purchases tied to yet further increases in production[156]. Interviews with manufacturers indicate strongly that this particular measure would provide a major incentive to export. The longer-run impact of such a policy change would be to reinforce the desired export-orientation of the sector, while the foreign exchange 'loss' – through the likely purchase of imported luxuries or payment for foreign holidays – would only account for 1 or 2% of the *increase* in foreign exchange earnings – a small price to pay. Finally, there is always the option of altering the current package of incentives.

One objection (from the international institutions) to this whole interventionist approach is that it is messy, cumbersome to administer, uncertain in its outcome and far too complex in relation to the alternative of abandoning controls, opening up the manufacturing sector to international competition and stimulating export expansion initially through a substantial (20–40%) devaluation of the Zimbabwean dollar followed by progressive and real annual depreciations of the currency. There are, however, a number of reasons why this latter approach would, in practice, be far less attractive than its advocates maintain.

One relates to the issue of uncertainty. The laissez-faire approach places major emphasis on current (static) international price differentials as the principal motor for export expansion. Zimbabwean evidence, however, confirms that factors other than price play a major part in determining export levels: long-term planning, quality factors and the acquisition of appropriate plant and technology, sometimes at variance with short-term comparative advantage indicators, can be crucial in building up an export business. In addition, as the World Bank has recently stressed, by taking the 'opening up' route, Zimbabwe would leave itself far more vulnerable to dumping and other trade practices by its trading partners, not least by South Africa. That this is far from an academic threat is confirmed by the unexpected 15 to 60% hike in duties and import surcharges announced by South Africa in August 1988 (*The Financial Gazette*, 19 August 1988) as well as specific action taken against particular Zimbabwean companies, such as the restrictions placed on South African imports of Monarch Products in late 1987[157].

As for the argument that a substantial one-off devaluation would lead to a major initial boost to exports, followed by a steady expansion assisted by continuous real depreciation of the currency, again there is little evidence to support this optimistic conclusion. Indeed, as already noted, the World Bank acknowledges that as a result of such a change it is 'very difficult to predict which manufacturing sub-sectors will enjoy rapid growth' (1987a: 70). As *rapid* growth of manufacturing and, implicitly, rapid export growth would require substantial amounts of foreign exchange for investment, there would clearly be a considerable lag between foreign exchange absorption and any dramatic rise in manufactured exports. It is thus doubtful if the substantial increase in foreign exchange resulting from the proposed devaluation/depreciation could be sustained without increasing foreign borrowing, a consequence which would only add to the risks of pursuing such a policy without any better guarantee of success than for the changes in the current export incentive system proposed here.

A final and related concern about the implications of 'opening up' the economy is that the removal of current controls would reduce significantly[158] the protective barriers which continue to provide a major incentive to further import substitution. Reducing the import bill has, of course, a similar beneficial impact on the overall foreign-exchange position to expanding exports – indeed a greater impact if, as has usually occurred, the import-substituted product has also been exported[159]. It should therefore be seen in conjunction with efforts to expand manufactured exports.

In conclusion, the overall argument here has not been that the necessary expansion of manufactured exports will be easy to achieve. Rather, it is that substantial progress can be made to achieve the desired goals by continuing to adapt the present system of export promotion, in conjunction with the other major policy proposals aimed at enhancing the incentive system and prudent management of the exchange rate.

Conclusions

The story of industrialisation in Zimbabwe is undoubtedly one of success. Among the main achievements are the following: widespread and sustained expansion; deepening of the industrial structure with the development of substantial inter-linkages within manufacturing and with other sectors of the economy; and the evolution of a manufacturing sector much of which appears to be internationally competitive. It is also apparent, however, that the successes achieved up to the present provide little guarantee that they can be repeated over the next half century – indeed over the next 10 years – unless changes take place and, *inter alia*, the policy environment is altered to address the substantial problems now facing the sector.

Since Independence, the performance of the sector has been characterised by a much greater and more enduring volatility than during any other six-to-seven-year period since the Second World War. On the supply side, shortages of foreign exchange for intermediate inputs and spare parts and for capital expansion present an ever-increasing constraint not only by severely restricting future expansion even in the short to medium term but, as a result of inhibiting maintenance and replacement investment, by eroding the very foundations of the country's manufacturing base. There is no doubt, too, that the inward-looking nature of the sector has accelerated since the mid-1970s and that as a result its contribution to national foreign-exchange saving and earning has deteriorated. There is nothing intrinsically wrong in the fact that manufacturing is an increasing user of foreign exchange; what is disturbing in the Zimbabwean case is that this has been occurring after a prolonged period of industrialisation and at a time when the capacity of the primary exporting sectors to earn more foreign exchange has itself been constrained.

Thus although Zimbabwe's manufacturing sector is both strong and diversified, the time has now past when it can be readily assumed that these strengths will automatically be maintained. It is the conclusion of this chapter that Zimbabwe's manufacturing industry *can* advance again on a path of secular expansion, but this can *only* occur if changes are made at the macro-level and if policies targeted directly at the sector are altered. Without such changes, the pessimistic predictions of stagnation and secular decline are likely to be confirmed.

It should be added, however, that even if policy changes to enhance manufacturing expansion are made, it is highly unlikely that over the next ten years the sector will prove to be the saviour which rescues the country from its serious economic and particularly foreign exchange problems – a role which increasing numbers of people, politicians and others, believe it might play. Steady expansion can be achieved but it is difficult to see how annual growth rates in excess of 5% can be *sustained* even if external influences prove more beneficial than appeared likely towards the end of the 1980s. Foreign exchange shortages are almost certain to remain a major constraint well into the 1990s, while *no* feasible strategy for the next five to ten years will be able to solve the country's major and growing unemployment problem.

To argue that changes are necessary, however, is by no means to concede that any one particular type of change should be advocated. A conclusion of the preceding discussion is that neither the type of policies outlined in the National Development Plan nor those being propounded by the World Bank are likely to achieve the targets set or to provide the basis for sustained expansion of the manufacturing sector over the next decade. Part of the reason for this is that these plans and proposals are based on a high level of ignorance, while the crude data that are available indicate both that key variables (upon which these projections are based) appear to be changing and that forecasting future performance remains a very inexact science. As Zimbabwe's statistics are among the most comprehensive in Africa, there are probably lessons here for other countries of the continent.

In spite of the gaps (and in part because of them), analyses of past performance and of alternative approaches for achieving the government's objectives for manufacturing, placing a high value on risk reduction, all point to the need to adopt a strategy rooted in the adaptation of the present system of interventionism rather than its abandonment. It is important, however, to make a clear distinction between an interventionist strategy *based* on the present system and the continuation of that system. If sustained manufacturing growth (even if not at very high levels) is to occur, it will only be in the context of agreed objectives at the sectoral and sub-sectoral level, and if some substantial changes in policies are implemented. Thus, the prevailing incentive structure *has* to be altered or else investment levels simply will not rise, no matter what the exhortations of government, and non-traditional exports will not expand at the pace necessary to begin to address the growing shortages of foreign exchange.

As for the laissez-faire alternative, the discussion has indicated that there are such serious problems with this approach that it offers even less hope for sustained growth while, at the same time, exposing the economy to extreme risk. Finally, however, and paradoxically, if the current interventionist system were to be maintained *unadapted and unchanged*, the growth rate of Zimbabwe's manufacturing sector over the next decade could well be lower than if the laissez-faire approach were to be followed.

Notes

1. For a fuller discussion of these issues see Riddell (1988a).
2. The Rhodesian Iron and Steel Commission was established in 1942.
3. For some discussion of the origins see Arrighi (1967), Irvine (1959), Barber (1961). More recent and comprehensive work is currently being done by Ian Phimister at the University of Cape Town. See, for example, Phimister (1987).
4. Strictly speaking, it was the manufacturing sector of 'Southern Rhodesia', for under international convention the country was not known as Zimbabwe until Independence in April 1980. Those living in the country after the Unilateral Declaration of Independence in 1965 called the country 'Rhodesia' until they again changed the name in 1979 to 'Zimbabwe Rhodesia'. For simplicity's sake the country will be referred to here as 'Zimbabwe' throughout.
5. Given the poor quality, or not infrequently the non-existence, of the national statistics of many African countries, these can be only rough comparisons; yet they would tend to underplay the contrasts between most SSA countries today and Zimbabwe of the late 1930s. Zimbabwean figures are estimated from Barber (1961: 98–115, 198–202); Irvine (1959: 324) and CSO (1955: 6); SSA statistics from the following sources: for the MVA/GDP ratio, UNIDO (1986a: Table 2), trade data from World Bank (1987a: 222–3) and employment data from ILO (1984: 255–65).
6. The value of the Zimbabwe dollar is determined with reference to a trade-weighted basket of 14 currencies; the weights are adjusted periodically. Recent trends are as follows for Z$1:

	£ sterling	US$	South African Rand
1980	0.664	1.586	1.183
1981	0.730	1.394	1.334
1982	0.671	1.088	1.167
1983	0.622	0.904	1.102
1984	0.571	0.666	1.316
1985	0.423	0.609	1.578
1986	0.405	0.596	1.314
1987	0.367	0.602	1.229
1988	0.311	0.555	1.254
1989 (May)		0.481	

7. It is far from easy to decide which products to include within the broad 'manufacturing' group and which, for example, to group within 'agriculture' and 'mining'. As can be seen from these different export figures, to classify cotton lint and ferro-alloys as manufactured products almost doubles the figure of total exports. A good discussion of these sorts of problems is contained in UNIDO (1986b: 47–57). This chapter follows the practice of the Central Statistical Office, Harare, and considers as 'manufacturing' all enterprises incorporated into the annual census of production. In broad terms this means that cotton lint and ferro-alloy production and exports *are* included in the definition of manufacturing but that the processing/manufacturing of other metals (such as tin, copper and nickel) are excluded from both the production and trade data for the manufacturing sector.
8. Throughout this chapter, both gross and net output *exclude* sales of goods not produced on the premises. Value added is defined as net output *less* payments for services.
9. As referred to in Note 7 above, data used in these calculations include ferro-alloys and iron and steel but exclude the production, export or import substitution of processed metals.
   The equation used was:

$$0 = \frac{0_1 \times \Delta DD}{(0+M)_1} + \frac{0_1 \times \Delta X}{(0+M)_1} + \left\{ \frac{0_2}{(0+M)_2} - \frac{0_i}{(0+M)_1} \right\} \times (0+M)_2$$

where O = Gross Output, DD = Domestic Demand, X = Exports, M = Imports.

The figures were calculated net of sales tax. Published international trade statistics are given as fob/for. For the purposes of the current analysis this was acceptable for exports but not for imports. Thus import data had to be changed to include the cost of freight and insurance (i.e. to be imports cif). IMF trade statistics use an arbitrary 15% increase to convert imports from fob to cif. This crude estimation was rejected because of the substantial variation in freight and insurance costs for imports coming from southern Africa (largely from South Africa) and those obtained from overseas. Unpublished data provided by the Central Statistical Office, Harare, showed that over 1984 and 1985 the cif value of imports from southern Africa averaged 10% a year more than their fob value, whereas the cif value of imports from overseas was 3% higher than their respective fob values. As the direction of fob imports for 1952/3, 1964/5, 1980/1 and 1982/3 could be found from published fob trade data, these increased cif amounts were added proportionately to the trade data reclassified into the 11 industrial sub-sectors. This gave a weighted increase of between 23 and 25% for all manufactured imports for these years. For the UDI years, estimates of trade direction were made based on the known direction of trade statistics for 1964/5 and 1980/1.

In Zimbabwe tariff levels have historically been typically low for manufactured imports because of the importance of Commonwealth preferences and the special trade agreement with South Africa (see Jansen, 1983 and Cole, 1968). Customs duties for most raw material inputs range from zero to only 5% of the cif value; at Independence Jansen estimated that weighted average customs duties and taxes on imports were less than 5%. With the inclusion of the 20% import surtax, the 1986 Commission of Inquiry into Taxation calculated that the average total tariff for all imported goods averaged only 21.1%, including an effective rate of over 60% for fuel, itself responsible for over 60% of the total; the average for machinery was 9.2% and for other intermediates 10.5%, again including the 20% surtax charge. (See Chelliah, 1986: 96–8.)

Estimates of the sources of growth for 1982 and 1983 were made with and without the inclusion of tariffs. As the overall resulting data did not vary by more than 1% from the data calculated without the inclusion of tariffs on imports (and because estimating cif imports *inclusive* of tariffs would have taken many weeks to complete) the current calculations do *not* incorporate the increases in imports due to tariffs. Hence, the overall data would tend (marginally) to under-estimate the importance of import substitution in decomposing the different elements of growth.

10. The figures contained here and those produced by the World Bank for 1965–79 in its Industrial Sector study of Zimbabwe (1987a: 12) differ quite markedly, except for sub-sectors 4 and 6. As the Bank provides no details of how its figures were derived it is not possible to compare the methodologies used.

11. As can be seen from the graph, positive export growth and domestic demand growth in excess of 100% are achieved because of the negative effect of import-substitution change.

12. Supported, if only marginally, in the contrast between the Federal and UDI periods when, respectively, the change in domestic demand rose from 36 to 60% of the total and the change in export growth fell from 10 to 9%.

13. I am grateful to Rob Davies for bringing this point to my attention. Davies illustrates his point by taking the hypothetical example of Zimbabwe establishing a tractor factory which leads to a halving of the number of tractors imported. Using the Chenery methodology this would show up as import substitution only in year one but surely, he argues, the tractors produced in year two should also be counted as import substitution. In other words, the import-substitution effects should be cumulatively assessed, although there would be a greater component of value judgment in the attempt to address this anomaly adequately.

14. For instance in July 1987, African Distillers announced plans to install new plant and technology with the objective of replacing all imported brandy with a locally manufactured product, at a saving over Z$0.5 m. Other recent major import-substitution projects include the Z$4 m. chemical plant of Hoechst Zimbabwe which in 1988 will have saved Z$1.5 m. in imports (*The Financial Gazette*, 20 November 1987 and 12 February 1988.) These initiatives are far from exceptional; it is rare for an announcement of similar initiatives not to appear in the Zimbabwe press at least every month.

15. Strictly speaking it is not 'all', for the trend is reversed for sub-sector 11. However, this grouping contains both a rag-bag of industries and, additionally, a grouping whose separate industries have changed significantly over the period.

16. While this tends to fly in the face of a good deal of the theory of the industrialisation process in Third World countries, in seeking an explanation for such a phenomenon one would also need to look into the respective price/profitability incentives in the two periods.

17. For foodstuffs (1), the differences were in fact only marginal. However, the contrast even for foodstuffs was greater in comparison with the other sub-sectors when the relative drop in export growth was very marked.

18. Cotton production was negligible in 1952/3 and was valued at less than Z$1 m. in 1964/5; by the end of UDI, however, production had risen to Z$70 m. Cotton lint exports were non-existent in 1952/3 and 1964/5 but had risen to Z$43 m. by 1978/9. For their part, ferro-alloy exports were valued at a mere Z$48,000 in 1953, rising to a still small Z$3.4 m. in 1964/5 and to a substantial Z$40 m. by the end of the UDI period (when, it should be added, difficulties of exporting during sanctions had led to stockpiling).

19. The growth and evolution of the capital goods sector has been researched and developed by Dr Dan Ndlela formerly of the University of Zimbabwe. See for example Ndlela (1985).

20. The structure of exports changed quite dramatically during the early part of the UDI period, especially during the first few years. Thus the straight line trend shown in Figures 10.5 and 10.6 does conceal some fluctuations especially in the three or four years immediately following UDI.

21. As gross output data for iron and steel, ferro-chrome and cotton lint production are not separately available, it is not possible to provide data of the export to gross output ratio excluding these products.

22. Hence rising manufactured imports over time would be a positive not a negative indicator of development.

23. Sub-sectors 1, 2, 3, 4, 5 and 8 are classified as the simpler, more consumer products while sub-sectors 6, 7, 9 and 10 are grouped as the more intermediate and capital goods sub-sectors.

24. Such a figure would be extremely difficult to compute for it would have to be based not only on the value of direct imports from different sources but also on the estimated foreign-exchange component of domestically produced goods, including – if it were to be accurate – the discounted foreign-exchange components of the capital equipment used in the manufacturing process, and of the energy utilised.

25. A comprehensive input/output matrix was constructed for 1964 and 1965 data by the Central Statistical Office in Harare. This was extrapolated forward to 1975 by Zimbabweans working at UNCTAD prior to Independence to provide a crude 10-year comparison. Currently the CSO are processing input/output data for 1981 but to date no large matrix has been published. Some of these data, referring particularly to transactions *within* the manufacturing sector, were used in the UNIDO (1986b) study.

26. The figures by sub-sector were as follows (UNIDO, 1986b: 70): (1)–2.4% imported; (2)–24%; (3)–23%; (4)–39%; (5)–14%; (6)–24%; (7)–52%; (8)–16%; (9)–41%; (10)–60%; 11–25%. The complex linkages existing between the industrial subsectors and between manufacturing and the other sectors of the economy are discussed most completely in UNIDO, 1986b, especially in Chapter 4 and Annexes A to F, pages 355 to 404.

27. The 1982 data were produced by a US team of consultants and graduate students under the leadership of a private independent consultant, Dr Doris Jansen.

28. Especially if one concurs with the widely-held view that because the 1982 calculations almost certainly use a substantially overvalued exchange rate (at least 15% too high) and because they fail to use shadow prices, they significantly underscore the degree of competitiveness. See Riddell (1983), Stoneman (1985), World Bank (1987a: 66).

29. Regrettably the available data do not permit one to test the hypothesis that Zimbabwe's manufacturing sector would have been even *more* competitive internationally in the absence of these inward-oriented policies.

30. This includes cotton lint, ferro-chrome and steel exports but excludes all other processed metal products. These figures were derived from published Statement of External Trade data and information provided by the Central Statistical Office.

31. That is, including steel and ferrochrome exports; if ferrochrome exports are excluded the proportion rises to 40%. For the 1980 data see Riddell (1981a).

32. The apparent dichotomy shown in the DRC indicators of a relatively high level of international competitiveness and the lower level indicated by these plant adequacy figures can, in part, be explained by the bias of DRC data. DRC data are an indicator of international competitiveness comparing domestic with *border* prices and because Zimbabwe's borders are located far from the coast, the respective DRC figures do not reveal industrial/sub-sectoral competitiveness in overseas markets which would have to take into account the double disadvantages of the land-locked geographical location.

33. I am grateful to Ian Phimister for these latter points which are covered more fully in his 1988 book entitled 'An Economic and Social History of Zimbabwe 1890–1948' (Longman).

34. From 1966 to the late 1970s, the ruling Rhodesian Front party never lost a single seat in the series of elections and by-elections that took place among the white electorate.

35. The effects were not all adverse; the war did lead to an increase in demand for war-related manufactures. In particular, demand for mine-proof vehicles was created while demand for uniforms and food for the military also expanded rapidly.

36. Figures are from the Confederation of Zimbabwe Industries Economics Research department.

37. It should be noted, however, that in the post-Independence period, price controls have become more all-embracing and many applications for price rises have been subject to long delays. In some

instances this has led to an erosion in profit levels, although work by the World Bank in 1988 and 1989 suggests that profit levels have remained high. ·

38. For recent sector-wide surveys of agricultural implement manufactures see CZI (1986) and Mazhar and Ndlela (1987).

39. Zimplow's *Annual Reports* (various), Tinto Industries' *Annual Report* 1983 and *The Financial Gazette* (supplement), 31 October 1986. Bulawayo Steel Products does not publish separate results in Zimbabwe; it is owned by the British firm Amalgamated Metal.

40. At least initially, the severe drought and related drop in domestic demand would, of course, have been an influence on short-term sales.

41. Bulawayo Steel Products as long ago as 1952.

42. The main imported input is sheet steel; however, in early 1988 it was expected that Tube and Pipe Industries would soon be rolling this product, reducing even further the import dependence of manufacturing – yet another example of contemporary import substitution.

43. Some forges and presses are made in Zimbabwe, for example by All Metal Founders, Hytech and D. Hadfield. I am grateful to Colin Stoneman for this point.

44. Standard Chartered Bank's corporate profitability index jumped from a value of 50 in 1978 to almost 200 in the year 1981, when the price control legislation was tightened.

45. For instance, in 1982, a 39% price increase was requested following a 25% rise in domestic steel prices (accounting for 80% of direct input costs) and an 18% increase was given after over six months delay. Similarly in 1985, a 20% price increase was granted following a 46% price rise application and this rise was only given at the end of the planting season when the annual purchase of agricultural implements had taken place.

46. Although partly related to the drought years, Zimplow suffered an after-tax loss of Z$22,000 in 1983, no profits were recorded in 1984 and for 1985 and 1986 an average after-tax profit rate 40% lower than that achieved in the period 1980–3 (and at *current* prices).

47. Zimplow reported a post-tax profit of Z$124,000 (2% of turnover), while Bulawayo Steel Products' profit level was about half that amount.

48. One needs to be especially wary of extending too far the argument either that because foreign exchange for capital investment has been at a low level for a decade or more or because machinery and equipment is sold it therefore needs replacing and replacing with *new* equipment. For instance, Bulawayo Steel Products maintains that even though most of its capital equipment is old it remains adequate to requirements for both domestic and export production; and of that which needs to be replaced there exists quite adequate second-hand equipment on the market. As for the argument from age, Bulawayo Steel Products are still using an 1897 press which is well maintained, quite adequate and certainly does not need replacing. Similarly, both Lemco and the country's largest tannery in Bulawayo have machines that are pre-World War I and neither company would wish to to see them replaced.

49. In the year ended September 1986 total turnover of Hunyani was Z$68.8 m., up from Z$39.8 m. in 1982, with after-tax profits of Z$6.9 m. in 1986 and Z$2.3 m. in 1982.

50. The numbers are 4,331 firms in the 1981–5 period compared with 4,002 in the period 1975–9. (*Quarterly Digest of Statistics, December 1986*, Table 26.1, p. 85.)

51. UNIDO estimates that, for foodstuffs, directly imported inputs constituted 2.4% of the total, compared to a sector-wide average of 25.3%. The next least-dependent sector was sub-sector 5, at some 14% (UNIDO, 1986b: 70).

52. In 1938/9, total food exports may have accounted for over 40% of total gross output but they only amounted to less than Z$500,000 m. (at current prices), with gross output valued at less than Z$1 m.

53. South Africa's action was partly in response to lobbying by South African companies and partly because Namibian factories were only working at 50% capacity. It was far easier, politically, for the South African authorities to concede to these pressures after rather than before Zimbabwe became independent.

54. Lemco changed its name from Liebigs shortly after Independence. Even more recently, it has been taken over by Unilever.

55. A new managing director took over after 1986 and the points raised here in no way reflect on his approach to the company; indeed, he appears to be fully aware of its export potential and is directly involved in pursuing this.

56. In this section, use is made of the CSO model and also data from UNCTAD (1980) and UNIDO (1986b) in the attempt to highlight, even if crudely, the changes in linkages over time.

57. For some reason, the available 1981/2 input/output data do not show the value of tobacco products used in the manufacture of tobacco see UNIDO (1986b: 136). The figure of Z$21 m. therefore underestimates the agro-industrial linkage for this sub-sector. Data provided by the tobacco industry suggest that this was valued at about Z$25 m. in 1981/2.

58. Information supplied by the meat canning industry.

59. These proportions are derived from the averages of the 1965 and 1975 input/output data – no reliable data are available for the post-1975 period.

60. Prior to Independence, the small-scale and communal areas were responsible for less than 10%

of marketed maize sales but by 1986 they accounted for over 40%, increasing total tonnage from less than 40,000 to well over 700,000 in the six-year period (averaged out to allow for drought years).

61. In its Industrial Sector Study, the World Bank erroneously states that 'Zimbabwe's fertilizer firms can meet most of the country's present fertilizer needs' (World Bank (1987a): 101).
62. Figures from World Bank (1987b, Volume I: 6 and 13).
63. The following tables of index values of imports and exports by different foreign currencies reveal the substantial differences between trade values in different currencies.

A. Index of the value of Zimbabwean imports, 1976 = 100.

	Zim $	SDR	US $	UK £	FRG Mk	SA Rnd
1977	101	93	97	86	86	98
1978	105	86	96	81	74	97
1979	143	116	131	100	96	131
1980	211	188	207	148	173	185
1981	266	288	229	205	218	266
1982	283	201	190	201	192	246
1983	277	171	155	180	180	227
1984	314	154	129	188	173	307
1985	378	151	143	166	147	446
1986	429	150	159	185	129	420
1987	455	139	170			
1988	559	154	192			

B. Index of the value of Zimbabwean exports, 1976 = 100.

	Zim $	SDR	US $	UK £	FRG Mk	SA Rnd
1977	97	89	93	82	82	94
1978	108	88	99	83	77	83
1979	124	100	114	87	83	114
1980	152	135	149	106	125	134
1981	170	146	146	131	139	170
1982	156	111	104	111	106	136
1983	198	123	111	129	129	162
1984	245	120	100	147	135	240
1985	298	119	113	131	116	352
1986	328	115	121	141	98	321
1987	365	112	138			

Note: Export data are for domestic exports, that is excluding gold sales.

Source: CSO, *Quarterly Digest of Statistics*, September 1987, Reserve Bank of Zimbabwe, *Quarterly Economic and Statistical Review*, Vol. 9, No. 3, September 1988 and Hawkins (1989).

64. Total official aid disbursements to Zimbabwe from all sources are estimated by the OECD's Development Assistance Committee to have been as follows:

Year	Total oda disbursements from DAC, OPEC and multilateral sources:	
	In current $m.	In fixed (1985) $m.
1980	170.4	
1981	212.3	
1982	215.8	213
1983	208.3	206
1984	297.5	301
1985	237.1	237
1986	224.8	183
1987	295.0	232

Source: OECD, *Development Cooperation 1987 and 1988 Reports*, Paris, OECD, 1988.

65. Preliminary data for the 1986 balance of payments show that the net outflow of profits and dividends had risen to Z$97.6 m.

    While it should be pointed out that the restrictions on remittance outflows imposed after Independence have applied only to pre-Independence investments and not to new foreign investment, there is little doubt that any policy of restricting dividend and profit outflow will concern potential new foreign investors and therefore provide a disincentive to foreign investment inflows. For a discussion of this and related issues see Riddell (1987b).

66. Until the change, importers were given licences for the fob/for value of imports; the foreign exchange (and local) costs of procuring the imports were automatically provided by the exchange authorities on production of the requisite papers. Given the acute foreign exchange shortages the system led to importers purchasing goods from the least fob/for source, even if it was on the other side of the world as the foreign exchange costs of shipping the goods would be paid for by the authorities with the importer only liable for the domestic price equivalent of these costs.

67. In April 1989, the government launched its new foreign investment guidelines (GOZ, 1989).

68. For an expansion of these points see Page and Riddell (1988).

69. For instance, a recent NRZ annual report recorded total outstanding loans as of mid-1986 at Z$441 m. of which Z$221 m. were foreign. Over 85% of these loans had been acquired after 1980. National Railways of Zimbabwe, *Thirty Seventh Annual Report 1987*, Bulawayo, December 1988, pp. 29–30.

70. In his July 1988 budget speech, Finance Minister Bernard Chidzero gave notice of his intention to introduce legislation limiting the amount of money the government will guarantee or borrow on behalf of its agencies.

71. The figures for the main parastatals have been as follows:

Parastatal	Accumulated Deficit, Z$ m. FYs 1980/1–87/8
Agricultural Marketing Authority[a]	1,584
National Railways of Zimbabwe	607
Air Zimbabwe Corporation	358
National Oil Corporation of Zimbabwe	161
Zimbabwe Steel Corporation	500
Post and Telecommunications Corporation	207
Zimbabwe Broadcasting Corporation	107
Electricity Supply commission	474
Zimbabwe Mining Development Corporation	200

Source: World Bank (1987b, Volume II: Annex III, p. 5).

Note: [a] Includes the Cold Storage Commission, the Dairy Marketing Board, the Grain Marketing Board and the Cotton Marketing Board.

72. In fact the aggregate deficit has been even higher than the trends in the recording of annual profits and losses because in some instances past losses have not been supported by the government. For example, in 1986, NRZ had an annual shortfall of Z$92 m., but because of a shortfall in previous years' payments its accumulated shortfall was over 30% higher at Z$123 m. For Air Zimbabwe in 1985/6 a current deficit of Z$23.2 m. contrasted with a cumulative uncovered deficit amounting to another Z$49.5 m.

73. In the first quarter of 1987/8, the central government budget deficit of Z$62.3 m. was financed by Z$46 m. foreign and Z$16.3 m. domestic resources (Reserve Bank of Zimbabwe, June 1987: 5).

74. Such a proposal was made in the 1982 World Bank initiated report by Dr Doris Jansen but the suggestion has subsequently been rejected by the government and by recent World Bank reports on the Zimbabwe economy.

75. In mid-1988, the total costs of rehabilitating ZISCO were put at Z$1 bn over a five to nine year period (see *The Financial Gazette*, 24 June 1988).

76. It should not be inferred from this statement that I am implying that the re-vamping of ZISCO should not take place.

77. There is going to be a far greater increase in the number of job-seekers in the next five years than in the past five years as in the latter period many potential job-seekers were absorbed in the rapidly expanded education system. For instance, between 1980 and 1986 total school enrolments rose by a staggering 113%, with secondary school places rising by over *600%* (*Quarterly Digest of Statistics, September 1987*, p. 5).

78. This has been particularly noticeable in Bulawayo.

79. This point has been reinforced with the appointment of Dr T. Masaya as the Deputy Minister of the reorganised and increasingly influential Ministry of Finance, Economic Planning and Development. In his academic studies, Dr Masaya has been one of the leading advocates of incorporating what he believes are predictable rainfall cycles into the planning process.

80. 1987 trade figures show that total exports to and imports from South Africa were valued at Z$548 m., 15% of total trade compared with total trade with the United Kingdom of Z$445 m. (12%) and with the Federal Republic of Germany of Z$346 m. (9%) respectively (C.S.O. *Stats-Flash, June 1988*).

81. The likelihood of this was a point point made by Mr Joshua Nkomo at the last meeting of ZAPU which dissolved the party following the agreement to amalgamate with President Mugabe's ZANU (PF) party.

82. Understood as the weighted average of the 14 currencies in the current basket.

83. The report continued: 'However, given the critical need for Zimbabwe to increase exports, there is a case for continuing the current practice of a gradual real effective depreciation of the exchange rate with the objective of gradually improving export competitiveness.'

84. The export expansion argument could apply with equal force to a currency which was already under-valued.

85. The effects of the export incentives from 1980 to 1985 and hence prior to the more recently introduced incentives, including the tax-free bonus, were as follows:

Year	Nominal Exchange Rate Z$/$	Effective Rate after allowing for export subsidy	Percentage Difference
1980	.643	.665	3.4
1981	.689	.689	0.0
1982	.757	.788	4.1
1983	1.011	1.078	6.6
1984	1.244	1.341	7.8
1985	1.612	1.738	7.8

Source: World Bank (1987a: 45).

86. For instance, sub-sectoral growth rates for the 11 manufacturing sub-sectors were contained in the Transitional Development Plan.

87. Not without importance, too, are the inconsistencies found in relation to these key aggregate numbers produced by the World Bank. For instance, in its November 1987 report p. 58 it states that in its reform case scenario the annual rate of increase of MVA in the years 1991–5 will be 4.8%; however, on p. 65 it states that this figure is 5%.

88. The first draft of which was written in 1984.

89. And hence at least in terms of recent years coinciding with the findings of the Kadhani and Green analysis (1985: 213).

90. See above and Robinson (1987), especially Table 4.15.

91. It is by no means easy to work out the relationship between manufacturing output and the imported inputs used in the production process. No accurate data are kept by the authorities and thus judgements have had to be made in deriving these figures.

The method used for the current exercise was as follows. For the years 1971–9, accurate data on imports obtained by manufacturers via Industrial Import Control were used, including those allocated as spares but excluding those under the heading 'replacement machinery'. To these figures was added a nominal 30% to incorporate allocations through Commercial Import Control but destined for the manufacturing sector. (This figure was based on discussions with senior officials from both Import Controls.) After Independence new facilities for obtaining imports were opened up, such as barter, commodity aid programmes and new and expanded export revolving fund facilities. Estimates of these flows have been made by the CZI, on the basis partly of government statistics and partly of fairly accurate surveys of manufacturers for the years 1981–3, again using particular assumptions about the (decreasing) quantities of imported material obtained via Commercial Import Control. The CZI data were used and checked against aggregate data from recent IMF reports. In this manner time-series data for the period 1971–86 of direct and indirect (non-investment-related) imports used by the manufacturing sector were drawn up.

It is, however, one thing to estimate the Z$ value of imports used by the sector and quite another to assess the currency's foreign purchasing power. To address this problem two steps were taken. First, the Z$ values of imports were changed into SDRs and Rands. Then each of these sets of figures was adjusted to allow for changes in export prices. For the SDR values, these were deflated by the International Financial Statistic Export Unit Value Index for industrial countries, and for the Rand by the 'Price, Home Goods Index', also published in the IFS statistics. Finally, these two sets of figures were divided into the index of manufacturing production for the respective years. The data from which the graph lines in Figure 10.18 are derived are as follows:

Year	Imp. inputs curr. pr. Z$ mn[a]	Imp. inputs curr. pr. SDR mn	Imp. inputs curr. pr. Rand mn	Export Unit Value Index Indst. cntrs 1989 = 100[b]	Home Goods pr. Index S. Af	Import to Z. manu-facturing SDRs	Import to Z. manu-facturing Rand	Index of Manu-facturing Output '80 = 100[c]	Ratio index of output over imported inputs SDRs	Ratio index of output over imported inputs Rand
71	94.6	130	156	32.2	34.2	380.2	484.5	72.6	19.1	15
72	97.7	138	162	37.5	34.4	368	470.9	81.4	22.1	17.3
73	112.3	154	190	45.3	39.1	339.9	486	87.4	25.7	18
74	168	250	296	56.4	45.6	443.3	649.1	93.8	21.2	14.4
75	119	163	159	62.8	52.8	259.5	301.1	91.6	35.3	30.4
76	128	178	171	62.6	60.9	284.3	280.8	86	30.2	30.6
77	129.9	165	169	67.7	69.4	243.7	243.5	81.2	33.3	33.3
78	116.3	132	144	76.3	76.3	173	188.7	79.2	45.8	42
79	185.9	209	231	88.1	87	237.2	265.5	87.2	36.8	32.8
80	274.6	341	325	100	100	341	325	100	29.3	30.8
81	330.2	396	442	96.2	115.2	411.6	383.7	109.4	26.6	28.5
82	250.9	247	293	92.8	132.2	266.2	221.6	108.7	40.8	49.5
83	237.1	205	261	89.7	148.8	228.2	175.4	105.8	46.3	60.3
84	321	218	422	87.5	165.7	249.1	254.7	100.7	40.4	39.5
85	394	220	621	87.2	179.5	252.3	345.9	112.2	44.4	32.4
86	462	225	607	99.3	213	226.5	284	115.4	50.9	40.5

[a] Author's estimates, based on official data.
[b] From IFS *Yearbook 1986*, and Vol. XLI, No. 1, January 1988.
[c] From CSO, *Quarterly Digest of Statistics*, September 1987.

92. For an assessment of OECD growth rates in the early 1990s by differing international agencies see Page (1988: 5).
93. For a more detailed discussions of the weaknesses of the National Development Plan see Robinson (1987).
94. It was released in May 1989.
95. This particular thrust is in broad terms similar to that advocated by Hawkins, the Professorial Head of the Department of Business Studies at the University of Zimbabwe. His proposals will not therefore be considered here separately except to say that in the broad context of liberalisation he additionally argues for some sort of two-tier exchange rate mechanism, not dissimilar to the South African system.
96. It adds 'over a limited number of years' (World Bank, 1987b, Vol. I: xx).
97. The Industrial Sector Memorandum maintains that it would be better 'to abolish price controls for industrial goods altogether' (1987a: 78).
98. It is true that the 1987 document does give a figure of 6% annual growth in domestic demand for the products of ZISCO steel but no explanation for this rate of growth is provided.
99. 'Reform of the foreign exchange allocation system is the key issue for medium-term structural change . . . It would have varying effects on different activities. In combination with exchange rate movement, the beneficiaries would be exporters, the bulk of agriculture, mining and much of manufacturing, including labor and natural resource-based activities, such as agro-processing, textiles, garments, ferrochrome, iron and steel and light engineering. The average impact on manufacturing would probably be neutral, but those parts of the sector that have enjoyed high levels of protection, such as consumer durables and automobile assembly, would suffer' (1987, Volume I: 38).
100. This is clearly a vast subject which cannot be fully debated here. For those who are interested in pursuing the issue further see 'the theory of the market' in Riddell (1987a: 161–175).
101. An example would be that of manufacturing and trading company, Surgimed, which began operating in 1982 and by 1988 was expected to have a turnover of some Z$5.6 m. The company applied for and received an allocation of foreign exchange which now far exceeds that received by long established companies and, it should be reiterated, this occurred at a time of sizeable reductions in allocations to both industrial and commercial firms.
102. Through destabilisation or transport disruptions.
103. This is not meant to imply that the NDP is better able to address the issue of unemployment, as the figures given above should indicate. As Robinson argues, 'the Plan is not destined to redress to any significant extent the existing structure of poverty and inequality in the country' (1987: 63).

104. *Trade and Financing Strategies For the New Nics: The Zimbabwe Case Study*, ODI Working Paper No. 23, July 1987.

105. On the question of rescheduling debt, Minister Chidzero has commented thus (*Southern African Economist*, April/May 1988):

> Rescheduling is not very easy for a country like Zimbabwe not only . . (because of) the bunching up of repayments over the next two to three years but also because certain of our policies would have to be addressed immediately in any rescheduling procedures in the Paris Club.

106. It could be assumed that the fall in domestic demand for the more sophisticated range of manufactured goods produced in the country would induce companies producing those products to attempt to export them. However, Robinson does not address this particular issue.

107. A start had been made, at least on the first issue, with the publication in May 1989 of the new investment regulations and the Investment Register.

108. Two exceptions are the chapter (12) on investment in the 1986 UNIDO report, the data from which are reproduced in the appendices of the World Bank's 1987 Industrial Sector Memorandum, and estimates from 1988/9 CZI survey work of replacement and new investment needs.

109. Not addressed in the document cited.

110. Capital stock figures from the early 1960s to 1982 were estimated in UNIDO, 1986b. For the purposes of the present exercise these have been updated to 1984.

111. Assuming the current (1980) weighting structure (see *Quarterly Digest of Statistics* September 1987, p. 46) is projected forward throughout this period.

112. The details of the trends in the volume index of manufacturing are as follows:

Sub-sector	mid-1987 index	1990 index @ 4.3% overall growth	Previous peaks reached	Projected 1990 indices in relation to previous peaks[a]	Annual increase in MVA in 1990 above previous peak
1	126.6	146.6	126.9	126.9	4.3
2	78.8	91.3	100.0	91.3	zero
3	200.5	232.2	200.5	200.5	4.3
4	108.2	125.3	128.4	125.3	zero
5	77.0	89.2	103.4	89.2	zero
6	113.4	131.3	113.4	113.4	4.3
7	115.0	133.2	121.8	121.8	3.3
8	141.4	163.8	141.4	141.4	4.3
9	98.6	114.2	104.8	104.8	2.7
10	84.0	97.3	178.4	97.8	zero
11	43.5	50.4	100.0	50.4	zero
Total	113.9	131.9[b]		119.8	2.8

Source: *Quarterly Digest of Statistics*, September 1987 and World Bank (1987,I).

Notes: [a] This column was calculated as follows: if the projected 1990 figure for MVA exceeded the previous peak then the previous peak was selected; if, however, the 1990 projected figure was lower then the projected number was selected.
[b] Using the weighting structure published in the *Quarterly Digest of Statistics*.

113. These, and subsequent, figures are based on the assumption of a 3% annual replacement cost of installed plant and equipment and a 10 year straight line replacement assumption for vehicles. See UNIDO (1986b: 339–40).

114. *In 1982 prices*, the annual investment requirements would be as follows, compared with the actual rates in the 1980–84 period:

> 1980–84   Z$169 m. a year   (achieved)
> 1988–90   Z$279 m. a year   (required to achieve annual increase of 4.3 % in MVA.)
> 1990–95   Z$450 m. a year   (required to achieve annual increase of 4.8 % in MVA.)

115. From a survey conducted by the Confederation of Zimbabwe Industries for the years 1983 to 1985, see Riddell and Nziyaludzu (1983).

116. The Riddell and Nsiyaludzu figures suggested that the foreign-exchange requirement of replacement investment was 37% and was 63% of the value of new investment. As we have seen, 49% of investment required in the period 1988–90 would be for replacement, falling to 35% in 1991–5.

117. In addition, as noted by Mike Humphrey, the scenarios outlined here assume no more complex inter-linkages than occurred in the past evolution of the manufacturing sector.

118. See UNIDO (1986b: 334). In this context it is also important to recall the discussion above, which indicated that manufacturing has become an increasingly efficient user of foreign exchange.

119. Z$89 m. annual average in 1980–84, Z$103 m. in 1988–90 under the alternative scenario compared with Z$140 m. under the policy reform scenario. The differences between the two growth paths by sub-sector are shown in detail in the table below.

Sub-sector	Replacement investment required Z$ m. 1988–90 @'82 prices (annual average) (A)	Annual new investment needed for 4.3% growth 1988–90 @1982 prices[a] (B)	Foreign exchange costs of (A) & (B) '82 prices (C)	Replacement investment required Z$ m. 1984 @1982 prices[b] (annual average) (D)	Annual new investment needed for 4.3% growth 1988–90 @1982 prices[c] (E)	Foreign exchange costs of (D) and (E) '82 prices (F)
1	21.2	20.8	20.9	19.8	30.0	26.2
2	12.5	0	4.6	11.7	0	4.3
3	12.2	17.5	15.5	11.4	25.1	20.0
4	4.2	0	1.6	3.8	0	1.4
5	3.8	0	1.4	3.6	0	1.3
6	7.0	9.8	8.8	6.5	14.1	11.3
7	18.8	19.8	19.4	17.6	2.6	8.2
8	8.9	24.7	18.8	8.3	11.3	10.2
9	45.0	48.8	47.4	42.0	4.7	18.5
10	2.9	0	1.1	2.7	0	1.0
11	1.1	0	0.4	0.9	0	0.3
Total	137.7	141.4	139.9	128.3	88.1	102.7

Source: *Census of Production 1984/85*, UNIDO 1986b, chapters 3 and 12.

Notes: [a] Figures based on uniform sub-sectoral growth of 4.3% a year to 1990 and 4.8% a year thereafter to 1995.
[b] Replacement investment levels will be lower in the alternative scenario because lower levels of new investment will lead to a lower capital stock in need of replacing.
[c] Figures are based on annual growth rates of 6% a year for sub-sectors 1–6, and of 2% a year for sub-sectors 7–11.

120. Calculated on the basis of the sub-sectoral use of imported to domestic inputs of the UNIDO report (1986b: 70).

121. The sub-sectoral details are as follows:

Sub-sector	Replacement investment required Z$ m. 1991–5 @'82 prices (annual average) (A)	Annual new investment needed for 4.8% growth 1991–95 @1982 prices[a] (B)	Foreign exchange costs of (A) & (B) '82 prices (C)	Replacement investment required Z$ m. 1991–5 @1982 prices (annual average)[b] (D)	Annual new investment needed for 4.8% growth 1991–95 @1982 prices[c] (E)	Foreign exchange costs of (D) and (E) '82 prices (F)
1	25.5	52.3	42.4	23.3	67.8	51.3
2	15.1	12.7	13.6	13.8	22.6	19.3
3	14.7	50.2	37.1	13.5	65.1	46.0
4	5.0	8.9	8.3	4.5	11.5	8.9
5	4.6	1.9	2.9	4.2	4.2	2.9
6	8.4	15.1	12.6	7.7	19.6	15.2
7	22.7	40.8	34.1	20.7	14.2	16.6
8	10.8	22.8	18.4	9.8	7.9	8.6
9	54.1	79.4	70.0	49.5	27.7	35.8
10	3.5	0	1.3	3.2	0	1.2
11	1.1	0	0.4	1.1	0	0.4
Total	165.6	284.2	241.1	151.4	240.6	207.5

Source: *Census of Production 1984/85*, UNIDO 1986b, chapters 3 and 12.

Notes: [a] Figures based on uniform sub-sector growth of 4.8% a year to 1990 for each industrial sub-subsector and on the assumption that this growth pattern also occurred from mid-1987 to 1990.

[b] Replacement investment levels will be lower in the alternative scenario because lower levels of new investment will lead to a lower capital stock in need of replacing.

[c] Figures based on annual growth rates of 6% a year for sub-sectors 1–6 and of 2% a year for sub-sectors 7–11 and on the assumption that this growth pattern also occurred from mid-1987 to 1990.

122. The per capita value of produce sold from the communal areas to official marketing boards rose from an average of Z$7.3 to Z$9.9 a head, at 1980 prices. (Figures from the *Quarterly Digest of Statistics*, December 1987, Table 11.1 and the *Census of Population*.)

123. The details are as follows:

Year	Average non-agric. wages (Z$) current prices	Average Annual Wage at 1980 Prices				
		Using the CPI for higher income families	Index 1980 = 100	Using the CPI for lower-income families	Index 1980 = 100	Average Index 1980 = 100
1980	2,535	2,535	100	2,535	100	100
1981	2,926	2,587	102	2,553	101	101.5
1982	3,643	2,912	115	2,684	106	110.5
1983	4,753	2,435	96	2,375	94	95
1984	4,755	2,567	101	2,676	106	103.5
1985	5,518	2,614	103	2,477	98	100.5

Source: *Quarterly Digest of Statistics*, December 1987, and *Stats-Flash*, February 1988.

Note: [a] Fourth quarter data estimated on basis of 1984 and 1983 trends.

124. As in practice the minimum wage rose from Z$840 in 1980 to Z$2,172 in February 1988 the loss of spending power was only 2.8%.

125. Official statistics on medium and high level earnings are not produced. However, such analyses are carried out periodically by private consulting firms. A recent survey (published in January 1988) by PE Consulting Group, covering 120,000 employees, found that basic salaries in manufacturing increased by only 8.6% in the year under review and that in the period 1982–7 salaries lagged 76.9% behind the CPI, with executive salaries a further 2.5% behind the CPI. (*The Financial Gazette*, 22 January 1988.)

126. Drink and tobacco are influenced significantly by excise duties; formal sector furniture tends to be oriented more to middle and higher-income than to lower-income groups (which tend to purchase more from informal sector outlets). The changes in sub-sectoral production have also, of course, been influenced by government spending which, in relation to education and health especially, has also raised the demand for cheaper consumer products.

127. The data in Table 10.22 give only a fairly crude, first-level, indicator of choices which could be furthered by a longer-term and co-ordinated policy on allocating foreign exchange for both raw material and investment purposes. As highlighted in the UNIDO report, one of the characteristics of Zimbabwe's manufacturing industry is the degree of inter-linkage between sub-sectors. These complexities clearly need to be incorporated into a longer-term perspective on foreign-exchange allocation. However in this regard two points need to be made. First, as the illustrative alternative illustrated, the main policy point is not so much to control allocations down to the last nut and bolt, clearly an impossible task. Rather the point to emphasise is that in a situation, preferably, of growth in *all* sub-sectors, higher levels of growth can and, it is argued here, should be encouraged and stimulated. Second, such a system could quite easily be adapted from the present system of foreign-exchange allocation and could be dramatically effective in easing this major constraint on future growth.

128. For a discussion of this point see Ndlela in Mandaza (1986: 157–9).

129. A foreign-exchange allocation system is needed where there are foreign exchange shortages, and it is believed a man-made rationing system produces a more rational system than a market-based one in which access to scarce foreign exchange is likely to be determined in some (perhaps large) measure by factors other than enhancing the productive process. In the recent but now defunct Zambian auction system, for example, access to foreign exchange was in large part determined by the availability of local currency that bidding firms had rather than on the basis of the importance of the products they were able to produce with the foreign exchange acquired (see Chapter 9).

130. Allocations are provided on a six-monthly basis and the amounts are frequently not known until the quota period has begun for raw materials, spares and sometimes even for investment goods.

131. Under such a regime there would still be no guarantee that foreign exchange would be available to manufacturers to the level they require.

132. In time, and if planning capacity allows, the two-year period could be extended forward to three or four years.

133. Donors' differing practices in this regard are shown by the content of some recent agreements. In March 1988, Norway announced it would provide the private sector with about Z\$30 m. in commodity aid over the next four years. In contrast, Sweden announced that some Z\$2.8 m. would be available for the year 1988/9 as from 1 July 1988, with no announcement about future commodity aid programmes. In the same month, the French had still made no announcement about the quantity of commodity aid they would offer for the coming year while the British, whose Z\$6 m. commodity aid scheme was to end in March 1988, announced that they could not say whether the scheme would be renewed in the coming year although it was 'unlikely'. (See *The Financial Gazette*, 11, 18, 25 March 1988.)

134. The proposal of a two-year high/low band for domestic users of foreign exchange does not carry such strictures. As the government has granted special provision to new investors since Independence in relation to profit and dividend remittances, there is widespread recognition among the investment community that these sorts of guarantees are meaningful and are therefore likely to adhered to be in the future.

It could be argued that discriminating in favour of new foreign investors in this way would work to the disadvantage of current industrialists as the pool of foreign exchange available for them is thereby diminished. To this legitimate complaint a number of points can be made. First, as new foreign investors are only to take advantage of such a system after agreement between government and current industrialists that this new investment is necessary (and therefore at least indirectly to their advantage) and that they are incapable of providing the country with these particular products, the unique contribution of the new investor should receive some recognition. Secondly, as it is highly likely that such investment will save foreign exchange through import substitution and/or increase foreign-exchange earnings through high levels of export earnings, it is quite possible that the net pool of foreign exchange will increase or, minimally, that the relative fall will be reduced once production has started after year one. Finally, if the policy is so successful that it is making a major dent in regular foreign-exchange allocations the time will have come to revise the system and make it less attractive.

The proposal is, apparently, similar in nature to the ten-year fiscal freeze operating in francophone Africa for large investment projects. I am grateful to Igor Karmiloff for this observation.

135. A 1987 IMF report on discussions with the Zimbabwean authorities stated that IMF staff 'encouraged the Zimbabwean representatives to phase out price controls as soon as possible'. The World Bank's Industrial Sector paper advocates the abolition of 'price controls for industrial goods altogether' once the country becomes open to outside competition.

136. An analysis of the 1982 edition of the publication *Products of Zimbabwean Industries* gives the following product manufacture breakdown:

Number of manufacturers	Number of products manufactured	% of total
1	3,110	50.4
1 or 2	4,381	71.0
1, 2 or 3	4,979	80.7
1, 2, 3 or 4	5,325	86.3
1, 2, 3, 4 or 5	5,553	90.9
6 to 19	555	9.0
20 or more	49	0.8

Source: Government of Zimbabwe, *Products of Zimbabwean Industries 1982*, Harare, Ministry of Industry and Energy Development, 1983.

137. The formula, devised in some cases over 15 years ago, allows a certain percentage mark-up over and above factory costs. However, the definition of factory costs is unclear and no allowance is made for changes in productivity following the acquisition of more efficient plant and machinery, more skilled labour or more efficient management.

138. In many instances this has been likened to a paper-chase with documents passing slowly upwards through a series of different committees until it eventually reaches an over-worked Cabinet for review and final approval. Of course one of the (almost certainly) deliberate outcomes of long delays is to operate a *de facto* temporary price freeze for the products concerned. As these occur in part because some influential government officials and ministers are (quite rightly) sceptical of the cost-plus basis for price increases, this particular reason for delays should fall away with the introduction of the proposed new formula.

139. Although a radical step to take, there is probably enough 'competition' among bread and mealie

meal manufacturers to enable these products to be removed from price control legislation, providing that there is some surveillance over potential price-fixing arrangements. The present discussion does not, however, specifically address the question of the merits of general price controls at the retail level.

140. For instance, in his 1988 report on the Industrial Development Corporation (IDC), the Chairman – who is also the Permanent Secretary of the Ministry of Industry – called both for increased investment incentives and for a 'timely review' of price applications put forward by IDC companies.

141. Certainly recent international evidence supports the contention that where developing countries have successfully pursued export-led growth their governments first followed active interventionist policies, that significant export expansion has tended to follow long periods of import substitution, and that the net effect of manufacturing on the balance of payments has also been negative for almost all developing countries (including, as with the other points, South Korea) over the post-war period of industrialisation. See Chenery et al. (1986) and Singer (1988).

142. Especially in Zimbabwe where monopoly production is so prevalent and where much plant and equipment is old, it would be naive in the extreme to assume that capital resources are mobile and adaptable.

143. See Riddell 1987b, section 3.2, for the major importance of this issue in a number of cases indicating the unreliability of price as a determinant of purchasing intention.

144. In relation to this point, issues such as dumping by South African or other supply sources and the higher costs of raw materials caused by having to use longer transport routes or by massive recent hikes in electricity charges would be pertinent.

145. Explanations could range from different types and ages of plant and machinery, different quality of labour force, different management capability, different ability to adapt, repair and maintain machinery, to different work practices and different labour relations records and attitudes.

146. Taking the extreme case of closing down firms or industries, a range of questions would need to be answered: what are the prospects for the plant, equipment and workforce to be absorbed else-where; would there be a short-/long-term loss of foreign exchange; would the foreign exchange costs of industries utilising the products of these manufacturing units rise and if so by how much, and to what extent would manufacturing and other exports be affected by such a move? (Clearly the economy will only achieve an absolute foreign exchange gain from closing down domestic production if the foreign exchange used to purchase the imported product is lower than the foreign exchange costs of production. In Zimbabwe, however, it is unlikely that such instances are widespread.)

147. Clearly where one firm has more modern (and it is assumed more efficient) plant it is likely to be able to produce at lower unit cost than a firm with older plant and equipment. Under the scheme envisaged, however, the former firm would have to show that it could produce at lower unit cost with the prevailing plant and machinery (for there would be no guarantee that foreign exchange would be available to update the equipment of the latter firm) or that it had sufficient capacity to satisfy at least local demand for a given period of time. The outcome of this process would be likely to be the absorption of smaller, older and less efficient firms by bigger, modern and more efficient ones. While such a trend would tend to raise the level of monopoly and oligopoly production in the country it would also lead to a smaller proportion of firms being able to survive simply and solely on the basis of supplying the relatively small domestic market: total domestic expenditure in 1985 amounted to $5 bn while latest available figures (for 1984) show that 45% of all formal sector manufacturing units had gross output levels of less than Z$500,000 (US$401,000) and only contributed 2% of total gross output of the manufacturing sector and with net output per employee less than half the sectoral average.

148. These would include a range of measures such as re-vamping of plant and equipment, worker and management re-training, increasing in-house management engineering capacity, altering the pattern of shift work, etc.

149. Some of these issues have been analysed in the three-volume 'Trade Liberalisation Study' commissioned by the government, submitted to it in late 1988 and upon which, in early 1990, it was still deliberating.

150. Exceptions will, of course, continue to manifest themselves. For instance if the rise in the price of nickel in the first four months of 1988 had been sustained throughout the year, it would have raised total export earnings by Z$200 m. over 1986 levels.

151. In part the problem has been created by the low level of replacement investment over the last ten years and in part because of the need to maintain a steady and high rate of annual growth over the next ten years.

152. It should be stressed that to the extent that the Zimbabwe dollar is 'overvalued' and exports are stimulated by export incentives, manufactured exporters in effect work with a dual exchange rate which operates to their advantage: imports are priced relatively lower so that more units of foreign exchange can be purchased with Z$1 while higher export prices are 'compensated' for by the financial incentive package which is currently in place.

153. These various incentives are well summarized, for example, in MBCA (1989).

154. For companies like Art Flooring and Super Canners which have exported between 70 and 100% of their manufactures, this sort of problem clearly does not arise.
155. This has happened already in the case of the textiles sub-sector where the most extensive investment programme in the early 1980s has led to the bulk of machinery now being capable of producing goods of a quality and at a speed adequate for penetrating of the European market. See Riddell (1990).
156. Under the post-November 1987 system, the increased allocation still has to be used to purchase produce to be used in the production process.
157. In July 1987, travel goods exports to South Africa manufactured by Monarch Products of Bulawayo were subject to an additional 115% 'dumping' duty by the South Africans resulting in an effective loss of Z$5 m. worth of exports between July and December 1987. While the 'dumping' duty was lifted in early 1988 following a successful appeal to the South African Board of Trade authorities, the management of Monarch Products acknowledge that it will be far from easy to begin again to penetrate the South African market and build up sales to previous levels.
158. And perhaps even eliminate these barriers, depending upon the degree to which laissez-faire principles were pursued.
159. An example here would be Lever Brothers, whose recent investments in plant and equipment led to new export sales in 1987/8 of Z$5.5 m.

References and Bibliography

Agricultural Marketing Authority (AMA) (1986), *Economic Review of the Agricultural Industry of Zimbabwe 1985*, Harare, AMA.

Arrighi, G. (1967), *The Political Economy of Rhodesia*, The Hague, Mouton.

Astrow, A. (1983), *Zimbabwe: a Revolution that Lost its Way?*, London, Zed Press.

Barber, W.J. (1961), *The Economy of British Central Africa*, London, Oxford University Press.

Cable, V. and Persaud, B. (eds) (1987), *Developing With Foreign Investment*, London, Croom Helm for the Commonwealth Secretariat.

Central Statistical Office (CSO) (various years), *National Accounts of Zimbabwe, National Accounts of Rhodesia, National Accounts of Southern Rhodesia* and *National Accounts of The Federation of Rhodesia and Nyasaland*, Harare, CSO.

—— (various years), *The Census of Production: Mining, Manufacturing, Construction, Electricity and Water Supply, Report on The Census of Industrial Production*, Harare, CSO.

—— (1986 and 1987), *National Income and Expenditure Report*, Harare, CSO.

—— (various years), *The Monthly Digest of Statistics, The Quarterly Digest of Statistics* and *Stats-Flash*, Harare, CSO.

—— (various years), *Statement of External Trade, Statement of External Trade by Commodity, Annual Statement of External Trade*.

Chavunduka G.L. (1982), *Zimbabwe, Report of The Commission of Inquiry into the Agricultural Industry under the Chairmanship of Professor G.L. Chavunduka*, Harare, Government Printer.

Chelliah, R.J. (1986), *Report of the Commission of Inquiry into Taxation under the Chairmanship of Dr R.J. Chelliah*, Harare, Government Printer, April.

Chenery, H.B. (1960), 'Patterns of Industrial Growth', *American Economic Review*, Vol. 50 (September).

—— Robinson, S. and Syrquin, M. (1986), *Industrialization and Growth*, New York, Oxford Univeristy Press for the World Bank.

Clarke D.G. (1975), 'The Political Economy of Discrimination and Underdevelopment in Rhodesia with Special Reference to African Workers 1940–1973', University of St Andrews, PhD Thesis (mimeo).

—— (1980), *Foreign Companies and International Investment in Zimbabwe*, London, Catholic Institute for International Relations.

Cochrane, E.D.D. and Donoso, R.H. (1987), 'Technology and Development Perspectives of the Chemical Sector of Zimbabwe', Harare (mimeo).

Cole, R.L. (1968), 'The Tariff Policy of Rhodesia', *The Rhodesian Journal of Economics*, Vol. 2.

Commercial Farmers' Union (CFU) (1986), 'The Agricultural Industry: An Overview of The Industry, The Need to Reduce Input Costs and The Provision of Adequate Essential Production Requirements', Harare, CFU, September (mimeo).

Confederation of Zimbabwe Industries (various dates), 'State of The Manufacturing Sector, Tri-Annual Survey', Harare, Confederation of Zimbabwe Industries.

—— (1986), 'Zimbabwe: Supply Survey of Agricultural and Horticultural Machinery For Soil Preparation or Cultivation', Harare, paper prepared for the International Trade Centre, UNCTAD/GATT in co-operation with the Secretariat of the Preferential Trade Area for Eastern and Southern African States (mimeo).

Department of Customs and Excise (1987), *Zimbabwe Customs and Excise Tariff Handbook*, Harare, Government Printer.

Department of Business Studies (various dates), 'Business Opinion Survey', Harare, University of Zimbabwe.

Government of Rhodesia, Minister of Trade, Industry and Development (1965), *Industrial Policy of the Rhodesia Government and How It Is Implemented*, Harare, Government Printer, 1 May.

Government of Zimbabwe (GOZ) (1983a), *National Manpower Survey 1981, Volumes I and III*, Harare, Ministry of Manpower, Planning and Development.

—— (1983b), *Transitional National Development Plan, 1982/83 to 1984/85, Volumes 1 and 2*, Harare, Government Printer.

—— (1986), *Republic of Zimbabwe First Five-Year National Development Plan, 1986-1990, Volume I*, Harare, Government Printer.

—— (1988), *Republic of Zimbabwe First Five-Year National Development Plan, 1986-1990, Volume II*, Harare, Government Printer.

—— (1989), *The Promotion of Investment: Policy and Regulations*, Harare, Government Printer, April.

Harris, P.S. (1974), *Black Industrial Workers in Rhodesia: The General Problems of Low Pay*, Gweru, Mambo Press.

Hawkins, A.M. (1987a), 'Industrial Policy in Zimbabwe', paper presented to the CZI Congress, Victoria Falls, July, reprinted in *CZI Industrial Review*, August.

—— (1987b), 'Zimbabwe's Socialist Transformation', *Optima*, Vol. 35, No. 4, December.

—— (1989) 'Time to Grasp The Nettle of Reform' in *Africa Economic Digest*, Zimbabwe Special Report, London, April.

Humphrey, M. (1989), 'An Ownership Profile of Zimbabwe's Manufacturing Sector', Harare, CZI Economics Department, April (mimeo).

Industrial and Process Engineering Consultants (Great Britain) in Association with Sir Alexander Gibb and Partners (1960), *Report on the Development of Manufacturing Industry within the Federation of Rhodesia and Nyasaland, July 1960*, Harare, Government Printer, C.Fed 161.

International Labour Office (ILO) (1978), *Labour Conditions and Discrimination in Southern Rhodesia (Zimbabwe)*, Geneva, ILO.

—— (1984) *1984 Year Book of Labour Statistics, 44th Issue*, Geneva, ILO.

International Monetary Fund (IMF) (1987), 'Zimbabwe: Recent Economic Developments', Washington DC, IMF, August (mimeo).

Irvine, A.G. (1959), *The Balance of Payments of Rhodesia and Nyasaland 1945-1954*, London, Oxford University Press.

Jansen, D. (1983), *Zimbabwe: Government Policy and The Manufacturing Sector*, A Study Prepared for the Ministry of Industry and Energy Development, Larkspur, California, Vol. I, *Main Report*, Vol. II, *Annexes*, (mimeo), April.

Kadhani, X.E. and Green, R.H. (1985), 'Parameters as warnings and guideposts: the case of Zimbabwe', *Journal of Development Planning*, No. 15, December.

Lewis, S.R. (1971), *Economic Policy and Industrial Growth in Pakistan*, London, George Allen and Unwin.

—— and Soligo, R. (1965), 'Domestic Resources and Fiscal Policy in Pakistan's Second and Third Year Plans', *Pakistan Development Review*, Spring.

Mandaza, I. (ed.) (1986), *Zimbabwe: The Political Economy of Transition 1980-1986*, Dakar, Codesria Book Series.

Mazhar, Y.K. and Ndlela, D.B. (1987), 'Technology and Development Perspectives of The Capital Goods Sector', Harare, (Draft mimeo).

Merchant Bank of Central Africa (MBCA) (1989), *Investing in Zimbabwe*, Harare, MBCA, May.

Ministry of Industry and Energy Development (1982), *Products of Zimbabwean Industries 1982*, Harare, Government Printer.

Muir, K. (1981), *Crop Production Statistics 1940-1979*, Department of Land Management, University of Zimbabwe, Working Paper 4/81.

Ndlela, D.B. (1981), *Dualism in The Rhodesian Colonial Economy*, Lund Economic Studies No. 22, Department of Economics, University of Lund.

—— (1985), 'The Capital Goods Sector in Zimbabwe', *Zimbabwe Journal of Economics*, Vol. 1.

—— (1986), 'Problems of Industrialisation: Structural and Policy Issues' in Mandaza.

Organisation of Economic Co-operation and Development (OECD) (1988), *Development Co-operation 1987 Report*, Paris, OECD.

Page, S.B. (1988), *Economic Prospects For The Third World, the 1988 Forecasts: Strategies for Industrialisation in the 1990s*, London, Overseas Development Institute, October.

—— and Riddell, R.C. (1988), 'Opportunities and Impediments to Foreign Direct Investment in Africa', Paper Prepared for the United Nations Centre on Transnational Corporations, London, Overseas Development Institute, July (mimeo) published in abridged form in *UNCTC Reporter*, April 1989.

Phimister, I. (1987), 'Industrialisation and Sub-Imperialism: Southern Rhodesian and South African Trade Relations Between The Wars', (mimeo). Paper presented to Oxford workshop on Alternative Development Strategies in Africa, September.

Ramsay, D. (1974a), 'Value Added at Constant Prices: Estimates for Rhodesian Manufacturing Industries and Some Observations', *The Rhodesian Journal of Economics*, Vol. 8, December.

—— (1974b), 'Productivity and Capital in Rhodesian Manufacturing', *The Rhodesian Journal of Economics*, Vol. 8, June.

Reserve Bank of Zimbabwe (various years), *Quarterly Economic and Statistical Review*, Harare, Reserve Bank of Zimbabwe.

Riddell, R.C. (1981a), 'Zimbabwe's Manufactured Exports and the Ending of the Trade Agreement With South Africa', Harare, Confederation of Zimbabwe Industries, December (mimeo).

—— (1981b), *Report of the Commission of Inquiry into Incomes, Prices and Conditions of Service under the Chairmanship of Roger C. Riddell*, Harare, Government Printer.

—— (1983), 'A Critique of "Zimbabwe: Government Policy and The Manufacturing Sector"', Harare, Confederation of Zimbabwe Industries (mimeo).

—— (1987a), *Foreign Aid Reconsidered*, London and Baltimore, James Currey and Johns Hopkins University Press.

—— (1987b), 'Zimbabwe's Experience of Foreign Investment Policy', in Cable and Persaud.

—— (1988a), *Industrialisation in Sub-Saharan African: Phase I, Case-Study, Zimbabwe*, Working Paper No. 25, London, Overseas Development Institute.

—— (1988b) 'Zimbabwe in The Frontline' in *Sanctions and South Africa*, Washington DC, Africa World Press.

—— (1989a) *Zimbabwe: Private Investment and Government Policy*, Washington DC, World Bank.

—— (1989b), *Zimbabwe: The Capital Goods Sector, Investment and Industrial Issues*, Washington DC, World Bank.

—— (1990), *Zimbabwe's Non-Traditional Exports to the EEC*, ODI Working Paper, London, Overseas Development Institute.

—— and Nsiyaludzu, D.F. (1983), 'Investment in the Manufacturing Sector: Projections to 1985 and Foreign Exchange Requirements', Harare, Confederation of Zimbabwe Industries, August (mimeo).

Robinson, P.B. (1987), *Trade and Financing Strategies for The New NICS: The Zimbabwe Case Study*, ODI Working Paper No. 23 London, Overseas Development Institute.

Singer, H. (1988), 'The World Development Report 1987 on the Blessings of "Outward Orientation": A Necessary Correction', *The Journal of Development Studies*, Vol. 24, No. 2, January.

Stoneman, C.S. (ed.) (1984), *Zimbabwe's Inheritance*, London, Macmillan.

—— (1985), 'Strategy or Ideology? The World Bank/IMF Approach To Development', Harare, University of Zimbabwe, Conference on Economic Policies and Planning Under Crisis, Paper No. 10 (mimeo).

—— (1988), *Zimbabwe's Prospects*, London, Macmillan.

—— (1989), 'The World Bank and the IMF in Zimbabwe', in Campbell, B. and Loxley, J (eds), *Structural Adjustment in Africa*, London, Macmillan.

Tobacco Industrial Council (1986), *Tobacco and Its Contribution To Zimbabwe*, Harare, Tobacco Industrial Council.

United Nations Conference on Trade and Development (UNCTAD) (1980), *Zimbabwe Towards a New Order: An Economic and Social Survey*, New York, United Nations.

United Nations Industrial Development Organisation (UNIDO) (1986a), *Africa in Figures, 1986*, Vienna, UNIDO, PPD.2, September.

—— (1986b), *The Manufacturing Sector in Zimbabwe*, Vienna, UNIDO, PPD/R.2, November.

Van Hoffen, M. (ed.) (1985), *Commercial Agriculture in Zimbabwe*, Harare, Modern Farming Publications.

Wood, A. (1986), 'Global Trends in Real Exchange Rates 1960–84', *Division Working Paper* No. 1988–1, Washington DC, International Economics Department, World Bank.

World Bank (1985), *Zimbabwe Country Economic Memorandum: Performance*, Policies and Prospects, Washington DC, IBRD.

—— (1987a), *Zimbabwe, An Industrial Sector Memorandum*, Washington DC, World Bank.

—— (1987b), *Zimbabwe: A Strategy for Sustained Growth, Volumes I and II*, Washington DC, World Bank.

Index